THE VISIONS OF
ISOBEL GOWDIE

*Magic, Witchcraft and Dark Shamanism
in Seventeenth-Century Scotland*

For Jamie, with love.

THE VISIONS OF
ISOBEL GOWDIE

Magic, Witchcraft and Dark Shamanism
in Seventeenth-Century Scotland

EMMA WILBY

sussex
ACADEMIC
PRESS
Brighton • Portland • Toronto

2 4 6 8 10 9 7 5 3 1

First published 2010 in Great Britain by
SUSSEX ACADEMIC PRESS
PO Box 139
Eastbourne BN24 9BP

and in the United States of America by
SUSSEX ACADEMIC PRESS
920 NE 58th Ave   Suite 300
Portland, Oregon 97213-3786

and in Canada by
SUSSEX ACADEMIC PRESS (CANADA)
90 Arnold Avenue, Thornhill, Ontario L4J 1B5

British Library Cataloguing in Publication Data
A CIP catalogue record for this book is available from the British Library.

Library of Congress Cataloging-in-Publication Data
Wilby, Emma.
The visions of Isobel Gowdie : magic, witchcraft, and dark shamanism in
    seventeenth-century Scotland / Emma Wilby.
p. cm.
Includes bibliographical references (p.   ) and index.
ISBN 978-1-84519-179-5 (h/c : alk. paper) —
ISBN 978-1-84519-180-1 (p/b : alk. paper)
1. Gowdie, Isobel, d. 1662? 2. Witchcraft—Scotland—History—17th
century. I. Title.
BF1408.G68 2010
133.4'30941109032—dc22

2009040229

Mixed Sources
Product group from well-managed
forests and other controlled sources
www.fsc.org Cert no. SGS-COC-2482
© 1996 Forest Stewardship Council

Typeset and designed by Sussex Academic Press, Brighton & Eastbourne.
Printed by TJ International, Padstow, Cornwall.
This book is printed on acid-free paper.

Contents

Contents

List of Illustrations

PAGE 7: 'Moray and Nairn' by Timothy Pont, c. 1590. Trustees of the National Library of Scotland.

PAGE 11: 'A fermtoun in the barony of Culbin, 1694'. From *The Culbin Sands, Fact and Fiction* (1992), reproduced here by kind permission of the author, Sinclair Ross, and the artist, Kris Sangster.

PAGE 38: Isobel Gowdie's first confession. Courtesy of Miss Elizabeth Rose, the trustees of Kilravock Castle Christian Trust and SCOTLANDSIMAGES.COM NAS: GD125/16/5/1/1.

PAGE 64: The trial of Anna Ebeler, *Relation oder Beschreibung* (. . .), Augsburg, 1669.

PAGE 89: Frontispiece to Peter Binsfield's *Tractat von Bekanntnuss der Zauberer und Hexen*. Stadtbibliothek/Stadtarchiv Trier; 'Witches' feast' and 'Witches transforming into animals' from Ulrich Molitor's *De Lamiis et phitonicis mulieribus* (1489). University of Glasgow Library, Department of Special Collections.

PAGE 106: Witness signatures from Isobel Gowdie's third confession. Courtesy of Miss Elizabeth Rose, the trustees of Kilravock Castle Christian Trust and SCOTLANDSIM-AGES.COM NAS: GD125/16/5/1/3.

PAGE 123: *The Legend*, by George-Paul Chalmers, 1864–7. Courtesy of the National Gallery of Scotland.

PAGE 152: Woodcuts from Janez Valvasor's *Theatrum Mortis Humanae Tripartitum* (1680–2).

PAGE 162: Ruins of Inshoch Castle, from the *Castellated and Domestic Architecture of Scotland*, Vol. II. By kind permission of Brill Publishing; Engraving by Georg Koler, with the inscription *In Solchem Habit gehendie 800 in Settin angekommen Irrlander oder Irren*, 1631. © The British Library.

PAGE 267: 'Sami shaman playing his drum . . .' From *En kortt Relation om Lapparnes Lefwarne och Sedher, wijdskiepellsser, sampt i manga Styken Grofwe Wildfarellser*, by Samuel Rheen, 1671, Uppsala: Harald Wretman, 1897. The University Library of Tromsø; Frontispiece to Doctor Faustus by Christopher Marlow. The Folger Shakespeare Library.

PAGE 285: 'The Angel Appearing to Ursula' by the Master of the Legend of St. Ursula, c. 1484–1515. The Wallraf-Richartz-Museum/Fondation Corboud Köln; photocredit: Rheinisches Bildarchiv Köln; Illustration from *Untersuchung der vermeinten und so genannten Hexereyen*, by John Webster, Halle 1719. Universitäts-und Landesbibliothek Sachsen-Anhalt in Halle (Saale).

PAGE 311: *Woden's Wilde Jagd* by Heinrich Heine, from *Nordische-Germanische Götter und Helden* . . . by Wilhelm Wægner, Leipzig, 1901. Kinder-und Jugendbuch-abteilung, Staatsbibliothek, Berlin.

PAGE 330: 'Aygnan and Kaagerre, aggressive spirits of the Tupi', woodcut from *Historia Navigationis in Brasiliam*, by Jean de Léry, 1580. John Carter Brown Library at Brown University; *Werewolf* by Lucas Cranach der Ältere, early 1500s.

PAGES 358–9: 'Witch with bow and arrow' from Ulrich Molitor's *De Lamiis et phitonicis mulieribus* (1500). University of Glasgow Library, Department of Special Collections; *The Triumph of Death* or *The Three Fates*, Flemish tapestry, probably from Brussels ca. 1510–20. The Victoria and Albert Museum; *Witch Riding Backwards on a Goat, Accompanied by Four Putti*, 1500–1, engraving by Albrecht Dürer. © 2010, Museum of Fine Arts, Boston.

PAGES 410–11: 'Witch embracing the Devil;, from Ulrich Molitor's *De Lamiis et phitonicis mulieribus* (1500). University of Glasgow Library, Department of Special Collections; Illustration from the *Misticall Marriage* by Francis Rous (1635). The Folger Shakespeare Library; *St Theresa intercedes for Bernardin Mendozy*, engraving by Schelte Boswert, after Peter Paul Rubens. © Museum of New Zealand Te Papa Tongarewa; gift of Bishop Monrad, 1869.

PAGE 439: *Michael the Archangel Fighting the Dragon*, probably 1497, woodcut by Albrecht Dürer. © 2010, Museum of Fine Arts, Boston.

PAGE 478: 'De ministero dæmonium' from *Historia de gentibus septentrionalis* by Olaus Magnus (1555). University of Glasgow Library, Department of Special Collections; 'Belial dances before Solomon' from *Das Buch Belial*. Bayerische Staatsbibliothek, Munich.

PAGE 541: First page from the score of 'The Confession of Isobel Gowdie' by James Macmillan, 1990. Reproduced by permission of Boosey & Hawkes Publishers Ltd.

The author and publisher gratefully acknowledge the companies and organizations detailed above for permission to reproduce copyright material. The publishers apologize for any errors or omissions in the above list and would be grateful to be notified of any corrections that should be incorporated in the next edition or reprint of this book.

Acknowledgements

I am very grateful to the depositor of the Gowdie manuscripts, Miss Elizabeth Rose, and to Sylvia Denton and the trustees of Kilravock Castle Christian Trust, for kindly granting permission to publish a new transcription of the confessions. I am also indebted to Julian Goodare, of the University of Edinburgh, for being so exceptionally generous with his time and knowledge; reading an early draft of the book and helping me with an endless list of queries on anything from the mysteries of covenanting spirituality to the mysteries of capitalization. I owe a debt of gratitude to my publisher, Anthony Grahame, for deftly accommodating a book that has turned out to be twice as long as originally intended. Special thanks must also go to Jonathan Barry and the Department of History at the University of Exeter, for supporting my research over the past four years.

I am much obliged to Diane Baptie, of the Association of Scottish Genealogists and Researchers in Archives, for providing me with a transcription of the confessions and other documents relating to John Innes, Harry Forbes and the Hay family, and for patiently helping me with numerous other questions. Thanks must also go to David Brown, Alan Borthwick, Alison Lyndsay, Leanne Swallow and Jean Crawford of the National Archives of Scotland for their help with the Gowdie manuscripts, and to Lynda McGuigan and Ian Riches for giving me access to the archives at Brodie Castle. I have valued support and advice received from others working in related fields, including John Finlay, Marion Gibson, Rune Hagen, Alaric Hall, Dietmar Knix, Diane Purkiss, Alasdair Raffe, Stuart Reid, Morgana Sythove and Sigurd Towrie. The inter-library loans department at Exeter University has also been unfailingly helpful and undaunted by the most obscure requests.

I am also obliged to Harry Gray, for trawling through Wick library in search of background information about Harry Forbes; to Andrew Coombs of Lochloy House, for good-naturedly digging out his old maps at very short notice; and to Mrs Halliday of Druim Farm, for an informative discussion about the Lochloy horizons. Thanks must also go to the staff at Nairn Museum, who were very helpful when I first came asking questions about Isobel four years ago and inadvertently provided me with the missing link that enabled me to track down the original confession documents.

Closer to home, I have valued advice from Andy Gurr and Pete Brickley, and encouragement from my brothers Ben and Joe, Jemma Inglis, Dave Gurr, PJ Gray, Joanna Redstone, John Sharkey, Karl Triebel and Tim Wellard. Vivid insights into contemporary storytelling traditions, courtesy of Michael and Wendy Dacre of 'Raventales', have also been much appreciated. Lastly, I am deeply grateful to my father, Roger, my mother, Annie, and to Jeremy and Sue Inglis, who have all been unfailingly generous and supportive, in a hundred and one different ways. Similarly, a huge thank you to my sons, Hamish and Dylan, for consistently lightening the dark shadows cast by Isobel's world. And of course to my husband Jamie, without whom not a single word of this book could have been written.

PART I

The Construction of
the Confessions

'I sent to Mr. Hari [Forbes] to com and wait on the witches;
to see if God would open ther hart to giv God glori,
and confess ther sins.'

Alexander Brodie of Brodie, May 1663

Introduction to Part I

I

Twenty miles east of Inverness, on the strip of lowland lying between the Cairngorm Mountains and the Moray Firth, lies an approximately mile-long, crescent-shaped scattering of small glacial hills. Some are spherical, others elliptical, and they rise from the flatlands like emerald green burial mounds. The last mound to the south, by the Nairn to Forres road, is called 'Macbeth's Hillock' and is traditionally deemed to be the place where the future Thane of Cawdor met the three weird sisters performing their uncanny divinations. The last mound to the north, known as the Downie Hill, is the place where Isobel Gowdie, the 'Queen of Scottish Witches' claimed to have feasted with the king and queen of the fairies.[1]

The events on Macbeth's Hillock are rooted in legend; the events on the Downie Hill are rooted in fact. In 1662 Isobel Gowdie, a woman from neighbouring Lochloy, gave a series of four confessions, ratified by a public notary and witnessed by a group of local dignitaries including the minister of Auldearn, Harry Forbes. After sinking into obscurity for nearly two hundred years the confessions emerged into the public domain in 1833, when a full transcription appeared in Robert Pitcairn's *Ancient Criminal Trials in Scotland*. Although the confessions quickly became celebrated, the original documents themselves disappeared for a further two centuries only to be rediscovered by the author during research for this book, in an uncatalogued box of papers once belonging to Isobel's landlord, John Hay, held at the National Archives of Scotland. Fully restored, all four confessions are now accessible to the general public for the first time.

II

Among academic historians and folklorists, Isobel's confessions are generally considered to constitute the most exceptional testimony to have been given by any witchcraft suspect in Britain, at any point in history. In 1833 Isobel's first transcriber, Robert

Pitcairn, stated that parts of her narrative were 'in all respects, the most extraordinary in the history of witchcraft of this or of any other country', and just over one hundred years later, in his *Calendar of Cases of Witchcraft in Scotland*, George Black echoed that 'This is the most remarkable witchcraft case on record in [the country] . . . The case of Issobell Gowdie is also referred to, in more or less detail, in every work relating to witchcraft in Scotland'.[2] Since this date, among scholars of witchcraft, Isobel's confessions have effortlessly maintained this pole position.

But Isobel has also enjoyed an equally high profile on a non-academic level. She is the subject of the acclaimed orchestral work, *The Confession of Isobel Gowdie*, that launched the career of Scottish composer James Macmillan in 1990. She has inspired novels, including the infamous *The Devil's Mistress*, by the nineteenth-century author John Brodie-Innes and more recently, *The Drowning Pond* by Catherine Forde; plays, with John Lawson's *The Witch of Auldearn* being performed in Nairn as recently as 2007; songs, one of the most well-known coming from The Sensational Alex Harvey Band; along with various radio broadcasts and public lectures.[3] Isobel is one of the few historical witches to appear in the *Oxford Dictionary of National Biography*, and her verses have been included in a recent anthology of early modern women poets. She is also the historical witch featured most frequently and prominently in Margaret Murray's influential and controversial work, *The Witch-Cult in Western Europe*, and as a consequence it could be argued that Isobel has influenced the ritual traditions of Wicca more than any other witchcraft suspect on record.[4]

But despite this notoriety, Isobel herself remains a mystery. Interest in her confessions has focused mainly on content, with scholars and popular writers alike using them as a type of archaic picture library to be mined for vivid snapshots of the weird and wonderful world of seventeenth-century witchcraft and fairy belief. However, the deeper dynamics and significance of the confessions remain unexplored. It is still unclear, for example, how much of Isobel's testimony came from herself, and how much from her interrogators; why her testimony differs so markedly from that of the hundreds of other witchcraft suspects who were interrogated in the early modern period; and most importantly, what she may have intended by many of the extraordinary things she claimed. The purpose of this book is to try and answer some of these questions.

III

But as an object of study, Isobel's confessions present us with a constant dilemma. On the one hand, the need to understand the woman and the interrogatorial process that gave rise to the confessions necessitates close historical analysis of social, political and religious issues peculiar to a small region of north-east Scotland in the mid-seventeenth century. But on the other, many of the passages in the confessions are so challenging that we need to roam far afield to find explanations: moving beyond Scotland, beyond the field of witchcraft and beyond historical methodologies altogether in order to explore avenues as diverse as Highland oral traditions, Amazonian shamanism, Corsican folklore, Christian mysticism, Nordic mythology, criminal psychology and contemporary North American dream research. And in mining these lodes, we find ourselves inadvertently developing, and therefore having to support within a broader context, hypotheses that are not only relevant to Isobel's confessions, but also to some of the key debates raging in the field of European witchcraft studies today.

This constant switch from micro-study to macro-study creates an unavoidable tension in the book. The biographical concerns restrict the detailed development of wider hypotheses while the need to develop wider hypotheses takes us deep into theory and away from the intimacy of an individual life. But in the end, we must navigate this conflict in the hope that our central protagonist would have wished it no other way. As her confessions testify, Isobel Gowdie was a woman whose existence was constrained by the market price of beef and linen, and by the boundary dykes of a small farm hamlet in north-east Scotland. But she was also, by her own reckoning, a woman who possessed powers over life and death itself, whose imaginative journeys transcended matter and geographical space, and for whom the abstract world of the mind was as real and important as the world of flesh and soil. It is hardly surprising, then, that an extended analysis of Isobel's confessions should mirror a similarly vertiginous paradox.

1

The Cottar's Wife

In 1662, the mile-long inlet named Loch Loy cut into the Moray Firth just two miles north of Auldearn, a small town situated roughly midway between Inverness and Elgin, and falling in the old Moray county of Nairnshire. At this time the term 'Lochloy' designated the whole area surrounding the sea loch, including a large deciduous woodland and the low hills leading up to where the main farm stands today. Then, as now, the panorama was sweeping. Southwards, in the distance, you would have seen the humped masses of Dava Moor and the Cawdor Hills sloping down into the wooded valleys of Darnaway, Lethen and Geddes before melting into the gently undulating lowlands – broken with patches of heath, copse and scattered glacial mounds – that ran northwards to meet the sea. The coastal strip (including the diminished loch) is now largely hidden beneath conifer woods, but in Isobel's time it would have shattered into long heaps of white sand dunes and beaches that extended eastwards into the Culbin Sands, and were later referred to as a 'miniature Sahara'.[1] Beyond this 'most singular landscape', as the sands were described in 1794, lie the waters of the Moray Firth back-dropped by the rising highlands of Easter Ross.[2] These features would have combined to give an impression, on a fair day, of wide expanses of glittering land, sea and sky encircled by a distant ring of blue mountains.

Although this coastal region brought curling winds and dramatic cloud formations, it also brought mild temperatures and low rainfall. In the 1650s the province of Moray was described as 'the most fruitful country in Scotland, and the common proverb is, that it hath fifteen days more of summer than any other part of the nation', while an eighteenth-century observer noted that the Nairnshire climate was 'almost as favourable as any in the kingdom'.[3] During this period wildlife was also prolific, with a commentator noting that in neighbouring Ardclach, in 1790, the 'woods and hills abound with moor-fowl, wood-cock, partridges, hares, foxes and some deer . . . [and] the otter and wild cat are frequently seen on the water's side'. At Nairn, meanwhile, the river teemed with trout and salmon, while 'haddocks, skate, cod, flounders, and some ling' were caught 'in abundance' in the coastal waters.[4] In Isobel's time, as now, the lowland soils between the Moray Firth and the Cairngorms were relatively fertile, with English angler Richard Franck being moved to admire the 'flourishing fields of Murrayland' when travelling through the region in 1658.[5]

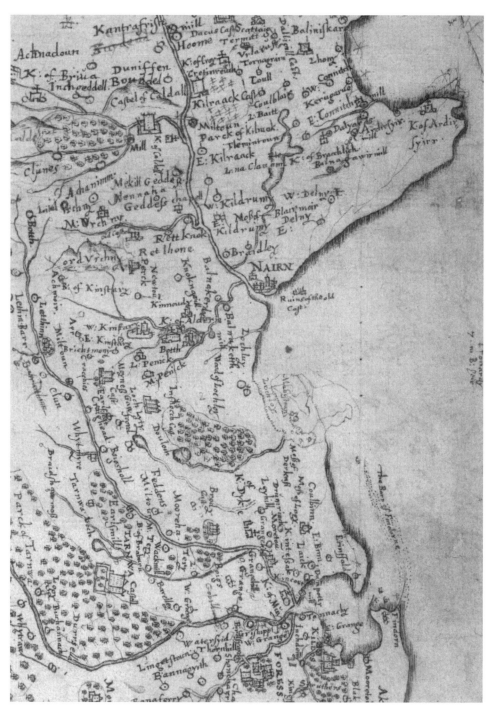

Section of the map of *Moray and Nairn*, drawn by cartographer Timothy Pont, c. 1583–96. The castles of Cawdor and Kilravock can be seen on the far left. In the centre near the coast we can see Nairn and Lochloy, and beneath these, the town of Auldearn. Inshoch Castle is clearly visible south of the Wood of Lochloy. Centre right we find Brodie Castle and the village of Dyke and, to the far right, the town of Forres.

In response to these relatively favourable conditions, rural Nairnshire would have been more highly populated than it is today. The stretches of heath and woodland between the mountains and the sea would have been interspersed with clusters of long, low thatched cottages irregularly grouped into farm hamlets or 'fermtouns', surrounded by the rough crenellations of ridge and furrow arable land, and beyond that, the pasture where the sheep and cattle grazed. The landscape would have been largely open, but zig-zagged across by muddy tracks and a few rudimentary stone or turf dykes and ditches.

During Isobel's lifetime the lands surrounding Auldearn and Lochloy were owned by a handful of families, all inter-related by marriage, who stationed themselves securely in stone castles, fortified houses and big farms on the tops of hills or down wooded lanes. Among the most prominent in the area were the Brodies, with the head of the family, Alexander, living at Brodie Castle four miles east of Auldearn, and one of his uncles, of the same name, living at the big house of Lethen just three miles south of the town. Also prominent, and living within an eight-mile radius of Auldearn as the crow flies, were the Rose family, who had their main seat at Kilravock Castle; the Dunbars, who had houses at Boath and Moynes; the Earls of Moray, who had a great castle at Darnaway; and the Campbells of Cawdor (home of the lairds of the Macbeth legend) who had their main seat at Cawdor Castle, less than three miles east of Kilravock. Lochloy, along with the lands of Park and other estates to the south and east of Auldearn, were owned by John Hay, nephew by marriage to Alexander Brodie of Brodie. In the mid-seventeenth century the Laird of Park lived at the Hays' principal seat, the Castle of Inshoch, which stood on a low hill to the south of Loch Loy. Other Hay family members lived at Newton of Park and Brightmony.

Isobel and John Gilbert

The fact that Isobel's trial confessions state that she was 'spous to Johne gilbert in lochloy', when taken in conjunction with the fact that the Laird of Park and his family feature prominently in her confessions, suggests that Isobel and her husband lived and worked on lands belonging to the Hays of Park. But we do not know exactly where they lived or their social status. Although a box of accounts, tacks and other papers relating to the Laird of Park's estates in the mid-seventeenth century survives, the earliest relevant document is dated 1677 (fifteen years after Isobel's trial) and none make reference to either Gowdies or Gilberts.[6] This could mean that Isobel's husband had been a joint tenant on Park's Lochloy estate, but had moved away prior to this date; the fact that Hay, like most landlords in the period, granted his tenants three-year leases would certainly have made such a move possible. But the more likely explanation is that, like the bulk of the rural population, John Gilbert was a cottar or labourer: a farm worker who was employed by tenants and therefore went unnamed in estate records. That both Isobel and her husband were without landed connections is further supported by the fact that neither Gilberts nor Gowdies appear in the Index to the Particular Register of Sasines for the sheriffdoms of Elgin, Forres and Nairn between 1617 and

1700. However we must set against this the fact that Isobel's claim to have helped her husband to sell 'beeff', 'nors noat vebis' and 'any uther thing' for 'silver and good pryce' at the local market suggests – as Diane Purkiss has pointed out – that they may not have found themselves at the very bottom of the social ladder. We can therefore speculate that John Gilbert was, at the very least, a cottar; that is, one of the large percentage of the rural population that worked for tenants on their holdings but 'were granted [by the tenant] a small portion of arable land and some grazing, usually with a cot house and a kale yard'.[7]

But even if we elevate Isobel and her husband to the status of reasonably-well-placed cottars or low-level tenants, it is important to remember that, as such, they would still have enjoyed a lifestyle more redolent of the current developing world than contemporary western Europe. Home would have been a classic fermtoun: a muddy area containing a scattered collection of cottages and barns, with hens and geese scratching in the dirt, steaming dung heaps, mangy dogs barking and ragged barefoot children. Isobel's cottage, maybe with an outhouse tacked onto the end, would have boasted low walls of turf, sometimes mixed with a bit of stone, overhung with a thatch of broom or marram grass. There would have been one central door, with perhaps a small unglazed window on either side, the latter being shuttered or blocked with hide or clothes in bad weather. One of the characters from Franck's *Northern Memoirs* (written in 1658) complained that, 'in my opinion [Scottish cottages] are but little better than Huts; and generally of a Size, all built so low, that their Eves hang dangling to touch the earth'; while in 1699, Edward Ward echoed that the houses of the poor were so small that 'it is no difficulty to piss over them'.[8] Even as late as 1794, James Donaldson, factor to William Ramsay of Maule, observed that in Nairnshire 'the habitations of the poorer tenants in the district . . . are mean, dark and dirty cottages built of turf, without order or connexion with each other'.[9]

If you stooped under the low door and entered Isobel's cottage, you would have come into an interior no more than four metres wide, with a floor of beaten earth, or of clay hardened over pebbles. In order to share precious heat, this space may have been divided in two by a low partition or piece of furniture to create an area for the family at one end and animals at the other. The long winter nights would have been punctuated by the shifting and snorting of cattle in the byre and the rustle of chickens roosting in the rafters. The fireplace was likely to have been in the centre of the room, built directly on the floor, backed by a flat stone against which the ashes could be banked. Smoke would have made its way upwards and filtered out through the thatch, or maybe a hole in the roof, the latter being sometimes topped with a rudimentary wooden chimney, perhaps made from an old bucket without a bottom.[10] Arching above your head, the fire-blackened wooden skeleton of the house would have been hung with baskets and creels, and with dried fish or meat, preserving in the smoke.

There would have been little furniture and few possessions. Like most in the period, Isobel and John Gilbert would probably have owned at least two chests, one for meal and another for clothes. They may also have owned one or two small wooden stools, although, as seventeenth-century minister James Kirkwood noted, in this period the poorer Scots generally sat 'about the Ground' around the fire.[11] The small number of kitchen pots and utensils would have been mainly wooden, supplemented by a few highly-prized metal objects like cauldrons and knives. In the corners of the cottage, sheepskins, or piles of straw or heather, perhaps shaped and sewn into rudimentary mattresses, would have been put to one side, ready to be slung around the fire at night to sleep on, though some of the wealthier may have possessed box beds, built onto the cottage walls like cupboards. Toilet facilities were chamber pots, pits in the earth, animal pens or local heaths, fields and copses.

Although basic, Isobel's cottage would have been eminently practical, being cool in the summer and retaining heat in the winter. And when the howling winds swept across the Moray Firth it would have provided good sound insulation. But it would also have been very dark. In the daylight hours, if it was fine, the interior would have been dimly lit by shafts of sunlight slanting in through the small windows, but in the evenings and on overcast winter days the only illumination would have been the fire, and perhaps a few cruisie lamps or flickering candles made out of resinous splinters of fir wood. The living area would also have been very smoky. Even if the cottage possessed a chimney, much of the fire smoke would have dissipated throughout the cottage and meandered its way up through the thatch; creating the impression, from the outside, of a 'smoking dunghill.'[12] In the 1720s Edward Burt noted that in the winter, poor Highlanders huddled close to the fire 'till their legs and thighs are scorched to an extra-ordinary degree; and many have sore eyes, and some are quite blind. This long continuance in the smoke makes them almost as black as chimney-sweepers'.[13] In the following century, gentlemen visitors to these turf cottages lamented that they were commonly given one of the few household chairs to sit on, as a mark of honour, but that the extra height only subjected them to the worse of the smoke. Burt also noted that when it rained, water frequently 'comes through the roof [of the cottage] and mixes with the sootiness of the inside, where all the sticks look like charcoal, [and] falls in drops like ink' onto the inhabitants below; while worms, dislodged from their homes in the turf walls and thatch, could also be airborne visitors.[14]

Isobel the Woman

So much for Isobel's home, but what of Isobel herself? We know nothing of her life before she married John Gilbert. Although it is likely that she was raised in the Auldearn area, it is impossible to determine where. Few references to 'Gowdies' survive in extant seventeenth and early eighteenth-century parish records relating to Nairnshire, and the surname has since all but disappeared from the county. Estate accounts lodged at Brodie Castle do indicate that in the mid-eighteenth century a number of Gowdies lived on the adjacent lands belonging to the Brodies of Brodie. A 'David Gowdie' is listed as a tenant, of the poorer kind, in 1728, 1735 and 1743, while in the 1770s a more substantial contingent of Gowdies (including a 'William' and a 'John') lived at a location termed 'Newlands'.[15] The fact that the place names mentioned by Isobel disproportionately favour the regions east and south-east of Auldearn that largely fell within, or abutted directly onto, the Brodie estates could suggest a link with

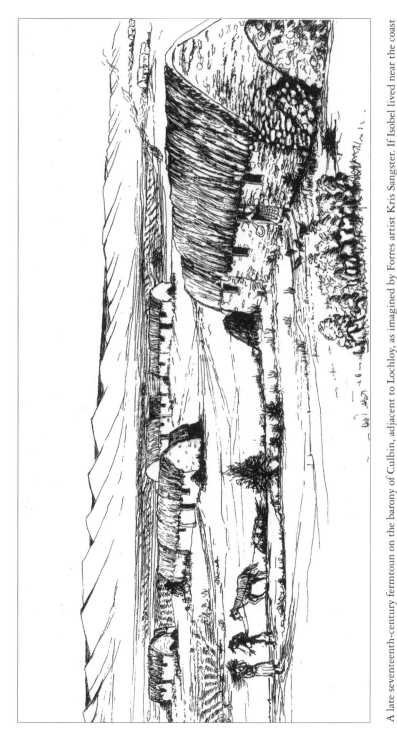

A late seventeenth-century fermtoun on the barony of Culbin, adjacent to Lochloy, as imagined by Forres artist Kris Sangster. If Isobel lived near the coast then her fermtoun was likely to have been back-dropped by similar dunes. One possible location is at the west end of the loch near Chapel Well, just below the road and opposite the present Lochloy House. In 1859 remains of a village – known to be extant until at least the early-seventeenth century – were uncovered here (*see* Bain 1928: 68).

these local Gowdies, but unfortunately there is no other evidence to support this speculation. Isobel's references to the Downie Hill, Hardmuir, Earlsmill, Boghole, Earlseat, the Muckle Burn, Moyness and Darnaway could just as easily have reflected any number of other factors: such as her husband's family, work-related matters, or the fact that if, like many women and children, she had accompanied cattle to their summer grazing at Edinkillie or Ardclach, she may have passed through some of these places on the way.

With regard to Isobel's age at the time of her trial, the records are also mute. The fact that she was married at the time of her interrogation puts her at about fifteen years minimum although, given the fact that in Scotland in this period the average age at marriage was around twenty-six to twenty-seven, it is more likely that she was closer to thirty than fifteen.[16] The fact that Isobel describes sexual experiences occurring fifteen years prior to the trial would also, if her memory reflected both real events and sexual maturity, put her well past puberty in 1662. We also do not know whether she had children. The confessions are silent on the subject and parish records of baptisms in Auldearn only survive from 1687 onwards. The fact that Isobel does not refer to any children, and the fact that, as we have noted earlier, no likely Gilbert descendants can be identified in later records, when taken in conjunction with Isobel's apparent openness and volubility concerning her private life, could be seen to indicate that she was childless. But the fact that many witchcraft records make no reference to the families of suspects means that we cannot assume this.

With regard to Isobel's appearance, we can only speculate once again. Following the nineteenth-century novelist John Brodie-Innes, popular writers have been fond of asserting that Isobel was young, handsome and red-headed; occult novelist Dennis Wheatley, for example, rhapsodising that 'she had exceptional beauty of face and body crowned by a mass of flaming red hair'.[17] This supposition, if not wholly poetic licence, may be derived from the fact that in her references to the sexual appetites of the Devil, Isobel seems to disassociate herself from 'all the old people th[a]t he cairis not for, and ar veak & wnmeit for him'. But to draw any conclusions about her physical appearance on the basis of such a statement is tenuous to say the least. In other matters, however, we can be a little more precise. We can be certain, for example, that however attractive she may or may not have been, Isobel would not have dressed like her illustrious neighbour, Margaret Innes, who was painted in 1662, soon after her marriage to the Laird of Kilravock. While Margaret posed before her portraitist in a blue silk gown and delicate white lace ruff, Isobel's main item of dress, worn over a coarse linen or woollen shift, would have been a heavy plaid of wool, about three yards long, and dyed in natural colours imitating 'those of the Heath in which they [Highlanders] often reposed'.[18] In fine weather, she would have set the plaid in folds and tied it around her waist with a belt to make a kind of skirt which hung halfway down the thigh, while in bad weather she would have worn it above her head, enveloping her whole body like an Old Testament matriarch. Unlike her eminent neighbour, Isobel would have possessed few changes of clothes and her plaid is likely to have not only doubled up as both dress and overcoat, but also as a blanket, with Edward Ward noting, in 1699, that while the Highland gentry go 'well enough habited' some of the poorer women 'have scarce any Cloaths at all, save part of their Bed-cloaths pinn'd about their Shoulders'.[19] In such constant use, these multi-purpose plaids carried sufficiently strong odours of wood smoke, animals and human sweat to offend fastidious urban observers, with Burt noting that when 'the plaid falls from the shoulder, or otherwise requires to be re-adjusted, while you are talking with them, [the Highlanders] toss it over again, as some people do the knots of their wigs, which conveys the offence in whiffs that are intolerable: of this they seem not to be sensible'.[20] Lice infestation is likely to have rendered Isobel's skin, as it did that of her contemporary Richard Franck, 'motled and dapled like an April trout'; and her knees, if Burt is to be believed, being 'exposed to all weathers' may have been 'tanned and freckled; and the joint being mostly infected with the country distemper . . . disagreeable to the eye'.[21] Beneath her plaid Isobel would probably have gone barelegged, or worn rough footless woollen stockings tied below the knee. In the winter and on Sundays she may have protected her feet with rude leather shoes or 'cuarans', but in the summer she may have gone without, with Ward noting that in the late-seventeenth century the poorer women 'go bare-foot'. This remark is supported by Burt's observation that even in the 1720s, many Highlanders were so unused to wearing shoes that when they put them on, once a week, to attend church they 'walk very awkwardly; or, as we say, like a cat shod with walnut-shells'.[22]

Isobel the Cottar's Wife

In seventeenth-century Nairnshire, as in the rest of Scotland in this period, agricultural methods were little different from those employed throughout the Middle Ages. And as a consequence, whether he was a tenant, cottar or labourer, John Gilbert's primary concern would almost certainly have been the growing and harvesting of grain which, on the Laird of Park's estates in this period, included bear (a form of barley), oats and a little rye.[23] Year in, year out, Gilbert would have worked his way through the seasons performing the sequence of tasks necessary to put food on his plate: spreading dung, ploughing, harrowing and sowing his arable strips; reaping, tying and stacking the ripened grain; transporting it to the barns to be threshed and winnowed; moving it on to the drying kilns; and then finally taking it to the mill or hand quern to be ground into meal. In between these activities, he would have devoted his time to the care, breeding and culling of Highland black cattle (used in the plough and for meat, milk, leather, horn and other by-products) and perhaps a flock of the traditional white-faced sheep (used primarily for wool). He may also have owned or maintained one or two small horses to carry packs and drag sledges and carts. His other chores would have included maintaining the dung heap upon which the fertility of the infields depended; cutting peat; building and re-building the walls of houses, barns and folds; burning field-stubble; cutting, turning and stooking hay from bogland or meadow; making and mending tools and harness; winding rope from horsehair and rushes; whittling arrows, carving bowls and spoons and weaving baskets.

Isobel would have been equally busy. Like all women of childbearing age, her main priority would have been the producing and raising of children. If Isobel was fertile, given the fact that, as Houston has recently shown, family limitation was seldom practised in Britain in this period and the average birth interval was approximately thirty months, we can assume that she would have spent much of her life either pregnant or breastfeeding, with the latter commonly continuing for at least a year after birth.[24] In which case, like the woman who visited Edinburgh cunning woman Jean Weir, sometime before 1670, she would commonly have gone about her business with 'ane chyld upon her back, and on or two at her foot'.[25] But whether or not she had children, for women like Isobel, child-rearing duties would have been incorporated into a ceaseless daily round of domestic chores. She would have been primarily responsible for the dairy work (milking cows and goats, and skimming and churning the milk to make butter and cheese) both to feed the household and sell at town; Burt noting that in the early-eighteenth century Highlanders arrived at their local markets with 'Two or three cheeses, of about three or four pound weight a-piece; a kid, sold for six-pence or eight-pence at the most; [and] a small quantity of butter in something that looks like a bladder, and is sometimes set down upon the dirt in the street'.[26] Isobel would also have been responsible for maintaining the fire and cooking, squatting over the hearth to turn bannocks over a griddle or hot stone, and preparing the standard oatmeal and vegetable broth that might be seasoned, on feast days or if an animal died unexpectedly, with some kind of meat. Living in a coastal area, Isobel would have supplemented this grain-based diet with fish and shellfish and, in times of need, she may even have mixed her bannock dough with blood drawn from the veins of cattle. Ale was also made at home, in large wooden vats, and she would have grown a few vegetables, like the ubiquitous colewort, in a 'kail yard' near the cottage.

Second to childcare and the preparation of food, Isobel's other priority would have been the production of cloth, both for personal use (ready-made cloth being too expensive for the poor) and to sell at market. The processes behind cloth manufacture were incredibly time consuming and laborious, this being the logic behind Burt's observation that eighteenth-century Highlanders who brought even 'a small roll of linen' or 'a piece of coarse plaiding' to sell at market would have been deemed 'considerable dealers'.[27] In the case of linen, for example, which the records indicate was being produced by the Laird of Park's tenants in Isobel's lifetime, the flax seed was sown in April in a patch of land near the house and hand-weeded throughout its growing period.[28] When ready, the flax heads would be harvested and then soaked and softened in a 'retting pool' before being beaten with wooden mallets, combed, and then spun into thread on distaffs. The latter was a time-consuming chore that was often performed in transit, folklorist Isabel Grant describing how the spinner 'wound the lint or wool round a longer piece of wood, the distaff, which she could carry in the crook of her arm so that she could spin as she moved about, herding cattle or walking to market, etc'.[29] The spun thread was then taken to a weaver, or woven at home in upright wooden looms that produced narrow lengths of cloth to be finally cut and sewn into garments. The long-drawn-out commitment involved in linen production is well expressed in the first half of a nineteenth-century folk song from Barra, in which a mother, startled with the ominous sight of a fairy woman washing her son's shirt, cries:

Is that the linen (shirt) I planted,
And the linen I plucked?
The linen I shrank,
And the linen I beetled?
The linen I softened,
And the linen I hardened?
The linen I heckled,
And the linen I combed?
Soft and elegant?
The linen I spun,
And the linen I wove?
The linen I steeped,
And the linen I washed?
The linen I decked,
And the linen I sewed?
The linen I bleached
On the grass of the green?
Ochone! ochone . . . ![30]

In addition to these major projects, Isobel would also have been responsible for many other supplementary chores: getting water from the burn or well; scouring pots; making baskets and rush lights; preparing herbal remedies; looking after fowl and any goats or pigs the household may own; herding and minding cattle; collecting sticks from the nearby Lochloy woods (as local women did in subsequent centuries); and visiting the local rivers and streams to wash clothes, the latter being a strenuous process that involved beating cloth upon rocks with a hard wooden beetle or trampling it with the feet. She is also likely to have walked to the nearby mosses to cut and transport peat, for even in the nineteenth century it was still not uncommon to see a local woman walking down the lanes with a hundredweight of peats in a creel on her back. At harvest time, along with all the other women in the farm village, Isobel's services are likely to have been called upon to swing a sickle or follow the cutters to lay and tie the corn into sheaves.

The sheer amount of domestic tasks to be performed, and the number of separate processes needed to transform flax seed into linen and barley grain into bannock, were so laborious that there would have been little opportunity for women like Isobel to do anything else with their hours. People always needed to eat and people always needed clothes and therefore, out of necessity, the same chores had to be repeated day after day, month after month, season after season. The fact that so many people worked on the Sabbath, despite the fact that they were forbidden to do so by the church, is testament to the weight of this constraint. Between 1613 and 1665, for example, the Elgin kirk session fined sabbath-breakers for activities as varied as hanging yarn, drying clothes, bringing fish into town and selling it, spreading muck, driving sheep, quern-grinding corn, running mills, threshing in barns, brewing ale, fishing for trout, brewing aqua-vitae or whisky and carrying loads by horseback, some of the latter 'laid on before sunrise' in an effort to escape censure.[31] The demands of this daily round also meant that women like Isobel would have spent the overwhelming majority of their waking hours in the fermtoun or its immediate environs; working in the dark, smoke-filled houses, the communal barns, the kail yards, folds, infields, outfields and pastures. As such, each farm hamlet amounted to what was, in many ways, a closed world, unaffected by outside events and powered by cycle upon cycle of inter-linked activity. Such conditions, occurring as they did throughout Scotland in this period, conspired to create particularly intense social microclimates.

The Outside World

But although the majority of Isobel's time would have been spent in the farm village and its immediate environs, her trial confessions suggest that she enjoyed some contact with the wider world. Although Lochloy, as part of the Moray Firth Lowlands, was cut off from the rest of Britain by the Grampian Mountains, it was not as remote as many regions of northern Scotland. Three towns were within easy walking distance: Auldearn was just over two miles to the south, Nairn just under three miles to the west and Dyke about four and a half miles to the east. A days ride beyond Nairn took you to Inverness, the capital of the Highlands, and a day's ride in the other direction, beyond Dyke, took you to Elgin, a town once grand enough to earn the sobriquet 'Rome of the North'. The long, straight roads that ran along the coast saw the coming and going of much land traffic between the two Northern cities of Inverness and Aberdeen. And along the coast, boats came into nearby Nairn, as they once did to Lochloy itself.

In her confessions, Isobel describes no less than thirty-four separate places, either cited as the location of events, or as the dwelling places of friends and acquaintances. All of the places named can be found on the map today and are situated, as the crow flies, within a five-mile circumference of Lochloy. While we cannot assume that Isobel was as well-travelled as her confessions suggest (for as we shall see later, it is highly likely that she wove fictional events into her narratives), we can assume that she visited a percentage of the places she described. The wakes, weddings, births and baptisms of relatives and friends would have taken Isobel out of the fermtoun, as would less formal social and church-based engagements. Similarly, although her fermtoun would have been largely self-sufficient, she would sometimes have sought out the services of the many shoemakers, smiths, weavers, tailors, millers, masons, square-wrights and dyers that lived in the parish.[32] In this context Isobel's claim to been familiar with the interior of Alexander Cumming's dye house in Auldearn, and to have sometimes gone to the town on 'som errandis to my neightbo[u]ris' seem believable, as does her claim to have gone down to the seashore to wait for the fishing boats to come in. Like the inhabitants of Dyke one hundred years later, she may have also walked to the sands to collect kelp or rake for cockles when the tide was out.[33]

Given the fact that her husband was involved in the selling of beef, cloth and other items for money, we can also speculate that Isobel may have attended some of the weekly markets in Auldearn and Nairn, to sell food or fuel and buy goods that could not be manufactured at home. Similarly, she is likely to have attended some of the bigger, annual markets and fairs. In 1796, for example, there were three such events in Auldearn, the biggest of which (dedicated to the town's patron saint, Columba) was 'frequented from far and near'.[34] In addition to trading, these events would have offered Isobel the opportunity to absorb new information and witness public spectacles. If she had attended the markets at Nairn, for example, she may have heard the gossip of the women from Fishertown, who used to sit below the town cross to sell their fish, or watched the punishments of criminals reserved – to maximise their function as a crime deterrent – for the days when the town was fullest.[35] If Isobel had been among the crowds at Nairn market in March 1660, she would have witnessed local weaver Donald McJames being forced to stand 'in tyme of open marcat in the jougs and ane clew of yarn in his arms' as a punishment for stealing 'six pounds weight of yarn of a plaiding web'.[36] Or she may have followed the crowds out to the Gallowhill, on the west side of town, to watch an execution, with Patricia Dennison noting that 'When an execution took place here [in Nairn] c.1660 all inhabitants of the town were ordered to attend, with arms.'[37]

The Belief Background: Christianity

In addition to sketching out a picture of the things Isobel may have done, we can also sketch out a picture of the things she may have believed. First and foremost, like almost every other individual living in Scotland in this period, Isobel would have considered herself to be a Christian. Christianity had been well established along the lowlands abutting the Moray Firth since at least the sixth century and by the fifteenth, the Catholic church had, as historian George Bain has emphasized, 'attained to a position of great magnificence' in the area.[38] The cathedral at Elgin with its colourful paintings of the Crucifixion and the Last Judgement was, according to one of its bishops, 'the mirror of the land and the glory of the Kingdom'.[39] The great abbey at Kinloss and the priory at Pluscardine, both – as the crow flies – within a fourteen-mile radius of Auldearn, were also prestigious and the town itself attained additional ecclesiastical status through being the benefice of the Dean of Moray.[40] St Ninian's Well, situated at Newton of Park, southwest of Auldearn, 'enjoyed great celebrity' in the Middle Ages and archaeological records indicate that there was once a chapel or oratory at Lochloy itself.[41] But despite, or maybe because of, the 'great magnificence' of Catholicism in this region, when religious reform, in the form of Calvinist-based Protestantism, swept through the country during the mid-sixteenth century, the new faith quickly took hold. The great ecclesiastical establishments at Kinloss and Pluscardine were demolished, local churches stripped of their images and shrines and Protestant ministers installed in every parish in the county. By the time of Isobel's trial, Nairnshire had not been offi-cially Catholic for nearly 100 years and there is no reason to believe that Isobel, like her parents and grandparents before her, did not consider herself to be a Protestant. What is far more difficult to assess, however, is what 'being a Protestant' would have meant to her.

The Protestantism of the Lairds

On the one hand, we know a good deal about what being a Protestant meant to the Nairnshire ruling class in this period. Like many of the Scottish elite, they were strongly attracted to Calvinism, with this attraction being rooted, in large part, in the fact that its essentially republican ecclesiastical structure provided an efficient blueprint for self-government which appealed to an independent-minded people who had always resented the idea of surrendering their authority to a centralized power, whether situated in London or Rome. But while many lairds throughout Scotland were persuaded by the new faith, among those from Nairnshire devotion was particularly fierce. The Nairnshire gentry were so committed to the cause that when successive English attempts to impose a more moderate Protestantism north of the border forced rifts between those who were prepared to negotiate a religious compromise with the English and those who were not, the Nairnshire lairds, almost to a man, sided with the latter camp. As such, they allied themselves with the religious extremists who, by virtue of their strict adherence to the presbyterian cause as set out in the National Covenants of 1638 and 1643, became known as 'covenanters'.

The covenanting zeal of the Nairnshire lairds is all the more notable for the fact that it flourished in relative isolation. The northern counties of Scotland tended to favour moderate Protestantism and Catholicism, and in this context Nairnshire, along with Caithness and the Orkneys, represented isolated pockets of religious extremism that bucked this trend. The covenanting zeal of the Nairnshire lairds is also notable for the fact that it remained strong for many decades after the re-establishment of episcopacy in 1661, despite the fact that after this date covenanting (or 'nonconformist') practices were officially illegal. Many ministers evicted from their positions because they refused to accept the new religious regime, came to Nairnshire to gain sanctuary, to the extent that the county, according to historian George Bain, became the 'asylum for the exiled Nonconformist ministers of the north.' [42]

It is highly significant that most, if not all of the lairds, ministers and elders either present at or involved in Isobel's interrogations, were ardent covenanters. The two men who are likely to have led the questioning, Harry Forbes and Hugh Rose (the ministers of Auldearn and Nairn respectively), were both devoted to the cause, with the former, as we shall see later, being hand-picked by local lairds for his covenanting piety and his principles evidently being so strong that he refused to accept episcopacy in 1663. Others present at the interrogations, including Alexander Brodie the Younger of Lethen, Alexander Dunbar the session clerk and schoolmaster of Auldearn, Sir Thomas Dunbar of Grange, Hugh Hay of Brightmony and John Innes of Edingeith, were also known to have similar sympathies. In 1670, for example, Lethen was fined by the court of Nairn for 'hearing vagrant preachers in his own house and not keeping the kirk', while Alexander Dunbar's nonconformist activities later saw him sent as a prisoner to the Bass Rock. [43] A number of those not listed as present at the interrogations, but who were still involved in the case, such as Alexander Brodie of Brodie, John Hay of Park and Hugh Campbell of Cawdor, were equally zealous. Brodie was possessed of such zeal that as a young man, in 1640, he stormed Elgin cathedral at the head of a group of accomplices and destroyed its priceless wall paintings, before he went on to win a seat on the general assembly and become one of the emissaries twice-entrusted to travel to the Netherlands to parley with the young Charles Stuart prior to his eventual crowning at Scone.[44] Isobel's landlord, the Laird of Park, was even more committed. After the re-establishment of episcopacy he harboured evicted ministers and was fined and imprisoned in Nairn tolbooth for illegally attending nonconformist meetings. At some point after 1656, his sister married the esteemed covenanting divine, Thomas Hogg, who lived with the family at both Inshoch Castle and the nearby farm of Knockoudie for many years after this date. In 1683–4 Park was imprisoned for thirteen months in the Edinburgh tolbooth and Blackness Castle as an accessory, eventually unproved, to the Rye House Plot.[45]

We are fortunate enough to gain direct insights into the private devotions of these Nairnshire lairds and ministers because a number of them committed their beliefs to paper. Hugh Rose, minister of Nairn, revealed his religiosity in a collection of personal writings, published in book form after his death under the title *Meditations on several interesting subjects* (1762); Sir Hugh Campbell of Cawdor disputed theological matters in his *Essay on the Lord's Prayer*, published in 1704; and Alexander Brodie of Brodie wrote lengthy diaries (published in full by the Spalding Club in 1863) that give us glimpses into both his spiritual life and that of his peers.[46] In these sources we find a faith which was both highly emotional and highly intellectual. A faith characterized by a disconcerting marriage between a passionate, often moving, devotion to God and an equally passionate self-loathing rooted in an obsessive preoccupation with sin. The primary religious observance for the Nairnshire covenanter, as for ardent Protestants throughout Scotland, was an intense introspection through which they attempted to identify sinful thoughts, feelings and actions, and then purify themselves of these through repentance. Through this repentance the individual came closer to the object of their devotion, that is, God or Christ; gained the comfort of knowing that their pious impulses identified them as likely members of God's 'elect'; and, rather more pragmatically, helped them to avoid the wrath that God reserved for recalcitrant sinners. This painstaking process of introspection and repentance was informed, at every level, by the reading of, and taking instruction from, the Bible, and by the faithful adherence to the doctrines and rituals prescribed by the church.

But the Nairnshire lairds did not only reserve their critical religiosity for themselves, but also directed it outward towards others. Since the Reformation in 1560, the Scots had prided themselves on having established a particularly pure form of Protestantism. In a sermon preached at the signing of the National Covenant in Inverness in 1638, for example, minister Andrew Cant claimed memorably that other Protestant nations 'had more of the antichrist than she [Scotland], she more of Christ than they: in their reformation something of the beast was reserved; in ours, not so much as a hoof'.[47] Twenty years later these traces of 'the beast' were still causing offence, with Alexander Brodie of Brodie noting, after attending divine service at Westminster Abbey in 1661, that 'I saw the superstition, bowings, external gesturs, heard ther singing, liturgie, affectation in vesturs, kneeling at the altar, bowing to the elements. Thes ar things which pleas not God'.[48] This conviction of religious superiority was interpreted as a God-given sanction to convert others, and flourished alongside the conviction that those that did not share their particular version of Christianity did not only deserve to be punished by the church, but also to languish in hell. In the hands of many Nairnshire covenanters, in other words, Protestantism became religious fundamentalism.

Isobel's Protestantism

But while we can get a good idea of how Protestantism was experienced by the men who prosecuted Isobel, it is far more difficult to assess how it was experienced by Isobel herself. The impetus behind the Reformation in Scotland, as historians frequently emphasize, came primarily from the ruling classes (with some subsidiary support from the middle classes) and it is still unclear how far the bulk of ordinary people rallied behind the cause. Although we know, for example, that in 1645 James Graham, the Marquis of Montrose, put the town of Nairn to the torch for being 'pro-Covenant', it is still difficult to determine how far his actions were a response to widespread covenanting sympathies among the population at large, and how far they were a response to the persuasions of a handful of leading townsfolk and lairds.[49]

Of some things however, we can be certain. We know that Isobel, like most of her contemporaries, would have been familiar with the inside of her local parish church, with this supposition being supported by her frequent references to the 'kirk of auderne'. And in Isobel's case, we can speculate that she may have been impressed. In the mid-seventeenth century the church of Auldearn stood, as it does today, on the summit of the motte of the old Castle of Pennick, which rises dramatically and steeply in the centre of the town. In Isobel's time this geographical pre-eminence would have been further enhanced by the fact that it was believed, by the locals, to be the site where the sixth-century missionary, St Columba, delivered his first sermons to the town's inhabitants. The church, now ruined but still visible, would have been a rectangular building of reddish stone, with low doorways, small arched windows, and a dim, flagged interior lined with the tombs of local gentry, carved with crude skulls and crossbones, sickles and sheaves of wheat. Outside the building the churchyard, which slopes steeply away from the church on all four sides, commands a breathtaking view embracing both the Moray Firth and the Bay of Cromarty, the whole panorama being encircled in the distance by a ring of purple mountains. Given its unique aspect, which still impresses today despite the encroaching modern houses and neat patchwork field systems, it is not hard to see why the Auldearn church and churchyard seem to have fired Isobel's religious imagination as deeply as did the fairy caverns under the Downie Hill.

As a parishioner of Auldearn, Isobel would have visited the church to witness the christening of her own children, should she have possessed any, or those of her friends and relatives. She would also have followed funeral processions as they wound their way up the steep hill for burial and probably have looked to its windswept graveyard as her own final resting place. Given the fact that there was a resident minister in the parish throughout Isobel's lifetime and that ministry in the town was strong, we can also consider it possible (though by no means certain) that every Sunday morning she put on her best shoes, if she owned any, and walked the two miles to attend divine service. Here, standing on the stone floor or sitting on a wooden stool, she would have listened to the minister deliver his sermons, heard Bible readings, chanted psalms, recited prayers and watched the rituals of repentance. And unless she had been refused the privilege through misconduct, once a year, around Easter time, she is likely to have made a special visit to receive communion. Through this attendance, Isobel would have become acquainted, and even familiar, with the two ministers who officiated at Auldearn during her lifetime: John Brodie (dean of Moray and also uncle to the zealous Alexander Brodie of Brodie), whose long ministry stretched from 1624 until his death in 1655; and Harry Forbes, who was then brought in to replace him and held the post until 1663.

There is also no doubt that Isobel would also have been aware of the church as a disciplinary body. As in all reformed parishes, law and order in Auldearn was maintained through both secular courts and the 'kirk sessions', that is, weekly hearings where the local minister and a group of elders (largely prominent tradesmen and landowners) convened to deal with breaches of church law ranging from adultery, fornication and theft to sabbath-breaking, blasphemy and magic. Isobel may well have found herself called up by the session to answer charges; for as Peter Maxwell-Stuart has noted, the breadth of the latter's disciplinary net meant that 'a large number of people in any given parish could expect to come before the session at some time in their lives'.[50] But she may also have resorted to them for help, with Margo Todd recently emphasizing that the sessions were often effective at resolving inter-personal disputes and functioned, at their best, as a type of early Social Services.

Inner Conformity

But although we can be certain that Isobel saw the church building as a sacred place and the body of the church as the arbiter of community ritual and discipline, this does not tell us about the nature of her personal faith. It does not tell us how far she understood the basic teachings of Protestantism and how far she developed the consciousness of sin, capacity for self-critical introspection and passion to know God, so crucial to the religiosity of the Nairnshire covenanters. Here, we are hindered by the fact that individuals like Isobel, who were of low status and generally illiterate or only partly-literate, did not leave written accounts of their spiritual lives. Like the overwhelming majority of her peers, Isobel did not keep godly diaries, pen meditations on 'interesting subjects' or compile feisty treatises on the Lord's Prayer in the manner of her educated neighbours Alexander Brodie, Hugh Rose and Hugh Campbell of Cawdor.

How far lay religiosity existed in the early modern period, and what form it took, is a matter of ongoing debate among historians. Traditionally, the latter have emphasized that since its emergence in Scotland in the sixth century, the Christian church had, as in other parts of Europe, been primarily concerned with maintaining social stability through the establishment of outward conformity. In other words, it was less concerned with what people thought and believed so long as they behaved properly. In Catholic Europe, as John Arnold has recently claimed, the church's primary consideration was 'the demand to do certain things . . . rather than the demand to know'; and even as late as the nineteenth century in Scotland, according Callum Brown, 'In so far as it was measured at all, religiosity was gauged negatively by demanding avoidance of misdemeanour rather than positively by demanding evidence of enthusiasm or inner piety.'[51]

But more recent historians have emphasized the fact that although outward conformity was important to the reformed church, in the early modern period ministers made more of an effort to encourage inner piety among their parishioners than had their Catholic predecessors, and that these attempts were more successful than has been generally acknowledged. University-educated ministers laboured to make their 'abstract, intellectual religion of the elite' accessible to largely illiterate congregations by dumbing down their sermons: simplifying language, enlivening their discourse with stories and allegories from the Bible and employing basic rhetorical techniques such as repetition.[52] They also sought to encourage lay piety through judicious use of the catechism, a small book that presented the basic doctrines of the reformed church in a question and answer format, and was specifically designed to be accessible. John Craig, author of the first Scottish catechism to come into common use, prefaced his 1581 work with the claim that: 'I have studied to be plain, simple, short, and profitable, not looking so much to the desire and satisfaction of the learned as to the instruction and help of the ignorant.'[53] The church aimed to distribute catechisms widely, with a 1649 act of the assembly commanding that every minister was, 'with the assistance of the elders of their several kirk-sessions, to take course, that in every house, there be at least one copy of the *Shorter* and *Larger Catechism, Confession of Faith,* and *Directory for Family Worship*'.[54] This ecclesiastical largesse was, in principle at least, followed up by annual home examinations in which the minister, visiting each family in turn, determined how well his parishioners understood their catechism, explained any queries they may have, and instructed them in prayer and family worship. These visits also gained extra bite from the fact that the church granted ministers the right to refuse annual communion to those who did not know their catechism well enough. There is no doubt that these duties were taken seriously in the Auldearn region. In March 1656, Alexander Brodie reminds himself to:

> mind to the minister [William Falconer of Dyke], that a day may be appointed to consider, how the peopl profit in knowledg. 2. What car[e] is taken in families to teach ther children and servants the grounds of religion; for mani ar slaik heer, great and small. 3. How the families may be visited, and inquiri taken, if they pray and examin ther famili. 4. To look out the overtours, interogatours, and questions set doun by the General Assembli for visiting families and catechizing.[55]

It is clear that the church's efforts to foster piety among the general laity were not wholly unsuccessful. As Margo Todd has recently emphasized, entries in kirk session records concerning requests for better access to sermon teachings give us glimpses of genuine religious enthusiasm. In Elgin in 1658, Marjorie Man, wife of a skinner, made a request 'desyreing the stap that goes in to the readers dask to sit in to hear the word becos scho hes ane impediment in her hearing'. In the same parish, five years later, local bailie John Dunbar asked to be able to 'erect ane seat in the roume betwixt James Hepburnes desk and the north church doore for the better hearing of God's word to him, his wyfe, children and servants'.[56] That some sermons clearly hit their mark is evinced by the fact that 'multitudes of all ranks would have crossed several ferries every Lord's day' to hear Robert Bruce preach, while his sermons delivered at Inverness allegedly drew people from as far afield as Ross and Sutherland. Alternatively, observers noted of John Welsh, John Knox's son-in-law, that 'no man could hardly hear him, and forbear Weeping: His Conveyance was so affecting'.[57]

Lacklustre Faith

But despite these advances, there is also much evidence that in the Auldearn region, as in the rest of Scotland, these valiant attempts to foster piety were an uphill struggle. Time and time again the Nairnshire covenanters bemoaned the ignorance and lack of proper devotion in their congregations. Brodie lamented that 'The tyms ar ill; [and] godlines litl regarded'; Hugh Campbell of Cawdor that 'the Generality of the people are so ignorant in matters of faith, and so far from the strict practice of moral dutys which the Laws of humane society require'; and Hugh Rose, the minister of Nairn, that:

> Men call the Bible a book of truth, but carry as if it were a romance made up of lies and stories. Oh, men do not believe, they do not rest upon the word of God as true, nor upon God as the God of truth that cannot lie. Why is the scripture so little read, so often read and heard in vain? Why are so many sermons preached, backed with scripture-authority, which do not prevail with sinners, but because Gods truth and veracity are not believed?[58]

The assessments of these men were not just the result of exaggerated fundamentalist imaginations. There is plenty of evidence to suggest that throughout seventeenth-century Scotland, and in the Highlands in particular, many ordinary people were ignorant even of the basics of Protestantism (that is, the ability to recite the Lords Prayer, the Commandments and the Apostles' Creed). In 1595 Perth's elders found that 'sundry within this congregation are found ignorant of the principles and grounds of religion notwithstanding that there is a yearly trial and examination'; while in 1608 the Innerwick session found 'the most part of the people wanted the commands, belief [Creed] and Lord's Prayer'.[59] Even the sons of godly lairds could fail in this respect, with diarist Alexander Brodie being shocked to find, in later life, that his ten-year-old grandson had never learned the Shorter Catechism.[60]

Some of this ignorance can be attributed to faults in the ministry. Then, as now, religious vocations did not always coincide with charismatic personalities or rhetorical skills, and sermons and explanations of the catechism were often lacklustre and dry. According to Brodie just about every minister in the Auldearn region suffered from this failing. He consistently complains about the shortcomings of William Falconer, minister of Dyke, and on two occasions subjects both Harry Forbes and Hugh Rose to the same treatment, claiming of the former that he 'kept a common form of catechizing, and this I thoght not edefying' and of the latter that his 'gifts be not great'. That Brodie's assessments were not wholly disingenuous, at least where Rose was concerned, is suggested by the fact that the latter, by his own admission, suffered from great anxiety while 'in the very performance' of public duties.[61] Conversely, Brodie's neighbour, Hugh Campbell of Cawdor, complained that ministers could fail their parishioners by delivering sermons which, despite the imperative to simplify language, were unintelligible; noting that young clergymen 'abounding in their own sense' sometimes used expressions 'which no man can make sense of. Some speaking what they understood not themselves, others what none of their hearers understood, better than the Commons do the Popish worship in an unknown tongue.'[62]

Similarly, though widely distributed, the catechism was not always as effective as desired. As anyone who has ever attempted to read a seventeenth-century Protestant catechism will know, even the shorter versions specifically designed to be 'short and profitable' for the 'help of the ignorant' can confound even the most enthusiastic intellect. It is hard to imagine what semi-literate Scottish peasants made of such texts, and one suspects that it was not very much. In addition, the annual ministerial examination designed to clarify these texts did not always take place with the regularity the church may have desired. In Elgin, in 1656, ministers declared that 'in respect of the numbers of their communicants and vastness of bounds' they 'could not doe their dutie in catechiseisng and visitatione of families and desyred the presbytry to tak it to their consideratione and ease them of their unsupportable burthen'.[63] Attempts to rectify the situation must have largely failed, for ministers were complaining of much the same thing over eighty years later.[64] We can assume that Harry Forbes and Hugh Rose, as ministers of Auldearn and Nairn, faced similar problems.

Disinterest and the Laity

But the prevailing religious ignorance among Isobel's contemporaries was not only the consequence of inefficient, lacklustre or over-obscure teaching. Many people seem to have been ill-informed for the simple reason that, as Brodie put it, they did not 'desir to know the Lord and be instructed'.[65] Some tried to avoid church attendance, and in order to counter this absenteeism the kirk stooped to the undignified lengths of sending out elders as 'searchers' to snoop around houses and fields, looking in windows and behind hedgerows to find those people who 'loathed that Exercise [divine service]'.[66] People also avoided communion – despite the centrality of the rite – and examinations on the catechism, the Elgin session being informed, in 1661, that 'many wilfullie absented themselves both from the Sacrament of the Lords Supper and also from the catechising frequentlie'.[67] The fact that parishioners were fined if they did not attend divine service also suggests that a proportion of regular attendees were likely to have been motivated by the desire to avoid censure, as much as by piety.

Levels of lay enthusiasm, or rather lack of it, were also reflected in church behaviour. Although some parishioners, like Elgin's John Dunbar, were so keen to catch every syllable of God's word that they asked to erect seats nearer to the pulpit, others were disciplined by the sessions for sleeping during divine service (with some even going so far as to lie down on the church floor). Several records also state that women were prohibited from covering their faces with their plaids, in case they may be tempted to doze off undetected.[68] At the other end of the spectrum, the congregation could express their lack of interest by becoming riotous, and by gaming, fighting and bringing dogs into church. In Elgin in 1632 three men were reprimanded for 'ther turbulent and loud speaches in the tyme of divyne service', while in 1650, a woman was reprimanded because 'in the midst of the last prayer [she] most contemptuouslie did ryse and raise up with hir a gryt number of men and wemen in tumultuous way so that the minister was forced to intermit prayer'.[69] In a Caithness parish, in the same decade, the sessions noted that 'some barbarous people does laugh at thes that sing the psalmes in ye kirk', and that many other 'ignorant people did slight the word, and wald be goeing in the church yaird in tyme of sermone'.[70]

Obviously, such behaviour does not indicate a lack of faith per se. Even if a parishioner, such as Isobel, had minimal knowledge of reformed doctrine, and even if she dozed off beneath her plaid during the sermon, or laughed at those who sang the psalms, this does not mean that she would have rejected Christianity or the reformed church. If she harboured overt criticisms of the latter, these were more likely to have been associated with the credibility of particular ministers, or reservations or confusions concerning certain aspects of doctrine, or dislike of certain elements of church law, as opposed to any lack of identity as a reformed Christian. But what these irreverent behaviours do suggest is that ordinary people like Isobel may have measured and inhabited their faith in very different ways to their ministers. As John Arnold says with regard to medieval lay religiosity, the fact that people were ignorant of Christian doctrines 'is not to suggest that they were any less "Christian" because of it. But it is to note that what constituted belief for these people, contrary to the pedagogic instincts of churchmen, was not essentially to do with the contents of prayers or the tenets of faith'.[71]

Folk Superstitions

Isobel's Protestantism, and that of many of her peers, would not only have differed from that of the lairds and ministers by virtue of its theological naivety, but also because it incorporated into itself a variety of unorthodox, or as they were often termed by Protestants, 'superstitious' beliefs and practices. Most of the latter were rooted in residual Catholicism that was itself, in turn, a more or less harmonious amalgam between the teachings of the early and medieval church and the non-Christian beliefs and practices that preceded them. In seventeenth-century Nairnshire, as in other Protestant regions in this period, residual Catholicism was predominantly derived from the memories and accumulated customs of the people themselves (as opposed to the ministry of recusant Catholic priests) and as such, we can subsume it here, along with other miscellaneous superstitious practices, under the term 'folkloric'. The unorthodox folkloric beliefs of the seventeenth-century Scots can be divided into two basic over-lapping categories: devotion to spirits (most notably saints, fairies and the dead) and attachment to magic.

Devotion to Spirits: Saints and Fairies

In the medieval period, devotion to the saints was widespread, and rooted in the belief that these deceased holy men and women could employ their supernatural power (or intercede with a higher spiritual being) to help their supplicants with a variety of issues; ranging from healing the sick and finding lost goods to protecting against enemies and bestowing general good fortune. Although the Protestant church condemned the petitioning or worshipping of any other being other than God as idolatry (a sin that contravened the first Commandment: *Thou shalt have no other gods before me*), there is plenty of contemporary evidence to suggest that throughout the seventeenth century many ordinary Scots continued to make pilgrimages to holy wells and springs and make offerings and prayers to saints. And despite the extremism of the local lairds, Nairnshire seems to have been little different in this respect. As late as 1671 Alexander Brodie recorded in his diary that he regretted trying to cure himself of the stone by drinking some water from a nearby holy well because the 'common peopl misunderstood and constructed it as if I placd som holiness in the well, or saints, or creaturs, and they took occasion to strenthen themselves in ther superstition'.[72]

Fairy belief was also widespread. Rooted in the animism of the pre-Christian Scots, fairy belief was perhaps most truly folkloric of all popular belief systems by virtue of the fact it had never been dispensed from the pulpit or systematized in texts, but had survived into the seventeenth century through purely oral transmission, handed down from generation to generation at the hearth and in the workplace. It is difficult to gauge the nature and intensity of early modern fairy belief because, with the exception of one slim volume written by Aberfoyle minister Robert Kirk in 1691, and scattered references in witch records and antiquarian writings, they went largely unrecorded; remaining hidden, to quote Larner's memorable phrase, in the 'secret, uncharted areas of peasant exchange' for a further 200 years before being uncovered and celebrated by nineteenth-century folklorists.[73] But nevertheless, contemporary research is increasingly emphasizing the fact that fairy belief was strong and widespread in the period, with Cowan and Henderson (*Scottish Fairy Belief*) recently stating categorically that 'What we can prove is that many Scots people, who lived mainly in the period from c.1450 to c.1750, had no doubt that fairies actually existed . . . They were a part of everyday life, as real to people as the sunrise, and as incontrovertible as the existence of God.'[74] Isobel's confessions, as we shall see, make it abundantly clear that fairy belief was thriving in seventeenth-century Auldearn.

In early modern Scotland the term 'fairy' seems to have covered a wide range of spirits and supernatural beings who were condemned, or whose existence was disputed, by the church. And among the most controversial of these were 'spirits of the dead'. Although the reformed church taught that the dead were not able re-appear to the living after death, people often claimed that they had seen deceased friends and relatives among the fairies or, less commonly, that a deceased friend or relative *was* a fairy. Both fairies and the spirits of the dead who consorted with them resembled saints in the sense that they were believed to possess supernatural powers and could be petitioned for a variety of benefits, but they differed from their holier counterparts in that they displayed more moral ambivalence and enjoyed a more ambiguous relationship with Christianity. This dissonance was further reflected in the fact that these categories of spirit did not live in heaven, but in fairyland or 'elphame', where they adopted a strange, simulacrum of human life: feasting under fairy hills, hunting with horses and packs of hounds, and following the fairy king and queen on their nocturnal processions through houses and across the night skies.

The Many Faces of Magic

Popular attachment to magic was equally strong and deeply rooted, although here some clarification of terminology is needed. Although distinctions have been made between magic and religion since classical times, among modern scholars the usefulness of the term 'magic' is hotly disputed. The current majority view, among historians, is that the term denotes anything defined as such by the reigning religious authorities; with the added qualification that in any culture, magical practices and beliefs tend to be less organised than those defined as religious. In other words, according to this definition, in early modern Scotland magic was whatever the church decided it was to be. But although this exposition is perhaps the most theoretically accurate, for our purposes there is still some mileage in the traditional, but now frequently discarded, view that magic can be distinguished from religion on the basis that it denotes a largely coercive as opposed to supplicatory method of dealing with the supernatural.

Many of the beliefs defined as 'magical' in witchcraft and sorcery records were coercive in the sense that they were based on an essentially animist conception of a connected universe: that is, the belief that everything that exists is linked by invisible and amoral occult forces, and that by moving one element you can mechanically affect another, although the distance between them be as great as that between a star and a herb; the flight of a crow and the hour of a man's death; or the agitation of a bowl of water and a storm at sea. In seventeenth-century Auldearn, as in any place where this world-view survives, it was believed that a man could gain benefit through the correct manipulation of these forces and correspondences. In other words, he could play the universe like a piano. The correct notes were chimed either directly through certain words or actions (which we can term here 'basic magic') or indirectly through commanding spiritual beings to create the effect by proxy (which we can term here 'spirit-aid magic'). In early modern Scotland the reformed church associated magical rites with both overt Catholicism and popular folkloric belief and practice, including commerce with spirits such as saints, fairies and the dead. But to its eternal frustration, it could not prevent many people from also approaching their Protestant devotions from a magical perspective: attending divine service and communion in the belief that this would automatically confer supernatural protection, and using reformed prayers in a mechanical or coercive manner.

Magical Specialists

While it was popularly believed that anyone could perform magical rites, certain individuals were seen to be specialists in the field, and as such were called upon to employ their superior abilities to benefit their communities. Among the ordinary laity, ministers were often credited with magical powers, for many made little distinction between the ability to perform miracles (defined by the church as acts of God) and the ability to perform magic. Many of the 'men, wives, bairns, rich, noble, and all others' who flocked to be blessed by the renowned minister, Patrick Simsone of Cramond, as he lay on his deathbed would not have quibbled or cared whether the power that flowed through the old man's hands had a 'miraculous' or 'magical' origin.[75] However, magical skills were also widely attributed to a variety of specialist lay folk. The latter went under a variety of names and were generally associated with particular areas of magical expertise, with distinctions often being made, for example, between 'charmers', 'seers', 'sorcerers' and so on. For the purposes of the present discussion we will be denoting all magical specialists, whatever their area of expertise, by the terms 'popular magical practitioners' and 'cunning folk' interchangeably. Although some scholars have associated the term 'cunning folk' with particular forms of magical practice, it remains useful as a less-corrupted variant of the generalist term 'wise man or woman', and shall be used in its broadest capacity here.[76]

While popular magical practitioners or cunning folk existed outside the umbrella of the church (not even possessing the 'extra-institutional role' of the mendicant minister or holy man) they could enjoy a surprising degree of popularity and authority in their community: assuming a particularly important role in the diagnosis and cure of sickness, the finding of lost goods, divination of the future and the performance of counter-magic. But despite the esteem in which they were often held, magical practitioners were also feared. Because the occult forces manipulated by the practitioner were, as we have already seen, morally neutral, and because many of the spirits with which they negotiated were morally ambivalent, any practitioner could theoretically direct these forces and spirits toward harmful as well as beneficent ends. As a consequence, although seventeenth-century cunning man Sandie Hunter, who also went by the nickname 'Hattaraik', was famous throughout East Lothian for 'his Charming and cureing of diseases in Men and Beasts', contemporary commentators noted that when he went from house to house begging 'none durst refuse Hattaraik an alms, rather for his ill, than his good'.[77] A similar paradox underpins the refrain, running through many witchcraft records, that the suspect is charged with both the 'laying on and taking off diseases'.[78] And of course it is here, where magical forces were at their most ambiguous, that the figure of the magical practitioner merged into that of the witch.

28

As with magic generally, in early modern Scotland it was believed that individuals could perform harmful magic or *maleficium*, either independently or with the help of spirits. In the former case, its effects were set in motion purely mechanically, through the performance of basic magical ritual (the latter ranging, in complexity, from a simple curse to the performance of lengthy physical and verbal rites). In the latter, they were engendered through gaining advice from, or through being in the company of, spirits (the latter predominantly, although not exclusively, being defined as demons, either in the sense of *a* Devil or *the* Devil). Beliefs surrounding spirit-aid *maleficium* had been of intense interest to the church since the early Middle Ages, and been progressively discussed, defined and systematized in theological works. As a result of these developments, by the early modern period, 'demonological witchcraft', as it has since been termed by historians, had widely come to be associated with two iconic events: the demonic pact (a bargain in which the witch gave her or his soul to the Devil and renounced Christianity in return for magical powers or benefits); and the witches' sabbath (a gathering of witches, in the presence of the Devil, where festivities were enjoyed and *maleficium* performed). But although beliefs about both basic and spirit-aid *maleficium* were widespread in early modern Scotland, the degree to which ordinary people, including Isobel, actually practised harmful magic or internalized elite demonological ideas, is something that we shall be returning to many times during the course of this book.

The War Against Superstition

This brief overview of the contemporary popular mind makes it clear that for women like Isobel, the teachings of the church would have occupied a mental landscape peopled with a wide variety of unorthodox beliefs. Protestant creeds jostled for space alongside Catholic prayers and charms; God and Christ competed for popularity with saints, fairies and the dead; and the pious exercises of prayer and repentance were performed alongside magical command and invocation.

But although this idiosyncratic, hybrid version of Protestantism may not have been a problem for women like Isobel, it was most definitely a problem for the reformed church. Isobel and her contemporaries had the misfortune to live in a period where, throughout Europe, the church was making unprecedented attempts to impose religious uniformity on the general populace. In Nairnshire, as in many parts of Scotland at this time, this acculturation process was achieved through emphasis on the conformity of worship and the censure of unorthodox belief and practice. This prohibition was directed toward all forms of residual Catholic belief and ritual, among them being the celebration of saints' days and holy days, visits to sacred springs and wells and the worship of or communication with saints, angels or the dead. Also pertinent, with regard to our analysis of Isobel, is the fact that the church also vigorously sought to censure all forms of magical practice, both basic and spirit-aid, beneficent and maleficent.

As repositories and disseminators of these beliefs and practices, magical practitioners were particularly vulnerable to this censure, and ministers and elders of the church were charged to be constantly on the look out for them. In the formula laid down for the visitation of kirks in the diocese of Dunblane in 1586, for example, inspectors were urged to 'inquire if there be any witches, sorcerers, passers in pilgrimage to chapels or wells, setters out of fires on saints' eves, or keepers of superstitious holy days'.[79] If ministers became alerted to a suspect, they pressed their congregations for more evidence about their activities. In 1661 the Elgin presbytery, cognisant of three magical practitioners operating in the locality, stated that they 'thought it fitte that intimation should be made by all the brethren from their several pulpits that if any person could clear any thinge of charmeing and witchcraft against the forsaid persons' they should come forward.[80] Some of those denounced as magical practitioners in kirk session minutes never appear in the records again and in these cases we can presume that insufficient evidence was compiled to bring a case against them. Others were brought before the session to be questioned in more detail, with more serious or complex cases being handed over to a higher authority, such as the presbytery or synod, the assizes, or locally-organised courts authorized through commissions. These – what seem to us – improbable crimes were taken very seriously, and according to the witchcraft acts of 1563 and 1604, both those who practised magic and those who consulted magical practitioners deserved the death penalty. In reality, those practitioners who were found guilty of performing purely beneficent magic often escaped with a fine, flogging, command to perform public penance and/or banishment from the parish. Those practitioners found guilty of performing witchcraft, on the other hand, were much more likely to receive a sentence of death.

Hunting Witches

In sixteenth and seventeenth-century Scotland, as in many other parts of Europe, there was an unprecedented increase in the number of men and women prosecuted for witchcraft, with the recent Survey of Scottish Witchcraft estimating that, on the basis of the sources currently available to us, at least 3,837 people were accused of the crime between 1563 and 1736 (although the real figure is likely to have been higher than this).[81] The numbers of Scottish persecutions and the savagery with which they were conducted did not reach the levels they did in some other parts of Europe, but nevertheless they were about four times the European average and were higher and more punitive than those taking place in England over the same period. The Scots' deeper commitment to religious uniformity, born out of their ideal to achieve a 'pure' form of Protestantism that contained 'not so much as a hoof' of the anti-Christ, is largely responsible for this difference in English and Scottish prosecution levels.

As in the rest of Europe, Scottish prosecutions came in waves, the most notable of these occurring in 1590–1, 1597, 1629–30, 1649–50 and 1661–2.[82] The reasons for these escalations are an ongoing matter of debate, but it is clear that they occurred in response to both national and local factors. Changes in legislation, political or military conflicts and even the weather, have long been argued to affect trial rates but recent micro-studies have increasingly emphasized that the predilections of individual ministers and landowners were also paramount. Whatever the political climate or success of the latest harvest, without the presence of a local authority figure prepared to take an accusation seriously and see it through the judicial process a witch trial could not take place.[83]

The years 1661–2 saw the final and most extreme wave of witchcraft prosecution in early modern Scotland. Although the severity of this wave still demands full explanation, many scholars have speculated that the collapse of the Commonwealth was likely to have played a role here. The English judges who sat alongside the Scots during the Interregnum were more lenient than the latter, with regard to both magic and witchcraft, and as a consequence fewer accusations were pursued. Furthermore, as Levack has emphasized, other changes to the judicial system, such as the disbanding of the privy council and stricter governmental supervision of local courts are also likely to have reduced the likelihood that a suspected witch would be brought to trial.[84] Given the fact that a reservoir of grievance and suspicion is likely to have built up over this period, it is speculated that when the Scots were left to their own devices after the Restoration this backlog, combined with the Scots' desire (on both a regional and national level) to re-assert control over their country, conspired to generate an increase in witch prosecutions. Although this unusually severe wave of persecution was felt most keenly in the East Lothian Lowlands, it also emerged in many other regions in Scotland, including the north-east, and a series of trials took place along the Moray Firth, from Inverness through to Elgin. The Auldearn region saw at least seven witches tried during this period, and among these was Isobel Gowdie of Lochloy.

Isobel's Route to the Pyre

The first record we have pertaining to Isobel's case is her confession, recorded in Auldearn on 13 April 1662, by the notary public, John Innes, and witnessed by the ministers of Auldearn and Nairn and at least twelve local lairds and church elders. The fact that these gentlemen had come together to question Isobel in the presence of a notary suggests that by this stage her case was already believed to be serious and that her interrogators were looking to secure a conviction. But the route that Isobel took to reach this point is less clear.

It is possible that, like most witchcraft suspects in the period, Isobel was first brought to the attention of the authorities through the accusations of a neighbour, although as we shall explore in more detail in CHAPTER SEVEN, it is also conceivable that her minister, Harry Forbes, or her landlord, the Laird of Park (or members of his family) may have been instrumental in bringing her to trial. The accusations are likely to have been raised, in the first instance, at the local kirk sessions that, as Stuart Macdonald has recently emphasized, were frequently responsible for setting the witch-prosecuting process in motion.[85] But since the session records for Auldearn have not survived from this period we cannot verify this. It is also possible that Isobel's accusers may have taken their grievance to their local laird or his officers, perhaps John Hay of

Park or Alexander Brodie of Lethen, at their local baron court (a franchise court that enabled a landowner to deal with estate issues, including disputes among tenants). Although we know that the Hays of Park had a baron court in this period, again no documentation for this period survives. But either way, upon accusation, Isobel would have been called in for further questioning.

Recent scholars such as Maxwell-Stuart have emphasized that witchcraft cases could take a long time to come to fruition, and it is highly likely that the initial accusations against Isobel were made some time previous to her first formal confession on 13 April. Although we have no evidence for this either way, it is perhaps pertinent that while in London on 24 March 1662 (nearly three weeks before this date) Alexander Brodie noted in his diary that 'I heard from Scotland that ther was a great discoveri of witchcraft in the parish of Dyke; and in my land, they had purposed evil against my son and his wyfe'.[86] Although Isobel does not mention Brodie's son or wife in her confessions, given the fact that Lochloy bordered on the parish of Dyke and that many of the accomplices and meeting-places described by Isobel are located in the latter parish, and given the fact that Brodie, as we shall see later, seems to have subsequently become involved in Isobel's prosecution, it is possible that this was an early reference to her case, or one of the suspects involved in it. In this context, given the fact that news of the 'discoveri' would have probably taken a number of weeks to reach him in London, we can speculate that accusations had been made and pursued well over a month before Isobel's first confession.

During these early days, Isobel would not necessarily have been in danger. Contrary to popular misconception, the majority of witchcraft accusations in Scotland, even during the waves of persecution, went no further than this stage. Upon further questioning and cross-examination of witnesses a suspect would be acquitted or, if found guilty of a minor crime, given a light reprimand. But if the case were considered serious enough to potentially warrant the death penalty, the suspect, if they had not been imprisoned already, would have been taken into custody and the inquiry taken on to the next stage. These more serious cases could either be referred on to the presbytery (if the initial hearings had occurred at the session) or pursued through a local investigation where 'ministers and elders went frequently with a notary to the place where the accused were confined and laboured to bring them to confession'.[87] Even at this stage, charges could still be dropped, but if the interrogators believed they had gathered enough evidence of the witch's guilt, they could either apply for the witch to be tried at the central court of justiciary at Edinburgh or one of the circuit courts which travelled round the country, or they could apply to the privy council to gain a 'commission of justiciary' which gave them licence to try the witch locally. The second option, being the cheapest, was the most common, and seems to have been the one pursued in Isobel's case.

Isobel's confessions are essentially the records of four formal interrogations, each about two weeks apart, that took place in Auldearn over a six-week period between 13 April and 27 May. At nearby Inshoch Castle, on the day after Isobel's first interrogation, one of the women she named as an accomplice, Janet Breadheid of neighbouring Belmakeith, also gave a confession. Although, like Isobel, Janet is likely to have undergone further interrogations only her first confession has survived among Hay's papers. It does not seem to have taken the interrogators long to become convinced of both women's guilt, for at some point between Isobel's first and last interrogations they sent some, if not all, of the confessions to Edinburgh to obtain a commission to try them. Six weeks after her fourth and final interrogation the following statements were written on the document bearing Isobel's second confession. On the reverse we have:

> Edgr 10 July 1662 Considered + found relevt be the justice dept Tak ceare of this peaper See the justice deputs judgement of it shove these to the Commissioneris.[88]

And below the confession itself, alongside the witness signatures, we have:

> hawing read & considered the confessions of Isabel gowdie within conteaned as paction with Sathan Renunciation of Baptisme, with dyvers malefices, I find that a co[m]mission may be verie justlie (*word unreadable*) for hir last tryall A Colville.

That Colville recommended the granting of a commission to try Isobel on this date is also supported by the following entry in the register of the privy council in July of the same year:

> Commission is direct to Sir Hew Campbell of Calder [Cawdor], shireff principall of Nairn, Hew Rosse of Kilraik [Kilravock], Thomas Dumbar of Grang, Alexander Dumbar of Both, William Dollace of Contray, William Sutherland of Kinstuir, Robert Cumin of Altar, David Dumbar of Dunfaill, the provest and baylies of Nairne, and Jon Stewart, shireff deputt of Murray, or any fyve of them, to to try and judge Jonet Braidheid and Issobell Goudy in Aulderne, who have confest witchcraft . . . [89]

The evidence strongly suggests that Alexander Brodie of Brodie, who was in Edinburgh during this period, was involved in Isobel's commission application. On 17 June the latter stated in his diary that: 'I read the depositions of Park's witches'. Four days later he followed this up with the claim that he was 'exercisd in ordouring the depositions of witches, and saw how grossli the Devel fooled thes poor wretches'; and on the next day he recorded that, '[I] met with Mr. Alex[ander] Colville, and conferrd anent witches'.[90] Although Brodie does not specifically mention Isobel or Janet by name, nor identify Alexander Colville as the justice depute, the timing of these events and the fact that he refers to the suspects as 'Park's witches', when taken in combination with his close links to many of the people involved in the prosecution, strongly suggests that the depositions Brodie referred to were those of the two Auldearn suspects. Moreover, Brodie's claim that his Auldearn kinsman 'Lethen' came to Edinburgh at around this time; that he dined with him three days before reading the depositions; and that he prayed with him to 'lay to hart the prevailing of the Devil by witchcraft' on the following day, points to the latter as a likely courier.[91] Brodie does not make it clear whether it was the older or younger Laird of Lethen who joined him in Edinburgh at this time, but either way, given the fact that the latter was present at Isobel's first interrogation we can assume that he received a verbal eye-witness account of the events that took place. The fact that Brodie was 'ordouring the depositions' suggests that either the Lethen lairds, the Laird of Park, or Harry Forbes had sought out his opinion and perhaps asked him to sort and present the confessions to Colville. This thesis draws support from the fact that Brodie enjoyed high status in the Auldearn area, and also from the fact that all four men sought out Brodie's help on a number of other occasions.[92] If these assumptions are correct, then we can presume that Isobel's and Janet's confessions reached Edinburgh as early as mid-June, less than three weeks after Isobel's last confession was made.

We do not, unfortunately, know what happened next, nor do we know Isobel's ultimate fate. Some historians have recently suggested that Isobel may have been acquitted on the grounds of mental instability. But as we shall reveal, the research undertaken for this book suggests that the most likely chain of events was that after Colville's report was brought back to Auldearn, in mid-July, Isobel and Janet were tried at a locally organised court, found guilty and sentenced to death.[93] Within the next few days, they were probably taken by cart to the Gallowhill, just outside Nairn, persuaded to make a show of public repentance and then strangled and burnt. While this is the most likely scenario there is an outside chance that Brodie's diary entry of 30 September – 'My Son went to Auldern to see the trial of the witch Bandon; who adheard to her confessions, and was condemnd' – may have referred to either Isobel or Janet under another name, if only for the reason that Bandon, like Isobel and Janet, seems to have controversially named the local school dame, Bessie Hay, as her accomplice.[94] But given the fact that witches were usually tried and (barring pregnancy) executed soon after the commission was granted, and given the fact that Bandon was tried over two months after the latter had been secured for Isobel's and Janet's trial and over four months after the former's last confession, this seems highly unlikely.

Isobel's Imprisonment

We can be almost certain that during the six-week period between her first and last confessions, Isobel was imprisoned. And given the fact that all four confessions state that they were given 'at Auldearn' we can assume that, like the witch Bandon three months later, she was restrained in the town itself; either in a barn or outhouse, the church steeple or, as was most likely, the local tolbooth. In the latter case, we can assume her prison to have been a rudimentary and badly-maintained building, as was its contemporary equivalent in Nairn, although in Isobel's case it seems to have been sufficient for its purpose. Unlike two witches held at Forres the following year Isobel did not, to our knowledge, break out of her prison and attempt to escape.[95]

We can be fairly certain that Isobel would have been kept in solitary confinement. For obvious reasons, she would have been prevented from making contact with any witchcraft accomplices, and this is probably why Janet Breadheid was interrogated and presumably imprisoned, at Inshoch. Contemporary documents recording how family members were fined for attempting to visit warded witchcraft suspects also suggests that she was probably denied contact, or only given severely limited contact, with friends and relatives.[96] Other interested parties, however eminent, would have been similarly restrained. When Brodie was asked to go down to visit the witch Bandon in Auldearn in October of the same year, he claimed that he 'had som reluctancie lest I should be found out of my line and calling . . . knowing that it was propper onli for thes that hav the commission'.[97] As Brodie's comment illustrates, it seems likely that the only people permitted open access to Isobel would have been those with the commission to try her, and any male 'watchers', should she have had them (the latter being further discussed in CHAPTER THREE). We can also assume that Isobel was periodically visited by the local minister, Harry Forbes, who may have been despatched by those involved to give her religious counsel, as he was with regard to two witches imprisoned in Forres the following year.[98] Despite these restrictions, however, we can speculate that a few clandestine visitors may have slipped through the net. Nairn burgh records reveal that eight years later, when John Smith was imprisoned in Nairn tolbooth on burglary charges, his accomplices Alexander Chisolm and George Houshold were both so anxious to persuade him not to confess to his crimes that they had 'severall tymes spoken him for yt effect under the silence of night throgh the prison door'.[99] Similarly, despite his scruples about not having the commission to try the witch Bandon, Brodie still went to Auldearn in an attempt to visit her, though unsuccessfully in this case.[100]

We know that during this period Isobel's solitary confinement was punctuated by at least four formal interrogations. The confessions list the presence of between eight and fourteen named witnesses apiece, all elders of the church, local lairds and ministers, many of whom also signed the confessions after they had been formally written up by the notary. But the fact that the confessions also list 'diverse utheris witnessis', 'many utheris witnesses' and, in Janet Breadheid's case, 'a great multitud of all sortis of uther persones' suggests that many more were present. We can assume that some of these were prosecution witnesses, that is, neighbours who may have first accused Isobel, or who had come forward with a grievance against her and who were called in to be questioned or confront Isobel directly with their accusations. Some named witnesses were clearly present at all, or nearly all, of her four interrogations, among these being the minister of Auldearn, Harry Forbes (present at all four); the minister of Nairn, Hugh Rose (present at least three); and Hugh Hay of Brightmony and John Weir of Auldearn (present at all four). Others, such as William Dallas, the sheriff depute of Nairn and Alexander Dunbar, the schoolmaster and session clerk of Auldearn, attended only one or two. We can assume that all of the interrogations took place, as did the second, at about two or three in the afternoon, allowing time for these many witnesses to travel in from the neighbouring estates and towns.

We shall be exploring the thorny question as to whether Isobel was tortured or maltreated in CHAPTER THREE. But even putting aside this issue for the moment, we are still left with rather a bleak picture. An illiterate farmer's wife, wrenched from her family, her fermtoun and her daily round of domestic activities, and thrown into a dark, barred room in Auldearn. Here, perhaps for the first time in her life, she was forced to endure extended periods alone, and her hands – accustomed since childhood to a ceaseless round of milking, kneading, digging, weeding and spinning – would have felt strangely still. Four times, we can see her scrabbling to her feet, defensively wrapping her dirty plaid around her, as she is shocked into alertness by the sudden intrusion, into her solitude, of a crowd of local men armed with quills and parchment and penetrating questions. Given the emotive nature of her subject matter, and the looming prospect of the death penalty, we can assume that the ensuing interrogatorial sessions were heated, noisy, and intense. These would have been the unfavourable conditions in which, on 13 April 1662, Isobel Gowdie, wife of John Gilbert of Lochloy, first opened her mouth and stepped into the history books.

2

The Confessions

Confession One

At Aulderne the threttein day of aprill 1662 yeiris In p[rese]nce of Master harie
fforbes mini[ste]r of the gospell at aulderne William dallas of cantrey Sh[e]reffe
deput of the Sh[e]reffdom of nairne thomas dunbar of graing allexr brodie yo[unge]r
of leathin allexr dunbar of boath James dunbar appeirant therof hew hay of brightmanney hew hay of newtowne william dunbar of clune and david smith and Johne
weir in auldern witnessis to the confession efterspe[cife]it spoken furth of the
mowth of Issobell gowdie spous to Johne gilbert in lochloy

The quhilk day In p[rese]nce of me Johne Innes no[ta]r publict and witnessis abownamet all under subs[cri]wand the said Issobell gowdie appeiring penetent for hir
haynows sines of witch craft and th[a]t she haid bein ower long in th[a]t service
w[i]thout any compulsitoris proceidit in hir confessione in maner efterfollowing: to
Witt:

as I wes goeing betuixt the townes of drumdewin and the headis: I met w[i]th the
divell and ther coventanted in a maner w[i]th him, and I promeisit to meit him in the

Spelling and punctuation are reproduced here exactly as found in the confessions. This lack of
modernization makes the text difficult to read, but is adopted in the belief that any intervention,
even one as simple as adding a comma or capital letter, could distort the original emphasis of what
is a very complex narrative. Having said this, in a concession to readability I have taken some liber-
ties with regard to presentation. First, although the confessional text is written as one continuous
narrative (*see* page 38) I have drawn attention to sudden changes of subject matter by using paragraph indentations, whilst still retaining original punctuation so the reader can see how the separated
sections were linked together in the original. Secondly, both here and in quotations from the confessions appearing in subsequent chapters, editorial comments and translations of obscure words are
italicized in round (as opposed to the more usual square) parentheses, to distinguish them from the
scribal shorthand omissions noted in square parentheses. Later quotations will also be referenced,
either in embedded parentheses or footnotes, by a page and line number (the latter counted down
from the top of the page) so that they can be easily located in the main confessional text. Anyone
wishing to read the confessions in an easier format can turn to the modernized, but still largely accurate, transcription found in Robert Pitcairn's *Ancient Criminal Trials in Scotland* (Edinburgh, 1833).

Isobel's first confession, given on 13 April, 1662. The text begins with a list of witnesses present at the top, and concludes with the notary's docquet and a selection of witness signatures.

night tym in the kirk of aulderne q[uhi]lk I did: and the first thing I did ther th[a]t night I denyed my baptisme, and did put the on of my handis to the crowne of my head and the uth[e]r to the sole of my foot, and th[e]n renuncet all betwixt my two handis ower to the divell, he wes in the readeris dask and a blak book in his hand: margret brodie in aulderne held me vp to the divell to be baptized be him, and he marked me in the showlder, and suked owt my blood at that merk and spowted it in his hand, and sprinkling it on my head said I baptise the Janet in my awin name, and w[i]thin a q[uhi]ll we all remoowed,

the nixt tym th[a]t I met w[i]th him ves in the new wardis of Inshoch, and haid carnall cowpula[tio]n & dealling w[i]th me, he wes a meikle blak roch man werie cold and I faund his nature als cold w[i]thin me as spring wall vater somtymes he haid buitis & somtymes shoes on his foot bot still his foot ar forked and cloven he vold be somtymes w[i]th ws lyk a dear or a rae,

Johne taylor and Janet breadhead his vyff in belnaketh (*blank*) dowglas and I my self met in the kirkyaird of nairne and ve raised an vnchristned child owt of its greaff, and at the end of breadleyes cornfield land just apposit to the milne of nairne, we took the s[ai]d child w[i]th the naillis af o[u]r fingeris and toes pikles of all sortis of grain and blaidis of keall and haked th[e]m all verie small mixed throw altogither, and did put a pairt therof among the mukheapes of breadleyes Landis and therby took away the fruit of his cornes etc and we pairted it among two of our coevens, q[uhe]n we tak cornes at lambes we tak (*crease in page – several words unreadable*) cornes ar full or two stokis of keall or therby and th[a]t giwes ws the fruit of the corn land or keal yaird whair they grew: and it mey be (*crease in page – several words unreadable*) yewll or pace, and th[e]n devyd it amongst ws

ther ar threttien persones in my coven, the last tym th[a]t owr coven (*rest of line obscured*) wer daunceing at the hill of earlseat, and befor th[a]t betuixt moynes and bowgholl, & befor th[a]t we ves besyd the meikle burne, and the uth[e]r coven being at the downiehillis we went from beyond the meikle burne and went besyd them to the howssis at the woodend of Inshoch and w[i]thin a qwhyll went hom to o[u]r howssis befor candlmas we went be east kinlosse and ther we yoaked an plewghe of paddokis, the divell held the plewgh and Johne yownger in mebiestowne o[u]r officer did drywe the plewghe, padokis did draw the plewgh as oxen qwickens wer sowmes a riglens horne wes an cowter and an piece of an riglens horne wes an sock, we went two s[eve]rall tymes abowt, and all ve of the coeven went still wp and downe w[i]th the plewghe, prayeing to the divell for the fruit of th[a]t land and th[a]t thistles and brieris might grow ther,

q[uhe]n ve goe to any hous we tak meat and drink, and we fill wp the barrellis w[i]th owr oven pish again, and we put boosomes in o[u]r bedis w[i]th o[u]r husbandis till ve return again to them, we wer in the earle of murreyes hows in darnvay and ve gott anewgh ther and did eat and drink of the best, and browght pairt w[i]th ws we went in at the windowes I haid a litle horse and wold say horse and hattok in the divellis name, and then ve vold flie away q[uhe]r ve vold be ewin as strawes wold flie wpon an hie way, we will flie lyk strawes q[uhe]n we pleas wild strawes and corne strawes wilbe hors to ws q[uhe]n ve put th[e]m betwixt owr foot, and say hors and hattok in the divellis nam, and q[uhe]n any sies thes strawes in whirlewind, and doe not sanctifie them selves, they we mey shoot them dead at our pleasur, any th[a]t ar shot be us, their sowell will goe to hevin bot ther bodies remains w[i]th ws, and will flie as hors to ws als small as strawes,

I wes in the downie hillis, and got meat ther from the qwein of fearrie mor then I could eat: the qwein of fearie is brawlie clothed in whyt linens and in whyt and browne cloathes etc and the king of fearie is a braw man weill favoured and broad faced etc ther wes elf bullis crowtting and skoylling wp and downe th[e]r and affrighted me,

whan we tak away any cowes milk we pull the taw and twyn it & plaitt it the vrong way in the divellis name, and we draw the tedder (sua maid) in betuixt the cowes hinder foot and owt betuixt the cowes forder foot, in the divellis nam and therby tak w[i]th ws the kowes milk, we tak sheips milk ewin so, the way to tak or giw bak the milk again is to cut th[a]t tedder, q[uhe]n ve tak away the strenth of anie persones eall and giwes it to an uth[e]r we tak a litle qwantitie owt of each barrell or stan (*stand?*) of eall & puts it in a stowp, in the divellis nam, and in his nam w[i]th owr awin handis putts it in amongst an uth[e]ris eall and giwes hir the strenth and substance & seall of hir neightbo[u]ris eall, and to keip the eall from ws th[a]t we haw no power of it is to sanc- tifie it veill, we get all this power from the divell & q[uhe]n ve seik it from him ve call him owr lord,

Johne taylor & Janet breadhead his wyff in bellnakeith bessie wilsone in aulderne and margret wilsone spows to donald callam in aulderne and I maid an pictur of clay to distroy the Laird of parkis meall children Johne taylor browght hom the clay in his plaid newk his wyff brak it werie small lyk meall and sifted it w[i]th a siew: and powred in water (*words obscured*) in the divellis nam & vrought it werie sore lyk rye bowt, and maid of it a pictur of the Lairdis sones it haid all the pairtis & (*markis?*) of a child such as (*word crossed out*) heid eyes nose handis foot mowth & litle lippes it wanted no mark of a child & the handis of it folded down by its sydis it wes lyk a pow, or a slain gryce, we laid the face of it to the fyre till it scrukned, and a cleir fyre round abowt it till it ves read lyk a cole, efter th[a]t we wold rost it now and then each day & th[e]r wold be an piece of it weill rosten, the Laird of parkis heall maill children by it ar to suffer if it be not gotten and brokin als weill as thes th[a]t ar borne and dead alreadie, it ves still putt in & takin out of the fyre in the divellis name, it wes hung wp wpon an knag, it is yet in Johne tayloris hows and it hes a cradle of clay abowt it, onlie Jon taylor and his wyff janet breadheid bessie and margret wilsones in aulderne & margret brodie th[e]r & I wer onlie at the making of it, all the multitud of o[u]r number of witches of the coevens kent all of it at our nixt meitting after it wes maid, and all the witches yet th[a]t ar untaken haw their awin poweris and owr poweris q[uhi]lk we haid befor we wer takin both etc bot now I haw no power at all,

margret kyllie in (*blank*) is on of the uth[e]r coven meslie hirdall spows to allexr ross in lonheid is on of th[e]m, hir skin is fyrie Issobell nicoll in lochloy is on of my coeven allexr elder in earleseat and Janet finlay his spows ar of my covens margret hasbein in moynes is on, margrat brodie in aulderne bessie and margrat wilsones th[e]r & Jean mairten ther and elspet nishie spows to Jon mathew ther are of my coven, the s[ai]d Jean mairten is maiden of owr coven Johne yowng in mebestowne is officer to owr coeven elspet chisholme and Issobell more in aulderne

magie brodie (*blank*) and I: went in to alexr cumings litthows in aulderne, I went in in the liknes of a kea, the s[ai]d elspet chishom wes in the shap of a catt Issobell mor wes a hair and magie brodie a catt & (*blank*) we took a thried of each cullor of yairne th[a]t wes in the s[ai]d allexr cuming his littfatt, and did cast thrie knotts on each thried in the divellis nam, and did put the thriedis in the fatt withersones abowt in the fatt in the divellis name and th[e]rby took the heall strenth of the fatt away th[a]t it could litt nothing bot onlie blak, according to the culor of the divell in qoes nam we took away the strenth of the ryt culoris th[a]t wes in the fatt,

all qwhilkis of the premissis swa spokin and willinglie confest and declairit furth of the mowth of the s[ai]d Issobell in all and be all things as is abow sett downe I the s[ai]d Johne Innes not[ar] publict haw w[ritti]ne thir p[rese]ntts and with the s[ai]dis witnessis abownamet haw sub[scrivi]t the samen in farder testimonie & witnessing of the premissis to be of weritie we haw sub[scrivi]t the samen w[i]th owr handis day yeir & place abowspe[cife]it

(Here follows John Innes's docquet – not transcribed)

Mr Hary forbes minister at auldEarn
ATTESTIS
WDallas off cantray S[he]reff deput
ATTESTIS
ABrodie witnes to the said confetione
Hew Rose Mini[ste]r att Nairne
ATTESTS the forsaid declara[tio]n
Hew Hay of Newtown   as to the prin[cipa]l Substantials
ATTESTES
George phinnie ^ ATTESTIS
     ^ In kirkmichael
W Sutherland off kinsterie
ATTESTS the s[ai]d confessione
Jo: weir in auldearne ATTESTS

(In margin – 'Jo Innes no[ta]rius publicus
Mr Hary forbes minister
of the gospel at ouldEarn
Hew Hay
George Phinnie)

Confession Two

Att Aulderne the third day of may 1662 yeiris abowt the houris of two or thrie in the efternoone or therby in p[rese]nce of master harie fforbes minister of the gospell at

aulderne Johne grant of (*moynes?*) Johne Innes of edingeich hew hay of Brightmanney
James dunbar apperiant of Boath williame dunbar off clunes (*written in the margin-* and
Johne weir in auldern) and divers utheris witnessis to thir confessione and declara[tio]ne
efterspe[cif]it spokin furth of the mowthe of Issobell gowdie spous to Johne gilbert in
Lochloy

The quilk day In p[rese]nce of Johne Innes no[ta]r publict and witnessis all
undersub[scri]wand the said Issobell gowdie professing repentance for hir former sines
of witchcraft proceidit in hir confessione in maner efter following To witt:

first I met w[i]th the divell betwixt the townes of drumdewin and the (*damaged*)
headis and ther he spak to me, and appointed me to meitt w[i]th him in the kirk of
aulderne q[uhi]lk I did in the night tym, and ther I denyed my baptisme and did put
the on of my handis to the crowne of my head and the uth[e]r hand to the soale of my
foot and renuncet all betwixt my two handis ower to the divell, the divell wes in the
readeris dask and an blak book in his hand, margret brodie hald me up to him to be
baptized be him q[uhai]r he marked me in the showlder and w[i]th his mowth suked
furth my blood owt of the mark and spowted it in his hand and sprinkled it on my head
and said I baptise ye Janet in my owin nam and w[i]thin a whyll th[ai]refter we all
remoowed,
      the nixt tym th[a]t I mett w[i]th him wes in the new wardis of Inchoch and ther
he h(*aid?*) carnell cowpula[tio]ne w[i]th me, and frequentlie thereftir at owr pleasur he
haid carnall dealling w[i]th me he ves a meikle roch man werie cold and I faund his
nature als cold within me as spring well water,
      efter th[a]t tym ther vold meit bot somtymes a coven somtymes mor somtymes les,
bot a grand meitting vold be about the end of ilk qwarter, thir is threittein persones
in ilk coeven, and ilk on of ws has a sprit to wait wpon ws and ve pleas to call wpon
him, I remember not all the spritis names, bot their is on call(*it?*) swein q[uhi]lk waitis
wpon the s[ai]d margret wilson in aulderne he is still clothed in grass grein: and the
s[ai]d margret wilson hes an niknam: called pikle neirest the wind, the nixt sp[ri]t is
called rorie who waitis on bessie wilsone in aulderne he is still clothed in yallow: and
hir niknam is throw the corneya(*ird?*) (*damaged – words missing*) The third spirit is called
the roring lyon (*word crossed out*) who waitis upon Issobell nicoll in lochloy and (*damaged
– words missing*) in sea grein, hir niknam is bessie rule, the fowrth sprit is called mack-
hector qwho (*damaged – words missing*) martein dawghter to the s[ai]d margret wilson,
he is a yowng lyk divell clothed still in gras(*s?*) (*damaged – words missing*) maiden to the
coven th[a]t I am of, and hir nikname is over the dyk w[i]th it becaws the dive(*ll?*)
(*damaged – words missing*) maiden in his hand nixt him q[uhe]n ve daunce gillatrypes
and q[uhe]n he vold lowp from (*damaged – words missing*) he and she will say ower the
dyk w[i]th it, the name of the fyft sprit is robert the r . . . (*damaged – words missing*) fadd
dun and seims to be a comander of the rest of the spirits and he waitts wpon margret
brodie in aulderne (*damaged – words missing*) is called thieff of hell wait wpon hir selfe
and he waits also on the s[ai]d bessie wilson, the nam of the sevinth (*damaged – words
missing*) the read reiver and heis my owin spirit th[a]t waitts on my selfe & is still clothed

in blak the aught spirit (*damaged – words missing*) robert the Jacks still clothed in dune and seimes to be aiged heis an glaiked gowked spirit the womans (*damaged – words missing*) th[a]t he vaitis on is able and stowt, the nynthe spirit is called Laing & the womans niknam th[a]t he waitis (*damaged – words missing*) is bessie bauld the tenth spirit is named thomas a fearie etc ther wilbe many uther divellis waiting wpon (*damaged – words missing*) maister divell bot he is bigger and mor awfull th[a]n the rest of the divellis and they all reverence him I will ken them all on by on from uth[e]ris q[uhe]n they appeir lyk a man,

Quhen we rease the wind we tak a rag of cloth and weitis it in water and we tak a beetle and knokis the rage on a stone, and we say thryse ower I knok this ragg upon this stone, to raise the wind in the divellis name, it sall not lye untill I please again (*damaged – words missing*) we wold lay the wind, we dry the ragg and say (thryse ower) we lay the wind in the divellis nam (*damaged – words missing*) ryse q[uhi]ll we or I lyk (*word crossed out*) to rease it again, And if the wind will not lye instantlie (*damaged – words missing*) we call upon o[u]r spiritis and say to him thieffe thieffe conjure the wind and caws it to (*damaged – words missing*) we haw no power of rain bot ve will rease the wind q[uhe]n ve please, he maid us believ (*damaged – words missing*) th[e]r wes no god besyd him,

As for elf arrow heidis, the divell shapes them w[i]th his awin h . . . (*damaged – words missing*) to elf boyes, who whytts and dightis them w[i]th a sharp thing lyk a paking neidle b . . . (*damaged – words missing*) I saw them whytting and dighting them q[uhe]n I wes in the elfes houssis they will haw we . . . (*damaged – words missing*) them whytting and dighting, and the divellis giwes them to ws each of vs so mony q[uhe]n (*damaged – words missing*) th[a]t dightis th[e]m ar litle ones hollow and bossis baked they speak gowstie lyk,

Qwhen (*damaged – words missing*) giwes th[e]m to ws he sayes shoot thes in my name and they sall not goe heall home, and q[uhe]n ve shoot thes arrowes (we say) I shoot yon man in the divellis name, he sall not win heall home, and this salbe alswa trw th[ai]r sall not be an bitt of him upon on lieiw, we haw no bow to shoot w[i]th bot spang them from of the naillis of owr thowmbes: som tymes we will miss bot if they twitch be it beast or man or woman it will kill tho they had an Jack upon them:

Qwhen we goe in the shape of an haire, we say thryse ower I sall gow intill a haire w[i]th sorrow and syt and meikle caire, and I sall goe in the divellis nam ay whill I com hom (*damaged – words missing*) (*in?*)stantlie we start in an hair, and when we wold be owt of th[a]t shape we vill s . . . (*damaged – words missing*) caire, I am in an hairis liknes just now, bot I salbe in a womans liknes ew . . . (*damaged – words missing*) when we vold goe in the liknes of an cat: we say thryse ower I sall goe int(*ill?*) (*damaged – words missing*) shot, and I sall goe in the divellis nam, ay q[uhi]ll I com hom again:, & if ve (*damaged – words missing*) we say thryse ower I sall goe intill a craw w[i]th sorrow and syt & blak (*damaged – words missing*) ay q[uhi]ll I com home again: and q[uhe]n ve vold be owt of thes shapes, we say: catt cat (*damaged – words missing*) send the a blak shott or blak thraw: I wes a catt or crow just now, bot I salbe (*damaged – words missing*) catt: catt: or craw: craw: goe send the a blak shot or a blak thraw:

Iff we in the (*damaged – words missing*) haire or any uth[e]r likenes etc goe to any of owr neightbo[u]ris howsis being witches, we we . . . (*damaged – words missing*) the goe w[i]th ws or me, and p[rese]ntlie they becom as we ar either ratis hearis crowes etc & goe (*damaged – words missing*) we wold ryd: we tak windlestrawes or beenstakis & put them betwixt owr foot and say thry(*se?*) (*damaged – words missing*) and hattok hors and goe, hors and pellatts ho ho: and immeditialie we flie away whair (*damaged – words missing*) and least owr husbandis sould miss vs owt of our bedes, we put in a boosom or a thrie (*damaged – words missing*) and say thryse ower I lay down this boosom or stooll in the divellis nam let it not ste . . . (*damaged – words missing*) com again: and immeditialie it seims a voman: before our husbandis: ve can not turn in the lik . . . (*damaged – words missing*)

Qwhen my husband sold beeff I used to put a swellowes feather in the hyd of the beast (*damaged – words missing*) putt owt this beeff in the divellis name, th[a]t meikle silver and good pryce com home, I did ewin (*damaged – words missing*) furth either hors noat vebis or any uther thing (*words missing*) put in this feather and said the (*damaged – words missing*) ower to caws the comodities sell weill etc (*damaged – words missing*) thryse ower: thus: owr lord to hunting he (*damaged – words missing*) marblestone, he sent vord to saint knitt . . . (*damaged – words missing*) he pat the blood to be blood till all upstood the lith to the lith till all took with our Ladie charmed hir deirlie sone w[i]th hir tooth and hir townge, and hir ten fingeris in the nam of the fath[e]r the sone and the holie gost, and this we say thryse over straiking the sor, and it becomes heall, 2lj for the beanshaw or pain in the heuch, Wee ar heir thrie maidens charming for the bean shaw, the man of the midle earth blew beaver Land seaver maneris of stooris the Lord fleigged the feind w[i]th his holie candles and yeird foot stone heir she sitts and heir shee is gon let hir nev . . . com heir again: 3lj for the seaveris (we say thryse over, I forbid the qwaking seaveris the sea seaveris the (*damaged – words missing*) seaveris and all the seaveris th[a]t ewer god ordained: owt of the head owt of the heart owt of the bak owt of the syd (*owt?*) of the kneis owt of the thieghes fra the pointis of the fingeris to the nebes of the toes owt sall the seaveris goe (*damaged – words missing*) to the hill som to the hap, som to the stone som to the stok in saint peiteris nam saint paullis nam & all the sa(*intis?*) of hevin: in nam of the fath[e]r the sone and the holie gost,

And when we took the frwit of the fishes from (*the?*) fisheris we went to the shore befor the boat wold com to it, and we wold say on the shore syd thrie s[eve]rall ty(*mes*) ower, the fisheris ar gon to the sea and they vill brang hom fishe to me they will bring them hom intill the boat bot they sall get of th[e]m bot the smaller sort: so we either steall a fish: or buy a fish or get a fish from them nowght an or ma: and w[i]th th[a]t we haw all the fruit of the heall fishes in the boat, and the fishes th[a]t the fisheris th[e]mseles will haw, wilbe bot froath etc

The first woyag th[a]t ewer I went w[i]th the rest of owr convens, wes (*word missing*) plewghlandis, and th[ai]r we shot an man betwixt the plewgh stiltis, and he p[rese]ntlie fell to the ground upon his nei(*se?*) and his mowth, and then the divell gaw me an arrow, and cawsed me shoot an vowman in that fieldis: q[uhi]lk I did and she fell down dead,

In winter 1660 q[uhe]n mr harie fforbes minister at aulderne wes seik: we maid an bagg: of the gallis flesh and gutts of toadis pikles of bear pairingis of the naillis of fingeris & toes the liewer of ane hair and bitts of clowts, we steipit this all together all night among watter and haked throw uth[e]r and whan we did put it among the water, satan wes w[i]th ws and learned ws the wordis following to say thryse ower ar thus: he is lyeing in his bed and he is lyeing seik and sore, let him lye intill his bed, two monethis (*damaged – words missing*) dayes mor 2lj let him lye intill his bed let him lye intill it seik and sore let him lye intill his bed two monethes thrie dayes mor, 3lie he sall lye intill his bed he sall lye in it seik and sore, he sall lye intill his bed two m . . . (*damaged – words missing*) and thrie dayes mor, q[uhe]n we haid learned all thes wordis from the divell, as s[ai]d is, we fell all dow(*n*) (*damaged – words missing*) kneis, w[i]th owr hear down ower owr showlderis and eyes, and owr hands lifted up and owr (*damaged – words missing*) the divell, and said the fors[ai]dis wordis thryse ower to the divell striktlie ag[ains]t masterie forbes (*damaged – words missing*)

in the night tym we cam in to mr harie forbes chalmer q[uhai]r he lay, w[i]th owr handis all sme . . . (*damaged – words missing*) of the bagg to swing it wpon mr harie q[uhai]r he wes seik in his bed, And in the day (*damaged – words missing*) number qwho wes most familliar and intimat w[i]th him, to wring or swing the bagg (*damaged – words missing*) not prevaill in the night tym against him: q[uhi]lk wes accordinglie done, Any of (*damaged – words missing*) comes in to yo[u]r howsis or ar set to doe yow ivill they will look uncowth lyk thraw(*n?*) (*damaged – words missing*) hurlie lyk and their clothes standing out

the maiden of owr coven Jean mairten (*damaged – words missing*) doe no great mater w[i]thowt o[u]r maiden, and if a child be forspoken, we tak the cradle (*damaged – words missing*) child throw it thryse and th[e]n a dowg throw it, and shakis the belt abow the fyre, (*damaged – words missing*) downe to the ground, till a dowg or a catt goe ower it th[a]t the seiknes mey com (*damaged – words missing*) catt

All q[uhi]lkis wer sua spoken furth of the mowth of the s[ai]d Issobell gowdie in all and be all thingis Johne Innes no[ta]r publict haw w[ritt]ine thir p[rese]nttis and with the witnessis abow and undernamet haw sub[scrivi]t day yeir moneth and place abowexprest in all pointis

(Here follows John Innes's notary's docquet – not transcribed)

Mr Hary forbes m . . .
&
Hew Rose . . .
Attests the for[sai]d
primo Subs . . .

hawing read & considered the confessions
of Isabel gowdie within conteaned as paction
with Sathan Renunciation of Baptisme, with
dyvers malefices, I find that a co[m]mission may
be verie justlie (*word unreadable*) for hir last tryall

AColuille

Hew Hay of newtoun
ATTESTES   Joh

George . . .
in Kirkmich . . .

Confession Three

At Aulderne the ffyftein day of may 1662 yeiris In p[rese]nce of master harie forbes
minister of the gospell at auldern, mr hew rosse minister at nairn, Johne Innes of
edinge(*ith?*), hew hay of newtoun, mr allexr dunbar schoolm[aste]r & session clerk
of aulderne, George Phinney in kirkmichaell and Jon weir and androw easie in
aulderne and many utheris witnessis to the confession efter sett down spoken furth
of the mouth of Issobell Gowdie spows to Jon gilbert in lochloy

The quhilk day In p[rese]nce of me Johne Innes no[ta]r publict and witnessis all under-
subs[cri]wand the said Issobell gowdie appeiring to be most penetent for hir
abominable sines of witchcraft most ingeniouslie proceidit in hir confessione therof in
maner efterfollowing To witt:

first as I wes going betuixt the towns of Drumdewin and the headis the divell met
w[i]th me, and q[uhai]r I covenanted w[i]th him, and promeisit to meit him in the
night tym in the kirk of aulderne q[uhi]lk I did, he stood in the readeris dask and an
blak book in his hand q[uhai]r I cam befor him and renuncet Jesus christ and my
baptisme, and all betuixt the soale of my foot & the crowne of my head I gaw frielie
wp and ower to the divell, margret brodie in aulderne held me up to the divell untill
he rebaptized me, and marked me in the shoulder, and w[i]th his mouth sucked out
my blood at that place and spowted it in his hand and sprinkling it wpon my head and
face he said I baptise ye Janet to myself in my owin nam, w[i]thin a whyll therefter we
all remoowed,
  and w[i]thin ffew dayes he cam to me in the new wardis of Inshoch, and ther haid
carnall cowpula[tio]n w[i]th me, he wes a werie meikle blak roch man, he will lye als
hewie wpon ws q[uhe]n he hes carnall dealling w[i]th us, als lyk an malt secke; his
memberis ar exceiding great and long, no mans memberis ar so long and bigg as they
ar: he wold be amongst us, lyke a weath horse amongst mearis he wold lye w[i]th ws
in p[rese]nce of all the multitud, neither haid we nor he any kynd of shame, bot especiallie he hes no sham w[i]th him at all, he wold lye and haw carnall dealling w[i]th
all enyie tym as he pleased, he wold haw carnall dealling w[i]th us in the shape of a
deir or any uth[e]r shap th[a]t he wold be in, we wold never refuse him,
  he wold com to my hows top in the shape of a crow, or lyk a dear or in any uther

shap now and then, I wold ken his woice at the first heiring of it, and wold goe furth
to him and hav carnall cowpula[tio]n w[i]th him,

the yowngest and lustiest woomen will haw werie great pleasur in their carnall
cowpula[tio]n w[i]th him, yea much mor th[a]n w[i]th their awin husbandis, and they
will haw a exceiding great desyr of it w[i]th him, als much as he can haw to them &
mor, and never think shame of it, he is able for ws th[a]t way th[a]n any man can be,
(alace th[a]t I sould compair him to an man) onlie he ves heavie lyk a malt seck a hodg
nature, verie cold as yce;

he wold send me now and (*then?*) to auldern som earrandis to my neightbo[u]ris in
the shape of ane hair, I wes on morning abowt the break of day, goeing to aulderne in
the shap of ane hair, and patrik papleyes servantis in kilhill being goeing to ther (*word
crossed out*) labouring, his houndis being w[i]th them, ran efter me being in the shape
of an haire, I ran werie long, bot wes feart being near at last to take my owin hous, the
dore being left open, I ran in behind an chist and the houndis followed in bot they went
to the uth[e]r syd of the chist, and I wes forcet to run furth again, and ran in to an
uth[e]r hows, and th[ei]r took leasur to say, hair hair god send the cair, I am in a hearis
liknes now, bot I sall be an vowman ewin now, hair, hair god send the cair, & so I
returned to my owin shap as I am at this instant again, the dowgis will somtymes get
som bytte of vs q[uhe]n ve ar (*word crossed out*) hairis, bot wil not get ws killed,

q[uhe]n ve turn owt of a hairis liknes to owr owin shap: we will haw the bytte and
rywes & scrattis in owr bodies, q[uhe]n ve vold be in the shap of catts, we did nothing
bot cry & wraw & rywing and as it ver wirrieing on an uth[e]r, and q[uhe]n ve com to
owr awin shapes again ve will find the scrattis and rywes on owr skins werie sor,

q[uhe]n on of vs or mor ar in the shape of catis & meitt w[i]th any of owr
neightbo[u]ris, we will say divell speid the, goe thow w[i]th me & immediatlie they
will turne in the shape of an catt & goe w[i]th ws,

Qwhen we wilbe in the shap of crowes, we will be larger th[a]n ordinar crowes, and
will sitt wpon brenches of treis, we went in the shape of rewkis to mr robert donald-
sones hows, the divell and Jon taylor and his wyff, went in at the kitchen chimney, and
went down wpon the crowk, it wes about Lambes in an[n]o 1659, they opened an
vindow and went all in to the hows, and gott beiff and drink th[ei]r, bot we did no mor
harme,

we went in to the downie hillis, the hill opened and we cam to an fair & lairge braw
rowme in the day tym, th[e]r ar great bullis crowtting & skrylling ther at the entrie;
q[uhi]lk feard me,

bot th[a]t q[uhi]ch trowbles my concience most is the killing of sewerall persones,
with the arrowes q[uhi]ch I gott from the divell, the first voman th[a]t I killed wes at
the plewgh landis, also I killed on in the east of murrey, at candlmas last, at that tyme
bessie wilson in aulderne killed on th[e]r, and margret wilson ther killed an uth[e]r, I
killed also James dick in conniecavell, bot the death th[a]t I am most of all sorrie for,
is the killing of william Bower in the miltowne of moynes, margret brodie killed an
vowman washing at the burne of tarres, Bessie wilsone killed an man at the bushe of
strutheris Bessie hay in aulderne killed an prettie man, called dunbar at the eist end of
the towne of forres as he wes coming out at an gaitt, margret brodj in aulderne killed

on david blak in darnvay, Janet breadheid spows to Jon taylor told me a litle befor she wes apprehendit th[a]t margret wilsoen in aulderne shot allexr hutcheon in aulderne, Janet breadheid shot Johne falconer in the park, the most of ws all wer ther at that tyme, bessie wilson killed on william man at burgie, margret wilson killed on Johne lees, and Janet breadheid killed a swyn at burgie

Bessie wilsone in aulderne, on an first monday of the reath, took an bagg maid of hairs lieweris, the flesh guttis and gallis of toadis naills of fingeris & toes, and swinged it on an young man called thomas reid, and he died,

Bessie and margret wilsones in aulderne Johne taylor and his wyff margrat brodie and I and the divell, wer togither and mr harie forbes minister of aulderne goeing to moynes the divell gaw margret brodie an arrow to shoot at him q[uhi]lk she did, bot it cam short & the divell cawsed tak it up again, and desyrit to shoot again bot the divell s[ai]d no: we wold not get his lyff at th[a]t tyme, the divell cawsed me to shoot at the Laird of park as he wes croceing the burne of the boath, bot I missed him,

we wold goe s[eve]rall howses in the night tym, we wer at candlmas last in grainge-hill, q[uhai]r we got meat and drink aneugh the divell sat at the heid of the table and all the coven abowt, that night he desyrit allexr elder in earlseat to say the grace befor meat q[uhi]lk he did, and is thus, we eat this meat in the divellis nam, w[i]th sorrow and syt and meikle shame we sall destroy hows and hald, bot sheip and noat intill the fold, litle good sall com to the fore, of all the rest of the litle store, & th[e]n ve began to eatt and q[uhe]n ve haid endit eatting, we looked steadfastlie to the divell and bowing owr selves to him. We said to the divell we thank the owr lord for this etc

the wordis which we spak q[uhe]n we maid the pictur for distroyeing of the Laird of parkis meall children, wer thus, In the divellis nam, we powr in this water among this mould, for land dwyning and ill heall, we putt it in into the fyre, that it mey be brunt both stik and stowre, it salbe brunt w[i]th owr will, as any stikle wpon a kill, the divell taught ws the wordis, and q[uhe]n ve haid learned them we all fell downe wpon owr bare kneyeis, and owr hair abowt owr eyes, and owr handis lifted up, looking steadfast wpon the divell, still sayeing the wordis thryse ower, till it wes maid, and then in the the divellis nam, we did put it in the miest of the fyre, efter it haid skrukned a litle befor the fyre, and q[uhe]n it ves read lyk a coale, we took it owt in the divellis nam, till it be brokin it wilbe the deathe of all the meall children th[a]t the Laird of park will ewer get, cast it ower an kirk it will not brak, q[uhi]ll it be broken w[i]th an aix, or som such lyk thing be a mans handis, if it be not so broken it will last an hundreth yeir, it hes an cradle about it of clay to preserw it from skaith, & it wes resten each uth[e]r day at the fyr, som tymes on pairt of it, somtymes an uth[e]r pairt of it, it vold be a litle watt w[i]th water & th[e]n rosten, the bairn vold be brunt & rosten, ewin as it ves by ws, it vanted no (*word crossed out*) mark of all the pairtis of an child, litle lippies etc and the handis of it folded downe by its sydis Jon taylor and Janet breadheid his wyff bessie & margret wilsones in aulderne & I my selfe w[i]th the divell wer onlie at the making of it, bot all the multitud of owr all o[u]r coevens got notice of it, at the nixt meitting, for all owr actis and deidis betuixt grett meittings most be given accompt of and notted in his book, at each grand meitting, bot all my owin coven gott notice of it werie shortlie, the divell him selfe cam to me to my awin hows, and bad me meitt him in Johne tayloris hows to help th[e]m to mak the s[ai]d pictur, all the coven did fflie lyk cattis beas hairis rewkis etc bot barbara ronald in brightmanney and I still read in an hors q[uhi]ch ve vold mak of a straw or beein staik, bessie wilsone wes still in the liknes of a rewk,

q[uhe]n we ar at meat or in any uth[e]r place q[uha]t[eve]r, the maiden of each coven sitts abow the rest nixt the divell and she serws the divell for all the old people th[a]t he cairis not for, and ar veak & wnmeit for him, he will be w[i]th hir & ws al, lyk a weath hors after mearis, and somtymes a man bot werie wilfull in carnall cowpula[tio]n at all tyms, and they ewin so, als wilfull and desirows of him, somtyms among owr selws we wold be calling him blak Jon or the lyk, and he wold ken it & heir ws weill aneughe, and he ewin then com to ws, and say I ken weill aneugh what ye wer sayeing of me, & th[e]n he vold beat and buffet ws werie sor, we wold be beattin if ve wer absent any tym, or neglect any thing th[a]t wold be appointed to be done, allexr elder in earlseat vold be werie oft beatin, he is bot soft, & could never defend him self in the least, bot greitt & cry q[uhe]n he vold be scurging him, bot margret wilson in aulderne wold defend hir self fynlie, & cast up hir handis to keip the stroakis off from hir and bessie wilsone wold speak croslie w[i]th hir townge, and wold be belling again to him stowtlie he wold be beatting and scurgeing ws all wp and downe, w[i]th tardis & uth[e]r sharp scurges, lyk naked gwhastis, and we wold be still cryeing, pittie, pittie, mercie, mercie, owr lord, bot he wold haw neither pittie nor mercie, whan he vold be angrie at ws, he wold girne at ws, lyk a dowge, as iff he wold swellow ws wp: somtym he vold be lyk a stirk, a bull, a deir, a rae, or a dowg etc and haw dealling w[i]th ws, and he vold hold wp his taill wntill we wold kiss his arce; and at each tym q[uhe]n ve wold meitt w[i]th him, we behoowit to ryse and beck and mak owr curtesie to him and we wold say, ye ar welcom owr lord, and how doe ye my lord etc

q[uhe]n ve wold tak the furit away of anie persones midden or dunghill, we wold say, thus, when we wold putt haiked flesh of an unchristned child dowgs and sheips flesh & pairingis of naillis etc al haked throw uth[e]r, we putt this in intill this ham, in o[u]r lord the divellis nam, the first handis th[a]t handles the brunt and scalded sall they be, we sall distroy hows and hald, w[i]th the sheip and noat intill the fold &litl sall com to the for of all the rest of the litl store

we killed an ox in burgie, abowt the sawing (?) of the day and we browght the ox w[i]th ws hom to aulderne and did eat all amongst ws, in an hows of aulderne, and feasted on it, tho the divell wold giw ws ther brawest lyk mo[ne]y th[a]t ewer wes coyned, w[i]thin fowr and twantie howris, it vold be bot hors muke,

alace I deserw not to be sitting heir, for I haw done so manie ivill deidis, espe[ci]allie killing of men etc I deserw to be reiven wpon iron harrowes & wors if it culd be devysit

and q[uhe]n we tak away the fruit of corns at Lambes we tak an wooll sheeir & cuttis or clips onlie thrie stakis of it & plaitis uth[e]r thrie rudis togither and sayes we cutt this corne in o[u]r Lord the divellis nam & we sall haw the fruit of it hom thus thryse ower, & so we haw the fruit of th[a]t field ewin so q[uhe]n ve tak keall or the lyk etc & we lay al vp till yewll pace or halie dayes & partis it among vs & feastis on th[a]t togither

Wpon the q[uhi]lkis all and sundrie of the premissis swa spokin & willinglie confest be the said Issobell gowdie I the s[a]d Johhne Innes no[ta]r publict haw wrettin thir p[rese]nttis & w[i]th the witnessis abow & under namet haw sub[scrivi]t the samen w[i]th owr handis day moneth place & yeir abow sett doun

(Here follows John Innes's docquet – not transcribed)

		Mr Hary forbes minister auldEarn ATTESTS
Jo: weir in auldearne ATTESTS	Hew Hay off newtown ATTESTES	Hew Rose Mini[ste]r At Nairne ATTESTS the fors[ai]d declara[tio]n as to the prin[cipa]l Substantial

George phinnie ^ ATTESTIS
^ in kirkmichael

(Signatures in margin:
J Innes no[ta]rius publicus
Mr Hary forbes
Hew Hay
George phinnie)

Confession Four

At Aulderne the twantie sevinth day of may 1662 yeiris In p[rese]nce of master harie forbes (minister at auldern *inserted*) patrik campbell of boath Mr Allexr Dunbar schoolm[aste]r and clerk of the session of aulderne George phinney in kirkmichaell hew hay of newtowne and Johne weir in aulderne witnesses to the confession of Issobell gowdie spows to Johne gilbert in Lochloy

The said day the said Issobell professing repentance of hir former sines of witchcraft and th[a]t she h[ai]d bein ower long in the divellis service without any compulsitoris proceidit in hir confession in maner efterfollowing Thatt is to say:

I aknowledg to my great grieff and sham th[a]t fyftein yeiris since I denyed fath[e]r son & holie gost in the kirk of aulderne, and gaw over my bodie and sowll to the divell he standing in the readeris dask of aulderne and an blak book in his hand, margret brodie in aulderne held me wp to the divell q[uhi]ll I did this, and q[uhi]ll he mark(ed) me one the shoulder and sowked out my blood th[e]rat, and spitted it in his hand and sprinkled it on my head and baptized me Janet in his owin nam:

efter th[a]t he h[ai]d carnall cowpula[tio]n w[i]th me in the new wardis of Inshoch, and still th[e]refter fra tym to tym at owr pleasur,

the names of the coeven: ar thes Bessie wilsone in aulderne Janet burnet ther elspet nishie ther margret brodie ther margret wilsone th[e]r Bessie hay th[e]r Jon taylor in belmakeith Janet breadhead his spows barbara ronald Issobell nicoll in lochloy: my self, w[i]th Jean mairten owr maiden & Jon yowng in mebestoun owr offi[ce]r

The names of owr divellis th[a]t waited wpon ws ar thes, first, robert the Jakis: Sander the read reaver Thomas the fearie: Swein: the roaring lyon: thieffe of hell wait wpon hir self, makhector, robert the rule: hendrie Laing and rorie, we wold ken th[e]m all on by on from utheris, som of th[e]m apeirit in sadd dun: som in grass grein, som in sea grein, som in yallow, the niknames th[a]t the divell gaw wnto ws were pikell neirest the vind, this wes margret wilsones niknam, Bessie wilsones niknam ves throw the corn yaird: Elspet nishies niknam ves bessie bald: Jean mairteins niknam q[uh]o ves maiden: is ower the dyk w[i]th it Bessie hayes niknam is able and stowt:

I haw sein the elf arrowes maid, the divell dightis th[e]m & the elf boyes quhytis them, we got ewrie on ws so many of th[e]m from the divell to shoot at men: I my self killed on w[illia]m bower at miltoun at miltoun (*sic*) of moynes this griews me mor th[a]n any thing th[a]t ewer I did, margret brodj killed an woman washing at the burn of tarras, Bessie wilson killed an man at the bush of Strutheris Bessie hay killed on (*blank*) dunbar at the east end of the town of forres coming owt at a gait, margret brodie shot at on david blak margret wilson killed on allexr hucheon in auldern, Janet bread-head now in prison killed Jon falconer in park ther wer thrie killed east the cowntrey at candlmes last I killed on margret brodie on & bessie wilson on, I shot on James dik in connicavell, margret brodie killed on w[illia]m crukshank margret vilson killed on Jon ley Janet breadhead killed a swyn: also she killed an uth[e]r man at burgie and bessie wilson killed on th[e]r namet w[illia]m man:

We killed an ox and brought it to Bessie hayes hows in aulderne and we did eat him th[e]r, I shot at the Laird of park as he ves crossing the burn of boath bot thankis to god now th[a]t he preserwit him, Bessie hay gaw me a great cuff becaws I missed him, margret brodie shot at mr harie forbes at the standing stones, bot she missed, & spierit if she sould shoot again & the divell said not for we wold not get his lyf at that tym,

we intentit s[eve]rall tyms for him, q[uhe]n he ves seik (*word crossed out*) Bessie hay Jean mairten the maiden bessie wilson margret brodie elspet nishie spows to Jon mathew & I my self met in bessie wilsones hows and maid an bag ag[ains]t him the bag wes maid of the flesh guttis & gallis of toadis the liewer of a hear, pikles of corn & pairings of (*naills – written above*) of fingeris & toes, we steipit al night among water, the divell learned ws to say thes wordis following at the making of the bag, he is lying in his bed & he is seik & sore, let him ly in till th[a]t bedd monethes two & dayes thrie mair, 2lj he sal ly in till his bed he salbe seik and sair, he sall lye in till his bedd monethes two & dayes thrie mair, & q[uhe]n we haid said this wordis we wer all on o[u]r kneyes o[u]r hair abowt owr showlderis & eyes holding wp o[u]r handis to the divell th[a]t it might destroy the s[ai]d mr harie, it ves intentit th[a]t ve coming in to his chalmer in the night tym we sould swing it on him, and becaws we prevailed not at th[a]t tym bessie hay undertook and cam in to his chalmer to wisit him being werie intimat w[i]th him, and she brought in of the bag in hir handis ffull of the oyll th[e]rof to haw swowng & casten drops of it on him bot ther wer som uth[e]r worthie persons w[i]th him at th[a]t tym, by q[uhi]ch god prevented bessie hay th[a]t she got no harm don to him, bot swang a litl of it on the clothes of the bed q[uhai]r he lay,

Jon taylor & his wyff Bessie & margret wilsones & I maid a pictur for the laird of parkis maill children Jon taylor brought hom the clay in his plaid newk, his wyff sifted it, we powred in vater in a cowg amongst it & wrought it sor & maid a pictur of it lyk a child als big as a pow it vanted no mark of the imag of a bairn eyes nose mowth litl lippies etc & the handis of it folded doun by its sydis the vordis th[a]t we s[ai]d q[uhe]n we maid it, ver thus we put this water among this meall for long dwynning & ill heall we put it in intill the fyr to burn them up both stik & stour it sal be brunt w[i]th o[u]r will as any stikill on an kill the divell sitton on an blak kist ve wer al on o[u]r kneyes and owr hair abowt o[u]r eyes looking on the divell stedfastlie & owr handis lifted vp to him saying the vordis ower & by this the bairns died etc

All this w[i]th a great many mor terrible things we the s[aid]is witnesses and no[ta]r haird the s[ai]d Issobell confes and most willinglie & penetent lyk speak furth of hir ovin mowth in witnes q[uhai]rof we haw sub[scrivi]t thir p[rese]ntis w[i]th o[u]r handis day yeir & place abow sett downe

Ita est Johannes Innes no [ta] rius publicus in fidem premissorum rogatus et requistus subscribo[rum] J Innes no[ta]rius publicus

Mr Hary forbes minister of the gospel at OldEarn ATTESTIS

Jo: weir in aulderne ATTESTS

George phinnie in kirkmichel ATTESTS

WSutherland off kinsterie ATTESTS

Hew Hay of newtowne ATTESTES

All:Dunbar Schoolmaster & Clerk to the Sessione of Oldearne ATTESTS

3

The Shadow of the Interrogator

What are we to make of these remarkable documents? For those who have no knowledge of witchcraft and fairy belief in early modern Scotland, they must seem virtually impenetrable. But even for those well acquainted with the subjects, they still present considerable challenges. In many ways they are no different from other witch-records from this period: like most, they contain descriptions of basic *maleficium* performed against neighbours; like many, they contain descriptions of demonological witchcraft; and like a significant minority, they include accounts of fairy belief and beneficent magic. But despite this conformity, Isobel's confessions remain profoundly demanding and complex on a number of levels. Emotionally, the reader is simultaneously attracted by their poetic beauty and intensity and repelled by their raw malevolence and strangeness. Intellectually, the attempt to understand how these fantastic narratives evolved out of standard judicial procedure generates endless questions. Did Isobel really say any of these things? If she didn't, then who was responsible for them and why were they written down? If she did, then why did she say them and what could she have meant by them?

For nearly 200 years, since they were first transcribed by Scottish historian Robert Pitcairn, any scholar who has read Isobel's confessions has been in the same predicament, and complex reactions undoubtedly lie behind oft-repeated terms such as: 'striking', 'startling', 'strange', 'powerful', 'extravagant', 'sensational', 'atypical', 'highly unusual', 'unrivalled', and most frequently of all, 'extraordinary'.[1] But while responses to the confessions have been diverse, as we have seen earlier, there has been no ambiguity surrounding their significance, with historians and folklorists either echoing George Black's view that they represent 'the most remarkable witchcraft case on record in Scotland' or John McPherson's more general acknowledgement of their 'supreme importance'.[2]

This importance lies in the fact that, as Maxwell-Stuart has recently noted, Isobel's confessions are extraordinary not in one, but in 'many ways' which, when taken together, combine to make them differ 'from all the others we have encountered'.[3] First, they are remarkable for their length and narrative form. Taken individually, the second and third confessions are among the longest on record and taken together all four constitute, to my knowledge, the longest collection of extant testimonial material relating to a single individual from a British witch-investigation in this period. The confessions are also, according to current historical research, the only witch-records to have been consistently recorded in the first person, and this feature, when combined with the fact that the narrative is also unbroken by any form of overt ordering or itemizing system, gives the impression of a flowing, personally-delivered monologue; an effect further intensified by the oft-repeated scribal observation, given with unique frequency and insistence, that she gave her confessions 'most willinglie' and 'without any compulsitoris (*compulsion*)'.

Secondly, the confessions are exceptional because they cover such a rich and varied range of subject matter. The folkloric material, particularly in relation to charming traditions and fairy belief, is arguably the most significant. With regard to the latter, the uniqueness of the content sets the confessions second only to Robert Kirk's famous treatise, *The Secret Commonwealth of Elves, Fauns and Fairies* as our most important documentary evidence for popular fairy belief in early modern Britain. It is with good reason that folklorist Katharine Briggs, a woman not without resources when it came to British fairy beliefs, claimed herself 'indebted' to Isobel for 'a description of life in the fairy hills'.[4] But folklore aside, Isobel's confessions are also notable for their demonological content. Not only do they contain what are arguably the most vivid and detailed descriptions of the demonic pact and witches' sabbath to have come down to us from a Scottish witch-testimony, but they also feature some of the more extravagant sabbath elements, such as sexual orgies, rarely found this side of the English Channel. After undertaking a comprehensive analysis of Scottish witchcraft cases, Christina Larner noted in 1981, that along with records relating to the celebrated Forfar witches, Isobel's confessions were those 'which most nearly parallel those of the continent'.[5] Moreover, while Isobel's confessions would be remarkable enough if they contained either the folkloric or the demonological detail alone, the fact that they contain these (in many ways diametrically opposed) elements simultaneously, and that the two are inter-meshed in a manner which defies simplistic interpretation, make her confessions truly unique, with Cowan and Henderson claiming in their recent study of Scottish fairy beliefs, that Isobel 'interspersed fairy and diabolical beliefs in her confessions of 1662 to a degree that is unrivalled in any other known witch trial'.[6]

Thirdly, Isobel's confessions are also noteworthy for their distinctive linguistic and narrative style. The detail, which is found in both demonological and folkloric passages, is legendary. Larner noted that, along with the material from Forfar, Isobel's confessions were 'quite exceptional in the richness of the detail which has been recorded', while Maxwell-Stuart echoed, more recently, that she 'goes into much more detail than is customary in her description of the Devil' and that 'when she comes to describe certain incidents, her attention to graphic detail is striking'.[7] The confessions also contain the highest number of charms, both malevolent and benevolent, found in any witchcraft record in Britain, and possibly Europe, from this period, with the tally amounting to an impressive twenty-seven.[8] This detail is further enhanced by the fact that it is woven into a narrative delivered with exceptional verbal fluency and dramatic flair. As we have seen earlier, when transcribing her records in 1833, Robert Pitcairn not only admired Isobel's 'singularly descriptive powers' but, with regard to one passage, went so far as to note that it was 'perhaps, in all respects, the most extraordinary in the history of witchcraft of this or any other country. Any comment would only weaken the effect of such very remarkable descriptions'.[9] In the subsequent century, folklorist John Macculloch suggested, rather less reverentially, that 'Isobel had a lively imagination as well as the gift of the gab, and her clerical judges drank in the vivid accounts'; Thomas Davidson that 'Isobel always seemed to do everything in a big way'; and Rossell Hope Robbins that her imagination was 'as powerful as Zola's'.[10] These views are echoed in George Bain's observation that 'The startling and strange feature of her evidence is that it reveals an elaborate system of incantation and devilry requiring considerable ingenuity even to imagine and suggest.'[11]

Lastly, Isobel's confessions are exceptional because they are one of the small minority in which the passages pertaining to harmful magic are so vivid and idiosyncratic that they point firmly beyond the artifice of the interrogators or the projections of neighbours to the possibility that the accused believed herself to be a malevolent witch. Comments such as 'we mey shoot them dead at our pleasur' and 'I haw done so manie ivill deidis, espe[ci]allie killing of men etc' persuaded Jeffrey Russell to conclude that 'it is probable that she believed what she was saying; her case is one of the clearest indications that people . . . could under the influence of prevailing beliefs come to believe themselves diabolical witches'. More recently, the folklorist Jeremy Harte has concluded that that Isobel 'does evil because she enjoys it', while Cowan and Henderson simply define her as a 'self-confessed witch'.[12]

It is by virtue of their many extraordinary features that Isobel's confessions are consistently featured in both academic and popular books on witchcraft. But as we noted in the Introduction to Part I, until now they have not yet been subjected to detailed study. No-one has attempted to examine, in any detail, the interrogatorial arena in which the confessions were forged; the question of how much confessional material can be linked to Isobel and how much to her questioners; and most importantly, what Isobel may have meant by many of the things she said. This kind of 'epistemological analysis', as we can term it here, is difficult at the best of times. With regard to any witchcraft testimony, historical distance from the event, the contamination of the sources and the elusive nature of the crime itself, make it difficult to understand how even the most conventional witchcraft confessions may have been created and what part even the most unimaginative suspect may have played in this creation process. But with Isobel's material, we are presented with an additional challenge. While every historian has their own perspective on her confessions, and these perspectives may vary widely, they all agree upon one fundamental thing – the confessions' extraordinary unusualness. As a consequence, when attempting to analyse Isobel's testimony we do not only have to explore what she said and why she may have said it, but we also have to explore why the things she said were so different from the things other witches said.

This overriding issue of unusualness is an important one, not just because unusualness is interesting in itself, but because it has been responsible for the fact that Isobel, more than any other witchcraft suspect on record, has been persistently dogged by accusations of insanity. Even at the time of her prosecution the privy council, having seen her confessions, cautioned the commissioners to make sure that she and her accomplice,

Janet Breadheid, were 'of sound judgment' and in 'nowayes distracted', and these suspicions have been repeatedly echoed since the confessions came into the public domain in 1833.[13] In 1857, Sir Walter Scott noted Isobel's 'derangement of mind' and memorably claimed that 'It only remains to suppose, that this wretched creature [Isobel] was under the dominion of some peculiar species of lunacy, to which a full perusal of her confession might perhaps guide a medical person of judgement and experience'.[14] In the following century, Macculloch described her testimony as 'delusions and erotic ravings'; Robbins asserted that she 'appeared clearly demented'; and even the normally-measured Katharine Briggs described Isobel's narratives as 'strange, mad confessions'.[15] Similarly, both George Bain and Thomas Smout, both balanced historians, dismissed Isobel's accounts respectively as 'horrible delusions' and 'insane fantasies'.[16] Although it is no longer the convention for historians and folklorists to pathologise witchcraft confessions in this reductive way, the view that Isobel was somehow mentally unstable persists. In 2005, in an introduction to a selection of folklorist John G. Campbell's works, Gaelic scholar Ronald Black drew attention to 'Isobel's ramblings' and claimed that she 'appears to have been a simple-minded young woman' whose imagination had been 'disordered' by the many tales of witchcraft she had heard. Similarly, in 2004 Harte noted her 'sad, crazy talk'.[17]

In Auldearn today, popular wisdom has it that Isobel may have suffered insanity as a result of contracting ergotism or, as it has been colloquially termed from the Middle Ages onwards, 'St Anthony's Fire', a disease caused by the *Claviceps purpurea* mycotoxin which, in its convulsive form, can cause a range of mental disturbances including mania, psychosis, delirium, dementia and hallucinations.[18] While any blanket association between ergotism and witchcraft prosecutions is generally dismissed by contemporary historians, in Isobel's case we cannot rule out the possibility completely. Rye grain, the primary vehicle that carries the ergot mycotoxin, was grown in several parts of Nairnshire, including some of Park's estates, in this period, and studies have shown that prior to the advent of modern pesticides most rye crops, wherever they were grown, are likely to have been infected with the fungus, with levels fluctuating in response to weather conditions and occasionally rising to degrees sufficient to cause local epidemics.[19] Moreover, that it may have risen to these levels in mid seventeenth-century Auldearn is strongly suggested by local minister Donald Mitchell's claim, a little over 100 years later, in reference to the adjoining parish of Ardclach, that 'St Anthony's Fire is a disease peculiar to the people of this place, both young and old'.[20] Isobel's claim to have kneaded clay 'werie sore lyk rye bowt (*meal*)' clearly attests to the fact that she herself consumed rye bread, and we can assume that being among the poorer Nairnshire residents she would have baked with the dark flour that so easily masked the presence of the red ergot-infected grain.

The Isobel-was-crazy hypothesis is further intensified by the fact that, mycotoxins aside, there has been a long historical association between witchcraft and insanity. The question as to whether some witchcraft suspects were mentally ill was often posed in the early modern period; and as the witch hunts went on, prosecutors and authorities became increasingly aware that false confessions could be produced through mental illness or disturbance (as opposed to the false confessions produced in response to the more esoteric disruptions of the Devil). Indeed, after the mid-seventeenth century it was not uncommon for the privy council to send cautions along with their commissions advising the judges to ensure that their suspects were not psychologically unstable. The very fact that such cautions were issued suggests that this distinction was sometimes abused by those either unable, or unwilling, to make it; mistakes undoubtedly exacerbated by the fact that mental illness, then as now, is so difficult to define. The black and white division of mentalities into 'sane' and 'insane' which characterized the early days of psychiatry is no longer tenable, and contemporary psychologists are more likely to identify mental illness as the presence of one or more 'psychiatric disorders' which can lie at any point along a scale of severity ranging from mild at one end to extreme at the other. Those with a disorder registered at the extreme end of the scale, such as morbid schizophrenics, are considered overtly insane in almost any culture, while those with conditions registered at the mild end are usually, depending on cultural mores, considered perfectly sane. Individuals suffering from a disorder that lies in the intermediate section of the severity scale (that is, it is extreme enough to disrupt their lives and cause unhappiness but not to prevent the development of positive relationships or some kind of integration into society) find themselves in an ambiguous position. Even today, these intermediate disorders are difficult to identify and manage, and there is no doubt that in the early modern period it would have been those who suffered from these, as opposed to the more overt forms of metal illness such as schizophrenia, who would have fallen foul of the judicial system.

From one perspective, these speculations are immaterial. It could be argued that, with regard to Isobel, the question of mental illness, whether ergot-induced or not, is largely irrelevant. And it is true that for general purposes, we can certainly enjoy the rich folklore and vivid detail of her confessions without needing to be precise about her psychological health. But if we wish to understand the woman behind the confessions, and why she made them, then such an assessment is important. It is even more pressing if we wish to use her confessional material as a building block upon which to construct larger hypotheses with broader cultural relevance. For these types of analyses, the place where Isobel sits on the 'psychiatric disorder severity scale' is directly proportional to the usefulness of her trial content. The nearer she is seen to be to the extreme end, the more her confessional content must be considered anomalous, and valuable only in the sense that it illuminates Isobel herself. The nearer she is to the mild end, the more this content can be seen to be representative of her peers, and more safely used as a basis on which to theorise about her wider community.

As a consequence of these factors, in the first half of this book our epistemological analysis of Isobel's confessions will tread two paths simultaneously. We will be approaching the confessions as we would any other from the period: using a variety of historiographical methods, including comparative analysis of other witchcraft records and cultural contextualization, to explore the factors that gave rise to her testimony. But at the same time our research will be responsive to the need to explore and explain the confessions' unusualness. Through attempting to identify, with some precision, exactly how and why Isobel's confessions were so unconventional, we will gradually peel away the extraordinary veneer that has historically acted, like a glamour, to obscure the woman behind them. Although this process cannot hope to provide any concrete refutation of the Isobel-was-crazy hypothesis it will, nevertheless, provide us with a finer feeling for the nature of her psychological state.

Voluntary Confession

We need to begin our analysis by taking a preliminary look at the core dilemma facing any investigation into witch-records: how far was the suspect's testimony freely given and how far was it coerced? Scholars frequently draw attention to the fact that Isobel seems to have produced her confession willingly, and indeed, among popular writers this has become something of a mantra, the name 'Isobel Gowdie' being seldom mentioned without a qualifying phrase along the lines of 'who gave her confession voluntarily' or 'who confessed without torture'. There are many causes for the emergence of this myth. Although references to voluntary confession such as 'ye freely confessed' appear in a significant minority of records from this period, Isobel's confessions are unique in that many words are used to make the point and the point is made frequently.[21] The first confession begins boldly with the claim that 'the said Issobell gowdie appeiring penetent for hir haynows (*heinous*) sines of witch craft and th[a]t she haid bein ower long in th[a]t service w[i]thout any compulsitoris proceidit in hir confessione' and concludes that it was 'spokin and willinglie confest'. The third and fourth confessions repeat these sentiments, with the last concluding dramatically that 'All this w[i]th a great many mor terrible things we the s[aid]is witnesses and no[ta]r haird the s[ai]d Issobell confes and most willinglie & penetent lyk speak furth of hir ovin mowth'.

The myth of Isobel's voluntary confession has also been fostered by the fact that, as already noted, her testimony is uniquely composed of relatively seamless descriptive passages delivered in the first-person, these two factors combining to create the effect of a continuous, stream-of-consciousness-like flow of dialogue that conjures up images of Isobel standing in Auldearn tolbooth boldly holding forth while the clerk frantically scribbled in an effort to keep up. But these anomalies are misleading. First, seamless narrative does not necessarily reflect seamless delivery. All early modern witchcraft interrogations, by virtue of being criminal investigations, involved questioning, but the clerks and notaries who recorded proceedings seldom reproduced the questions asked, preferring instead to conflate question and answer into single statements. In other words, an interrogator/suspect exchange along the lines of 'Did you meet the Devil?' 'Yes' would have been recorded by the clerk as 'She met the Devil'. In the majority of records we can detect the presence of these invisible questions through the way the narrative is ordered, most commonly through itemization (with sections of text being prefixed by phrases such as 'Item, filed and convict for') or the use of repeated expressions such as 'She confessed that' or 'You were delated by so and so for' etc.[22] But in a minority of cases these ordering methods are so inconsistent or subtle that they hardly intrude upon the text at all, and Isobel's confessions can be numbered among the most extreme in this category. A similar judgement can be made with regard to the first-person issue. Although most witchcraft confessions are recorded in the third person, and most trial dittays in the second, we do find individual statements, or even on occasion longer passages, recorded in the first person.[23] Although, as we shall explore in more depth later, the fact that Isobel's confessions are recorded consistently in the first person is unique, the fact that it occurs at all can be seen, like the absence of ordering, to represent an extreme example of an established norm as opposed to something without precedent. In other words, we cannot point to a seamless, first-person narrative as sure evidence that Isobel's confessions were freely given.

But there remains one last factor, with regard to the voluntary confession issue, that is more difficult to dismiss. As touched on earlier, Isobel's confessions are notable for the fact that a wealth of personal and folkloric references are woven deeply into all four confessions; references that are frequently so colourful and idiosyncratic that we can be certain that they came from Isobel herself. Colloquial nicknames such as 'pikle neirest the wind' and 'over the dyk w[i]th it', and vivid descriptions of 'bossis baked' elf boys 'whytting and dighting' elf arrows were definitely not put into Isobel's mouth, in the form of questions, by her interrogators. This assumption still does not give licence to assume that her confessions were voluntary (for just because information clearly came from a witchcraft suspect does not mean that it was freely or willingly given) but on the other, it strongly suggests that Isobel was substantially involved in the creation of the confessions. But how involved, and in what way, is a more complex question. And in order to answer it we need to stand back and look at the mechanics of early modern witch-interrogation from a wider perspective.

Coercive Interrogations

In the early modern period a large number of women, and to a lesser extent men, confessed to having committed the crime of witchcraft, and ever since historians have struggled to explain why. It is difficult for the post-Enlightenment mind to understand how an individual could stand in a courtroom before the massed members of their community and confess to having made a pact with Satan, or to having performed a ritual or charm which caused the death of a child, knowing full well that in doing so they sealed their own death warrant. Although historians have long been aware of the rationales which lay behind early modern witchcraft belief, and been aware that people could believe themselves capable of causing magical effects, when analysing witchcraft testimonies they have traditionally focused on the phenomenon of 'false confession', in the assumption that the accused was coerced or somehow enticed into accepting responsibility for a crime that they did not commit.

There is no doubt that witchcraft suspects were pressurized to make confessions in seventeenth-century Scotland, although there is ongoing dispute among contemporary scholars over how to define and assess the nature and frequency of the methods of coercion used. Acts coming under the general definition of 'torture', as it would be understood today, could range from the use of instruments specifically designed to produce pain such as the thumbscrews or the iron boot, to less formal practices (often not defined in the period as torture proper at all, but subsumed under the general terms 'maltreatment or ill-usage') such as beating, shaving, pricking and, most commonly of all, sleep-deprivation.[24] The use of these coercive methods was largely unregulated, with Edinburgh University's Survey of Scottish Witchcraft recently concluding that 'In theory, torture was only to be used with the permission of the state; however in reality it would seem that torture was frequently used without any official permission. It was not until after the 1661–2 period of high level witch accusations that the privy council issued a declaration that torture was only to be used with its permission.'[25]

There is no doubt that suspects gave false confessions in order to obtain relief from such coercion. Before her execution at Edinburgh in 1596, Alison Balfour denied her previous testimony claiming that she had been tortured 'out of all remembrance of guid or evill' and that 'upoun promeis of hir lyffe, and guid deid be the said Persoune, falslie, aganis hir saull and conscience, sche maid that Confessioun, and na uthirwyis'.[26] Similarly, in Pittenweem in 1705, after observing the maltreatment of a group of local witchcraft suspects, an observer commented:

> the Minister and Baillies imprisoned these poor Women, and set a Guard of drunken Fellows about them, who by pinching and Pricking some of them with Pins and Elsions, kept them from sleep for several Days and Nights together; the Marks whereof were seen by severals a month thereafter; this cruel Usage made some of them learn to be so wise, as acknowledge every Question that was ask'd them; whereby they found the Minister and Baillies well pleas'd, and themselves better treated.[27]

But while coercive interrogatorial methods certainly occurred, assessing their frequency and extent is more difficult, for they were not generally recorded. Recent research suggests that the use of specific instruments of torture, such as the thumbscrews or the boot, was infrequent but that maltreatment was likely to have been common or even, according to some assessments, routine. Certainly, in reference to witchcraft suspects tried by 'Gentlemen, and others in the Country', prominent Scottish lawyer Sir George Mackenzie lamented in 1678 that 'Most of these poor creatures are tortur'd by their keepers, who being persuaded that they do God good service, think it their duty to vex and torment poor Prisoners'.[28] Similarly, nearly twenty years later Scottish scholar George Sinclair echoed that 'it is commonly believed that many innocent Persons have suffered as Witches, especially such as have been Tortur'd to a Confession'.[29]

There is also evidence that false confessions were made even when coercive interrogatorial methods were not employed. Some innocent suspects clearly pleaded guilty in the hope of leniency or, more unusually, because conviction was for some reason seen as preferable to release. Mackenzie claimed, for example, that a witchcraft suspect 'told me under secrecie' that:

> she had not confest because she was guilty, but being a poor creature, who wrought for her meat, and being defam'd for a Witch she knew she would starve, for no person thereafter would either give her meat or lodging, and that all men would beat her, and hound Dogs

at her, and that therefore she desired to be out of the World; whereupon she wept most bitterly, and upon her knees call'd God to witness to what she said.[30]

As we shall explore in more depth in CHAPTER NINE, contemporary research into the psychology of false confession suggests that even when imprisoned and interrogated in relatively benign conditions, perfectly sane criminal suspects can cave in under the authoritative convictions of their interrogators and the pressure of evidence lodged against them, temporarily losing faith in their own ability to judge what they may or may not have done and finally accepting the allegations made against them. The fact that it was not uncommon for witchcraft suspects to subsequently deny or retract previous confessions also supports this thesis; psychologists having identified recantation as one of the core characteristics of this form of false confession.[31]

Remaining 'Obstinat'

While it is undoubtedly probable that a substantial number of witchcraft suspects confessed to having performed crimes they did not commit, this does not mean that we can dismiss all confessions, or even all the parts of an individual confession, as false; nor that we can simplistically cast the (always male) interrogator in the role of powerful orchestrator and the (usually female) witch as a helpless victim. The truth, as always, was more complex. Ongoing research into Scottish witchcraft records suggests that it was common for suspects to consistently refute accusations of witchcraft. In 1981 Larner asserted that 'Given the pressures upon the suspects during their imprisonment it is remarkable that so many of them asserted their innocence to the end'; while more recently, in his analysis of the 1661–2 wave of persecutions, Maxwell-Stuart emphasized that 'people did not always automatically cave in to whatever pressures may have been exerted to get them to confess and conform' and that, with regard to gender dynamics, 'Scottish women were by no means overawed by male authority, and we shall find them fully prepared to resist it when they thought it was unjust or unfair'.[32] Such resistance could even be maintained in the face of severe coercion. Earlier in this chapter we cited an account from Pittenweem (1705) to illustrate how false confessions could be elicited through maltreatment. But interestingly, this account could just as easily be used to illustrate the opposite. As we have seen, the writer claimed that as a result of much 'cruel Usage . . . some of them [the suspects] learn to be so wise, as acknowledge every Question that was ask'd them'. But the phrase 'some of them' indicates that a number of the suspects were able to resist these pressures; a fact corroborated by the author's subsequent observation that 'Notwithstanding of all this [cruel usage] some of the more Foolish, continued, as the Minister said, hardened in the Devil's service'.[33] Similarly, in Caithness in 1719, three accomplices named by witchcraft suspect Margaret Nin-Gilbert remained obstinate, the sheriff depute of Caithness writing that 'there are other three defamed by her who continues incarcerated, but notwithstanding of great pains taken upon them, cannot be brought to any confession'.[34]

These perspectives are supported by the growing acknowledgement among histo-

rians that witch-interrogators were not as narrow-minded and bent on conviction as
has traditionally been assumed. By the mid-seventeenth century the vein of caution and
scepticism that was to contribute towards the demise of witch trials in the subsequent
century, and which was so eloquently put to paper by Scot and Weyer in the previous,
was clearly evident on many levels of Scottish society. Indeed, in April 1662 the privy
council were sufficiently concerned about the dangers of coerced and false confessions
to issue a declaration urging that witchcraft testimony be procured 'without any maner
of tortur or other indirect meanes used' and that 'at the tyme of their confessions they
[the suspects] were of right judgement, nowayes distracted or under any earnest desyre
to dy'.[35] How seriously such reservations were taken is well illustrated in the following
account from Sinclair, which describes how prosecutors in mid seventeenth-century
Lauder rather farcically attempted to persuade a woman suspected of concocting false
testimony to retract her confession. 'Intelligent persons', the text reads:

> began to be jealous of the truth of that confession, and began to suspect, that out of the pride
> of her heart, in a desperate way, she had made up that confession to destroy her life, because
> she still pressed to be cut off with the rest upon Munday. Therefore much pains was taken
> on her by Ministers, and others, on Saturday, Sunday, and Munday morning, that she might
> resile from that confession . . . yea, it was charged home upon her by the Ministers, that
> there was just ground of Jealousie, [and] that her confession was not sincere . . .[36]

But it was not only enlightened ministers, scholars or privy councillors who possessed
such refined sensibilities. Recently, scholars like Todd and Maxwell-Stuart have
asserted that the landowners and businessmen who sat on the kirk sessions in the early
modern period could be equally discriminating. As members of the local community,
they argue, sessions members were usually well aware of the interpersonal tensions that
lay behind witchcraft accusations, and made considerable attempts to solve the causes
of discord rather than jump to assumptions of witchcraft. Todd notes that 'contemporaries were well aware that interpersonal conflict very often lay behind charges of
witchcraft' and that 'the vast majority of witchcraft charges in kirk session books were
answered by mediation of a quarrel rather than pursuit of presumed sorcery'.[37] She then
goes on to suggest that during the waves of national witch-panic, rather than
succumbing to conviction-hysteria, the sessions actually increased their caution:

> in nearly every case the individual bringing the charge of witchcraft was made to apologise
> to the woman (or more rarely the man) so labelled, even when the slanderer was male and
> of higher social status . . . In the midst of a real witch craze in 1626–7, the Dysart session
> punished any slander of witchcraft with unusual severity, given the serious outcome of crim-
> inal pursuit.[38]

Obviously the kirk sessions, as arbiters of minor crimes, had more luxury to take their
time and exercise leniency than an assize court, or a locally convened court held under
a commission of justiciary, both of which usually examined cases for which there was
a strong body of evidence against the accused and therefore a higher prior presumption

of guilt. But even these more serious cases may have been negotiated with a lighter hand than might be imagined. As the Survey of Scottish Witchcraft has revealed, most of the records that emerged between 1563 and 1736 contain no record of the sentences given to named witches. However, of the 305 individual cases where the latter is known, it is notable that roughly a third of the accused did not receive the death penalty. This is only a tentative figure and, as Goodare has emphasized, subsidiary evidence can be marshalled to either elevate or lower it.[39] But as it stands it represents a level of restraint, even in the years that saw the highest numbers of convictions. Having said this, in Isobel's case the prognosis was likely to have been less favourable. Most of the 305 trials used to arrive at this figure took place at the central justiciary court, whereas those held at the less regulated locally-organized courts, where investigations fuelled by personal vendetta were more easily cloaked, and maltreatment (as Mackenzie lamented) less policed, the death sentence was likely to have been more frequent.[40] Indeed, although they acknowledge that their figures are based on limited evidence, Larner and her fellow researchers have argued that justiciary court acquittal rates were at least 50 per cent higher than those at locally convened courts and that, as Levack has recently re-emphasized, 'in more than 90 per cent of all the trials conducted by local commissioners the accused were convicted and executed'.[41]

Isobel's Interrogation

As this brief overview indicates, in mid seventeenth-century Scotland witchcraft investigations spanned a wide spectrum: with interrogatorial methods ranging from the heavily coercive to the restrained, and suspects from the easily intimidated to the stoically defiant. The question we must now ask is, where, on this spectrum, can we place Isobel and the men who questioned her?

Our first point of interest is the fact that Alexander Colville, the justice depute who recommended the granting of the commission for her trial, was clearly well aware of the miscarriages of justice that could occur in witchcraft interrogations.[42] In June 1662, when discussing (what we have assumed to be) Isobel's case with Alexander Brodie, Colville cautioned the latter that the allegations of accomplices could not always be believed 'becaus the devel can mak appeirances fals' and that 'the mark is not infallible, because phisicians think by natural means the flesh may be deadnd and feeling taken away'.[43] The fact that Colville was considered, by his contemporaries, to be a man of 'great sagacity and knowledge as to Witches', suggests that this caution reflected wider opinion among his peers. Similarly, when the privy council issued the commission to try Isobel and Janet Breadheid in mid-July they also included the following note of reservation:

> quhilk commission conteanes these qualities, that if they [Janet Breadheid and Isobel Gowdie] shall be found guilty of the said cryme upon voluntar confessions without any sort of torture or other indirect meanes used or that malefices be legallie instructed and proven against them, and at the tyme of their confessions they were of sound judgement, nowayes

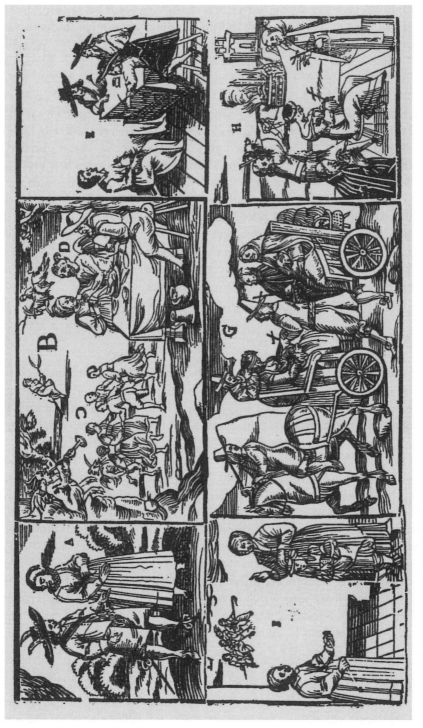

This set of woodcuts illustrates a mid seventeenth-century witchcraft trial, in this case that of Anna Ebeler, who was tried in Augsburg in 1669. Read from left to right, the images provide a chronological account of the witch's story, from her first meeting with the Devil to her prosecution. The final two images depict Isobel's probable fate – being transported by cart to the place of execution, exhorted to repent and then burnt to ashes on a pyre.

distracted or under any ernest desyre to die, and that they reiterat and renew ther former confessions judicially, that then and in that case and no otherwayes, they cause the sentence of death to be execute upon them conform to the lawes of this realm.[44]

The privy council issued such cautions relatively frequently after the April 1662 proclamation, but not across the board, and therefore it is difficult to assess how far, in Isobel's case, it was sent out as a routine precaution or knee-jerk response to the recent proclamation, and how far it reflected the fact that there was something about her confessions that made the privy councillors suspect that either mental illness or undue coercion may have been involved.[45]

But if the privy council did indeed have suspicions with regard to torture or maltreatment in Isobel's case, were they justified? The evidence is mixed. On the one hand, there is no doubt that the vein of judicial caution that ran through Scotland in this period also took a course through Nairnshire. Alexander Brodie, who was on the commission to try a number of witches during the 1660s, and who also, according to John Barrett, 'led opinion' among the Moray gentry, clearly believed that suspects should not be physically mistreated.[46] In relation to Isobel Elder and Isobel Simpson, who were tried for witchcraft in Forres in 1663, Brodie wrote: 'It troubld me that ani constraint should hav bein usd to them; that they should hav bein beaten.' He also seems to have been anxious that questioning be conducted with integrity claiming, with regard to the same case, that:

> I again and again beseech the lord to mak truth appear, and bring it forth to victori; to guid the Judges, and to giv them understanding; to guid us, that we be not blinded with carnal passion or prejudic, or mistak; to open the harts and mouths of thes poor wretches; and to ordour this matter to his glori.[47]

Brodie's scruples also came to the fore when, the previous year, some tenants came to him bearing witchcraft accusations against two local women, Sandie Hardie and Margaret Clerk. Clearly taking the case to heart, the laird went home that evening and prayed that 'Let the Lord cleir and goe befor us. I desir'd that noe sinful piti or respect might blind upon the one hand, nor misguided zeal on the other.'[48] Similarly, with regard to the questioning of the witch named Bandon, who was tried in Auldearn several months after Isobel, Brodie wrote 'I neither would press her to tell, nor yet hinder her, onli exhort her to doe nothing ignorantli or out of ani sinistrous end, by respt. [respect], passion, anger, reveng, prejudic, or the lyk.'[49] The fact that Brodie consistently referred to witchcraft suspects as 'poor creaturs' as opposed to enemies of God or servants of Satan suggests that his scruples were rooted in compassion as well as intellectual discernment.[50]

It is also clear that Brodie was not alone in his reservations. The case of Forres witches Elder and Simpson seems to have been difficult for all concerned, largely because the two women first gave full confessions and then later retracted them. But rather than seizing upon the women's recantations as a sanction to increase interrogatorial pressure, a number of commissioners responded by pulling back from the fray, making it difficult, on more than one occasion, to mass a quorum. According to Brodie, Sir Robert Innes of Moortown 'was so scrupolous that he would scarc meit, but resolvd not to vote', while Thomas Dunbar of Grange, having declined one meeting, only reluctantly appeared at the trial itself, and when there, voiced resistance to the giving of the death penalty.[51] Indeed, reservations ran so high among the commissioners that Brodie had cause to note that 'ther be not that zeal in them as [to] this wickednes', with this loss of impetus finally provoking him to send one of their number 'to the Bishop to communicat with him, and to get his advic' for the 'encouradgment of thes imployd'.[52] This lack of zeal may have been rooted, in part, in the fact that the perceived mishandling of witchcraft interrogations seems to have been openly criticized in the region; a situation that bred an anxious self-consciousness about the whole process. When Elder and Simpson were condemned, for example, Brodie hesitated to get involved in a dispute about who should be responsible for their subsequent care because 'I desird not to be lookd on as the pursuer of thes poor creaturs, and therefor left it on them.'[53] We can speculate that similar misgivings may have underpinned his resistance to Alexander Colville's attempts, in 1662, to 'hav me on a particular commission'.[54] It is likely that scruples such as these also lay behind the fact that Nairnshire witchcraft interrogators did not routinely procure confessions. Several of the witchcraft suspects known to us did not plead guilty. Brodie's tenants Sandie Hardie and Margaret Clerk, for example, 'denied soe vehementlie that we could get noe clearnes', and the fact that his diaries do not mention their case again suggests that it was dropped. Similarly, as we have already seen, although Elder and Simpson made full confessions when they were first interrogated, they later 'denied all that they had confessd' and despite efforts to urge them otherwise, 'died obstinat'.[55]

Purging the Land

But this evidence of restraint is counterbalanced by evidence of a very different kind. It is clear that, despite their scruples about the interrogatorial process, during this period the Nairnshire gentry nurtured a very real fear of witches. As seen earlier, in March 1662, in what may have been an early reference to Isobel's case, Brodie recorded in his diary that 'I heard from Scotland that ther was a great discoveri of witchcraft in the parish of Dyk; and in my land, they had purposd evel against my son and his wyf.' The fact that Brodie concluded this entry with the claim to be 'exercisd under this, and the mani troubls that myself and my poor freinds wer involvd and plungd in' suggests that he took the threat of witchcraft seriously, as do his comments made three months later, after reading Isobel's and Janet's confessions:

> Among other things I am desiring this day to lay to hart the prevailing of the Devil by witchcraft. Oh! that's a sadd token of displeasur, quhen Thou permitts him to deceav, tempt, and to prosper, and that his visibl kingdom taks issue expressli. As if thou hadst given up that place wher I had my residenc, and the inhabitants of it, to be the Devel's propertie and possession, what comfort can I hav in it? Shall I not bemoan . . . Sathan's

success, the spreding of sin, the destroying of so mani immortal souls? And even in that place quhair I live.[56]

The Nairnshire gentry did not only consider witchcraft to be a genuine threat, but they were also sensible of their responsibilities, as custodians of the godly society, to seek to eliminate it when uncovered. Brodie, for example, rounded off the above diatribe with the chilling soliloquy: 'what does this say to me? Oh teach! teach for thy nam[e]'s sak! Discover in the mean tym mor, and destroy as thou discovers his [Satan's] works. Let the land be purgd and not given over, for thy nam'.[57] Five days later, after having discussed the case with Colville, his evangelistic fervour was again renewed, and he pledged to himself:

> my hand shall still be lifted up to God for mercie to the land in this particular, and that he would glorifi himself in discovering and destroying all thes and other works of the Devel; may rais up zealous and able men, and with inlarged and of good understanding for this end: and that he would not giv over the land to be posest by devels . . . [58]

Such sentiments and preconceptions undoubtedly obscured judgement. It is certain, for example, that physical coercion was used against some Nairnshire suspects. The fact that Brodie was concerned that Isobel Elder and Isobel Simpson may have been beaten suggests that they probably were, with the evidence pointing to the fact that their original confessions, which they later recanted, had been generated as a result of this abuse. It is also clear that Nairnshire interrogators were capable of sending witches to their death, even when guilt was ambiguous. Although Brodie knew and disapproved of the fact that coercion had been employed to obtain Elder and Simpson's original confessions; and although the women vehemently retracted their initial confessions; and although he was anxious not to be 'blinded with carnal passion or prejudic, or mistak' when interrogating them; and although some of his fellow commissioners had severe doubts about the women's culpability, Brodie still clung tenaciously to his original assumption of guilt throughout the proceedings. Indeed, unlike his fellow commissioner Thomas Dunbar of Grange, his belief that the women were culpable seems to have been hardened, as opposed to softened, by their recantations, leading him to lament, 'I was in great darkness anent the matter, being desirous that sin might be discoverd and punishd on the one part; ther denial, difficulti of proving, and the restriction of the commission, on the other part, straightning.'[59] Like many men in his position, including the minister from Pittenweem we met earlier, Brodie justified his presumption of guilt through a chilling circular logic, concluding that it was the Devil – and not the truth – that lay behind their protestations of innocence: 'The poor creaturs wer found guilti, and condemned to die', he noted, relatively compassionately, before adding ominously 'The witnesses agreid clearli and fullie; but Sathan hardnd them to denie. Let the Lord overcom ther obdurednes in His due tym.'[60] Similarly Brodie's plea, during prayer, that 'noe sinful piti or respect might blind' his judgement suggests that a belief that sympathy could sabotage the search for truth may have also been an efficient way to suppress emotional qualms.[61]

In the last analysis, despite his evident capacity for compassion and despite all his introspective agonizing about what course of interrogatorial action was right or wrong, Brodie's religious ambition and visceral human fear, articulated through the intellectual machinery of Protestant fundamentalism, was more powerful than his commitment to either the nuances of the law, or, ultimately, his commonsense or empathy. Nowhere is this mentality more chillingly expressed than in a diary entry recorded on 8 October 1662. In reference to a case in which Brodie seems not to have been involved, and to suspects whom he seems not to have known, the laird could still claim, 'I heard that at Invernes ther was non of the witches condemnd, and I desird to consider this and be instructed. This, if God prevent not, will be of veri ill example.'[62]

So much for Brodie, but what of the men who actually interrogated Isobel? In the first instance, we can assume that they shared similarly complex views. As we saw in the last chapter, as the ruling inhabitants of an isolated covenanting stronghold the lairds of Nairnshire, already bound by blood and marriage, were more tightly bound by religious and political views than those inhabiting less religiously extreme, or more religiously diverse, Scottish counties. We can add to this the fact that Brodie was not only one of those who 'led opinion' among the Moray gentry but he was also intimate with, if not related to, many of the men present at Isobel's interrogation. William Dallas of Cantrey, Thomas Dunbar of Grange, Alexander Dunbar of Boath, John Stewart the sheriff depute of Moray, Alexander Brodie of Lethen, Auldearn schoolmaster Alexander Dunbar, Harry Forbes and Hugh Rose were all in frequent contact with Brodie, as were the commissioners not present at the interrogations, including Sir Hugh Campbell of Cawdor, sheriff principal of Nairn and Hugh Rose of Kilravock.

But while we can assume Brodie's views on witchcraft prosecution to have represented the general tenor of Isobel's interrogation, within this mean there would have been variations of opinion. We can speculate, for example, that some of the men present may have brought more scruples to the table than Brodie would have done, had he been present. Thomas Dunbar of Grange, who witnessed Isobel's first interrogation, was not only related to Brodie by marriage but also became one of his lifelong friends. A close neighbour, based near Forres, Grange joined the latter in his ongoing battles for religious independence after the Restoration and visited him in the weeks before his death.[63] But although he was a staunch covenanter who shared many of Brodie's views, the Forres laird seems to have exhibited more discernment than the latter during the controversial trial of Elder and Simpson, with Brodie complaining, as we saw earlier, that Grange declined to be present at a meeting of the commissioners and only reluctantly appeared at the trial itself, where he 'was [still] not clear; albeit he consented to the asiz, yet he was avrs [averse] from the sentenc of death'.[64] Though we have little information about Grange, Brodie's diaries hint at some of the qualities that may have lain behind these scruples. The fact that Brodie followed his claim that the Forres laird was 'avrs from the sentenc of death' with the comment 'I desird to be touchd with som human affection towards thes wretched creatures, and bewail their sin and miserie' suggests that his guilt in this respect may have been provoked by visible evidence of Grange's compassion. The fact that, later in the same passage, Brodie expressed an anxiety 'not to be lookd on as the pursuer of [the witches]' could also point to self-consciousness in the face of his friend's reservations. Grange's capacity for empathy is also hinted at in Brodie's claim that, when he was embroiled in an emotional dispute with a neighbour that evoked 'resentment . . . passion and heat' on both sides, reconciliation commenced when the neighbour 'was, by the persuasion of Grang and others, induced to com to me, and professd som kindnes'.[65]

We can speculate that the recently-installed minister of Nairn, Hugh Rose, who was present at three, and possibly all four, of Isobel's interrogations, brought similar sentiments to the proceedings. As a local divine, with an interest undoubtedly sharpened by Isobel's claim that his parishioner, Janet Breadheid, was her primary accomplice, Rose is likely to have been directly involved in the questioning process. This speculation is supported by the fact that his name sits high on the list of witness signatures, and is generally inscribed alongside that of Isobel's minister, Harry Forbes. More than one historian has noted that Hugh Rose merited respect, with Craven, in his *History of the Episcopal Church in the Diocese of Moray*, claiming that he was 'accomplished and worthy' and considered to be 'a person of great knowledge and integrity'.[66] The fact that Rose's *Meditations* periodically divert – more markedly than the writings of godly contemporaries like Brodie and Katharine Collace – from conventional preoccupations about personal and peer salvation into vivid evocations on the sufferings of the poor and the powerless, also suggests that he was a compassionate man.[67] Even more relevant to the case in hand is the likelihood that Rose combined these attributes with sound judicial scruples. As Levack has recently noted, a good proportion of the injustices that took place at locally-convened trials resulted from the fact that the lairds, magistrates and elders who conducted the proceedings were 'almost always legally untrained' and therefore more likely to gloss over or exploit the law's many loopholes and grey areas.[68] It is all the more pertinent here, then, to note that before he became 'enamoured of divinity' Rose was an accomplished student of law. His enduring respect for the profession is suggested, not only by the fact that his later writings are filled with legal terminology and metaphor but also by the fact that he alone, of all the witnesses who signed Isobel's confessions, took the trouble not only to follow his signature with the word 'attests', but also with the more legally-precise: 'attests the forsaid declareation as to the principal Substantial'.[69] That Rose did not only retain a commitment to legal propriety, but also a more abstract and profound respect for the truth – in all its elusiveness – is suggested by the fact that the subject emerges as a recurrent theme in his later writings. 'Sometimes we are very remote from truth' he muses in a typical passage from his *Meditations*, 'sometimes we border upon it, but do not come its length: sometimes we think we have it, and are mistaken; sometimes we think we have it, and yet doubt as in suspense. How little it is that man as man can certainly know!'[70]

We can also speculate here, though more tentatively, that Rose may have combined this 'great knowledge', compassion and legal integrity with a level of intellectual discernment concerning witchcraft. The crime was clearly not an enduring preoccupation for the minister, for he does not mention it in his later writings, though he is certainly eloquent enough about other threats to the godly society. Although we can read little into this in itself, it is interesting, in this context, to note that while studying law at Leyden, Rose befriended fellow student George Mackenzie; a man who later rose to pre-eminence as Lord Advocate (also holding the position of justice depute between 1661–3). Mackenzie has gained esteem among historians for being unusually measured with regard to witchcraft, for despite believing in the reality of the crime and maintaining that it should be punishable by death he was openly sceptical about false confession and vigorously condemned the maltreatment of witchcraft suspects.[71] Although we do not know how close Rose and Mackenzie's friendship was, that there was a friendship at all suggest a certain amount of psychological compatibility, and on this basis we could speculate that Rose may have shared some of Mackenzie's scruples regarding false confession. Certainly, as we shall explore in more detail in CHAPTER FIVE, Rose read widely enough and reflected deeply enough to encounter and give thought to current trends of enlightened scepticism. And this deliberation would have been sharpened by the fact that, as his later writings clearly indicate, Rose was not only a man who was painfully aware of the limitations of human knowledge and the problems generated through unexamined opinion or bias, but he was also a man who was capable – almost to the point of procrastination – of seeing both sides of an argument. It is unlikely that the author of the following sentences would have passed over contemporary debates about the nature of witchcraft and the dangers of false confession without giving them careful consideration:

> Man is but man; his judgment is but short, shallow, fallible. Though naturals appear the same to the organs of the external senses, yet how differently do the same positions appear to the judgement of different beholders? To speak nothing of education, humour, prejudice, faction, contradiction, (any of which may bias severally), there is somewhat in mens very judgments which makes as great a difference of opinions, as there is of faces . . . How differently do men judge of one and the same tenet? It is truth with one, an error with another; its is truth for one with one argument; it is reputed truth by another, for another argument.[72]

But while these perspectives on Rose are valid, and paint a genial picture, they must not be over-emphasized. Unlike Mackenzie, Rose's measured progress through the legal profession was interrupted by a call to God that the former, who took a more middle road when it came to religious matters, found hard to understand. In the preface to Rose's *Meditations* Robert Rose claims that 'nothing could surprise the great Sir George Mackenzie more than Mr Rose's resolution of becoming the clergyman, knowing his extraordinary abilities as a lawyer'.[73] Although Rose's covenanting principles were flexible enough to allow him to accept episcopacy, like the majority of his Nairnshire kinsmen he believed it his moral duty to purge the land of all forms of superstition and ungodliness, Brodie stating tellingly, on one occasion, that:

> I spok with Mr. Hugh Ross [Rose] anent the corruptions of the church, and corrupt naughtie men admitted to the ministeri, nobiliti corrupt, and degenerat, and general ignoranc and negligenc reigning, and Poperi, implacablnes of good men to one another, decay of godliness and pieti, and growth of profannes and errour. Thes are tokens of God's wrath.[74]

In conclusion, whatever integrity, compassion and 'extraordinary abilities as a lawyer' Rose brought to Isobel's interrogations, these attributes may well have been undermined, as they so clearly were in Brodie's case, by evangelistic fervour.

To this caveat we can add the fact that although men like Grange and Rose may have been generally more cautious than Brodie with regard to witchcraft convictions, there is evidence that others present at Isobel's interrogations may have been less. The most influential of these was likely to have been the minister of Auldearn, Harry Forbes. Forbes did not only attend every interrogatorial session, but his name headed both the lists of those present and the witness signatures recorded at the beginning and end of every confession. Forbes's involvement was undoubtedly fuelled, in large part, by the fact that as Isobel's local minister he was expected to take a prominent role in the interrogatorial proceedings. But a closer analysis of the circumstantial evidence also suggests that his prominence may have been underpinned, on a deeper level, by a particularly ardent preoccupation with the crime for which she was charged.

It is notable, for example, that apart from a brief mention of a witch who was 'letten loos' in February 1655, Alexander Brodie's references to witchcraft all post-date Forbes's arrival in Auldearn and that when they do emerge, they relate to cases in which the minister was directly involved. Moreover, after Forbes had left the parish in 1663, Brodie does not mention witchcraft again, even in passing. We can read little into this in itself, for there could be many factors at play here. There are large gaps in Brodie's diaries (the most significant being between from October 1656 to July 1661 and July 1663 to January 1671) and the absence of reference to cases after 1663 could reflect the nationwide decline in prosecutions after this date. But on the other hand, supporting evidence invites us to speculate that this pattern reflected the fact that Forbes was more zealous than Brodie where witchcraft was concerned, and that to a certain extent he mobilised the latter in this respect. We have clear evidence, for example, that Forbes did not only share Brodie's fear of witchcraft and his belief that it was it his duty to purge it from his community, but also that, more unusually for an educated man, he believed that he had been a victim of witchcraft himself. In July 1655, several months after Forbes took up his seat in Auldearn, Brodie recorded in his diary that:

> Mr Hari [Forbes] told me what work he had with witches, ther lifting him, and bowing his bodi together in his bedd; ther confessions, and Sathan's own, that they could doe him no harm; made his image of wax, but could not hurt him. Oh! what confimation was this to my soul to beleev in God al sufficient, and not to turn asyd to crooked paths.[75]

Whether this account referred to current or previous events shall be explored in more depth in CHAPTER SEVEN, but it is sufficient to identify it here as clear evidence that the Auldearn minister nurtured an acute and visceral fear of witches. Other entries in Brodie's diaries support this view. In 1655–6 the Dyke laird was visited several times by a local woman named Cathrin Hendrie who believed herself to be tormented by the Devil. The woman was clearly educated and pious, and Brodie took much time attempting to solve her dilemmas. But although he offered up many explanations for her distress, at no time over this period did he suggest that her troubles may have been brought on by witchcraft. It is all the more interesting, then, that when he finally discussed the case with Forbes in January 1656, the latter immediately diagnosed witchcraft as the cause, with Brodie noting: 'I went to Auldearn. I communicated with Mr. Jos. and Mr. Harie anent Cathrin Hendrie and her goodman, how it was that they both should be so afflicted and terrified: they thoght because she had been charmed, she oght to disclaim solemnlie that confederacie.'[76] What this passage clearly reveals is that Forbes saw witchcraft where others did not. And if a man such as Brodie, who did not jump to accusations of witchcraft in cases such as these, and who had scruples about the way he implemented judicial procedure, could sway toward an assumption of guilt during interrogations, then we can presume that Forbes would have been even more likely to do so. As opposed to approaching Isobel, as his contemporary Thomas Dunbar of Grange may have done, with the presumption that she was innocent until proven guilty, he is more likely to have assumed that she was guilty unless proven innocent, and to have felt no compunction in pressing her, as he pressed Brodie to do with Cathrin Hendire, to 'disclaim solemnlie that [witchcraft] confederacie'. As we shall see in CHAPTER FIVE, Forbes certainly succeeded in eliciting confessions out of other reluctant suspects.[77]

But these perspectives, though ominous, do not mean that we can dismiss Forbes as a paranoid bully. As we shall explore in CHAPTER FIVE, there is evidence to suggest that he was both a deep thinker and a patient, empathic listener. Moreover it is clear that however single-minded his views, he was not always as skilful in imposing them onto witchcraft suspects as he may have wished. A year after Isobel's trial, when Elder and Simpson were imprisoned at Forres, Brodie sent Forbes to try and encourage them to deny their recantation and adhere to their original confessions, his diary entry stating: 'I sent Mr Hari to com and wait on the witches; to see if God would open ther hart to giv God glori, and confess ther sins.' But the fact that the women were burnt 'obstinat' at Forres the following day roundly indicates that Forbes was unsuccessful in his attempt.[78]

With regard to the other men present at the interrogations, we have little direct information, although there is scattered evidence to suggest that a number of them may have veered toward the Forbes end of the Forbes/Brodie/Grange continuum we have constructed here. The views of Alexander Brodie the younger of Lethen, who was present at Isobel's first confession, were probably similar to those of his cousin, Alexander Brodie of Brodie, with whom he shared private worship and sought spiritual guidance. Indeed, the fact that after the Restoration Lethen boldly hosted and attended illegal conventicles, despite being jailed for these activities, while Brodie cautiously abstained, suggests that he was more headstrong, and probably more religiously dogmatic than his older kinsman.[79] Similarly, when we explore John Hay of Park and his family in more detail in CHAPTER SEVEN, it will become apparent that, by virtue of their kinship with the zealous laird, both Hugh Hay of Newtown (present at all four of Isobel's confessions) and Hugh Hay of Brightmony (present at three) may not only have veered towards Forbes's more extremist views, but may also have had significantly more influence on Isobel's interrogations than their placing on the witness lists suggest. But although this evidence is suggestive, as our analysis of Grange indicates, we must be careful not to simplistically assume that either intimacy with Brodie or strong covenanting sympathies always translated into bigoted witch-persecution. Schoolmaster and session clerk Alexander Dunbar, who was listed as present at two of Isobel's interrogations and who, as we shall see in CHAPTER FIVE, may also have been involved in committing them to paper, remained a zealous nonconformist minister throughout his whole life and provided Brodie with, as one commentator put it, 'one of the strongest friendships of his life'. However, Bain's enigmatic claim, in his *Lord Brodie: His Life and Times*, that 'we know in after years he [Dunbar] disbelieved entirely in witchcraft', although frustratingly unreferenced, raises the possibility that even as early as 1662 the zealous young schoolmaster nurtured scruples similar to those so clearly displayed by Grange.[80]

How these different characters interacted and operated during the interrogation process can only be surmised. Though rooted in similar ideologies and environment, and more often than not related by marriage or blood, these men were all individuals with their own unique intellectual and emotional perspectives, and we cannot assume that, with regard to Isobel's case or any other, they always displayed a united front. For example, although Grange seems to have been an empathic, reasonable man with a capacity for peace-keeping and negotiation, we can speculate that relations between himself and Harry Forbes may have been cool. In October 1662, while the latter was still toying with the idea of accepting episcopacy, Brodie wrote, 'I did speak to Grang anent Mr. Harie's presentation [to the dean]' but 'found him not soe sensible of his [Forbes's] position as I expected'.[81] Although Brodie's entry confirms that Grange eventually 'yeilded to giv him [Forbes] a presentation', it is possible that his help did not arrive, or had been unsuccessful, for in the following year Grange and his neighbour Alexander Dunbar of Boath presented another man to the dean in Forbes's stead, a course of action which caused Brodie to 'mourn under this and be affected.'[82] As we shall see when we explore Forbes's character in more detail in CHAPTER SEVEN, a number of reasons could have lain behind the possible *froideur* between Grange and Forbes, but given the fact that by the time these events occurred the two men had been involved in a number of witchcraft trials together (including those of Gowdie, Breadheid, Elder, Simpson and probably Bandon, Nic Ean Vane and Mc Gillivorich) it is tempting to speculate whether, on these occasions, a clash between Forbes's interrogatorial zeal and Grange's more measured approach contributed toward this antipathy.[83] This perspective is supported by the fact that if Grange had harboured any misgivings about Forbes, or the judicial procedure at Isobel's interrogations in general, he is likely to have expressed them openly. As we have seen earlier, during the trial of Elder and Simpson the following year, he declined from commissioners' meetings despite the fact that his absence 'hindred' proceedings and frustrated Brodie, and was not afraid to advertize his aversion, in this case, to the sentence of death.[84] We could interpret the fact that Grange only attended Isobel's first interrogation as evidence that the fastidious laird did not want to get involved in a case that was so clearly led by Forbes's prior assumption of guilt. Speculating even more wildly, we could also entertain the possibility that similar reservations lay behind the fact that Grange's fellow commissioner, Alexander Dunbar of Boath, who conspired with him to present Alexander Stewart to the dean in place of Harry Forbes, was also only present at Isobel's first interrogation.

Isobel's 'Voluntary Confession' Qualified

If these labyrinthine investigations into witchcraft prosecutions in contemporary Nairnshire tell us anything, they tell us that with regard to the tenor of Isobel's inter-rogations, we cannot jump to any conclusions. We can fairly safely assume that she was not subjected to specific instruments of judicial torture (such as thumbscrews or the boot), but that it is quite possible that she was beaten and/or pricked, shaved and subjected to sleep-deprivation at some stage in the proceedings. The extremity to which this maltreatment may have been taken, however, is not at all clear. On the one hand, we can speculate that some of the covenanting extremists involved in Isobel's prosecution would have been predisposed to presume her guilt and would therefore have pressed hard for confession, with those who believed themselves to have been the victims of witchcraft, such as Harry Forbes, being particularly zealous in this respect. But on the other, we can also fairly safely assume that these men would have tempered their zeal with a certain level of compassion and intellectual discernment. Because they are likely to have been aware of the types of precautions advised by the privy council, and of the fact that any indecent fervour to convict or marked abuse of suspects would be openly criticised, any physical or psychological maltreatment that may have taken place is unlikely to have spiralled out of control. More specifically, the presence of judi-cious and compassionate men like Hugh Rose and Thomas Dunbar of Grange – who also nurtured, in Rose's case at least, considerable knowledge of the law – would have tempered proceedings with a level of legal propriety that restrained, or at least soft-ened, any interrogatorial excesses that took place. Taking all of these factors into account it is probably fair to say that although pressures, and possibly severe pressures, were undoubtedly put on Isobel to confess, we cannot automatically assume that they would have been abusive enough to force a strong-minded individual to confess some-thing that they did not want to confess, or force a suspect to withdraw a retraction once it had been made.

In conclusion, these perspectives suggest that John Innes's claim that Isobel confessed 'willinglie' and 'w[i]thout any compulsitoris' need not have been an outright lie. But they also suggest that his claim can only be accepted in conjunction with signif-icant caveats. We can accept the statement only if we take into account the fact that she may have 'willinglie' confessed *after* having been mistreated, and perhaps severely. We can accept it only in the sense that, to our knowledge, during the six-week period on record, she did not 'vehemently deny' or recant the charges laid against her, as did her neighbours Hardie, Clerk, Elder and Simpson the following year. We can accept it only on the understanding that a confession given 'w[i]thout any compulsitoris' is not necessarily a true one, for as we have seen, false testimony can be generated in benign, as well as overtly coercive, conditions. And lastly, we can accept the statement only on the understanding that, given the degree of interrogatorial preoccupation with witchcraft and concomitant tendency to assume guilt, Isobel's confession was likely to have been closely directed. In other words, when Isobel 'willinglie' confessed, she willingly confessed to a series of specific, and possibly very detailed, questions put to her by Forbes et al.

The Questioning Process

In our attempt to assess what contribution Isobel made to her confessions, we must now explore, in more detail, the kinds of questions she may have been asked. Our efforts to trace the pattern of these invisible directives are hampered by the fact that, as we noted earlier, Isobel's confessions were recorded as seamless, first-person narratives, without any form of visible ordering system. But if we examine the confessions closely, we can hazard some guesses. Swift changes of subject matter, for example, particularly when marked by commas (which the clerk used as full stops) or capitalized words, are likely to indicate the presence of questions. Indeed in many places these subject changes are so defined that they have been used, both by Pitcairn and myself, to structure the transcribed text into paragraphs. In the places where these changes 'turn on a comma' we can go so far as to speculate the exact point at which a question may have been asked, as in the following examples:

> he vold be somtymes w[i]th ws lyk a dear or a rae, [POSSIBLE QUESTION HERE] Johne taylor and Janet breadhead his vyff in belnaketh (*blank*) dowglas and I my self met in the kirkyaird of nairne . . . (39/12)

> and we vold say, ye ar welcom owr lord, and how doe ye my lord etc [POSSIBLE QUESTION HERE] q[uhe]n ve wold tak the furit away of anie persones midden or dunghill, we wold say . . . (49/26)

> we haw no power of rain bot ve will rease the wind q[uhe]n ve please, [POSSIBLE QUESTION HERE] he maid us believ (*damaged – words missing*) th[e]r wes no god besyd him, [POSSIBLE QUESTION HERE] As for elf arrow heidis, the divell shapes them w[I]th his awin h . . . (*damaged – words missing*). (43/16)

We can also gain a more general, but ultimately more rewarding, idea of the overall pattern of questioning that generated the confession narratives through looking at the general shifts between different categories of subject matter. Taking the confessions as a whole, we can order the latter between two continuums: the first running from harmful magic (*maleficium*) through to beneficent magic, and the second from what we can term 'demonological lore' (specific reference to stereotypical ideas about the Devil as they are found in elite writings) to 'fairy lore' (beliefs about fairies rooted in popular traditions). The second continuum is more complex than the first, because most of confessional content sits somewhere between the demonological and fairy lore extremes, forming what we can term here 'intermediate' or 'fairy-related' material: that is, material which represents fairy lore conflated, to a greater or lesser extent, with demonological belief. This picture is rendered even more complex by the fact that certain motifs and subjects move up and down this continuum between different confessions, or even within the same confession. Magical flight, for example, can emerge in one paragraph relatively undemonized and therefore closer to the fairy lore end of the continuum, and then several lines further down the page, appear demonized and therefore closer to the demonological end.

Interrogatorial dynamics can be detected in the fact that all four confessions commence with a closely written description of the demonic pact, after which they drift into intermediate material or fairy lore, and occasionally beneficent magic, before, after a greater or lesser amount of time, swinging back to either demonological lore or *maleficium*. In the longer confessions, this cycle is repeated more than once. This swing back and forth is likely to reflect the pattern of questioning. As a cottar's wife, Isobel would have possessed a deeper knowledge of fairy belief and beneficent magic than her educated interrogators. The latter, on the other hand, would have possessed a deeper knowledge of demonological theory than Isobel, and a stronger desire to establish whether or not she had performed *maleficium* and/or made a pact with the Devil. As a basic rule of thumb, then, we can assume that close questioning from the interrogators at the beginning of each trial was largely responsible for the descriptions of the demonic pact; Isobel's answers were largely responsible for the subsequent swing towards fairy lore and beneficent magic; and directive interrogatorial questioning was the impetus behind the shifts back to demonology and *maleficium*. Significantly, as the four confessions progress, the tenor of the material moves closer to the maleficent and demonological ends of the spectrum, so much so, that by the fourth confession we find barely any fairy lore or beneficent magic at all. From this perspective, we can assume that Confession Four represents a distillation of the interests of the interrogators. Interests which include, in the order in which they appear: meeting and making a pact with the Devil; participating in the witches' coven; causing harm through shooting elf arrows and performing *maleficium* against Harry Forbes and the Laird of Park.

The Questions Themselves

Although the specific questions that generated this ebb and flow between demonological and fairy lore are essentially invisible, we can nevertheless hazard some speculations. For example, with reference to Brainerd and Reyna's recent overview of criminal-suspect interrogations, it is fairly safe to assume that they fell into one of the following three overlapping categories:[85]

Specific-closed: Specific and suggestive questions that demand a 'yes' or 'no' answer and require very little input from the suspect. An example would be: 'Did you make a pact with the Devil in the churchyard at Auldearn?

Specific-open: Specific and suggestive questions that are open-ended, in the sense that they demand a multiple-word answer as opposed to just a 'yes' or 'no'. An example would be: 'What *maleficium* did you perform with your coven?'

General-open: Less suggestive questions than the above, and also delivered with less expectation of a specific kind of answer. An example would be: 'What else did you do on that night?'

If we superimpose theoretical templates of each category of question onto two passages from Isobel's first confession, one from the fairy lore end of the continuum and the other from the demonological, we can get a finer feeling for the types of questions that Isobel may have been asked and when. The first passage is taken from her description of meeting the Devil:

> he wes a meikle blak roch man werie cold and I faund his nature als cold w[i]thin me as spring wall vater somtymes he haid buitis & somtymes shoes on his foot bot still his foot ar forked and cloven he vold be somtymes w[i]th ws lyk a dear or a rae . . . (39/9)

By superimposing our three questioning templates over this passage we generate three potential scripts.

Specific-closed:
Q. Was the Devil a tall, black, rough/hairy man?
A. Yes.
Q. Was his nature cold within you, like spring-well water?[86]
A. Yes.
Q. Did he sometimes have boots or shoes on his feet?
A. Yes.
Q. Were his feet forked and cloven?
A. Yes.
Q. Did he come to you in the form of a deer or a roe?
A. Yes.

Specific-open:
Q. What did the Devil look like?
A. He was a tall, black, rough/hairy man.
Q. What was his nature like?
A. It was cold within me, like spring-well water.
Q. What were his feet like? Were they forked and cloven?
A. Sometimes he had boots and sometimes shoes on his feet, but they were still forked and cloven.
Q. Did he come to you in animal form?
A. He would be sometimes with us like a deer or a roe.

General-open:
Q. What was the Devil like?

A. He was a tall, black, rough/hairy man, very cold. And I found his nature as cold within me as spring-well water. Sometimes he had boots and sometime's shoes on his feet, but still his feet are forked and cloven. He would be sometimes with us like a deer or a roe.

Here it is clear that the last option, the general-open, does not work, for the sentences are too stereotypical and stilted to have been delivered as a continuous verbal response. As we would expect, given the fact that there would have been a high level of inter-rogatorial interest in the demonic pact, the first option, the specific-closed, is viable. But although generally convincing, it does not wholly account for the idiosyncrasies that pepper the passage. Although the interrogators would undoubtedly have been interested to determine whether the Devil had cloven feet, and whether his penis was cold, it seems unlikely that they would have asked 'Did the Devil wear shoes or boots?' or 'Was the Devil's nature as cold as spring-well water?' Such details were simply not necessary or conventional. Here, we get a far more convincing script if we combine the specific-closed template with the specific-open template. This conflation gives us the close questioning necessary to generate stereotypical testimony coupled with the level of openness necessary to foster the emergence of anomalies.

The second passage, also taken from Confession One, details Isobel's feast at the Downie Hill with the king and queen of the fairies:

I wes in the downie hillis, and got meat ther from the qwein of fearrie mor then I could eat: the qwein of fearie is brawlie clothed in whyt linens and in whyt and browne cloathes etc and the king of fearie is a braw man weill favoured and broad faced etc ther wes elf bullis crowtting and skoylling wp and downe th[e]r and affrighted me . . . (40/5)

As it deals with fairy lore, we would not expect this passage to have evolved through very close questioning. And indeed, if we superimpose the specific-closed template onto the passage it simply does not work:

Q. Did you go to the Downie Hill?
A. Yes.
Q. Did you get meat from the queen of the fairies?
A. Yes.
Q. Did you get more than you could eat?
A. Yes.
Q. Was the queen of the fairies brawlie clothed in white linens, and in white and brown clothes etc?
A. Yes.
Q. Was the king of the fairies a braw man, well-favoured and broad-faced etc?
A. Yes.
Q. Were there elf bulls rowting and skoylling there?
A. Yes.
Q. Did they frighten you?
A. Yes.

It would be tempting, on the basis of the idiosyncrasy of the material, to go to the other extreme and suppose that the passage was produced through a single general-open question:

Q. Did you visit the fairy folk?
A. I went to the Downie Hill and got meat there from the queen of the fairies, more than I could eat. The queen of the fairies is brawlie clothed in white linens, and in white and brown clothes, &c. The king of the fairies is a braw man, well favoured, and broad-faced, &c. There were elf bulls rowting and skoylling up and down there which frightened me.

But while this option is more convincing than the specific-closed option, it still does not account for the jarring narrative shift between the description of the fairy feast to that of the fairy queen and king's appearance, nor for the fact that the latter is described so systematically. But if we combine this general-open questioning with specific-open questions, we have a template that is much more convincing, as it accommodates both the folkloric elements and the slightly stiff, almost mechanical list of physical observations:

Q. Did you visit the fairy folk?
A. I went to the Downie Hill and got meat there from the queen of the fairies, more than I could eat.
Q. What does the queen of the fairies look like?
A. She is brawlie clothed in white linens, and in white and brown clothes, &c.
Q. Was the king of the fairies there?
A. Yes.
Q. And what does he look like?
A. He is a braw man, well favoured, and broad-faced, &c.
Q. Did you see anything else there?
A. There were elf bulls rowting and skoylling up and down there which frightened me.

We shall be returning to the questioning process many times, from different perspectives, in later chapters of the book, but at present it is sufficient to note that on the basis of this simple experiment we can speculate that Isobel was likely to have been asked a variety of specific-closed, specific-open and general-open questions in varying combinations throughout the interrogations. Specific-closed questions would have been more frequent during the generation of the demonological passages and general-open during the creation of the passages dealing with fairy lore. But overall the category of question most commonly used throughout the interrogations is likely to have been the specific-open. That this was the case is supported by the fact that specific-open questions are also prominent in the few extant witchcraft records featuring fairy lore that retain direct evidence of interrogatorial prompting. Some examples of the former, as they emerged in the trials of Ayrshire cunning woman Bessie Dunlop (1576) and Appin cunning man Donald McIlmichall (1677), can be found at the beginning of CHAPTER FOURTEEN.[87]

But although this simple experiment has enabled us to argue that Isobel's testimony was primarily forged through specific-open questioning, it also enables us to be a little more specific about the nature of Isobel's responses. Specific-open questions, by definition, require more than a 'yes' or 'no' response, but they can still be answered relatively briefly. An enquiry such as 'And what other *maleficium* did you perform with your coven?' could be dispatched with a simple 'I don't know' or 'Nothing, we went home'. But what is clear from this analysis is that Isobel did not dodge the questions that were put to her in this way, but answered readily and in some detail. This verbosity is further intimated by the fourteen etceteras peppered throughout the text, the most famous of which curtail Isobel's descriptions of the fairy king and queen, in the Downie Hill passage quoted earlier. We shall be exploring these omissions of text in more detail in CHAPTER FIVE, but at this stage it is sufficient to note that their presence strongly suggests that Isobel provided her interrogators with more information than they cared, or were able, to write down; an interpretation strengthened by Innes's attestation, at the end of Confession Four, that 'All this w[i]th a great many mor terrible things we the s[aid]is witnesses and no[ta]r haird the s[ai]d Issobell confes'. The likelihood that Isobel's responses to the specific-open questions put before her were not only loquacious, but also energetic and creative, is particularly evident in the rhyming-charm passages found in Confession Two. On the one hand, the fact that each charm is prefaced with an introductory line of the 'When-we-do-that-we-say-this' variety suggests prosecutorial prompting. If we convert these lines into questions, we find ourselves with a convincing interrogatorial script: 'Qwhen we goe in the shape of an haire, we say' becoming 'What do you say when you go into the shape of a hare?'; and 'Quhen we rease the wind we tak a rag of cloth . . . we say' becoming 'What do you say when you raise the wind?' and so on. But on the other hand, the number and idiosyncrasy of the lines that follow these initial phrases, which in one case produce a charm no less than ninety-seven words long, leave us in little doubt that Isobel was largely responsible for the richness and diversity of the rhymes themselves. Such observations suggest that although we can only accept the fact that Isobel confessed 'willinglie' in conjunction with significant caveats, we can also assume that she contributed significantly to the generation of her confessions.

4

Interweaving Worlds

Having explored the ways in which Isobel's confessions may have been created, we can now move on to look at their content. And we will begin this process by sketching out a detailed overview of their subject matter. This will give us a firm grasp of the confessional material before we move onto the more wide-ranging and theoretical analyses later in the book, but it will also enable us to begin a more precise assessment of the confessions' unusualness. By sorting Isobel's subject matter into categories and then cross-referencing it with other witchcraft records we will be able to assess how common or uncommon, and therefore how 'normal' it may have been. Throughout this process we shall be keeping in mind the question as to whether the unconventionality or otherwise of Isobel's subject matter can reasonably be interpreted as suggestive of mental illness.

The analysis will take place within certain perimeters. In the last chapter we argued that Isobel's confessional content can be helpfully visualised as spanning two continuums: the first running between maleficent and beneficent magic, and the second between demonological and fairy lore. In this chapter we will be working with this model, but with some adaptations for the sake of clarity. First, the maleficent/beneficent magic continuum will be limited to basic, as opposed to spirit-aid magic (with beneficent charms being subsumed here under the 'basic' category). Spirit-aid magic, being inseparable from descriptions of fairies and the Devil, will be discussed within the context of the demonological/fairy lore continuum. Isobel's maleficent charms, being highly complex, will be passed over altogether here and discussed in CHAPTER EIGHT, where we shall examine Isobel's self-confessed malevolence in more detail.

Maleficium

Isobel's confessions are dominated by descriptions of *maleficium* performed against named individuals, and in this respect they are completely standard. The fact that Isobel directs most of her harmful magic towards authority figures (Harry Forbes, her minister, and the Laird of Park, her landlord) as opposed to her peers is less usual, but still not uncommon. While the majority of records describe *maleficium* being directed towards individuals of a similar, or slightly higher, social standing to the accused, a significant minority cite authority figures as targets. In her attempts to harm Harry Forbes therefore, Isobel was behaving no differently from Renfrewshire witch Marie Lamont (1662) who claimed to have attempted to have performed *maleficium* by fetching 'wyt sand from the shore, and cast[ing] it about the gates of Ardgowand, and about the minister's house'. Or from the group of women who, in the same area over thirty years later, were alleged to have 'roasted the effigy of Mr. Hardy, a clergyman, after having dipt it into a mixture of ale and water'.[1]

The methods Isobel used to perform her *maleficium* were also standard. Take, for example, the following passage from the first confession, in which Isobel states that she and her companions:

> met in the kirkyaird of nairne and ve raised an vnchristned child owt of its greaff, and at the end of breadleyes cornfield land just apposit to the milne of nairne, we took the s[ai]d child w[i]th the naillis af o[u]r fingeris and toes pikles of all sortis of grain and blaidis of keall and haked th[e]m all verie small mixed throw altogither, and did put a pairt therof among the mukheapes of breadleyes Landis and therby took away the fruit of his cornes etc. (39/15)

The strategic placement of charmed objects or concoctions was standard magical procedure in the period, whether the effects intended were for good or ill, and it was quite logical for Isobel and her companions to rationalize that they could reduce the fertility of their neighbour's land by placing their potion in his dung heaps, as a type of anti-compost. Three years prior to Isobel's interrogation, in the Moray village of Duffus, John Russell claimed that his neighbour had 'taken a calf's guts and laid [them] upon his land, and thereafter his ox fell down in the plough'; while nine years earlier the Elgin kirk session recorded that local man William Duncan claimed to have 'found a piece of flesch in his corne rig and that yeir his corne grew not weill' – an act that was attributed to his neighbour, Janet Hossack.[2] Such maleficent rituals were the mirror image of beneficent ones, such as the rite used by Orkney cunning woman Jonet Reid (1643), who advised a man to put some charmed moss into his corn stack 'affirmeing that it suld mak him keip the profeit of his cornis, so that none suld be abill to tak it from him'.[3]

Similarly logical would have been Isobel's claim that to prevent Harry Forbes from recovering from his sickness she and her companions 'maid an bagg: of the gallis flesh and gutts of toadis pikles of bear pairingis of the naillis of fingeris & toes the liewer of ane hair and bitts of clowts' and attempted to 'wring or swing the bagg' upon him as he lay in bed (44/43). Smuggling charmed potions or objects into a victim's house was a reasonably common allegation in witchcraft cases. Thresholds were a common target, but beds were not unknown; with the trial dittays of Bute witches Margaret and Katherine Mc Cuillem (1662) describing how they 'did put witchcraft about hallowday last under Mr. John Stewart minister his bed'.[4] Again, these maleficent rituals were direct inversions of beneficent practices, with Stirling cunning woman Isobel Bennet, for example, claiming in 1659 that when curing paralysis caused by bewitchment she 'washes such persons with water brought forth from the hollows of the sea, and takes a little quantity of meal and strews it in the four corners of their bed' and then adds 'a small bit of the shoe of a horse which had been ridden by the fairies, a hook, and a piece of raw meat'.[5]

While Isobel's basic potion components (grains of wheat, nail parings, animal flesh and so on) were all common ingredients in magical charms of the period, her claim to have used the flesh of an 'vnchristned child' raised 'owt of its greaff (*grave*)' is much more unusual (39/15). Nevertheless, a handful of similar references can be found in contemporary witch-records, two of the most notable dating from the same year as Isobel's. In January 1662, Bute cunning women Jenat McConochie and Elspath Galie were alleged to have laid 'some pocks of witchcraft' under a neighbour's threshold and 'that the thing they put in the pocks is the mooles of ane unchristened bairnes threid nailes'; while in Forfar, Helen Guthrie and others famously 'reased a young bairne unbaptized, and took severall pieces therof, as the feet, the hands, a pairt of the head, and a pairt of the buttock, and that they made a pye thereof', the eating of which was supposed to have given them the power to resist confession.[6] Although these kinds of specific references to the magical use of unchristened children are few, less demono-logically stereotypical references to the magical use of dead body parts and grave paraphernalia (such as bones, flesh and grave mould) are found relatively frequently in Scottish witchcraft and sorcery records, and later folkloric sources, most commonly in relation to healing. The dittay relating to the 1597 trial of Aberdeenshire cunning woman Isobel Straquhan, for example, states 'It was deletit that the said Isobel passit to the Kirk of Dyce, and gatherit ane number of deid folkis baines [bones], and seyndit [washed] thame in water, and tuike the water and weische Willeam Symmer in Haltoune of Fyntrey (he beand seik).'[7]

Isobel's claim that she performed her *maleficium* through image magic was also not anomalous, with allegations that suspects had created human forms out of clay or wax (the former being known in Gaelic as the *corp creadh*) for magical purposes appearing in a significant minority of records. The trial of Jonat Leisk in Aberdeen, 1597, provides us with a long account that approaches Isobel's in its detail and precision. Leisk was accused of making a wax 'picture' of her enemy, Walter Cruikshank, 'within thy awin houss at the Furde of Fortrie, and pat the same on ane spitt nichtly, fra four hours eftir-nune quhill ten hours at ewin, or thairby, turning the same at the fyre, melting the same awey; and as the wax meltit, at that same tyme and hour, sua his body meltit be sueting'. Details illustrating the strange contiguity between the wax image and the bewitched man then go on to occupy a further thirteen lines.[8] Alternatively, an account from Paisley in 1676 describes how a group of witches used image magic, as did Isobel and her companions, to harm the local laird; allegedly sticking pins into wax and clay forms modelled in his likeness, the former being bound 'on a spit, and turned . . . about before the fire'.[9]

That Isobel claimed to have performed *maleficium* against the (presumably innocent) children of an enemy, as opposed to directly against the enemy themselves may seem particularly chilling. But again, a significant minority of witch-records contain similar allegations, with attacks against the children of lairds and ministers featuring in a number of other cases.[10] It was also common, both in the seventeenth and later centuries, for individuals to curse each other's progeny; indeed, in his *Curses, Charms and Talismans* Gilbert Lockhart goes so far as to claim that 'a promise that in a particular family son should never succeed father' was 'the most popular form of malediction' in the Scottish Highlands.[11] It is likely that this emphasis reflected anxieties surrounding high infant mortality, and the fact that in a society heavily dependent on inter-generational support and primogeniture children, and male heirs in particular, represented the familial Achilles' heel.

The wide variety of other, more peripheral, types of *maleficium* described by Isobel were also standard, appearing relatively frequently in the same or similar forms, both in witchcraft records and later collections of Scottish folklore. Isobel's claim that she gained milk through drawing 'the tedder (sua maid) in betuixt the cowes hinder foot and owt betuixt the cowes forder foot' echoed traditional folk belief (where the practice was attributed to both witches and fairies), and appears in a number of witch-testimonies. Her claim to raise and lay winds through wetting and drying a rag is an uncommon, but wholly logical, variation of the common sympathetic magical practice of agitating bowls of water in order to create a storm or, even more specifically, sinking a wooden cup in a dish of water in order to make a ship sink.[12] Her claim that she 'took the heall strenth' of Alexander Cumming's dye vat by tying 'thrie knotts on each thried' pertains to the common practice of knot magic, which again could be used to help or harm: the tying and untying of three knots on a rope or cord, for example, being a widespread method of raising and laying winds.[13] With regard to descriptions of basic *maleficium* overall, the emphases found in Isobel's confessions are also standard. In most witch-records from the period, accounts of causing sickness and death to humans or animals or both are most prominent, with those of causing harm to domestic or agricultural processes, such as drawing milk, spoiling ale or taking fertility being secondary, and Isobel's are no different in this respect.

Basic Magic: Good

In addition to descriptions of basic *maleficium*, Isobel's confessions contain a collection of healing charms and rituals, with most of these being clustered in the second confession. In this respect they fall within the substantial minority of witch-records that contain references to beneficent magic. The charms and rituals Isobel describes are all standard, with close variants appearing in other witch-records, contemporary antiquarian writings and later folkloric collections. The following incantation for healing sores, which Isobel claims to have recited three times while 'straiking the sor', makes reference to 'our Ladie' and concludes with the phrase 'in the nam of the fath[e]r the sone and the holie gost'; both elements illustrative of the survival of the Catholic remnants in post-Reformation Scottish charming traditions:

> owr lord to hunting he (*damaged – words missing*) marblestone, he sent vord to saint knitt

. . . (*damaged – words missing*) he pat the blood to be blood till all upstood the lith to the lith till all took with our Ladie charmed hir deirlie sone w[i]th hir tooth and hir townge, and hir ten fingeris in the nam of the fath[e]r the sone and the holie gost. (44/16)[14]

Another of the charms cited by Isobel reflects the widespread practice of healing through sickness transferral, that is, the belief that an individual can be cured through diverting their sickness onto something or someone else. This charm also displays the word-repetition and strong internal rhythms so characteristic of popular charms:

3lj for the seaveris (we say thryse over, I forbid the qwaking seaveris the sea seaveris the (*damaged – words missing*) seaveris and all the seaveris th[a]t ewer god ordained: owt of the head owt of the heart owt of the bak owt of the syd (*owt?*) of the kneis owt of the thieghes fra the pointis of the fingeris to the nebes of the toes owt sall the seaveris goe (*damaged – words missing*) to the hill som to the hap, som to the stone som to the stok in saint peiteris nam saint paullis nam & all the sa(*intis?*) of hevin: in nam of the fath[e]r the sone and the holie gost. (44/24)

Variations of this particular charm, adapted for different ailments and citing different transferral objects, emerge in other witch-records and source material from the period. In *The Secret Commonwealth*, for example, Kirk cites a very similar version, which involves 'assigning a place for the Evil' that is causing disease and distributing 'a Third [of it] on waters, a Third on woods, a third on the Brown Harts of the Forrest, and a third on the grey stones.'[15] Isobel also describes a ritual, based on the principle of transference, in which sickness is diverted from a bewitched child onto its cradle belt and finally onto a dog or cat (both of the latter being common recipients of transferred sickness in the period):

and if a child be forspoken, we tak the cradle (*damaged – words missing*) child throw it thryse and th[e]n a dowg throw it, and shakis the belt abow the fyre, (*damaged – words missing*) downe to the ground, till a dowg or a catt goe ower it th[a]t the seiknes mey com (*damaged – words missing*) catt. (45/22)

Isobel's claim that the child's cradle belt was employed as a conduit to divert sickness onto an animal is also echoed in other witchcraft and sorcery records. After visiting a local cunning man for help in 1625, the parents of a sick child from Ellon 'returned home and by his advice made a grave under the child's cradle, in the place where the cradle was rocked. They cut the cradle belt in nine pieces and took a quick [live] cat and the cradle belt cut as aforesaid and buried them in the grave.'[16] Isobel's emphasis on the ritual passing of the sick person through the object of transferral is similarly conventional. In a typical example from 1623, a man named Thomas Greave was accused of attempting to heal William Beveridge of 'ane grevous seiknes, be causeing him pas throw ane hesp of yairne thre severall tymes; and thairefter burning the said hesp of yairne in ane grit ffyre'.[17]

The variety and sure-footedness of the charms and rituals described in Isobel's confessions tempt us to draw comparisons with the testimony of witchcraft suspects known to have been beneficent magical practitioners or cunning women, like Agnes Sampson and Bessie Dunlop. In this respect, Isobel's confessions suggest that instead of merely being an individual onto whom the ability to perform magic had been projected by her anxious community, she was a self-conscious magical practitioner. This speculation is supported by the fact that Isobel claims to have healed a bewitched child, for the ability to perform counter-witchcraft was predominantly associated with cunning folk. Although unusual in its intensity, the overt malevolence described in Isobel's confession does not contradict this thesis, in principle at least. As we noted earlier in the book, on a popular level magical power was seen as a neutral force that could be employed to either beneficent or maleficent ends and, as we shall be discussing in more detail in later chapters, there is evidence to suggest that people sometimes petitioned cunning folk to perform *maleficium* against their enemies and that cunning folk sometimes obliged. This conflation between beneficent and maleficent magic is one of the main reasons why so many cunning folk found themselves called up on charges of witchcraft, and why so many witch-records include descriptions of beneficent magic. But the interface between magical practitioner and witch is very hard to navigate. The extent of a magical practitioner's malevolence, or to put it another way, the balance between healing and harming magic that they may have maintained in their general practice, is almost impossible to determine from witch-records because the interrogators were so much more interested in maleficent magic than they were in beneficent. In other words although Isobel's confessions emphasize harmful magic, in her general practice healing magic may have been far more prominent.

Subject Matter: Demonology

Throughout Isobel's confessions, descriptions of basic *maleficium* and beneficent magic are interspersed with references to 'demonological witchcraft', that is, witchcraft performed through meeting and collaborating with the Devil. Again, in this respect they are not unusual. Although, as Joyce Miller has recently pointed out, demonological elements are not as common in early modern Scottish witch-records as is often assumed (an issue that we shall be exploring in more depth later in the book) they nevertheless appear in a substantial minority of cases.[18]

In many of the records containing demonological witchcraft, a description of the demonic pact is often one of the first items listed, and Isobel's case is no different in this respect, with all four confessions beginning in this manner. The pact that Isobel describes is also largely conventional, reproducing a stereotypical sequence of the core events that emerge in accounts throughout Scotland: the witch meets the Devil when she is walking alone, or is introduced to him at the witches' sabbath ('as I wes goeing betuixt the townes of drumdewin and the headis: I met w[i]th the divell'); the Devil is a tall, black man ('he wes a meickle blak roch man'); the Devil offers to help the witch and/or to meet her at the sabbath ('I promeisit to meit him in the night tym in the kirk of aulderne q[uhi]lk I did'); at this first meeting, or later at the sabbath, the Devil asks the witch to renounce her Christianity through placing one hand on her head and the other on her foot and surrendering everything between to him ('and the first thing I did ther th[a]t night I denyed my baptisme, and did put the on of my handis to the crowne of my head and the uth[e]r to the sole of my foot, and th[e]n renuncet all betwixt my two handis ower to the divell'); the Devil gives the witch a mark ('and he marked me in the showlder'); the Devil gives the witch a new name (he said 'I baptise the Janet in my awin name'); the Devil has sex with the witch, either at this or a later meeting, or at the sabbath ('the nixt tym th[a]t I met w[i]th him ves in the new wardis of Inshoch, and haid carnall cowpula[tio]n & dealling w[i]th me'); and finally, the Devil's penis is cold ('I faund his nature als cold w[i]thin me as spring wall vater') (37/14). The uniformity of Isobel's pact narrative can be further illustrated by comparing it with another standard account, found in the records relating to Forfar witch Margaret Hoggan, who was tried in 1662:

> ye freely confessed that three years since bygane in harvest was the first time Sathan appeared to you in the . . . coming out of Carnbo, when he desired you to be his servant, whilk ye confessed to do, and put ane of your hands to the crown of your head and the other to the sole of your foot and delivered all to Sathan's service. Likeways ye confessed that Sathan desired you to renounce and forsake your Baptism whilk ye lykways did, and immediately after your renunciation of your baptism he gave you a new name calling you Kathrine Mahoun and Sathan's name was David Mahoun. Lykways ye confessed that Sathan had copulation with you, and that his body was cold and his seed also, and said he was an uncouth man with black cloathes and ane hood on his head, and he said to you that ye should never want but have enough.[19]

However although Isobel's pact is stereotypical, it also contains some notable anomalies. Her claims, for example, that in giving her his mark the Devil sucked blood out of her shoulder and that she was 'held up' to be baptized by him are, to my knowledge, unique. But the uniqueness of these comments must be considered alongside the fact that in Scottish witchcraft records as a whole, descriptions of the demonic pact, though often stereotypical, are seldom uniform. One or more core events are frequently missing, elements may appear in a different order or with different emphases and, of most significance here, many descriptions contain either personal or circumstantial detail that is unusual or unique. Only Agnes Murie, for example, claimed that after making the demonic pact the Devil 'had the use' of her body 'at the foot of the round knowe at the back of the yards of Tulliebole'; only Jonet Howat claimed that when the Devil was healing her painful shoulder he kissed her affectionately and called her his 'Bonny Burd'; and only Margaret NcWilliam claimed that, in giving her his mark, the Devil 'griped her about the left hench quhich pained her sorely and went away as if it [he] were a grene smoak'.[20] The strangeness of Isobel's pact anomalies is also lessened by the fact that they are not wholly illogical within a broader context. Her blood-sucking Devil can be seen as a variant of the blood-sucking animal familiar (although this stereotype was rare in Scotland), while her description of being held up for baptism mirrored conventional baptismal ritual in the region.[21]

Isobel's claim that she did not only meet the Devil when alone, but also in the company of a group of men and women (both in the church where the pact was made and in various other town or countryside locations) is also relatively standard. Demonologically-themed witch-records commonly describe communal gatherings (termed 'witches' sabbaths' by historians) situated at various points along a continuum that ranged from informal meetings, that predominantly focused on feasting and dancing, through to more formal affairs that resembled the more subversive and cere-monial sabbaths described in Continental witch trials, at which the demonic pact, sexual relations with the Devil and/or *maleficium* were often performed more self-consciously and publicly. A significant minority of Scottish accounts, like those given by Isobel, also combine some or all of these elements into a kind of mobile witches' sabbath. Here, a group of witches, sometimes in the company of the Devil and/or in the form of animals and sometimes by virtue of magical flight, travel from house to house, gaining access through chimneys, doors and windows or, more fantastically, through keyholes and cracks. Once inside, the company feasts on the food and wine stored there and/or performs *maleficium*, most commonly through bringing sickness or death on the inhabitants. In 1658, Alloa witch Margret Duchall claimed that she and her companions met at the 'bletching burn' and then:

> after they war turned all in the liknes of cattis, they went in over Jean Lindsayis zaird Dyk and went to Coudans hous, whair scho declared, that the Devil being with tham went up the stair first with margret tailzeor Besse Paton and elspit blak who had ane pok with som th[ing] in it lyk peas meall, and they strawed it on tuo of coudons bairnes, qch scho granted was the death of tham both. . . . [on another occasion] she was at ane meeting in the cuningar, quhair they war all altogidder dancing.[22]

While Isobel's confessions resemble many other witch-records from the period in the fact that they combine both informal and formal sabbath elements, where her case differs markedly from the norm is in the matter of proportion. In the majority of records, the more formal, Continental elements are relatively minimal and fragmen-tary. But in Isobel's case they are comprehensive and dominant. Isobel claimed, for example that witches in the Auldearn region formed groups (which she termed 'covens') which periodically met in the presence of the Devil at the quarters ('efter th[a]t tym ther vold meit bot somtymes a coven somtymes mor somtymes les, bot a grand meit-ting vold be about the end of ilk qwarter, thir is threittein persones in ilk coeven'). She also claimed that there was disciplinary ritual ('[our deeds are] given accompt of and notted in his book, at each grand meitting'/ 'we wold be beattin if ve wer absent any tym, or neglect any thing th[a]t wold be appointed to be done'); and a hierarchy ('the maiden of each coven sitts abow the rest nixt the divell'). She claimed that her coven made obeisance to the Devil and kissed his behind ('and at each tym q[uhe]n ve wold meitt w[i]th him, we behoowit to ryse and beck and mak owr curtesie to him'/'he vold hold wp his taill wntill we wold kiss his arce'); and that they periodically engaged in promiscuous sex ('he wold lye w[i]th ws in p[rese]nce of all the multitud, neither haid we not he any kynd of shame'). She claimed that the coven members were waited on

The breadth of Isobel's testimony is reflected in the fact that it covers most of the activities depicted in the compendium of witch-practices in the frontispiece to German bishop Peter Binsfield's *Tractat von Bekanntnuss der Zauberer und Hexen* (1592). From left to right we have the witch surrendering herself to the Devil, flying to the sabbath, raising storms and harming crops, cooking babies in a cauldron and exchanging embraces with the Devil.

Two other classic witch-activities, feasting and transforming into animals, are also included in Isobel's testimony. These two images are taken from Ulrich Molitor's *De Lamiis et phitonicis mulieribus* (1489).

by personal demons ('and ilk on of ws has a sprit to wait wpon ws and ve pleas to call wpon him'); that the Devil helped them to perform *maleficium* ('the divell held the plewgh . . . and all ve of the coeven went still wp and downe w[i]th the plewghe, prayeing to the divell for the fruit of th[at]t land and th[a]t thistles and brieris might grow ther'); and that coven members attended and left the sabbath in animal form by means of magical flight ('all the coven did fflie lyk cattis beas hairis rewkis etc').[23]

But although the high levels of Continentalism in Isobel's sabbath passages are unique, as Larner has noted, other witch-records, such as those from Forfar and Alloa, come very close to Isobel's in this respect.[24] It is also significant that, in terms of subject matter alone, nearly all of the more sensational or ceremonial elements of Isobel's sabbath can be found represented in at least one other Scottish witch-record from the period. Other covens meet according to the calendar; other witches worship the Devil and kiss his behind; other covens have a hierarchical system that includes an officer and a maiden; other witches are served by named personal spirits in the service of the Devil; other covens perform *maleficium*; and other witches travel in animal form to their meetings. Even the sexual promiscuity that the Devil displayed so vividly in Isobel's accounts is also intimated in other records, though not so graphically.[25]

Subject Matter: Fairy-Related

The fact that Isobel does not only claim to have encountered the Devil, but also claims to have encountered fairies is also not unusual. A significant minority of contemporary witch-records contain references to fairy belief, with the majority of these describing direct encounters. Similar accounts are also echoed, with relative frequency, in kirk session records. But any attempt to cross-reference and contextualize Isobel's fairy beliefs in more depth in order to assess their unusualness encounters an immediate obstacle. Despite the fact that Isobel's testimony has been consistently lauded as an unprecedented mine of information about contemporary fairy belief, there are only three occasions in her long confessions where she specifically mentions fairies, or the equivalent 'elves', by name. The first is the famous passage in Confession One where she states: 'I wes in the downie hillis, and got meat ther from the qwein of fearrie'; the second is the reference to a spirit named 'thomas a fearie' during the long list of familiar spirits described at the beginning of Confession Two; and the third is in the notable passage, again in the second confession, where Isobel claims to have been 'in the elfes houssis' and seen 'elf boyes' shaping and trimming 'elf arrow heidis'. The second two references are repeated in the summing up in the fourth confession (with 'thomas a fearie' reappearing as 'Thomas the fearie'), while the first is merely alluded to in the third. Aside from these references, the majority of Isobel's subject matter provides no terminological indications that, so far as she or anyone else was concerned, it related to the fairy belief matrix. Moreover, the fairy references that do occur are so tightly bound up with demonological lore that it is often difficult to untangle the two sets of belief. As a result of this, before we can begin to assess the unusualness of Isobel's fairy belief, we must first spend some time attempting to identify it.

Identifying the Fairy Belief

The elements of Isobel's confessions most commonly believed to reflect contemporary fairy belief are those concerned with magical flight. As mentioned in CHAPTER ONE, the fairies were believed to gather in troupes or 'wandering courts' that travelled about, often by night, feasting in houses, under hills and in the open countryside.[26] Although they could reach their destinations on horseback or by foot, these troupes were also believed to travel by virtue of magical flight either in the form, or in the company of, a whirlwind. We shall explore this 'fairy host', as it is generally termed, in much more detail later in the book, but it is sufficient to note here that in the early modern period and later, it was believed that both living and dead humans could be swept up by this airborne fairy train. Newborn babies, particularly if they had died before they were baptized, were commonly believed to swell its numbers, as were those who had been shot or killed by the fairies or had otherwise died a violent or premature death. Living souls, on the other hand, could be swept up at any time, whether awake or asleep. In 1588 Fifeshire cunning woman Alison Peirson summed up this belief in her claim that 'quhene we heir the quhirll-wind blaw in the sey, thay [the fairies] wilbe commounelie with itt, or cumand sone thaireftir: than Mr Williame [her familiar] will cum before and tell hir, and bid hir keip hir and sane hir, that scho be nocht tane away with thame agane'.[27] Similarly, in Elgin in 1629, Cristan Nauchty 'confessit scho was three severall tymes away [to fairyland], ilk tyme aucht dayis away, and scho wes taine away with a wind'.[28]

On the one hand, we cannot automatically assume that the descriptions of magical flight that so dominate Isobel's confessions relate to this fairy belief matrix. As we have seen earlier, in this period magical flight was not only a core component of contemporary fairy lore, but also of the demonological stereotype of the witches' sabbath. Witches, and Continental witches in particular, frequently claimed to have flown in groups to their nocturnal rendezvous, often in the form of animals and/or in the company of the Devil, and a number of Scottish witchcraft suspects and victims clearly state that it was the Devil and not the fairies who carried them away in a whirlwind.[29] Isobel's flight experiences, moreover, do contain some clear demonological credentials, most prominent of these being the fact that at no time does she state directly that she flew with or was carried through the air by the fairies, claiming instead that her airborne companions were an assortment of neighbours (whom she termed her 'coven') and the Devil.

But on the other hand, despite these demonological references, there are three concrete indications that suggest that, however Isobel conceptualised her airborne adventures on a personal level, they were very closely associated with contemporary beliefs surrounding the fairy host. First, we have her manner of travel, with Isobel famously stating of her coven that:

> and then ve vold flie away q[uhe]r ve vold be ewin as strawes wold flie wpon an hie way, we
> will flie lyk strawes q[uhe]n we pleas wild strawes and corne strawes wilbe hors to ws
> q[uhe]n ve put th[e]m betwixt owr foot, and say hors and hattok in the divellis nam, and

q[uhe]n any sies thes strawes in whirlewind, and doe not sanctifie them selves, they we mey shoot them dead at our pleasur . . . (39/42)

Although they merged into popular witch lore, beliefs surrounding magical flight on plant stalks were primarily associated with the fairy host and those who accompanied them. In the well-known poem by sixteenth-century Scottish poet Alexander Montgomerie (which is believed, by folklorists, to reflect elements of popular belief) this manner of flight is vividly described:

Into the hinderend of harvest, on ane alhallow evin,
When our goode nichtbouris [fairies] ryddis, if I reid richt,
Sum bucklit [mounted] on ane bunwyd [flax stalk] and sum on ane bene,
Ay trippand in trowpis fra the twie-licht;
Sum saidlit ane scho aip [she-ape] all grathit [clad] into grene,
Sum hobling on hempstaikis, hovand on hicht [rising on high]
The king of pharie, with the court of the elph quene
With mony alrege [eldritch] incubus, ryddand that nicht.[30]

Such beliefs were still going strong in many parts of Scotland 300 years later, with a nineteenth-century observer noting, for example, that 'It is popularly believed all over Galloway, that the Fairies grow them [Bowlock or 'Ragwort'] for horses; and when they require a steed to bear them on a journey, they select a big bowlock and change it into a horse at the word of command'. Indeed, in this region these beliefs were so strong that 'no farmer almost would cut them [the Bowlock plants] till after Halloween, for fear the Fairies had need of them'.[31] Similar motifs emerge frequently in traditional Scottish stories and legends. In the tale of 'The Black Laird of Dunblane', collected in the nineteenth century, the protagonist was coming home one night from Alloa when he met a group of fairies who invited him to 'go with them'. Upon his acceptance of their offer 'They mounted bundles of windlestrae, and he a plough-beam left in a furrow', after which, 'Crying "Brechin to the Bridal" they flew thither through the air on white horses'.[32]

The second feature of Isobel's magical flight sequences indicative of fairy lore is her claim that when she and her coven set off on their airborne adventures they would cry 'hors and hattok in the divellis nam' or '(hors?) and hattock hors and goe, hors and pellatts ho ho' (44/4). Similar phrases were occasionally associated with witchcraft, and in a sermon given at the trial of the Paisley witches in 1697, minister James Hutchison stated that when a person 'falls among' a company of witches 'accidentally and is surprizd . . . they say "up and away" or "mount & flee" and he sayes that too and he flies with the rest to this or that countrey'.[33] But the fact that taking off or levitation cries emerge strongly in contemporary and later fairy belief (with phrases such as 'Up horsey' and 'Rise, rise, rise' peppering folk tales and anecdotes), strongly suggests that these motifs were ultimately fairy-derived.[34] The likelihood that Isobel's 'hors and hattok' cry was a regional fairy anthem is further supported by a letter sent by Scottish professor of divinity James Garden to the Wiltshire antiquarian, John Aubrey, in 1694.

Here Garden records a local anecdote, allegedly stretching back at least three generations, in which a predecessor of the Laird of Duffus (a village roughly twenty miles north-east of Auldearn), was walking in the fields near his house when:

> he heard the noiuse of a whirlewind & of voices crying horse and hattock (this is the word which the Fairies ar said to use when they remove from any place) wheruopon he cried [horse and hattock] also & was immediately caught up and transported through the aire by the Fairies to that place, where after they had drunk heartily he fell asleep, & befor he awoke the rest of the company were gone. & had left him in the posture wherin he was found.[35]

Garden also informed Aubrey that the tutor of the current heir of Duffus had told him, in conversations on this theme, that when he was a schoolboy at nearby Forres around the middle of the seventeenth century, boys playfully used the phrase 'horse and hattock with my top!' to conjure eddies of wind to lift their spinning tops.[36] We cannot rule out the possibility that the phrase could have leaked into both the Duffus anecdote and the Forres schoolboys' vocabulary via Isobel's confessions. Not only were Duffus and Forres close to Auldearn geographically, but both the laird referred to by Garden and his father were friends and dining companions of Alexander Brodie. And knowing the latter's interest in witchcraft, and his penchant for speculating about current events, we can consider it likely that colourful witch-testimonies such as Isobel's formed the meat of more than one after-dinner conversation.[37] However, tantalising as this possibility is, it is far more likely that Isobel used the phrase because it was in common usage in the period; this thesis gaining support from the fact that in the nineteenth century it could be found as far afield as the Shetland Islands, and in more than one variant. An anecdote recorded by Ernest Marwick describes how:

> A man dwelling in Houll, Mid Yell [in the Shetlands] one night before going to bed, stepped outside in his shirt and drawers, and saw a band of trows [fairies] going by him. They were saying some words, and he repeated after them:

> Up hors, up hedick
> Up will ridn bolwind
> An I kin I's reyd among yu
> (And I know I'll ride among You).[38]

The third feature of Isobel's magical flight sequences indicative of fairy lore is her claim that, while airborne astride her corn straw horse, she shot arrows at passing humans and animals ('and q[uhe]n any sies thes strawes in whirlewind, and doe not sanctifie them selves, they we mey shoot them dead at our pleasur') (40/1). This belief has little correlation with demonological stereotypes of the witches' sabbath, but is firmly rooted in contemporary beliefs surrounding the airborne adventures of the fairies. In its search for sustenance, the fairy host was believed to scour the land, commonly taking the goodness or 'foyson' of grain, milk and other foodstuffs. But it was also believed to hunt humans and animals. In order to make their kill, the fairies used what were commonly termed 'elf arrows' or 'elf darts'; tiny projectiles fashioned in fairyland and identified, by the common folk, with the prehistoric flint arrowheads found then, as now, in many parts of Scotland. Thus armed, the fairies roamed the countryside, entering into fields, barns and houses to, in the memorable words of one seventeenth-century eyewitness, 'seek a prey'.[39] If the humans and animals that crossed the fairies' path did not protect themselves through blessing (that is, 'saining') themselves or being blessed by someone else, the fairy darts would cause them to sicken and/or die. According to some contemporary accounts, after hitting their targets the fairies leapt upon the bodies of their victims and sucked their carcasses dry, while later tales and anecdotes emphasize the fact that the elf-shot victims were carried away by the fairy host.[40]

With regard to Isobel's confessions, the most significant element of this belief matrix was the fact that humans could be swept up by the host and called upon to function as fairy archers. In 1699, Welsh cartographer Edward Lhuyd noted, for example, that in many parts of Scotland it was believed that the fairies called on humans to shoot their arrows because they could not perform the task themselves: 'their Opinion is' Lhuyd wrote to a friend in Yorkshire, 'that the Fairies (having not much Power themselves to hurt Animal Bodies) do sometimes carry away Men in the Air, and furnishing them with Bows and Arrows, employ them to shoot Men, Cattle, &c.'[41] The writings of nineteenth-century folklorists confirm that this belief was still widespread 150 years later, where, according to one contemporary informant, 'good sensible' men were often swept up by the fairy host.[42] The following anecdote, recorded by John Francis Campbell, is one of many:

> An old highlander declared to me that he was once in a boat with a man who was struck by a fairy arrow . . . [later] a man, whom the fairies were in the habit of carrying about from island to island, told him that he had himself thrown the dart at the man in the boat by desire of *them* [the fairies]: '*they* made him do it'. My informant evidently believed he was speaking truth.[43]

The House-to-House Visits

The connections between magical flight and beliefs surrounding the fairy host in Isobel's confessions are so strong that they enable us to draw another, less obvious, component of Isobel's subject matter under the fairy lore umbrella. As we have seen, in the early modern period it was believed that the fairy host did not only spend its time feasting in fairy hills and hunting, but that it also engaged in house-to-house processions, sweeping in through keyholes and chinks in doors and windows and feasting on the food and drink left by hearths and in cellars. Although, like elf-arrow lore, these beliefs are better documented in nineteenth-century sources, we have some early modern references. Orkney cunning woman Katherine Jonesdochter (1616), for example, being able to state firmly that she saw the 'Trowis [trolls/fairies] ryse out of the kirkyeard of Hildiswick, and Holiecross Kirk of Eschenes, and on the hill called Greinfaill' and that they came to any house where there was 'feasting, or great mirrines and speciallie at Yule'.[44] This aspect of fairy behaviour is also amply reflected in tales and legends, both collected from the period and later. In the tales describing the adventures of the Laird of Duffus and the Black Laird of Dunblane mentioned earlier, the protagonists claimed, respectively, that they were swept across the English Channel, by the fairies, to drink from the 'French King's Cellar with a silver cup' and carried to a 'mansion where a banquet was prepared, and ate and drank, invisible to the guests. Then crying, "Cruinan to the dance!" they [the fairy company] passed out again through the keyholes "like a sough of wind" and went in the same way to Cruinan.'[45] Lore surrounding the processional activities of the fairy host is complex and varied, and we shall be exploring it in much more depth later in the book. But it is sufficient here to note that in the context of the fairy-relatedness of Isobel's confessions as a whole, the house-to-house visits she describes, in which she feasted and drank wine in her neighbour's cellars, can be linked as convincingly to the processional activities of the fairy host as to the demonological sabbath. This ambiguity is a prime example of the crossover between demonological and fairy lore found throughout Isobel's confessions. In some places the overlap is simple to identify, and it is possible to separate the two categories of belief; but in other places, as in this instance, the beliefs are so tightly interwoven that it is difficult to separate the two.

Assessing the Fairy Belief

Having established the areas of Isobel's confessional material which can be justly related to fairy belief, we can now return to our original task as laid out at the beginning of this chapter, that is, to analyze comparatively the subject matter in relation to other witchcraft confessions of the period in order to assess how conventional it may have been. In many respects, much of the fairy lore contained in Isobel's confessions is standard, in the sense that it appears, in some form or other, in a significant number of other fairy-related records from the period. Accounts of participating in fairy revels, for example, were common, and Isobel's claim to have feasted in a 'fair & lairge braw rowme' under the Downie Hill was little different to Appin cunning man Donald McIlmichall's claim to have encountered 'a great number of men and women within the hill quhair he entered haveing many candles lighted'; or Stirling cunning woman Isobel Watson's claim to have been taken by the fairies to a 'fine house where there were many people' beneath the earth.[46] Descriptions of participation in fairy-related magical flight are more unusual, but a scattering exist, although in most cases they are brief and flight is usually intimated as opposed to being spelt out, emerging in statements such as, 'the fairie had taken hir away to Messindiu wher she slept all night' and '[she was] takin away be the fair folk'.[47]

With regard to the shooting of arrows, Isobel's confessions are less standard. While a number of records describe how suspects have harmed or killed humans or animals through shooting fairy darts, Isobel's claim to have shot these arrows in association with the fairy host is more unusual, but precedents do exist. As we shall explore in more detail later in the book, Isobel's statements in this regard can be particularly likened to those made by a group of women tried in Bute, in 1662, who claimed to have seen each other in the company of the fairy host and, as one suspect put it, travelled 'with diverse others . . . on a voyag from Corsmore overseas to Kerramorrie in Kingarth and ther killed a bairne of Donald Moir Mc Kawes . . . and that for effectuating heirof they took a boy out of Patrick Glas house being a coosine of his and that it was the said boy that shot the child'.[48] Isobel's claim that the fairies were 'hollow and bossis baked' also emerges in other testimonies, most notably those of Cristan Nauchty (Elgin, 1629) and Jonet Boyman (Edinburgh, 1572): the latter claiming that the fairy-like spirit she encountered 'was waist behind lyke ane stik'.[49]

But in addition to these correspondences, Isobel's confessions also contain a large number of details that are unique. Despite the fact that they derived from contemporary fairy lore, Isobel's descriptions of conjuring 'wild strawes and corne strawes' into horses; of crying 'hors and hattock in the divellis nam' as she levitated into the air; of witnessing elf arrows being whittled by elf boys; and of shooting and killing passing humans while airborne were not recorded in any other records, either for witchcraft or sorcery, during the whole of the early modern period. Other details, such as the chanting of charms while flicking fairy darts from thumbnails and seeing elf bulls 'crowtting and skoylling' at the gates of fairy hills are, to my knowledge, unique to the whole of Scottish folklore.

This contradictory pattern of both conventionality and uniqueness can also be found in relation to the areas of overlap between demonological and fairy lore. On the one hand, the fact that Isobel's confessions should contain such an overlap is standard. Although some witchcraft confessions contain fairy beliefs relatively free of learned ideas about demonological witchcraft, in the majority of confessions the two are intertwined. But on the other hand, Isobel's confessions are unique in the degree to which they interweave so many different aspects of fairy and demonological lore so tightly and in so many different ways, to the extent that at least half of her testimonial material could be said to fall within this overlap category. The confessions suggest that so far as Isobel was concerned, the group of men and women (or 'coven') with whom she went into houses in the form of animals and performed *maleficium* were the same men and women with whom she mounted fairy steeds and hunted with elf arrows. Similarly, the group in whose presence she made the demonic pact and had sex with the Devil was the same group with whom she went 'daunceing at the hill of earlseat' and feasting in the 'braw' room under the Downie Hill with the king and queen of the fairies. As they progress, the confessions chart a swinging motion back and forth between the demonologically stereotypical witches' sabbath and gatherings with the fairy host, with the coven acting as the connective vehicle. In this respect, more than any other, Isobel's confessions are truly unique.

Subject Matter and Sanity

Through this chapter we have gained a basic overview of the subject matter contained in Isobel's confessions and this will stand us in good stead later in the book. But where does it leave us with regard to the confessions' unusualness? The analysis of the content on the beneficent/maleficent magic continuum undertaken in the first half of the chapter, although not complete (an examination of the maleficent charms being still to come), uncovered nothing that could not be found, either in the same form or as a variant, in a number of other witch-records of the period, with most of the material being common. The analysis of the content on the demonological/fairy lore continuum was more complex, but ultimately yielded similar results. The perceived unusualness of the material was clearly diminished by the fact that precedents could be found, in either witch-records or contemporary and later folklore, for nearly all the content falling into this category. The fact that the confessions also contained a handful of unique references was also, within the context of other witch-records, conventional.

But on the other hand, Isobel's confessions have emerged as leading the handful of Scottish witch-testimonies in which the level of rare or anomalous material is exceptionally high. And when we stand back and look at our findings from a distance it is clear that Isobel's confessions attain this pole position not so much because of the nature of their subject matter, but because of the *amount of it*. As we have seen, most of the Continental-type details are not without precedent when taken individually, but they seem so simply because there are so many of them; the fairy lore is not anomalous in itself, but appears that way because so many disparate beliefs are accumulated into the one narrative; and the overlap between demonological and fairy lore is not surprising per se, but becomes so because such a variety of lore is described so frequently, and in such microscopic detail, that the crossover between these elements becomes greatly magnified.

At this point in our research, we have no explanation for this multiplicity. It could be argued that these high levels of anomaly are representative of mental illness. But such a conclusion is premature. While the high incidence of stereotypical Continental-type detail in the confessions could indicate that Isobel seized on the demonological beliefs suggested to her by the interrogators and incorporated them into her testimony to a degree that was inappropriate, even for the seventeenth century, this interpretation is challenged by the fact that in other parts of Scotland, such as Forfar, witch-testimonies containing high levels of Continental-type detail were made by large groups of suspects simultaneously. And unless we are prepared to brand all of those involved in these cases as mentally ill, then we cannot fairly level the accusation at Isobel. By the same logic, we could argue that the elevated levels of fantastic and dramatic fairy beliefs in the confessions might also have been suggestive of some kind of incongruous response. But we must set against this the fact that, barring one or two exceptions, all of the fairy beliefs she described were rooted in conventional folklore absorbed at the hearth by every man, woman and child in seventeenth-century Scotland. Indeed, even Isobel's most sensational claims, such as her assertion that she flew through the air with the fairy host and shot elf arrows at passers-by, were calmly made by perfectly 'good' and 'sensible' Highlanders over 200 years later.[50] Similarly, we could interpret the high level of demonological/fairy lore overlap as indicative of mental confusion (with the inability to distinguish between disparate phenomena, for example, being characteristic of some forms of psychosis). But we must set against this the fact that the two categories of belief were commonly conflated by both interrogators and suspects in the period; with some records clearly indicating that contemporaries could be confused, as Isobel was, about the connection between witches' sabbaths and fairy revels.[51] In conclusion, because mental illness does not emerge clearly as a causative factor, the unusual breadth and multiplicity of Isobel's confessional content still requires explanation.

5

Curious Minds

Our continuing attempts to explain the quantity and diversity of Isobel's subject matter, and our more general intention to explore both the unusualness and epistemological status of her confessions, can now be furthered by changing direction and approaching the narratives from a different perspective altogether. This change of direction involves moving away from looking at the types of things Isobel said, to looking at the way that she said them. As we noted at the beginning of CHAPTER THREE, Isobel's confessions are remarkable not only for the breadth of subject matter they cover, but also for the fact that these subjects are described in such detail and with such narrative flair. These 'stylistic features', as we can term them here, are not unique. Many witchcraft and sorcery records are detailed, particularly with regard to basic magical techniques, with the dittays of Orkney cunning woman Katherine Craigie (1640), for example, devoting over 600 words to describing how she performed a single healing ritual.[1] Alternatively, although descriptions of communication with spirits are not generally so methodical and precise in their exposition, a number of highly-detailed examples exist, such as those given by Alison Peirson, Agnes Sampson and Bessie Dunlop.[2] A significant minority of witchcraft and sorcery records also display considerable narrative flair. Fifeshire cunning woman Alison Peirson (1588) claimed evocatively that when 'thay [the fairies] come verry feirfull sumtymes, and fleit [scared] hir verry sair, and scho cryit quhene thay come'; Aberdeenshire cunning man Andro Man (1598) conjured up vivid images of the Devil being 'cassin in the fyre becaus he dissavis wardlingis men', and the fairy queen and her train riding 'upon quhyt [white] haicknayis' and eating at 'fair coverit taiblis'; while Bute cunning woman Jonet Morison (1662) described how a spirit clothed in white addressed her with the grandiloquence of an Ossian sage, telling her 'thow art a poor woman and beggar among a cumpanie of harlots, goe with me and I'll make the a Lady and put the in a brave castall quhair thou shalt want nothing and I will free the of all the poverties and troubles thou art in'.[3] Many other records, such as those relating to Edinburgh suspects John Fian and Euphame MacCalzean and Orkney cunning women Marable Couper and Jonet Reid, also display fluid narrative styles.[4]

But although Isobel's confessions are not unusual in the fact that they contain these stylistic features, they are unique in the degree to which they do so. Their detail, for example, is legendary. Many witches claimed they had made a *corp creadh*, but none described the process with such forensic relish as Isobel. In her case, the image was not just made out of clay, but made out of clay that had been brought to Janet Breadheid's cottage in the corner of a plaid and then broken up 'werie small lyk meall and sifted . . . w[i]th a siew'. And the *corp creadh* did not just resemble a child, but possessed 'all the pairtis & (*markis?*) of a child such as (*word crossed out*) heid eyes nose handis foot mowth & litle lippes . . . & the handis of it folded down by its sydis' (40/26). Similarly, many witches named their accomplices, but few also described where they lived, who they were married to and what they looked like: Meslie Hirdal, for example, was not just listed as herself, but as 'meslie hirdall, spows to allexr ross in lonheid is on of th[e]m, hir skin is fyrie' (40/40). A small number of witchcraft and sorcery suspects cited charms used to heal the sick, but none cited anywhere near as many as Isobel, nor such a wide range. Not only do her confessions provide us with charms for healing, but they also provide us with charms for making a *corp creadh*, stealing fish, raising winds, administering poisons, gaining success at market, levitating in fairy whirlwinds, shooting elf arrows and transforming into animals.

Similarly, the linguistic and narrative flair of the confessions is unparalleled. Although the detail is scrupulous to the point of seeming obsessive, it is never bland or dry, and no witchcraft or sorcery record from throughout the early modern period contains comparable levels of descriptive vocabulary, vivid imagery and dramatic tension, or manages to knit these elements together with as much fluidity and immediacy. The Devil is not just heavy, he is as heavy as a 'malt secke'; his penis is not just cold, it is as 'cold w[i]thin me as spring wall vater' (39/11). Isobel's fellow coven member Bessie Wilson does not just argue with the Devil, but 'wold speak croslie w[i]th hir townge, and wold be belling again to him stowtlie'; the Devil does not just beat Isobel and her companions, he 'wold be beatting and scurgeing ws all wp and downe, w[i]th tardis & uth[e]r sharp scurges, lyk naked gwhastis'; and Isobel does not just run away from her neighbour's hounds but 'ran werie long . . . (*and*) wes feart being near at last to take my owin hous, the dore being left open, I ran in behind an chist and the houndis followed in'.[5]

The Men with the Pens

In order to find some explanations for these stylistic features, we will begin by turning our attentions away from Isobel and directing it toward her interrogators. Historians analysing Isobel's confessions have never given sufficient weight to the fact that she was not their sole author. Witchcraft records do not only reflect what the suspects themselves said, but also the types of questions they were asked and the way these questions and the responses they provoked were recorded by clerks and notaries. And in Isobel's case, the documentation relating to her neighbour, Janet Breadheid – although only amounting to a single confession – provides us with evidence that a percentage of the stylistic features characteristic of Isobel's confessions can be firmly attributed to the men who interrogated her.

Many of the men present at Isobel's interrogations (including the ministers Forbes and Rose) were also present at Janet's, which took place at Inshoch castle the day after Isobel had given her first confession. Janet's testimony was also authenticated by the same notary, John Innes. As we shall be exploring in more depth in CHAPTER FIFTEEN, some of the passages in Janet's testimony, such as those describing the making of the *corp creadh* and the performance of the demonic pact, are so similar, in terms of both subject matter and style, to those of her Auldearn counterpart, that we can assume that some kind of crude read-out-and-assent process occurred. In other words, Janet's interrogators read out Isobel's versions of these events, which had been given the day before; asked her if she had been present; and in response to her 'yes' recorded Isobel's words as if it they had been Janet's own. Little else could account for the fact that the women's narratives do not only share the same phrases, but even the same idiosyncratic metaphors and similes. But on the other hand, there are many other passages in Janet's confession (such as her descriptions of being initiated into witchcraft by her mother-in-law and of her solitary trysts with the Devil while her husband was working 'in the morning at the plewgh') that bear no relation to Isobel's confessions subject-matter-wise and can therefore be assumed to have come directly from Janet herself. The stylistic similarities between these passages and Isobel's narratives cannot be attributed to Isobel and neither – unless the two women shared uncannily similar modes of expression – can they be attributed to Janet. We can therefore assume them to have been of inter-rogatorial origin.

The interrogator-derived stylistic features that emerge most strongly from this comparison are those of linguistic precision and graphic detail. And nowhere are these elements more vividly illustrated than in the women's lists of coven members. The readiness with which Isobel seems to have listed things (including not only coven members but also nicknames and the arrow-slain) has been remarked upon by scholars, with Maxwell-Stuart observing that 'Another notable characteristic of Isobel's narra-tive is her evident pleasure in listing names.'[6] But whatever Isobel's eagerness in this respect, it was comprehensively dwarfed by Janet's. The latter's list of coven members was not only as detailed as Isobel's, but was considerably longer, incorporating a cool forty-three names in comparison with Isobel's twelve. This difference, combined with the fact that Janet was clearly referring to a coven that existed in the past, as opposed to the coven that she currently participated in with Isobel, makes it abundantly clear that her list was not merely the result of a read-out-and-assent to the list that Isobel had given on the previous day. In this case, the only viable explanation is that the graphic detail and linguistic precision that is so marked a feature of these lengthy roll calls derived from exceptionally close prosecutorial questioning. Moreover, the fact that similarly precise detailing occurs throughout the confessions suggests that this level of questioning was not just reserved for inquiry into the identity of coven members, but was a consistent feature of both women's interrogations.

But such an assumption is larger than the sum of its parts. Close questioning was a requirement of the interrogator's job, whatever the crime being investigated, with the burglaries committed by local resident John Smith, for example, being painstak-ingly investigated, down to the last rifled chest and forced door, at his trial at the burgh court in Nairn in 1677.[7] But in Isobel's case what is significant is that this attention to detail is exhibited across a wide range of subject matter that derives from both extremes of the beneficent/maleficent magic and demonological/fairy lore continuums, and in relation to events that seem to have had very little connection to the core crimes for which she was being charged. This wide-ranging interrogatorial interest is supported by our conclusion, in CHAPTER THREE, that even when Isobel was discussing fairy encounters, her examiners explored her claims with specific-open questions. In other words, when she stated that she had met the fairy king under the Downie Hill, instead of passing over the subject as irrelevant, or bending it into to something more demonologically significant by asking specific-closed 'Was the Devil there?' or 'Did the fairy king ask you to make a pact?'-type questions, the interrogators responded to her claims by enquiring: 'And what did the king of the fairies look like?'

The Doctrine of Repentance

To a certain extent, we can attribute these high levels of close and rigorous questioning to the fact that Isobel was interrogated in a covenanting parish. Since the Middle Ages it had been considered important, from a legal perspective, to gain full confessions from witchcraft suspects for the simple reason that, given the invisibility and unprovability of the crime, the absence of an admission of guilt made it difficult to secure a conviction. But religious zeal also played an important role here. Recent scholars have noted that the spiritual vocation played a more complex role in early modern witch-persecution than has previously been acknowledged, and that much of the religiosity of the process was bound up with a belief, central to both the Protestant and Catholic faith, in the value of repentance.

Throughout the Middle Ages the Catholic church taught that if an individual confessed and repented, they would be saved (that is, God would forgive them and after death their soul would go to heaven and enjoy eternal bliss); but that if they did not, they would be damned (that is, God would not forgive them and after death their soul would go to hell and endure eternal torments). According to this doctrine, it was never too late to gain God's mercy, and from this perspective the attempts to make felons repent when standing before the gallows were not just public spectacles aimed at emphasizing church authority, but also genuine efforts to give the condemned man or woman one last shot at salvation. For Scottish Protestants, whose Calvinist-based faith strongly emphasized the notion of 'predestination', the doctrine of repentance was equally charged but considerably more complex. Predestination referred to the belief that since the beginning of time God had decided who was going to be saved and who was going to be damned; that no man or woman could know for certain which category they fell into until their death; and that however good or bad they may have been during their life on earth, God's decision was irrefutable. Such a premise (which necessitated unbelievably complex theological gymnastics to circumnavigate the fact that it contradicted many passages in Holy Scripture) did not compel the reformed church to forgo repentance as a religious observance, but meant that in the absence of 'ticket to salvation' status it had to be underpinned by different rationales; with repentance being sold, among other things, as a means of avoiding God's wrath; accessing the comfort of the sacraments; publicly reinforcing godly mores; and gaining spiritual encouragement, in the sense that the ability to fully and genuinely repent was believed to be a sign (though not complete assurance) that an individual was one of the saved. There is some evidence that seventeenth-century Scottish ministers, being pragmatically aware that the prospect of averting damnation was a powerful deterrent to sin, glossed over the subtleties of predestination from the pulpit, and were aided in their attempts by the fact that reformed catechisms were less emphatic on this issue than, given the theological importance of the doctrine, they should have been.[8] Ministers may also have avoided these subtleties because they themselves could not quite relinquish the idea that salvation was to some degree conditional, these anxieties finding formal articulation in the works of contemporary theologians like Jacobus Arminius. Certainly Brodie saw cause to complain in 1653 that his local minister, William Falconer, 'preached on Isa. lviii. 8., and said, The Lord's promises were conditional' and the Covenant of Grace 'not absolute'.[9]

These religious beliefs about the value of repentance translated directly into the arena of witchcraft prosecution. Coercive interrogators were not all sadistic bigots, merely seeking to purge their communities of 'devilish practices' and see witches burnt and sent to hell as fitting reward for their years of demonic service, but in many cases were under the genuine impression that through persuading the suspect to confess her sins they worked in her best interests. This convoluted, but nevertheless sincere brand of ministerial compassion is clearly visible in a sermon given by David Brown, at Paisley in 1697, in which he tries to entreat some seemingly-impenitent witches, who were scheduled to be executed the next day, to repent. Brown's exhortations also serve as another example how, despite Calvin's emphasis on the doctrine of predestination, some reformed ministers continued to imply that salvation was something that could be earned:

> We are come to you, when ye are within a few hours of eternity, to intreat you, before ye perish forever, to embrace the offers of Christ. For, first, ye go aback from the remedy if ye close not with Christ; for though now conscience be secure, yet it will rise like a roaring lion at the last; and though *ministers would weep over you*, as if we were seeking from you some great thing for ourselves, yet ye will stand it out. What will conscience say when the Devil will be at the gallows foot ready to harle you down to hell? And no sooner in hell, but conscience will say, when God sent his ministers to you, ye believed the Devil and would not yield to Jesus Christ [my italics].[10]

And as Lyndal Roper has recently emphasized with regard to German material, the core belief (fundamental to both Catholic and Protestant theology) that divine favour or forgiveness was reserved for genuine penitents only meant that, for witchcraft interrogators, the religious vocation did not only involve persuading suspects to make confessions, but also involved persuading them to make their confessions as full and honest as possible. Roper argues that while interrogators were, of course, seeking accounts of demonic pacts, witches' sabbaths and *maleficium*, their pursuit of the authentic and heartfelt confession meant that they were not happy with simple assents to specific-closed questions (aka 'Did you make a pact with the Devil' 'Yes') or stereo-typical accounts clumsily cobbled together from bits of demonological lore gleaned from the pulpit, fireside or market-place. But rather, they would continue to question and question, and in some cases torture and torture, for weeks at a time until they obtained an account that contained enough realism, coherence and personal detail to persuade them that it was genuine.[11]

Repentance in Nairnshire

The religious fervour that swept through early modern Europe during the Reformation meant that, with regard to witchcraft prosecution, both Catholics and Protestants could pursue the genuine confession with equal commitment. But within this generality, in some denominations, some regions and some minds, the doctrine of repentance played a more prominent role than others, with reformed Scotland being one of the places where it gained particular pre-eminence. Not only, as we saw in CHAPTER ONE, was repentance one of the recurring themes in the private spiritual introspections of pious men like Alexander Brodie, but teachings and rituals surrounding the doctrine also formed a prominent role in divine service. As Todd has recently emphasized, when women like Isobel attended church on the sabbath they did not only listen to sermons or readings and chant psalms and prayers, but also witnessed lengthy and elaborately-staged rituals of public penitence. In every reformed church in the country, a special stool or bench was installed prominently near the pulpit, and those found guilty of minor misdemeanours by the kirk session were required to proceed theatrically through the nave to the stool, and then sit there for the duration of the service displaying signs of their sin, such as sackcloth, or a piece of paper bearing written details of their crime. At some point during the proceedings, the penitents were required to kneel before the congregation, recite their crimes aloud and plead for forgiveness for their sins and, depending on the severity of their case, some would be required to repeat the whole process on several consecutive Sundays. These proceedings were often emotive and highly-charged, and were such a prominent part of the service that they have led Todd to conclude that public repentance was 'arguably the central ritual act of protestant worship in Scotland'.[12] Such public humiliations may seem cruel or farcical to modern eyes, and elements of sadism, voyeurism and exhibitionism were likely to have been involved on all sides. But, as Todd has emphasized, the sentiments behind them could also be altruistic and sincere. That the men who sent penitents to the repentance stools could be genuinely concerned for their charges' souls, as opposed to just administering punishments and setting examples, is clearly attested to by the fact that they looked for evidence of genuine penitence, and heeded the church's warning not to accept confessions given in either a mechanical, 'careless and jocund' or 'contemptuous and arrogant' manner.[13]

With regard to Isobel, what is interesting is the fact that in covenanting parishes like Auldearn, where kirk discipline was at its most extreme and austere, the doctrine of repentance was likely to have been particularly prominent. As we have seen, the ministers who led Isobel's interrogations, Harry Forbes and Hugh Rose, were both highly-motivated men of covenanting sympathies. Forbes's devotion to presbyterianism was so extreme that he refused to acknowledge episcopacy in 1663, and Rose's writings clearly reveal that, though he was able to bend his principles sufficiently to accept the bishops, he possessed a deeply religious and evangelistic mind. We can suppose that, with these two ministers at the helm, the desire to act in Isobel's best interests through eliciting as full and genuine a confession as possible was a primary motivation throughout her interrogations. And evidence from the manuscripts themselves bears this out. The notary, John Innes, begins every confession by emphasizing Isobel's penitence. The first states that she confessed 'appeiring penetent for hir haynows sines'; the second that she did so 'professing repentance for hir former sines'; the third that she confessed 'appeiring to be most penetent for hir abominable sines'; and the fourth, that she did 'most willinglie & penetent lyk speak furth' her testimony. Similarly, Janet Breadheid's confession also begins with 'professing repentance for hir former sinnes [she confessed . . .]'. References to the penitence of the suspect is relatively common in witchcraft records, but it is not uniformly found, and seldom so prominently, these factors suggesting that Isobel's interrogators considered it particularly important. Equally persuasive is the fact that repentance, in all its painful, introspective glory, was demonstrably important to the young minister of Nairn, Hugh Rose. As this passage from his *Meditations* illustrates, Rose, like fellow minister David Brown, clearly consorted with the belief that salvation was something that could be earned:

> That thou art guilty, yet thy case is not desperate. Has not God sworn by himself, that as he lives, he delighteth not in the death of a sinner, but rather, that he should return and live? Has he not promised to the wicked penitents, that though their sins be as scarlet, they shall be white as snow, though they be red like crimson, yet they shall be as wool?[14]

The prominent role that repentance played in Rose's personal spirituality is also evident in the following passage, where he urges that:

> We should bewail our predominant sins, and master-idols, which rob God of our hearts and homage. We should acknowledge the sins of our temper and particular inclinations. The sins of commission, in doing forbidden evil; the sins of omission, in neglecting commanded good; the sins of our station, relation, our not furthering good, or hindering evil, when either lay in our power; the spiritual sins of our hearts, their hypocrisy, spiritual pride, unbelief, are not to be passed by: our idle (that is, hurtful) words, thoughts, and ill intentions, even unprosecuted bad resolutions, are to be taken notice of. Oh what a large field for confession! how much exact trial, depth of humiliation, and even large time it would take to go about it rightly![15]

We can speculate that Rose, motivated by the heartfelt belief that God 'promised to

The witness signatures as they appear in Isobel's second confession, made on 3 May, 1662. As in the first and third confessions (and that of Janet Breadheid) the signatures of local ministers Harry Forbes and Hugh Rose are prominently placed either adjacent or close to each other (here appearing on the far right). On the left we can also see John Innes's docquet.

the wicked penitents, that though their sins be as scarlet, they shall be white as snow', pressed Isobel hard to 'bewail her predominant sins and master-idols'. Given the fact that, with regard to his personal sins, Rose sought to leave no stone unturned, we can assume that he was similarly rigorous on Isobel's behalf, working hard to peel away her layers of response, as he did with his own conscience on a daily basis, attempting to uncover layer upon layer of increasingly subtle sins in order to reach the kernel of naked truth and true remorse at their core. And we can also suppose that Rose was sorely challenged in this respect. For it is hard to imagine that, in his three short years as a minister, he had ever come across such a 'large field for confession' as the one brought to him by Isobel Gowdie.

Curious Minds: Harry Forbes

But although a commitment to the doctrine of repentance is likely to have played a role in Isobel's interrogations and undoubtedly generated close and persistent questioning, we cannot assume this to have been the whole story. Protestant fervour was not exclusive to Nairnshire, and plenty of witchcraft prosecutions took place in other covenanting regions without producing records as graphically detailed and linguistically precise as Isobel's. But if we combine these perspectives with a closer examination of some of the characters involved in the interrogations, then a more nuanced and persuasive picture begins to emerge.

In CHAPTER THREE we drew attention to the fact that Harry Forbes considered himself to have been a victim of witchcraft as early as 1655, when he first arrived in Auldearn; and that, as illustrated by the case of Cathrin Hendrie, he was quicker than some of his peers to diagnose distressing symptoms as being due to witchcraft. As a consequence, we can assume it likely that Forbes's ministerial zeal to generate a full and genuine confession for the sake of Isobel's soul would have been intensified by his preoccupation with, and fear of, the crimes for which she was charged. But Brodie's diaries suggest that Forbes's attentions may have also been sharpened by other factors. We know, for example, that he was well educated. In this period prospective ministers needed to complete a degree and then become a student of divinity under the auspices of a presbytery for several more years (being tested each year as to their progress) before being considered suitable to be licensed. At present we do not know which presbytery Forbes studied under, but we can confirm that he was awarded his MA at King's College, Aberdeen, in 1634.[16] There is also some evidence to suggest that Forbes was not only well educated, but also interesting. A big fish in a small pond, Alexander Brodie knew many of the great and the good and the very well informed, and he did not spend time with anyone, and particularly social inferiors, lightly. Not only was he impatient with ignorance, especially in ministers (with the unfortunate William Falconer, minister of Dyke, frequently being the butt of his barbed retorts), but he was also painfully cognisant of the dangers which careless use of time posed to the soul. It is therefore telling that on several occasions Brodie spent many hours discussing religion and politics with Forbes. Moreover, the two men did not just discuss practical matters, such as the rights and wrongs of 'secluding the profane from prayer' or 'baptizing promiscuouslie', but also more abstract issues. On one occasion, for example, they plumbed 'the darknes we ar under, the mani great misteries in religion, and how litl they ar knowen'; and on another, the theological complexities of free will.[17] These discussions began when Forbes first arrived in the parish in 1655 and continued until he left eight years later, with Brodie recording as late as 1663 that 'Mr Hari Forbes was with me this day. We wer observing something of the Lord's ways, his soverainti, wisdom, unsearchablnes of his ways, and that "His judgements wer a great deep, past finding out."'[18] On no occasion does Brodie record having comparable discussions with the minister of his home parish, William Falconer, the diaries suggesting that he only met with the Dyke clergyman out of necessity to discuss practical issues.

These observations intimate that although the ever-critical Brodie complained about Forbes on occasion, and although Forbes was clearly less measured than many, at least where witchcraft was concerned, he possessed sufficient powers of contemplation to attract the Brodie laird. That Forbes was both intellectually curious and able can also be inferred from other sources. The fact that his elder brother, William, was also a clergyman (who served at Innerwick in Caithness from 1640 until his early death in 1646), increases the likelihood that Forbes came from a zealous and bookish household and that he learnt his skills of theological disputation during his formative years around the childhood dinner table. The fact that he did not receive his first permanent ministerial position until Auldearn, nearly twenty years after his graduation, could also be significant here. Although, as Julian Goodare has pointed out, this slow career trajectory could illustrate limited abilities, Forbes's decades without the exacting demands of a ministerial post may have offered increased opportunity for private study; particularly if, like many ministers, he worked as a schoolmaster or tutor while waiting to be placed.

Whatever the nature and genesis of Forbes's intellect, Brodie's diaries also suggest that the capacity for abstraction was not the minister's only attraction. In July 1655, Brodie spent the best part of the day talking with Forbes, recording in his diary that 'Efter dinner we went forth, Mr. Hari and I, quhen I did rehears to him how the Lord had dealt with me from the year 1632 until this day.'[19] Brodie's detailed rehearsal seems to have gone on through the afternoon until supper (the substance of the intercourse being recorded assiduously, over a number of pages, in the diary) before being rounded up with prayer and, after supper, more theological discussion. At no other place in his diary does Brodie record such giving such a lengthy personal declaration, and at no other place does he describe the early death of his 'beloved' wife ('the delight of my eys') in such detail, or with such evident emotion – both factors suggesting that Brodie's unburdening was a profound one.[20] It is possible that Brodie chose to pour his heart out to Forbes because he was a new minister, needing instruction, but it is also reasonable to speculate that he did so because the minister was not only a keen thinker, but also a skilled and empathic listener; this thesis being supported by the fact that, as we have seen, Brodie maintained an affection for Forbes throughout his eight-year incumbency.

Then, as now, this diverse range of psychological attributes was unlikely to have been common, and that it existed in Isobel's primary interrogator would go some way toward explaining the unusualness of her confessions. Like many interrogators, Forbes's desire for the genuine confession and his visceral fear of witchcraft, would have motivated him to question closely, but his developed listening skills may have provided Isobel with greater-than-average space in which to articulate her responses, and his empathic manner may have stimulated higher-than-average levels of emotional disclosure. Moreover, while he was likely to have pressed Isobel very hard on demonological matters (with the pact passages, as we saw in CHAPTER THREE, bearing clear signs of specific-closed questioning), we can also speculate that in other places Forbes's fascination with 'the mani great misteries in religion' may have seduced him into running with some of her more exotic answers and following where they led, as opposed to immediately diverting them onto something more demonologically or legally relevant. This perspective on Forbes supports the view, argued in CHAPTER THREE, that Isobel's confession was primarily elicited through specific-open questions. From this angle, it is easy to imagine that when Isobel claimed to have met the king of the fairies, the Auldearn minister may have responded with the question: 'And what did the fairy king look like?'

Hugh Rose

With regard to Hugh Rose, we can sketch out a similar picture. We do not know whether the Nairn minister was particularly preoccupied with witchcraft, but as illustrated earlier in this chapter, we can safely assume that his zeal to generate the genuine confession necessary to secure salvation is likely to have provoked him to question Isobel closely. We can also speculate that this attention to detail would have been intensified by his legal training. As argued in CHAPTER THREE, despite his defection to the world of faith, as a one-time law student with a 'genius' for the profession, Rose seems to have maintained a strong respect for judicial propriety and we can assume that however religiously-inspired his investigations, they would have been sharpened by his scruples regarding the pursuit of impartial truth, his commitment to precise and rational interrogation and his developed ability to see both sides of an argument.

But there is also evidence to suggest that, as with Forbes, Rose also brought more abstract qualities to the table. Although, like all covenanters, he adhered to a rigid doctrinal code and held the firm conviction that his version of God's word was closer to the truth than anyone else's, as we have seen in CHAPTER THREE, Rose was not immune to the complexities of human existence and seems to have nurtured, as Macdonald wrote in 1875, a 'decidedly speculative turn of mind'.[21] Conveniently for us this mind is exhibited in the series of essays published after his death, under the telling title *Meditations on several interesting subjects*. As is appropriate for a seventeenth-century clergyman, these writings grapple with a wide range of theological considerations, but their narrative style and range is telling. The writings of men and women who immersed themselves primarily in the Bible and related commentaries, such as those of Katharine Collace or, to a lesser extent, Brodie, have a distinctive quality, derived from the fact that their phraseology, imagery and allegory are all drawn from the same curtailed field of theological discourse. But Rose's speculations, though they focus on religious conundrums, display a far wider ideological palette than the former works, drawing on vocabulary, metaphor and allegory from the natural sciences, philosophy, history and the study of law. Rose himself inadvertently reveals the causes of this intellectual promiscuity in the following passage which, being so vivid, is worth quoting in full:

> Love of philosophy, study of human things, have made me less studious of the scripture and divine matters; they have diverted my heart. What riches are to the covetous, and pleasures to the voluptuous, such have often been studies of that nature to me. They have enhanced my heart and time, they have got in upon me when I should have been serious in duty to God. As they have been my delight, so I may say, that not seldom have they been my snare. I have longed impatiently, and been itchingly curious after the novel speculations of this luxuriant age; to know the cause of this and the other secret in nature, to know this and the other man's opinion about it; and though I neither found satisfying solidity nor truth, yet the newness and wittiness has caught me. How have I wished, fought, expected, and longed for such writings with impatience! how overjoyed when I got them! how disrelishing were interruptions! how have I thought time tedious till I might return to them! The time has been, when, upon the sabbath, I have longed for the week-day, that I might have the restraint taken off, and I get liberty to use them. It was then with me as with the covetous that cried, When will the sabbath be over, that they might set forth their corn to sale?[22]

These glimpses into Rose's mind tempt us to speculate that his efforts to secure Isobel's full and genuine confession may not only have been motivated by his devotion to legal exactitude, or his ministerial desire to bring her to God through repentance. By virtue of his 'itchingly curious' temperament and his impatient desire to fathom 'this and the other secret in nature', Rose may have flattered Isobel with unusually rapt attention and creative questioning, following her 'diverting' claims to their unknown destinations rather than attempting to constrain them within something more judicially relevant or conventional. In 1662, Hugh Rose was still a young and passionate man, with life's mysteries spreading, tantalisingly unexplored, before him, yet to be dulled and familiarized by age. When faced with Isobel's claim to have encountered the king of the fairies Hugh Rose, like his fellow minister Harry Forbes, simply may not have been able to resist asking: 'And what did the fairy king look like?'

John Innes

Isobel's confessions would not only have been influenced by the men who asked her questions, but also by the men who committed her answers to paper. Although more than one person may have been involved in this process, there is no doubt that the man ultimately responsible for recording Isobel's interrogatorial proceedings would have been the public notary. As a kind of freelance law agent, in this period the Scottish 'no[ta]r publict' was called on to record and authenticate legal transactions: drawing up formal documents, complete with the signatures of witnesses, which then constituted official documents or 'instruments' that provided accurate and legally-binding records of what had taken place. The notary who oversaw both Janet's and Isobel's interrogations was John Innes. Every confession begins, very properly, with a statement along the lines of 'The quhilk day In p[rese]nce of me Johne Innes no[ta]r publict' the suspect 'proceidit in hir confessione'; and ends with a variant of the following: 'declairit furth of the mowth of the s[ai]d Issobell in all and be all things as is abow sett downe I the s[ai]d Johne Innes not[ar] publict haw w[ritti]ne thir p[rese]ntts and with the s[ai]dis witnessis abownamet haw sub[scrivi]t the samen'. Innes's intricate docquet is also reproduced at the foot of every document (*see* page 106).

But although these references ensure that Innes is a dominant presence throughout Isobel's confessions, the man himself is largely a mystery. We do have one initially promising, but ultimately frustrating, lead. By the mid-seventeenth century notaries were largely concerned with drawing up 'instruments of sasine', that is, documents relating to land transactions, with copies of these instruments being generally recorded in protocol books. Against all the odds, of the two protocol books that survive from Elgin (the administrative centre of Moray) in the period from 1658–64, one belongs to Isobel's John Innes, despite the fact that at least ten notaries were likely to have been working in the Elgin area at any one time and despite the fact that few protocol books survive from this period.[23] Even more pertinently, Innes's book was begun in June 1662, one month after he recorded Isobel's final interrogation and while she was presumably still alive and imprisoned in Auldearn. But despite these propitious circumstances, the book yields nothing directly about Isobel's case. At this late period notaries did not usually set down criminal interrogations in their protocol books, and Isobel's case is neither recorded nor mentioned, with the book being filled with conventional instruments of sasine involving local lairds.

That said, however, the book does tell us that Innes was living in Auldearn in June, and this encourages us to speculate that he was a local man. The Innes were a large, influential Moray family, led by Sir Robert Innes who held a seat near Forres, with a notable branch also being found at Leuchars, three miles south of Elgin. John seems to have been an extremely popular name among the seventeenth-century Innes, with almost every other laird or laird's son bearing the name, and attempting to identify Isobel's notary among them is like looking for a needle in a haystack (with a 'John Innes of Edingeich', for example, being listed as present at Isobel's second and third interrogations). But we can nevertheless speculate that he was likely to have been the younger son of a minor local laird who had been forced to take a profession, or the elder son of a non-landed lesser branch of the Innes clan. We can also be fairly sure that, whatever his exact origins, coming from seventeenth-century Moray he was likely to have been well educated and of good social standing. According to Jane Thomas, notaries from the Elgin area enjoyed higher status than those living in other regions of Scotland in this period. Not only were they unusually prosperous, appearing in the Elgin maintenance rolls of the 1640s and 50s as one of the most highly-taxed groups, but they were also unusually politically active, with their involvement in both burgh and kirk sessions work being far higher, percentage-wise, and their length of public service far longer, than that of other occupational groups.[24] Innes's protocol book also reveals that, like Rose, he was relatively young (no older than 36 years old) and that he had been sworn in as a notary in November 1661, four months prior to Isobel's first interrogation. This timing means two things: first, that he had obviously come to the office later in life than many of his peers and therefore probably enjoyed a prior profession; and secondly, that Isobel's may have been the first case, and almost certainly the first criminal case, he had taken on as a fully-qualified notary.

But although we have few further biographical details about the man himself, on the basis of what we know about his profession, we can identify some of the ways in which Innes is likely to have shaped Isobel's testimony. It is likely, for example, that he functioned as the clerk at her interrogations. We cannot rule out the possibility that, as George Bain has proposed, local session clerk Alexander Dunbar performed this func-tion. As a young graduate and trainee minister who was soon to pass his trials before the presbytery with distinction, and who was later to become one of Brodie's closest friends and spiritual allies, Dunbar would certainly have been up to the task.[25] But although the young clerk may have played some kind of role in proceedings (perhaps at the initial shorthand recording stage), the fact that notaries were obliged to draw up their formal documents or the basis of their own notes and that, by virtue of their recording skills, they often worked as clerks in the period, makes Innes the much more likely candidate. The fact that Dunbar was only listed as present at Isobel's last two confessions and not listed at Janet's, and that where he does appear, it is as a witness, further supports this thesis.[26]

Seated strategically in the tolbooth, in a position where he could clearly hear both Forbes's and Rose's questions and Isobel's answers, Innes would have recorded inter-rogatorial proceedings in shorthand on loose sheets of paper, after which he would have gone home and reworked the notes into the neatly written legal documents which have come down to us today. When they were completed, he would have sought out the signatures of a number of the men who witnessed the interrogations as verification that the documents presented an accurate account of what had taken place. These same docu-ments, or a duplicate copy, would have then been sent on to the privy council in Edinburgh. The shorthand notes that Innes took down were intended to be an accurate reflection of all that took place during the questioning. In a guidebook for the notarial profession published in 1740 under the title *Ars Notariatus*, it is stated that although the notary is required to be knowledgeable of the law, 'his Duty lies chiefly in noting what is said and done between and among Parties, without adding any Thing of his own, and to put it in a formal Instrument' and that he 'ought to make Attestation for no other Thing than what falls under the Senses of his Body, and which he distinctly perceives'.[27] This necessity for accuracy demanded the putting aside of the self and personal opinions; the *Ars Notariatus* going on to quote Nicolas Everard's observation that: 'Notaries are as a Pyot or Parrot caged in their Master's Lodgings, which speak without knowing what they say'.[28] The practice of reading confessions back to suspects for their corroboration, and of obtaining the signatures of witnesses, all served to support these aspirations to accuracy. It is also worth noting here, in respect of Isobel's confessions, that this attention to detail could extend to subtle idiosyncrasies of expression. Like their counterparts in England, the best Scottish judiciaries would have striven to be 'long-minded, to endure the rusticity and homelinesse of common people in giving evidence after their plaine fashion and faculty, in time, and multitude of words, happely with some absurdities of phrase and gestures, nor impatient towards their foolish affected eloquent tearmes'.[29] The best notaries reflected this 'long-mindedness' in their work; with William Angus noting that in this period the notary 'frequently [had] to take down verbatim the words uttered by parties in the proceedings before him, and one finds the vigour and directness of colloquial speech in pleasing contrast with the more formal and stilted legal phrases of the instrument'.[30]

But as in so many areas of life, reality often failed to reflect such lofty ideals. First, in compiling their accounts, early modern notaries did not simply record testimonies and declarations word for word, they shaped what was said. In his analysis of the Forfar trial confessions, historian Joseph Anderson states that when witches were interrogated: 'they [the interrogators] seem to have plied them with questions, the notary taking down the substance of the admissions made in reply to these interrogatories. The results of repeated questionings, brought together and reduced to a sequential form in one document by a notary, were called a confession.'[31] The necessity of reducing the 'substance of the admissions' to a 'sequential form' would have involved transforming disjointed exchanges, recorded in shorthand during the interrogation, into a flowing narrative. It would have been the notary who transformed questions and answers into single statements. And it would have been the notary who inserted connective words and phrases to join one answer to another to create the effect of a continuous speech: turning, for example '"Did the Devil ask you to renounce your Christianity?" "Yes" "Did he give you a mark?" "Yes" into 'She confessed that the Devil asked her to renounce her Christianity and then gave her his mark.' In this drawing-together process the notary would have enjoyed a certain amount of leeway. In addition to conflating question and answers, he would have needed to change their order and add or subtract words and phrases to ensure narrative sense and flow. This was a highly-skilled art, particularly with regard to complex testimony such as that often given in witchcraft trials, and there is no doubt that some notaries were better at it and more scrupulous about it, than others. Maxwell-Stuart, for example, draws attention to a poorly-written witchcraft confession recorded at some presbytery hearings in Stirling in 1590, claiming that the account, which quickly degenerated into 'a near-incoherent ramble through entirely disparate pieces of information' may point to 'a failing of the clerk himself . . . [the accused] was providing a great deal of information, and it is quite possible that the clerk was not skilled in the art of precis and so failed to produce a decent, well-structured account for the presbytery records'.[32]

On the basis of these perspectives, we can be in no doubt that the superior narrative form and style of Isobel's confessions is directly attributable to the professional skills of John Innes. He clearly possessed the scribal ability to record the detailed questions and answers that swung back and forth between Isobel and her interrogators quickly and efficiently. But he also possessed the literary skill and linguistic precision to mould these details into coherent sentences, arrange these sentences into cohesive paragraphs and to invest the whole testimony with narrative rhythm, pace and fluidity. Although, as we have seen, the interrogators are likely to have been rigorous in their questioning and Isobel seems to have been forthcoming in response, Innes's notarial abilities were clearly of a high enough standard to enable him to match everyone involved nearly every step of the way. Interestingly, his protocol book hints at these superior abilities. Although standard in that it contains predominantly instruments of sasine, the wording of which accorded with the standard formats laid down in contemporary style books or formularies, in a period when spelling was not standardized and in which clerks commonly spelt the same word differently in several places in a text, Innes's spelling is unusually consistent. This feature, as genealogist Diane Baptie has pointed out, points to him not only being well-taught, but also possessing good concentration and probably a scrupulous nature.[33] We can speculate that this level of diligence was encouraged from a young age; certainly, in this period, other members of the Innes family were urged to prize this particular virtue. In 1673 John Innes of Leuchars, near Elgin, advised his son (also named John) to 'Learne I pray yow to be sober painfull vigelant and diligent above all things for diligence passes all sheame and ane man diligent in his calling shall not be ascheamed to stand beforr kings, for diligence maketh Riche.'[34]

But with regard to Innes's involvement in Isobel's case, there remains one last consideration. As noted in CHAPTER THREE, Isobel's confessions are unique in the sense that they were written in the first person throughout. And as the notary, Innes was almost certainly the individual responsible for this anomaly. Why he should have made such a decision is obscure. We can suppose that it was made in response to the fact that Isobel and Janet gave their confessions 'most willinglie', but there are many other cases of suspects confessing, or described as confessing, freely or willingly without their words being recorded in the first person. Searching around for other explanations, we can speculate that, as a newly qualified notary, and a man who may not have recorded a witchcraft interrogation at this level, Innes may not have been versed in protocol. The Innes-as-ingénue hypothesis, as we can term it here, also gains support from the fact that, in the absence of other explanations, it goes some way towards explaining why he recorded so much of Isobel's testimony, and with equal attention to detail, whichever end of the demonological/fairy lore continuum it related to. Not being familiar with witchcraft interrogations, and by implication, the demonological writings in which some of his interrogatorial peers were clearly well-versed, Innes may have lacked the prior suppositions that would have predisposed him to precis Isobel's fairy belief out of existence in his drawing together and summing up.

We can further speculate that, as was probably the case with Forbes and Rose, Innes's attention to detail may have also been motivated by interest for interest's sake. Although we have no direct evidence to support this supposition, we do have an interesting reference to play around with. In his entry on the Innes family in his book *Scottish Clans and Tartans,* historian Ian Grimble notes that 'The 19th Baron [of Innes] shared the interest of James VI in witchcraft, and was alleged to have entertained the Queen of Elphin.'[35] Barring further research this statement must remain a mystery, for it does not appear, to my knowledge, in any archive relating to the Moray Ineses. But given

the fact that Grimble was not prone to making wild claims, and that his solid dispu-
tations on clan history seldom embark on arbitrary forays into folklore, we can assume
that it was not fabricated out of thin air. One possible explanation might be that, as an
enthusiastic collector of oral history based in the north-east, Grimble gleaned the allegation orally. As such, the source could have been rooted in anything from a genuine
memorate to little more than a local legend, such as the one cited earlier concerning
the fairy-whirlwind experiences of Innes's neighbour, the Laird of Duffus. But whatever the source or accuracy of the reference, it is pertinent here that the 19th baron's
son was Brodie's father-in-law, and a man who continued to have close contact with
both Brodie and other local gentry (including the Earl of Moray and the Laird of Duffus)
until his death in 1656, only six years before Isobel's interrogation. Moreover his son,
in turn, went on to become one of Brodie's closest lifelong friends. Given the fact that
John Innes the notary is likely to have been related to the Moray Inneses, even if only
tangentially, and given the fact that the 20th and 21st lairds had such close contact
with some of those involved in Isobel's interrogation, we can speculate that the tale of
his kinsman's encounter with the 'Queen of Elphin', should it have been current in the
region in this period, would have reached his ears. Certainly, given the stature of the
19th Innes patriarch, the tale is likely to have made an impression on the notary, and
to have made Isobel's fairy-related claims all the more interesting.

The role of Innes in recording Isobel's confessions also deserves particular emphasis
here because, where it has been commented on, it has generally been criticized. It is
standard for scholars to lament that the scattering of etceteras found in both Isobel's
and Janet's confessions indicate a clerical laziness, narrow-mindedness or lack of interest
that has left us all bereft. With regard to those appearing in the famous passage
describing Isobel's feast with the fairy king and queen, for example, Robert Pitcairn
noted that 'It is a thousand pities that the learned Examinators have so piously declined
indulging the world with the detailed description of these illustrious personages.'
Similarly, in 2005 Maxwell-Stuart notes wearily that 'The clerk is a nuisance with his
"etc". He uses it a number of times during the record, and one cannot tell whether he
was too impatient to note all the details Isobel was providing, or inclined to censor the
narrative when it was becoming too prolix for his taste.' Diane Purkiss expresses similar
frustrations, lamenting that 'Sometimes one could travel back in time just to wring the
clerk's neck.'[36] But while these sentiments are understandable, they are misleading. It
is true that, by general witch-record standards, Isobel's and Janet's confessions do
contain an unusually high number of etceteras (fourteen and two respectively), but it
is just as likely that these represent clerical scrupulousness as opposed to negligence.
The fact that the etceteras are not only found in passages relating to fairy belief, but
also in passages relating to the more legally relevant animal metamorphosis, *maleficium*
and worship of the Devil, strongly suggests that Innes did not omit material because
he considered it uninteresting, irrelevant or distasteful, but simply because he was
receiving more information from his suspect than even he could deal with. The two
etceteras in the following passage from Confession Three, for example, cannot be tritely
attributed to lack of interest in the subject matter, which was surely demonological
enough to satisfy the most Devil-obsessed interrogator:

somtym he vold be lyk a stirk, a bull, a deir, a rae, or a dowg etc and haw dealling w[i]th ws, and he vold hold wp his taill wntill we wold kiss his arce; and at each tym q[uhe]n ve wold meitt w[i]th him, we behoowit to ryse and beck and mak owr curtesie to him and we wold say, ye ar welcom owr lord, and how doe ye my lord etc. (49/22)

From this perspective, Innes's penchant for etceteras suggests that, unlike many clerks, he was sufficiently fastidious to acknowledge and record the places where his abilities failed him. Furthermore, even if we retain the view that impatience, disapproval or a lack of interest did indeed underpin Innes's omissions, it is fair to argue that his achievements far outweigh his failures and that the quality of what he did record far outstrips the loss of what he did not. There is little doubt that the wealth of vivid detail so characteristic of Isobel's confessions could not have come down to us in the form that it has without the exceptional scrupulousness and literary skill of John Innes. And for that we are most definitely in his debt.

Isobel's Contribution

We have speculated that some of the stylistic features characteristic of Isobel's confessions can be attributed to the interventions of Forbes, Rose and Innes. It could also be argued that these perspectives on interrogatorial involvement provide us with an answer, or at least partial answer, to the question posed at the end of the last chapter: why do Isobel's confessions span such a diverse range of subject matter and why do they contain so much of it? For it is not difficult to see how the intellectual curiosity, developed listening skills and literary abilities that produced such high levels of graphic detail and narrative flair are also likely to have unearthed, pursued and recorded a wide and diverse range of topics.

Taken together, these perspectives certainly go some way toward explaining the unusualness of the confessions, and reduce the need to reach for the Isobel-was-crazy hypothesis to account for them. But as always, things are a little more complicated than this. Neat as such a conclusion might be, we cannot place everything at the interrogators' door. If we return, once again, to our comparison between Isobel's and Janet's confessions, we find evidence to suggest that Isobel may have played a much greater role, both in terms of stylistic features and subject matter, than our argument up to this point has suggested. Until now we have focused on the fact that both Isobel's and Janet's confessions contain similar levels of graphic detail and linguistic precision, and that these features can be attributed to the interrogators. But it is equally important to note that the confessions are not stylistically identical. With the exception of those passages that were likely to have been influenced by Isobel's testimony (such as those concerned with the demonic pact and the *corp creadh*), Janet's narrative differs from those given by Isobel in a number of ways. Although it shares their commitment to graphic detail and linguistic precision, it lacks their pace, their profusion of adverbs, adjectives and similes, their dramatic moments of direct speech, their vivid imagery and their intellectual energy. Similarly, Janet's narrative does not contain the breadth and depth of subject matter found in Isobel's, or their vertiginous and fluid sweep from fairy lore to demonology, or their kaleidoscope of vibrant images relating to the fairy world, or their profusion of lively and idiosyncratic charms. In the last analysis, although rich in the context of Scottish witch-records as a whole, Janet's confession seems markedly pedestrian when set side by side with those of her Lochloy counterpart.

Unlike the attention to detail and linguistic precision, these differences cannot be attributed to the influence of either the interrogators or the notary. While we cannot rule out the possibility that the inferiority of Janet's confession is attributable to the fact that John Innes may have compiled it on a 'bad writing day', it is far more likely that it differed from Isobel's because the latter's delivery possessed a verbal flair, intellectual energy and diversity of subject matter that Janet's lacked. But in acknowledging that Isobel may have contributed to her confessions in this way, we are faced with a barrage of new questions. Why did Isobel make these contributions when Janet did not? How unusual may her contributions have been? And, to return to the questions posed in CHAPTER THREE, can they be interpreted as symptomatic of the fact that, unlike Janet, Isobel suffered from some form of psychiatric disorder?

Isobel the Tradition-Bearer

It is here that a passing remark by Peter Maxwell-Stuart, in his rich analysis of the Scottish witch-panic of 1661–2, provides us with a fruitful avenue of exploration. In reference to Isobel's case the latter claims 'I suspect that the principal reason it differs from all the others we have encountered is that she was a Highlander and thus steeped in the living oral tradition that is so much a part of Gaelic culture.'[37] Whether or not Isobel was a Highlander is open to debate. The name Gowdie (also commonly spelt as 'Gaudie' or 'Goudie' in the period) is not of Gaelic derivation and is generally considered to have been a medieval import derived from the Old English 'Gold', with some tracing it to Scandinavia and others to Spain and Italy.[38] Similarly, none of Isobel's coven members, including her great ally, Janet Breadheid, bore specifically Gaelic names. There is also no indication, although we cannot rule out the possibility altogether, that Isobel's testimony was delivered in Gaelic. As was normal for the period, Innes recorded the confessions in a mixture of English and Scots (the vernacular English) spelling and vocabulary. But if his text represented a translation from the Gaelic, undertaken by either a translator or by Innes himself, you would not expect the vocabulary to be as varied, colourful and vernacular (ie: 'glaiked' and 'gowked') as it appears in the text, nor would you expect the charms to rhyme in such an effortless and consistent manner.

But the fact that Isobel probably gave her testimony in Scots, and did not bear a Gaelic name, does not rule out the possibility of Highland kinship. Owing to its proximity to the Cairngorm Mountains to the south, Nairnshire was a border region, that is, a region where, to a varying extent, Highlanders and Lowlanders inhabited the same territory. This intimacy was mirrored in the fact that, by the eighteenth century, Nairn was considered to be an eastern gateway to the Highlands, famously being the place where Samuel Johnson, on his progress along the Moray Firth from Aberdeen, first 'saw peat fires, and first heard the Erse language'.[39] The strength of Highland presence elsewhere in the region is similarly attested to by the Forres presbytery's reference, in 1676, to the 'rud, barbarous and ignorant Irish people . . . betwixt Archlach, Calder, and Moy'; and by Gaelic scholar Charles Withers's claim that, even as late as 1706–7, 'for the parishes of Nairn, Ardclach, Cawdor, and Edinkillie religious administration in Gaelic was "absolutely necessary"'.[40] Given this cultural melting pot, Isobel could easily have been part-Gael. North-eastern ballads often sang of the inconvenient romances which sprang up between Lowland girls and their Highland sweethearts, and such dalliances could have flourished in the Nairnshire parishes. It is worth noting in this respect that although we have absolutely no evidence of such, we cannot rule out the possibility that Isobel's mother, whose maiden name is unknown, was of Gaelic descent.

But even if Isobel did not inherit Gaelic blood, just through living in seventeenth-century Auldearn she would have come into close contact with Highland culture. The constant need for bilingual ministers in these regions well into the eighteenth century is clear evidence that many Highlanders could not speak English or Scots and that many Lowlanders could not speak Gaelic, with this dilemma being immortalized in James VI's alleged boast, to some of his English courtiers, that he 'had a toun in Scotland – the toun of Nairn – so big that the people at the one end did not understand the language spoken by those at the other end'.[41] But a certain level of bilingualism was vital in an area where Highland/Lowland trade was important. In Inverness in 1704, for example, it was noted that in one parish over 900 people spoke both languages, while fifty years later Burt noted of the city that 'although they speak English, there are scarce any who do not understand the Irish Tongue; and it is necessary that they should do so, to carry on their Dealings with the neighbouring Country People; for within less than a Mile of the Town, there are few who speak any English at all'.[42] Although we cannot draw firm conclusions about the nature of this bilingualism (with Withers, for example, recently lamenting of the period that 'there is very little evidence about the actual geography of the language, the nature of the language itself, or the ways in which Gaelic and English were used in particular social situations by those people able to speak both'), we can nevertheless assume that it generated a high level of cultural transmission.[43] Not only did bilingualism facilitate business transactions (with Highlanders selling their cattle at Lowland markets and Lowlanders negotiating grazing rights on the summer shielings and so on) but it also assisted the sharing of medical knowledge (with some witch-trials describing how Lowlanders resorted to Highland cunning women for medical help); the dissemination of news and gossip; and the exchange of folk literature, in the form of songs, stories, ballads and so on.[44] This intimate cultural exchange would have been intensified by the fact that the parishes along the Moray Firth, being trapped between the sea and the Grampian Mountains to the south, were relatively cut off from the cosmopolitan influences of the central Lowlands around Edinburgh and Glasgow.

With regard to the discussion in hand, the fact that Isobel lived in this microclimate of intense and relatively isolated cultural interaction, could be significant. Since they first began seriously recording and studying oral traditions in the late-eighteenth and nineteenth centuries, scholars have noted that folk literature from the north-eastern Lowlands, particularly Aberdeenshire, is among the best in Scotland. Indeed, with regard to balladry, Buchan goes so far as to claim that 'Northeast balladry constitutes the richest regional tradition in Britain.'[45] Whether or not such a claim persuades, there is no doubt that Aberdeenshire provided over a third of the Scottish ballads in Child's famous nineteenth-century collection and that the Scots language, as spoken by the north-eastern Lowlanders, is known for its 'remarkable richness and distinctiveness', combining, as it does, an original Anglo-Saxon Northumbrian dialect with a vivid inclusion of Gaelic, Norse, French and Flemish loan words.[46] With regard to oral traditions, this richness and distinctiveness was probably fostered, as in other border regions of Scotland, through a particularly close Highland/Lowland interaction, with Morayshire folklorist Robert Jamieson (1780–1844) pointing out the similarities, in methods of oral recitation, between 'Lowlanders in the North of Scotland' and 'the Highlanders and Irish'.[47] As a consequence, although we do not know whether Isobel inherited Highland blood or whether she spoke Gaelic, with regard to the question of whether she was 'steeped in living oral tradition', it is clear that being an inhabitant of Auldearn in the seventeenth century would have been qualification enough.

But although we can entertain this conclusion as a possibility, how and in what manner Isobel's oral heritage may have contributed towards the unusual stylistic and content-related features of her confessions, is more difficult to establish. As a consequence, we propose here to take a diversion into the whole subject of Scottish oral literature and performance in general. This diversion may appear, in the early stages, to be an unnecessarily comprehensive one, but it will serve several purposes simultaneously. First, it will help us to gain a sense of the degree to which Isobel may have contributed to the unusualness of her confessions. Secondly, it will also enable us to revisit, from a different perspective, the interrogatorial motivations and interventions of the men who questioned her. And thirdly, through giving us a deeper insight into the contemporary oral mind, it will lay the foundations for some of the discussions developed later in the book: specifically CHAPTER EIGHT, where we explore Isobel's maleficent charms; CHAPTER NINE, where we explore to what degree Isobel's confessions related to true or false events; and CHAPTERS TWELVE to EIGHTEEN, where we emphasize, from a shamanistic perspective, the vast gulfs that existed between elite and popular imaginations in seventeenth-century Nairnshire.

6

'Q[uhe]n I wes in the elfes houssis'

The [traditional Scottish] texts, of story, song, proverb or riddle, have a vigour, a directness, and a concrete vividness; they can be both precisely factual and soaringly fantastical,
sometimes in the same sentence. They avoid linguistic superfluity but can dwell on the
telling detail; they eschew psychological introspections but can embody in the narrative
action or the proverb's phrase highly accurate perceptions of universal human behaviour.[1]

Although recent scholars have emphasized that the written word played a more significant role in early modern Britain than has been previously supposed, there is little
doubt that until the late-eighteenth century, when printed works became more
numerous and widely available, and the late nineteenth, when literacy levels began to
rise significantly, it fed into an essentially oral culture. Although we have few sources
directly relating to this culture as it existed in seventeenth-century Scotland, we can
speculate about it on the basis of the wealth of oral literature gathered and recorded by
nineteenth-century Scottish folklorists. Despite the fact that the latter were collating
their material over 150 years after Isobel's lifetime and that oral culture, being a
dynamic art form, changes in response to current events and the influences of individual
tellers, these later collections can still be seen as generally reflective of early modern
traditions. Although in constant flux, traditional oral literature has always been stabi-
lized by a strong vein of conservatism and scholars have often marvelled at the extent
to which individual works can remain relatively unchanged over many generations. The
fact that oral lore was passed primarily between the old and the young effectively
enabled a ballad, song or story to stride undisturbed through the centuries in seventy-
year boots, with nineteenth-century folklorist Alexander Carmichael claiming, for
example, that 'In 1860, 1861, and 1862 I took down much folk-lore from Kenneth
Morrison, cotter, Trithion, Skye . . . [he] told me that the old men, from whom he heard
the poems and stories, said they had heard them from old men in their boyhood. That
would carry these old men back to the first half of the seventeenth century.'[2]

It is difficult for the modern Western mind to appreciate the complexity and diversity of pre-modern folk literature and the many and various ways in which it was
integrated into daily life. Almost all communal gatherings, whether seasonal celebrations, life-cycle rituals, markets or evenings around the fire, would have been

accompanied by the sharing of songs, ballads, stories, rhymes, riddles, anecdotes and proverbs. In the absence of radio, television – or even, for the most part, books – oral literature was a valuable currency, and it was a widespread tradition for guests or those who made a living through travel, such as tinkers or drovers, to contribute a speech, song or anecdote as they passed through a community. 'When a stranger appeared', recalled David Stuart of his childhood in the eighteenth-century Highlands, 'after the usual introductory compliments, the first question was, "Bheil dad agad air na Fheinn?" ("Can you speak of the days of Fingal?") If the answer was in the affirmative the whole hamlet was convened, and midnight was usually the hour of separation.'[3]

But oral performance was not just reserved for special events and long winter evenings, it was also woven into the fabric of everyday life itself, being commonly used to alleviate the monotony and rigour of farming and domestic chores. In nineteenth-century Fife an observer noted that when the women 'go to gather bait they tell tales', while in 1782, an English servant complained that on the Isle of Skye the common folk wasted much time 'telling idle tales and singing doggerel rhymes' and that 'all kinds of labour is accompanied with singing: if it is rowing a boat the men sing; if it is reaping the women sing. I think that if they were in the deepest distress they would all join in a chorus'.[4] As in tribal cultures today, work songs were most widely developed among women. And sung charms, which had the double advantage of both occupying the mind and magically enhancing the process in hand, were particularly favoured. Both songs and charms possessed cadences that reflected their practical usage, with the rhythmic pounding of the butter churn, for example, being clearly heard in the following verse recorded by George Sinclair in 1685:

> Come Butter Come,
> Come Butter come,
> Peter stands at the Gate,
> Waiting for a Butter'd Cake,
> Come Butter come.[5]

Lifelong exposure to oral lore would have affected the way young minds developed, and it is difficult for the modern Western mind, so used to 'seen' literature, to appreciate the developments which occurred in response to literature that was solely 'heard'. Thrown into slings on their mothers' backs, children would have been swung back and forth to the rhythm of reaping, churning and waulking songs from the moment of birth, and before they were a year old they would have spent hundreds of hours by the fire-side listening to ballads, songs, and stories being performed into the night. As they learnt to understand language, they would also have learnt how to listen. No child who, like the boy from early nineteenth-century Uist, sat listening to a story 'mute and motionless for the best part of the night' would wish to miss the punch line through a careless lapse in attention.[6] From the moment they could string together a phrase or hit a note, children joined the communal chorus of song that accompanied both work and play and later, as their minds matured, they rose to the intellectual challenges of riddling and the invention of lyric verses or humorous rhymes. As a consequence of this immersion, even the most isolated and illiterate seventeenth-century peasant was likely to have had a larger vocal range, a wider vocabulary and a better command of language than many university-educated twenty-first century Britons.

The Fireside Bards

But while general verbal facility was, by the standards of today, very high, there were certain individuals who, whether through natural ability or inclination, became specialists in the field. Prominent among these were the professional, formally-trained bards who earned their living either travelling through the land or in residence under a single employer where, according to folklorist Joseph Nagy, they occupied themselves with 'the oral transmission and performance of traditional prose tales' and 'the composition of verse celebrating . . . [their] patrons and detailing the genealogy and lore of families and tribes'.[7] Although enjoying an ancient lineage, by the seventeenth century the numbers of professional bards were in serious decline.[8] But running beneath this network was another, equally old and deep-rooted, which has been termed by modern storytellers the 'fireside tradition'. Instead of being formally trained, fireside bards learnt and developed their skills within the confines of the fermtoun. And instead of earning a living through their craft, they worked on the land or plied a trade like their peers and shared their verbal expertise with their friends and neighbours (or the communities they passed through on business) for free, or in exchange for goods such as grain or tobacco. Illiteracy and motherhood were no barrier to this tradition and although the profession was still male-dominated, it was not unusual for a woman to gain a reputation as the village bard (baird a' bhaile). Unlike its professional counterpart, the fireside tradition remained vibrant well into the nineteenth century: Grant noting that in the early modern period there emerged a remarkable surge in fireside poetry composition, and that by its peak in the mid-eighteenth century, notable bards had emerged 'from every rank in life, the kinsfolk of chiefs and tacksmen, ministers and schoolmasters, a cattleman, a slater, crofters. They included men and women and some, even among the most distinguished poets, were illiterate.'[9] Indeed, enthusiasm for the art was so widespread that in the eighteenth century a Highland minister's wife could observe that 'In every cottage there is a musician and in every hamlet a poet'.[10]

Although fireside bards are stereotypically associated with dimly-lit cottages and long winter evenings, their skills were also valued during the working day. In 1859 one of J. F. Campbell's Islay acquaintances sent him a song that she claimed to have heard 'an old ploughman of my father's sing very near sixty years since. He had a great collection of tales and songs, and often have I stood or sat by him in winter when kiln-drying corn, or in summer when building a peat stack, listening to what was to me so fascinating in those days.'[11] Indeed, drying corn seems to have been such a monotonous task that in the early decades of the century some village bards were offered grain to entertain their neighbours while they completed the task.[12] But although it could be sought out to alleviate the drudgery of work, oral performance could also be sought out

A storytelling circle, as portrayed by Scottish artist George-Paul Chalmers in the 1860s. Though Chalmers was painting two hundred years after Isobel's trial, rural cottage interiors and the dynamics of storytelling would have changed little in the intervening period.

purely for itself. Despite the fact that 'every hamlet had its poet', people would travel distances to hear a performer of skill: nineteenth-century Uist farmer Donald MacCraw remembering how, as a child, he and his companions would often walk 'six or seven miles in the snow' in the pursuit of a good storyteller.[13]

The Bardic Skills

Like the formally-trained bards, fireside performers enhanced their natural abilities through the development of specific skills. The most prominent of these was the ability to memorize large amounts of prose and verse. In the mid-nineteenth century J. F. Campbell noted that Donald Maclean of Ardnamurchan 'recites his tales without the slightest hesitation, although in some cases their recitation occupies a couple of hours . . . Mclean's is a remarkable instance of the power of memory in the uneducated, shewing that it is quite possible to retain and recite, with perfect accuracy, compositions which would form a volume.'[14] As a result of these abilities, Campbell notes, 'one good story in the mouth of a good narrator, with a good audience, might easily go rambling on for a whole winter's night, as it is said to do'.[15] Even as late as 1986, Nagy could still claim confidently that 'until recently' tellers 'with amazingly large story-repertoires could be found among Gaelic-speaking peasants and fishermen in Ireland and Scotland'.[16] In memorizing this material, fireside bards acted as librarians, quite literally storing the oral heritage of their communities in their heads, a function that has earned them, among folklorists, the sobriquet of 'tradition-bearer'. Memory skills were equally important for those bards who did not only remember and recount oral literature verbatim, but also improvised on known texts and in some cases, composed new ones. We shall be exploring the dynamics of extempore composition and improvisation in some detail in CHAPTER EIGHT, but it is worth noting here that when oral performers composed and improvised stories, ballads and songs, they did not do so in a mental vacuum. Not only did they mine a wide vocabulary and an extensive knowledge of folklore, but they also drew on a memorized store of standard word groupings or phrases that were employed as component parts to be arranged and rearranged to serve the performer's purpose in different combinations.[17]

Whether they composed from scratch, improvised on known texts or memorized verbatim, oral performers also needed to master the skills of repetition, with Buchan claiming that when encountering Scottish folk literature 'The linguistic feature that first strikes the reader is likely to be the frequency of repetition, of words, of phrases, of sentences, and even of whole episodes'.[18] Through mastering the skills of repetition (and the closely connected skills of listing) the oral performer achieved a variety of aims simultaneously. He rested his memory and gave himself space in which to recall or invent the next line or stanza; he provided his audience with a period of emotional or mental respite before they needed to engage with the next passage; and he improved the pace, flow and dramatic tension of his piece. The ways in which repetition can punctuate and intensify a tale is well illustrated in the following story, taken down from a Barra fisherman who claimed to have learnt it from his father around the turn of the eighteenth century:

> 'What good did it do thee to slay the people, and that I will kill thee,' said the great warrior at their head. 'If I had come out, from my meat and from my warmth, from my warmth and from my fire, thou shouldst not kill me.' He and the warrior began at each other. They would make a bog of the crag, and a crag of the bog, in the place where the least they would sink they would sink to the knees, in the place that the most they would sink they would sink to the eyes. The great warrior made a sweep with his glave, and he cut the head off Innsridh MacRigh nan Sealg.[19]

Many oral performers were also adept at rhyming and versifiying. Although these skills are now associated primarily with children, as Buchan observed in 1984, in the pre-modern period they occupied 'a significant place in the life of the adult community, and one which deserves more attention than so far received'.[20] Not only was rhyming a genre in itself, but it worked its way into nearly all forms of oral literature, including songs, ballads, proverbs and riddles. Particularly pertinent in relation to Isobel's confessions is the fact that in older Scottish sources, rhyming also frequently found its way into prose, with Bruford noting that in the early modern bardic manuscripts of the Gaelic romances, 'Dialogue is sometimes carried on in verse: the normal procedure in that case is to give the gist of the conversation or speech in prose before saying that a poem was made out of it and quoting it. The device is inspired by the poems in Old Irish tales . . . The normal pattern of mixing prose with verse was probably established by the "Three Sorrows" which, it is suggested, were worked over by a single hand some time before 1500.'[21] That this fusion of genres was incorporated into fireside oral performance in pre-modern Scotland is attested to by eighteenth-century observers, and by the fact that many recorded versions of popular folk tales known to have been extant in seventeenth-century Scotland, such as 'The Black Bull of Norroway', 'The Wall at the Warld's End', 'Rashie Coat' and 'Child Roland', have also come down to us in this format.[22]

Oral performers also possessed a good command of descriptive language, whether in the form of adjectives and adverbs, or stock phrases, metaphors and similes. This resource could be employed to 'impress the audience with the author's command of language' with Bruford noting, for example, that the alliterative phrases used to construct the runs in Gaelic romances 'though roughly rhythmic, are open-ended, so that on occasion up to thirty adjectives may follow one noun'.[23] But more importantly, descriptive language generated valuable atmosphere, realism and dramatic effect, enabling a performer to take a tale or ballad that had been heard many times before and craft it into a thing of vividness and immediacy. The following memorate, recorded in Aberdeenshire at the turn of the nineteenth century, illustrates how pithy verbs, adjectives, adverbs and similes could be used to transform a stereotypical narrative event (in this case, meeting the Devil) into a viscerally real experience:

> and ae Setterday nicht that I wis awa' on the rig it wis into Sabbath afore I cam' hame, an' jist as I wis gyaun up the chaumer stair to ma bed, there wis Sawtan, in the shape o' a muckle

black cauf, stan'in' glowerin' at me wi' the twa muckle een o' him burnin' like can'les in's heid, and I can tell ye the sicht gar't the caul sweat come oot o' me, and I've been a cheenged man ever sin' syne.[24]

When highly descriptive language is combined with the vibrancy of direct speech, the impression is further intensified, as in the following version of 'Rumpelstiltskin', recorded in Dumfries:

'Goodwife o' Kittlerumpit, ye weel ken what I come for – stand and deliver!' The wife pretends to greet sairer than before, and wrings her nieves, and fa's on her knees, wi': 'Och, sweet madam mistress, spare my only bairn, and take the weary soo!' 'The deil takle the soo for my share,' quo' the fairy; 'I come na here for swine's flesh. Dinna be contramawcious, hizzie, but gie me the gett instantly!' 'Ochon, dear leddy mine,' quo' the greetin' goodwife; 'for-bear my poor bairn, and take mysel!' 'The deil's in the daft jad,' quo' the fairy, looking like the far-end o' a fiddle; 'I'll wad she's clean dementit.'[25]

With regard to our analysis of Isobel, it is interesting to note that although dramatic intensity, of the kind illustrated above, is found in oral literature throughout Scotland, some scholars have identified it as a 'hallmark' of some north-eastern oral genres. With regard to balladry, for example, Buchan notes that:

Though phlegmatic and ostensibly unemotional, the northeasterner has a strong sense of the dramatic; in pre-Reformation times Aberdeen was the Scottish burgh most renowned for its plays and pageants. And the hallmark of the old northeastern ballads is that they are dramatic, the best of them integrating lyric emotion and narrative event within powerfully dramatic wholes. Here, perhaps, is one key to a psychological understanding of why the Northeast folk liked their ballads . . . In this society the ballads served a cathartic function, for they provided a dramatic yet disciplined outlet to the emotions denied regular expression by dour, canny, undemonstrative, northeastern folk.[26]

But for the fireside bard, capacious memories, wide repertoires and good verbal and rhyming skills would have amounted to nothing without mastering the skills of delivery. In the hands of an expressive performer, even the most bland, unsophisticated tale could become compelling, emotive and as J. F. Campbell put it, 'sharper and deeper' in the telling.[27] In contemporary Britain, where oral traditions have fallen into decline, story delivery is generally associated with the cheery, parental tones employed for children's bedtime stories, or the gentlemanly Queen's English deployed by actors for audio books or radio broadcasts. But the manner of oral delivery in pre-modern Scotland would often have been different, as illustrated by folklorist Robert Jamieson's account of hearing 'Child Roland' (a variant of 'Jack and the Beanstalk') as a boy, in the late-eighteenth century. The tale, which was told by a tailor who was working in his father's house:

was recited in a sort of formal, drowsy, measured, monotonous recitative, mixing prose and verse, in the manner of the Icelandic sagas; and as is still the manner of reciting tales and *fabulas aniles* in the winter evenings, not only among the Islanders, Norweigans and Swedes, but also among the Lowlanders in the North of Scotland, and among the Highlanders and Irish . . . of the *verses* which have been introduced, I cannot answer for the exactness of any, except the stanza put into the mouth of the king of Elfland, which was indelibly impressed upon my memory, long before I knew anything of Shakespeare, by the odd and whimsical manner in which the tailor curled up his nose and sniffed all about, to imitate the action which 'fi, fi, fo, fum!' is intended to represent.[28]

Songs and ballads, when well delivered, could have an equally powerful impact. In 1799 an observer noted that Scottish working songs 'seem to invigorate every nerve in their [the singers'] bodies', while thirty years earlier Irish poet Oliver Goldsmith remembered that 'The music of our finest singer is dissonance to what I felt when our old dairy-maid sung me into tears with Johnny Armstrong's Last Good-Night or the Cruelty of Barbara Allen'.[29] Anyone who has heard traditional singers like Aberdeenshire's Jeannie Robertson can recognize that in the hands of an accomplished vocal performer, the simplest tunes and lyrics can generate profound emotional effects. Highland delivery would often have been more akin to that of the contemporary Sufi performer than that of the jolly, rosy-cheeked-folksinger stereotype. Voices would not have been restricted by the pursuit of the 'pleasant' sound and in order to express emotions, and particularly the emotions associated with suffering or longing, singers would push their voices out of their comfort range and disregard the limitations of the classical octave. During his tour of the Highlands in the early-nineteenth century, John Leyden noted that the reaping songs, which were even then beginning to die out, sounded like 'the screaming of sea-gulls'; while Burt noted that a century earlier women reapers 'keep time together, by several barbarous Tones of the Voice'.[30] The 'heart-rending [graveside] lamentations' of the *bean-chaointe*, or keening-women, would have been equally uncanny.[31]

Isobel as Bard

Recent research into literacy levels in mid seventeenth-century Scotland suggests that the mean illiteracy level for adult males in rural parishes was 80 percent, with the levels among women being supposed considerably higher.[32] Although this figure is only approximate and is likely to underestimate reading ability, particularly with regard to women, taken in combination with the fact that Isobel's confessions contain few of the biblical and literary references representative of the contemporary literary mind, it enables us to assume, with a fair degree of certainty, that she was illiterate. We can also safely assume that she would have been well acquainted with oral lore and that, like the majority of her peers, she possessed a degree of native verbal facility. But the stylistic flair and breadth of subject matter displayed in Isobel's confessions invites us to go one step further than this, and speculate that her oral skills may have been more highly developed than average and that, as a consequence, she may have functioned as some kind of oral performer. Exactly what kind of oral performer is impossible to tell, for theoretically the term can be applied to an individual who tells a tale occasionally through to someone who tells them frequently and is consistently sought out for their performance abilities. But nevertheless, we can speculate that Isobel stood somewhere on this oral performing continuum.

This hypothesis enables us to look at some of the confessions' stylistic features from a new perspective. Their use of descriptive language is a prime example. The text seldom employs one noun, when two, three or four would do: the Devil is 'lyk a stirk, a bull, a deir, a rae, or a dowg etc'; and when Isobel's coven members were transformed into cats they had 'the bytte and rywes & scrattis in owr bodies'. The confessions also consistently employ powerful and vivid verbs, often in multiples: the Devil was 'beat-ting and scurgeing'; elf bulls were 'crowtting and skrylling'; and the elf boys were 'whytting and dighting'. Adjectives and adverbs also appear with remarkable frequency, again often in multiples: she went into a 'fair & lairge braw rowme'; those intent on harm 'will look uncowth lyk thraw (n?) (*damaged – words missing*) hurlie lyk and their clothes standing out'; the Devil was 'bigger and mor awfull' than the other Devils and 'his memberis (*limbs*) ar exceeding great and long'; while those copulating with him had 'a exceeding great desyr of it'. The confessional text is also peppered with alliteration and assonance, with Isobel's coven, for example, doing 'nothing bot cry & wraw & rywing and as it ver wirrieing on an uth[er]'. Similes and metaphors are also abundant, with Isobel noting that the Devil has a 'hodge nature, verie cold as yce', that Margaret Wilson's helping spirit wore clothes that were 'grass grein', and that the *corp creadh* shall be burnt 'as any stickle wpon a kill (*kiln*)'.

As noted already, although individual words or even phrases may have been inserted into the text by Innes to enhance the sense of a passage, and many undoubtedly found their way there via the wording of the questions, it is unlikely that either he or the interrogators were completely responsible for this diverse and colourful cacophony of descriptive words and phrases. There simply would have been no reason for them to elaborate Isobel's testimony in this way. However until now, it has been difficult to comprehend why an individual on trial for her life and charged with such antisocial crimes would find either the time or inclination to embroider her testimony with so many superfluous rhetorical details. But once we bring the possibility that Isobel was an oral performer into the equation, this incongruity lessens. As some kind of *baird a' bhaile*, or village bard, Isobel is likely to have had a larger-than-average reservoir of descriptive words and phrases to hand, and to have been accustomed to weaving them into narrative demanded by, and delivered before, an audience. Although, during inter-rogations, Isobel was delivering her narrative under arrest before a band of legal prosecutors as opposed to at a ceilidh before her family and friends, it is unlikely that her affinity with language and her skills of oral delivery would have been wholly suppressed; for whatever else the interrogators were doing, they were still asking her to tell a story. This thesis is also indirectly supported by the fact that the 'vigour', 'directness' and 'concrete vividness' of the descriptive language found in Isobel's confes-sions, and the way they navigate effortlessly between matters 'both precisely factual and soaringly fantastical, sometimes in the same sentence', conforms perfectly to Buchan's summary – quoted at the beginning of this chapter – of the core characteristics of traditional Scottish literature.[33]

The Isobel-as-oral-performer hypothesis also sheds light on the characteristic fluidity and pace of her narrative that, like her use of descriptive words and phrases, is so much more marked than that of her accomplice, Janet Breadheid. If we look closely, we can see that this effect is partly created through the skilful use of repetition: words or groups of words being used over and over again to knit phrases, sentences or passages together. In the following passage from Confession One, for example, the impression of narrative flow is created through the use of the repetitive connectives 'and before' and 'went':

> the last tym th[a]t owr coven (*rest of line obscured*) wer daunceing at the hill of earlseat, and befor th[a]t betuixt moynes and bowgholl, & befor th[a]t we ves besyd the meikle burne, and the uth[e]r coven being at the downiehillis we went from beyond the meikle burne and went besyd them to the howssis at the woodend of Inshoch and w[i]thin a qwhyll went hom to o[u]r howssis. (39/25)

It could be argued that notarial skills were likely to have been responsible for the fluidity of this passage. The interrogators may have asked Isobel a series of 'And where did your coven go next?' questions and Innes, clearly an able scribe, may have taken her disjointed answers and knitted them together with appropriate connectives. But we must set against this assessment the fact that retrospective listing, of the kind that appears here, is not suggestive of sequential questioning, with the interrogators being much more likely to have asked 'And where did your coven go next?' than 'And where did your coven go before that?' Moreover, the possibility that this passage accurately, or relatively accurately, reflected Isobel's manner of delivery is further supported by the fact that other confessional passages contain repetitive phrases that are far less likely to have come from the interrogators. In the following two extracts, both taken from Confession One, the phrase 'in the Devil's name' (here italicised) is illustrative:

> we took a thried of each cullor of yairne th[a]t wes in the s[ai]d allexr cuming his littfatt, and did cast thrie knotts on each thried *in the divellis nam*, and did put the thriedis in the fatt withersones abowt in the fat *in the divellis name* and th[e]rby took the heall strenth of the fatt away th[a]t it could litt nothing bot onlie blak, according to the culor of *the divell in qoes nam* we took away the strenth of the ryt culoris th[a]t wes in the fatt . . . (41/5)

> whan we tak away any cowes milk we pull the taw and twyn it & plaitt it the vrong way *in the divellis name*, and we draw the tedder (sua maid) in betuixt the cowes hinder foot and owt betuixt the cowes forder foot, *in the divellis nam* and therby tak w[i]th ws the kowes milk. (40/10)

Although not impossible, it is unlikely that the interrogators constantly interrupted Isobel's testimony with the query 'And did you do that in the Devil's name?' It is also unlikely that Innes, in response to her assent, dutifully inserted the phrase in full after every relevant statement to give the impression of continuous delivery. As with the passage about coven meetings cited above, it is far more likely that this repetitive device reflected Isobel's natural manner of speech.

The Isobel-as-oral-performer hypothesis would also go some way towards explaining the dramatic intensity of the confessions. Whatever event Isobel describes, whether making the *corp creadh*, raising winds, flying through the air or feasting at the sabbath, her accounts leap out of the page with a sharp, almost urgent, emotional tension. In the following passage, for example, she employs descriptive words, repetition, listing and direct speech to create a scene of almost burlesque theatrical intensity, of the kind displayed in the Dumfries 'Rumpelstiltskin' version cited earlier:

> somtyms among owr selws we wold be calling him blak Jon or the lyk, and he wold ken it & heir ws weill aneughe, and he ewin then com to ws, and say I ken weill aneugh what ye wer sayeing of me, & th[e]n he vold beat and buffet ws werie sor, we wold be beattin if ve wer absent any tym, or neglect any thing th[a]t wold be appointed to be done, allexr elder in earlseat vold be werie oft beatin, he is bot soft, & could never defend him self in the least, bot greitt & cry q[uhe]n he vold be scurging him, bot margret wilson in aulderne wold defend hir self fynlie, & cast up hir handis to keip the stroakis off from hir and bessie wilsone wold speak croslie w[i]th hir towynge, and wold be belling again to him stowtlie he wold be beatting and scurgeing ws all wp and downe, w[i]th tardis & uth[e]r sharp scurges, lyk naked gwhastis, and we wold be still cryeing, pittie, pittie, mercie, mercie, owr lord, bot he wold haw neither pittie nor mercie, whan he vold be angrie at ws, he wold girne at ws, lyk a dowge, as iff he wold swellow ws wp. (49/11)

The speculation that Isobel may have been an oral performer also helps to explain the unprecedented number of rhyming charms that emerge in the confessions. On the one hand, as we have seen in CHAPTER THREE and shall explore in more depth later, it is highly likely that the latter were produced in direct response to close interrogatorial prompting. In Confession Two, for example, the charms frequently and formulaically illustrate magical activities previously described in prose, with descriptions of rituals performed to raise winds, concoct potions and make *corp creadh*, for example, being neatly followed by renditions of the verses chanted when performing them. A pattern that strongly suggests that the latter emerged in response to: 'And what did you say when you rose winds, concocted potions and made the *corp creadh*'-type questions. But on the other hand, as also noted earlier, it is clear that although they were interrogator-prompted, the body of the charms themselves came from Isobel. And in the context of the present discussion, we can speculate that Isobel's evident responsiveness to this type of prompting derived from the fact that, as an oral performer, the process of swinging back and forth between prose descriptions and reflective rhyming stanzas, and of interspersing first or third person prose narrative with bursts of versified direct speech, would have been very familiar to her.

Isobel the Performer

The Isobel-as-oral-performer hypothesis also enables us to look at the confessions' unique range of subject matter from a new perspective. We have already argued that the preponderance of listing was attributable to interrogatorial scrupulousness. But the long tally of the arrow-slain found in her confessions (and which are largely absent from Janet's) demand further explanation. Although we can speculate that Forbes et al. asked plenty of 'And who else did you kill with your elf arrows?'-type questions, and that Isobel possessed the verbal facility to meet their demands, the readiness, and even relish, with which she seems to have responded to this macabre line of questioning remains hard to rationalize. Indeed, Isobel's lists of arrow-slain – like the one below taken from Confession Three – are among those confessional passages most conducive to mental illness as an explanatory hypothesis:

> the first voman th[a]t I killed wes at the plewgh landis, also I killed on in the east of murrey, at candlmas last, at that tyme bessie wilson in aulderne killed on th[e]r, and margret wilson ther killed an uth[e]r, I killed also James dick in conniecavell, bot the death th[a]t I am most of all sorrie for, is the killing of william Bower in the miltowne of moynes, margret brodie killed an vowman washing at the burne of tarres, Bessie wilsone killed an man at the bushe of strutheris Bessie hay in aulderne killed an prettie man, called dunbar at the eist end of the towne of forres as he wes coming out at an gaitt, margret brodj in aulderne killed on david blak in darnvay, Janet breadheid spows to Jon taylor told me a litle befor she wes apprehendit th[a]t margret wilsoen in aulderne shot allexr hutcheon in aulderne, Janet breadheid shot Johne falconer in the park, the most of ws all wer ther at that tyme, bessie wilson killed on william man at burgie, margret wilson killed on Johne lees, and Janet breadheid killed a swyn at burgie. (47/37)

Although we shall be exploring Isobel's arrow-shooting passages in much more detail later in the book, with regard to the present discussion it is sufficient to note that her lists of victims become less anomalous if we take into account the fact that in this period an accomplished oral performer was likely to be experienced in giving lengthy roll calls of the arrow-slain. Traditional ballads and tales frequently featured famous archers and their exploits, and generally relished the numbers of arrows shot and victims killed. The exploits of John MacAndrew, for example (a member of the watch who lived near Dulnan around 1670), generated many stories 'of his wonderful prowess with the cross-bow', with one such describing how, when defending himself against angry reivers, he 'climbed into his tree, and picked off every one of his would-be assassins with his bow and arrow before they were able to rush him'.[34] Similarly, the famous ballads 'The Battle of Otterburn' and 'The Hunting of the Cheviot', both of which depict the English vs. Scots Battle of Otterburn (1388), and variants of which are believed to have been well-known in Scotland by the mid-sixteenth century, are paeans to death by arrow and sword. In a seventeenth-century broadside copy of the latter (which, though poor, was claimed by Addison to have been 'the favorite ballad of the common people of England'), stanzas 48–53 run:

With stout Erle Percy there was slaine
Sir John of Egerton,
Sir Robert Harcliffe and Sir William,
Sir James that bold barron.

And with Sir George and Sir James,
both knights of good account,
Good Sir Ralphe Rebbye there was slaine,
whose prowesse did surmount.

For Witherington needs must I wayle
as one in doleful dumpes,
For when his leggs were smitten of,
he fought upon his stumpes.

And with Erle Dowglas there was slaine
Sir Hugh Mountgomerye,
And Sir Charles Morrell, that from feelde
one foot would never flee.[35]

In an essentially warrior society, such grim roll calls would not only have been the preserve of oral performers, but would also have emerged in more general discourse. When writing an account of his genealogy in 1676, Isobel's educated neighbour, John Innes of Leuchars, identified his ancestors not only by name, but by the nature of their death in battle and the identity of their killer, at one point stating that: 'This Collonell Gordons father wes ane John Gordon sone to John Gordon off Kadenbanno brother to ane Gilbert Gordon off Ardmackyer who wes father to William Gordon who fell in to be Laird of Gight after the slauchter of Sir George Gordon who wes killed att the windmill of Dundie be the Laird of Tullie Forbes who killed eache other at that place.'[36]

The Nicknames

The Isobel-as-oral-performer hypothesis can also shed light on the uniquely idiosyncratic and colourful nicknames she attributes to fellow coven members and their familiar spirits, and which include: 'pikle neirest the wind', 'throw the corneya(*ird?*)', 'roring lion', 'bessie rule', 'mackhector', 'over the dyk w[i]th it', 'thieff of hell', 'read reiver', 'robert the Jacks', 'able and stowt', 'bessie bauld' and 'Thomas the fearie'. While it would be tempting to suppose that this wildly inventive list was underpinned by some form of mental instability, it becomes immediately less anomalous if we take into account the fact that the use of aliases is a characteristic feature of tight-knit traditional cultures in many parts of the world – with Maxwell-Stuart noting that they were 'very common among the Border reivers' in the early modern period – and that, as an oral performer, Isobel would have readily recalled established names and possessed an inherent advantage when it came to inventing new ones.[37] In his study of contemporary Scottish travelling communities (that retained their living oral culture well into the twentieth century), folklorist Timothy Neat notes that nicknames were often vivid and humorous, reflecting the travellers' tendency to 'decorate, humour, vitalise and subvert conventional descriptions, rhythms and associations. Like cartoonists they leap on the odd and peculiar, they characterize and personify.'[38] Characters from stories, songs and ballads were also frequently called upon in order to make a point. Interestingly, many of the nicknames Neat recorded bear more than a passing resemblance to those listed by Isobel three centuries earlier:

> Wooden Sleeves, Love-in-a-Close, Twa Holes in a Blanket, The Big-ma-Hungry, The Waterbottle, Half-a-Shirt, Meg-and-the-Moneyfeed, Forty Pooches, Fish-Airse, Pishy Jean, Hieland Scrogg, The Sheep's Heid, Laughter, The Rockingham Tea-pot, Alec-was-his-Granny, The Little Dancer, The Four-eyed Blister, Crazy Horse, Lang Cauld and Hungry, The Galoot, The Wild Colonial Boy, The Scoots, Kettle-heid, The Half-Hangit Ministair, Burnt Bonnet, Cauld Stane, White Iron Kate, Wee Grassie Mouse, Quarry Yaks.[39]

That Isobel's nicknames were, like those of the Neat's travellers, rooted in real-life characteristics is confirmed by her claim, in Confession Two, that the maiden to her coven was called 'over the dyk w[i]th it becaws the dive(*ll*?) (*damaged – words missing*) maiden in his hand nixt him q[uhe]n ve daunce gillatrypes and q[uhe]n he vold lowp from (*damaged – words missing*) he and she will say ower the dyk w[i]th it'. And on this premise, we can also speculate as to the internal logic of some of the other nicknames Isobel cited. Elspeth Nishie may have been known as 'bessie bauld (*bold*)' because she was indeed a forceful character. Certainly the way in which she seems to have bludgeoned her daughter-in-law, Janet Breadheid, into practising witchcraft would support this. Bessie Hay, on the other hand, may have been termed 'able and stout' because she was large and capable (or not, as the case may be); the 'able' part being particularly interesting in the light of the fact that, as we shall see later, she was likely to have been the same Bessie Hay recorded as the 'dame' of Auldearn school in the Kilravock papers.[40]

As they did for Neat's travellers, other names may have reflected characters from contemporary oral lore. The nickname that Isobel gives to her own familiar spirit, the 'read reiver', is particularly significant here. A French pirate of similar name ('the Red Reiver') plays a prominent role in the life of William Wallace, the medieval warrior whose exploits were a popular subject of both oral, written and printed ballads throughout Scotland from the Middle Ages onwards. Moreover, Isobel's casting of the Red Reiver as her familiar spirit would have been an eminently rational one, for after being captured by Wallace the pirate pledged the Scot allegiance, became his boon companion and thereafter 'loved' him 'with so true a heart, Whate'er befel would never from him part'.[41] Similarly, we can speculate that the name of the seventh spirit, 'Thomas the fearie', was rooted in lore and belief surrounding the legendary thirteenth-century prophet, Thomas Rhymer, who was reputedly enticed into fairyland by an amorous queen of the fairies. Popular throughout Scotland since the medieval period, the Rhymer did not only inspire many ballads and stories, but was also considered to be a living presence, with Aberdeenshire cunning man Andro Man claiming, in 1598, that when he visits fairyland 'Thomas Rymour is their'.[42] The Rhymer's relevance, so far as Isobel was concerned, is also supported by the fact that, even as late as the nineteenth century, people from the north believed that he enjoyed an association with Tomnahurich Hill, the famous fairy mound in Inverness.[43] It is also possible that 'mack-hector' had a similarly auspicious origin. One of the most famous and bloody battles in northern Scotland took place between Highlanders and Lowlanders at Harlaw, west of Aberdeen, in 1411. Here, the renowned warrior and Highland chieftain Hector Roy Maclean of Duart, or 'Red Hector of the Battles', died in single combat: an event so legendary that ballads on the subject are still performed in Scotland today.[44] Alternatively, a character named Hector (usually associated with the classical warrior) is also found in some versions of the traditional Galoshins plays recorded in the eighteenth and nineteenth centuries and it is reasonable to suppose that he may have featured in earlier versions.[45] Although these plays were banned by the reformed church, there is evidence from kirk session records that they were performed clandestinely up until the 1630s in the Elgin region and such performances would still have been within some living memories during Isobel's lifetime.[46] Some of Isobel's nicknames may have also taken their inspiration from less folkloric sources. We can assume, for example, that the terms 'roring lion' and 'thieff of hell' came from the pulpit. The former, which derived from St Paul's famous description of Satan, was a favoured contemporary image, being frequently employed in sermons and also used, more than once, by Alexander Brodie. The latter, or a close variant thereof, was also widely employed; it also being notable (in the context of our analysis of the origins of Isobel's 'Thomas the fearie' figure) that a variant of the name appears, in the form of the 'foul fiend of hell', in medieval versions of *The Romance and Prophecies of Thomas of Erceldoune* (aka Thomas Rhymer).[47] Speculating more wildly, we can entertain the possibility that although 'Black' was a common name-prefix in the period, the nickname 'Black John', which Isobel's coven gave to the Devil, and to which he took so much offence, could have been a humorous jibe drawn from contemporary anecdote heard at market or by the hearth concerning the infamous Highland bandit John Dow Gare, otherwise known as 'Black John the Left-handed', who terrorized the north of Scotland with his band of twenty men during the mid-seventeenth century.[48]

The Sexual Scenes

The possibility that Isobel was an oral performer also enables us to re-configure the way we look at her famously graphic descriptions of sex with the Devil. On the one hand, the high level of detail in these descriptions can, as in other parts of the confessions, be attributed to close interrogatorial questioning. But the fact that Isobel seems to have responded so compliantly and explicitly in this, the most sensitive of subject areas, still demands explanation. We shall be exploring this issue more deeply later in the book, both in relation to further revelations about Harry Forbes's character and recent research into the phenomenon of false confession, but in the present context it is worth pointing out that the Isobel-as-oral-performer hypothesis can provide us with some preliminary insights here.

Through their art, fireside oral performers and composers were called upon to reflect all aspects of early modern peasant life, including sexual attitudes and practices. And in this period, despite the prurience of the reformed church, these attitudes were often candid and matter-of-fact. In farming communities the mating of animals would have been a matter of both familiarity, importance, and general conversation. Isobel's observations, in Confession Three, that the Devil's possessed a 'hodg nature'; that he 'wold be amongst us, lyke a weath horse amongst mearis'; and that 'neither haid we nor he any kynd of shame' were blunt, but no more blunt than the way in which her husband, as a man who reared or helped to rear cattle and horses, may have talked about the latest exploits of a prize bull or stallion. Similarly, at a time when whole households often shared the same floor space around the fire at night, the sexual act was less private and mysterious than it came to be in later centuries. Protestant women, moreover, were not always as reverent about the matter as some pious ministers would have liked, with the minister of Kinghorn, for example, coming across the wife of one of his parishioners 'in the fields' as she took 'a horse band and knit it to her belt with the one end between her legs and got on upon another woman as if she had been a man'.[49]

Although some folklorists have chosen to overlook this aspect of Scotland's oral traditions, there is no doubt that performers and composers naturally encapsulated these robust sexual attitudes and experiences in their sentences and verses, with Henderson noting that traditional 'bawdry' presents a 'large and entertaining part of our Scottish ballad heritage' and Buchan, that many folksongs 'are imbued with a strong and natural sexuality' and betray a 'fresh and healthy eroticism'.[50] Also pertinent to Isobel is the fact that some poems and ballads relating to Thomas Rhymer portray a protagonist who was easily as sexually voracious as her Devil, with Cowan and Henderson noting, in their discussion of the extant medieval texts, that:

> Lust knows few limits and he [Thomas] lay with her [the fairy queen] seven times under the Eildon Tree, his willing partner coquettishly remarking that he obviously enjoyed their love-making since it had lasted all day long: 'I pray thee, Thomas, let me be!'[51]

A similarly blunt, humorous sexuality can be found in the Aberdeenshire song, of unknown age, titled 'The Cuckoo's Nest':

> There is a thorn bush in oor kail-yard,
> There is a thorn bush in oor kail-yard.
> At the back o thon bush there stands a lad and lass,
> And they're busy, busy herry-in' at the cuckoos nest.
>
> It is thorned, it is sprinkled, it is compassed all around,
> It is thorned, it is sprinkled, and it isn't easy found.

> She said: 'Young man, you're plundering;' I said it wasnae true,
> But I left her wi' the makin's o a young cuckoo.[52]

Such sentiments were also expressed higher up the social scale. In the late-sixteenth century, Scottish poet Robert Sempill composed a candid verse based on the controversial trial of Fife cunning woman Alison Peirson (1588), who claimed that the bishop of St Andrews, Patrick Adamson, had sought her out for magical aid. The poet claims that after imprisoning Alison in his castle the bishop:

> Closing the door behind his back
> And quietly to her he spak,
> And said his tool was of no worth:
> Loosing his breeks he laid it forth.
> She sained it with her holy hand,
> The pure pith of the prior's wand:
> When she had sained it twice or thrice,
> His rubigo began to rise:
> Then said the bishop to [his] 'John Bell',
> Go take the first sight of her yoursel.
> The witch to him her vessel gave,
> The bishop's blessing to receive.[53]

The Miraculous Plough

The Isobel-as-oral-performer hypothesis can also illuminate the famous 'plough of frogs' passage found in Confession One. To my knowledge this passage, which Pitcairn elevated as 'the most extraordinary in the history of witchcraft, of this or any other country', is unique both among witchcraft records and Scottish folklore as a whole and, like Isobel's lists of the arrow-slain, is so fantastic that it is tempting to assume that in order to have produced it she must have been mentally unstable:

> befor candlmas we went be east kinlosse and ther we yoaked an plewghe of paddokis, the divell held the plewgh and Johne yownger in mebiestowne o[u]r officer did drywe the plewghe, padokis did draw the plewgh as oxen qwickens wer sowmes a riglens horne wes an cowter and an piece of an riglens horne wes an sock, we went two s[eve]rall tymes abowt, and all ve of the coeven went still wp and downe w[i]th the plewghe, prayeing to the divell for the fruit of th[a]t land and th[a]t thistles and brieris might grow ther. (39/30)

But this passage becomes less anomalous if we take into account the fact that contemporary oral performers, and particularly those who were concerned with tales of the supernatural, would have been accustomed to delivering detailed accounts describing the magical transformation of objects: particularly the small into the large and the mundane into the magnificent and vice versa. In traditional stories relating to both fairies and witches, for example, eggshells and sieves are commonly turned into (or function as) boats, plant stalks and broomsticks into airborne steeds, rags into silks and silks into rags, hovels into palaces and palaces into hovels. This theme is also reflected in the fact that, in both Janet's and Isobel's confessions, the Devil's gifts of money frequently morphed into something less tangible: the latter lamenting that 'tho the divell wold giw ws ther brawest lyk mo[ne]y th[a]t ewer wes coyned, w[i]thin fowr and twantie howris, it vold be bot hors muke' (49/35). The fact that in the above-quoted passage, Isobel claims to have used 'quickens' (dog-grass) to make 'soames' (an image which mirrors her claim to have used corn straws to make fairy steeds), also suggests that her plough had fairy connections. Tom Thumb, a popular folkloric character also celebrated for his affiliations with the fairy folk, and whose widely-printed exploits were almost certainly based on oral tradition, was similarly inventive.[54] In a chapbook printed in Edinburgh in 1682 the text reads that:

> Now after this, in sowing time
> His Father would him have,
> Into the field to drive his plough,
> and therewithal him gave
> A whip, made of a barley straw,
> To drive the cattel on.[55]

This connection is further reinforced by the fact that although images of supernatural, animal-drawn, vehicles are seldom featured in witch-testimonies (the only other account, to my knowledge, being an Aberdeenshire cunning man's description of the fairy queen 'rydaying on a hackneyis'), they are a common feature of folk literature concerning fairies.[56] The tale in which the fairy godmother transforms a pair of mice into horses and a pumpkin into a carriage is well known to all of us. Similar equipages appear in some versions of the Tom Thumb legend. One typical mid eighteenth-century chapbook account states that 'Tom grows in Favour with the King, who buys him a Coach drawn by six Mice', while later versions attribute a comparable vehicle to the fairy queen.[57] Other tales and ballads depict similarly fantastic variants. In the following rhyme, taken from a traditional Aberdeenshire ballad about an elf knight, it is a robin, as opposed to a mouse or a frog, who pulls the miniature cart:

> And bigg a cart of stone and lyme,
> Robin Readbreast he must trail it hame.
> Thou must barn it in a mouse-holl,
> and thrash it into thy shoes soll.[58]

Animal Metamorphosis

The Isobel-as-oral performer hypothesis also enables us to normalize her descriptions of animal metamorphosis which arguably exceed, in both detail and vividness, those found in any other witchcraft record from the period. We have little information about contemporary folk beliefs on this still little-understood subject, or how these beliefs may have integrated into magical practice, and it would be all too easy to assume that elite demonological stereotypes, absorbed by Isobel prior to or during interrogation, underpinned her descriptions of how her coven travelled to their meetings in the form of crows, hares and cats.

But her references become less anomalous if we take into account the fact that many contemporary oral performers would have been familiar with dispensing vivid, detailed accounts of human shape-shifting prowess. Stories and ballads collected in the nineteenth century frequently describe humans – and particularly humans who become involved with the fairies or other supernatural beings – transforming into animals without any reference to witchcraft or the Devil. Many plots feature heroes who, on being pursued by an enemy (whether a magician, fairy man, ogre or giant and so on) transform themselves into different shapes to elude capture. The ballads 'Tam Lin' and 'The Twa Magicians', both of which contain the stanza structure indicative of early origin, are illustrative. In the former the eponymous hero, held fast in the arms of his human lover, undergoes a number of transformations in order to escape the enchantments of the fairy queen, including that of an adder, a 'bear sae grim', a 'lion bold', a red-hot band of iron and a 'burning gleed [flame]'.[59] Meanwhile, in 'The Twa Magicians' a woman and an amorous 'coal-black smith' play a dangerous game of cat-and-mouse: she turns herself into an eel, he turns himself into a trout; she turns herself into a duck, he turns into a drake and so on until interestingly, with regard to the case in hand, some variants echo the common witch-transforms-into-a-hare motif cited by Isobel in Confession Three:

> She turnd hersell into a hare,
> To rin upon yon hill,
> And he became a gude grey-hound,
> And boldly he did fill.
> O bide, lady, bide, &c.[60]

A wealth of literary precedent can also be found for Isobel's claim that both she and the Devil favoured the form of the crow. J. F. Campbell, for example, observed that in the nineteenth-century Highlands it was possible to find 'a great many versions' of 'The Tale of the Hoodie' – a story in which a woman marries a man who spends his days in the form of a man and his nights in the form of a Royston crow.[61]

A Taste for the Fantastic

The possibility that Isobel was an oral performer also sheds light on why the folkloric references in her confessions so consistently relate to the fantastic and the supernatural. Scholars of oral literature have emphasized that, however wide their repertoire, most fireside bards developed areas of expertise. As Buchan has shown with regard to north-eastern balladry, men generally favoured warrior epics and histories, and women romances and tales of the supernatural.[62] But within this divide there were many permutations. The folklorist Duncan Anderson described, for example, how in the nineteenth-century village of Sillerton the miller concerned himself with 'the miller world and the water kelpie'; the blacksmith 'dealt chiefly with feats of manly strength that he had witnessed'; the cobbler, Sandy Simms, related stories 'that very graphically brought out the pawky character of Scottish humour'; and Jean Barden, the old woman who 'occupied a small cottage in the village square' and was the 'pre-eminent' story-teller of the village, specialized in stories, songs and ballads that explored the macabre and the uncanny.[63]

On the basis of her confessional content, we can speculate that, like many north-eastern female performers, Isobel was drawn to tales of romance and the supernatural. We can also speculate that, like Jean Barden of Sillerton, she possessed the kind of fierce and provocative imagination that predisposed her to specialize in the darker aspects of these genres; and that these preoccupations made an impact on her friends and neighbours. In Barden's case, although she lived (as would have Isobel) in 'a humble apartment . . . [with] only an earthen floor' she made such an impression on the young Duncan Anderson that even fifty years later he was moved to wax lyrical about the fact that:

> the horrible in what was human, and the blood-curdling in what was supernatural . . . [were] the commodities in which she dealt. Nor was her stock of these by any means limited, as kelpies, goblins, fairies, brownies, elves, ghosts, wizards, witches, and sundry others of a kindred nature, were to her household words . . . Then, in addition melancholy songs and ballads, all invariably of a lugubrious character, and covering a wide field of weird literature, her vivid imagination, and her peculiar faculty of finding suitable words to express her meaning, would alone have made her remarkable in any community.[64]

Unexplained Factors

The Isobel-as-oral-performer hypothesis does not, of course, answer the more complex questions surrounding why she should have claimed to have personally performed so many of the fantastic and impossible acts described in the confessions. For answers to these more epistemologically challenging questions we must wait until later in the book. But it does make the way she expressed her claims less anomalous, and in doing so goes some way towards explaining the unusualness of her confessions and further mitigating the Isobel-was-crazy theory. But before we can accept, or at least entertain, this hypothesis, we still need to address one outstanding difficulty. Given the fact that early modern Scotland was, for the uneducated majority, an essentially oral culture, we can assume that a considerable percentage of the general population possessed good verbal skills and were well acquainted with a wide range of oral lore. We can also assume that a sizeable minority of the latter possessed significantly higher-than-average verbal skills and functioned as fireside bards. In this context, it would be wholly illogical to suppose that over this whole period Isobel was the only female oral performer ever to have been interrogated for witchcraft. But if this is the case then why do we not have any other confessions like hers?

It could be argued that location played a role here. As we touched on in the last chapter, some historians have suggested that Isobel's confessions were 'different from all the others we have encountered' because she was a Highlander or, as we qualified, heavily influenced by Highland culture. Because witch prosecutions were less common in the Highlands than in Scotland as a whole, we could speculate that elite demonological lore may have made fewer inroads into the popular mind in these regions and that witch testimonies, when they did emerge, would have contained higher levels of folklore than those garnered in the Lowlands. Similarly, because the Highlanders' oral traditions were rooted in the Irish Gaelic, we might expect these their confessions to be more dramatically intense and verbally grandiloquent than those derived elsewhere. And these expectations are, to a certain extent, supported by the evidence. The majority of the records that come closest to Isobel's, with regard to richness of folkloric detail and stylistic flair, come from the Highlands and Islands, or the regions abutting them. But as an explanatory hypothesis, location is only partially satisfactory. First, there are enough richly-detailed records from the southern regions of the country, such as those relating to Bessie Dunlop, Agnes Sampson and Janet Boyman, to indicate that Lowland oral traditions (even those from parishes close to Glasgow and Edinburgh) were quite capable of generating witchcraft confessions containing a high level of folkloric references, dramatic tension and descriptive power. This is supported by Lizanne Henderson's recent argument that Highland and Lowland witchcraft beliefs did not differ to the extent previously supposed.[65] Secondly, and more significantly, even within the sub-category of records clearly influenced by Highland culture, Isobel's stand out as unique. Although the richly-textured testimonies of the Aberdeenshire, Forfar or Bute witches, for example, contain much folklore and vivid detail, they do not equal Isobel's with regard to sophistication of language and narrative style, nor in depth and range of subject matter.

Returning to the Men with the Pens

But if we turn away from speculations about location and return to the men who interrogated Isobel, we can find some possible answers to these questions. In the last chapter we argued that a percentage of the graphic detail and linguistic precision of Isobel's confessions, and to a certain extent their wide range of subject matter, might have been attributable to interrogatorial influence. We argued that through a variety of motivations – ranging from fear of witchcraft, religious zeal and respect for judicial propriety, to intellectual curiosity and a desire to plumb 'the mani great misteries in religion' – the men who interrogated Isobel questioned her closely on a wide range of issues. We also argued that this spirit of inquiry, when combined with developed listening skills and an empathic manner, may have encouraged Isobel to open her heart and mind and prompted her interrogators to accommodate and run with her contributions, as opposed to constantly reining them in to make them conform to stilted demonological stereo-types. And finally, we argued that the notary, John Innes, possessed the scribal abilities, scrupulousness, and perhaps also interest in Isobel's revelations to record these complex proceedings in meticulous detail and draw them together into a fluid narrative whole. But if we take this white-hot furnace of interrogatorial attention and skill and intro-duce into it, as our raw material or *prima materia*, not an ordinary witchcraft suspect, but a witchcraft suspect who also happened to be a voluble oral performer, then we find ourselves with an alchemical reaction that would have been considerably more potent than the sum of its parts.

This reaction would have been both a product of the people involved and a product of the times. Although there was a close interaction, or seamless continuum, between elite and popular culture in early modern Scotland, Protestantism, and extreme Protestantism in particular, often compromised this dynamic. Through their devotion to covenanting theology, lairds and ministers could easily cut themselves off from their largely illiterate, more religiously-moderate tenants and parishioners. The more that deeply pious men like Hugh Rose or Alexander Brodie immersed themselves in the Bible and other religious works, and the more they constrained their actions within the template of what was considered godly – that is, introspection, prayer and the enforce-ment of parochial discipline – the more distant their lives became from those of the ordinary people who, despite the liturgical changes of the Reformation, generally farmed, celebrated, practised magic, sang songs and told stories much as their ances-tors had done for many centuries before them. This conflict of interests generated disdain in the former (with Brodie noting that the Dyke parishioners were 'boring', 'ignorant' and 'dead and dull') and defensiveness in the latter.[66] Cautious of censure and ridicule, many common folk would have withheld their hearts and minds from their local lairds, ministers and prominent townsfolk, in a way that they may not have done from their Catholic predecessors a hundred years earlier.

We can get a keen sense of the extent of this cultural gulf by looking at the diffi-culties that nineteenth-century folklorists encountered when attempting to penetrate the popular mind. Even this late, when increased schooling had lessened the educa-tional gap between the rich and the poor, it was difficult for 'outsiders' to glean information about popular beliefs and traditions. Foreigners met with obvious prob-lems, with Kathleen Raine noting in 1976 that the late nineteenth-century American folklorist, Evans-Wentz, was fed 'inauthentic' fairy lore which 'any bard or crofter would tell a foreign visitor to whom he wished to be polite while at the same time refusing to be "drawn"'.[67] But native Scots also met with resistance. The following description of Carmichael's charm-collecting skills, given by his friend Kenneth MacLeod, only serves to highlight the difficulties that less fortunate folklorists faced. 'Others', Macleod notes, 'could get the heroic tales and ballads, the things which were recited in public at the *ceilidh*; only Alexander Carmichael could have got the hymns and the incantations, the things which were said when the door was closed, and the lights were out . . . Not all of what he learned was written down, or if written down, has been preserved; many curious rites, embodied in unusual language . . . were revealed to him under a strict pledge of secrecy.'[68] Even Carmichael's contemporary John Francis

Campbell, one of the most diligent and sympathetic champions of Gaelic culture, claimed that 'In the Highlands, as elsewhere, society is arranged in layers, like the climates of the world . . . dwellers in the upper and lower strata of society, everywhere, know as little of each other's way of life, as the men of the plain know of the mountaineers in the snow.'[69] If penetrating the popular world-view was difficult for these sympathetic and relatively open-minded Scotsmen, who were asking their questions in a century when no-one was put to death for giving an unorthodox answer, then how much more difficult would it have been for ministers and lairds operating in the repressive seventeenth century to gain access to the inner worlds of the poor?

Given this scenario, we can speculate that when Hugh Rose, Harry Forbes et al. found themselves interrogating an oral performer who was willing to talk relatively freely and eloquently about her magical beliefs and experiences, they found themselves looking through a window onto what was essentially an unknown and largely unimagined world. And we can also speculate that, given their decidedly speculative turns of mind, they were fascinated by what they saw. Although covenanting theology was fundamentalist in the sense that it refused to accommodate any other ideologies, in the mid-seventeenth century it flourished alongside the beginnings of an elite interest in the beliefs and practices of the common folk; a movement that would reach its apogee in the work of the great nineteenth-century folklorists. This interest seems to have been more commonly kindled in the hearts of religious moderates such as James Garden, Robert Kirk, James Kirkwood and John Beaton. But at the same time, it was not incompatible with fervent and committed Protestant ministry. In the Invernesshire parish of Kirkhill, in 1677, local elders reported to the presbytery that their minister, James Fraser, was not only zealous in 'catechising the people, and his other ministerial duties' but he also 'went in and out among them, not only as their spiritual guide and temporal advisor, but also as one deeply interested in their manners and customs, and in the Gaelic legends and lore, which he noted mentally as he rested within their turf huts'.[70] Indeed, Fraser's knowledge in this area was considered to be so great that, when touring the Highlands, Welsh antiquarian Edward Lhuyd applied to him for information about local sights and customs. In the context of the present discussion, Fraser's interest in his parishioners' folkloric beliefs and practices is all the more notable for the fact that he moved in the same social circles as some of the Nairnshire lairds involved in Isobel's trial, most notably attending the wedding of Sir Hugh Campbell of Cawdor in 1662 in the company of the Laird of Lovat.[71] Although it is a bit far-fetched to suppose that Harry Forbes, with all his prejudices and fears, ever rested in Isobel's turf hut and listened in a 'deeply interested' manner to her accounts of Gaelic legends and lore, given the fact that he swam in the same social and cultural pool as men like Fraser, it is not unreasonable to speculate that something akin to Fraser's fascination was ignited, in the mind of the minister and his companions, during the Auldearn interrogations. The fact that the confessional text bears signs of close questioning, and that Innes stated, quite overtly, that Isobel '*most ingeniouslie* proceidit in hir confessione therof in maner efterfollowing [my italics]', directly intimates as much.

We can assume that this interest was also partly responsible for the confessions' unique stylistic features. We have noted that John Innes was a scrupulous notary, and that he recorded Isobel's words with exceptional linguistic precision and attention to detail. But what we have not yet emphasized is the degree to which he recorded descriptive and dramatic words that were not in any way relevant to, as Hugh Rose put it, the 'principal Substantialls' of the case. For example, Innes dutifully recorded Isobel's account of Bessie Hay's familiar spirit, but it was arguably above and beyond the call of duty for him to record not only the spirit's name ('robert the Jacks') and his appearance ('clothed in dune and seimes to be aiged') but also two additional adjectives ('glaiked gowked') to round off the description. Similarly, while Innes carefully noted Isobel's claim to have seen fairy bulls 'at the entrie' of the Downie Hill, for legal purposes no-one really needed to know that they were 'great' bulls; that they were 'crowtting and skoylling'; and that they did so as they went 'wp and downe'. Equally, although the courts may have welcomed the knowledge that Isobel's clay image was the size of a head ('pow'), did they really need to know that it was *also* the size of a sucking pig ('slain gryce')? And it was surely outside Innes's professional remit to punctuate Isobel's long description of the superior sexual prowess of the Devil with what seems to have been a bracketed phrase of her direct speech: 'alace th[at] I should compair him to an man' (47/7). Such examples could go on and on. The fact that Innes incorporated such a high level of judicially superfluous rhetorical flourish into Isobel's confessions could merely indicate scrupulousness, but it could also indicate that both he, and probably her interrogators, were not only struck by the things she said, but also by the way she said them.

That Innes and his companions should have shown such interest in Isobel's verbal skills is not as surprising as it may at first appear. The evidence suggests that most, if not all, of the men who questioned Isobel were born and bred in the region. The Inneses, Brodies, Hays, Campbells, Dunbars, Roses et al. were all local families and although we do not know Harry Forbes's provenance, the fact that Forbes is a common Aberdeenshire surname, and that both he and his brother attended university in Aberdeen, strongly suggests that he also came from the north-east.[72] As a consequence, these men would all have been influenced, to a greater or lesser extent, by the fact that the rich and vibrant oral traditions of northern Scotland were not just the preserve of the uneducated. As in other parts of the country, up until the Reformation many of the great families of Moray would have maintained links with their indigenous bardic heritage and the Roses of Kilravock, Brodies of Brodie and the Hays of Inshoch are all likely to have entertained professional bards at their castles, spent long hours listening to romances and histories and ensured that their children were thoroughly instructed in the rhetorical arts. While these pre-Reformation lairds would have been primarily concerned with the more sophisticated renditions in classical metre composed by formally-trained bards, some are likely to have also developed a taste for more popular fare. Jacqueline Simpson has argued that the sixteenth-century poet, Alexander Montgomerie, would have assumed that his audience were familiar with popular tales about the fairy rides, and even King James V was nurtured, by his tutor Sir David Lindsay, on traditional tales such as the 'The Red Etin'.[73] From the Middle Ages onwards nationally-acclaimed novelists and poets, such as Walter Scott and Robert Burns, openly took inspiration from popular oral traditions.[74]

As covenanters, Isobel's interrogators would have rejected much traditional oral lore on religious grounds. Not only would the subject matter of the romances, histories, marchen, fables, humorous tales, rhymes and songs been seen as ungodly, but the aesthetic enjoyment derived from wordplay would have been condemned as a carnal pleasure that distracted the soul from the true and lasting satisfactions to be found only in God. But despite these condemnations, many covenanters retained a love of language and an acute sensibility to the manner in which it was delivered. This sensibility was one of the reasons why, in reformed Scotland, ministers took so readily to the high rhetoric and evangelistic emotionalism of the scriptures and the psalms, and why such value was placed on passionate delivery and extemporization in sermonizing. Indeed, as we have seen earlier, some notable divines, such as John Welsh, seemed to have earned their reputations for their ability to stimulate the tear ducts as much as the intellect.[75] That Nairnshire lairds and elders would have nurtured an abiding respect for the skills of rhetoric is also suggested by the nature of the festivities that accompanied the marriage of Sir Hugh Campbell of Cawdor and Lady Henrietta Stewart in January 1662. Many of the men involved in Isobel's trial, including Brodie of Lethen, Thomas Dunbar of Grange, Hugh Hay of Brightmony and local ministers Rose and Forbes, were likely to have been present at the event (with Brodie, despite being in London at the time, deeming it sufficiently important to note in his diary). Despite the fact that the majority of these men were covenanters, it is significant that at this prominent event traditional versification and wordplay still provided the meat of the after-dinner entertainment. The Gaelic-legend-and-lore-loving minister James Fraser, whom we met earlier, witnessed the proceedings and afterwards noted:

> The gloves and contract ribbans being distributed in state, we had a most solemn feast, wedding rather than a contract dinner. In the afternoon the wits of the house gave anagrams and accrosticks in writ to the bride, and I judged Lovat gave the most apposit of all, Henreta Stuart, an tru sweet hart: which, with the accrosting pertinent verse, was applauded, the bridegroome, Sir Hugh, the greatest poet in Murray, being the most competent judge in that case.[76]

Although he was unlikely to have deserved the latter accolade, Hugh Campbell's *Treatise on the Lord's Prayer* attests to the fact that he enjoyed a comfortable affinity with language and the skills of rhetoric. The diaries of Alexander Brodie are similarly suggestive. In moments of high emotion, for example, Brodie frequently strung together three or more adjectives where one or two would have sufficed, as in: '[I am] a reeling, unstable, staggering, unsettled, luke-warm creature' and 'Oh keep me from these unsober, distempered, mad, unruly thoughts!' He could also make good use of dramatic repetition, at one point lamenting 'when I would hate, I cannot; when I would love, I cannot; when I would grieve, I cannot; when I would desire, I cannot'.[77] But what is interesting with regard to Isobel is the fact that the writings of both Campbell and Brodie, highborn and educated as they were, appear pedestrian and colourless when placed alongside those of her interrogator, Hugh Rose, minister of Nairn. In page after page of his *Meditations*, Rose produces fluid and rhythmic prose consistently dense with adjectives, metaphors, similes and proverbs. Vain thoughts 'grow up like hemlock in the furrows of the field' and are 'but fancies, fictions, idle, spider's webs, woven out of our own bowels' which 'run up and down unsettledly, as atoms in the sun-beams'. Man is 'is born to trouble as the sparks fly upward' and mortal speculations are 'canglings anent moonshines, and contests for our own shadows'.[78] In his ruminations on damnation and salvation, as in his descriptions of the merits of confession and dangers of worldly knowledge quoted in the last chapter, we find many of the oral performing skills identified in Isobel's confessions, with a strong emphasis on repetition. Indeed, some of these passages are so potent they suggest that if anyone deserved the accolade of 'greatest poet in Murray' it was the young minister of Nairn, not the Laird of Cawdor. In the following passage on hell, you can almost hear Rose's rhetoric thundering down from the Nairn pulpit:

> there is no beam, not a hair-breadth for their hope to fix upon. Eternity is the adjunct of their misery, both in the whole, and in the parts. They are to be miserable throughout eternity; they are to be without God throughout eternity; they are to burn throughout eternity; they are to be lashed by conscience throughout eternity; they are to be tormented by Devils throughout eternity. If they can hope for the period of eternity, they may hope for the end of these. But eternity is endless, else it were not eternity. When thousand thousands and millions of millions of ages are passed, their torments will be no more ended, than at the first beginning.[79]

Rose was present at three – at least – of Isobel's interrogations. And as a local minister (also personally responsible for Isobel's accomplice, Janet Breadheid) he was likely to have been involved in, and at times led, the questioning. With men like Rose at the helm, it is tempting to speculate that in the Auldearn tolbooth in 1662, an unlikely chord of sympathy was struck between Isobel Gowdie, the illiterate farmer's wife, and her university-educated interrogators. A poet will always respond to a poet, whatever the subject of their discourse and wherever that discourse takes place. And Rose, Innes, Forbes et al. may have chosen to listen closely to Isobel's words and record them diligently not only because they were legally bound to, or because they were anxious to convict, or even because they were 'itchingly curious' about the 'mani great mysteries in religion' – but simply because they were moved by her skills of rhetoric. While their intellects strove to condemn Isobel's claims as delusions of the Devil or, at best, 'idle spider's webs woven out of her own bowels', as sons of the north-east, their hearts and aesthetic sensibilities may have responded to them in a very different way.

As a consequence, with regard to stylistic features and subject matter, we do not need to call on theories of overt mental illness to explain the unusualness of Isobel's confessions. We can, instead, point to a variety of contributory factors: oral performing skills, respect for rhetoric, religious zeal, fear of witchcraft, awareness of judicial propriety, close questioning, patient listening, curious minds and significant notarial abilities. None of these factors would have been unique and many of them were not even unusual, but the evidence suggests that the extraordinariness of Isobel's confessions lies in the fact that all of these factors converged together in the same place and at the same time.

7

The Men of Constant Sorrows

In the last three chapters we have identified many of the factors that may have contributed towards the unusualness of Isobel's confessions, and towards the perception that she could have been mentally ill. But while these perspectives have deepened our understanding of Isobel's case, with regard to both unusualness and mental illness the most incriminating evidence still lies before us. All witchcraft records, by definition, describe acts of *maleficium* and Isobel's are no different in this respect. But hers are highly unusual in the degree to which the *maleficium* is so apparently 'self-confessed'.[1] In the majority of confessions and trial dittays the descriptions of harmful magic are so tightly woven into a web of accusation, counter-accusation and interrogatorial intervention that it is difficult to hear the voice of the suspect and thereby assess the degree to which they contributed towards the descriptions of the crimes alleged against them, or how far they acknowledged their guilt. It is only in a minority of cases, as in the records of Jonet Rendall (Orkney, 1616) and Isobel Haldane (Perthshire, 1623), that the record-wording is such that we can be fairly certain that the suspect (whether voluntarily or under coercion) contributed to the descriptions of *maleficium* and/or openly confessed to having performed it.[2] And of this minority, Isobel's case is the most extreme. Not only do her confessions provide us with the most startlingly wide array of maleficent acts found in testimony from a single individual, but they also provide us with some of the most detailed and lengthy admissions of self-guilt to be found in any British witchcraft record from the early modern period. Consequently we cannot abandon, or even ameliorate, the Isobel-was-crazy hypothesis without finding an explanation for this malevolence.

On the one hand, our investigations in the previous chapter have already enabled us to refine this picture. As with other parts of her testimony, it is likely that some of the descriptive detail that gives Isobel's *maleficium*-accounts such power and immediacy can be attributed to exceptionally close and attentive questioning and recording as opposed to maliciously-compulsive detailing on the part of Isobel herself. But on the other hand, as illustrated in CHAPTER THREE, there is no doubt that Isobel contributed here. We can be certain with regard to the making of the *corp creadh*, for example, that although her curious interrogators may well have asked 'Where did you get the clay from?', the information that 'Johne taylor browght hom the clay in his plaid newk (*the fold of his plaid)*' was highly likely to have come from Isobel. Similarly, although Forbes et al. may have pressed her for details as to how she made the image, it is unlikely that they provided the technical description of the clay-slaking process found in the confessions, nor the observation that the reconstituted clay needed to be 'vrought . . . werie sore lyk rye bowt (*rye meal*)'; the latter sounding suspiciously like the kind of metaphor that would have been used by a farmer's wife who knew, from bitter experience, that rye flour, containing little gluten, had to be kneaded hard before it could be made into efficient dough. Isobel's complicity with regard to these descriptions of specific *maleficium* is further supported by the fact that her statements of contrition, recorded in the third confession, do not sound like forced shows of repentance simulated to please her interrogators. Her lament that 'alace I deserw not to be sitting heir, for I haw done so manie ivill deidis, espe[ci]allie killing of men etc I deserw to be reiven wpon iron harrowes & wors if it culd be devysit' sounds fresh and real, as does her bleak confession that 'the death th[a]t I am most of all sorrie for, is the killing of william Bower in the miltowne of moynes' (49/37; 47/40).

The Perimeters

There is clearly much to unravel here, and the next two chapters will be concerned with exploring Isobel's alleged *maleficium* from a variety of different angles. But the analysis will, at this juncture, be curtailed within tight perimeters. The *maleficium* described in the confessions can be roughly divided into two overlapping, but nevertheless reasonably distinct, categories. The first, which we can term 'specific *maleficium*', is directed towards named persons. The second, which we can term 'non-specific *maleficium*', is directed either at unnamed persons or is seemingly arbitrarily aimed at named persons, as in the arrow-shooting scenes. As a general rule of thumb (although there are several exceptions to this), specific *maleficium* is basic and non-specific *maleficium* is performed with spirit-aid. Both categories of maleficent magic are described in a close, detailed narrative style and accompanied by rhyming charms.

In the present chapter, we will be focusing on Isobel's specific *maleficium* only. While the question of her non-specific *maleficium* needs to be addressed, particularly with regard to the question of her sanity (arbitrary malevolence being more suggestive of mental illness than malevolence that can be clearly linked to a grievance), we have not constructed a wide enough theoretical framework at present to consider this gainfully. A fuller explanation of Isobel's non-specific *maleficium* must be deferred until our exploration of shamanism in Parts II and III. In addition, in the present chapter we will be concentrating on actual (that is, physically performed) as opposed to imaginary acts of specific *maleficium*. With regard to the question of Isobel's sanity, the question of whether she literally performed the maleficent acts she described or only imagined that she had done so is largely irrelevant, for both options could have been rooted in mental illness. But we will be considering them separately here. Like non-specific *maleficium*, imagined *maleficium* can only be properly discussed within a more complex conceptual framework and will therefore be deferred until CHAPTER NINE, where we will be examining Isobel's confessions with reference to false confession. In the next two chapters, then, we will be restricting our analysis to the question: did Isobel physically perform any of the specific *maleficium* she described, against her named victims, prior to her arrest and interrogation?

The attempt to assess the 'reality' of Isobel's *maleficium*, even when circumscribed within such tight perimeters, is not a simple one and gains very little direction from the work of contemporary historians. Although many books have been written on the subject of witchcraft and magic in the past fifty years, they generally focus on the function of witchcraft beliefs for the accuser (arguing that witchcraft accusations helped to resolve inter-personal tensions) and the prosecutor (arguing that witchcraft prosecutions offered an opportunity to enforce conformity and control) as opposed to their relevance for the accused. The issue as to whether, or to what degree, witchcraft suspects actually believed themselves to have performed basic *maleficium* remains inexplicably overlooked; either being passed over altogether or briefly mentioned en route to something else. Even the increasing awareness, over the past couple of decades, that the use of torture and coercive questioning was less successful than previously thought and that suspects were often significant co-authors in their own confessions, have not yet altered this emphasis, with attention now lighting upon the suspect's fiction-making exploits during interrogation as opposed to whether they had performed any of the crimes alleged against them.

Where conclusions have been drawn with regard to this issue, the general position is that *maleficium* was 'attributed' as opposed to actual, with Éva Pócs claiming, in 2000, 'The question arises: did malefactor witches par excellence live out the role of witches? Were they aware of the assumed maleficium? Did they internalize an identity as witches? Research has asked these questions in various ways and contexts and the answer is usually no.'[3] Alternatively, as recently as 2008 Lauren Martin and Joyce Miller noted, with regard to Scottish witchcraft research, that 'there has been a degree of reluctance thus far [among scholars] to consider that some of the accused may indeed have been guilty of attempting to cause harm'.[4] Those scholars who do accept that some suspects may have 'internalized an identity as witches' tend to see this process as anomalous and occurring in those individuals who are in some way psychologically isolated from the rest of their peers, with Robin Briggs, for example, acknowledging in passing that a minority of witches may have considered themselves capable of practising *maleficium*, but then portraying these women as unfortunate victims who were 'manipulated into playing a part' of maleficent witch in response to cultural projection.[5]

The tendency to resolve this issue briefly, and usually in the negative, is surprising, not least because the discipline of history is largely occupied with charting the manifestations and consequences of human aggression, and has no trouble acknowledging and even rationalizing within its context, the massacres of Oliver Cromwell or the legal mutilation of children. On one level, we can attribute this 'resolution in the negative' to scholarly rigour (that is, to a credible reluctance to extrapolate from contaminated sources). And it is certainly true that any concessions to having performed *maleficium* found in witch-records cannot be automatically assumed to refer to real events, because of the possibility that the testimonies were coerced. But while these scruples are admirable, they have also stifled the field of research. To conclude that because we cannot prove that a witchcraft confession or dittay recorded the performance of malefic magical acts we must therefore assume it did not, is simply incomplete logic. It is also possible that these easy assumptions may be rooted in an unconscious cultural bias. Post-Enlightenment mentalities, unschooled in the subjective reality of magical thinking, may find it easier to rationalize how an individual might slaughter in the heat of battle, or execute a child in response to the letter of the law, than rationalize how they could create a clay image and slowly and carefully roast it before a fire in order to cause the death of an enemy. It conclusion, it could be argued that despite all the scholarly attention which early modern witchcraft has received over the last fifty years, in some respects maleficent magic still remains taboo.

Nature's Threats

While Isobel's confessions contain descriptions of *maleficium* directed at a number of people, with regard to specific *maleficium* they are essentially dominated by two magical acts: the making of the *corp creadh*, designed to harm the heirs of the Laird of Park; and the potion-magic, designed to harm the minister of Auldearn, Harry Forbes. Lengthy accounts of the former appear in the first, third and fourth confessions, while the latter appears in the second and fourth. Whatever the degree of Isobel's contribution to these accounts, we can suppose that their prominence in the confessions reflected pre-existent tensions, and so we will begin our analysis by exploring the relationships that may have existed between Isobel and these two men. In order to do this, we must spread our net wide. Isobel's interactions with Park and Forbes were conducted within a very particular social and environmental context, and unless we understand this context we cannot properly analyze any hostilities that may have developed between them. This diversion to look at the bigger picture will temporarily take us away from the question in hand, but it will enable us to return to it later in the chapter, far better informed. It will also give us a good grounding from which to analyze Isobel's non-specific *maleficium* in CHAPTER TWELVE.

In early modern Nairnshire all social relationships were conducted within an arena of physical hardship and emotional suffering that is very difficult for modern Western mentalities to grasp. Although, as we noted in CHAPTER ONE, the region was one of the mildest and most productive in the country, this plenty was relative and by modern standards life was still astonishingly hard. Despite the reasonable fertility of the soil, adherence to primitive agricultural methods, over-farming and vulnerability to bad weather meant that crop yields often fell short of demand. The first half of the seventeenth century was generally better than the previous, but there were still 17 years of dearth in Scotland before 1660, many concentrated between 1630–1650, with 1650–1, a period corresponding with Isobel's lifetime, being a double year of shortage. Great rains, such as those that fell in 1655, damaged crops severely, as did flooding from the sea and sandstorms, to which the Nairnshire coast was particularly vulnerable.[6] Some time before 1661 Robert Gordon of Straloch wrote that 'time has changed the appearance of [Nairn] and the sea has partly destroyed with sandbanks and partly washed away a good part of the highly productive land'; while in 1663 Brodie lamented that 'Nairn was in danger to be quitt lost by the sand and by the water'.[7] These concerns were horribly realized thirty-one years later when large parts of the estate of Culbin, only a few miles east of Lochloy, were completely overwhelmed with sand in a single night.[8]

The threats posed by the physical environment were intensified by the fact that, in a subsistence economy, there was little slack in the system when things went wrong. In a bad year, a solicitous laird opened his barns, but his supply was ultimately dependent upon the same weather conditions as everyone else and could soon run dry. And when this happened there was quite simply no food and people starved to death. How imminent starvation must have been to Isobel and her contemporaries is illustrated by the fact that during the four-year-long countrywide drought that occurred at the end of the seventeenth century, up to 15 percent of the total population of Scotland is estimated to have either died or emigrated to avoid death.[9] And despite its 'flourishing cornfields', Moray did not escape. Dennison notes that Nairn may have suffered as keenly as Aberdeen, where the population fell by over a fifth, while Sinclair Ross recalls the 'harrowing tales of the poor starving to death in the streets of Elgin'.[10] A famous account given by Sir Robert Sibbald in 1699 – about Scotland in general – describes how:

> for Want, some Die by the Way-side, some drop down on the Streets, the poor Sucking Babs are Starving for want of Milk, which the empty Breasts of their Mothers cannot furnish them: Every one may see Death in the Face of the Poor, that abound everywhere; the Thinness of their Visage, their Ghostly Looks, their Feebleness.[11]

Even without failed harvests, vulnerability to disease caused by chronic malnutrition and poor sanitation meant that epidemics still swept through the population on a regular basis and infant mortality was high. It would have been highly unusual, for example, for a woman not to have lost at least one child in infancy, and commonly more. Contemporary medical provision could not conquer such challenges. Officially trained doctors were few and far between and although, by 1670, there was a doctor resident in Nairn, many Moray parishes were not so lucky. Even as late as the 1790s an observer noted of Rathven, in nearby Banffshire, that 'no doctor has found it worthwhile to settle this parish'.[12] The poor, for whom the services of the physicians where they did exist were too expensive, resorted to either apothecaries or magical practitioners. Although the latter were often as effective as the physicians, without the benefit of modern drugs their treatments were limited. Livestock, which was such a valuable source of dairy produce, meat, hides and wool was also vulnerable to disease, and without enough hay to see them through the long winters, cattle often died, or became so weak that with the arrival of spring they quite literally had to be carried out into the fields, in a process known as 'lifting'. Even the nourishment gained in the Highland pastures or 'shielings', to which the herds were driven each summer, was often insufficient, a contemporary noting in 1796 that Auldearn cattle returned from the shielings 'in as wretched a condition as they are sent'.[13]

The popularity of the allegory of the Dance of Death throughout the Middle Ages and into the early modern era reflected the fact that in pre-industrial Europe life was tenuous. In this woodcut, one of a series published in Janez Valvasor's *Theatrum Mortis Humanae Tripartitum* (1680–2), death stalks the farmer at his plough.

Nor did the rich escape. In another woodcut from Valvasor's series a nobleman's fine sword, handsome clothes and grand house cannot protect him from death's insistent grasp.

These conditions bred an uncomfortable intimacy with death. Brodie could remark in 1676, with sadness but also a relative lack of surprise, that one of his tenants, John Brodie, 'died this day; his wyf, and 2 children, or 3, having died few days befor . . . This is the second poor tenant that I did intend som thing for, and they did not enjoy it, but wer prevented by death.'[14] But neither did the rich escape. Brodie's niece, who married John Hay of Park, and was mother to the male heirs allegedly targeted by Isobel and her coven, died 'in the flour of her age'. Similarly, Margaret Innes, who married the Nairnshire Laird of Kilravock in 1662 (and whose fine clothes we compared so favourably with Isobel's plaid in CHAPTER ONE) passed away after only fourteen years of marriage, and after having lost four of her seven children in infancy.[15] In this context, it is not difficult to see why Hugh Rose, who was also Margaret's friend and kinsman, claimed to have been 'a man of constant sorrows and acquainted with grief' and to have 'known multitudes, many younger, older, equals, translated by death from time to eternity; some leisurely, others suddenly'.[16] As we saw earlier, Harry Forbes also came face to face with the grim reaper relatively young, losing his bother William less than six years after his graduation.

Human Threats

But for Isobel and her contemporaries, the sufferings generated by bad weather and lack of food and disease were compounded by more human threats. The Moray Lowlands, with their 'flourishing cornfields', were rich compared to the mountainous regions to the south, and for many centuries the Highlanders (or 'Irishes', as they were commonly termed) had come down from the hills with bands of men to plunder the coastal regions. The threat was considered to be so great that, like many Lowland lairds throughout Scotland, the Roses of Kilravock resorted to paying the Highlanders not to attack their lands.[17] The following letter, written in 1691, in which Sir Hugh Campbell of Cawdor tells the Laird of Park about some raids that took place while he was visiting Inshoch in the latter's absence, vividly evokes the immediacy of the Highland threat:

> ther came two or three parties off Hielanders, one of them caryed away a great many cattell out of Aitnoch and caryed away above ane hundred head of cattel. The partie was strong, betwixt fiftie and threescore . . . The nixt partie fell upon my lands in the more and in the breas off Altherg, when I was at Inshoch and caryed such cattel as they found quit away; about thirtie head and four peice of horss. The third partie fell upon my lands off Boath, but then I was at home, and sent my sone Archie and the lightest lads I hade after them. They were overtaken in the breas of Strathherrick and brought back. One of their boyes was likewayes catcht and brought prisoner. And just as this letter is a writting I have advertisement from severall friends off the brea of Strathnairn that ther is a partie of five or six score Lochabber men past by them, who is like may make ane onset this night somewhere in our breas. If we knew where, we would endeavour to buckle a touch with them.[18]

Some Highland raiders became self-styled outlaws or reivers who travelled about the countryside at the head of a group of armed men and saw cattle-raiding as legitimate warfare. As we saw in the last chapter, during Isobel's lifetime John Dow Gare, or 'Black John the Left-handed', 'troubled all the North with excursions, and never traveled without 20 stout fellowes attending him well armed, [and] put a tax uppon townes and villages as he went through, and made all compon with him, bribing him with loane and soumes of mony'.[19] Closer to home, Sir Hugh Campbell of Cawdor, although affronted when Highlanders stole his livestock when he was at Inshoch, was happy to protect – and receive rents from – notorious cattle reiver Callum Beg, who lived on his lands near Findhorn, despite the fact that Beg 'made his name the terror of the district' and engaged in 'periodical descents on the lowlands, uplifting the very pick of the cattle'.[20]

But during the 1640s, Isobel and her contemporaries did not only have to cope with the threats of disease, starvation and Highland raids. They also had to contend with the fact that during the first half of the seventeenth century their woods, pastures and moors became the arena for a different order of suffering altogether. By 1644 the religious and political conflicts between England and Scotland which, as we noted in CHAPTER ONE, led to a split between more extreme presbyterians (who supported the 1638 and 1643 National Covenant and Solemn League and Covenant) and the more moderate Protestants who were prepared to negotiate a settlement with Charles I, sparked into open warfare, generating what has come to be known as the 'Scottish Civil Wars'. Between 1644 and 1646 these, what can be loosely termed 'royalist' and 'covenanting' armies, met in a series of skirmishes, battles and sieges in various parts of Scotland, from Dumfries to Carbisdale, and passing regiments, with their ranks of pikemen 'substantiouslie accompturit with jack and plait, steilbonnet, sword, bucklair . . . and a speir [spear] of sax elne long [16ft] or thairby', and colourful musketeers with 'twa cullouris, ane drum and ane bag pipe' would have been a common sight in many parts of Scotland.[21] But in February 1645, when royalist armies, under James Graham, Marquis of Montrose, amassed at Elgin, these military activities directly impacted upon the peoples of Nairnshire. Montrose's hungry army scoured the region for food, plundering the estates of the local covenanting lairds, including those of the Dunbars of Grangehill, Kinnairds of Culbin and Inneses of Forres. Closer to home, the estates of Alexander Brodie of Brodie were plundered and his uncle, Brodie of Lethen, saw his house 'besieged and his cattle driven off to feed the king's soldiers.'[22] This unrest rumbled on for the next few months until, on 9 May, they erupted into something more significant. This latest development was not a skirmish between the armed men of Cawdor and 'five or six score' cattle-raiding reivers, or even a clash between regional militia and an enemy regiment dispatched to plunder local estates. This was the 'centrepiece' of the royalist campaign: a battle so distinctive that, according to one observer, the like had 'never been seen in the low country'; a battle so large that nearly five thousand men came head to head and many hundreds lost their lives; a battle so bloody that all chroniclers, whether royalist or covenanting, emphasized 'the sheer ferocity of the fighting'; and a battle so memorable that ballads about it were still being sung in the streets of Aberdeen into the first decades of the twentieth century.[23] And what is so pertinent, with regard to

Isobel, is the fact that this battle was fought just one and a half miles from Lochloy, on a sloping field by the drying kilns just outside the town of Auldearn.

Isobel and the Battlefield

The Battle of Auldearn occurred seventeen years prior to Isobel's interrogations, and we cannot be certain where she lived or how old she was when it occurred. However, if the dates can be believed, Isobel's claim that she covenanted with the Devil in the church of Auldearn 'fyftein yeiris since' would indicate that she was living in or near the town in the mid-1640s. We can also speculate that she would either have reached adulthood or been approaching it by this time. As we calculated in CHAPTER ONE, she was likely to have been between thirty and fifty at the time of her trial, and this would put her at thirteen, at the very youngest, in 1645.

Should she have lived near Auldearn at this date, Isobel would certainly have been exposed to the battle. She may well have seen the royalist army arrive on the evening of 8 May, and set up its headquarters at Boath, the Dunbar seat north of Auldearn on the road to Lochloy. She may have witnessed the officers and foot soldiers who sought shelter in the surrounding cottages and barns, cooking their supper and sharpening their pikes in readiness for battle. In the early hours of the following morning, she might have heard the covenanting army, led by Sir John Hurry, approaching on the Nairn road and the 'thundring report' as they cleared their muskets in order to load; a noisy mistake which alerted the enemy watch and cost them the advantage of surprise.[24] She may have seen the horizon darken as Hurry's bowmen 'let fly their arrows with deadly effect' and heard the pounding of hooves as the royalist troops 'run throw' their enemies 'killing and goaring under foot'.[25] During the day-long battle, she might have cowered in her turf cottage while Montrose's cavalry swept through the covenanting army 'like a whirlwind' and caused them to fall 'thickly, mown down like grass'; and heard the distant screams as the royalist infantry 'keiping together and following the charge of the horsemen, did tear and cut them in pieces, even in rankes and fyles, as they stood'.[26] She may have seen the straggling covenanters being hunted down and killed as they tried to escape on the road to Nairn – for no quarter was given and no prisoners taken – and seen the flames reaching up into the night sky as both Auldearn and Nairn were put to the torch. In the days after the conflict she might have watched the long baggage train, carrying the many wounded, heading for the security of Bog of Gight Castle; and have ventured into Auldearn itself, skirting past the blooded streets and fields and watching as the hundreds of corpses were buried below the churchyard wall at the northwest corner and in the patch of wasteland now known as Dead Men's Wood. Standing here, she could also have witnessed the burial of John Hay of Kinnudie, the 'tall powerful' uncle to the old Laird of Park, who had been violently cut down by Montrose's major general with 'one sweep of his broadsword'.[27]

After Montrose had swept his troops back to Elgin and then on to the Spey, Isobel – along with all the inhabitants of Nairnshire – would then have encountered new challenges. Flushed with victory, contingents of Highlanders, pragmatically fusing their newly-found royalist cause with their long-held taste for Lowland plunder, continued to harry the estates of the Moray covenanters. The Dyke estates of Isobel's neighbour, Alexander Brodie, which had already been plundered prior to the Battle of Auldearn, were plundered again, and more than once, with Brodie later telling Harry Forbes that during these years 'we fell befor the wild Irishes six tyms without anie interruption . . . my hous, and my mains and bigging was brunt to the ground, and my estat made desolat, and noe place left me, nor means to subsist'.[28] The Brodies of Lethen also suffered successive attacks. In 1645 they were besieged by both Montrose and Huntly, and in the latter case the Lethen family and friends (including the young Alexander who was later present at Isobel's first interrogation) defended their strong house for over three months before they finally capitulated to the Marquis and his Highland forces. Even as late as 1654, Brodie notes that the royalist Earl of Glencairn 'burnt the corns and houses of Leathin'.[29] The dramatic events of 1645 were summed up in the Act of Parliament drawn up in 1647, by which Lethen gained recompense:

> In the yeere 1645, his hous of Lethen, was beseidged be James Grahame and his adherents, wha, not able to prevaill, brunt his haill barnes, barneyairdis, and cornes, plunderit the haill insight and plenishing of his baronie, and took away eight hundreth oxin and kyne, eighteine hundreth sheepe and goates, two hundreth horses and meares: Lykeas therefter the laite Marques of Huntlie, and his sones, with two thousand fute and horse, beseidged the supplicantis hous of new, be the space of twelff weekis, Wha, being dissapoynted and inraged throw the loss of many of their men, at last did utterlie burne over againe the said supplicant his haill landis. Wherupone their wes abone the number of eight scoir persons, and left not ten of them to remain upone the saidis landis: And about half a yeere therefter, the Hielanders took away all that wes left upone the ground.[30]

We have no evidence that the Park and Lochloy estates were plundered over this period, but given the Hay family's covenanting sympathies, it is highly likely. It is also probable that the Hay widows and the young heir of Park were among those who took refuge at Lethen during Huntly's three-month siege. Certainly Brodie, who was stuck in the garrison at Inverness for the duration, claimed that 'all my friends were taking shelter' there.[31]

The poorer inhabitants of the region would also have suffered. As John Barrett has recently noted, although Montrose's and Huntly's forces targeted the barns and cellars of the big houses, peasants 'were not ignored by foraging Royalists'.[32] Faced with a band of armed men, Isobel and her neighbours would have had a stark choice: either comply with the army and surrender their precious animals and corn or face the destruction of their livelihoods, with Brodie noting gravely that the royalists 'left neither to eat, nor sow, nor plogh in many places, wher they reaceau'd not obedeinc'.[33] Even if Isobel and her peers had emerged from these raids with anything left in their pastures, folds and barns, they may have felt duty bound to share it with the less fortunate. After Lethen was ransacked in 1654, Brodie gave 'a stack of oats and straw to his [Lethen's] poor people' and lower down the social scale, tenants, cottars and labourers linked to families living on plundered estates are likely – within their means – to have done the same.[34]

But even after 1645, when the worst excesses of the wars had passed, Isobel's troubles would still not have been over. On the one hand, Montrose's defeat in 1646, and the corresponding parliamentarian victories in England, meant that the Nairnshire lairds had come out on the winning side, and as we have already seen, they lost no time in petitioning parliament for compensation for their plundered estates. Over the next few years Isobel and her contemporaries saw the towns of Nairn and Auldearn, and the estates of Lethen and Brodie, rebuilt. Farmsteads were repopulated, livestock numbers regenerated and fields re-sown. But this peace was short-lived. Although the covenanters had supported the parliamentarian cause, they became increasingly frustrated with the latter's refusal to accede to their religious demands and this frustration sent them, ironic as it may seem, back into negotiations with the monarchy (hence Brodie's role as commissioner in the diplomatic efforts that brought Charles II to be crowned at Scone). This defection, unsurprisingly, precipitated them into military conflict with their erstwhile allies, the parliamentarians, by whom they were finally defeated in 1652. In response to this insurgence, and cognisant of the pockets of royalist dissent still simmering in the Highlands, Cromwell sent forces to Scotland under General Monck, and the country was effectively under military occupation for the next nine years. For the inhabitants of Moray, one army had been replaced by another. Cromwell built a citadel in Inverness out of stones plundered from Kinloss Abbey, and sold to him by Alexander Brodie of Lethen. Detachments of soldiers were also stationed at Elgin, Darnaway and, closer to home, Nairn and Lethen, in addition to being billetted in the surrounding cottages and fermtouns.

During this period Isobel, like all the inhabitants of Nairnshire, would have suffered the brooding tensions of a country under occupation. In some ways, the Cromwellian rule brought welcome stability, and on the surface, an equable truce. Brodie invited English officers to his castle to discuss religion and even, at times, share worship, while local women found love with soldiers.[35] The English judges who shared the administration of justice were more moderate, with regard to magical traditions, than the Scottish, and this benefited those men and women who were, like Isobel, wedded to less orthodox Christian practices.[36] But in other ways it was a tense and uneasy alliance. English soldiers were not always the most genial of guests, and many nurtured deep prejudices born of centuries of English/Scottish conflict. The following account, though derived from a religiously-moderate English officer stationed in Scotland at the end of the seventeenth century, vividly sums up the contemporary English presumption that the Scots were both primitive and simple-minded:

here [in Scotland] is great store of Fowl, indeed, as foul Houses, foul Sheets, foul Linnen, foul Dishes, Pots, Trenchers, Napkins, &c. . . . For their Butter and Cheese, I will not meddle withal at this time, nor no Man else at any time that loves his Life . . . The Air might be wholesome but for the stinking people that inhabit it; the Ground might be fruitful, had they the Wit to manure it . . . As to their Religion, it is such a Hodge-podge, there is no describing it . . . They hold their Noses, if you talk of Bear-baiting, and stop their Ears, if you speak of a Play . . . The men of old did not more wonder that the great Messias should be born in so poor a Town as Bethlehem, than the World may wonder at, that England should have a Race of Kings from such a cursed Countrey as Scotland.[37]

The impositions of the English were further reinforced by the burden of Monck's heavy taxation, which caused Brodie to lament, in 1655–6, 'the strait of poor people for the new burden of excyse' and 'the encreas of burthens on the poor land, without ane mitigation or relief'.[38] These privations then went on to outlive the Commonwealth, with Brodie noting, when travelling through Lincolnshire en route to London in 1661, that the former was a 'large beautifull countree, not straitnd with the povertie that my nativ soil was under'.[39] Subsistence living, Highland raids, civil war, military occupation and crippling taxes: these, then, were the factors that formed the backdrop to Isobel's relationships with the Laird of Park and Harry Forbes.

Isobel and the Laird of Park

As with any bond based on social inequality, the relationship between a Moray laird and his tenants (the latter term, as it is used in this section, covering both tenants proper and the cottars and labourers who worked for them) was an ambiguous one at the best of times. If a laird was sympathetic and fair, the latter could be treated well enough. Although Brodie, for example, was often exasperated by his tenants (at many points lamenting their 'ungodliness, lying, [and] perjury') he seems to have been reasonably compassionate, as illustrated by his attempts to help the unfortunate John Brodie and his family, and his evident sorrow at their untimely deaths.[40] Similarly, when the house of Lethen was besieged by Huntly in 1645, Brodie worried about Lethen's 'poor people' and lamented: 'I could not tell what to advise the poor tenants to do.'[41] But there was also great potential for abuse. In the late-seventeenth century an English traveller noted that in Scotland 'The Nobility and Gentry Lord it over their poor Tenants, and use them worse than Gally-Slaves . . . Every Laird (of note) hath a Gibbet near his House, and has Power to condemn and hang any of his Vassals; so they dare not oppose him in any thing, but must submit to his Commands, let them be never so unjust and tyrannical.'[42] This indictment is obviously an exaggeration and tinged with anti-Scottish sentiment, but it can still be seen as representative of the worst abuses of the system, as reflected in the old Gaelic proverbs: 'An alder lord will twist an oak tenant' and even more evocatively, 'Slippery is the flagstone at the great house door'.[43] Nine years before Isobel's interrogations, Brodie lamented a general 'rigour to tenants' and 'straitned[ness] to the poor', and it is clear that these were not isolated cases, with similar abuses landing, less than thirty years later, right on his doorstep. In 1680, despite his father's compassionate example, Brodie's son, James, recorded in his diary that 'I conferrd with Calder [the Laird of Cawdor] on bussines of my oun . . . [and] He told me he heard I was severe to tennents.'[44] Moreover, although James pledged, on hearing this criticism, 'to tak this [Cawdor's] warning, and to reflect upon the ground of it', four years later he was still confessing that 'In dealing with depauperat tennents I am apt to be sever.'[45]

The two core demands that the laird made of his tenants proper were rent and labour. Rent was usually paid twice a year to the laird's tacksman, both 'in kind' and in the form of money (the latter largely gained through selling goods at market). Labour, on the other hand, could be called on at anytime. The Laird of Park's estate accounts reveal, for example, that a man who took the lease of Meickle Penick in 1678 had to pay him fourteen bolls of bear, three Scots pounds, seven capons, two hens, six poultry, six cuts of yarn and had to lead peats and carry grain to the port of Findhorn or Nairn at his own charge.[46] These multiple demands were often oppressive. It was difficult for tenants to part with hard-won grain and livestock, as old proverbs like 'Ane to saw, ane to gnaw and ane to pay the laird with' attest.[47] It was also hard for them to walk away from their own crops in order to harvest those of the laird. As Sinclair Ross emphasizes, in reference to the seventeenth-century barony of Culbin, east of Lochloy:

> The most resented part of a tenant's rent was the time spent in providing a certain number of days' work on the Laird's home farm, usually in ploughing and at harvest time. This work took priority over work on the tenant's own holding. Each tenant had to cut, dry and deliver a stated number of loads of peats to the Laird each summer, and in winter, after threshing the corn, deliver their own grain rent to the Laird's storehouse or to a specified market. The estate's mill was also maintained by the tenants as part of their dues and they were bound to have their own grain ground there. With all these additional tasks imposed on him, the tenant had little time to concentrate on his own holding, while the Laird, having all the necessities of life delivered to his door, was loathe to change the system.[48]

Stressing the System

Pertinent to our analysis of the relationship between Isobel Gowdie and the Laird of Park is the fact that, at times of stress, the delicate relationship between a laird and the people who lived and worked on his land could easily become strained. And for the peoples of Nairnshire, on all social levels, few times were more stressful than the first half of the seventeenth century. Religious divisions became increasingly extreme, driving covenanting landowners to be more contemptuous and condemnatory of their generally more doctrinally-moderate tenants than those who came before and after them. In addition, while economic and political conditions placed many Scottish lairds under financial stress during this period, in the 1640s and 50s the monetary demands of the civil war, and Monck's subsequent taxes, hit the Nairnshire gentry particularly hard. Although Lethen, for example, claimed compensation after his estates were plundered by Montrose and Huntly, he was still feeling the repercussions in 1662, Brodie noting that he 'seimd much weighted with his burdens, and the condition of his effairs, and seimd as inclind to sell somwhat of his estats'. In the same year, Hugh Campbell of Cawdor also experienced 'distress in his effairs'.[49] Given the fact that any laird's prime source of revenue was his land, when financial troubles arose he would naturally increase his demands on his tenants, whether it be for victuals, money or labour; a pattern reflected in the sour old proverb 'The yield of the land is according to the laird'.[50] Given the fact that in the harsh aftermath of the civil wars, both tenants and the cottars and labourers who worked for them would have been primarily concerned with filling their own barns with corn and feeding their own children, as opposed to filling the barns and feeding the children of the laird, we can assume that in the years leading up to Isobel's trial, tensions between the Nairnshire lairds and their tenants ran high. These tensions would have been exacerbated by the fact that, as Barrett notes, although peasants 'were not ignored by foraging Royalists' they 'fell beneath notice when losses were assessed'.[51]

But what is particularly significant with regard to Isobel is the fact that for the tenants of the Laird of Park this already tense situation would have been exacerbated by yet another factor. While many lairds suffered financially as a result of the civil wars, the monetary troubles of the Hays of Park and Lochloy had deeper origins. As early as 1635 a document states that Park's grandfather David, his father John, and several local lairds 'mett to consider of the Laird of Parkis burdingis, and to give thair advys and countnance for defraying therof, and preyventing the incres of the samyn'. The cost-cutting measures decided at this time included the younger laird moving into Inshoch with his family and a limited number of servants:

> First, the laird of Park elder, his burding of debt is fund to be nyn thowsand merkis, and his frie rent, by the deanes dewis, will be ellevin scoir bolluis victuell, by the maynes of Inschoche estimat to threscoir, quhairof it is condescendit that the maynes and fourtie bollis of the rediest of his rent of Lochloy sall be intromittit with be him and his ladye, with the haill custoumes and service of thair estate for mantennance of thair hous; and the rest, extenden to nyn scoir bollis sall be taken upp be the young laird, the said Alexander Dunbar in lochloy and Hew [. . .] as factors specially nominat to that effect, and the annuellis of the said nyn thowsand merkis being payit therewith, the reste to be imployit for defraying of the burding, and thay to be comptabill therfoir.
>
> Item, that the young laird come into his fatheris house, with his wyff, childring, ane servand man and ane servand woman, and be intertenit thair; and to enter at Witsonday 1635, and to give in of his estate yeirlye, twa chalderis victuell for thair sustentatioun, and to pay ane chalder victuell of the same crope betuix and the first of Junii nixt and the uther chalder of the nixt crope betuix thence and Candlemes nixt, and this conditioun betuix them to indure als long as they keip ane familye.[52]

But these economizing measures were clearly not effective, for thirty years later David Hay's grandson John – the Laird of Park named in Isobel's confessions – still struggled with the same insolvency. Between the late 1650s when he came of age, and his death sometime in the 1690s, Hay struggled to keep his estates afloat through borrowing widely and using his lands as security. The boxes of Park's papers held at the National Archives of Scotland and the Hay archives held at Brodie Castle, contain between them huge numbers of bonds and discharges relating to his debts, while Bain also notes that:

The sheriff court books of Nairn are crowded with bonds registered against the estate of John Hay of Lochloy, by his procurator John Dallas, burgess of Nairn. He appears to have borrowed money freely from all sorts and conditions of people. Amongst others, old Bailie Tulloch advanced him considerable sums . . . The lairds of Brodie, Lethen, Clava, and Boath were large creditors.[53]

The fact that Hay was not served heir to his father's estates until 1679, close to two decades after he had reached the age of twenty-one, also suggests that he was trying to evade debts. After the Restoration, Park's finances were additionally drained by ongoing charges for nonconformist worship and a £200 fine resulting from the 1660 Act of Indemnity, which required those who had fought against the king to make good, and for which he spent five months in gaol in 1666.[54] Twenty years later, matters were approaching a critical point. Creditors were pushing harder for legal action in order to recoup their loans and in 1684 James Brodie recorded that 'I had heard som dais befor of the stat and condition of the Laird of Park, and that he was neir to breaking'.[55] Although in 1690 Park delayed the inevitable through successfully petitioning parliament – gaining protection from any attempts to bring legal action against him for a three-year-period – in the first decade of the eighteenth century his creditors successfully took his son, Major William Hay, to the court of session, which finally forced a judicial sale in 1710.[56] In this way, the lands which had passed down the Hay bloodline since they were first gifted by William the Lionheart in the twelfth century, were lost. And within little more than a hundred years, as if uncannily in accordance with Isobel's ill wishes, Inshoch castle had fallen into ruins and the Hays of Park and Lochloy sunk into oblivion.

We have little information as to how Park's imminent bankruptcy impacted upon the tenants, cottars and labourers who lived on his estates, the documentation being mute on this point. But the likelihood that the impact was negative is raised by the fact that Park's financial straits certainly brought him into conflict with his peers. In 1671, for example, his desperation to benefit from a patronage involving Pennick (an estate adjoining Inshoch) seems to have severely threatened his relationship with his uncle, and fellow beneficiary, Alexander Brodie. The details of this transaction are unclear, but it seems that Park was pushing Brodie for a part of Pennick to which the latter considered he had no right. After a series of fraught exchanges, in which Brodie perceived that Park 'was picking a quarrel with me', he recorded in his diary:

> I did meit with Park, at Penick . . . The best want not ther failings. He took exception at that which I writ, that nothing but our corruptions neided interupt our friendship. He movd to have that he might hav the land beneth the way; yet he had past from it. This man is an exercis to me . . . I see it difficil, and almost impossibl to retain this man; yet I desir that nothing may separat me from him in the Lord.[57]

We also have evidence that with regard to employees, Park was reluctant to part with money. His bill of account to Harry Forbes in 1662–3 clearly indicates a resistance to pay for anything unless he absolutely had to; a trait that would not have endeared him

The ruins of Inshoch Castle, once home to the Hays of Lochloy and Park. The castle fell into disuse in the eighteenth century. This is the place where, on April 14, 1662, Harry Forbes, Hugh Rose and others interrogated Isobel's accomplice Janet Breadheid.

The Highland soldiers that fought at the Battle of Auldearn would have resembled the infantrymen depicted in this 1631 engraving by the German artist Georg Koler, and which is thought to portray Scottish mercenaries in the service of the King of Sweden, Gustavus Adolphus, during the Thirty Years War. Indeed, many of the mercenaries who served Adolphus went on to fight in the Scottish Civil Wars thirteen years later.

to Forbes given the fact, as we shall see later, the minister was himself in dire financial straits.[58] What also emerges clearly from the records is the fact that Park possessed an almost preternatural ability to ignore the requests of creditors. In the following letter, written to Park in 1666, the frustrations of the author, Alexander Dunbar, are obvious:

> There is some money serve be you this several yeares bygone by your two severall bonds, which I have sent for at several ocasions, but has receaved no satisfactione, yet I resolve to spaire you till the nixt tearme of whitsonday . . . the last tyme he was at your, it was promised to be sent him in eight days after but I find it was not . . . I forbear to enlarge only my love rememberit to your self and relations, Your loving friend and servant A Dunbar.[59]

With regard to his relationships with tenants, such evidence is ominous. If Park was able to cut himself off from feeling the material distress he caused his relatives and peers, with whom he ate and fought and worshipped, then we can safely assume that he was also able to distance himself from the material distress he caused the poorer men and women who lived and worked on his lands, and from whom he was so clearly separated by status, religion and education.

Park's inability to empathise with others may have been rooted in desperation, for a man whose neck is on the block finds it difficult to worry about anyone else. But the evidence also suggests that this quality may have been rooted in character as well as circumstance. Despite the fact that Brodie helped him gain the commission to try Isobel and Janet in June 1662, later in the same year Park still found cause to take him to task. Although Park's grievance may have been justified (for the causes of the quarrel are not noted) Brodie's patent bemusement regarding his confrontation is palpable and, considered alongside his previous description of their conflict over Pennick, suggests that the young laird may have possessed a petulant and perhaps even paranoid nature, with Brodie noting that: 'Park took journey south. He enquird why I was jelous of him; and I told him, I found him and his wyf alienated from me and my family, and I had born respect to him as much as to anie. He cleard himself, but exprest that he could not doe to my famili that which he would do to me.'[60] Brodie's son James expressed similar bemusement, in response to Park's grievances, nearly twenty years later, claiming in December 1680 that, 'I greive to be coming off in anie mistak with Park, albeit the Lord knows how I have bein willing to carie fair with him. Yet dare I not justifie my self in anie thing.'[61] Shades of petulance can also be detected in Park's ability to openly denigrate close peers and family members, despite the fact that most were creditors and many seem to gone out of their way to be patient with him, with James Brodie noting with obvious disquiet in 1684 that: 'I cam in by Miltoun; heard of Park's expressions of me and my friends . . . [he said of us] that becaus we had gatherd and com to som welth, and wer swelling, therfor we wer vain and lifted up'.[62]

Although these references are obscure (with the details of the disputes between Park and his peers never being fully explained), and we can draw little from them in isolation, they become clearer when examined in conjunction with what we know about Park's childhood. There exists no genealogical tree of this branch of the Hay family, but piecing together evidence from marriage contracts, sasines, gravestones and contemporary writings we can confirm that between 1640 and 1643, when the young John Hay was still an infant, his grandfather David, his father John and his uncle William all died in quick succession.[63] After which the deceased John and William's younger brother, Hugh, stepped in and managed the estates until the infant laird came of age, only a few years before Isobel's arrest. As a result of these events, the young John Hay and his siblings (the evidence points to at least one brother, named Hugh and one sister, named Anna) would have grown up without a father and been raised by women – their mother Jean Cuming and grandmother Marie Rose – who undoubtedly mourned long and hard.[64] Given this unfortunate chain of events, we can suppose that it would have been very difficult for the Hay widows not to have treated the fatherless heir with kid gloves, and perhaps to have inadvertently given him an elevated sense of his own importance.

This peculiarly intense upbringing did not necessarily make Park an unpleasant man. Brodie's descriptions of his conflict with him over Pennick indicate that he had genuine affection for the younger laird: the former hoping, at one point, 'that my friendship and lov to him [Park] should outwear houses and enjoyments heir, and the rocks. Lord! I speak this in the singlnes of my heart Thou knows.'[65] That the young laird was held in some esteem is also suggested by the fact that Alexander Dunbar, whom we met earlier, waited so long before he called in his debt, and that he called it in with such restraint; while Park's exceptional hospitality toward nonconformist ministers, despite the personal risks involved, also earned him gratitude and respect (with here, his material insecurity perhaps sharpening his spiritual resolve).[66] Hugh Rose's claim, in his genealogical history of the Roses of Kilravock, that 'The sones [of Park's grandfather, David Hay] had each in their dispositions something peculiar and different; but all were well favored, prettie gentlemen, and in good repute where they lived' is also suggestive here, though it is unclear whether Rose used the term 'sones' in a general or specific way.[67] But although it would clearly be unjust to leap in and pronounce Park unlikeable, we can speculate that his unusual childhood may have fostered a higher-than-average degree of narcissism; a character trait that would go a long way towards explaining both his petulance and his ability to ignore creditors. We can also speculate that a fatherless childhood, spent in a house of mourning, and over-shadowed by the threat of financial ruin, may have generated tendencies to both hard-done-by-ness and perhaps paranoia; with the demise of the former lairds of Park constantly hanging, like the Sword of Damocles, over his young head. All three qualities would be consistent with his difficulties with Brodie and none would have boded well for 'desperat tenants' like Isobel and John Gilbert.

Park and Witchcraft

But the plot thickens yet further. For Park's relationship with his tenants may not only have been complicated by the stresses of war, financial insolvency and childhood trauma but also by a very different, and in Isobel's case highly relevant, factor. As a zealous covenanter, Park disapproved of adherence to all forms of superstitious and magical practice and was, like many of the local lairds, present on the commission of various witchcraft trials in the early 1660s.[68] He was also likely to have been aware that, by virtue of his position, he was vulnerable to maleficent attacks by resentful tenants. Rumours of such events were certainly part of popular currency in Scotland in this period. When Robert Douglas, a landowner near Auchintulloch, Loch Lomond, became unstable and killed a neighbour in 1664, it was 'weill knouine to all the countrie about the place wher he leivid' that he did so 'in a distraction bewitchd as is alledgd by some highlanders there for his strict exacting of the customes deu to the Castle of Dumbarton'.[69] Similarly, in Paisley nearly twenty years later, the whole region was awash with the news that local woman Bessie Weir and her neighbour, an under-miller named John Stewart, had confessed to having made a *corp creadh* in order to harm the local laird, George Maxwell; the former because Maxwell 'had not entered her husband to his harvest service', and the latter 'to revenge the taking of his mother Jennet Mathie' on charges of witchcraft.[70] But while most lairds would have been aware that they could theoretically become targets for witchcraft, we have reason to believe that the young Park would have been particularly sensitive in this respect. As we have seen earlier, the laird's childhood was blighted by the fact that his grandfather, father and uncle had all died in quick succession, within three years of each other. But with regard to Isobel, these unfortunate deaths become even more significant when we take into account the fact that they were openly attributed to witchcraft.

Park's Other Witches

The facts of the matter are all laid out, in black and white, in the register of the privy council where, in 1643, it is recorded that a woman named Agnes Grant was 'apprehendit for the murther be sorcerie and witchecraft of David Hay of Park [and] Johne and William Hayis, his sones'.[71] We also know that the trial was a memorable one, the account stating that many of the onlookers, among whom emotions clearly ran high, wished to add their own grievances to those for which she was already being tried. A letter sent to the privy council along with the request for permission to try her, detailed the proceedings as follows:

> wee war so pressed be them [the onlookers] that wee resolved to heir [the accusations of] sum that war present; wha being callit befoir us, deiplye sworne with upholdin handis in the audience of the pannell and assyse, they gave in sindrie delationes whairof the pannell confest the most pairt bot with feirfull execrationes aganes the delatouris [accusers]. Theis ditteyes ar not mentionat in the rolment of court, bot wee thoght it expedient to represent them to your lordshipes in a by paper. This wretchit creature hes bene ever and as yit is of ane exceding ivill reporte, and there have bene monye vehement presumptiounes exhibited to us that schee hes bene acessorie to dyverse divilische practices.[72]

We do not know how far the Hay family, including the newly-widowed Marie Rose and Jean Cuming, and the surviving brother, Hugh Hay, credited these accusations, but it is likely that they took them very seriously. Given the fact that Grant was charged and – if Janet Breadheid's reference to the case it to be believed – executed for the crime, and that even men as educated and sober as Alexander Brodie believed that witches could target and harm their families, we can be certain that the young laird would have grown up nurturing the suspicion (and probably the firm conviction) that the tragic deaths of his grandfather, father and uncle were caused by witchcraft. Certainly, Janet Breadheid's confession suggests that this was the view among the local population, for not only does she reiterate the fact that Agnes Grant had been burnt for attempting 'to destroy the lairdis of park and lochloy', but also implicates another local woman: stating confidently that 'it wes Keathrin Sowter that wes brunt that (*killed/shot?*) William Hay the last Laird of Park's brother'. We can also speculate, though here more tangentially, that the suspicion that the male lairds had died through unnatural causes may have been intensified by the fact that their wives Marie Rose and Jean Cuming survived their unfortunate husbands by many years, with the former not dying until 1672 at the grand old age of eighty-eight.[73]

Given these events, it is of course highly significant that Isobel claimed to have committed essentially the same crime as Agnes Grant (that is, the murder of the heirs of the Laird of Park) and it is hard not to suspect that her assertion was somehow connected to Agnes's high-profile conviction. This suspicion gains further confirmation from the fact that, although the evidence is not completely clear on this point, the man listed in the confessions as 'hew hay of brightmanney', and who was present at all four of Isobel's and Janet's interrogations, is likely to have been the younger brother of the deceased John and William who had managed the Park estates until the infant John Hay had come of age.[74] There is also a possibility that the 'W Sutherland off kinsterie' listed in Janet's and two of Isobel's confessions was related to the John Sutherland who attended Grant's trial in 1643 and put his name to the letter of complaint sent to the privy council. Given the fact that, second to Inshoch, Newton of Park was the most prominent Hay estate, we can further speculate that the 'hew hay of newtoun' who witnessed all four of Isobel's confessions may have been John Hay's younger brother; solicitously present here in his absence. There is obviously a can of worms here and we shall explore it in more depth in CHAPTER NINE, when we look at Isobel's testimony in the context of false confession. But at present it is sufficient to note that the young Park and his family are likely to have nurtured a heightened fear of witchcraft and that this fear is likely to have rendered them particularly sensitive to any perceived hostility from the men and women who lived and worked on their lands. This touchiness would also have been exacerbated by the fact that, given contemporary political upheavals and the family's financial insolvency, levels of tenant-hostility on the Park estates are likely to have been generally high. Moreover, in the years leading up to Isobel's trial, these tensions would have increased dramatically when, in the late 1650s, the young Park married Brodie's niece and the family began to generate new male heirs for the first time since the three tragic deaths in the early 1640s. In such a heated environment, it is not difficult to see how smouldering suspicions of witchcraft, when they arose, could have been quickly fanned into flame. Whichever way you look at it, the odds were stacked against good relations between Isobel Gowdie and the Laird of Park. For a poor, superstitious, magic-practising tenant such as Isobel, the flagstones would have been very slippery at the Inshoch Castle door.

Mr Harry Forbes, Minister of Auldearn

With regard to Harry Forbes, matters would have been equally complex. In this period the relationship between parishioner and minister was, like that between tenant and laird, an ambiguous one at the best of times. On the one hand, seventeenth-century congregations could clearly value and develop great affection for their ministers. The writings of Aberfoyle minister Robert Kirk, for example, reveal a man who was genuinely fond of his parishioners and it is clear that they returned his affections by confiding in him; an intimacy that bequeathed us the unparalleled riches of *The Secret Commonwealth of Elves, Fauns and Fairies*.[75] James Fraser, minister of the Invernesshire parish of Kirkhill, who we met in the last chapter, seems to have been equally esteemed. During a presbyterial visitation of the parish in 1677, William Mackay notes that the 'elders declared themselves satisfied with his doctrine, living, and conversation' and emphasized that Fraser:

> was so 'panefull' in visiting the sick, catechising the people, and his other ministerial duties, 'that they were affrayed that he should thereby shorten his own days in all likelihood.' In visiting the sick he, doubtless, gave them the free benefit of that medical knowledge of which he made use in the parish 'Herbal' and 'Experiments of Phisick and Chirurgery,' and which he had probably acquired from his father. The session-book tells us that he provided so well for the poor of the parish that crowds of hungry strangers flocked to the church at his annual distribution of money and meal. In discipline he was firm, but just. The 'Bill of Mortality' and *Polichronicon* show that he knew his parishioners and the inhabitants of the surrounding districts by name and headmark.[76]

However there is also ample evidence that ministers were frequently resented. Nowhere is this fact more simply and convincingly portrayed than in the following extract from Craig's Catechism of 1581, where the value of ministerial teaching is emphasized:

> A. God has established this order in His Church because we need continually to be instructed.
> Q. What follows from this?
> A. The ministers or pastors are needful for us.
> Q. But they are commonly neglected and despised?
> A. He who despises them, despises God and his own salvation.[77]

One of the primary reasons why reformed ministers were 'commonly neglected and despised' was because they attempted to impose strict moral codes upon their congregations, and possessed, through the kirk sessions, the means through which to enforce them. Many of the poor, for whom sickness and death were an ever-present threat,

167

instinctively adopted a 'live and love while you can' approach to life that made the pleasures of worldy existence more – as opposed to less – sweet. And for them, the church's
condemnation of many basic celebratory activities such as dancing, singing, playing
music and drinking, were widely resented. The church's alternative life-prescription –
self denial – did little to make amends. Hugh Rose's cry 'let me live to God, in studying
him in his works of creation and providence; in prayer, meditation, watching, in self-
examination, in self-denial, in the mortification of my woeful unhappy lusts' would not
necessarily have appealed to men and women like Isobel and John Gilbert, who came
home from a back-breaking day's work in the out-fields looking forward to a jug of ale
and an evening of song.[78] Nor are they likely to have sympathized with the spiritual
distress Brodie experienced after catching himself taking pleasure in a country walk.
'In going about the fields', he notes in his diary in May 1656, 'I found the hart apt to
rys with carnal delight in feilds, grass, wood &c. This I desird the Lord to guard me
against, that such decaying, corruptibl, poor comforts, steal not away my heart.'[79]
Popular resistance to reformed austerity is aptly reflected in proverbs such as 'Hard as
is the factor's rule, no better is the minister's'. Or, even more boldly, 'God has not said
all thou hast said'.[80]

The ministerial vocation was rendered even more unpleasant by the fact that many
people seem to have expressed their resentments of the ministry openly. Margo Todd
notes, for example, that in the first half of the seventeenth century 'There are surprisingly numerous instances of parishioners standing and interrupting sermons and
prayers, supposedly to disagree with the teaching, but often because they had endured
quite enough denunciation of their sins'.[81] Some were so affronted by the prohibitions
of their minister that they even resorted to physical violence. In 1608, when Alexander
Mortimer was denounced by the minister for lighting a midsummer bonfire, he
resorted to 'taking his hat off his head and striking him on the fact therewith'.[82] Given
that Brodie saw cause to lament, with regard to Auldearn, that 'I observd the decay of
religion as generalli, soe particularli in this place, and desird to mourn under it', we
can assume that similar sentiments were harboured among Forbes's congregation.[83]
This was certainly the case in adjacent parishes. In 1653 George Balfour, the minister
of Ardclach, lamented 'the deplorable condition of the people under his charge by
reason of many heinous and fearful sins daily increasing and abounding among them,
as also of their untowardness and unwillingness to submit themselves to discipline
grounded upon the inequity of the time'; while several decades later, an equally despon-
dent Hugh Rose echoed: 'Oh remember, that being a gospel-minister, though briars
and thorns should be with me, and I dwell among scorpions, I should not be
dismayed'.[84]

But for Forbes, newly arriving in Auldearn in 1655, this inherently ambivalent
minister/congregation relationship would have been complicated by several additional
factors. First, we have the fact that even before he had formally taken up the ministry
in the town he had been exposed to overt congregational hostility. On 15 April 1655,
on the day that he buried his uncle John Brodie (Auldearn's former minister), Brodie
wrote the following entry in his diary:

That sam day that he was buried, Mr Heri Forbes was nominated Minister in Auldearn. I observed the Lord's wisdom. 1. He humbl'd me and others micle by the fear we had of Moynes his opposition, for he had been counseld to protest. 2. The Lord's kindnes in confounding ther counsel, and carying on the nomination so farr with consent that non contradicted it, albeit som were non-liquets.[85]

Although, three days later Brodie noted that 'We kept the Presbytrie anent the cal to Mr. H. Forbes . . . They agreed on it in the end unanimouslie in the Presbyterie', the fact that some were not happy with Forbes's instalment is suggested by a subsequent entry (written nearly a month later) stating that, 'I heard that som of Auldearn said they wer forc'd to subscriv the letter [objecting to the instalment of] . . . Mr Hari. The Lord consider and bring forth good of this; for we ar at our wit's end; readi to sink.'[86] The details of this matter (and the nature and purpose of this particular letter) are not clear, but we can assume that these disagreements were rooted in the complexities of the election process. Theoretically, during this period congregations were allowed to choose their own ministers by vote, out of a number of candidates sent by the presbytery, with each candidate having to prove their worth through preaching to the congregation in turn. In reality, however, decisions were often swung in a less-than-democratic manner by the wishes of the local elite. In Forbes's case, the evidence suggests that Brodie and others put pressure on both the presbytery and congregation to accept him, despite the fact that some (seemingly using John Moynes as a mouthpiece) disputed it. That Brodie, on the recommendation of the newly-installed minister of Kiltearn, Thomas Hogg, was instrumental in choosing Forbes is suggested by his claim, as early as February 1655, that 'I wryt to Mr. Thomas Hogg, and exhorted him to faithfulness; and desired to be informed anent Mr. Hari Forbes'.[87] This interpretation is further supported by the fact that Brodie was clearly not adverse to throwing his weight around when he had a mind to, as evinced by a diary entry in June of the same year, which states that friends had told him 'they wer feared for my oppression, and I swayd judges and took two parts of my will'.[88]

Whether this resistance to Forbes's instalment was purely fuelled by objection to the rigged nature of the election, or whether personal antipathies towards the minister also played a role is difficult to tell. We certainly have no reason to believe that he was an overtly unpleasant man. As we surmised in CHAPTER FIVE, not only was he likely to have been a deep thinker and a good listener, but he also seems to have possessed the emotional maturity to make real friendships. That Brodie nurtured a genuine affection for Forbes is clearly illustrated in his claim, on hearing that the latter might lose his position in 1662, that 'I heard of Mr Hari his straits, and desir to bear burthen with him'.[89] The evidence also suggests that – among his covenanting peers at least – Forbes could inspire respect. As we have seen, Brodie's attentions are all the more notable for the fact that he did not suffer fools gladly and was, as Bain expressed it, 'a keen judge of character' who 'readily distinguished between those who were worldly, self-seeking or conceited, and those who were earnest and noble-minded'.[90] The fact that Forbes may have been championed by Thomas Hogg, a minister who was still remembered and revered in the Auldearn region over 200 years later for his 'clear intellect, solid judgement, high-toned spirituality of mind, firmness of character, and courtesy of demeamour', is also suggestive here.[91] More direct confirmation can be gleaned from the fact that, as we shall explore in more depth later, local covenanter Katharine Collace – a woman as spiritually-ambitious and hard-to-please as both Brodie and Hogg – clearly stated in her memoirs that Forbes was 'highly reputed for piety' and 'highly esteemed among us'.[92]

But our sources also suggest that while Forbes could inspire affection and respect in some, he could inspire dislike in others. Particularly pertinent in this respect is the fact that the Auldearn congregation was not the first to resist his taking up the ministerial post in their parish. Prior to his arrival in the town, Forbes had spent over four years as a temporary minister in Wick, Caithness. And that he did not endear himself to all of his parishioners during this period is indicated by the fact that when, in 1655, he was nominated to take a permanent post, several members of the congregation vehemently protested, with the presbytery minutes of 22 August stating that: 'That day compeered Francis Manson in Wick with the Mistres of Ulbister & gave in a paper affecting pretended reasons why they would not have Mr Hary Forbes to be th[ai]r Minister in th[ai]r owne name and in the name of severall oth[e]rs of the said paroch.'[93] As with the conflict in Auldearn, the exact reasons behind this resistance are unclear, but our knowledge of all the parties involved suggests that religious differences may have played a role. Protestant ministers, like their godly parishioners, varied in their levels of religious extremism, and it is clear that Forbes represented the 'without so much as a hoof [of the anti-Christ]' end of the reforming continuum, this being one of the reasons why he appealed to the equally fundamentalist Nairnshire lairds and ministers. As a consequence, Forbes was among the extremist minority who refused to accept episcopacy after the Restoration and were therefore forced to resign their posts.

Such religious rigidity may have caused some problems in Wick. The circumstances that led to his posting there were, by all accounts, unusual. In 1650 the whole of Caithness presbytery, in a dramatic series of events, had been deposed in one fell swoop for complying with the royalist commander, Montrose, and a number of ministers, including Forbes, were drafted in to temporarily fill the vacant posts.[94] Although the presbytery's capitulation to Montrose seems to have been secured largely through intimidation, there is no doubt that, as in many parts of Scotland, the general population nurtured wider sympathies with the moderate Protestantism underpinning the royalist cause. As we saw in CHAPTER ONE, in contemporary Caithness some parishioners laughed at those who sung the psalms in church, and wandered irreverently into the churchyard 'at tyme of sermon'. But as the following comments by Craven indicate, this watery presbyterianism was not limited to the lowest rungs of Caithness society:

> Notwithstanding all the efforts of the clergy, it is certain enough that at this time Caithness was 'in a state of semi-barbarism, with the spirit of superstition . . . clinging to her with desperate tenacity.' Even elders, when charged for offences on the Lord's day, gave as an apology that they had entirely forgotten what day it was . . . There were great numbers of

alehouses, and it is to be feared that both old and young, when congregated in these, got drunk, quarrelled and fought, and so gave large business to the session.[95]

That ungodliness was rife in the county and that Forbes was likely to have met with limited success whilst there, is corroborated by Brodie's comment, shortly after Forbes had settled in Auldearn, that 'I prayd with Mr. Harie. 1. We mentiond the seed that had been soun in Cathnes, thoogh it should not appeir for mani years, yet that it might in due tym tak som effect.'[96] Caithness's ongoing need for reformed ministry is also indicated by Brodie's belief that without Forbes, it would quickly degenerate: 'In this matter of Mr. Harie Forbes, Lord' prayed Brodie again, 'I remitt the bridling, curbing, restraining of Cathnese's wickednes to Thee, for quhen thou calls him [Forbes], thou art bound to tak the care off them.'[97] Speculating more widely, we can also entertain the possibility that Forbes's task may have been hampered by the fact that the minister he replaced, John Smart, seems to have been well-liked. Having officiated at Wick since 1638, he was still living in or near the town six years after his dismissal and was evidently esteemed by his peers (who claimed he 'walked Christianlie as became him' and that they 'knew nothing scandalous in him'). Forbes's extremism, in this context, would have been rendered all the more grating for the fact that he imposed it having stepped into a martyr's shoes.[98]

In the last analysis, whatever the reasons that lay behind the resistance to Forbes's incumbency in both Caithness and Auldearn, we can be fairly certain that it would have left its mark upon him – particularly if it had been expressed aggressively. Although we have no evidence of the latter, there is no doubt that reformed congregations were not inhibited in this respect, and could express their disapproval over ministerial appointments overtly and even physically. In 1644, for example, members of one Lanarkshire congregation objected so strongly to the presbytery's choice of minister that they prevented access to the church through 'ramforcing' the 'doores of the kirk with clog stones and others the like materialls'; while on another occasion they 'violently stayed' the prospective minister from entering the pulpit, while the ringleader assured him, boldly, 'Howbeit yow be compared to a dog, yow sall not bark heir.'[99] Although Forbes's reception was unlikely to have been this dramatic, whichever way you look at it, he would have begun his ministry in Auldearn sensitized to parishional hostilities. And this would have made him highly defensive from the start.

Forbes, Magic and Witchcraft

With regard to Forbes's relationship with Isobel, what is also significant here is the fact that these tensions and hostilities could easily have played themselves out through the dynamics of witch-prosecution. One of the important functions of the reformed minister was to police magical practices, whether beneficent or maleficent, both through preaching and at the kirk sessions. In 1659 for example, in response to reports of magical practices, the presbytery of Deer in Buchan appointed 'several brethren to intimate from their pulpits that none of their congregations use such diabolical practices, and that they endeavour to convince them of the sinfulness of the same, and that they beware thereof or of any charmings, under the pain of the highest censures of the Church, that so henceforth none may pretend [claim] ignorance.'[100] There is no doubt that these 'intimations' were resented. John Guthry so angered several members of his congregation by preaching against 'superstition and fortune-telling' that they refused to properly acknowledge him in the street, one of them claiming that 'it was not the duty of the pastor to charge his people with witchcraft, sorcery, [or] turning of the riddell, and to utter calumnies against his flock'.[101] Meanwhile, the magical practitioners themselves were cautious, particularly given the severity of the punishments potentially involved. After performing a divinatory service, Kirkcudbright cunning woman Janet Miller (1658) – whose minister was a covenanter – told her client that the consultation 'should be kept close, especially from their minister, of whom she said he threatened to cause burn me for a witch; but (honest man), it is a wonder how he keeps his feet among them for there are more [magical operators] about him than he realises'.[102]

While we do not know precisely what views Forbes held concerning beneficent magic, as we have seen in CHAPTER THREE, he seems to have been very conscious of the threats posed by witchcraft and was quicker to diagnose it as a cause of symptoms, than some of his contemporaries, even when alternative explanations were available. We also know that he had considered himself to have personally been the victim of a magical attack, telling Brodie, only two months after his arrival in Auldearn in July 1655, about 'the work he had with witches' and how they had been 'lifting him, and bowing his bodi together in his bedd' and making 'his image of wax'.[103] As noted in CHAPTER THREE, whether Forbes's disclosure related to an attack that had occurred before or after his arrival in Auldearn is unclear, for Brodie does not tell us the names of the witches, nor the time or place where the attack supposedly occurred. But it is surely pertinent here that a number of entries in Brodie's diaries over this period suggest that witchcraft accusations were emerging in the Auldearn region at this time. Only two weeks before Forbes told Brodie about his witch-experiences, the latter, after dining with Moynes and Lethen, had 'spok of familiar spirits, divination, and witchcraft, and wer enquiring into the reasons of the Lord's great jealousie against that sin above anie other'.[104] And the fact that Brodie laments, with more than usual vigour, 'a land and a people that ar dround in sin and ingodlines' over this period, suggests that this discussion may have been prompted by local events.[105] That these events may have been specifically located in Auldearn can be further speculated from Brodie's claim that on the day after he spoke about witchcraft with Moynes and Lethen 'Park came to me, and we conferrd and soght the Lord together for our own souls, and for our families, and for that desolat place of Auldearn.'[106] This evidence of a possible 'mini witch panic' still does not tell us whether Forbes's perceived witch-attack related to present or pre-Auldearn events, for although the minister could have precipitated the panic through claiming that he was being attacked by local witches, he may merely have been prompted to share past witch-experiences with Brodie in response to the fact that witchcraft allegations were being made by others in the Auldearn region at the time. Nevertheless, that Forbes could have considered himself to be the victim of witchcraft within only two months of his arrival in the parish, does fit with the psychological profile we have developed here on a number of levels. As argued earlier, Forbes arrived from Caithness already sensitized to congregational hostilities and this sensitivity would have been reinforced by the poor reception he received in Auldearn. It would have been logical, given what we know of the man, for this sensitivity to manifest as an exaggerated fear of *maleficium*.

But whether or not the allegations made by Forbes were current, given the fact that he believed himself to have been a victim of witchcraft and was quick to identify its effects in others, we can be certain that he emphasized the evils of the crime from the Auldearn pulpit and that local magical practitioners were well aware of his opinions on the matter. Indeed, as speculated in CHAPTER THREE, the pattern of witchcraft reference in Brodie's diaries suggest that Forbes may have been the prime motivator in raising awareness of the crime in Auldearn post-1655, on both a popular and elite level. That Forbes's passion and influence in this respect did not generate high profile legal prosecutions – so far as we know – until 1662, after he had been resident in the parish for seven years, may not have been for want of trying. As we saw in CHAPTER ONE, historians have speculated that the 1661–2 surge in witchcraft trials reflected a build-up of resentment against suspects who had escaped prosecution under the more lenient English administration of the law prior to the Restoration. Certainly, Forbes could have pursued allegations of witchcraft and sorcery at the Auldearn sessions prior to this date, but it would have been harder for him to effect prosecutions. And it is therefore quite possible that his personal suspicions concerning witchcraft may have grumbled along at a largely sub-clinical level throughout the late 1650s and that, like many other ministers and lairds, when the legal system changed he seized his chance to gain satisfaction of the women, including perhaps Isobel, who had been a thorn in his side for many years.

Forbes's Big Secret

Thus far, the picture we have painted of Forbes is that of a man who was not only locked, as were many of his contemporaries, in an ambiguous and confrontative relationship with his parishioners, but one who was also more-than-usually sensitive to hostility and more-than-usually ready to confront his parishioners over allegations of witchcraft. But while these factors point to a high degree of anxiety and intensity, there is evidence to suggest that his position was further complicated by the fact that during his time in Auldearn he grappled with a number of pressing personal problems. First, like Park, the minister seems to have endured almost constant financial insolvency. The evidence suggests that neither he nor his brother inherited any land, there being no listing for them in the Sasine Index for Aberdeenshire, Banffshire and Moray, and whatever employment the former had undertaken in the intervening years since his graduation seems to have brought him little financial gain. As early as 1655, just after Forbes had been sworn in, Brodie wrote that he 'was informd of Mr H. Forbes his scarciti of money, and was displeasd with myself for not giving him som'; and other sources suggest that his fortunes did not improve, with Bain noting that after Forbes resigned his post 'Poor man, he seemed to be in great straits as regards his worldly circumstances, and all the efforts of Denoon, the burgh officer, and the magistrates were needed to make him pay his merchant's accounts'.[107] Similarly, an extant bond indicates that by 1663 he had been forced to borrow 700 merks from his niece Margaret, daughter to his long-deceased brother William.[108] In the two years leading up to Isobel's trial in 1662, these financial worries would have been increased by the threat of losing his livelihood as a result of the reinstatement of episcopacy. Certainly, between 1662–3 Forbes was deeply troubled by the necessity to either take or reject the oath to accept the new regime, with Brodie claiming, on more than one occasion, that he 'spok with Mr. Hari, and did see his exercis and trial [in this matter]'.[109] In the end, Forbes went with his principles and resigned his commission in 1663, from whence he went to Nairn, and then into obscurity in England. A passing diary entry by Brodie in 1678 ('Sir Lod. Gordoun cam heir this night. He told me he had sein Mr. H. Forbes in England. I considered this, and was humbld') suggests that he did not end up in the best of circumstances.[110]

But while Forbes's financial insolvency was likely to have put added strain on an already-tense relationship with his congregation, there is also evidence to suggest that his ministry in Auldearn may have also been aggravated by a conflict of a different kind altogether; a conflict that causes us to review the whole picture of Forbes we have constructed to date. In a nutshell, there is a slender but ultimately persuasive piece of evidence to suggest that during his residence in Auldearn, Forbes entered into an adulterous relationship with a servant. The story runs as follows. In the 1650s an educated and attractive young covenanter in her early twenties, named Katharine Collace, lived at the Bridge-end of Inshoch, near Auldearn, for four years, having been invited there by the Lady of Park to teach her daughters needlecraft.[111] In later life Collace – who Macdonald describes as a person of 'great force of character and fervent piety' – grew to be a considerable spiritual authority in her own right (even advising men such as Brodie on matters of the soul) and her godly memoirs were duly published in full in 1735.[112] In them she claims that while staying at Auldearn she:

> met with a sore blow from a Christian acquaintance and neighbour, who through emulation (I being noticed (though most undeservedly) by some fearing God, more than that person was) proved such an affliction to me that I was either necessitate to leave the place or suffer the way of God to be reproached.[113]

Katharine followed this rather obscure statement by describing how she then moved to Forres, where, with the benefit of hindsight and 'more occasion of privacy' she was able to acknowledge her own culpability in the troubling affair and isolate the event that had precipitated it:

> I found out the occasion for it to be the conversing with one highly reputed for piety, who took a liberty in his conversation which I could never go in with; but, having such an esteem of the person, his practice had some secret influence upon me, that put me out of that degree of tenderness the Lord had brought me to. That which blinded me, that I saw not this before,

was 1. I thought I was neighbour-like with these who were highly esteemed amongst us; and so I might soon be, for they were grossly departing from God, which afterwards appeared. 2. I was kept somewhat lively as to love towards the people of God, zeal for the cause of God, freedom in prayer. And this Satan suffered me to go on in, and likewise kept them in my eye, so that I might not suspect myself, and that he might by insecurity undermine me and draw my heart from God, I not being in an universally good frame.[114]

Particularly relevant to us here is the fact that in what is thought to be the oldest manuscript version of Katharine's memoirs (found in the Wodrow MSS), the author inserts the following paragraph after the phrase 'one highly reputed for piety, who took a liberty in his conversation which I could never go in with':

> This was Mr Hary Forbes minister of Auldearn whose wife had troubled her so to leave that place, and the said Mr Hary fell in adultery with his servant afterward as was thought, though Mrs Ross [Collace] sets not down their names nor this passage.[115]

Two eighteenth-century manuscripts of the memoirs simply clarify Collace's reference to 'one highly reputed for piety' with the note that 'she said Mr Hary'.[116]

There are problems with this reference: the accuracy of the Wodrow version cannot be verified and Collace's narrative, being discreet to the point of obscurity, is open to a number of interpretations. But taking the Wodrow additions and Collace's comments together we can nevertheless collate two plausible versions of events. First, we can speculate that Collace was a witness to a growing romantic attachment, which later became physical, between Forbes and his servant that she tolerated until, careful of Collace's reputation, Forbes's wife 'troubled her to leave that place'. From this perspective, the 'liberty' in the minister's conversation which Collace 'could never go in with' may have been some open reference to this relationship. Secondly, and more controversially, we can speculate that, in the light of the fact that Forbes was capable of adultery, the 'liberty in his conversation' which Collace could never 'go in with' was a direct proposition, to Collace, of a sexual nature. This second interpretation would explain, perhaps better than the first, why Forbes's wife was so keen to see her gone. Furthermore Collace's barely intelligible earlier claim that she 'met with a sore blow from a Christian acquaintance and neighbour, who through emulation (I being noticed (though most undeservedly) by some fearing God, more than that person was)' could suggest that Forbes's wife was also jealous of Collace because her husband was attracted by her piety.

The fact that Harry Forbes, the minister who had come to 'sow Christ's seed' in Auldearn, and a man who had the ear and protection of some of the most powerful covenanting figures in the county, committed adultery with a servant and possibly sexually propositioned other women, is a surprising revelation that invites us to speculate about his relationship with Isobel from new angles. What immediately springs to mind, of course, is that it may have some bearing on the fact that the confessions that Forbes elicited from Isobel contain the most detailed and explicit sexual passages to have come down to us from any witch-record, from anywhere in Britain, during the early modern period. While a proper analysis of the role that Forbes's sexual inclinations may have played in Isobel's interrogation will be deferred until CHAPTER NINE, when we look in more detail at the questioning process with regard to false confession, we can hazard a few speculations as to how his secret may have impacted on his pre-trial relationships with Isobel and the other members of the Auldearn congregation.

On the one hand, it is unlikely that Isobel was directly affected by Forbes's adultery. The possibility that she had been the servant who was the object of his attentions and that this generated the mixture of vivid sexual detail and enmity towards Forbes found in her confessions cannot, of course, be ruled out, but is unlikely and not supported by any of the evidence. However the tensions generated by Forbes's adultery may have impacted on her indirectly. Adultery was common enough in the period, and ministers, as everyone knew, were not exempt from this failing, with old Highland proverbs consistently emphasizing the fact that – both before and after the Reformation – clergy failed to live up to their own moral standards, as in 'It's a fine day when the fox preaches', 'The nearer the kirk, the faurer frae grace', 'It is not the priest's first story that should be believed' and, particularly relevant to the case in hand, 'It is his own child the priest baptizes first.'[117] But the high moral tone taken by the covenanters meant that, for them, the sin of adultery was particularly dangerous; the higher a minister elevated himself above the rest of humanity, the further he had to fall. The fact that Forbes succumbed to temptation, despite the extremism of his faith and his status as minister, suggests that his romantic or sexual nature must have been very strong.

But even more surprising is the fact that Forbes seems to have succeeded in hiding his sexual indiscretions from those around him. Brodie fails to mention them and, knowing his character, it is highly unlikely that he would have continued to be intimate with the minister had they been known to him. Similarly, Collace makes it clear that Forbes's advances corrupted her all the more because he was 'highly reputed for piety' and that 'having such an esteem of the person, his practice had some secret influence on me'. That Forbes presented an outward image of piety, during the 1650s at least, is further indicated by the fact that Thomas Hogg – a man of exacting spiritual principles whom Collace revered as her 'spiritual father' – is unlikely to have recommended Forbes for the Auldearn incumbency, or worshipped with him (as he did in November 1655 at Brodie Castle) if any whisper of sexual scandal had reached his ears.[118] Forbes's congregation seems to have been equally oblivious. As Todd has illustrated, reformed congregations were just as capable of vociferously protesting against the immorality of incumbent ministers as they were of protesting against the appointment of unwanted ones, and we can fairly confidently assume that if the minister's adultery had been common knowledge at this time, the Auldearn parishioners would have complained about it.[119] Indeed, those who had objected to his initial instalment may have been particularly keen to throw the first stone.

Forbes, then, carried a heavy secret. And unless we are to believe that his piety was a complete sham, we must speculate that he negotiated a powerful conflict between his religious zeal and his romantic or sexual drives. The way this conflict impacted upon his parishioners would have depended on how he managed it. Given the austerity of the covenanting doctrine, the most obvious scenario is that Forbes conformed to the stereotype of the 'repressed repressor', aggressively attempting (and sometimes failing) to control and suppress his own adulterous desires and, in the process, aggressively attempting to suppress the adulterous desires of others; a task that would not have been at all difficult, given the fact that adultery and fornication topped the list of crimes managed by the kirk sessions. Forbes may also have attempted to disassociate himself from his clandestine physical desires by attributing them to the Devil, a projection which could have caused him to exaggerate Satan's influence in the world and fuel his fear of magic and witchcraft. Simultaneously, through focusing on the role of the Devil as the seducer of witches, he would have gained the liberty to openly express an interest in the sexuality that he found so compelling and yet strove so hard to repress in himself. Either way, there may have been a deeply personal element to Forbes's exhortation, to his congregation in June 1663, to heed the words of Psalm 51:7: 'Wash me throghli, and I shall be clean; cleans me, and I shal be whiter then the snow.'[120]

But it is also possible that Forbes did not wrestle with his adulterous desires as energetically as might be expected and that, as countless clergymen have done before and since, he allowed himself to act upon them – perhaps even on a regular basis – by somehow justifying them to himself. This justification could have amounted to little more than avoidance, for despite all his intellectual energy, Forbes could have circumnavigated the manifold theological and moral issues that his actions raised by simply not thinking too much about them. It is also possible that, if Forbes was one of those reformed ministers who leant towards Arminianism and nurtured more traditional notions concerning repentance and salvation, he may have used his faith like some kind of 'forgiveness cash-dispenser': appealing to God every time he succumbed to the pleasures of the flesh, expressing remorse, considering himself to have gained absolution and then walking away 'throghli' washed and 'whiter then the snow' only to commit the same crime all over again. This pragmatic approach toward forgiveness was certainly adopted by some less godly parishioners on a daily basis.

But there is also another option. While many ministers harboured Arminian sympathies in this period, the fact that Forbes was among the minority unable to modify their Calvinism sufficiently to accommodate episcopacy after the Restoration, suggests that he may not have been among them. And if we assume this, then we must give some consideration to the controversial, but ultimately quite persuasive, possibility that Forbes was not only anti-Arminian but that he leaned toward antinomianism. Present in various forms from the earliest days of Christianity, antinomian beliefs – which, through various theological justifications, release an individual from the obligation to adhere to any form of moral law – emerged to particular prominence during the Reformation in response to Protestant theologies surrounding salvation. The Calvinist doctrine of predestination, in particular, when taken to its logical extreme, sailed dangerously close to these heretical beliefs, with critics arguing that the conviction that the elect had been chosen out of God's 'free grace and love, without any foresight of faith or good works or perseverance' implied that that no form of behaviour, however good or bad, would affect salvation status.[121] Heated debates about antinomianism featured in many of the religious controversies that emerged in sixteenth and seventeenth-century Europe, and although it remained heretical and did not become the official doctrine of any major Protestant sects, antinomian views were undoubtedly held, and even taught, by individual Protestants throughout the period.

Forbes was certainly both speculative and well-read enough to have engaged with the antinomian ideas that would have been circulating, in various guises, in Scotland at the time, and if he had taken them on board they undoubtedly would have made it easier for him to succumb to sexual temptation. On a basic level, they would have sanctioned his adultery on the rationale that if he was one of the saved then his sins would not affect his predestined path to heaven, while if he was damned they wouldn't matter because he was going to hell anyway. If Forbes was convinced (as his richeous stance suggests he was) that he was one of God's elect, then he may have gained further comfort from the more extreme antinomian belief that, by virtue of being God's chosen people, the elect were literally incapable of evil: it being 'as impossible . . . to recognize the existence of evil in themselves as in God. For in truth, they were part of the divine'.[122] Taken to its extremity, this theological position stretched the Protestant emphasis on the supreme authority of man's personal relationship with God to its ultimate distortion. When deciding on a course of action, extreme antinomians were not obliged to look to moral law or social convention, but only to the 'divine grace acting within them'. And this divine grace expressed itself through 'impulse', in the sense that: 'what they wanted to do was right and should be done'.[123] Unsurprisingly, this type of self-deification, however cogently argued, could lead a man or woman into some very perilous places. As David Stevenson emphasizes:

> the dangers of their beliefs were obvious. If to act on any impulse that stirred them was right, they 'were left alone and defenceless in the world of their own instincts and desires. Given their premises, it was hard to escape the conclusion that every one of their whims was a divine impulse. For how could they dare to resist the will and the power of the spirit exerted in them?' Not only were they free to obey every impulse, they were obliged to do so.[124]

Although there is no direct evidence to support the argument that Forbes was an antinomian, Collace's intimation that the minister was attracted by her 'piety' certainly suggests that the minister did not dissociate his adulterous desires from his religious vocation, as does the fact that his unwelcome advances were made 'in an environment 'lively' with 'zeal for the cause of God' and 'freedom in prayer'.[125] The seemingly self-possessed and open way in which Forbes propositioned the zealous and theologically-informed Collace would also suggest a confidence born of robust inner belief. Collace would, after all, have taken much more convincing, in the matter of adultery, than an illiterate serving girl. This interpretation would also explain why Forbes's wife seems to have tolerated, or at least not blown the whistle on, his indiscretions, perhaps being held in unwilling thrall, on the question of their morality, by her husband's intellectual superiority. It also helps us to understand how Forbes could have squared his hidden adultery with his pious ministerial aspirations. Stevenson's speculations on the antinomianism of Edinburgh siblings Thomas and Jean Weir (both of whom combined outward piety with a hidden life of sexual immorality, for which they were executed in 1670), certainly give us an insight into how Forbes may have negotiated his double life:

> The assumption that this was so [that is, that they were antinomians] would explain much in their [the Weirs'] lives. Their crimes would then not be crimes, for they could do no wrong. Their godliness and devotion to the covenants would not be hypocrisy if they were convinced that they had received divine grace and were justified in all they did. The fact that they kept their crimes secret and outwardly obeyed moral law would be merely a matter of expediency to guard themselves against the reprobate who did not understand the divine will so well as they did . . . Thus the seemingly unbearable tension between their private and public lives may be reconciled.[126]

That Forbes nurtured this kind of profound antinomian conviction would also help to explain how he managed to persuade stern critics like Brodie and Hogg – who were, as we have seen in CHAPTER FIVE, ever on the alert for insincere spiritual motivations – of his moral integrity, despite his adulterous private life. According to this hypothesis, Forbes's impression of piety would have been convincing precisely because it was rooted in the fact that he genuinely believed himself to be pious.

Ultimately, in lieu of further information, we do not know which of the above explanations, or combination of explanations, best applied to Forbes. But as it stands, the evidence strongly suggests that, so far as his family, friends and parishioners were concerned, the minister's duplicity and capacity for psychological evasion made him a very dangerous man.

The Repercussions

In the last analysis, we do not know the specific events that led to the breakdown of relations between Isobel and Harry Forbes and the Laird of Park. As in so many cases, the nuances of the interactions between authority figures and the poor, when taking place outside the law courts, were not deemed worthy of recording and are absent from the historical documents. But we do know that severe social and environmental pressures of the kinds we have described at some length in this chapter, can put an unimaginable strain on human relations. And in such heated, intense arenas threads of causality can easily lead to blame. To take a simple example. If a tense and paranoid Forbes had hauled Isobel's mother or aunt or sister up before the sessions on charges of magical healing or witchcraft, and the unfortunate woman had been whipped through the streets of Auldearn or banished from the town 'nevir to returne under the pane of death', or even 'bund to a staik and hangit to the death and burnt to asches' – who would Isobel have held responsible? God? The king of the fairies? The Devil? Or the man who had denounced her relative from the pulpit, ordered her arrest and led the interrogations against her?[127] More seriously still, if a beleaguered, self-interested Laird of Park had urged his tacksman to coerce John Gilbert or the tenant he served for his full quota of grain rent in a poor year, and grain supplies in the Gowdie household had then run out in March instead of April, and Isobel's children were, as a result of this, less well-nourished than usual and during one of the frequent epidemics some of these children had died – who would Isobel have blamed? Even if she had never met the Laird of Park personally, it is easy to see how she could have traced responsibility for her children's deaths to his door. These types of grievance, stacked one on top of the other, season after season, year after year, and even generation after generation, would have created literally unbearable resentments. And if women like Isobel nurtured such resentments, then what did they do with them? Would they have, to return to the original question posed at the beginning of this chapter, expressed them through the performance of *maleficium*?

8

The Ethics of Malevolence

We cannot begin to explore the question as to whether Isobel and her contemporaries expressed their resentments through the performance of *maleficium* without first understanding the fact, largely foreign to modern Western mentalities, that in early modern Scotland many people considered it quite appropriate for an individual to express resentments through revenge. In the late-sixteenth century, the anonymous author of *The Historie and Life of King James the Sext* lamented that the Highlanders 'ar sa crewall in taking of revenge that nather have thay regarde to person, eage, tyme, or caus; sa ar thay generallie all sa far addictit to thair awin tyrannicall opinions'; while over a century later, in 1726, the traveller Edward Burt complained that: 'The ordinary natives are, for the most part, civil when they are kindly used, but most mischievous when offended, and will hardly ever forgive a provocation, but seek some open or secret revenge.'[1] These are extreme examples, the former tinged with prejudice and the second with condescension, and Jenny Wormald has illustrated that negotiation and settlement, based on the principle 'of compensation rather than retribution' played a far more prominent role in Highland feuding than has often been assumed.[2] But nevertheless, they reflect a general truth. Despite the lamentations of the church, the censure of the courts and the fact that, according to Wormald, 'men still desired to die in their beds', the essentially warrior mentality of the Scots' Celtic and Germanic forebears still held sway, particularly in the Highlands, and many believed that it was a slur on an individual's valour, family honour and pride to allow an offence to pass without retribution.[3] Trial testimonies testify to this tough logic, with Renfrewshire man William Fergison claiming in 1650, for example, that Margaret Finalson told him to tell her enemies that 'if anything ailed hire [Margaret], hire sones perhaps would be sholdiers, and if they took not amends of it, it mycht be that the nynetten degree of her kind would revenge it'.[4] The importance of the Scottish revenge-ethic is also vividly illustrated in oral and written literature, particularly verses and stories charting the exploits of the medieval warrior, William Wallace. Accounts of Wallace were incredibly popular, with the earliest printed version of his adventures (the late fifteenth-century epic poem by the medieval bard 'Blind Harry') going through no less than twenty-three editions between 1508 and 1707, with Hamilton's 1722 adaptation going on to become, according to Elspeth

King, 'the most commonly owned book in Scotland, next to the Bible'.[5] This tome, proudly displayed on cottage bookshelves and undoubtedly recounted from memory by countless fireside bards, is in many ways one long, passionate and bloody hymn to the satisfactions of revenge, with verse upon verse reinforcing the fact that 'A fierce revenge bends ev'ry warrior's bow, And steely vengeance sends him to the foe'.[6] In the following passage, for example, Wallace responds to the discovery that his wife has been killed by the English:

> To thee I swear, this sword I'll never sheath,
> Till I revenge my dearest, dearest's death.
> Heavens! what new toils of death and war remain!
> Rivers of floating blood and hills of slain!
> But steel'd with rage, to slaughter let us fly,
> And for her sake there shall ten thousand die.[7]

Although the revenge-ethic could prolong suffering through precipitating bitter cycles of hatred, it survived because it could also serve a purpose. Working with the my-pain-is-eased-by-causing-my-enemy-pain dynamic, it provided a more immediate and simply-executed route to emotional relief than the abstract principle of forgiveness counselled by the church. Moreover, as a sign of strength, successfully executed retribution could deter an enemy from further aggression, in the short term at least, thereby fostering intermittent social stasis. From this perspective, revenge acted as a form of self-defence. Although in the contemporary West it is, quite rightly, *de rigueur* to condemn revenge and support diplomatic solutions to conflict, it is important to remember that, as psychologist Steven Pinker has noted, the modern ability to resist vengeful impulses may have more to do with improved living conditions and the fact that 'life has become longer and less awful', than with evolved ethical sensitivities. As Pinker emphasizes (in reference to the work of James Payne), 'when pain, tragedy and early death are expected features of one's own life' – as they certainly were in early modern Europe – 'one feels fewer compunctions about inflicting them on others'.[8]

In this context, it is not unreasonable to assume that if Isobel or someone dear to her had suffered or was suffering as a result of actions taken by either the Laird of Park or Harry Forbes, that she would have considered it perfectly logical to resolve the matter through self-defensive revenge. But as a woman and a farmer's wife, what were her options in this respect? There is no doubt that some men in her position may have resorted to physical violence, whether expressed through direct attack or indirectly through the theft of cattle or goods and so on. Many men seem to have gone about primed for defensive action by carrying swords and daggers (Highlanders, for example, taking weapons into church well into the eighteenth century) and spent their leisure time developing prowess at arms; with ministers like John Welsh condemning those 'who used to go to the Bow-Butts and Archery, on Sabbath Afternoon'.[9] The warrior attributes of physical courage and skill with weaponry, whether longbow, musket or blade, were still core male aspirations of the time, and the ways in which men like Wallace could 'dang out' their enemies' brains and leave their 'mangled' bodies 'welt'ring in their gore' with a single swing of their broadswords were the meat of many proud verses.[10]

But for women like Isobel, danging out brains and leaving enemies sweltering in gore was not a viable option. Although we have examples of women expressing their frustrations physically in this period, with witchcraft trials sometimes describing them striking officers and physically resisting arrest, realistically, unless her alleged feuds with Park and Forbes were linked to wider inter-clan disputes or the interests of more powerful allies with manpower at their disposal, there would have been little to gain through physical violence. There would also have been little to gain through recourse to the disciplinary authorities. Although the kirk sessions could be very adept at resolving community tensions, their reach was still limited, and complaints against authority figures such as ministers and lairds were hindered by the fact that these were the very people who presided over both the sessions and their secular equivalents, the barony and sheriff courts. Moreover, if the individual who sought justice was a magical practitioner, or even just an individual who just did not generally conform to covenanting mores, they would have stood outside the law at the best of times, and any attempt to obtain legal redress would have been even more doomed to failure. There was cold truth in the old Gaelic proverb 'He that quarrels with the gentry is a miserable man.'[11]

But there was a third, more viable, form of recompense that was freely available to both men and women in the period, whatever their financial or social status. It was a form of recompense that is particularly relevant in Isobel's case, because it was one for which women, and particularly verbally-gifted women, were supremely qualified. For however powerless and however outside the law a woman may have been, no one could prevent her from exacting her revenge through the use of words.

The Weapon of Words

In early modern Scotland, a centuries-old interaction between warrior mentalities and vibrant bardic traditions had given rise to two distinct but overlapping traditions of ritualised, public, verbal aggression. Flyting, which was the less malign of the two, involved a staged bout of colourful, reciprocal insult-calling between aggrieved parties. Cursing, which is what we are concerned with here, was far more serious, and involved an individual openly and verbally wishing harm upon their enemy. It is hard for the modern Western mind to understand the potency behind the verbal malediction or curse, but at a time when it was widely believed that both speech and action could, through occult emanations, manipulate the physical world either directly or through application to a supernatural being, the spoken word was a formidable force, underpinning the efficacy of not only the curse but also the larger cultural edifices of charming, oath-swearing and of course, prayer itself.

The result of a uniquely creative fusion between aggression and verbal skill, traditional Scottish cursing reached a level of sophistication unparalleled elsewhere in the British Isles. In *Curses, Lucks and Talismans*, Gilbert Lockhart claimed that

'Cursing on the grand scale, as distinguished from occasional blasphemy, is more commonly encountered among Gaels than among the Saxons . . . The best Curses of all are to be found in the Highlands of Scotland'.[12] Maledictions featured prominently in the prophecies of popular figures like Coinneach Odhar and Thomas Rhymer, and emerged in songs, ballads and tales. They were also a feature of general verbal interchange. The Larger Catechism of 1648 found it necessary to condemn 'all sinful cursing, oaths, vows, and lots'; while Brodie, along with many other pious men of his day, lamented that 'profannes, lying, cursing, whordoms, loosnes in words and conversation' was everywhere.[13] Two centuries later, the practice was still widespread enough for the folklorist John Gregorson Campbell to compile a list of over twenty-four curses that 'are of common use'.[14]

While the reformed church took a severe view of cursing it also, ironically, reinforced contemporary belief in its efficacy and the validity of its use as a vehicle of moral retribution. The Old Testament, newly-translated into English for the edification of the people, gave parishioners access to some of the most blood-curdling imprecations that have ever been committed to paper, with Deuteronomy, in particular, devoting many chapters to charting the dire consequences of being condemned by God's wrath. In Chapter 28, verses 15–22, to pick a typical passage, Moses tells his people:

> But it shall come to pass, if thou wilt not hearken unto the voice of the Lord . . . Cursed shalt thou be in the city, and cursed shalt thou be in the field. Cursed shall be thy basket and thy store. Cursed shall be the fruit of thy body, and the fruit of thy land, the increase of thy kine and the flocks of thy sheep. Cursed shalt thou be when thou comest in, and cursed shalt thou be when thou goest out . . . The Lord shall smite thee with a consumption, and with a fever, and with an inflammation, and with an extreme burning, and with the sword, and with blasting, and with mildew; and they shall pursue thee until thou perish.

From here on, the myriad methods through which God would wreak revenge on those who disobeyed his word are listed for a further forty-five blistering verses before concluding with the promise that persistent sinners would be banished to Egypt and sold as slaves. Similarly, in Chapter 32, verses 23–5, the eloquent Moses claims how a spurned God will proclaim:

> I will heap mischiefs upon them; I will spend mine arrows upon them. They shall be burnt with hunger, and devoured with burning heat, and with bitter destruction: I will also send the teeth of beasts upon them, with the poison of serpents of the dust. The sword without, and terror within, shall destroy both the young man and the virgin, the suckling also with the man of gray hairs.

In the reformed church, Yahweh's penchant for cursing was bluntly emphasized as a way of intimidating parishioners to conform. The Larger Catechism's exhortation that 'Every sin, even the least . . . deserves His wrath and curse, both in this life, and that which is to come' was standard, as was its warning that man needs to repent in order to 'escape the wrath and curse of God due to us for the transgression of the law'.[15] Such condemnations entered into general godly discourse, with Brodie blithely noting, during private prayer: 'Cursed be they that love not the lord Jesus.'[16]

In the early modern period popular curses were seldom recorded for their own sake, with scholarly interest in this aspect of folk culture not really developing until the nineteenth century. But because men and women who used curses were often suspected of witchcraft, and the alleged use of curses was seen as supporting evidence in the case against a witch, they were often recorded in witchcraft records. Here they are usually short and pithy, but through the vivid employment of metaphor and imagery they really pack a punch, with examples such as: 'the devill grind the said Robert as small as gunn powder among the mill wheeles'; 'within few dayis his bones sould be raiking about the bankis'; 'I would give a pennanc of my flesh for all my dayes to have amends of the'; 'tho shooe hade twentie bairnes there would never one live of them'; and 'I ask God and our dear Lady that the next child Isobell Murray shall bear to her husband be like a wedder [sheep]'.[17] Other curses could be more long-winded. Although the old Gaelic proverb laments 'Its little we complain though we suffer much', there is no doubt that some people, when they suffered, complained a great deal indeed. The following curse, that allegedly 'brust forth' from the loquacious Orcadian Thomas Cors in 1643, would not have been out of place in Deuteronomy:

> thow art the highest man that ever thow salt be! Thow ar going to shear thy corne, but it sall never doe yow good! Thow art going to sett hous with thy wyff – ye sall have no joy on of on uther! Ye sall not keip yow and hir, ye sall have such ane meit-will and sall have nothing to eat, but be fain to eat grass under the stanes and wair [seaweed] under the bankis.[18]

Curses could also be reinforced through physical actions, with falling on the knees or shaking the hair loose being the commonest accompaniments. After a dispute with neighbour William Holland, Orkney woman Helen Wallis allegedly 'tore the curtch off her head: and put it under her belt, shook her hair about her ears, ran to the Lady Chapel hard by, and went thrice about it upon her bare knees, praying cursings and maledictions to light upon the said William'; while in 1633, Orkney witch Bessie Skebister was charged that her victim 'has nevir bein weill since ye curst hir, or sheuk your hair lous'.[19] The following account of a progeny curse, recorded by the nineteenth-century folklorist J. G. Campbell, illustrates just how dramatic and intimidating the physically enacted public curse could be. During an altercation with some Tiree villagers a tinker's wife:

> Threw off her cap and allowed her hair to fall over her shoulders in wild disorder. She then bared her knees, and falling on them to the ground, in a praying attitude, poured forth a torrent of wishes that struck awe into all who heard her. She imprecated: 'Drowning by sea and conflagration by land; may you never see a son follow your body into the graveyard, or a daughter to mourn your death. I have made my wish before this, and I will make it now, and there was not yet a day that I did not see my wish fulfilled,' etc.[20]

It is of course difficult to determine how far the curses that appear in witch-records reflected genuine practices and how far they were merely attributed, that is, fabricated by angry neighbours eager for conviction. But the possibility that the former represented some kind of social reality is supported by the fact that scholars largely uninvolved in witchcraft paradigms have associated cursing with two factors that also happen to be among the defining features of the stereotypical witch: being powerless and being female. With regard to powerlessness, both Campbell and Lockhart state that cursing was a socially-sanctioned method through which those who were materially disadvantaged could gain revenge on an enemy that it would otherwise be impossible to defeat. This dynamic is powerfully illustrated in the following traditional waulking song, in which a woman who has been raped by her brother anticipates the warped justice she will receive at the kirk sessions the following day. 'Tomorrow I go before the session', she laments, 'there will be few to take my part and many more to do me injury. The minister will be standing there. Sickness take him – even if it be the fever and he never rises again!'[21] In addition, the traditional belief that an undeserved curse could not harm you but a deserved curse could, gave the procedure a rudimentary moral sanction, with this ethos clearly enabling a mid seventeenth-century Elgin woman to curse her neighbour with a clear conscience: the presbytery records stating that 'sitting doun on her bear knees [she] had oftin prayed God to curs her iff she had don wrong to the said Jannat and God to curse the said Jannat iff she had wronged her'.[22] The moral unease that the threat of the curse could instil in the rich and powerful – however disadvantaged the deliverer – is well illustrated in the following diary entry, recorded by Brodie in 1671: 'A poor man did meit me, which fel doun on his knees. The dislyk of the postur did mak me hast from him, and quhen I returned, he was gon. I was chalendgd for not supplying him.'[23] Meanwhile, the association between cursing and women has been rationalized by Campbell as illustrative of the fact that pre-modern women (presumably by virtue of their social status and physical limitations) were more accustomed to 'impotent rage'. But also pertinent here is the fact that recent research into gender-related differences in brain function has confirmed that, as a result of structural differences resulting from prenatal exposure to sex hormones, women's verbal memory skills and (with regard to certain tasks) verbal fluency, are superior to those of men.[24] Therefore we can add to Campbell's insight the fact that women were more likely to have used curses, not only because it was one of the few options open to them, but also because, by virtue of their generally higher verbal facility, they were simply very good at it.

Isobel's Beautiful Curses

In Isobel's case it is pertinent that the twenty-four maleficent rhymes that form such a prominent part of her narrative can be seen to conform, in many ways, to contemporary popular cursing traditions. In her second confession Isobel states that she and her companions attempted to harm Harry Forbes by reciting:

he is lyeing in his bed and he is lyeing seik and sore, let him lye intill his bed, two monethis (*damaged – words missing*) dayes mor 2lj let him lye intill his bed let him lye intill it seik and sore let him lye intill his bed two monethes thrie dayes mor, 3lie he sall lye intill his bed he sall lye in it seik and sore, he sall lye intill his bed two m . . . (*damaged – words missing*) and thrie dayes mor . . .

She also states that the charm was accompanied by what we can now identify as traditional curse ritual, concluding the above passage with:

q[uhe]n we haid learned all thes wordis from the divell, as s[ai]d is, we fell all dow(n) (*damaged – words missing*) kneis, w[i]th owr hear down ower owr showlderis and eyes, and owr hands lifted up and owr (*damaged – words missing*) the divell, and said the fors[ai]dis wordis thryse ower to the divell striktlie ag[ains]t masterie forbes (*damaged – words missing*). (45/8)

But although Isobel's maleficent charms are undoubtedly linked to popular cursing traditions, they differ from those found in other witch-records, and from the curses recorded by later folklorists, in one key respect. The traditional curse, as found in the latter sources, is usually a public affair, performed within earshot of the intended victim in spontaneous response to an affront and reported by witnesses or observers. But Isobel's curses seem to have been performed out of earshot of their intended victims, with no reference to the affront that may have stimulated them and, most notably of all, are not reported by external witnesses but by Isobel herself. This type of 'private cursing', as we can term it here, seldom appears in witchcraft records or indeed any other contemporary documentation relating to popular belief. And this leaves us with two options. Either we can deduce that, as modelled by Isobel, it seldom appears in the sources because it was not very common, and that her devotion to this art was highly anomalous; or we can deduce that it seldom appears in the sources because it was a covert tradition – by definition unobserved and unrecorded; only becoming visible in Isobel's case because she was unusually loquacious and her interrogators exceptionally curious and facilitating.

In exploring this question, we are hampered by the fact that, while recognized as a historical phenomenon, private cursing practices have received little attention from historians. Although some have argued that they were likely to have been more common than the evidence suggests (Kieckhefer noting, with regard to the Middle Ages, that because private curses 'would be uttered in secrecy . . . they probably show up in the court records much less often than they were actually used'), the lack of proof has generally inhibited speculations as to their nature and extent.[25] But nevertheless, it is possible to gain insights into this dilemma by way of the back door as it were, through circumventing cursing, witchcraft and the early modern period altogether, and taking a different route entirely. In the nineteenth century folklorists collected a wide range of charms used by contemporary Highlanders, and a surprisingly large number of these were concerned with protecting humans, animals and land from the harmful effects of the 'evil eye'. Beliefs surrounding the evil eye can seem patently ridiculous to modern Western mentalities, but in early modern Scotland, as in most pre-industrial societies throughout the world, inter-personal conflict gained an ominous intensity through the widespread conviction that harm-bringing occult emanations could be directed through the eyes. In other words, someone who didn't like you could physically harm you simply by looking at you with evil intent. Nineteenth-century sources reveal that the evil-eye-averting charms employed by contemporary Highlanders generally worked on the rationale of magical transference. Just as magical practitioners claimed to cure the sick by transferring maladies onto something else, so Highlanders protected themselves from the malevolent emanations of the evil eye by deflection. Many such averting charms involved diverting the sent evil onto natural objects, such as rocks, woods or animals, but the overwhelming majority also involved sending it directly back to the sender, as if reflecting it back to them in a mirror. What is particularly relevant to our study of Isobel is that the latter charms, which can be termed 'evil-eye-reversal charms', resembled curses in the sense that they listed, often in vivid and forensic detail, all the harms which the returned evil would wreak on its human target. In a typical example that, according to J. G. Campbell, was used 'with slight variations on the part of different individuals' in nineteenth-century Tiree, ten of the charm's thirty lines are devoted to listing its devastating effects:

> Whoever has thee under lock
> Of eye or malice or envy,
> On themselves may it fall –
> On their goods and on their children,
> On their juice and on their fatness,
> On their long white ground,
> On their choicest herd,
> Their white-backed cows,
> Their sheep
> And pointed goats.[26]

Some of these charms, as in the following extract recorded by Campbell's contemporary Alexander Carmichael, depict this deflection of sent evil with surprising brutality:

> May it lie on their back-head joints,
> May it lie on their back-leg sinews,
> May it lie upon each one of those things in the world
> That these people love better than all else.[27]

With regard to Isobel, what is particularly significant is that these evil-eye-reversal charms were essentially private affairs. Unlike the classic curse, they were not performed in public, in response to a direct affront. Nor were they performed in the presence of the aggressor. As a method of deflecting from a distance harm delivered from a distance, they were most frequently performed in the home or close to the persons or objects that needed protection. And as such, evil-eye-reversal charms can be seen to represent a popular tradition of private cursing.

Again, the very private nature of this tradition makes it difficult to assess its prevalence. But the large numbers of evil-eye-reversal charms collected by folklorists from all parts of the Highlands strongly suggests that they were relatively widely used. Support for this view can also be garnered from a more unlikely quarter. One of the primary motivations driving the nineteenth-century Scottish folklorists was the desire to celebrate Highland culture, and particularly oral traditions, in the face of both imminent extinction and English condescension. As a consequence, some folklorists – the most notable being Alexander Carmichael (*Carmina Gadelica*, 1900) – have been accused of manipulating their sources in an effort to elevate their literary value and increase their aesthetic and romantic impact: adding lines, improving metres and rhymes and so on. More recent scholars, such as John MacInnes, have ameliorated ongoing criticisms of Carmichael's work, but what is significant here is that whatever the degree of the latter's manipulations, if his purpose in writing, as Ronald Black has recently articulated it, was 'to display the Gael in the best possible light', then it would surely have been against his interests to advertize either the number or malevolent content of evil-eye-averting charms uncovered during his research.[28] It is very telling then, in this context, to note that the *Carmina Gadelica* contains no less than thirty-three vivid and aggressive charms specifically concerned with deflecting the evil eye, with many other charms making reference to evil-eye beliefs.

Given the fact that evil-eye-reversal charms were being performed in Carmichael's time, it is hardly surprising to find that they were also performed in previous centuries, though here the evidence is fragmentary. As early as the tenth century, Aleffric, the abbot of Eynsham, condemned the popularity of what he termed 'cursing charms', while charms against the evil eye can also be found in fifteenth-century Scottish manuscripts.[29] In 1774, the minister George Low observed that in the Shetland Isles 'They are afraid of hurt either in person or goods from the evil eye, and have particular ceremonies to avert the malignity of it, but pretend to make a great mystery of their rites.'[30] We also find occasional examples in witchcraft records. The trial dittays of Bute cunning woman Margaret NcWilliam (1662) state that 'she confesses haveing the charme for ane ill ey quhilk she repeited over in the yrish language but that she made no use thair of but to her selfe only'; while in Orkney in 1616, Jonet Irving allegedly confessed to the court that the Devil had told her 'if she bure ill-will to onie bodie,' to look on them 'with opin eyis and pray evill for thame in his name'.[31] Some of these charms clearly deflected sent evil onto both inanimate objects and the men or women deemed responsible for sending it. The following seventeenth-century example from Robert Kirk, which we have already encountered in CHAPTER FOUR, is standard:

> HE that gives warmth and prosperity, turn from thee all hill-Envy, (or Fayrie-Envy) all Son-malice, all man-malice, all Woman malice, my own malice with them; as the Wind turns about the Hillock, Thy Evil Turne from Thee a Third part on this Man, and third part on that Woman, a Third on Waters; a Third on Woods, a third on the Brown Harts of the Forrest, and a third on the grey stones.[32]

Another contemporary charm, recorded in 1650 and allegedly cited by Fifeshire woman Marion Cunningham 'each night when she went to bed', is also strongly suggestive of the human-targeting evil-eye-reversal charm:

> Out throw toothe and out throwe tongue,
> Out throw liver and out throw longue,
> And out throw halie harn pan;
> I drank of this blood instead of wine;
> Thou shalt have multifire all thy dayes syne,
> The bitter and the baneshaw
> And manie evil yt no man knowes.[33]

Isobel's Evil-Eye Charms

Isobel's maleficent charms differ little in tone, intention or language from the private evil-eye-reversal charms found in both early modern and nineteenth-century sources. In some cases, the similarities are very close indeed. For example, an extract from a nineteenth-century verse concerning the deflection of sent evil back onto a person's livestock or land, reads:

> Tis my prayer each evening
> Both Sunday and week-day
> That the she-fool be stowed
> With the rabble of the graves;
> Shortened be the life
> Of herself and her people,
> Her goats and her sheep,
> Her stock and her kine:
> Be they stolen and plundered,
> Be they blasted and burned![34]

Some of Isobel's verses also target the farm and livestock of the intended victim, and employ comparable metre, phraseology and imagery in order to do so. Isobel claimed to have recited the following words (set out here in stanza form to facilitate comparison) when placing 'haiked flesh' and 'pairingis of naillis' into her neighbour's dung hill to 'tak the furit away':

> we putt this in intill this ham,
> in o[u]r lord the divellis nam,
> the first handis th[a]t handles the
> brunt and scalded sall they be,
> we sall distroy hows and hald,
> w[i]th the sheip and noat intill the fold

&litl sall com to the for
of all the rest of the litl store. (49/29)

But although situating Isobel's cursing charms under the general umbrella of evil-eye-reversal charms makes it easier to accept that they may have been 'genuine' (in the sense that she may have performed them, in private, prior to arrest), in order to take this hypothesis fully on board we still need to negotiate the problem of reciprocity. Although evil-eye-reversal charms have, in all periods, been condemned by the church, among the common folk they were justified as self-defensive responses to magical aggression. It was, to put it bluntly, a simple case of 'an evil eye for an evil eye'. But Isobel's cursing charms do not seem to have been simple deflections or reversals of magical attack. The primary targets of Isobel's verbal malice were Harry Forbes and the Laird of Park, and whatever offences these men had committed against Isobel we can be sure that they were not – and that Isobel would have known that they were not – magical ones. Therefore, by cursing Forbes and Park Isobel diverted from the rationale that underpinned the evil-eye-charm template by responding magically to a non-magical offence.

But if we stand back and consider the problem within the context of cursing traditions in general, this difference dissolves. As we have explored earlier, public curses were a form of magico-verbal revenge used when more direct forms of retaliation, such as physical force, were not possible or desirable. And as a consequence they were characteristically used by the poor against the rich or the physically weak against the physically strong, in defence against material wrongs such as the refusal of alms, the demanding of extortionate rents, miscarriages of justice and so on. Given the fact that public cursing, from this perspective, was characteristically a magical response to a generally non-magical offence, then there is no reason why private cursing could not have operated in the same way. If an individual could mutter cursing charms, in private, to deflect sent harm onto an individual believed to have threatened them through evil-eye emanations, then they could just as logically mutter charms, in private, to harm an individual believed to have threatened them in some other way. And on the back of these speculations we can argue that, as opposed to being anomalous in this respect, Isobel's confessions give us a unique insight into a dark, and generally neglected, dimension of pre-modern Scottish charming traditions.

Ritual *Maleficium*

This diversion into cursing traditions has provided us with a partial answer to the question posed at the beginning of the last chapter: did Isobel and her companions express their resentments through the performance of maleficent magic? By virtue of the fact that it was believed to cause harm by manipulating occult forces, cursing can be classified as a form of verbal *maleficium*; and by arguing that Isobel may have genuinely performed the cursing charms recorded in her confessions we have, in effect, argued that she performed some of the *maleficium* described.

But in giving Isobel's verbal *maleficium* the green light, as it were, can we now go on and do the same for the physically-enacted *maleficium* with which it was so closely entwined? In other words, if we can accept that Isobel may have voiced a curse to harm an enemy, can we also accept that she may have beaten wet rags to raise winds, cast knotted threads to sabotage dye vats, made potions to steal fertility and roasted clay figures in order to kill a child? In approaching this question we confront the same obstacle as in our analysis of the charms: the very private nature of the crimes described. At no point in Isobel's confessions do we find any references to the fact that her phys-ically-enacted *maleficium* was witnessed by outside observers. With the exception of her accomplice, no-one seems to have stood before the interrogators and claimed that they had seen Isobel making a *corp creadh* or brewing maleficent potions.

The fact that Isobel's physically-enacted *maleficium* was not witnessed is wholly standard. In the majority of witchcraft records, as they emerged throughout early modern Europe, maleficent acts were alleged as opposed to empirically observed. Indeed, according to Norman Cohn, it was this 'almost unprovable' nature of grass-roots *maleficium* that ensured that, despite being practised throughout the Middle Ages, it remained outside the law courts until it was gathered up by the momentum of the early modern witch hunts.[35] This lack of proof is also, of course, largely responsible for the historiographical reluctance to engage with *maleficium*-performance as a genuine historical phenomenon.

But from our perspective, having entertained the possibility that Isobel may have performed the verbal *maleficium* described in the confessions, the admission that she may have also performed the physically-enacted *maleficium* described alongside it is only a small step away. Verbal and physical magical rites were often indistinguish-able in the period by virtue of the fact that they were usually performed together, coming as a mutually beneficial magical double act. Charms were usually accompa-nied by physical ritual, and physical ritual was usually accompanied by charms, with Maxwell-Stuart going so far as to state, in reference to early modern Scotland, that 'Charming involves the use of both words and actions – without words, the actions are much less effective and indeed such an operation cannot be accounted as "charm-ing"'.[36] The articulation and strengthening of a charm through physical ritual did not just extend to the use of movements and gesture, but also to the use of ritual objects, and Scottish witch-records contain many descriptions of magical practitioners mut-tering charms over stones, cords and other objects, and placing them in certain places, to imbue them with magical power. The same fusion of charm, action and object runs throughout Isobel's confessions, in relation to both beneficent and maleficent magic. We have already seen that in order to take away the fruit of her neighbours' dunghills she did not only place concoctions of minced flesh and nail pairings inside them but also chanted maleficent verses as she did so; in order to help her husband gain a good market price for his beef she did not only 'put a swellowes feather in the hyd of the beast' but also accompanied this action with the words 'putt owt this beeff in the div-ellis name, th[a]t meikle silver and good pryce com home'; and in order to raise winds, she and her companions did not only 'tak a rag of cloth and weitis it in water' and then 'tak a beetle and knokis the rage on a stone' but also chanted, thrice over, 'I

knok this ragg upon this stone, to raise the wind in the divellis name, it sall not lye
untill I please again'.

But while it is relatively easy to assume that beneficent charms were associated with
physical ritual, can we assume the same for the maleficent? In one sense, the immediate
answer is yes. As we have seen earlier, the potency of the public curse was traditionally
enhanced through the simple but powerful physical ritual of falling to the knees and
shaking the 'hair lous'. We also have evidence – though here more fragmentary – that
physical ritual was traditionally incorporated into the private curse. Norman Cohn
notes, for example, that in medieval Europe people performed charms in conjunction
with the physical manipulation of ritual objects to divert evil from their own possessions onto those of someone else, claiming that in the early medieval German lawbook,
the *Corrector*:

> The confessor's questions show that peasants often practised sorcery to improve their own
> position at their neighbour's expense. Swineherds and cowherds would say spells over
> bread, or herbs, or knotted cords, which they would then deposit in a tree or at a road-fork;
> the object being to direct pest or injury way from their own animals and on to other peo-
> ple's . . . There is no doubt that these things really were done . . . [37]

It could be argued that while the evidence certainly suggests that evil-eye-averting
charms could be performed in conjunction with physically-enacted ritual, with regard
to the possibility that Isobel's more complex and specific maleficent acts, such as
making the *corp creadh*, reflected genuine magical practices, we must remain cautious.
Although discoveries of *corp creadh* have been recorded in Britain since the early
medieval period – with the *Inverness Courier* reporting as late as 1879 that one had
been found in a stream on the Black Isle, across the Moray Firth from Nairn – the fact
that these findings have been intermittent and usually unsubstantiated, and that, in
the absence of witnesses, they cannot be categorically linked to maleficent magical
intent, means that they must be viewed with circumspection.[38] But nevertheless, in
considering this problem we must bear in mind the fact that the difference between
the private curse or evil-eye-reversal ritual and the performance of image magic is
ultimately one of degree, not substance. If a woman wished to gain revenge on an
enemy through targeting their descendants, then the making of a *corp creadh* may have
been a more complicated method than the public curse, but the intent and rationale
behind it would have been the same and no essential moral distinction would have
divided the two. From this perspective, it could be argued that the fact that the *corp
creadh* took a long time to execute, and that it required a chilling level of premedita-
tion and involved more risk than the public curse, was ultimately a matter of
functionality as opposed to ethics. Witchcraft records, such as those pertaining to
Orkney cunning woman Katherine Bigland (1615), suggest that many of the most
powerful magical rituals, whether designed to heal or to harm, involved careful preparation and took time to execute, and it is wholly logical that, as one of the most
potent methods through which to disable an enemy, the *corp creadh* should have been
work-intensive.[39] In this context, it could be argued that those women who rose to its

challenge were merely displaying seriousness of intent as opposed to degraded moral sensibilities.

Maleficium: A Woman's Work

This hypothesis regarding Isobel's *maleficium* also has relevance for the wider debate about *maleficium*-performance in this period. Historians of witchcraft have consistently emphasized that in Britain, as in many parts of Europe, maleficent magic was primarily associated with women at the mid-to-lower end of the social scale. Much time and energy has been spent trying to identify the reasons for this stereotype, with conclusions ranging from simple misogyny, to the cultural resentment of burdensome widows, to the projection of fears about motherhood and child-rearing onto lying-in maids and so on.[40] While these factors all have a role to play, our research into Isobel's *maleficium* suggest that scholars may not have paid enough attention to the fact that this stereotype may have evolved simply because it was true.

Our inquiry into Isobel's working life in CHAPTER ONE emphasized how, like most low-status women in the period, she lived a life that was tightly curtailed. Although she may have attended church on Sundays, accompanied her husband to markets and visited friends and family in local farmsteads and towns, the demands of subsistence-level farming meant that she would have spent the overwhelming majority of her days chained to the cottage and its environs. Here, she would have spent her waking hours performing time-consuming and repetitive practical tasks such as cooking, milking, butter and cheese-making, waulking, spinning, washing clothes and so on. And as emphasized earlier, if a woman in this situation wished to protect herself or her family against an aggressor through self-defensive revenge, then her options were limited. All direct responses (such as physical violence or seeking satisfaction through the courts) were either unlikely to succeed or risked dangerous repercussions. And if the aggressor were, as in Isobel's case, of significantly higher social standing, then these dangers were multiplied. From this perspective it is not difficult to see how, when a woman such as Isobel sought to choose a method of self-defence, *maleficium* would have emerged as a serious contender.

It is notable here that all the commonest maleficent magical techniques described in witch-records from the period are firmly situated in the women's sphere. The curse, as we have seen, gave voice to women's enhanced verbal skills. The maleficent touch or look gave expression to their facility for tactile relationships and their sensitivity to body language. And traditions involving potion-making, mincing flesh, tying knots and moulding clay images and so on all reflected the dextrous skills of the hearth. Equally significantly, most of these techniques would not have necessitated setting a foot outside of the cottages, barns and kail yards that defined the woman's domain. The female-friendly nature of these practices supports the possibility that *maleficium*-usage was not only a projected fantasy invented by learned male mentalities or paranoid neighbours, but that it constituted a complex nexus of covert magical practices traditionally exploited by women.

But if we are to entertain the possibility that *maleficium* was genuinely performed in seventeenth-century Scotland, then we must also acknowledge the fact that in order for the practice to have survived into this period it must have carried psychological benefits. Historians consistently and correctly emphasize that witchcraft accusations (through the dynamics of projection and accusation and then punishment and/or un-witching ritual) worked as a means of defusing the strong inter-personal tensions that developed in tight-knit communities operating at subsistence level. However, the general tendency to overlook the question as to whether and to what extent *maleficium* was actually practised, has obviated the need to explore the latter's therapeutic bene-fits. But if you look for them, these benefits are easy to find. Like any ritual, the verbal and physical components of *maleficium*-performance would have given the practitioner immediate emotional relief, as would the attribution of any misfortune later befalling the victim to the *maleficium* performed. Similarly, the ensuing sense of satisfaction and resolution (that is, of having restored moral equilibrium and made things right) may even have worked, as did witchcraft accusation and prosecution, as an intermittent peace-keeping dynamic that helped to maintain the emotional stability of early modern village society. A wronged woman who believed, however erroneously, that she had righted the wrong done to her through covert *maleficium*, would have been less likely to stir up trouble than one who considered her desire for vengeance unfulfilled. Moreover, this method of expressing and managing tensions may have also been partic-ularly suited to the female temperament. Biologically designed to nurture the young, women do not inherit, to the same degree as men, the capacity to inflict and witness the effects of physical aggression, and therefore in seeking to defend themselves they are more disposed to seek other methods. Whether or not she was a mother, Isobel was unlikely to have been able to harm any child, even the child of her enemy the Laird of Park, directly. But causing the death, at a distance, of a baby she did not know but who she considered might grow up to tyrannize her, would have been far less difficult. Particularly if she believed herself or her peers to have lost their own children as a direct result of Park's severity.

Communal *Maleficium*

Although we can now argue that Isobel could potentially have performed some of the basic *maleficium* described in her confessions, before we can accept this possibility seri-ously we need to accommodate one last element: the fact that she claimed to have performed it in the company of others. While it is not too difficult to imagine Isobel reciting cursing charms as she knelt down alone beside her bed, like Fifeshire woman Jonet Hutton, or even to imagine her concocting potions in the dark corners of her cottage when everyone else was out working in the fields, it is much harder to imagine her doing these things as part of a group. With regard to the *corp creadh*, for example, are we really supposed to believe that Isobel, along with Margaret and Bessie Wilson, met Janet Breadheid at her house in Balmakeith; that Janet's husband, John Taylor, arrived back with some clay in the fold of his plaid; and that together they painstak-ingly minced, sieved, kneaded and moulded the clay into an image of a small child? And are we supposed to believe whenever the Laird of Park's wife gave birth to a new son, the five of them reconvened around the Breadheids' hearth, took the image from where it hung on a knag and roasted it in the fire? For such an occurrence to have taken place, Auldearn would have to have harboured a far more open acceptance of *maleficium* than has been heretofore imagined. And because such a level of approval seems so unlikely, it is tempting to assume that Isobel's claims to having made the *corp creadh* were false; an assumption which, in turn, reflects negatively on the reality status of all the other specific *maleficium* described in the confessions.

The problems posed by the alleged commonality of Isobel's basic *maleficium* are relevant to Scottish witchcraft in general, for accounts of maleficent magic performed by small groups of family and/or friends emerge with notable frequency in contemporary witchcraft records. But although such accounts are common, this issue remains largely unexamined by historians. The fact that scholars have generally dismissed the question of whether and to what extent *maleficium* may have been performed on the grounds of source contamination, means that secondary questions as to whether this *maleficium* may have been performed communally do not even have a chance to get off the ground. And while there is no scope to give this complex question the attention it deserves in the present book, in order to explore Isobel's claims in this context we need to give it some consideration here.

In Isobel's case, it is significant that an account of making the *corp creadh* is also found, almost word for word, in Janet Breadheid's confession. We have already argued, in CHAPTERS THREE and FIVE, that the similarities in phraseology between the two women's accounts strongly suggest that Janet's version, made the day after Isobel's, was the result of a read-out-and-assent process through which the interrogators took Isobel's account and fed it back to the assenting Janet. But although this scenario suggests that Janet confirmed Isobel's version of the event, it does not dispute her claim to have been involved in it. Although the former's *creadh* account is very similar to Isobel's, it contains small but significant differences that suggest that she was actively involved in its construction. Janet's claims that she 'brought hom the water in a pig, owt of the rud wall' and that she sometimes hid the clay image 'under a chist' are absent from Isobel's account from the previous day. And it is Janet, not Isobel, who first claimed that the ritual was performed with the accompaniment of charms; was spoken on their knees with their hair loose; and was taught to them by the Devil. Moreover, Janet sometimes goes into more detail than Isobel concerning the use of the image. While Isobel merely states, in her first confession, that after making the *corp* 'we wold rost it now and then each day & th[e]r wold be an piece of it weill rosten . . . it ves still putt in & takin out of the fyre', Janet stated:

> (*we*) layed it up and steired it not untill the nixt bairn (*word crossed out*) wes borne, and then
> within half an yeir efter that bairn ves borne (*we?*) took it owt again out of the cradl and
> clowt, and vold dip it now & th[e]n among water, and beck and rost it at the fyre each
> uth[e]r day once, as ve did ag[ains]t the uth[e]r th[a]t ves dead untill th[a]t bairne (*damaged
> – words missing*). (545/38)

Of course, the fact that both Isobel and Janet may have contributed to their accounts of communal *maleficium* does not necessarily mean that they genuinely performed it together, for as we shall explore in the next chapter, there are many methods through which criminal interrogators can persuade people to make false confessions. But on the other hand, we cannot rule out the possibility completely. It is easy for the modern Western commentator to overlook the fact that for the poor in seventeenth-century Scotland almost everything was done communally. People slept together, ate together, worked together, played together and worshipped together; and even the most private moments, such as courtship, sickness, birth and death, were intensely communal affairs. Hardly surprisingly, people also performed magical rituals as a group. In 1623 cunning woman Isobel Haldane confessed to the Perth sessions that she had performed a healing ritual involving three cakes, and that she 'made a hole in the crown of every one of them, and put a bairn through every cake three times, in the name of the Father, Son and Holy Ghost. *There were women present* who put the said bairns thrice backward through every cake, using the same words [my italics].'[41] Similarly, when Orkney cunning woman Jonet Reid (1643) tried to cure John Kirknes of the 'boneshaw', her treatment, which involved massage and incantation, was performed in the presence of both John's wife and a servant girl, the latter being asked to participate by 'repeating everie word after her at her direction'.[42] In this context, we have no trouble in accepting that when Isobel stated 'and this *we* say thryse over straiking the sor, and it becomes heall [my italics]' that she was referring to a ritual that had been performed in the company of others.

But while we can accept the notion of communal rituals performed to generate magical healing, can we also accept the notion of communal rituals performed to cause magical harm? This is a difficult and controversial question, but in approaching it we must bear in mind the fact that because the reformed church prohibited all superstitious rituals, by the seventeenth century most magical healing or divinatory rituals had been forced underground, and had effectively become clandestine activities that involved a conspiracy of secrecy between participants. In Aberdeen in 1597, for example, John Ramsay claimed that when he visited Helen Fraser at her house in Aiknishill, to 'seik releif of his seiknes', the cunning woman said 'sche wald do quhat in hir lay for the recoverie of his health: bot willit him to keip secret quhatsoevir sche spak or did, and that becaus the warld wes evill, and spake na gude of sic medicinars'.[43] Similarly in Orkney, in 1643, Andrew Brown claimed that Marion Peebles successfully cured him of a sickness, but that when 'he fell again in the sd sicknes wors than befoir, and paynet away with sic extremetie of sicknes, that he sent you againe, desyring meat out of your hand; and after long intreatie, ye wald not cum to him with it, least your witchcraft and charmes again sould cum to lyt'.[44] Moving up the social scale, three magical practitioners allegedly commissioned by Ross-shire gentleman Hector Monroe (1590) to cure his sick brother, left the house before they could finish their treatment because they feared that if they remained there any longer Hector's disapproving father 'wald haif apprehendit thame'.[45] As a consequence, many of these healing rites took place under cover of darkness, with accounts consistently stating that the clandestine deeds were done 'efter sun setting', 'befor sun rysing', 'undir silence and cloud of night', 'quhen the starrs wer in the firmanent', and with people returning from their magical escapades 'befoir any of the house war risen out of thair beddis'.[46] The horror expressed by the participant in the following event, which seems to have been an attempt to gain parts of a dead body for occult purposes, indicates how far people were prepared to flout church teachings in order to achieve their magical aims. The trial dittays of Aberdeenshire cunning woman Jonet Wishart, in 1597, state that a witness claimed:

> being in thi service in tym of hervest, gangand to Gordonismyln to grind cornis to the hewkis with the, a pairt being ground in the nicht, thou [Wishart] and scho [the witness] returning eftir midnyght, past out of the commoun way cuming throw the Linkis the get to the gallowis, quhairat the woman was grytlie effreyit, and refusit to gange; yit thow urgit hir nocht to feir in thi cumpanie, so that sho was forsit to cum fordwart, quhair thow brocht hir to the gallows, and schew hir that thow suld learn hir ane lessoun suld do hir gud all hir dayis; and ane deid mann being hinging thair, baid hir hald his futt, quhill thow cuttit af pairt of all his memberis, quhairat the womann was stricken with sic feir, feill deid, and refusit to mell with sic thing; quhairupon thow forsiblie stretit hir be hir aitht, nevir to reveill, or than thow suld instantlie gar hir dee.[47]

With regard to communal acts of *maleficium*, it is equally important to remember that the interconnectedness of human lives, particularly among the poor, meant that the sufferings that affected one often affected many. The combined oppressions of the Highland raids, the civil wars, the English occupation and the Laird of Park's looming bankruptcy would not just been felt by Isobel, they would have been felt by all of Park's tenants and by the cottars and labourers who worked for them, for they all farmed the same lands, ground their corn in the same mills and saw their rents make their way to the same place. We can assume, of course, that the majority of Park's tenants would have negotiated his demands, however oppressive they may have been, without resorting to *maleficium*. But it is reasonable to speculate that if any did choose the latter path they would have sought courage in numbers. An individual embarking on a cattle raid in the company of others as part of inter-clan dispute would have felt less fear and guilt than if they stole a neighbour's animal privately in response to purely personal vendetta. Similarly, the anxieties associated with the performance of self-defensive *maleficium* would have been ameliorated if the latter were enacted communally in response to collective grievances and aims. The numbers sanctioned the act.

The fact that the performance of *maleficium* was not always conducted in isolation, but was facilitated through community consent or participation, is also supported by the small minority of records that indicate that some individuals may have genuinely resorted to magical practitioners in order to be protected from, or avenged upon, enemies. Although these accounts, as with all those found in witchcraft records, cannot be assumed to depict events that actually took place, they depict community-dynamics that are inherently feasible. For example, as Peter Maxwell-Stuart has shown, a series of trials from Aberdeenshire in 1590 provide us with a detailed and compelling picture of a man (named William Leslie) who, with the help of his servant, applied to various local cunning women in the hope of finding one who would accept his commission to magically harm the Laird of Boquhane, with whom he had recently quarrelled. As Maxwell-Stuart argues, the integrity of the account is supported by the fact that the first woman approached (Barbara Kaird) seems to have refused the job through ties of obligation to the laird's family 'rather than revulsion at the suggestion that she murder him by magic'.[48] Similarly, the fact that the woman who allegedly accepted the commission – renowned local healer Janet Grant – was not charged for this particular crime, but was found guilty of accepting similar commissions from other clients, also suggests that this cluster of trial records may have reflected genuine crimes as opposed to interrogatorial presumptions based on unfounded witness-allegations. Small details, such as the fact that when Grant was engaged to kill cattle belonging to local resident William Ross she was allegedly paid 'half a scraped hide and twenty silver shillings by one John Adie' are also suggestive here.[49]

Even more pertinently, evidence that *maleficium* was performed to client-demand is also found in the confession given by Isobel's accomplice and neighbour, Janet Breadheid. In the first instance, Janet asserts confidently that 'Agnes grant who wes brunt on the (*damaged – words missing*) hill of (*blank*) gott hyre from elspet monro to destroy the Lairdis of park and lochloy' (544/44). That the statement can be taken at face value, and that women like Agnes Grant were indeed 'hired' to perform *maleficium* in the Auldearn region in the period, is further supported by Janet's later claim that 'it wes keathren sowter th[a]t wes brunt th[a]t (*verb missing here*) w[illia]m hay the Last Laird of parkis broth[e]r for on gilbert kintey' (545/18). As we shall be exploring later in the book, both the missing verb and the words 'for on' render the meaning of this last statement obscure, but here it is pertinent to note that Robert Pitcairn, who tran-scribed Janet's confession in 1833, assumed that the missing verb related to some kind of magical harm and that 'for on' meant 'at the instigation of'; changes that would make the statement read 'and it was Katherine Sowter that was burnt that destroyed William Hay the last Laird of Park's brother at the instigation of Gilbert Kintey'.[50]

There is no reason to suppose that these *maleficium*-demanding and *maleficium*-performing events could not have been communal affairs. When William Leslie went to Barbara Kaird he did not travel alone, but brought his servant, Bessie Roy, along with him. When Janet Grant took on the job of destroying the Laird of Boquhane she travelled to Robert Swapis's house in Crethie in order to make and roast a *corp creadh*, and we can suppose that the master of the house, or at least some family members, were present while she was there. In one high-profile late sixteenth-century case that took place in Ross-shire, Katharine Ross, the Lady Fowlis, did not only allegedly hire at least two magical practitioners to dispatch various members of her family, but at times she joined them at magical work which included both poison-brewing and making a *corp creadh*. On one memorable All Hallow's Eve, according to the dittays, Ross allegedly helped the women to cast elf arrows at a carefully-moulded clay image of the victim, with the records noting emphatically that 'thow [Ross] wes present, and saw and hard this done'.[51] Such accounts cannot, of course, be taken as definite indications that these events took place, but by the same token they cannot be dismissed out of hand. And taken together they suggest that, with respect to Isobel's communally-performed *maleficium*, we must retain an open mind. If we can accept her statement: 'this we say thryse over straiking the sor, and it becomes heall', as representative of a group healing ritual, then we should at least entertain the idea that her statement: 'we maid the pictur for distroyeing of the Laird of parkis meall children', may also have reflected a genuine event.

The Elite Magic Connection

The assertion that early modern witches may have actually performed *maleficium* is so controversial and difficult to prove that – in order to press the case – we have been forced to develop a complex argument based largely on inference and probability. But if we spread our net wider and move a little higher up the social ladder, we find some additional – and considerably more concrete – evidence to support the claim. The plethora of elite magical grimoires that emerged throughout western Europe from the early Middle Ages onwards frequently, and without apology, contained charms and rituals designed specifically to cause harm, either for the magician's personal gain or at the behest of clients. Norman Cohn, for example, notes that although non-harming rituals were the 'commonest' listed in these texts they:

> were not the only ones. Causing disease, deafness, blindness, insanity; provoking men to theft and murder, producing putrid wounds, leading to death within three days; burning the magician's own enemies – these are true *maleficia*, and all of them figure amongst the 'offices of the spirits' . . . some demons specialized in producing wars and battles, sinking warships, demolishing walls, burning towns to the ground.[52]

Similarly, after noting that 'Later medieval books of magic are seldom shy about giving straightforwardly harmful formulas', Kieckhefer summarizes a description of a maleficent ritual involving a wax image that makes Isobel's *corp creadh* rite seem positively pedestrian by comparison:

> A fifteenth-century *Liber de angelis, annulis, karecteribus et ymaginibus planetarum* (*Book of angels, rings, characters, and images of the planets*) in the Cambridge University Library contains an experiment called *Vindicta Troie* (*Vengeance of Troy*), which can be used to arouse hatred or to cause bodily harm or even death. The procedure calls for the making of an image on the day and in the hour of Saturn, in the name of the person to be harmed. The image must be made of wax, preferably from candles used at a funeral. It should be made as ugly as possible; the face should be contorted, and there should be hands in place of feet and vice versa. The victim's name should be inscribed on the forehead of the image, the name of the planet Saturn on its breast, and the seals or characters of Saturn between its shoulders. The operator should call upon the spirits of Saturn to descend from on high and afflict the named victim. The image should be fumigated with various substances, including human bones and hair, then wrapped in a funeral cloth and buried in some unclean place, face downward. If the magician wishes to harm any particular member of the victim's body, there are instructions for binding the corresponding member on the image with a funeral cloth and piercing

the image with a needle; to kill the victim, the magician should insert the needle into the spine, from the head down to the heart.[53]

Of course, in the absence of witnesses, these accounts do not prove that such rituals were actually ever performed. But because they emerge consistently throughout the centuries, and more significantly, because they were not produced in a coercive arena, scholars cannot – and do not – automatically dismiss them as interrogatorial projection. As a result, although reluctant to commit themselves with regard to extent, most scholars in the field acknowledge that some elite magicians were likely to have performed maleficent magic, both for personal gain and to client demand. Surprisingly, this scholarly consensus has had little impact on the 'Did witchcraft suspects really perform *maleficium*?' debate. And yet its relevance here is immediately obvious. If the relatively well-educated and moneyed sectors of society could stoop to the performance of maleficent magic, then it is likely that those lower down the social scale – who had to struggle against even greater odds with even less resources – would also have done so. The fact that elite magicians recorded their *maleficium* in texts while popular magical practitioners did not does not reflect any difference in degrees of practice, but merely the fact that the illiterate majority seldom committed any of their beliefs, rituals and experiences – whether magical or otherwise – to paper.

Conclusions

In the last analysis, we cannot assert that Isobel definitely performed the various types of *maleficium* described in her confessions. But we can conclude that she may have done so. And we can also argue that, in the context of contemporary mentalities, she may have considered these actions to be rational and just. Certainly the evidence suggests that in seventeenth-century Auldearn, as in the rest of Scotland in this period, behind the closed doors of turf cottages and hidden from the eyes of ministers, the levels of shame and guilt associated with maleficent magic may not have been as high as historians generally assume. This conclusion goes against the trend of current thinking which, as we illustrated at the beginning of this chapter, tends to the view that on this social level *maleficium* was generally attributed as opposed to performed. But is it really so untenable? We must remember that the huge majority of people, from university-educated men sitting in their libraries and castles to the isolated Highlanders who had barely seen the inside of a church, believed that individuals could and did attempt to gain vengeance on their enemies through the performance of maleficent magic. There is no doubt that, in fearful response to these beliefs, *maleficium* was often attributed, and as in parts of Africa and Asia today, gross human abuses and injustices occurred as a result of projection and scapegoating. But to assume that there was nothing at the heart of it; to assume that the whole of Europe was, for over 300 years, suffering some form of inverted 'Emperor's New Clothes' syndrome that caused it to become obsessed with the identification and elimination of an always-imaginary crime, is premature. After all, these people were there at the time and we were not. As we have begun to explore in this chapter, and shall be exploring in more depth in CHAPTERS TWELVE and THIRTEEN, for modern historians the 'Did witchcraft suspects really perform *maleficium?*' question must be considered in the light of the fact that conditions of life were very different in the early modern period and that people behaved very differently because of it.

9

Wonderful Lies

In the last five chapters we have explored Isobel's confessions from a variety of perspectives in order to identify and explain why they are so different from other witch-records of the period. With regard to the Isobel-was-crazy hypothesis raised in CHAPTER THREE, our analysis suggests that although we cannot dismiss the possibility out of hand, the fact that we have been able to find such a wide array of alternative explanations, other than mental illness, to explain the unusualness of her confessions means that we can fairly safely assume that she was not overtly insane. This conclusion is also supported by more circumstantial considerations. It is difficult to imagine how judicious men like Hugh Rose and Thomas Dunbar of Grange would have taken Isobel so seriously, over a six-week period, in an environment where, as we have seen, witchcraft interrogations were under scrutiny and criticism, if she had been displaying obvious symptoms of mental illness. Isobel's relative sanity is also supported by the fact that her confessions corresponded, in many ways, with that of Janet Breadheid and that, for legal purposes, the two women were considered together. The fact that Isobel seems to have shown genuine contrition for her witchcraft and expressed this contrition in a manner that suggests she fully understood church teachings on sin and the value of repentance, also points to a sane mind, as does the fact that she seems to have been a magical practitioner of some years standing. These views are further supported by the fact that although, as we saw in CHAPTER THREE, it is quite possible that Isobel suffered from ergot-poisoning at some point in her life, the theory that ergot-induced mental instability was responsible for the strangeness of her confessions does not stand up to scrutiny. As Frederick Burwick has recently argued with regard to French poet Gérard de Nerval, although the symptoms of severe ergotism can persist for many weeks, cases acute enough to precipitate the mental effects associated with insanity, such as delirium and dementia, are inevitably accompanied by dramatic physical symptoms such as vomiting, diarrhoea, livid skin colour, fever, painful muscular contractions in the extremities, severe itching and tingling, convulsions and so on.[1] If Isobel had been suffering these kinds of physical symptoms (whether as a result of a recent infection or a relapse) it is difficult to see how she could have endured six weeks of questioning and imprisonment, or how her interrogators, even if they were not familiar with medical opinion on the matter, could have overlooked or discounted them.

But although we can conclude that overt insanity, whether ergot-derived or otherwise, was unlikely, we cannot rule out the possibility that Isobel suffered from some mental condition that was situated near enough the mild end of the severity scale for her interrogators to assume her 'of sound judgement' but far enough away from it to place her outside the commonplace. A condition that caused her to, when placed before a group of exceptionally curious and attentive interrogators, produce testimony that stands out from that given by most other witchcraft suspects in this period. Some form of bipolar condition, that generated periods of mania interspersed with periods of depression and suicidal impulses, could arguably fit Isobel's template. Returning to ergotism, we can also entertain the possibility that this low-level mental instability could have been caused or compounded by the 'various mental derangements' that can plague those who have contracted, but survived, a severe bout of the disease.[2] But we must remain cautious here. Barger's analysis in *Ergot and Ergotism* suggests that although severe attacks can cause permanent dementia and/or relapses characterized by convulsions and mental disturbance, the long-term mental after-effects are commonly 'dullness', 'stupidity' and intellectual 'backwardness', with Barger noting that after infection 'Minor nervous defects, spasms and a dull intellect may persist for a long time in the adult'.[3] Although it is highly possible, given her rye-eating habits, that Isobel had contracted ergotism as a child and that this had affected her mental development, when reading her testimony a 'dull intellect' is not something that immediately springs to mind. It is also important to remember that whatever the causes, nature, and degree of Isobel's hypothetical mental illness, as some form of intermediary condition it may have marked her out from her peers, but need not have prevented her from maintaining positive relationships and integrating into the Auldearn community. Nor would it have prevented her from being a fireside bard or magical practitioner. Indeed, as we shall explore in more detail in later chapters, in most cultures and historical periods throughout the world, artistic and magical work comes naturally to those who are predisposed to be unusually intense and live their lives on a psychological knife-edge.

But Why Did She Confess?

But if we now put aside, or at least ameliorate, the Isobel-was-crazy hypothesis we find ourselves faced with a new set of questions. If Isobel was, as we can loosely term it here, 'relatively sane', then why did she stand up in the tolbooth before Harry Forbes, Hugh Rose and the rest of the gathered company and confess to having engaged in such a wide range of malevolent, fantastical and incriminating activities? Some parts of the confessions generate these questions more than others. We can fairly safely assume that the passages in which Isobel describes using magical rituals and charms to cure sickness and generate success at market may have referred to genuine experiences. And on the basis of the perspectives developed in the last two chapters we can also entertain, if not fully accept, the idea that some of Isobel's specific *maleficium*, such as making the *corp creadh* and the maleficent potion, were also accounts based on magical rituals performed prior to arrest. But it is altogether more difficult to draw the same conclusions with regard to the more fantastic demonological and fairy-related passages. To put it simply, if Isobel were relatively sane then why did she claim to having performed so many acts that were physically impossible, such as making pacts with the Devil, riding in fairy whirlwinds on horses made out of corn straws and shooting at and killing seemingly innocent passers-by with elf arrows shot from the nails of her thumbs?

Our alternative-to-insanity explanations are of no further help to us here. In response to exceptionally persistent and attentive questioning, for example, fireside performing skills and a wide knowledge of oral lore might have equipped Isobel to describe animal metamorphosis or flight with the fairies with confidence and eloquence. But it would not have predisposed her to recount them in the first person or attribute them to neighbours. To claim that the 'splendid fellow' from the traditional 'Tale of the Hoodie' turned into a crow is very different from claiming that '*I* turned into a crow'. [4] And to state that the legendary Laird of Duffus had been swept away by the fairies was very different to stating that Bessie Hay, who was alive and well and working in the Auldearn school at the time, had also suffered the same fate. Here, having finally peeled away the extraordinary veneer that casts such a distracting spell over Isobel's testimony, we find ourselves confronting the questions that lie at the heart of all witchcraft confessions, whether short or long, simple or complex, extraordinary or ordinary: how far did witch-testimony relate to the suspect's 'real' experience, and why did witches confess what they confessed?

Retrospective Fiction Making

In order to tackle these questions, we need to move back into the arena of interrogation. As we saw in CHAPTER FIVE, recent scholars have emphasized that the motivations behind witch-prosecutions were more subtle than has previously been supposed, with Lyndal Roper, in particular, arguing that interrogators were not just happy to superimpose stereotypically demonological ideas onto defenceless suspects weakened by torture and maltreatment, but wished to elicit full and genuine confessions, both to establish the correct legal details of the case and to facilitate the witch's full repentance. Roper maintains that although interrogators were looking for incriminating events like the demonic pact and sex with the Devil, they were not happy for these subjects to be confessed in a parroted or unconvincing way, and spent much time and energy seeking out those realistic, personal details that suggested that the events had actually taken place. As a consequence of this interrogatorial zeal, witchcraft suspects, worn down by imprisonment, questioning and torture, soon learnt that if they were to convince their inquisitors that their confession was genuine and thereby bring their ordeals to an end, they had to weave their demonological themes into a 'personal story' that contained accurate and convincing details from their own life. Roper claims that:

> She [the suspect] had to provide those details which only she could know. Her description

of the Devil had to be vivid enough to persuade interrogators that she really had encountered him, and to do this, she had to incorporate her story about the Devil into the tissue of everyday life. This is what makes the confessions such remarkable documents. To an extent, they conform to the broad outlines of what a sound grounding in the principles of demonology might have led one to expect a witch to say. But they are peppered with detail drawn from the witch's own experience and coloured by her own emotions.[5]

Roper and other scholars mining the same vein have argued that as a consequence of this interrogatorial prerogative, even the most demonologically stereotypical witch-craft records can give us genuine insights into the personal lives of the accused, frequently highlighting female anxieties surrounding childbirth (labour and lying-in), child-rearing (lactation, wet-nursing, infant sickness) and sexuality (pre-marital sex, abortion, adultery, incest).[6] They have also emphasized that witch-records do not only give us insights into general areas of anxiety, but also into specific life-events. Roper argues, for example, that the series of confessions given by German witch Appolonia Mayr, in 1686, masked an episode of infanticide:

> The Devil had promised that if she killed her child, her lover would marry her. She had strangled the infant at a little hill beyond the Lech bridge, just before the small town of Friedberg . . . Describing the birth and murder, she said, 'The Evil Spirit left her no peace. It was only a moment, the Devil touched it [the child] as if he were a midwife, it happened quite quickly that the child came out. She strangled it immediately with the hand, and she felt no pain in the delivery.' Then Appolonia walked on: 'She left it lying quite naked, uncovered, and unburied . . . The Devil did not go with her, but remained staying by the child, and she did not look back.'[7]

Alternatively, Roper claims that the series of confessions given by Appolonia's fellow countrywoman Regina Bartholome sixteen years earlier, masked an adulterous relationship:

> Bartholome confessed that she had lived with the Devil as man and wife. Aged 21 when she was interrogated by the Augsburg Council, she had met the Devil five years before. She recalled that the Devil was clad in silken hose with boots and spurs and that he looked like a nobleman. They enjoyed trysts twice weekly at a tavern-bakery in Pfersee . . . He promised her money, but she had received barely 6 Kreuzer from him, and even that had turned out to be bad coin. In return for this meagre reward, Regina had signed a pact with the Devil for the term of seven years. She had forsworn God and the Trinity, and she had taken the Devil – her lover – as her father in God's stead.[8]

Roper maintains that in both cases the confessions were essentially remembered real-life crimes that had, over the process of various interrogations, been gradually demonized by both the accused and their inquisitors in a process which was both coerced and voluntary. The testimonies given by Regina Bartholome, for example, were not freely given, but 'emerged, with considerable resistance, over the course of eight sessions of interrogation both with and without torture and its threat'. But on the other hand, Regina was not merely bludgeoned into confessing, and seems to have brought the Devil into the picture unprompted, in 'an extraordinary, voluntary admission', claiming that he visited her in her cell after she had first been imprisoned by the council. Once the Devil was mentioned however, as Roper notes, her prosecutors became increasingly interested in the role he may have played in her experiences, and as subsequent interrogations progressed he was placed further and further back in the series of events until he was present, with biblical inevitability, at her initial seduction.[9] The net result of this painstaking, painful, but chillingly creative process was a fantastical and in many ways stereotypical account of communication with the Devil, with a genuine life-experience at its core.

Isobel's Life: The Long View

Following Roper, we can assume that Isobel wove her own personal story into her confessions and that the latter can be decoded to give us some insights into her world. Putting aside, for the moment, the epistemological questions raised by the supernatural and demonological confessional elements, it is immediately clear that Isobel's testimony is scattered with realistic detail and provides us with a kaleidoscope of images that paint a vivid and comprehensive picture of the sights, sounds and feelings that must have informed her daily life.

It was, without a doubt, the life of a Nairnshire cottar or farming tenant's wife. We are shown, among other things, the ploughing of land and the harvesting of grain. We are shown sheep being sheared, cows being milked, stallions put to mares and oxen being slaughtered. We are taken out into the hills and glens to see sheep and cattle folds, men hunting with hounds in the early morning and women beating clothes at the fast-running burns. We are taken to the forests where sticks are collected to be shaped and whittled, to the beaches where women gather waiting for the fishing boats to come in, and to the markets where the farmers sell horses, cattle and cloth. We are shown the rooms where yarn is swirled in great vats of black and sea-green dyes and where ale is stored in wooden barrels. We are taken inside Isobel's cottage to see its small shuttered window, to see its chimney-hole high up in the blackened rafters and to hear the crows cawing on the thatch above. We are shown her fire crook, her three-legged stool, her wooden chests, her pillow, her plaid, her broom standing in the corner and her bags of precious things hanging on pegs, safe from harm. We see her mincing sheep's flesh and colewort, kneading rye dough, baking scones and roasting sucking-pigs in the red-hot coals of the fire. We are shown Isobel and her companions taking each other by the hand to dance the gillatrype, plaiting corn stalks at the feast of Lammas and dividing grain at Yule. We see them mumbling charms around sick beds, congregating in the church to watch their infants being raised for baptism and gathering around cottage hearths to share grievances about their landlords and ministers. And running through this kaleidoscope of days we have glimpses of the emotions that both illuminated and darkened them: the satisfactions of food, the joys of sex, the elation of dance, the admiration of a well-dressed woman or a handsome man, the humour of an apt nickname, the pleasure of a well-turned phrase, the energy of the chase, the dark thrill of skilfully-aimed revenge, the visceral terror of being hunted like an animal or beaten with cords and flails, and the biting fear of fevers, infections and the deadly stealth attacks of elves.

Looking at Isobel's confessions from this perspective also enables us to speculate as to the real-life events that may have informed some of the more obscure events described in the confessions. The prominence of elf-arrow heads in the narrative, for example, may not only be linked to the fact that they featured in local folklore, but also to the fact that the ancient flints with which these arrows were commonly associated throughout Scotland were unusually plentiful along the sandy beaches of this section of the Moray coast; this plenty reflecting the fact that these game-rich coastal areas were exploited by generations of prehistoric hunter-gatherers.[10] Just as local nineteenth-century families spent their weekends hunting for arrows on the Culbin Sands (with Nairn Museum displaying such finds to this day) Isobel and her peers are likely to have come across the small flint heads as they cut peat near the shore, collected shellfish at low tide or walked along the dunes to neighbouring Maviston to meet the fishing boats.[11] We can even speculate, though here more wildly, that Isobel's unique claim that her coven flicked the arrow heads from 'the naillis of owr thowmbes' enjoyed similarly prosaic origins. Writing about her childhood in Nairn in the early-twentieth century, Margaret Bochel wrote that one of the most popular summer games was that of marbles or 'boolies':

> There were several games played with boolies [marbles]; the first was often played on the way home from school in the strannies or drainage gullies on the High Street. One player threw a boolie forward and the others took it in turn to try and hit it; the first to hit it won the bool. Another game was played on the many dirt closes or lanes in the Fishertown; this time a shallow hole was carved out of the soil . . . the object of this game was to get the boolie in the hole from a predetermined distance . . . Mothers made little cloth bags with drawstrings for holding the boolies.[12]

Given the fact that marbles was a popular child's game in early modern Scotland, we can safely assume that it would have been familiar to Isobel and her childhood companions, although, living over two centuries earlier, they would have manufactured their marbles themselves, fashioning them out of clay and baking them in the fire. Building on this, we can also assume that both Isobel and her early twentieth-century counterparts would have been familiar with what a recent book on the game terms the 'time-honoured [marble-shooting] method' of 'knuckling-down'; a technique that involves placing the ball on the forefinger of the knuckled hand and flicking the marble from the thumbnail.[13] On the back of this, we can entertain the possibility that Isobel's claim to have shot elf arrows from her thumb nails may have drawn on childhood memories of squatting on the dirt road between Lochloy and Nairn knuckling-down clay marbles with the local boys. Indeed, given the numbers of arrowheads scattered among the sand dunes adjacent to the Nairn-Lochloy road it is also not beyond the realms of possibility that shooting arrowheads from thumbnails may have become, for some local children, a local variant of marble play.

The search for realism could also illuminate the references to magical flight that emerge so prominently in Isobel's confessions. On the one hand, Isobel's vivid descriptions of her coven flying as 'strawes in a whirlewind' and of arrow-slain bodies flying 'as hors to ws, als small as strawes', could have been drawn from oral literature concerning fairy whirlwinds. But they could also have gained some of their vigour from personal experience. The laborious job of threshing grain, for example, would have often fallen to women, and since she was a young girl Isobel would have been familiar with the sight of clouds of corn straws massing, floating and dispersing in the shafts of sunlight slanting through the doors and openings in the dark threshing barns. On the other hand, living near the dunes along the Moray Firth shoreline and traversing them in order to reach the shore, she would also have been familiar with the sight of sand, dried grass and other debris being swept up by eddies and whirlwinds. An account given by Elgin resident John Martin, who encountered a sandstorm on the neighbouring Culbin dunes in 1860, clearly indicates how easily local people could link these natural whirlwinds, at the moment of experience, to fairy lore. Walking along the dunes, on a day with westerly gales, Martin was met by:

> such as powerful blast of wind that came sweeping round the corner of the (sand) hill, as seemed to be a work altogether beyond the common operation of nature. So violent and tormenting were those attacks, that I could not help thinking that the fairies must have leagued together to punish me for entering their domains. Whether the fairies took part in the affair or not, I am not prefered to affirm, but coming out of the gorge I felt as though a dozen thongs were lashing me with great force around the body, and I actually felt as if the points of them had reached upwards and were twitching my face. Ropes of sand are generally spoken of with a degree of contempt, but really when they operate like the thongs of Culbin, they are not to be despised.[14]

Isobel's claim that the Devil 'wold be beatting and scurgeing ws all wp and downe , w[i]th tardis & uth[e]r sharp scurges, lyk naked gwhastis' may also have been coloured by her experiences of being scourged by 'ropes of sand' as she traversed the dunes along the Lochloy coast (49/19).

The Close-Up

While the confessions, read in this manner, can give us a general impression of Isobel's daily life, they can also hint at the specific events and relationships that may have influenced her. Others have certainly attempted to decode Isobel's confessions in this way. Diane Purkiss, for example, concludes that the passage describing feasting with the king and queen of the fairies in the Downie Hill indicates that Isobel was a woman who suffered from chronic hunger and a lack of status:

Given Gowdie's stress on the queen's fine clothes, or the king's, we might see this as a fantasy of dining with the great, or perhaps as a traditional piece of hospitality extended to a poor woman by a rich family. This would not be incompatible with seeing the story as a fantasy version of such hospitality, in which the social barriers of class are broken by the anomalousness of the supernatural, so that Gowdie can dine with the fairy king and queen almost as their friend as well as their dependant; certainly, her attempt to describe their accoutrements in detail implies an identification with their elevated social status. It is suggestive that the fairies give Gowdie meat, for meat suggests upper-class and celebratory meals. The fact that the fairy court is surrounded by 'elf bulls' is equally significant, for in the Scottish Highlands cattle were a sign of wealth, as well as a source of meat; bulls mean a lord's house. However, Gowdie may simply be using the term as a synonym for food in general. If so, this is indeed a fairytale, for English folklore is full of stories about peasants who gain advancement in great or little ways by association with the fairies.[15]

Purkiss's conclusions have been recently echoed by John Callow, who argues that, 'Rather than speaking for a prior folk culture, Gowdie's wild imaginings can be more accurately viewed as articulating the concerns and frustrated desires of a poor and frequently hungry woman who wished for plentiful meat to feed upon'.[16] Scholars have further speculated that Isobel's confessions reflect not only hunger and low status, but also powerlessness. Callow speculates that they reveal 'a level of social and sexual freedom which was all too lacking in the hierarchical, and kirk dominated, Scotland of the mid-seventeenth century', while Purkiss interprets Isobel's claim to have shot elf arrows as some kind of wish-fulfilment, noting that: 'If meat is what Isobel wants, a fantasy projection by a woman who is chronically hungry, are the arrows also a projection of power by a woman who is chronically powerless, but perhaps angry?' Peter Maxwell-Stuart also takes up the Isobel-as-powerless baton with his suggestion that the decidedly authoritarian Devil-figure who dominates her confessions could have reflected a dictatorial, and possibly violent, male known to her in real life.[17]

While such interpretations can come across as reductionist, particularly if they are presented in isolation as the ultimate raison d'être behind Isobel's confessions, there is no doubt that they catch a truth. As our analyses in CHAPTER SEVEN revealed, Isobel lived through hard times. Not only was she likely to have witnessed the carnage of the Battle of Auldearn and the tensions of the siege of Lethen, but she also endured the ongoing threat of Highland aggression, the condescension of the occupying English military regime, the disciplinary repression of religiously-fundamentalist elders and ministers, the privations of subsistence-level farming and onerous demands for rent and labour from an increasingly-desperate landlord. And as we argued in CHAPTER EIGHT, it may well have been Isobel's sense of powerlessness in the face of these oppressions that motivated her to defend herself and her family through *maleficium*. Similarly, the fact that Isobel's Devil-figure is such a vibrant and coherent piece of characterization also supports Maxwell-Stuart's suspicion that he was modelled on a real-life acquaintance. In a patriarchal culture where men could, to a certain extent, legitimately beat their wives and daughters, Isobel's vivid accounts of being whipped and scourged by the Devil take on an ominous significance above and beyond a memory of local sandstorms or the storyteller's capacity for dramatic exaggeration and raise the possibility that she had, at some point in her life, suffered violence at the hands of a father or husband. The judicial authorities may also have played a role here. Whippings were a standard form of punishment, and there is no doubt that Isobel would have witnessed, and perhaps even been a victim of, such events. Reserved for market days to maximize impact, these disciplinary proceedings would certainly have been long-drawn out and theatrical enough to fire the most sluggish imagination.[18] In 1743, for example, the sheriff court of Nairn ordered 'common thief' Margaret Davidson to be banished from the shire on pain of death. But first, she was to have her ear cut off at the tron before being 'carried to the bridge of Nairn under a sure guard and a hangman at her back, and there and then to be stript to the middle, and when so stripped to receive six strokes upon the back with a whip from the hangman, the like number at the cross of Nairn, the like number at the Horologe Stone, and the like number at the foot of the Gallows'.[19]

In the same vein, we could speculate that the Devil's prominent sexuality reflected the fact that the tall, authoritarian male who dominated Isobel's life was also sexually predatory and perhaps promiscuous. Such a figure could have been her husband, John Gilbert, but it could just as easily have been someone else. As we noted in CHAPTER SEVEN, adultery and fornication were consistently the most frequent crimes to come before the kirk sessions in this period, with Todd observing that 'Session books from every parish are dominated by cases of fornication and adultery, with occasionally lurid accounts of couples caught in the act, abundant depositions by suspicious neighbours or witnesses, and vigorous grilling of suspects about times and places.'[20] Certainly, despite its covenanting aspirations, the Auldearn region seems to have been no different in this respect, with Brodie lamenting that when he attended a session meeting at Dyke, in 1672, he witnessed not just a trickle or stream but a 'flood' of 'profannes, perjuri and adulteries'.[21] As Stevenson has shown with regard to Aberdeen in the 1650s, illicit sexual activity would also have increased in response to the influx of English soldiers into north-eastern cities and towns.[22] Similarly, the endemic warfare of the 1640s and 50s would also have encouraged sexual openness, on the 'why put it off when you may die tomorrow' ethos that so unsettled middle England during the first and second world wars. As we have seen in the previous chapter, in these heated times even respected ministers like Harry Forbes turned their attentions from their godly wives to their servant girls.

Of course, we also cannot rule out the possibility that Isobel's graphic accounts of demonic sex masked something more sinister. In the following passage, Isobel states that her sexual encounters with the Devil were consensual ('we wold never refuse him') and at several points during the confessions she claims that they were also pleasant. But some of the phraseology, such as 'he will lye als hewie wpon ws . . . enyie tym as he pleased' raises the possibility that a level of coercion was involved. In the following passage, the sexual activities of Isobel's coven are undoubtedly orchestrated by the Devil's needs:

and w[i]thin ffew dayes he cam to me in the new wardis of Inshoch, and ther haid carnall cowpula[tio]n w[i]th me, he wes a werie meikle blak roch man, he will lye als hewie wpon ws q[uhe]n he hes carnall dealling w[i]th us, als lyk an malt secke; his memberis ar exceiding great and long, no mans memberis ar so long and bigg as they ar: he wold be amongst us, lyke a weath horse amongst mearis he wold lye w[i]th ws in p[rese]nce of all the multitud, neither haid we nor he any kynd of shame, bot especiallie he hes no sham w[i]th him at all, he wold lye and haw carnall dealling w[i]th all enyie tym as he pleased, he wold haw carnall dealling w[i]th us in the shape of a deir or any uth[e]r shap th[a]t he wold be in, we wold never refuse him. (46/23)

Here, of course, we could speculate a fantasy-response to the trauma of rape. There is no doubt that during periods of both chronic and acute warfare incidences of rape rise, and sometimes dramatically. Reports in mid sixteenth-century kirk session minutes and justice court records attest to the relative frequency of the crime in this period.[24] Some of these incidents were rooted in clan antagonisms, with the tenants of the Laird of Balvenie, for example, seeking help from the law to protect themselves against the rival Clan Gregor in 1649: the privy council register stating that the supplicants complained that for several years past 'we have monie tymes suffered dyvers oppressiones and ryotts, boith in our bodies, guides and geir, as also by ravishinge of our women, maried and un-maried, by certane savadge, laules and broken men of the Clangregor and their accomplishes'.[23] The presence of Cromwellian soldiers during the Interregnum, many of them quartered in local houses, also engendered rape accusations. Similarly, it may be no coincidence that, by her own reckoning, Isobel's first sexual encounter with the Devil took place in 1647, a date that came fast on the heels of the Scottish civil wars.

Made in the Tolbooth, circa 1662

But while we can fairly safely assume that during interrogation Isobel wove elements from her own life-story into her stereotypical accounts of meetings with the Devil and travelling with the fairies, the complex processes through which Isobel's violent father, husband or lover was transformed into the 'beatting and scurgeing' Devil, or through which her experiences of threshing corn or walking through sandstorms were transformed into flying through air on corn straws with the fairy host are far less easy to explain.

Scholars working in this field, prominent among them being Roper, have applied themselves to this question in various ways. On the one hand, they suggest that in a bid for leniency and in order to bring the sufferings of imprisonment, torture and repeated interrogations to an end, suspects simply told their questioners what they felt they wanted them to say. In other words, knowing that the interrogators wanted a realistic account of carnal relations with the Devil, they gave them a realistic account of carnal relations with the Devil, and pragmatically drew on their own sexual experiences in order to do so. As Purkiss notes, 'When you are being asked questions by a man who has the power of life and death over you . . . you are probably going to try to say *some-*

thing. But people cannot talk about what they don't know, but only about what they know.'[25]

Purkiss and Roper also emphasize that this, what we can term here, 'retrospective fiction-making process', was more subtle than simple coercion. Employing psychoanalytic perspectives, Roper argues that the suspect's willingness to confess was not just motivated by the fear of torture or desire for leniency, but was the result of a deeper exchange between suspect and questioner; an exchange that followed a similar psychological dynamic to that which traditionally arises between a therapist and their patient. During the witchcraft interrogation, as in therapy, the flattering attentions of the interrogator set up a chain of transference, counter-transference and projection through which the suspect could express unresolved anxieties and thereby achieve emotional release. Roper notes

> It is the individual's inner conflicts which are projected into fantasy and acted out in relations with others. Because these conflicts are intolerable and unresolved, they are constantly repeated and re-enacted. Interrogation for witchcraft, we might say, offered the accused a theatrical opportunity to recount and restage these linked conflicts – and what better audience than the rapt ears of the council's representatives and executioner?[26]

According to Roper, this process of interrogatorial disclosure was deeply reciprocal. Just as the skilled therapist adapts his counselling approach to the individual idiosyncrasies of each patient, so the interrogator, probing the psychology of the witchcraft suspect in search of the authentic confession, would sense where and in what manner he should direct his questioning in order to obtain the fullest and most genuine emotional response. The suspect, on their part, being bound to their interrogator through projection and transference, would tend to channel their emotional release through the avenues made available to them by their confessors. As Roper states, 'The projections of the accused on to the interlocutor allow deeply buried emotional experiences to be expressed. As she or he begins to know the interrogator and unconsciously to identify with his needs, so it becomes possible for her to produce the kind of story he wants to hear.'[27]

We can see, then, how the interrogations that took place in the Auldearn tolbooth may have acted as a pseudo-therapeutic arena through which Isobel accessed and unlocked 'deeply buried emotional experiences'. As argued in CHAPTER FIVE, the men who probably led the interrogations, Harry Forbes and Hugh Rose, were likely to have been skilful questioners and good listeners who were genuinely interested in what Isobel had to say. And these empathic attentions may have acted like a key which efficiently – perhaps more efficiently than any of them ever anticipated – unlocked the emotional conflicts that tensioned Isobel's inner life.

The dynamics of this unlocking process can be most clearly traced in the scenes describing sex with the Devil. While the single scene in Confession One is detailed but essentially conventional, the scenes in Confession Three, recorded nearly a month later, are far more complex and contain higher levels of demonological detail, idiosyncrasy and emotional intensity. Working with Roper's paradigm, this progression suggests that over this four-week period, insinuating and quite possibly sympathetic questions of the 'How and when did you have sex with the Devil?' type may have caused Isobel to increasingly retrieve, express, and elaborate upon buried memories of sexual experience. Such questions would have come easily to ministers who were, as Todd notes, well used to the 'vigorous grilling of suspects about [the] times and places' where they may have committed fornication or adultery.[28] This hypothesis gains further support from the fact that, as noted in CHAPTER SEVEN, few men would have better equipped or more deeply motivated to make such investigations than Isobel's minister, Harry Forbes. Not only was he a good listener and profound thinker who was concerned with the 'deep mysteries' of religion, but he was also a man whose own romantic or sexual passions were powerful enough to subdue his godly inhibitions and lead him into adultery. As such, we can speculate that he was deeply drawn to exploring the sexual dimension of Isobel's life-story and gained vicarious excitement, and perhaps some form of emotional release, from eliciting her disclosure. If we combine this portrait of Forbes with the thesis that, as an oral performer specializing in romance and the supernatural, Isobel may have been unusually articulate and forthcoming on the subject of sexual relations between humans and spirits, then we come some way towards explaining why Isobel's interrogations managed to generate the most graphic and powerful sex-with-the-Devil scenes recorded in any early modern British witchcraft record. This hypothesis is further reinforced by the fact that, as her local minister, Forbes would have been the individual primarily responsible for engineering Isobel's repentance through full and genuine confession, and it is likely that he paid her additional visits at the Auldearn tolbooth during the intervening weeks between her first and third interrogations. Certainly, he visited the witch named Brandon when she was warded in Auldearn nine months later. And during these intimate, probably one-to-one, sessions Forbes may have gradually teased out, image by image and metaphor by metaphor, the full-blown sexual scenarios that explode, as if from nowhere, onto the pages of Confession Three.

But Did She Do It?

Using the retrospective-fiction paradigm, we are able to identify all the elements necessary to explain how Isobel's personal story and the interrogators' demonological theories could have been woven together to construct her confessions. But this analysis still leaves one crucial question unanswered. If Isobel was truly coaxed into constructing a web of retrospective fiction, then how far did she, and by implication any confessing witch, actually believe in the truth of the wonderful lies she described? In other words, although Isobel may have been persuaded to express repressed memories of sexual experience through the conceptual vehicle of stereotypical demonic seduction – did she, at any point in the interrogations, actually believe herself to have had sex with the Devil? Or if Isobel, with the encouragement of her interested interrogators, managed to skilfully weave her memories of sandstorms, threshing barns, and folktales into a description of airborne flight to the sabbath – did she, at any point in the interrogations, actually believe herself to have flown through the air to witches' meetings astride a corn stalk?

In trying to find an answer to this question, the theories of Roper et al. are less helpful. While Roper admits that, in respect to some confessions, 'some' witches 'may well have come to believe they truly were the Devil's own', and that by the time of her confession, German witch Margaretha Minderlin seemed 'to have self-consciously adopted the identity of the witch' such comments are no more than asides.[29] More commonly, historians working with the retrospective-fiction paradigm tend to avoid or gloss over the question with ambiguous comments. Purkiss, for example, notes that 'If asked to produce a story under pressure, people will draw on stories they have heard, stories they have read, stories they have already told, stories they think others will believe'; while Robin Briggs concludes that 'it was all too easy for them [witchcraft suspects] to turn their own experiences into the kind of stories required, translating them into the language of the diabolic, and describing their repressed wishes as if they had been murderously effective in reality'.[30] While both comments are insightful, neither gives us any indication as to whether the suspects themselves believed the 'stories' they were so elaborately and obligingly constructing.

But since the core historical texts relating to the retrospective-fiction paradigm were written in the mid 1990s–early 2000s, there has emerged a significant body of scientific and psychological research, yet to be seriously mined by scholars of witchcraft, that not only reinforces and to a certain extent repackages the theories of Roper et al., but also takes them in a new direction. With regard to the matter in hand, this research enables us to explore the question of 'Did Isobel really believe the things she confessed?' with far more depth and precision than was possible even as recently as ten years ago. And therefore, in order to move more deeply into the truth of Isobel's complex fictions, we will now take a detour into the emerging research surrounding the phenomenon of 'false confession'.

False Confession

The human capacity to make false confessions in courts of law has been observed since classical times, but it is only since the late-twentieth century, when scientific advances such as DNA testing and video evidence have been able to categorically prove, beyond any shadow of doubt, that some individuals did not commit the crimes they claimed to have committed, that the subject has gained a high profile and generated significant research funding. This interest has also been fuelled by widely-publicized sexual abuse cases, where it has been proved that therapists adhering to the 'recovered-memory paradigm' (that is, the belief that the patient's mental distress is caused by the fact they are repressing traumatic memories) have coerced individuals to confess to abusive events that did not actually take place.

Following the classification system devised by psychologists Kassin and Wrightsman in 1985, and which has since been widely accepted by researchers, false confessions can be divided into three basic categories: 'voluntary', 'coerced-compliant' and 'coerced-internalized'.[31] Voluntary false confession is primarily associated with either protecting the guilty or non-responsibility (caused by mental illness or the consumption of mind-altering substances). Coerced-compliant and coerced-internalized false confessions, on the other hand, are more complex and while they are associated with certain mental conditions or tendencies, such as low self-esteem and high-anxiety, they pertain to individuals generally considered sane.[32] Given the fact that there is no indication that Isobel gave her confessions in order to protect anyone else, or that she was overtly insane or under the influence of mind-altering substances, we will be concentrating on the last two categories of Kassin and Wrightsman's classification.

Coerced-compliant and coerced-internalized confessions overlap considerably, but there is also a clear distinction to be made between them. In the case of the coerced-compliant confession, the innocent suspect claims to having committed a crime even though they do not remember having done so. This kind of false confession can be made either with or without belief. In the case of the without-belief variant, a suspect goes along with what they think the questioner wants to hear and admits guilt despite the fact that they do not believe that they have committed the crime, because they think that this will improve their situation in some way, with the hope for leniency being the commonest motivator. In the case of the with-belief variant, at some point during the interrogation the suspect 'caves-in' and accepts that they committed the crime for which they are accused even though they do not remember doing so, presuming they performed it because the person interrogating them said so. Both types of coerced-compliant confession are strongly dependent on momentary factors: in the first case, promises of leniency and in the second, psychological mood. As psychologists Charles Brainerd and Valerie Reyna note, because promises may not always be delivered and moods generally pass, these types of confession are characteristically followed by changes of heart, making recantation a 'determinative feature of a coerced-compliant confession'.[33]

The coerced-internalized confession, meanwhile, is something very different. Here, the innocent suspect does not accept that they committed a crime that they can't remember; they accept they committed a crime because, during the process of the interrogation, they develop vivid memories of having performed it. The existence of a memory phenomenon whereby, as Brainerd and Reyna put it, 'normal people are possessed of positive, confident memories of things that never happened to them', is difficult to grasp, but in the last two decades, a 'broad-based outpouring of research' into the subject has generated startling clinical results.[34] Although researchers are still unsure as to the psychological and somatic mechanisms behind the phenomenon, since they were first put forward in the early 1900s theoretical models of how the process works have become increasingly sophisticated, with 'opponent-process' theories being currently popular. The latter hypotheses are too complex to explore in this book, it being sufficient to note here that they are based upon the idea that memory itself is a 'reconstructed phenomenon' (that is, the result of a process that requires co-operation from different parts of the mind) and that false memories are created when factors such as fear, stress, suggestion, misinformation and so on cause the parts of the mind which construct memories to interact in a non-standard way.[35]

Given the fact that the concept of false memory is so difficult to grasp, before we move on to examine it in the context of Isobel's confessions some recent studies will be explored here in a little more depth. Of the highly persuasive research into false memory that has emerged in the last two decades, a selection of experiments led by psychologists Ira Hyman (1995) and Stephen Porter (1999) are illustrative. In the first, Hyman invited students to participate in an experiment that was seemingly-devised to establish how well people remember childhood experiences. After gathering together (from correspondence with parents) a collection of childhood memories relating to each of his participants, Hyman met them individually and described a number of their childhood experiences to them. But in each case Hyman deliberately included two false experiences (an exciting birthday party and a hospital visit, both at age five) alongside the genuine ones gleaned from parents. As you would expect, during this first interview most of the participants remembered details about the true episodes, but not about the false ones. Hyman then asked his participants to go away and do 'memory work' in order to try and recover details of some of these experiences, including one of the false ones. By the second session 20 percent of the students remembered details about the false episode, and had often attached surprisingly rich 'supporting memories' to the memory 'shell' that had been given to them by Hyman. Encouraged by these results, Hyman then repeated the experiment over three sessions, using only negative childhood episodes and putting a stronger emphasis on memory work. As before, no students remembered the false episodes in the first session, but by the second, 18 percent remembered the false experience and by the third this number had risen to 26 percent.[36] In a similar, but more complex experiment performed by Porter et al., which was based on purely traumatic childhood events and was more coercive (participants were told that 'if they failed to recover memories of an experience, they were probably not working hard enough'), no less than 56 percent of the subjects experienced false memories of a childhood event implanted by the experiment-leader.[37]

What has emerged prominently from these and similar studies is the fact that although, in the more coercive experiments like Porter's, some people produced false memories in the first session, in most cases the development was accumulative, with Brainerd noting that 'false memories for complex events tended to emerge across experimental sessions, rather than appearing suddenly, in finished form, during the first experimental session'.[38] Equally importantly, the experiments revealed that people were more likely to develop false memories around the familiar, as opposed to the unfamiliar, with Brainerd claiming that 'subjects would be most likely to generate rich supporting memories of false memories that referred to situations with which they were familiar and for which they would therefore possess strong gist memories. Consistent with this hypothesis, subjects who discussed personal knowledge during the first interview that was relevant to the false experience were more likely to remember the experience later and supply supporting details.'[39] For example, in one recent study led by Pedzek (1997), a mixed group of Catholic and Jewish students were all given the same false memories, one of them involving an embarrassing event which occurred at communion, the other involving an incident which occurred at a shabbat. The results, as paraphrased by Brainerd, were as follows: '31 percent of Catholic students displayed false memories of the communion incident, with only 10 percent displaying false memories of the Shabbat incident. In contrast, 14 percent of the Jewish students displayed false memories of the Shabbat incident, with none displaying false memories of the communion incident.'[40]

Although both coerced-compliant and coerced-internalized confessions can theoretically occur in any situation, outside specially-devised clinical trials they most notably appear in either criminal interrogations or therapeutic sessions, in the latter case most commonly emerging where the therapist works with the recovered-memory paradigm. Both situations frequently contain a number of the core factors necessary to generate false confession: high levels of stress (in criminal investigations the tensions of arrest and threat of punishment and in therapeutic exchanges the tensions of disclosure and the distressing symptoms that prompted the patient to seek help in the first place); power imbalance (with regard to the matter in hand, both the detective and therapist have more status, power and knowledge than the suspect or patient); a strong prior assumption of guilt on the part of the questioner, based on what is considered to be compelling evidence (the detective suspects the individual to have committed the crime and the therapist believes the patient is repressing hidden trauma); claims, by the questioner, to have superior knowledge of the hidden event and how to identify it (the detective has material evidence, witness reports and so on and the therapist has knowledge of the psychological dynamics of repression); and most significantly of all, the repetitive and persistent use of misinformation (as in: 'You walked into the jewellery shop at 8.30') or suggestive questioning, whether of the specific-closed variety (as in: 'Did you walk into the jewellery shop at 8.30?') or the specific-open (as in: 'When did you walk into the jewellery shop?').

Isobel's False Confession

These perspectives support the view, already attested and explored by Roper et al., that witchcraft testimony would have been generated in conditions very conducive to the development of false confession. In Isobel's case, all the core elements were certainly present: the stressful situation, the power imbalance, the strong prior assumption of guilt, the interrogator's claim to superior knowledge and, of course, very close, suggestive questioning. But although we can speculate on the basis of this that Isobel's narratives may have been, in part or whole, 'false confessions', it is more difficult to determine exactly what category of false confession they may have been. Following Kassin and Wrightsman's classification system, we can assume that they would have fallen into one of three categories: the without-belief coerced-complaint confession (that is, Isobel pleaded guilty to the crimes alleged against her knowing that she was innocent, in the hope of leniency); the with-belief coerced-compliant confession (that is, Isobel caved in and accepted that she may have committed the crimes alleged against her, although she could not remember doing so); and the coerced-internalized confession (that is, Isobel came to believe that she had committed the crimes, on the basis of strong false memories generated during interrogation and imprisonment). In the remainder of this chapter, we will be dividing Isobel's confessional content into three categories: (1) Demonological elements and specific *maleficium* (restricted here, as in the last two chapters, to the basic variety). (2) Charms (both maleficent and beneficent). (3) Fairy-related material. And in each case we will assess which of the three types of false confession emerges as the most convincing. While such an analysis can only be highly speculative, it generates new perspectives on the confessions and gives us a fuller sense of how they may have been created.

Demonological Elements

Unsurprisingly, the passages that lend themselves most readily to explanatory theories of false confession are those which describe either specific *maleficium* or stereotypical demonological events such as the demonic pact and the witches' sabbath. As argued in CHAPTERS THREE and SEVEN, these passages do not only deal with the subjects that most concerned the prosecutors, but they also contain the strongest evidence of close and persistent interrogation, an evident presumption of guilt and a high level of specific-closed questioning. Although, as we argued in the last chapter, Isobel's descriptions of specific *maleficium*, such as making a *corp creadh* to kill the heirs of Park, mixing maleficent potions to kill Forbes and sabotaging Alexander Cumming's dye vats may have been based on real magical practices undertaken before arrest, their context, as with the more fantastic demonological passages, also suggests that false confession may have been involved.

But if this was the case, then what kind of false confession? First, we cannot rule out the coerced-compliant option. With regard to the without-belief variant, Isobel could have pleaded guilty to the crimes alleged against her, even though she knew she was innocent, in a desperate bid for leniency. As argued in earlier chapters, the men who interrogated her were capable of compassion and she may have learnt quickly that if she told them what they wanted to hear and satisfied their thirst for detail they were kinder; perhaps providing better food, more visits and most importantly, forbearing from any maltreatment (watching, pricking, beating and so on) they may have initially adopted in order to loosen her tongue. Alternatively, in the case of the with-belief option, in response to the intense and coercive interrogatorial conditions, Isobel may have become scared and disorientated early on in the proceedings; lost faith in her own ability to judge reality, either past or present; and finally caved in and acknowledged having performed the crimes alleged against her, even though she did not remember having done so. In both cases we can speculate that, as an oral performer, her imaginative abilities and verbal skills may have rendered her more qualified than many to weave disparate strands of suggestion and real-life experience into vivid and coherent false narratives and to deliver them with dramatic conviction and rhetorical skill.

But although we cannot rule them out, both coerced-compliant options remain unconvincing on a number of levels. Although they could reasonably account for the admissions of guilt Isobel made during the first interrogation, particularly given the fact that, as we saw in CHAPTER THREE, Isobel was quite possibly maltreated in some way, it does not account for the fact that she stood by these admissions, and in some cases elaborated upon them, in the second, third and fourth. As Brainerd has noted, recantation is a 'determinative feature' of the coerced-compliant confession. Once maltreatment ceases or promises of leniency are not delivered or mood changes, and an individual has a chance to reflect on their self-incriminatory testimony, they often become at pains to deny it. This certainly seems to have been the case with Forres suspects Isobel Elder and Isobel Simpson in 1663. As we saw in CHAPTER THREE, the evidence suggests that the two women made their first confessions after being beaten, only to later retract them and then hold to their retractions in the face of mounting interrogatorial exasperation. If we were to entertain either of the coerced-compliant options in Isobel's case, we would have to accept that she made her false confession during her first interrogation on 13 April, and that subsequently, over the whole of the following six-week-period (much of which would have been spent alone in the tolbooth, with plenty of time to reflect on what she had said), she never experienced a change of heart that caused her to regret her incriminatory fictions and retract. Alternatively, we would have to accept that if she did retract at any point, her prosecutors or keepers managed to successfully coerce her to acknowledge her guilt all over again; re-adhere to her previous false testimonies; and build upon them at the next interrogation, without any contrariety or loss of descriptive precision or tone.

But moving onto our last option, the coerced-internalized false confession, we find ourselves contemplating an altogether more convincing scenario. According to this hypothesis, Isobel described performing the demonic pact or making the *corp creadh* because, over the course of her imprisonment and interrogation she developed 'firm, confident' memories of these events having taken place. Those unfamiliar with the phenomenon of false memory might find it difficult to imagine how Isobel could possibly have fabricated consistently detailed, vivid and crime-specific memories of such fantastic and incriminatory events. But these kinds of fabrications are wholly congruent with recent research. In order to illustrate this, we will embark on a short case study; cross-referencing, in some detail, the sex-with-the-Devil component of Isobel's demonic pact and sabbath scenes with a well-documented and high-profile twentieth-century sexual abuse case grounded on false-memory recollections.[41]

In 1992, in Missouri, USA, a sane but 'highly strung' nineteen-year-old girl named Beth Rutherford went to a therapist because she was having difficulty sleeping. The therapist, who worked with the recovered-memory paradigm, asked her if she had been sexually abused. Believing herself to enjoy a happy and normal relationship with her parents she vehemently denied the suggestion. The therapist did not respond by withdrawing his allegations but merely emphasized that her symptoms fitted those of sexual abuse victims. In Beth's second session with the therapist she admitted that she sometimes had violent dreams in which her father attacked her with a knife. Again, she was told that although she had no memory of it, these types of dreams were symptomatic of sexual abuse. After this Beth's therapy sessions were increasingly focused on the attempt to recover her repressed memories of this alleged abuse and a variety of techniques were used. The latter can be summarized (with Brainerd's illustrative commentary in parentheses) in the following list. (1) The interpretation of behavioural symptoms (Beth was told that 'the fact that she was an A-student in high school was a sign that she had been abused'). (2) Age regression (she was 'instructed to relate memories of childhood experiences . . . [and] the counselor then interpreted those reports in ways which were consistent with sexual abuse. When Rutherford described a storage shed in one home, for instance, this was transformed into a place in which she had been tied up and where objects had been inserted in her body'). (3) Interpretation of the behaviour of others (her accounts of activities involving her parents were interpreted so as to support the sexual abuse story, so for example, 'when Rutherford related a story of writing cheques with her father to pay bills when she was 9 years old, her counselor characterized this as evidence that her father was treating her as a spouse, rather than as a daughter, and that he preferred Rutherford over her mother'). (4) Dream interpretation ('as the emphasis on sexual abuse increased, Rutherford began having dreams with intense sexual content, dreaming, for instance, of occasions on which she and her friends were raped while her father watched . . . The counselor informed her that the dreams were true memories and that her mind was using the mechanism of dreams to reveal the reality of her abuse'). (5) Forced accusation and confrontation ('the counselor urged Rutherford to confront her parents and to openly accuse them of abusing her. Rutherford was urged to take these steps on the ground that they were essential if she wished to heal the damage that had been caused by the abuse'). These techniques were so effective, summarizes Brainerd, that after two and a half years of counselling Beth:

> had recovered highly specific 'memories' of repeated sexual abuse by her father between the ages of 7 and 14, including being sodomized by him with a curling iron and being raped by him with a fork and scissors. Among other memories, she recalled being twice impregnated by her father. Upon discovering she was pregnant for the first time, she remembered that her father had used a coat hanger to perform a painful abortion on her . . . She also remembered her father cutting her and licking the blood from her body.[42]

Although he pleaded innocent to all charges, as a result of his daughter's accusations Beth's father was dismissed from his job and she was advised, for her own self-protection, to sever all contact with her parents. But several years later, in a dramatic follow-up to this traumatic train of events, Beth became reunited with her family and, collectively coming to believe that her abuse-memories had been false, they filed suit against the therapist for malpractice and defamation. As part of their case, Beth's family cited the fact that her father had undergone a vasectomy and therefore could not have impregnated her. Even more significantly, Beth had a gynaecological examination which 'revealed not only that she never been pregnant but that, indeed, she was still a virgin'.[43] Unsurprisingly, the Rutherfords won their suit.

It is not unreasonable to speculate that the sexual content of Isobel's demonological passages, which was not only sensational but also increasingly incorporated both stereotypical and idiosyncratic sexual details as the interrogations progressed, may have been generated as the result of a similar process. As argued earlier, although sex with the Devil was a standard feature of the demonic pact and witches' sabbath stereotype, for personal reasons Harry Forbes was likely to have been particularly interested in this dimension of Isobel's experiences and was therefore likely, as did Beth Rutherford's therapist, to have energetically pursued it, both at the four main interrogations and also at the private one-to-one meetings that may have taken place inbetween them. In addition, as the following list illustrates, although Forbes was involved in a criminal investigation and Beth's therapist was involved in a therapeutic one, the functional similarities between early modern concepts of the Devil (as they were understood by reformed ministers like Forbes) and twentieth-century concepts of the unconscious (as interpreted by adherents of the recovered-memory paradigm) mean that the two men may have approached their respective tasks in very similar ways. (1) Both would have embarked upon proceedings with the unimpeachable conviction that destructive forces, independent of personal will, exist in the subject's mind: for Beth's therapist this dark force was the unconscious and for Harry Forbes it was the Devil. (2) Both men believed that this force had the ability to hide the truth from their subject: Beth's therapist believed that the unconscious could conceal and disguise traumatic memories while Harry Forbes believed that the Devil could manipulate and trick the mind with illusions. (3) Both men believed that their subject needed to uncover the truth beneath this false veneer through full and honest disclosure: Beth's therapist would have told her that 'talking about your memories of abuse and reliving them will help you to overcome them' while Forbes would have impressed upon Isobel that only a fuller, genuine, confession would enable her to break free from the Devil's clutches and make her peace with God.[44] (4) Both men believed they possessed superior knowledge of the way this destructive force – the unconscious or the Devil – was causing harm to their subject than the subject themselves: Beth's therapist managed to convince her that her unconscious was repressing memories of incest with her father in order to protect him and prevent her own cure, while Forbes, in accordance with general demonological thinking of the time, is likely to have told Isobel that her inability to remember her crimes or unwillingness to confess (should this have occurred) denoted the fact that the Devil was blocking her memory or 'stopping her tongue' to prevent genuine confession.[45] (5) Both men would have facilitated his truth-unearthing process by gleaning personal details from their subject; re-defining them in accordance with their conceptual paradigms and behavioural checklist and then reflecting this back to them. Beth's therapist would have told her that symptoms x, y or z indicated that she was sexually abused by her father while Forbes may have told Isobel that the red mark on her shoulder meant that she had made a pact with the Devil, or the English soldier with whom she had committed adultery was the Devil in disguise and so on.

In both cases, these interrogatorial processes would have created the same psychological effect: kneading the psyche like dough and causing it to become pliant and responsive. And through this intimate, reciprocal investigative process Isobel may have begun, as did Beth, to generate false recollections of the crimes levelled against her and contextualise them within a bed of 'rich supporting memories' drawn from her own life experience. Just as Beth spontaneously recalled vivid, detailed memories of having sex with her father, so Isobel may have spontaneously recalled vivid, detailed memories of having sex with the Devil: memories that amalgamated genuine – and maybe previously repressed – memories of sexual experience, personal sexual fantasies (perhaps influenced by oral literature concerning amorous relationships between humans and spirits), and stereotypical images of sex with the Devil, as suggested by Forbes. Given the fact that under the manipulations of her therapist Beth became so convinced of the truth of her false memories that she was able to directly and publicly accuse her innocent father of violent episodes of sexual abuse, it is not unreasonable to suppose that Isobel (whose memories, by the way, appear almost prosaic when set side by side with Beth's) became so convinced of the reality of her carnal transgressions with the Devil that, despite the fact that they were completely false, she was able to describe them fully and confidently at the crowded interrogations in the Auldearn tolbooth.

We can posit a similarly intricate, multi-authorial genesis for the passages describing basic specific *maleficium*. With regard to the making of the *corp creadh*, the circumstantial evidence is particularly compelling. First, we have the fact that Isobel's interrogations were led by a minister who believed that he had personally been attacked through the deployment of maleficent image magic. Secondly, we have the fact that, as we saw in CHAPTER SEVEN, many, if not all, of the interrogators and witnesses at Isobel's trial would have been aware of the notorious trial of Agnes Grant, the woman accused of murdering the Laird of Park and his two sons nineteen years earlier. Thirdly, we have the fact that two of the men most likely to have been traumatized by these events – surviving son Hugh Hay of Brightmony and his fatherless nephew, Hugh Hay of Newton – were present at all four of Isobel's interrogations. Fourthly, we have the fact that Forbes and his fellow prosecutors would have examined Isobel in the apprehensive knowledge that Newton's brother – John Hay – was married and producing male heirs for the first time since the three tragic deaths nearly twenty years ago. Given this hotbed of anxiety, it is not difficult to see how Isobel could have been subjected to particularly focused and coerced-closed questioning on the matters of both image magic and the fortunes of the Lairds of Park. Certainly, in a crucible of this intensity, joint interrogatorial preoccupations could have generated enough 'When did you make an effigy in order to harm the heirs of Lairds of Park?'-type questions to provoke Isobel into producing false memories of the alleged event. And knowing what we know about Isobel, it is also not difficult to see how she, for her part, could have drawn on personal experience to create 'rich, supporting memories' to underpin this core fictional event. Memories of sitting around the fire kneading flour, turning scones and roasting meat; of working clay into marbles, child's dolls, or domestic pots; of witnessing, or even participating in, the performance of clandestine magical ritual; and of hearing whispered gossip, passed around the dark cottage hearths of Auldearn, about how local women Agnes Grant and Katherine Sowter had used *maleficium*, with devastating success, to bring down the heirs of Park nearly two decades earlier. In the light of the perspectives drawn in CHAPTERS SEVEN and EIGHT, we can also consider the possibility that Isobel's false *corp creadh* memories may have been rooted in something more concrete. At some point prior to her arrest she may have genuinely attempted to harm either the Laird of Park or someone else through making a clay image and roasting it before the fire. The event may not have conformed, in every particular, to the confessional account, but would have rendered up a wealth of raw material. Isobel's memories of a rite performed alone or with different people, or of a rite begun and aborted, or of a rite merely planned without being executed could, under interrogatorial pressure, have been drawn into false-memory constructs, where they fused into something altogether grander, and finally gave rise to the sophisticated, detailed *corp creadh* accounts that emerge in the confessions.

Rhyming Charms and False Confession

With regard to Isobel's rhyming charms, explanatory theories of false confession are equally persuasive, although the complexity of the genre means that the issue takes more unpacking. As we have seen in CHAPTERS THREE and FIVE, the textual context of the rhyming charms strongly suggests that they were generated in response to direct questioning of the 'What charm did you recite when you did x, y or z?' variety. On the one hand, this does not necessarily mean that they were false. Charming was widespread in the period and Isobel would have almost certainly possessed a collection of charms for personal use and for use in her capacity as a magical practitioner, should she have been one. And on this basis, as argued in CHAPTER FOUR, we can fairly safely assume that the five beneficent charms cited in the second confession were genuine, that is, inherited charms used by Isobel prior to arrest. Similarly, although the question of the genuineness of the maleficent charms is more controversial, we still cannot rule out the possibility completely. First, we can fairly safely assume (as we cannot with regard to many of the prose passages) that these charms came, largely fully-formed, from Isobel herself. Even if the interrogators had badgered Isobel with rhyme-prompting questions, these would not have been word or phrase specific, and would have been constructed along the lines of 'And what charm did you say when you made the *corp creadh?*' as opposed to 'Did you say "we put this water among this meall for long dwynning & ill heall etc" when you made the *corp creadh?*' Secondly, as argued in CHAPTER EIGHT, because these charms conform to contemporary curse and evil-eye-averting charm templates we cannot rule out the possibility that they were inherited verses recited during the performance of maleficent magical acts.

But against the latter possibility, we must set the fact that the maleficent charms display a number of anomalies which, although not significant individually, when taken together strongly suggest that some, or all, of them may have been false in the sense that they were not only delivered, but also made up, in response to interrogatorial prompting. It is significant, for example, that in the first confession Isobel's richly-detailed prose accounts of making the *corp creadh*, feasting in cellars and stealing the fertility of her neighbour's land contain no references to charms at all, but that by the fourth confession (after Isobel's capacity for rhyme production had become fully evident) all four accounts have become illustrated or accessorized with appropriate and often unerringly crime-specific charms. The rhyme that Isobel claims, in the third confession, to have used when making the *corp creadh*, for example, accurately reflects the ritual she described so memorably in prose four weeks before:

In the divellis nam, we powr in this water among this mould, for land dwyning and ill heall, we putt it in into the fyre, that it mey be brunt both stik and stowre, it salbe brunt w[i]th owr will, as any stikle wpon a kill. (48/24)

It could be argued that the crime-specific quality of Isobel's charms signifies little because it is quite standard for traditional charms of all types to contain versified descriptions of the chain of the events they are intended to instigate. But in Isobel's case, the sheer numbers of crime-specific charms produced, seemingly on demand, to accompany so many of the maleficent acts described in the confessions, however large or small, mundane or fantastic, strongly suggests that they may have been made-to-measure in response to interrogatorial suggestion. This possibility is supported by the fact that Isobel's charm-generating capacities do not seem to have distinguished between standard and physically-possible acts of basic *maleficium* and the more fantastic and physically-impossible acts of fairy-related *maleficium*. In other words, any concession to the possibility that Isobel's *corp creadh* charm may have been genuine, on the premise that she may have conceivably made the *corp creadh* itself, is sabotaged by her equally confident claim to have used charms when shooting elf arrows while flying through the air astride corn straws (as in, 'I shoot yon man in the divellis name, he sall not win heall home').

The possibility that Isobel made up her charms in response to interrogatorial suggestion is also supported by the fact that they are markedly more simple, both in vocabulary, style and form, than the beneficent charms cited. Again, in itself this is not significant: traditional maleficent charms are often less sophisticated and formal than beneficent (a difference partly that may be rooted, in part, to the fact that the latter were influenced by Catholic prayer and liturgy). But in Isobel's case, the maleficent spells cited flaunt such a rough, colloquial, and at times clumsy, assortment of phrases and half-rhymes that they evoke the informality and emotional spontaneity of the hastily-composed curse or flyghting insult as opposed to the memorized verse-charm. We can further add to these idiosyncrasies the fact that Isobel's charms borrow from, and mimic, one another to an unusually high degree. The three charms which she claimed to have used when metamorphosing into animal form, for example, share many of the same phrases. To transform into a hare Isobel chanted:

I sall gow intill a haire w[i]th sorrow and syt and meikle caire, and I sall goe in the divellis nam ay whill I com hom (*damaged – words missing*).

To transform into a cat:

I sall goe int(*ill?*) (*damaged – words missing*) shot, and I sall goe in the divellis nam, ay q[uhi]ll I com hom again.

To transform into a crow:

I sall goe intill a craw w[i]th sorrow and syt & blak (*damaged – words missing*) ay q[uhi]ll I com home again. (43/32)

Again, such inter-borrowing signifies little in itself, for traditional charms, songs and ballads often share phrases, rhyming couplets and even whole stanzas, particularly if they are concerned with the same subject matter, with this repetition reflecting the process of adaptation and improvising upon a theme that lies at the very heart of traditional oral transmission. From this perspective, the similarity between these animal metamorphosis charms could be simply attributed to thematic congruence. But on the other hand, the way that these charms are presented, neatly one after the other in quick succession, evokes the picture of Isobel frantically hashing and re-hashing the same charm in an attempt to meet her interrogators' 'And what do you say when you turned into a hare/cat/crow?'-type demands. That something like this may have been the case is supported elsewhere in the testimony. In Confession Three, for example, Isobel claims that at Candlemas, Alexander Earleseat recited the following charm when the coven sat down to eat at Grangehill:

> we eat this meat in the divellis nam, w[i]th sorrow and syt and meikle shame we sall destroy hows and hald, bot sheip and noat intill the fold, litle good sall com to the fore, of all the rest of the litle store. (48/18)

Later in the same confession Isobel recites a different charm, which she and her companions used when placing a potion-bag into their neighbour's dunghill, to draw off the fertility. Interestingly, it contains virtually the same last four lines (highlighted here in italics) as the one spoken by Alexander Earleseat:

> we putt this in intill this ham, in o[u]r lord the divellis nam, the first handis th[a]t handles the brunt and scalded sall they be, *we sall distroy hows and hald, w{i}th the sheip and noat intill the fold & litl sall com to the for of all the rest of the litl store.* (49/29)

These two charms are concerned with two very different magical acts and therefore their similarities cannot, as with the animal metamorphosis charms, simply be attributed to thematic congruence. Moreover, the fact that both charms accessorized magical rituals previously described without accompanying charms, and that both emerged in close proximity to each other (the second half of the third confession), strongly suggest that improvisation was involved. While it is, of course, conceivable that during the third interrogation Isobel coincidentally remembered, at around the same time, two charms associated with two different magical acts that just happened to share a very similar stanza, it is just as likely – indeed it is more likely – that their similarities reflect the fact that both were composed by Isobel, in response to interrogatorial prompting, during the same bout of questioning.

But perhaps the most persuasive evidence supporting the Isobel-made-up-her-charms-during-interrogation hypothesis is the degree to which her charms make reference to the Devil. With one exception, these references appear in the form of the phrase 'in the Devil's name', and the phrase appears in no less than eleven of the twenty-seven rhymes as well as in a number of confessional prose passages. In itself, the term is not unique. Scattered references suggest that it was part of contemporary speech, and it found its way into at least one other witchcraft record, with Agnes Wobster's trial dittays (Aberdeenshire, 1597) stating that she 'cumand to George Mitchellis houss, in Auchtidonald, quha haid ane lamb keddie, and, at thy incumming, the keddie lap upon the, quhom to thow said, in Deuillis name, that it was so wantoun, for it supit mair milk nor thow did'.[46] While it is difficult here to tell whether the phrase in question came from Agnes, her accuser, or her interrogators, a 1655 entry in the Caithness presbytery records strongly suggests that the term was sometimes used in popular magical invocations; the minutes claiming that local fisherman John Gills was commanded to 'stand in sackcloth, and [be] put in the joggs' because 'being at sea, the rest of the boat getting fishe and not he, [Gills] Did throw over his hook, saying, "If thou slay not in God's name, slay in ye devill's name."'[47] That the phrase enjoyed popular usage is corroborated by its appearance in a number of ballads and stories: with the northeastern ballad of 'The Twa Sisters', in which a miller plays a violin made out of human bones before the king, concluding dramatically with the stanza: 'Now pay the miller for his payne/And let him bee gone in the divel's name.'[48] But although the phrase appears in reported speech and song, and even in the occasional witch record, it is not, to my knowledge (though examples may exist), found in any of the hundreds of traditional rhyming charms or curses recorded in Scotland from the seventeenth century through to the nineteenth. Although charms and curses frequently invoke powers 'in the name' or 'for the sake' of a spirit or deity the invoked spirit is seldom the Devil.

Given this scarcity, the fact that the phrase 'in the Devil's name' appears so frequently throughout Isobel's rhyming charms is truly unusual. And this anomaly can be interpreted in two ways. On the one hand, we can take the confessions at face value and conclude that the phrase was a pre-existent feature of Isobel's repertoire of maleficent and/or evil-eye-averting charms, and that prior to her arrest her magical practice had revolved heavily around invocations of the Devil. This possibility (which at this stage in our research seems too fantastic to be credible) will be further explored in CHAPTER SEVENTEEN. But on the other hand, we can conclude that because Isobel's interrogators were primarily interested in the role of the Devil in her magical practice, and questioned her suggestively to this effect, she specifically wove the colloquial phrase 'in the Devil's name' into her rhyming charms. The indiscriminate, and at times excessive, way the phrase is scattered throughout the confessions supports the latter view. It is promiscuously tacked onto the ends and beginnings of many different types of charm – both long and short, complex and simple, basic and fairy-related – and is found facilitating magical acts as diverse as raising winds, transforming into animals, stealing fertility and levitating on corn straws.

Popular Versifying

That Isobel may have been capable of making up charms in response to interrogatorial questioning may seem unlikely, but it is in fact wholly congruent with what we know about seventeenth-century popular culture, and oral performers in particular. As we briefly explored in CHAPTER SIX, rhyming occupied a significant place in the cultural life of early modern Britons. But this interest did not only extend to memorizing and listening to rhymes, but also to rhyme composition. In Scotland, as in England, 'the inventing and retaining of rhymes was commonplace at all social levels. Versifying not only preserved a variety of useful knowledge, but also provided a standard form of entertainment.'[49] Also interesting, with regard to Isobel, is the fact that these and associated skills were often attributed to women, with Kirkwood noting, in the late-seventeenth century, that Highland women were 'good at vocal music; and inventing of Songs'.[50] Both fireside and classical bards would also have been accustomed to versifying upon current events as well as epic heroes and fictional worlds. In early nineteenth-century Galloway, as in other parts of Scotland in this period, 'Almost every village used to have a kind of Poet in it, that made sangs about anything aboon the common that was gaun on at the time; some of them were very clever at it.'[51]

But if we are to accept the possibility that Isobel composed her rhyming charms in response to interrogatorial interest, we also need to consider where and when this composition may have occurred. It could, theoretically, have taken place during her solitary confinement. There is no doubt that by the time Isobel began rhyme-making in earnest (from the time of the second confession onwards) she had been warded for at least two weeks. That was plenty of time for a quick mind, already in possession of verbal skills and a wide range of oral lore, to mix, match and adapt the charms she already knew into those variants recorded in the confessions. But on the other hand, we must also consider the possibility that Isobel composed her rhymes during the interrogations themselves, despite the fact that, at first glance, this seems unfeasible. That a woman who had endured weeks of solitary confinement and community humiliation would have been able to stand in a crowded room on trial for her life and possess either the inclination or the wherewithal to compose a wide array of colourful, crime-specific rhymes on demand, seems patently far-fetched. But this picture becomes far less improbable when considered in the light of the fact that the ability to make up or 'extemporize' verse on the spot was, among peoples of all ranks of society and levels of education, one of the most prized verbal skills in early modern Scotland.

In a recent study Adam Fox noted that early modern England 'was a society in which it was quite normal to sit around the fire or the workbench improvising and extemporizing on a theme . . . Such habits have been all but forgotten in subsequent centuries.'[52] The situation was little different in Scotland. Folklorist Isabel Grant claimed that pre-Modern Highlanders 'had to a high degree the gift of improvising verse' and that there 'are many anecdotes about this talent'; while Martin Martin noted that in the Western Isles in the late-seventeenth century 'several of both Sexes have a Gift of Poesy, and are able to form a *Satyr* or *Panegyrick ex tempore*, without the assistance of any stronger Liquor than Water to raise their Fancy'.[53] Similarly, in his seminal work *The Ballad and the Folk* Buchan claimed that improvisation played a far more prominent role in ballad-singing than has previously been acknowledged, claiming that 'the oral poet re-creates each story at each performance, during each performance' and that every time a performer sings a ballad he embarks upon a 'process of re-composition' or 'disciplined improvisation' in which he becomes performer and composer at the same time.[54] Interestingly, as with rhyming generally, extemporization was particularly associated with the natural and quick verbal skills of women, with Will Walker, who helped Child collect his ballads in nineteenth-century Aberdeenshire, claiming that 'we must remember that improvisation and impromptu adaptation were far more common among rural maidens and mothers in Scotland, during the centuries that are past, than they are now'.[55] As with women's oral performance in general, rhyme production often accompanied the household tasks that dominated the working day, with Grant noting that, when fulling cloth in the Hebrides, 'part of the fun [for the participating women] was the making up on the spur of the moment of couplets about the company and their friends'.[56]

The possibility that Isobel may have composed her rhyming charms during inter-rogation becomes even more compelling when we take into account the fact that extempore versifying, as it emerges in traditional oral cultures, is much easier than the modern literate mind generally assumes. As Kittredge wryly noted in 1904, 'Improvisation in verse is a lost art among us, and we instinctively regard it as a very special mark of exceptional genius. But this is a serious misapprehension. It survives in full vigor among the folk in most countries.'[57] Similarly, with regard to traditional Scottish ballad singing, Buchan claims that the oral poet 'can compose rapidly in performance, because he has learned the phrases and rhythms of poetic language, the language of tradition, which he can think in almost as easily as we can think in the phrases and rhythms of our prosaic language'.[58] Although some critics have argued that Buchan overestimates the role that improvisation, as opposed to memorization by rote, played in ballad transmission, his work provides us with valuable insights into the extemporization process.[59] Buchan emphasizes that the improvisational abilities of the poet lie in the fact that he has memorized a 'method of composition' as opposed to an intact ballad with a set number and order of stanzas.[60] He also emphasizes that this technique consists of many different skills, prominent among them being the ability to memorize and quickly access a large pool of words which rhyme or half-rhyme. This affinity with the shared properties between groups of words also generates the capacity to alliterate lines at speed and exploit assonance. The ability to store and manipulate formulaic phrases, similes and metaphors (such as the classic 'berry brown steed', 'leaf green wood' and 'rose red lips') is also crucial, for these can then be stacked one upon the other, like building blocks, in an infinite number of ways. Also important is the capacity to 'carry a rhyme' through the clever use of 'inessential lines' (that is, lines that do not rhyme or contribute to the narrative) and to take advantage of the crucial split-seconds of thinking space which they give the inventing mind. According to Buchan, the ability to memorize the overall 'structures of balladry', in a manner that is both 'spacial as well as simply linear and sequential' is also central. Through his knowledge of 'certain structural-mnemonic rhythms and patternings', such as 'balances and paral-lelisms, contrasts and antitheses, chiastic and framing devices' and 'various kinds of triadic groupings', the improvising poet can 'marshal his material compactly but not rigidly' and develop his story-line with flexibility but within a firm aesthetic frame-work.[61]

Buchan emphasizes that in traditional oral cultures these methods of composition would have been learnt in the earliest years of infancy alongside the development of language, and that because they were internalized at such a fundamental level they would not have been employed consciously, but would have been brought to bear in the same unconscious, largely effortless way that we employ the grammatical forms and phrases of normal language. As scholar of oral literature Albert Lord emphasizes: 'The speaker of this language, once he has mastered it, does not move any more mechanically within it than we do in ordinary speech. When we speak a language, our native language, we do not repeat words and phrases that we have memorized consciously, but the words and sentences emerge from habitual usage. This is true of the singer of tales working in his specialised grammar.'[62] Kittredge, meanwhile, goes so far as to claim that 'Improvisation in verse . . . is well known to be far less difficult, in itself, than the art of speaking extempore in well-turned prose sentences.'[63]

In this context, the argument that Isobel may have been able to compose her rhyming charms during interrogation is no longer surprising. Her maleficent verses contain all the core building blocks necessary for improvised performance and, more significantly, the nature of their component parts, and the ways in which they were put together, are not overly complex by the standards of the period and would have been within the reach of any skilled extempore poet. Rhymes (such as, sair/mair, will/kill, hald/fold); alliteration (such as, 'seik and sore' or 'sorrow and syt'); inessential lines ('and this salbe alswa trw'); and formulaic phrases ('ay q[uhi]ll I com hom again') would all have been easily sourced and constructed. The fact that Isobel could have produced such a performance in a crowded room while fielding suggestive questions is also not as surprising at it seems. Many folklorists and scholars of oral tradition have observed that traditional extempore performance is at its best in a communal situation and when generated in response to the interests of an attentive audience. This interactive dynamic is vividly described by J. F. Campbell, who noted, in the mid-nineteenth century, that when contemporary Highland women went about their chores they frequently composed extempore, particularly to entertain or tease passers-by. He also observed that this process often involved one particularly skilled girl or woman taking the role of composer while the rest served as the chorus: 'The composer', he notes, 'gives out a single line applicable to anything then present, and the chorus fills up the time by singing and clapping hands, till the second line is prepared. I have known such lines fired at a sportsman by a bevy of girls who were waulking blankets in a byre, and who made the gun and the dog the theme of several stanzas.'[64] We can speculate that, by virtue of her verbal skills and ready wit, Isobel may have taken a prominent role in communal extemporization, and that when the women of the Lochloy fermtoun gathered to reap grain in the fields, wash clothes by the burns or work in the threshing barns, her voice may have been accustomed to leading the throng. In this context, Isobel's interrogation may have provided a macabre, inverted simulacrum of these domestic group-composing experiences. Just as Campbell's group of waulking-girls incorporated references to guns and dogs in their extempore versifying to entertain a passing sportsman, Isobel may have incorporated references to the Devil and maleficent magic to please and impress Harry Forbes and his companions.

Coerced-Compliant Rhyming

But if some or all of Isobel's maleficent charms were falsely confessed, in the sense that they were composed or adapted during the six-week interrogatorial period, then, returning to Kassin and Wrightsman's classification system, what category of false confession may they have been? On the one hand, as with the demonological and specific-*maleficium* passages, we cannot rule out the coerced-complaint option. With regard to the without-belief variant, if Isobel was an oral performer skilled at extempore versifying, then in a bid for leniency she may have quickly learnt to play her trump card to her advantage, producing quick and vivid – but knowingly false – rhymes on a range of demonic and maleficent themes to satisfy her questioners' desire for a full and genuine confession. Such displays of verbal prowess may have served other purposes. At times, Isobel's natural pride in her oral abilities may have merged into vanity, and made it difficult for her to resist flaunting her rhetorical skills before an admiring interrogatorial audience. On a more profound level, she may also have found that the respect and fear that such displays generated went some way toward softening the humiliation of her predicament. This type of without-belief coerced-compliant composition could have taken place during interrogation or solitary confinement, although on balance the former seems more likely. That Isobel extemporized her incriminating charms in the heat of the moment, drunk on the attention of her questioners, is far more persuasive than the picture of her sitting alone in the tolbooth clear-headedly and premeditatedly composing a variety of rhymes in order to falsely confess them at her next interrogation. We could also consider the possibility that Isobel recounted her charms as part of a with-belief coerced-compliant confession, psychologically caving in under prosecutorial pressure to the extent that when the interrogators told her she had used a charm to accompany a maleficent ritual she believed them and obliging produced a made-to-measure example.

But both hypotheses are unconvincing. The without-belief option demands that we accept, without recourse to the Isobel-was-crazy hypothesis, that for a four-week period from her second interrogation, when she first began rhyming in earnest, until her last, Isobel consistently made up rhymes that she knew were false to accompany maleficent magical acts that she knew she had not performed, without ever once regretting or reneging on her decision. The with-belief option, meanwhile, demands that we accept the quixotic possibility that, on four consecutive occasions, Isobel did not only psychologically cave in under interrogatorial pressure and acknowledge and believe that she had performed the crimes alleged against her even though she couldn't remember having performed them, but that she simultaneously, during these moments of psychological meltdown, found the motivation and wherewithal to extemporize the charms that she had supposedly performed when she committed the maleficent acts that she couldn't remember performing.

Coerced-Internalized Rhyming

Once again, as with the demonological and specific-*maleficium* passages, it is the coerced-internalized confession that provides us with the most convincing scenario. On the one hand, the idea that Isobel's rhyming charms could have been some kind of false-memory recollection is countered by the fact that the latter are usually generated through persistent, event-specific questioning of the type which is unlikely to have taken place with regard to Isobel's versifying. Although there is no doubt that Harry Forbes et al. were interested in her rhymes – as we have argued earlier, they did not only record them meticulously but also seem to have asked charm-prompting questions – as witchcraft interrogators it was ultimately the crime, not the rhyme, that concerned them and their questioning would have reflected this. For example, the wording of the third confession strongly suggests that the interrogators included a 'What charm did you use when performing the ritual?'-type question when asking her about the *corp creadh*. But having already gained Isobel's unequivocal assent to having performed this ritual at her first confession over four weeks earlier, it is unlikely that their subsequent questions about accompanying rhymes would have been asked with the level of conviction, repetition and specificity necessary to stimulate the development of false memories. This lack of interrogatorial commitment or zeal with regard to rhyme-retrieval is also evinced by the fact that on at least two occasions, Innes cuts short his list of charms with one of his tired etceteras. Also inconsistent is the fact that, as we illustrated earlier in the chapter with regard to Beth Rutherford, false memories are usually generated piecemeal, as the result of an intimate dialogic exchange between authority and subject. And although this pattern makes sense with regard to Isobel's densely textured prose passages, it stands at odds with her verses, which seem to spring eager, fully-formed, and unequivocally 'Isobel-ish', from the pages of her confessions.

But despite these contraindications, other factors strongly support the coerced-internalized option. As we explored briefly in CHAPTER SEVEN, for ordinary people like Isobel, rhyming charms were an absolutely integral feature of magical ritual, whether maleficent or beneficent. And in this context, it is therefore reasonable to suppose that had she been closely questioned about a specific maleficent act, such as making the *corp creadh*, and responded to this questioning by developing 'rich supporting' false memories surrounding the event, that some of these memories may have been concerned with accompanying charms. In other words, the rhyming charms emerged as a kind of 'false-memory by-product' of the interrogatorial process; though not themselves the object or direct product of persistent questioning, they appeared alongside the false memories of the events that were.

In order to get a better insight into how such a process could have occurred we can return again to the skills of verbal improvisation. As we have already argued, if Isobel had been a fireside bard she would have come to the interrogation with an efficient memory packed full of rhyme components and with the techniques of composition necessary to string them together, extempore, in a theoretically infinite number of ways. But this ability to extemporize may not have needed to operate consciously. As noted previously, Isobel would have acquired the techniques of rhyme composition in early childhood, alongside the development of language itself, and by adulthood rhyming couplets and stanzas may have come as easily as sentences until she did not 'move any more mechanically within it [the poetic language] than we do in ordinary speech'. We can therefore speculate that the techniques of rhyme composition operated on such a deep cognitive level that she was able to experience herself, quite literally, thinking, fantasising and dreaming in rhyme; and that this process, like those of thought, fantasy and dream, occurred independently of conscious will. Just as the musical composer, deeply absorbed in a particular work, finds himself spontaneously generating refrains, or the philosopher, contemplating a specific problem, wakes up one morning with the crucial step of an argument fully formed in his head, so Isobel, during the long nights of solitary imprisonment, or the tense, chaotic hours of interrogation, with the intensely-suggestive descriptions of the events alleged against her running constantly through her mind, may have found that the false memories she spontaneously generated in response did not only manifest as images and spoken conversation but also as complete, fully-formed, rhymes. In other words, to all intents and purposes, the rhymes made up themselves. Although these perspectives are highly speculative, it is hard to find another hypothesis that adequately accounts for the contradictory impression, running through all four confessions, that Isobel both composed her rhymes extempore during interrogation or imprisonment and yet also genuinely believed, throughout the whole six-week confessional period, that she had used them in the ways described.

Fairy Lore and False Confession

If we now move into our final category of subject matter, the fairy-related passages, we find the conclusions equally compelling and equally ambiguous. On the one hand, the fact that Isobel's fairy lore, which appears in its purest state in Confession One, becomes progressively demonized as the interrogations progress strongly indicates the production of false confession in response to suggestive questioning. In the first testimony, for example, Isobel mentions shooting arrows at people with her coven but makes no mention of the Devil being present; in the second she describes how the Devil was present at the manufacturing of the arrows and that he placed the completed weapons into her hand; while in the third the Devil plays an even more proactive role, getting actively involved in a dispute with Margaret Brodie and other members of the coven over whether or not she should shoot the Laird of Park. The increasingly prominent role played by the Devil can be directly attributed to interrogatorial interest, and specific-closed questioning, of the 'Was the Devil with you when you shot the elf arrows?' type. We can also detect the signs of false confession both in the fact that almost every fairy-related description of group magical flight dissolves, either in the same or subsequent confession, into a depiction of group *maleficium* or the witches' sabbath, and in the fact that the tenor of the confessions moves gradually, over the period of the four confessions, towards the demonological end of the demonological/fairy lore spectrum.

With regard to what type of false confession was involved, once again, as with all the other categories of subject matter we have looked at, it is the coerced-internalized option that emerges as the most persuasive. Although we cannot rule out the possibility that Isobel's fairy lore emerged as with or without belief coerced-compliant responses, it is hard to accept that Isobel made up such consistently vivid and idiosyncratic folkloric beliefs (either knowingly, to please her interrogators, or through psychological cave-in) for six weeks, without doubt or attempts at recantation. But on the other hand, it is not at all difficult to imagine how persistent, suggestive questions of the 'Was the Devil with you when you shot the elf arrows?' type would have, either during the heated crucible of the interrogation itself or during the long hours of solitary confinement, worked their way into Isobel's dreams and daydreams until they manifested as vivid and confident false memories. This option would fully account for the fact that Isobel's fairy lore becomes progressively demonized over the six-week interrogatorial period.

If Isobel's fairy-related passages were indeed rooted in false memories, it is likely that, as with the maleficent charms, these memories emerged as by-products to questioning about other matters. Although seventeenth-century witchcraft prosecutors were often interested in fairy beliefs, in most trials this interest was subordinate to the main interrogatorial focus: that of discovering whether the suspect had made a pact with the Devil or performed *maleficium*. As noted in CHAPTER FIVE, in Isobel's case Forbes, Rose, Innes et al. seem to have been more-than-usually curious about her fairy-related experiences, just as they were more-than-usually curious about her ability to produce charms, and their speculative minds ensured that when Isobel referred to it they did not immediately repress or demonize her accounts. But nevertheless, the evidence suggests that theirs was still a subsidiary interest. The fact that fairy beliefs, along with charms, play a far smaller role in the final 'summing up' confession than they do in the previous three, is telling here. As is the fact that, as argued in CHAPTER THREE, the more overtly fairy-related passages do not betray signs of having been produced in response to high levels of specific-closed questioning, and there seems to be no consistent interrogatorial focus with regard to fairy beliefs when they do appear. Indeed, some of the latter seem to have interested Forbes et al. so little that, after their first appearance, they sink without trace. All in all, with regard to fairy belief, the interrogatorial response seems to have been one of interested response rather than initiation.

But although fairy belief may have only been a subsidiary interest, the relative responsiveness of Isobel's interrogators in this respect, when combined with persistent questioning about demonological matters or specific *maleficium*, may have been enough, in her case, to allow fairy-related false memories to flourish. Our analyses into the confessional subject matter in CHAPTER FOUR suggests that in Isobel's mind beliefs about demonological witchcraft and beliefs about fairies were deeply intermingled, and that when she called up an idea or image about the Devil and his cohort of witches there was frequently some kind of fairy belief fused with, or grafted onto, it. As a consequence, we can speculate that where false confession was concerned, the development of false memories about one subject was unlikely to occur without the development of false memories about the other. In Isobel's case, for example, ideas about witches' sabbaths seem to have been deeply amalgamated with ideas about fairy gatherings, and so when – in response to persistent questioning about when and where her witches' sabbaths took place – she finally generated vivid false memories of having attended witches' sabbaths, these fictitious meetings spontaneously occurred beneath fairy hills guarded by elf bulls and in the presence of fairy kings and queens.

False Confession: The Unanswered Questions

In conclusion, with regard to Isobel and false confession, the coerced-internalized option emerges as the most persuasive, in all four interrogations and in relation to all three categories of confessional content. But having said this, as an explanatory hypothesis it still remains problematic on a number of levels. As we have seen earlier, the evidence suggests that false memories are typically generated over a period of time in response to intense and highly-suggestive interrogatorial or therapeutic interchanges. But this stands at odds with the fact that, as we have noted many times before, many of Isobel's demonological, specific *maleficium* and fairy-related passages emerge fully developed in her very first confession. Indeed, it is noteworthy here that, barring the addition of the odd charm and an increased involvement of the Devil, her descriptions of making the *corp creadh*, of feasting with the fairies and (with the exception of the sexual element) performing the demonic pact, vary very little after this date. Therefore, in order for the coerced-internalized hypothesis to stand, we are left with little option but to assume that Isobel underwent interrogations conducive to false-memory generation before she gave her first recorded confession.

On the one hand, this is a distinct possibility. As noted in CHAPTER THREE, Isobel's case was probably a long time brewing. She is likely to have been questioned prior to her formal incarceration and interrogation in Auldearn after 13 April, either at the kirk session or a local tenant's court. Moreover, if Brodie's diary reference to a 'great discoveri' of witchcraft 'wher I live' in the spring of 1662 did indeed relate to Isobel's case, then it is possible that she was being intensively questioned as early as 10 March. And being a full month before her first formal confession, this would have allowed plenty of time for false memories to develop. But on the other hand, the fact that these prior questioning sessions remain wholly unsubstantiated means that we cannot jump to any conclusions here. To this note of caution, we must add the fact that the false-memory hypothesis would probably not only depend upon Isobel having been questioned before 13 April, but also on her having been imprisoned. Although research has shown that individuals can be encouraged to generate false memories without being held under arrest, memories involving serious self-incriminatory elements are much more likely to be produced by those suffering the disorientation and stress of enforced confinement.

That we should maintain a level of caution, where the false-memory hypothesis is concerned, is also supported by closer analysis of the fairy-related passages. As our previous discussion has shown, it is not difficult to see how fairy lore could have become woven into demonological lore as Isobel's four interrogations progressed, or how fairy beliefs could have emerged as a by-product of questioning about demonological issues.

But we must set against this the fact that both of these processes involve a movement from demonological material towards fairy lore that runs counter to the core-gravitational pull of the text. As we have seen earlier, putting aside the initial demonic pact scenes (which are quite clearly grafted onto the beginning of each confession) the directional energy of Isobel's narrative consistently runs from pure fairy lore through to demonology, both internally within each confession and within the four confessions as a whole. In Confession One Isobel's accounts of visits to fairyland and elf-arrow shooting are only minimally linked to demonological ideas, while, by the third, they are deeply entwined with images of the Devil, the sabbath and the witches' coven. As a consequence, the hypothesis that Isobel's fairy belief emerged as a by-product of demonologically-themed false memories must somehow account for the fact that in the majority of cases demonological belief seems to have been grafted onto fairy belief, as opposed to the other way around. In other words, the fairy belief came first. Therefore, however energetically we argue that interrogatorial questioning along the lines of 'Was the Devil with you when you shot the elf arrows?' generated false memories of the Devil being present when Isobel shot elf arrows, the fact that she claimed to have shot the arrows in the first place still requires explanation.

As a corollary of this, we also need to explain why Isobel's fairy belief emerges so powerfully and coherently in her very first recorded confession. We argued earlier that Isobel could have developed vivid and detailed false memories on a range of subjects by the time of her initial formal interrogation because she had been questioned, and perhaps imprisoned, prior to this date. But this hypothesis is more convincing with regard to the demonological and specific-*maleficium* passages than to those dealing with fairy belief. If, as we argued earlier, fairy-related false memories were likely to have evolved as by-products to intense questioning about demonological matters, then you would expect them to be more intertwined with demonic elements at their point of emergence. And while this intertwining is clearly visible in Isobel's second, third and fourth confessions it is largely absent from the first, where the fairy belief emerges as largely distinct from demonological themes. Indeed, the thematic integrity and narrative organisation displayed in the fairy lore passages in Confession One strongly suggests that they emerged without distortion, in the same dramatic but unforced manner in which fairy-related stories, ballads and anecdotes would have emerged from Isobel in her role as fireside bard in the fields and cottages of the Lochloy fermtoun. These various caveats do not challenge the value of false confession as an explanatory hypothesis per se, for the evidence strongly suggests that false-memory generation played a role in the creation of all four of Isobel's confessions, and in relation to a wide range of their subject matter. But they do leave us with some significant unanswered questions.

PART II
Shamanistic Perspectives

A truly great storyteller begins to see visions of the characters
and the stories. Sometimes it happens that a storyteller
must become a shaman. The characters become
internalized in you. You call the spirits
of the stories often enough and
at last they force you.
Borbak-ool Saryglar, Tuvan shaman and storyteller

Introduction to Part II

At the end of the last chapter we concluded that although theories of false confession can help us to understand how Isobel's confessions may have evolved, certain features of the confessional text still demand fuller explanation. In particular, the passages dealing with fairy belief in Confession One leave us with a number of outstanding questions. And in order to find some answers to these questions we must now embark on a change of direction – temporarily moving away from seventeenth-century Scotland and into the field of anthropology.

In his groundbreaking work on the folkloric origins of the witches' sabbath (*Ecstasies*, 1989) Italian historian Carlo Ginzburg cited Isobel's testimony (along with that of one other Scottish witch) as an example of the persistence of shamanistic beliefs and practices into early modern Britain.[1] Subsequent to this high-profile debut, this proposed link between Isobel and shamanism has been widely entertained, particularly on a popular level, with a recent anthology of early modern women poets being able to assert confidently that her confessions represent 'a whole substrate of Scottish rural fantasy, roleplaying, shamanism, and residual pagan belief'.[2]

But among academic historians, this link is an ambiguous and by no means unchallenged one. This ambiguity is rooted largely in the fact that the link between shamanism and witchcraft is itself controversial. Though posited in various ways since the nineteenth century, it first became the subject of serious international debate in the late 1960s, with Ginzburg's pioneering research into a series of early modern trial records from Friuli, in Northern Italy.[3] Analysing the records in some detail, Ginzburg concluded that they provided evidence of a local fertility cult, termed the *benandanti*, that participated in seasonal visionary rites which were, over a period of a hundred or so years, progressively demonized by prosecutors into the stereotypical witches' sabbath. Ginzburg argued that although the *benandanti's* rites were Christianized, they were rooted in shamanistic beliefs and practices of pre-Christian origin. In his follow-up work, *Ecstasies*, he broadened his hypothesis to argue that European beliefs surrounding the witches' sabbath were the result of a complex and profound cultural fusion between widespread beliefs and fears concerning marginal cultural groups and visionary folkloric traditions of pan-Eurasian and pre-Christian origin centred on the 'matrix of all possible narratives': the 'journey of the living into the world of the dead.'[4]

Ginzburg's theories have received a mixed response. While few scholars have accepted his work uncritically, many, particularly on the European Continent, have been persuaded by his general approach, and have worked to modify and develop his hypotheses in a wide range of contexts, incorporating under the term 'shamanistic' certain types of encounters with individual spirits and other supernatural experiences.[5] Hungarian scholar Éva Pócs has arguably made the most significant contribution here, with her investigations into 'several thousand pages of records, that pertain to the Hungarian witch hunts of the sixteenth to the eighteenth centuries' leading her to claim decisively that '[Ginzburg's] findings were confirmed by our detailed research'.[6] Pócs's work has convinced many, with Valerie Kivelson echoing, in her review of *Between the Living and the Dead* (Pócs 1999), that 'If one needed further proof of Carlo Ginzburg's connections between witchcraft belief and shamanic practice . . . Pócs's Hungarian material certainly provides that evidence. Hungarian trials made those connections specific'.[7] This 'shamanistic paradigm', as we can term it here, has been so influential that it is now discussed or at least referenced in most books on early modern witchcraft and has become widely accepted on a popular level.

But despite this enthusiasm, many historians of witchcraft, particularly in Britain and America, have been resistant to Ginzburg's hypothesis, and in spite of recent research by Pócs et al., Robin Brigg's 1996 observation that '[Ginzburg's] ingenious interpretation has not found much support among other historians' arguably still holds true.[8] This resistance has evolved, in part, in response to the fact that Ginzburg and several other scholars mining the same vein, have not only been eager to identify the presence of shamanistic beliefs and practices in early modern Europe, but also to trace their unbroken genesis back through time, with Ginzburg taking his readers on a dashing, labyrinthine journey across successive centuries, cultures and continents in pursuit of pre-Christian origins. For many historians, this emphasis is at best unhelpful and at worst misleading. Commenting on Ginzburg's theory on the pagan antecedents of the witches' sabbath, for example, Briggs, again, notes that 'it does not seem to be very helpful in relation to the situation during the sixteenth and seventeenth centuries. Whatever the origins of the belief system, by this time it had developed an internal logic which related it to a nexus of ideas about witchcraft rather than those about dead ancestors.'[9] Behringer, on the other hand, labels Ginzburg's 'survivalist' claims 'to have discovered a mythic essence that supposedly survived over centuries or even crossed millenia without losing any of its vital force' as 'exagerrated'; while folklorist Linda Degh criticizes Pócs for 'attempting to reconstruct the original from decomposed rudiments' before going on to protest: 'But what was the "original"? Pócs evaluates her data from the vantage point of the reconstructionist's ivory tower'.[10]

Resistance to the shamanistic paradigm is also fuelled by the fact that many scholars find it difficult to negotiate the idea that European shamanistic practices, of palpable pre-Christian origin, could have persisted into the early modern period. Here, Ginzburg's reliance on the *benandanti* is consistently singled out for criticism. While scholars do not generally challenge the shamanistic credentials of the Friulian cult (the evidence is simply too strong for this) many argue that the *benandanti* were an exception, rather than the rule, with Briggs, again, summarizing that 'most scholars have seen the *benandanti* as an exceptional local case rather than the tip of a submerged iceberg' and that 'There are hints of similar beliefs elsewhere, but nothing remotely as complex or systematic as this strange corpus of folklore'.[11] Although scholars such as Henningsen and Pócs have subsequently argued that experiential belief-matrices of similar complexity to those of the Friulian cult existed elsewhere in Europe in this period, the ambiguities surrounding this material means that the dispensing-with-the-*benandanti*-as-an-anomaly view persists, and has enabled many scholars to avoid engaging with Ginzburg's attempts to argue that, as Kieckhefer puts it, 'What happened in the case of the *benandanti* becomes the model for understanding the witch trials generally.'[12] As a consequence, as recently as 2008 Julian Goodare could still claim that 'Historians have agreed that this [Ginzburg's *benandanti* research] was extraordinary, but they have not really known what to do with it. Was the *benandanti* cult unique and exotic, or would all pre-industrial peasants turn out to have had similar beliefs and even cults, if only we had the evidence? And what connections were there with more familiar witchcraft beliefs?'[13]

These criticisms surrounding the *benandanti* correctly highlight the ambiguity that stands at the core of the shamanistic hypothesis: how far were contemporary 'shamanistic narratives' (that is, descriptions of encounters with spirits or spirit worlds displaying shamanistic characteristics) sets of themes, motifs, and images about visionary travel into the world of the dead, inherited from the pre-Christian past, and how far were they expressions of living, experiential traditions? This ambiguity is highly resistant to analysis, and has been compounded by the fact that Ginzburg, to the frustration of his critics, was himself unspecific on this point, with Kieckhefer complaining in his 1992 review of *Ecstasies*, that 'When Ginzburg writes about the actual trials, he remains unclear about how far he would want to extend his conclusions. Would he want us to assume that Johannes Junius of Bamburg was (or was seen as) a shaman? That the accused at Salem were bearers of archaic shamanistic tradition?'[14] Similarly, in *Between the Living and the Dead*, Pócs discusses this epistemological dilemma head on, but only to emphasize its elusiveness, stating that:

> The dilemma that has haunted research [into the sabbath] is whether it was an experience or narrative, communication with the dead or literary topos? We have to assume a permanent duality and interrelationship between the two possibilities, as researchers of religious visions have done for a long time in connection with visionary literature.[15]

While Pócs, Ginzburg et al. are happy to work with this ambiguity, their critics are not. But although the latter caution, quite reasonably, that the survival of shamanistic beliefs and motifs cannot be assumed to be indicative of the survival of experiential shamanistic traditions, their caution all-too-frequently implies the negative. In other words, it is all too often inferred that because there is a lack of clear evidence that visionary experience took place, it must be assumed that it did not. On the shamanistically-themed lore surrounding the Wild Hunt that persisted throughout the Middle Ages, for example, French historian Robert Muchembled concluded that 'It was neither a pure survival of Germanic religions . . . even less was it a survival of real shamanic practices. At most, it may be that traditions uprooted from their place of origin retained a sufficient symbolic power to evoke powerful images in a Christian world, so enriching diabolic imagery and adding to its contradictions'.[16] Other scholars respond to this ambiguity by avoiding the experiential question entirely and discussing early modern shamanism purely in terms of residual 'beliefs', 'ideas', 'themes' and 'stories'. Michael Bailey, for example, claims that fifteenth-century demonologist Johannes Nider 'reveals that *ideas* of night flight or spiritual transportation to a nocturnal gathering . . . may well have been relatively widespread especially among European peasantry as a vestige of some archaic form of shamanism'; Robert Thurston notes, of accounts describing travel with the fairies or the dead, that 'the elite mounted a "frontal attack" on these *old stories* and twisted them into malicious reports'; and Edward Cowan reminds his readers that Ginzburg 'suggested that night flights taken to diabolical sabbats constituted, however distorted they were, a very ancient *theme* . . . It may be suggested that *beliefs* surrounding the sojourn in Fairyland shared a similar origin or root'(my italics throughout).[17]

But by avoiding the issue of the experiential dimension of folkloric beliefs scholars are faced with a dilemma. If they accept that shamanistic beliefs and themes informed accounts of travelling to the witches' sabbath or fairyland but deny the persistence of a ritual and visionary dimension to these beliefs, then they need to explain why so many witchcraft trial records contain highly personal and idiosyncratic claims to have experienced or witnessed these events; accounts that, as in Isobel's case, cannot be wholly attributed to interrogatorial coercion. Even more difficult to explain are the many descriptions of fairy and ghost encounters that emerged outside the coercive arena of witchcraft prosecutions and are therefore even less amenable to explanatory models of false confession. The references to people who claimed to have encountered spirits of the dead or to 'ride with the fair folk' that appear with relative frequency in antiquarian writings and kirk session and presbytery records throughout seventeenth-century Scotland still demand explanation.[18]

Those historians who wish to avoid the shamanistic paradigm, but who at the same time need to account for the fact that many encounter-narratives seem to contain some kind of experiential or visionary dimension, generally opt for more conventional and neutral terms such as 'fantasy', 'imagination' and 'dream'. In his influential *Witches and Neighbours*, for example, Briggs claims that, 'The detailed accounts of the pact and the sabbat evidently reflect the everyday cultural and social concerns of their tellers, however fanciful the imaginary packaging may appear. They also reaffirm the creativity and significance of human *fantasy*, through which the juxtaposition of real and *imaginary* worlds took place [my italics]'.[19] But in most cases the nature or epistemological status of this 'fantasy' or these 'imaginary worlds' are elucidated no further. The conclusions reached by the minority of British scholars who have explored the issue in any detail, such as Briggs, Roper and Purkiss, are curtailed within the psychoanalytic paradigm. Roper, for example, claims provocatively that 'In many cases, works of demonology were written not before their authors had been involved in a witch hunt, but after the experience, as they sought to come to terms with what they had heard and seen and pass on their knowledge. As a result, witches' confessions were not just the product of the demonologists' fantasies – indeed, one might say that works of demonology were also the product of the witches' fantasies.' But subsequent lines reveal that by 'witches' fantasies' Roper predominantly means those fictions constructed in a false confessional response to the pseudo-therapeutic arena of interrogation.[20]

The problem with the terms 'imagination', 'fantasy' and 'dream' is that they are very general, covering a wide spectrum of subjective experiences which may or may not relate to visionary phenomena and which can range from the simple daydream through to the mystery of false confession or the numinous intensity of the full-blown waking vision. More significantly, historians seldom explicitly state what they mean by these terms, and this leaves them dangerously open to under-interpretation. In our rationalist Western culture, a dream is 'just' a dream, while the default positions for the terms 'imagination' and 'fantasy' lie somewhere between the pages of a novel, the images on a painter's canvas and – on an experiential level – the neuroses of the psychiatric patient. But none of these associations come anywhere close to expressing the complex and powerful ways in which visionary experience can emerge within and impact upon pre-industrial and non-literate cultures.

The dangers of this type of under-interpretation can be seen in the work of Norman Cohn. Though generally celebrated for his criticism of the theories of Margaret Murray (which we shall be exploring in more detail later), and his stimulating research into the elite contribution to beliefs surrounding the witches' sabbath, Cohn is also one of the few British scholars to have given the experiential dimension of witch-beliefs more than a passing acknowledgement. As early as 1971 he identified the folkloric themes surrounding travel into spirit worlds that lay behind the sabbath stereotype, empha-sizing that:

> it is clear that already in the Middle Ages some women believed themselves to wander about at night on cannibalistic errands, while others believed themselves to wander about, on more benign errands, under the leadership of a supernatural queen. Later, after the great witch-hunt had begun, some women genuinely believed that they attended the sabbat and took part in its demonic orgies: not all the confessions, even at that time, are to be attributed to torture or the fear of torture.[21]

Writing before the shamanism paradigm had gained widespread currency, Cohn employed the terms 'imagination' and 'fantasy' to explain this phenomenon. Witch and fairy figures 'belonged to the world of popular imagination, particularly peasant imag-ination' and, in the case of witchcraft confessions, 'collective fantasy has simply taken possession of the minds of certain women, to the extent that they believe themselves to be night-witches'.[22] As they are understood in the West today, these terms were simply not robust enough to do justice to Cohn's theories and this, combined with the fact that, post-*Ecstasies* (translated into English in 1991) Ginzburg's shamanistic hypothesis effectively monopolized and polarized the debate, meant that Cohn's notable contribution towards our understanding of the experiential dimension of early modern witchcraft has often been overlooked, particularly in popular circles.

The encounter-narratives of early modern cunning folk and witches may well come under the general dictionary definition of 'fantasies', but if this is the case, then we are dealing with something that is very different from what is generally understood by the term in the West today. We are dealing with fantasies that were constructed and experienced by a wide number of people; fantasies that were believed, by those who experienced them, to be wholly real; fantasies that were so robust that they could be described, often decades after the event, with intense emotion and in forensic detail; and fantasies that, however exotic and fantastic the subject matter, were often dictated, at their core, by a strikingly matter-of-fact and pragmatic functionalism. The following account, sandwiched unceremoniously between entries concerned with fines for sabbath-breaking and fornication in the 1629 Elgin kirk session records, is illustrative:

> Compeirt Cristan Nauchty and confessit scho was three severall tymes away, ilk tyme aucht dayis away, and scho was taine away with a wind and knew no man bot Johne Mowtra and ane Packman quho wer dead lang ago, and that they two strak hir. Scho confessit ther wer ma in hir cumpany quhom scho kend no, above ane hundreth. Ther faces seimed whyt and as lane but ther backis wer boss lyk fidles.[23]

Even more significantly, we are dealing with fantasies that were considered so authoritative that men and women would administer herbs and perform healing rituals for their sick children according to their representations. Margo Todd reveals, for example, that members of Perthshire cunning man John Gothray's community clearly believed that the latter's imagined encounters with a spirit of the dead qualified him to act as an unofficial doctor; while Gothray, in turn, was in deadly earnest when he told his local presbytery that he had been:

> 'taken away by the fairies in a harvest evening and among them got kindness of a little lad who called himself his brother and showed him how he himself was taken away by them, being but a month old.' Having stayed with the fairies for some time, he was released with a gift for his trouble, in the form of healing power, renewed periodically by visits from 'that little lad who comes to him once in a month and shows him such and such herbs and tells him for what use they serve'.[24]

It is plain that as they are generally understood in the West today, and as they are employed by the historian, the terms 'fantasy', 'imagination', or 'dream', do not sufficiently evoke the type of phenomenon we are dealing with here. And in the face of this inadequacy, the language of shamanism clearly has something to offer. However controversial, shamanistic terminology elevates the visionary functions of the human psyche to a different level: a 'shamanistic experience' evokes a far more profound and nuanced set of associations than that of fantasy, imagination or dream. Indeed, it is the aspirational, and in the wrong hands pretentious, nature of these associations that has helped to fuel historiographical resistance to shamanism as an explanatory hypothesis.

But what is precisely evoked by these shamanistic terms is a more complex question. By replacing the term 'fantasy' with that of 'shamanistic experience', we are in many ways exchanging an inadequacy for an uncertainty. As with all terminology associated with shamanism, the word brings with it a huge number of problems, and these largely centre on the fact that among scholars there is no consensus about what 'shamanistic experience' or, more fundamentally, 'shamanism' itself, actually means. This problem is further compounded by the fact that – until very recently – scholars working with the shamanism hypothesis have seldom set out their own understanding of these terms in any detail, and as a consequence the latter have been all too easily misinterpreted by critics who have then employed their own, equally undefined, terms by way of challenge; a cyclical exchange which has built layer upon layer of misunderstanding.[25] The term 'shamanistic experience', for example, can be used to indicate altered states of consciousness undergone either in the presence or absence of visionary phenomena; it can refer to the altered states generated by specifically Siberian magical practitioners; it can be used as a more general term to describe the experiences of any group who undergo trance, at specific times, with shared ritual intentions; or it can be used to describe a solitary encounter with an individual spirit that has no links with group ritual or traditional culture at all. Any of these definitions, in turn, can be applied to experiences with or without traceable thematic links to paganism, inside or outside official religion, and restrained or unrestrained by temporal or geographical boundaries. Derivatives of the terms associated with shamanism are equally ambiguous: 'shamanistic substrate', 'vestigial shamanism', 'shamanistic tradition', 'shamanistic ideas', 'shamanistic traits', 'shamanistic soul journeys' and so on, are still liberally used by both proponents and critics of the shamanistic paradigm but without any clear consensus as to what these terms actually mean.[26]

Given these problems, it is evident that if we are to examine Isobel's confessions in the context of shamanism, then we need to define our terms clearly. But at this stage off-the-peg definitions – however clear and precise – will be of limited use. Both the impoverishment of terminology associated with visionary experience and the confusions and prejudices surrounding the language of shamanism have their roots in deep cultural attitudes. Attitudes which, being largely unconscious, cannot easily be shifted by neat definitions. In the wake of the Enlightenment and the Industrial Revolution, modern Westerners inherit ways of thinking and standards of living that dramatically separate us from the lives of our early modern ancestors, and nowhere is this existential gulf more dramatic than in the arena of visionary experience. Unless we attempt to bring these differences to the forefront of consciousness, and understand them more profoundly, any analysis of shamanistic belief and practice in early modern Europe will be of limited use.

Given these considerations, we will begin our enquiry into the links between Isobel's confessions and shamanism by going right back to basics. We will spend some time examining the nature and function of visionary experience in pre-industrial cultures, both in contemporary non-European societies and early modern Britain, and in exploring how these experiences have been traditionally articulated within shamanistic paradigms. This process will help us to arrive at a more informed definition of shamanism and will also soften some of the unconscious cultural attitudes that so commonly distort our view of the subject. Although this task will, in its early stages, take us a long way away from Isobel, and her interrogations in Auldearn, it is only by acquiring this deeper knowledge of shamanism that we can gainfully consider the role it may have played in her confessions.

10

An Old Way of Seeing

In this chapter we will be primarily concerned with the human capacity to manufacture mental imagery and the term we shall use to denote the act of witnessing this imagery will be *visionary experience*. As it is used here, this term will cover the following overlapping phenomena: (1) All imagery produced during waking states, from mild (as encountered during the proverbial 'day dreaming') through to intense (as encountered in active imagination and waking visions). (2) All imagery produced during sleep states, from normal dream impressions through to vivid flying or lucid dream phenomena. (3) All imagery produced during semi-waking visionary states, such as hypnagogic and hypnopompic imagery (characteristically accompanied by sleep paralysis). (4) All imagery associated with experiences traditionally defined as 'paranormal', including out-of-body encounters and remote viewing.

Although wide-ranging, the term 'visionary experience', as it is used here, will be more epistemologically exact than the terms 'fantasy' and 'imagination', as they are generally employed by historians of witchcraft, in the sense that it will specifically designate an *experience*, that is, an actual perception of visionary phenomena at a given moment in time. As a consequence, the term will include false-memory recall occurring during or between witchcraft interrogations but not 'fantasies' or 'fictions' constructed during interrogations that did not involve direct perception of envisioned phenomena. In addition, because the term will be primarily employed in relation to shamanism, it will carry certain emphases. (1) It will denote forms of visionary experience at the more intense end of the spectrum, particularly vivid, lucid dreams, active imagination and waking visions. (2) It will not, unless specified, make any material distinction between 'dream' or 'vision': the definitive emphasis being on the frame of mind in which an individual enters and inhabits a visionary experience and what they do with it, as opposed to its precise psychological definition. (3) It will give rise to the derivative adjective 'envisioned', which will frequently be employed in reference to spiritual agencies, as in 'envisioned helping spirit' or 'envisioned Devil'. These terms will not imply the existence of these spirits per se, but will designate a visionary phenomenon defined by the beholder as such.

While the capacity to produce visionary phenomena is a universal feature of the human mind, the significance placed upon these phenomena, and the ability to produce them, differs widely according to culture and historical period. As a general rule, visionary experiences are more highly valued in pre-industrial cultures and less in industrialized: a contemporary Amazonian or African tribe will hold them in far higher esteem than the populations of western Europe or North America. The reasons behind this divergence are many, but they can be subsumed under two main categories: lifestyle and belief.

Lifestyle

One of the reasons why visionary experience is more highly valued in pre-industrial than industrial societies is simply because, in the former, it is more common. The importance of this fact, which is so simple that it is often overlooked by historians, cannot be overstated. Over the past century psychologists have confirmed that the traditional association between asceticism and visionary experience, fundamental to all religious traditions, is a wholly rational one: physical and mental stress alters physiology and creates the conditions in which visionary states are more likely to occur.[1] In pre-industrial societies, what we can term here 'naturally-occurring asceticism' is widespread. Chronic and acute under-nourishment and exposure to high-levels of disease are commonly combined with long and physically-hard working hours that push the body to its limits.[1] Similarly, exposure to sickness and death, and the threat of sickness and death, are a constant burden, with the traditional, tight-knit societal structure ensuring that the sufferings of relatives and neighbours, particularly children, are commonly witnessed first-hand. By contrast, although fully industrialized societies have their own stresses, their levels of under-nourishment, disease and mortality are comparably low and work seldom drives an individual to the limits of physical endurance. Moreover, the dominant societal structure, that is, small nuclear families living largely independently of each other, means that the suffering of others, when it does occur, is relatively easy to avoid. Few adults in the modern West will have witnessed a child die; but most adults living in a pre-industrial society would – many times over. As a result, modern Westerners are far less likely to be subjected to the physical and psychological stress levels conducive to the generation of visionary experience.

Belief

The second reason that visionary experience is more highly valued in pre-industrial societies is not rooted in lifestyle, but in mentality. Industrialized cultures are underpinned by the Enlightenment paradigm that advocates an essentially mechanistic, materialist view of the universe that dispenses with the necessity for transcendent occult forces, spirits, or a creator God. Human endurance is seen to be primarily dependent upon access to technology; and visionary experiences, being seen as physiologically-induced creations of mind, are deemed incidental to survival. But in pre-industrial cultures, grounded in an animist world-view, the universe is seen to be dependent upon the activities of multifarious spiritual forces and entities; human endurance is seen to be primarily dependent upon the manipulation of, and intercession with, these forces; and visionary experiences, as the *sine qua non* method of encountering them face-to-face, are deemed central to survival.

That visionary experiences should be considered the optimum method through which to encounter supernatural agencies in most parts of the globe and in all periods of human history, is no coincidence. Following the pioneering work of anthropologist Edward Tylor, many scholars have speculated that belief constructs concerning spirits emerged directly out of the human capacity for visionary experience. In other words: in the perennial dialectic between visionary experience and the belief in spirits, the visionary experience came first.[2] The theory, which helps us – perhaps better than any other – to gain a sense of the primacy of these experiences in pre-industrial cultures, runs thus: In the absence of any other explanation early man rationalized his dream and vision experiences as an encounter with an objectively real parallel reality. His observation that in dream and vision people and places were not restricted by the physical limitations of normal waking existence (being able to appear and disappear, fly, or metamorphose into other forms) gave birth to the idea that although they resembled waking life phenomena, the beings who lived in this parallel reality possessed a supernatural status, that is, they were 'spirits', and the dimensions they inhabited were 'spirit worlds'. His observation that when he entered this world, he too was freed of these restrictions, gave birth to the idea that a part of the human being can detach itself from the body and enter the spirit worlds and that when it does so, it possesses the same powers as the spirits themselves (this separable part being defined as the spirit or soul). His observation that sometimes, during dreams and visions, he seemed to inhabit some kind of corporeal form, gave rise to the idea that the separable soul is, or can clothe itself in, a supra-physical or 'subtle' form of similar substance and properties to those possessed by spirits. And finally, but perhaps most significantly, his experience of meeting figures resembling dead relatives and friends in dream and vision gave rise to the belief that, on death, the separable soul leaves the body and goes to live in the spirit world for ever.

Despite the fact that this theory has been around for a long time, and despite the fact that over the past half century there has been a small, but steady, increase of interest in the subject of visionary experience among scholars in the fields of anthropology, psychology, and religious history, it remains difficult for many modern Western researchers to appreciate the prevalence and primacy of the visionary experience in pre-industrial cultures. As a consequence, before we progress onto our analysis of shamanism we will try to illustrate this primacy in a little more depth. Our analysis will draw primarily on contemporary and recent anthropological material pertaining to indigenous pre-industrial societies from the Americas and northern Asia. These societies shall be referred to as 'tribal' to distinguish them from the traditional pre-industrial societies of early modern Europe.

The Pre-Industrial Vision

Anthropological studies have revealed that in cultures where visionary experience is highly valued, it is considered to be as real as the perceptions of normal waking life. Indeed, as anthropologist Jackson Lincoln has observed, in some cases it is regarded 'as having a greater reality value than an actual experience.'[3] In addition, as Barbara Tedlock has recently emphasized, while modern Western thought sees visionary reality and everyday reality as two distinct modalities, in tribal cultures the two are inextricably interconnected or overlapped in a 'unified spatio-temporal frame of reference for all self-related experience'.[4] As such, events in one modality are believed to directly affect events in the other. Men from the Brazilian Kalapalo tribe, for example, try to keep each other awake on the night prior to a wrestling competition, 'lest they dream of a bad action that would then cause that action in waking life'. Conversely, the North American Zuni and Hopi believe that 'good' dreams must remain untold and kept 'inside the heart and silently' (because speaking of them would counteract their potency) while 'bad' dreams must be told out, and the teller undergo ritual catharsis, in order to avert their ill effects.[5] The epistemological symbiosis between visionary and normal physical reality permeates all forms of tribal discourse and anthropologists have described how, because dream sharing is often unframed in speech (that is, the teller does not state that 'now I am going to describe a dream experience'), they have found themselves listening to an anecdote for a long time before realising that it was a dream-recounting as opposed to a real-life event.[6] This symbiosis is encouraged by the segmented sleep patterns common in pre-industrial societies (with the increased time spent in the heightened and meditative nocturnal inter-sleep periods intensifying the interplay between visionary and waking consciousness), and by the fact that in the absence of efficient artificial lighting, many waking hours are spent in darkness or the half darkness of dawn and twilight.[7] The ritual ingestion of hallucinogens practised, to a greater or lesser extent, in most indigenous societies, also plays a significant role here.

While these societies view visionary experiences as real, this does not mean that they consider them to obey the same rules, or that they should be interpreted using the same criteria, as normal waking events. In most tribal cultures, dream and vision experiences are interpreted in two very different ways. As in some modern Western schools of thought, they can be analyzed symbolically according to some kind of sign system. If a Mongolian Naga dreams of fire, for example, it means he can anticipate a large family, or if a North American Kwakiutl dreams of lice he can anticipate sickness and so on.[8] But where the mentality of the Naga or Kwakiutl tribesman differs from that of most contemporary Westerners is in the fact that dreams and visions can also be interpreted literally, that is, by treating 'the manifest content directly without seeking latent meanings'.[9] According to this mode of interpretation, if your dead grandfather appears in a vision offering you his hand, it is not a symbolic representation of your grandfather offering you his hand, it is your dead grandfather offering you his hand. Or if you dream that you are flying across a mountain range, you are not dreaming of flying across an image of a mountain range that actually represents something else, you are actually flying across a mountain range. In most tribal societies the symbolic and literal interpretative modes are not mutually exclusive and can be employed at the same time, in reference to the same dream. For example, as William Morgan notes, 'when a Navajo dreams that he is dead, he means that in his dream, he was in the next world with the spirits of the dead. To be there and to come back is not necessarily a bad dream; but if the dead beckon to the dreamer or he shakes hands with the dead, it means that he is going to die.'[10]

This lack of concern for the dichotomy between 'real' and 'unreal', 'material' and 'immaterial', 'symbolic' and 'literal' does not mean that the approach to dream analysis and classification in tribal societies is not sophisticated. In fact, as Benjamin Kilborne emphasizes, 'whereas it is commonly believed that thought systems have evolved from simple to complex, according to some sort of progression toward increasing complexity, dream classification apparently is most elaborate in cultures other than those associated with the modern Western rationalist tradition'.[11] Most tribal cultures believe, for example, that humans possess at least two souls, or more accurately 'capacities of soul' (with up to seven not being unusual), with a common distinction being made between some form of 'free soul' which leaves the body in dreams and a 'body soul' which leaves the physical body at death. Different souls have different capacities and compositions of subtle body and can be associated with contrasting forms of visionary experience. Distinctions are also made between different kinds of dream or vision experience, with some possessing spiritual significance and others not, with this analysis usually being made on the basis of a subjective reaction as opposed to an externally-imposed classification system. Among the Crow Indians, for example, 'one [dream/vision] experience thrills and thereby convinces the beholder that he is in communication with the supernatural, the other does not'.[12] In many traditional societies a value-distinction is also made between vision and dream, with the former usually, although not always, being considered the most significant. Among the Crow again, dreams are divided into 'ordinary dreams without religious significance' and 'dreams that are reckoned the full equivalent of visions'.[13]

Because they believe that the visionary world presages benefits and dangers that can be gained or avoided through the correct waking response (whether through the simple act of keeping a dream untold or complex ritual involving the whole community) tribal societies attach great importance to the skill of dream and vision interpretation and a range of specialists emerge to meet this need. But the importance attached to the visionary modality does not only generate the need for specialist dream and vision interpreters, but also specialist dream and vision experiencers. In the majority of tribal cultures throughout the world, certain individuals are marked out, often when they are quite young, as possessing greater-than-average capacities for visionary experience. These individuals are then encouraged to develop these capacities in order to benefit not only themselves, but also their community – becoming, in effect, living conduits between their tribe and the visionary world. And it is this professional visionary who is so often termed the 'shaman'.

The Shaman

The term 'shaman' is a controversial one. Initially employed by early anthropologists to refer to a specific category of magical practitioners from Siberia, the term is now widely used to denote similar practitioners from a variety of cultures around the world. This application of an originally culture-specific term to a more general usage has caused problems with regard to definition, with disagreements among scholars over whether certain features, such as soul flight or possession, or certain types of altered states of consciousness, should or should not be listed among the core characteristics of shamanism. As a consequence, in both popular and scholarly treatments of the subject, definitions of shamanism range from the very narrow, such as '[shamanism is] the religion of certain peoples of northern Asia' to the very general, such as '[the shaman is] a religious specialist who uses supernatural power in curing' or 'The only defining attribute [of shamanism] is that the specialist enter into a controlled ASC [altered state of consciousness] on behalf of his community'.[14] Moreover, ongoing research into the subject and the continuing employment of new paradigms means that new definitions of the phenomenon emerge frequently, and that any discussion of shamanism or shamanistic phenomena needs to begin by clearly setting out which definition is being employed at any given time.

The definition being used here will fall into two parts: one dealing with epistemological characteristics and the other with interpretation and rationale. First, we shall be defining the shaman as a magical practitioner who enters into an altered state of consciousness characterized by the experience of visionary phenomena. This definition over-simplifies a complex subject, for the altered states associated with shamanism can involve a wide range of inter-related sensory modes, frequently incorporating sight, sound and physical sensation simultaneously and powerful shamanistic experiences can take place in the complete absence of visionary phenomena. But nevertheless, visionary experience does emerge from the anthropological literature on shamanism as the most prominent sensory modality. And this pre-eminence, when considered alongside the fact that visionary experience seems to have also been a prominent feature of European shamanistic beliefs and practices, as they may have existed in the early modern period, is sufficient to justify this emphasis here.

Secondly, with regard to how the shaman and his community interpret and rationalize these visionary experiences, we shall be working with the 'reasonably narrow and precise' definition devised by psychologist Roger Walsh (reproduced here with additional clarifying comments in square brackets):

> Shamanism can be defined as a family of traditions whose practitioners focus on voluntarily entering altered states of consciousness in which they experience themselves or [phenomena defined by them as] their spirit(s) traveling to other realms [or places] at will, and interacting with other entities in order to serve their community.[15]

This definition suffers from the fact that, like all those relating to non-Siberian shamanism, it is ultimately subjective, with Walsh himself emphasizing that 'Of course, this definition will not satisfy everyone or include every conceivable shaman. Judging from the enormous number and range of definitions, no single one can.'[16] But nevertheless it is useful in that it employs shamanism as a non-culture-specific term, without making it so broad as to lose form and distinctiveness, enabling us, as Walsh goes on: 'to focus our investigations on a clearly distinguished group of practices and practitioners that almost all researchers would agree are indeed shamanic'.[17] According to this definition, when taken in conjunction with our previously-stated emphasis on visionary experience, the derivative term 'shamanistic' does not refer to phenomena associated with some kind of ambiguous generalized altered state of consciousness – but to visionary states that are, wherever and whenever they are found, associated with the family of traditions concerned with direct, largely voluntary, and controlled interaction with spirits and spirit worlds on behalf of community, as defined here by Walsh.

The Shaman's Experience

The shaman experiences spontaneous or induced altered states of consciousness through a variety of ritual means, which commonly include asceticism, physical or mental activities involving monotonous focus such as dancing or drumming, and the use of psychoactive substances. These ritual methods can take place in public or private, and with or without dramatic ceremony. The altered states of consciousness induced can vary from mild forms of waking trance, in which the shaman remains in control of his body and engages with visionary phenomena while remaining aware of the outside world, to deep trance (often distinguished as 'ecstasy') in which bodily control is absent and awareness of surroundings is drastically reduced or disappears altogether.

In the early days of anthropology, shamans were typically associated with the most extreme of the latter states, psychologically defined as 'cataleptic trance', in which the dissociated body becomes rigid and immobile. This emphasis partly derives from the fact that ritualised catalepsy is often dramatic to watch, as illustrated in a classic account from the turn of the twentieth century, in which the Native American Paiute shaman, Bobby Dodd, attempts to cure a sick person by retrieving his soul from the spirit world. Dodd begins by singing a song and then asks four or five men to stand in a circle holding a rope around the sick person, after which he:

> walked around for about thirty seconds, then he'd start losing his breath. He breathed heavily until he couldn't get any more air. Then he stopped, raised both hands over his head, and rang his rattle against his left hand, so people knew he was going to fall. His power made him stiff as a log. He'd fall into the men's arms . . . Then everybody would be quiet while the doctor was asleep (in trance). The doctor's spirit flew up after the spirit of the sick person, leaving his body behind . . . When Bobby Dodd came back, he'd start to shake. This showed that his power was strong . . . He'd be all stiff. Two guys would lift him and set him on his feet, still stiff as a log.[18]

The shaman believes that through these trance experiences he can communicate directly

with spirits, either by calling them to him or travelling to meet them through sepa-
rating his soul (or more accurately one of his souls) from his body and journeying into
their spirit worlds. Shamans usually develop an intimate relationship with one or more
spirits, traditionally termed 'familiar', 'helping' or 'guardian' spirits by anthropologists. These helping spirits, as we shall term them here, can appear in a variety of forms
and are often identified with souls of the dead or animals. They act as mediators between
the shaman and the supernatural world, performing a wide range of functions from
dispensing medical advice to assisting spirit-world travel. In many cultures the envisioned appearance of the helping spirit heralds the commencement of the shamanic
vocation, as described in this classic initiatory vision account derived from a Native
American Paviotso:

> She [the shaman-to-be] dreamed that he [her dead father] came to her and told her to be a
> shaman. Then a rattlesnake came to her in dreams and told her to get eagle feathers, white
> paint, wild tobacco. The snake gave her the songs that she sings when she is curing. The
> snake appeared three or four times before she believed she would be a shaman. Now she
> dreams about the rattlesnake quite frequently and she learns new songs and is told how to
> cure sick people in this way.[19]

Also characteristic of shamanism, though by no means a universal feature, is the fact
that the journey to and from the spirit world is frequently experienced as some form
of flight, either alone or in the company of other spirits and in either human or animal form. Among the Turkic-speaking peoples of Siberia, for example, the shaman
can fly to the spirit world in the form of a bird, or astride his drum, which acts as a
magical steed and is often described as a horse.[20] Recent research suggests that the
prominence of flight experiences in the shamanistic visionary experience is likely to
reflect the biological functioning of the human brain: with the positive association
between flight experience and lucid dreaming (that is, the sensation of being aware
and in partial control while dreaming) having been confirmed by a number of recent
studies.[21]

But whatever their nature and characteristics, however they are defined and wherever in the world they occur, the shaman's experiences are underpinned by the same,
essentially very simple, rationale: the need to benefit his community. Given the material imperatives of pre-industrial life, the benefits sought are primarily practical and
most of the shaman's time is taken up with propitiating, battling or negotiating with
spirits in order to facilitate physical survival: protecting the tribe (through predicting
enemy raids, planning attacks on rival groups and so on), ensuring they have enough
food (through locating crops, weather control etc.) and most importantly of all, healing
the sick. But although the shaman's imperative is practical, it simultaneously fulfils a
religious or spiritual function. In his search for practical magical help, the shaman
glimpses hidden supernatural realities and is able to bring back information about the
appearance and topography of spirit worlds and the desires and intentions of the beings
that live there. As such, he fulfils the role played by the religious mystic in the world's
developed religions while at the same time providing the kinds of practical help that,

in the modern West, would be more readily associated with the doctor or the policeman.

The Deeper Experience

But while it is simple enough to outline the shaman's role in his community, it is much more difficult to penetrate the subjective nature of the shamanistic experience itself. Although, as we have seen, physical and psychological stress can be conducive to the generation of visionary experience, it is also the case that shamans have been traditionally associated with particular character traits: often being described by anthropologists as 'highly-strung', 'melancholy', 'tense' or any other of the myriad terms used to describe individuals who are not mentally ill but who, as Marjorie Balzer puts it, live 'a very intense inner existence'.[22] As a reflection of this, the initiatory visions that mark the commencement of the shaman's vocation do not only emerge in response to stresses provoked by external factors – whether induced, (through asceticism, drugs etc.) or accidental (through bereavement etc.) – but also through psychosomatic illnesses or psychotic breakdowns that seem to emerge spontaneously and are therefore less easy to explain. In addition to being unusually intense, shamans are also believed to belong to that minority of the population (recently estimated at 4 percent) defined as 'fantasy-prone', that is, they 'fantasize a large part of the time' and 'typically "see," "hear," "smell," "touch," and fully experience what they fantasize'.[23] Either under instruction or alone, the shaman then develops this naturally occurring ability through shamanic practices that serve to progressively increase the clarity, vividness and substantiality of the imagery invoked. Recent evidence suggests that this 'mental imagery cultivation', as Richard Noll has termed it, induces psychological mechanisms that increase the sense that internally-produced images have an independent, objective existence. In other words, the more an individual evokes envisioned phenomena through shamanistic methods, the more 'real' they seem to become.[24]

But the shaman does not only work to increase the vividness and tangibility of mental imagery, he also works to increase his capacity to control it. Initiatory visions are often experienced as overwhelming and disorienting, but over time and with practice the shaman develops the ability to enter into and/or influence visionary states at will. Rather than emulating the dictatorial control of the puppeteer, this shamanistic command resembles a partnered dance; a reciprocal push and pull between the desires of the visionary and the autonomous contents of the dream or vision (a dynamic which, in waking trance, is reflected in the push and pull between internal imagery and external impressions). In the following passage, Tedlock vividly evokes this dynamic, as it emerges in the state defined by psychologists as 'lucid dreaming':

> The dreamer is simultaneously aware of being asleep and removed from the external world and of being awake and receptive to the inner world. In that paradoxical space between sleeping and waking, as the lucid dream takes shape out of dreaming consciousness there exist complex sensory crossovers, or synesthesias, that are visual, auditory and tactile. These

interrupt the narrative flow of a dream and fuse dreamer to imagery in such a way that the dream is experienced as simultaneously fearful and joyful. Because of the mix of emotion and thought, a lucid dream leaves the dreamer with an expansive thrill or numinous feeling . . . [lucid dreaming] ranges from a quasi-lucid state in which one is aware of dreaming but unable to control the content of one's dreams to being able to enter the dream space and affect the dream's outcome.[25]

Another feature of shamanism is the fact that the visionary does not only learn how to control an induced or spontaneous visionary state at the moment of experience, but also gains the ability to influence, in advance, the type of experience he will have. Many psychological studies have shown that specifically-themed dreams can be generated in response to certain stimuli. And we are all familiar with the saying, here articulated by psychologist Montague Ullman, that 'If the analyst is a Freudian, the patient tends to dream in Freudian symbols; if the analyst is a Jungian, the patient dreams in Jungian archetypal symbols' and so on.[26] Given the fact that shamans generally enter into visionary states with specific prior intentions – whether these be to find a cure for a particular illness, meet a certain spirit or travel to a designated place in the spirit world – it comes as no surprise to find that they develop the ability to induce envisioned events that reflect these intentions. This 'incubation' process, as it is often termed, can be so precise that, as Cahuilla shaman Ruby Modesto was told by her mentor: 'You can tell yourself ahead of time where you want to go, or what you want to see, or what you want to learn.'[27]

A Different Kind of Vision

Thus far, the shamanistic visionary experience is relatively accessible to the modern Western mind. Most of us have experienced exceptionally intense dreams at some point in our lives and a significant number will have experienced moments of lucidity or flight during these experiences. Many of us may have a sense of how specifically-themed dreams can be induced, even if it is just through noticing how an impression, pre-occupation or event experienced in the day can emerge in dream experience the following night. And the minority of people who work with mental imagery cultivation – such as magicians, neo-shamans, imaginal psychologists and those studying dreams in laboratory conditions – will also know, from personal experience, that through inner work lucidity can be increased, and internally-produced imagery can become more vivid, controllable and 'real'. But nevertheless, there are aspects of the shamanistic experience that remain largely inaccessible to modern Western mentalities, however sympathetic they may be.

The first is concerned with belief. In the culturally-diverse West, the majority view is that internally-produced images are mental creations which, though they may serve a purpose in normalizing brain function or relieving personal anxieties, can only have a subjective reality and do not influence either the wider community or the physical world. Even the minority of people who work with mental imagery in the belief that it possesses some kind of objective reality or functions as a portal to some type of supra-normal knowledge or power (whether a deity, transpersonal self or archetype), do so in the knowledge that their view is only one, and a marginal one at that, among a number of alternatives. As a consequence, for these people the belief that an image is objectively real, or that it functions as some kind of portal to something supra-normal, lives directly alongside the knowledge that others might dismiss it as completely unreal and a portal to absolutely nowhere at all.

But for the shaman, crucially, there is no such ambiguity. Shamanism originally emerged and remains at its most influential, in small, relatively closed, communities that share a homogeneous belief system in which the importance and objective reality of visionary phenomena is unchallenged. As a consequence, the tribal shaman believes that his visionary experiences are important and real because this is the only view available to him. The ways in which such conviction, undisturbed by the existence of alternative explanations, might affect the creation of, and response to, visionary experience is difficult to grasp. Also difficult for us to grasp is the impact that such convictions can have on a young mind. There is a world of difference between the five-year-old tribal child who, after having a powerful nightmare, is questioned seriously about every detail by his parents and elders, told that the dream may be the presence of a dead ancestor bringing a valuable message from the spirit world and encouraged to perform certain ritual actions in response – and the five-year-old Western child who has a vivid nightmare and is told by his parents, however compassionately, that the dream is meaningless and that he should go back to sleep and take no notice of it at all. The ways in which these children respond to visionary experience, from this point in time onwards, will be radically different.

It is also difficult for the modern Western mind to appreciate how the shaman's experiences are affected by accountability. The shaman enters into visionary experience in the belief that the actions he performs there will produce real, visible outcomes in the physical world: through his efforts he will, quite literally, be able to make a wound heal and corn grow. In the West, by contrast, the cultivation of visionary experience is predominantly concerned with psychological outcomes: the resolving of personal anxiety, the pursuit of self-development and the search for spiritual enlightenment. Of the minority who work with specific, practical outcomes in mind, only a percentage will deal with life-threatening illnesses and they will generally do so in conjunction with conventional medical care or in situations where such care has proved ineffective. Few contemporary European or North American visionaries, then, can enter into the mentality of the shaman for whom it is a regular occurrence to be called to attend a gravely sick child in the knowledge that, in the absence of any alternative, the hopes of the child and its family will be pinned on what takes place during his dream or vision. Few can understand what it must feel like for him to embark on a visionary journey to locate distant herds in a time of famine, knowing that the actions of the tribe's hunters and thereby the survival of the whole community will be dictated by the phenomena he encounters and the decisions he takes while doing so. Few can really appreciate the fact that for the shaman, the success of his visionary experience is not judged by the beauty of its imagery, the intensity of its accompanying ritual, or even the profundity of the insights gained, but by hard, cold, observable facts: Was the sick child cured? Was the herd where the shaman predicted it would be? This pragmatic accountability means that the shaman enters into a dream or vision experience with a unique level of emotional intensity, mental intention and commitment to his method; and it is virtually impossible for modern Westerners to judge what effect such forces may have on the visionary capacities of the human mind.

It is also difficult for us to appreciate the degree to which the shaman's visionary experiences are moulded by what anthropologist Jackson Lincoln has termed 'culture-patterning'. Working in the early-twentieth century, Lincoln was the first to make a categorical distinction between two different kinds of visionary experience: one primarily reflecting culture (which is deliberately sought out) and the other primarily reflecting the individual (which appears spontaneously in sleep). Using the term 'dream' to cover both waking and sleeping visionary experience, he defines the two types of experience as follows:

> the pattern dream or vision represents the culture's demand on the individual, and its manifest content reflects the culture first, and secondarily individual psychology. The individual dream, however, represents the individual in his relation or non-relation to the culture, and its manifest content reflects his psychology first and secondarily his culture.[28]

Although Lincoln's categorization system has been criticized as overly simplistic, particularly with regard to his differentiation between sought-out and spontaneous visionary experiences, his distinction between culture-patterned and individual dream/vision content remains a useful paradigm and shall be employed here.[29]

Under intensive exposure to specific cultural influences any human mind is theoretically capable of producing specifically-themed dreams in response, with this capacity being most evident, in the modern West, in therapeutic situations. But among the general population, some societies are more likely to generate culture-patterned dreams than others. In the developed world, where communities are divided into numerous subcultures, and within these, largely independent nuclear family units, and in which every individual has access to a wide extra-community knowledge base through which they can develop highly-personal and idiosyncratic world-views, visionary experiences are more likely to be individual. But in small, interdependent tribal communities that share a uniformity of lifestyle, aspiration and belief and where everyone is exposed to the same closed pool of imagery and symbolism, visionary experiences are more likely to be culture-patterned. In these communities, culture-patterns are absorbed by osmosis through oral literature and physical ritual impressed frequently and consistently upon young minds from an early age: a process that conspires to persuade a tribe member to dream what his culture expects him to dream. A prime example of this is the initiatory vision. Anthropologist R. F. Fortune has shown that since they were too young to remember, boys from the nineteenth-century Native American Omaha tribe were exposed to myths, stories, anecdotes, songs and rituals that reminded them that, as they grew toward adulthood, some of them would experience a vision in which a 'Supernatural Patron' offered magical powers that would, in some cases, be strong enough to enable them to become shamans. They knew the names of the beings that might appear to them, the forms they might appear in, where they lived and the types of powers they were likely to bestow. As they became older, these boys were deliberately sent on ritual quests to precipitate these encounters: at seven or eight they were dispatched in groups, to selected spots, with their faces 'covered with clay by their parents'; and after puberty, to sacred places where they were expected to meditate and fast, in solitude, for four days and nights.[30] Given this attention to detail it is hardly surprising that, either during formal rituals or spontaneously during daily life, a significant minority of Omaha boys found themselves experiencing the requisite visions.

Because dream and vision experiences possess this highly absorbent quality, in societies without written texts they also function as vehicles through which cultural traditions are preserved. Noll argues that 'What is often understated in discussions of nonliterate societies by modern observers is that the cultural mythology is a *living* one. There are no written sources to validate religious beliefs, only the repeated, ritualized, reexperiencing of the sacred'. In this way, he continues, the vivid visionary journeys of the shaman operate as an 'imagery mnemonic for the retention of mythological beliefs and other culturally relevant materials in a nonliterate society'.[31] From this perspective, the shaman who remembers complex mental maps of interlocking spirit worlds does not only do so because they have been described to him but also because he has personally visited them.

Anthropologists have also observed that in order to give voice to these complex and vivid experiences, and to maximize their magical effect, shamans often possess highly developed verbal skills, with folklorist Georgii Kurbatski noting that they 'have a much larger vocabulary than do ordinary people, a vocabulary that describes the vast worlds they encounter on their voyages and reflects structures and concepts long forgotten among non-shamans'.[32] As Kira Van Deusen has recently illustrated with regard to Turkic Siberia, this mutual reliance on the partnership between language and imagination means that in traditional cultures the vocations of oral performer and shaman often overlap. Similarly, like many traditional fireside bards, the shaman often composes his charms, songs and stories extempore, with Van Deusen noting that, 'Shamans create song-poems spontaneously, both in trance and in ordinary states of consciousness'.[33]

But while the ability to memorize and accurately recount culture-patterned visionary experience is a core shamanistic skill, invention can also play an important role here. As Lee Irwin has recently argued, the value of the culture-patterned visionary experience lies not only in its ability to retain mythology and tradition, but also in its ability to invigorate and rework it. The individual who 'dreams what his culture expects him to dream' does not only witness a stereotypical narrative, but witnesses a stereotypical narrative imbued with a powerful personal resonance, containing those intimate, idiosyncratic details that make it his alone. The adolescent Omaha boy who encounters a Supernatural Patron in the guise of his dead grandfather meets a spirit that is wholly particular to him: it is his grandfather who appears in the vision, talking to him in the special way that only his grandfather did. Carrying unique power and immediacy, these personalized culture-patterned visionary experiences feed directly back into culture and in so doing energize and reshape the religious traditions of the community. As Irwin elaborates, with regard to Native American Indian traditions:

> Because of the unbound nature of dream and visionary experience, and because of the religious sanctions surrounding the vision encounter, the results of the vision can act as a source for an ongoing transformation of religious thought and behaviour. The conventional attitude that dreams and visions are 'stereotyped' experiences strictly reflecting cultural norms is not supported by the ethnography. The innovative and creative aspects of the visionary experience provide a context for new interpretation and understanding that is generally congruent with existing social patterns. Yet they also provide a means for more individualized interpretations that come to have highly personal and idiosyncratic meanings. It is this dialogical relationship between the social form and the visionary content that provides a context for collective transformations.[34]

Visionary Experience in Early Modern Scotland

Armed with this brief overview of how visionary experience is perceived and utilized in contemporary tribal cultures, we can now move on to consider the phenomenon in relation to early modern Europe. We will begin by exploring how far early modern attitudes toward visionary experience reflected, and how far they diverged, from the basic anthropological template sketched out above. This analysis will be curtailed, in its initial stages, within certain perimeters. First, we will be employing a simple comparative approach only. The complex question as to what extent correspondences between early modern European and contemporary tribal beliefs may be construed as evidence of the survival of pre-Christian belief and practice into the early modern age does not fall within the remit of this book. Secondly, this analysis will begin without reference to either demonological encounter-narratives (that is, narratives containing references to demonological witchcraft) or fairy-related encounter-narratives (that is, narratives containing references to fairies or associated spirits). Given the fact that these are so controversial with regard to the question of shamanistic experience, these sources will be drawn into the analysis later in the chapter when a general overview of visionary traditions in this period has been established. Thirdly, by way of caution, it must be emphasized that our source material is heavily biased in favour of the elite minority. For insights into any subjective experience in this period, whether visionary or otherwise, we are largely dependent upon the observations of the relatively small number of individuals who possessed the capacity, leisure time or inclination to commit them to paper. As Steven Kruger recently noted with regard to medieval dream accounts: 'Different dreamers, of distinct social status, education, and experience, must have used their dreams in varying ways, but only the dreams of those able to record their experience, and only the dreams they thought worthy of presentation, survive.'[35]

As we have explored in CHAPTERS ONE and SEVEN, early modern Europe was an essentially pre-industrial culture, and as in similar cultures worldwide, the physical and psychological stresses conducive to visionary experience (as caused by factors such as chronic and acute food shortages, hard physical labour, vulnerability to sickness and high mortality levels) were ubiquitous. As a consequence we can assume, as we have done with regard to tribal societies, that visionary experiences were more common than they are in Europe today. Certainly, the links between visionary experience and phys-iological stress, so clearly evident in many tribal shamanic narratives, can be identified in many seventeenth-century dream and vision accounts, with one of our most dramatic examples coming from Moray covenanter Katharine Collace who, as we have seen earlier, was intimate with both the Hays of Park and Harry Forbes. Collace claimed that over a nine-month period, while resident in Auldearn in the 1650s, she encoun-tered both Christ and the Devil in a series of powerful visual and auditory hallucinations. But it can surely be no coincidence that these visions occurred during a period when she was not only 'for the most part . . . sick', but had also recently lost 'two fine children' (one of whom was 'overlaid by his nurse') fast on the heels of losing two others, in Ross, before her arrival in Auldearn.[36]

We can also presume that the ingestion of mind-altering substances played a role here. Alcohol was consumed on a daily basis in all levels of society. It is hard not to suspect, for example, that an excess of spirits played a role in the spirit-encounters of Major Wilkie, the Scottish soldier described in Baxter's *Certainty of the World of Spirits* as: 'a scholar of considerable learning; he would drink too much, and had the signs of a heated brain, but no failing of his reason perceivable' but 'confidently affirmed, that he continually saw good and evil spirits about him, and that he had a good genius [familiar spirit] and an enemy'.[37] Similarly, in a period when crops were grown without the benefit of modern pesticides and people could not afford to be too fastidious about what they ate, the prevalence and ingestion of hallucinogenic plant toxins, like the mycotoxin ergot, would have been much higher than they are today. It is also possible, though difficult to establish with any certainty, that some contemporary magical prac-titioners may have deliberately employed psychoactive plants, such as henbane, in a ritual capacity. Long evenings in poorly-lit rooms, and in shadowy, dusk-filled barns and fields, would also have played a role in nurturing the visual imagination, as would the fact that, as Roger Ekirch has recently emphasized, the interaction between the waking and visionary modalities would have been intensified by the segmented-sleep patterns common throughout Europe in this period. Ekirch argues that:

> Until the modern era, up to an hour or more of quiet wakefulness midway through the night interrupted the rest of most Western Europeans . . . [during which they] reflected on the dreams that typically preceded waking from their 'first sleep'. Not only were these visions unusually vivid, but their images would have intruded far less on conscious thought had sleepers not stirred until dawn. This historical implications of this traditional mode of repose are enormous, especially in the light of the significance European households once attached to dreams for their explanatory and predictive powers.[38]

Given these general conditions, we can assume that, as in tribal cultures, the relatively high incidence of visionary experience in pre-modern Europe helped to render these experiences more culturally significant. Even as late as the nineteenth century, as Judith Devlin has argued with regard to France, the 'prevalence and popularity of tales about extraordinary visions' could be attributed to the fact that 'hallucinations were probably more common in the last century than now . . . [and] Part of the explanation for the interest people had in this area of experience and for the importance they attached to it is probably due to the fact that it was relatively common'.[39] We can assume that similar levels of incidence underpinned the fact that, as Kirkwood observed, the late seventeenth-century Highlanders 'greatly observe[d] Dreams'.[40]

But in early modern Europe, visionary experiences were not only considered significant because they were relatively common, but also by virtue of the belief system that underpinned them. Like contemporary tribal societies, the overwhelming majority of early modern Europeans believed that spirits possessed an objective reality; that they enjoyed supernatural powers that could influence the world of men; and that visionary experience was a direct method of negotiating with these spiritual beings, face to face, for the benefit of both self and community. Similarly, as in tribal societies, the visionary and non-visionary modalities were considered to be part of the same unified spatial-temporal reference, with Pócs arguing, in reference to early modern Hungary, that 'the alternative world that appeared in visions or dreams was part of "normal" existence and . . . there was a path between the two. The smooth continuity of events and the web of cause and effect interwove between the two worlds and the motions of both were seen as the same reality.'[41] Nothing but a heartfelt belief in the direct link between these two worlds could have motivated a Bute woman to deem it relevant, when Jonet Morison was tried for witchcraft in 1662, to testify that two years previously 'she took a dreaming of Jonet Morisone in her bed in the night, and was afrighted therewith and, within half ane hour after wakning, her young child took a trembling a very unnaturall lyke disease quhair of he died'.[42] Like their tribal counterparts, early modern Europeans made distinctions between visionary experiences that were 'only dreams' and those that were believed to be genuine encounters with the supernatural, and they generally considered waking visions to be more significant than dreams.[43] Beliefs in the existence of subtle or astral bodies that could leave the body, often in some kind of flight, during visionary experience were also prevalent although, as we shall explore later, highly controversial. As in tribal societies, these widespread convictions concerning the existence of spirits and spirit worlds, when combined with a lifestyle-induced susceptibility to visionary experience, fostered ways of experiencing and interpreting the world that are difficult for the modern Western mind to appreciate. According to Carolly Erickson, in her monograph on the 'extraordinary perceptual significance attributed to the visionary imagination' in the medieval period:

> The perceived reality of the enchanted world predisposed the medievals to special habits of sight. Put another way, belief in a densely incorporeal population that could be glimpsed under special conditions affected the quality of their visual perception. Their sight was different from ours in kind; accepting a more inclusive concept of reality, *they saw more than we do* [my italics].[44]

Dream Interpretation

As in tribal societies, in early modern Europe interpretations of visionary experience could be both symbolic and literal. Evidence of the former is vividly illustrated by Edward Lhuyd's claim, in the late-seventeenth century, that if a Highland seer sees a man 'with fish [scales] over his hair and his clothes, he is to be drowned; bloody, if he is to be wounded; in his shroud if he is to die in his bed; with his sweetheart on his right hand if he is to marry [her], but on his left hand if he is not'. It is also intimated by later sources, with the inhabitants of nineteenth-century Fife, for example, believing that to dream of rats or eggs was unlucky (because eggs denote disputes and rats, enemies) while to dream of the loss of teeth or fingers indicated a death.[45] Evidence of symbolic interpretation can also be found among the early modern elite, with Alexander Brodie, in December 1662, interpreting an intense dream, in which he found himself sitting on a dunghill, as representative of worldly downfall:

> I thoght I was in the Cougat at Edinburgh, and ther was sitting on a dunghill, and was looking stedfastli on a gibbet befor me; and a sister or freind of Sir Jhon Nisbet's did com and speak with me, and bad tak me up . . . But if by this the Lord be shewing me that He intends to humbl me, and to bring me low, even to the dunghill, let His will be don.[46]

The many 'dream books' that were widely circulated throughout Europe in this period, and which enabled the reader to decode dream images by a variety of methods including date, phases of the moon, random openings of the Bible or definitive sign systems and so on, attest to the popularity of this form of symbolic analysis.[47]

But even more significant, in the context of the present discussion, is the fact that in early modern Europe, as in contemporary tribal cultures, visionary experience could also be interpreted literally. A wide variety of sources, including the Bible, legends of the saints, theological works, dream-vision narratives, poetry, and the anecdotes and polemics contained in the ubiquitous pamphlets, bear testament to the belief that objectively real spirits could be encountered face to face through visionary experience. At no point does the early eighteenth-century pamphlet recording how Richard Brightly, a minister near Salcraig, 'fell into a trance' while praying and was 'warned of his death by an angel' question the objective reality of the spirit encountered.[48] Similarly, in Dyke over fifty years earlier, Cathrin Henrie sought out Brodie's help because she was clearly convinced that it was Satan himself, in person, who had repeatedly approached her in visionary form 'sometymes in the shape of some friend, or [sometimes] her brother'.[49] In 1775 Moray minister Lachlan Shaw claimed that in previous centuries 'Apparitions were every where talked of and believed', and noted that reports of sightings of the spirit *Maag Moulach*, who appeared in the form of 'a Young Girl, whose left hand was all hairy' were taken so seriously by the Moray synod that it issued frequent orders to the presbyteries of Aberlaure and Abernethie 'to enquire into the truth' of her appearances.[50] Visions of the dead were also taken literally. One of the most popular books in eighteenth-century Scotland, George Sinclair's *Satan's Invisible World Discovered* (1685), was filled with accounts of the dead allegedly returning to visit their friends and relatives. Similarly, Shaw noted that in seventeenth-century Moray it was widely believed that 'Ghosts or departed souls, often returned to this world . . . That Children dying unbaptized wandered in woods and solitudes, lamenting their hard fate, and were often seen.'[51]

But whether the interpretation was symbolic or literal, like their tribal counter-parts, the early modern Europeans believed that visionary experiences could be vehicles through which individuals could gain supernatural knowledge and power. The dead, from their vantage point beyond the grave, were believed capable of relaying impor-tant messages to the living: Shaw noting that in Moray, as in the rest of Scotland, they served to 'to warn their friends of approaching danger, to discover murders, to find lost goods, &c.'[52] The gravity with which such messages were taken is vividly illustrated by the fact that when four Orkney widows, in 1666, encountered dream-images of their husbands who had recently died at sea, their experiences were taken so seriously as messages concerning possible murder that the kirk session ordered that the men's graves be disinterred in the hope of discovering 'evidence of tampering or foul play'.[53] Among Protestants, as Walsham, Todd and Landsman have emphasized, dreams and visions were often celebrated as messages or 'providences' from God himself, often in the form of predictions, designed to bring spiritual guidance and comfort: the latter noting, in reference to 'voices and visions', that 'the legends of the covenanters were filled with tales of supernatural signs of divine approbation of the martyrs and heroes of the day and divine retribution against their adversaries'.[54] Certainly, as we have seen earlier, even the down-to-earth Brodie believed that his dream of sitting on a dunghill was a prophetic message from God: as evinced by his claim that, 'if by this the Lord be shewing me that He intends to humble me . . . let His will be done'.[55] Over fifty years after Brodie recorded this dream in his diary, a pamphlet published in Edinburgh in 1719 celebrated the fact that, while praying in his corn yard, pious Scottish farmer William Rutherford encountered an angel that 'opened up to him strange visions unknown to the inhabitants of the earth' and revealed 'the dreadful wrath that is coming on Britain, with an eclipse of the gospel, and the great death that shall befall many'.[56]

Visionary Specialists: Interpreters and Shamans

Given the value attributed to visionary experience in the early modern centuries, it is no surprise to find that, as in tribal societies, a range of visionary specialists emerged to manage and facilitate them. With regard to dream interpretation it was the clergy, as the designated experts in all things spiritual and supernatural, who were deemed to be the official port of call, and the seriousness with which they were encouraged to take this responsibility is reflected in the fact that, as Stuart Clark has recently noted, the interpretation of dreams and 'divination in general – was a preoccupation of the vast literature of religious guidance that accompanied the Protestant and Catholic Reformations'.[57] But people also resorted to lay spiritual mentors, with Cathrin Hendrie, for example, seeking guidance from Brodie when troubled by visions of the Devil. The interpretative skills of lay spiritual mentors were particularly important for the members of unorthodox sects, who resorted to them in preference to the conventional ministers who did not share their particular brand of Christianity.[58] Even more interestingly, given our thesis here, is the fact that dream and vision analysis was also commonly undertaken by magical practitioners. Elite magicians and astrologers frequently advised on these matters, with some (commonly known as 'dream interpreters' or 'oreinomancers') making it their professional speciality. On a popular level, this function was often performed by cunning folk, with sixteenth-century English witchcraft sceptic Reginald Scot condemning 'those witches, that make men beleeve they can prophesie upon dreames'.[59] The trial dittays of Orkney cunning woman Jonet Reid, for example, describe how she was sought out by a man troubled by apparitions of his recently deceased wife: the records stating that 'Robert Sinclair in Gerssand, being efter he haid married his secund wyif, sore trublit in his sleip with apparitiounes of his ffirst wyiff, which vexit him and disquietit him verie much, he was advysit be yow [Jonet] to goe to his first wyfis grave, and to chairge hir to ly still and truble him no moir.'[60] Folk songs and ballads also attest to the interpretative skills of cunning folk. In 'Fair Margaret O' Craignaritie' (collected in the north-east in the mid-nineteenth century), a woman is troubled by recurring dreams:

> Three times on end she dreamed this dream
> Which troubled sore her mind
> That from that very night and hour
> No comfort could she find
>
> But she sent for a wise woman
> Who lived near that part
> She being called the instant came
> That lady to comfort
>
> She tauld to her the dreary dream
> With the salt tear in her e'e
> Thinking that she would read the same
> Her mind to satisfy.[61]

But again, as in tribal societies, it was not only those who were skilled at interpreting dreams and visions who were valued, but also those who were skilled at experiencing them. Many early modern Scots clearly believed that their dreams and visions were relevant to others as well as themselves and felt duty bound to relay them, or the message they contained, to their wider communities. During his visionary trances, Salcraig minister Richard Brightly was not only given a personal message regarding his forthcoming death by an angel, but he was also told by Death himself – 'riding in triumph on a pale horse' – to 'warn the inhabitants of the earth of the wrath to come'. Brightly seems to have duly divulged his experiences to his congregation with almost farcical theatricality: the pamphlet recording his experiences describing how he 'afterwards ordered his coffine and grave to be made, and invited his parishioners to hear his last sermon, which he preached the Sunday following, having his coffine before him, and then declared his visions'.[62] Similarly, reluctant visionary William Rutherford, at the behest of his envisioned angel, allegedly rushed off to call the local minister and 'four honest men' to witness his trances, 'that the world might have nothing to object' when he relayed his apocalyptic message about 'eclipse of the gospel, and the great death that shall befall many'.[63] As temporary hotlines to supernatural power such visionaries were, as in tribal societies, frequently petitioned with requests for information or aid. When the ten-year-old daughter of godly Perthshire farmer Donald McGrigor experienced a series of visions involving angels in the late-seventeenth century, her family and neighbours (who saw her visions as a 'mercifull dispensation of Providence') clustered around her and pressed her with questions to ask the angels on their behalf. Her mother beseeched her to inquire 'what came of young children not baptized' while her father demanded that she ask the spirits 'Whether the indulged ministers did well in accepting the indulgence' and, even more specifically, whether a minister recently executed for murder really did have 'any hand in the childe's blood who was murdered'.[64] Visionary knowledge was so esteemed and sought after in the period that, as Margo Todd has recently argued, reformed clergy even publicized their access to it as a means of luring people away from superstition and over to the godly cause:

> Their visionary aspect certainly helped ministers to win a devoted following. The more extraordinary a preacher's prophecies, the more likely he was to gain what one might as well call 'groupies', often women, who sought out their pastors constantly, followed their counsel blindly . . . and, most significantly, emulated them. Like the holy men of an earlier era, the ministers inspired visions and miracles among their lay followers, spawning a whole second tier of saints with remarkable access to supernatural power.[65]

Early Modern Shamans

It is not unreasonable to argue that the activities and experiences of many of these early modern visionaries fall, to a greater or lesser degree, under the definition of shamanism that we are employing here (*see* page 252). Some of these visionaries (such as William Rutherford, Richard Brightly and the Perthshire farmer's daughter) arguably performed, what we can term here, a 'semi-shamanistic function', in that although their visionary experiences were communally beneficial, their access to them was temporary and occurred largely independently of their conscious will. But others seem to have performed a more comprehensive shamanistic role, in the sense that they generated relatively-controlled visionary experiences seemingly at will, on a regular basis, and in response to community demand.

Surprising as it may seem, during the Middle Ages, these more fully-functioning shamanistic practitioners could be commonly found within the church itself. The gaining of spiritual knowledge through intentioned visionary experience was an enduring component of many Christian contemplative traditions, and medieval visionaries, both cloistered and uncloistered, clearly invoked such experiences in response to

This woodcut from a Swedish manuscript, dated 1671, depicts a Sami shaman using a circular drum inscribed with magical symbols to enter trance and communicate with his familiar spirits. As was common in the period, the Christian artist portrays the shaman's familiars as evil demons.

Although they worked within a different tradition, contemporary European magicians engaged in very similar activities. In the well-known frontispiece to Marlow's *Doctor Faustus*, the magician invokes the demon Mephistopheles using a ritual circle composed of magical symbols.

petitions for help and advice on both practical and spiritual matters.[66] But after the Reformation, and particularly in Scotland, the shamanistic practitioners most likely to be consistently generating visionary experience in response to community demand worked within the magical traditions. Despite their intellectualism, neoplatonist magicians maintained the centrality of the visionary experience through the magical conjuration of spirits and performed invocations in response to client requests for aid.[67] On a popular level, a similarly concrete shamanistic role was often assumed by cunning folk. In Scotland, many of the latter built their reputations around their capacity to perceive the 'invisible world' through dream or vision, commonly employing the facility to seek out the wishes of the dead, divine the future, locate lost goods and diagnose or heal the sick. While many cunning folk emphasized the spontaneity of their visionary encounters, the records suggest that some advertised their ability to specifically generate them in response to client demand. The fact that these popular practitioners were widely termed 'seers' or those with 'second sight' confirms the centrality of the visionary experience in their practice. Similarly, the fact that seers of some description were to be found in just about every parish in the country from the early modern period through to the nineteenth century confirms the importance of visionary magical traditions for the pre-industrial Scots.[68]

Although scattered and sparse, the evidence suggests that both within and without the curtilage of orthodox Christianity and on both an elite and popular level, shamanistic and semi-shamanistic practitioners could encounter dream and vision phenomena in a range of trance states. Kirk describes how a seer could obtain visions while in company, merely pausing in his work to 'stare a little strangely' or break off conversation to 'look oddly'; while early seventeenth-century traveller Martin Martin claimed that 'At the sight of a vision, the eye-lids of the person are erected, and the eyes continue staring until the object vanish.'[69] The trial dittays of Orkney seer Jonka Dyneis (1616), alternatively, state that when her husband was in trouble at sea she was found 'standing at hir awin hous wall, in ane trans, that same hour he was in danger; and being trappit, she could not give answer, bot stude as bereft of hir senssis; and quhen she was speirit [asked] at quhy she wes so movit, she answerit, gif our boit be not tynt, she is in great hazard – and was tryit so to be'.[70] Others seem to have encountered their visions during classic shamanistic catalepsy. In 1717 John Gardner, a minister from near Elgin, allegedly 'fell into a trance . . . and lay as if dead, to the sight and appearance of all spectators, for the space of two days'. The pamphlet describing his experiences claims that it was only after he had been committed to his coffin that he awoke and 'being carry'd home, and put in a warm bed, he in a little time coming to himself, related many strange and amazing things which he had seen in the other world'.[71]

Visions: the Growing Scepticism

But although the seventeenth-century Scots resembled those living in tribal societies in that they valued and utilized visionary experiences, their essentially animist perspectives were simultaneously modified by the rationalist intellectual traditions that would, over the following five centuries, gradually revolutionize the belief constructs under-pinning attitudes toward visionary experience as a whole. These traditions, which by the seventeenth century had been present in elite discourse for at least five hundred years, had their roots in Ancient Greece and Rome where classical thinkers, in their boundless enthusiasm to subject all phenomena to epistemological analysis, had been the first to make the crucial conceptual shift from asking 'What does this dream mean?' to 'What is a dream?' In attempting to answer this question, Aristotle, Heraclitus, Macrobius, Calcidius et al. examined visionary experience through the emerging dualist conviction that the universe, and all the phenomena contained within it, could be gainfully divided into opposing forces or elements, such as spiritual/material, sacred/mundane, real/not real and so on.[72]

Classical thinkers were products of their time, and they did not deny that dreams and visions could be direct encounters with spiritual realities, but they also argued that they could be rooted in purely psychological and somatic factors. In other words, an envisioned angel could be 'real' if it appeared in a dream of spiritual or divine origin, but 'unreal' if it appeared in a dream manufactured solely by the psychological func-tion of memory, or by some form of physical disturbance. These ambiguities were energetically grappled with by ecclesiastics and intellectuals throughout the Middle Ages and into the early modern period. And while these thinkers could assume a variety of extreme positions, the majority tended to the moderate view that visionary experi-ences fully spanned the mundane/divine continuum, with most falling in the middle range.[73]

These rationalist theories about visionary experience automatically affected ways of thinking about the spirits and spirit worlds with which they were so profoundly linked. The traditional animist view that spirits possessed bodies of subtle matter survived into the early modern period, with writers like Kirk still claiming that spirits had 'light changeable . . . bodies of congealed air' that were 'somewhat of the nature of a condens'd cloud'.[74] But as early as the fifth century the rationalist dichotomy between 'material' and 'spiritual' had given rise to the idea that spirits were non-material in essence (having 'neither hands or feet, neither appearance, shape or matter') and the non-mate-riality of spirits became part of Catholic doctrine at the Lateran Council of 1215.[75] But although, from this point on, the church maintained that spirits were immaterial and that there was 'nothing of them therefore that we can perceive and comprehend', the persistent belief that they could appear, in visible form, during visionary experience still required explanation, and this epistemological challenge was widely taken up in theological and scientific writing from the fifth century through to the early modern period.[76] Two main theories emerged: the first maintained that although spirits were essentially immaterial, they could assume a body at will by clothing themselves in material elements; the second, favoured by influential writers like Augustine, main-tained that spirits, being immaterial, manipulated the imagination so that the human perceived them to be in bodily likeness. The fourteenth-century visionary contempla-tive Birgitta of Sweden claimed that Christ told her:

The vision that you see does not appear to you just as it is. For if you would see the spiri-

269

tual beauty of the angels and the souls of the saints, your body would not be sufficient for seeing it . . . If, on the other hand, you would see the demons just as they are, either you would live with much pain or you would die suddenly because of the frightful sight of them. Therefore spiritual things appear to you as if they were corporeal.[77]

This view that the envisioned image is false, but that the spiritual agency working behind it is real, can be seen to represent a mid-way point between the tribal animist belief that envisioned spirits have an independent, objective reality and the modern rationalist view that they are unreal figments of the imagination. This paradigm can be seen to mark the beginning of the modern conception of the imagination as a purely psychological function, at this stage still bound up with the belief that it was connected to the actions of supernatural agencies.

But with regard to the ontology of early modern spirits, the plot thickens yet further. By courtesy of rationalist dualism, the Christian world-view did not only divide envisioned phenomena into material and spiritual, but also into 'good' (of God) and 'bad' (of the Devil). Both good and bad spirits were believed to possess the ability to manipulate the imagination, but in the early modern period it was the Devil's activities in this respect that received an unprecedented amount of scholarly attention. Theologians and intellectuals emphasized, over and over again and at great length, how the Devil could use his imagination-manipulating skills to distract the holy from their spiritual path, tempt them into sin, gain their immortal souls and, in the case of witches, lure them into an open alliance with him. To this end, the Devil was imputed to create visions of beings and landscapes so compelling and numinous that they were hard to resist, and his alleged skills in this field meant that many contemporaries, from both sides of the Catholic/Protestant divide, found themselves challenged in this area. Despite being one of the most experienced and respected visionary mystics of her age, for example, Saint Teresa of Ávila often found it difficult to determine whether a seemingly-beatific vision was created by God or the Devil, while Martin Luther, although a different kind of mystic altogether, begged God not to send him dreams because he was afraid that he could not judge whether they were true or false.[78]

But in the early-seventeenth century, the status of envisioned spirits was subjected to a further and far more prescient threat: the question of the reality of spirits themselves. The challenge came from two directions. First, were the Protestant assertions that purgatory did not exist; that the soul went directly to heaven or hell on death; and that spirits of the dead could not roam the world or be encountered, visually or otherwise, by the living. Although this doctrine did not deny the existence of spirits per se, nor their ability to be encountered through visionary experience, by denying the existence of this particular category of spirits the Protestants dealt all spirits a mortal blow. Dream and vision encounters with deceased friends and relatives are not only common, but they are also among the most emotionally intense, realistic and meaningful types of visionary experience accessed by humans: indeed, according to the visionary-experience-gave-rise-to-the-belief-in-spirits theory discussed earlier in this chapter, it was the impact of these encounters with images of the dead and the attempt to understand them, that provided much of the impetus and emotional rationale behind theories about subtle bodies and, more significantly, the afterlife itself. Any grieving seven-teenth-century housewife who was told by her minister, or anyone else, that a powerful and personally-affecting vision of a dead husband, parent or child was illusory – whether a product of purely physiological factors or the manipulations of the Devil – did not only find her sense of subjective emotional conviction irrevocably undermined, but also found herself only a small step away from suspecting that all other visionary experiences, however realistic and profound, were also false. Such suspicions, accumu-lating over lifetimes and generations, gradually eroded confidence in the status of the visionary world. It is no accident that in the early modern period ardent Protestants were generally more likely to be sceptical of the reality of dream and vision phenomena than those of more moderate religious convictions.[79]

The other challenge to the existence of spirits emerging in this period was more abstract, but ultimately more damaging, and came in the form of a swathe of the new, what we can loosely term, 'materialist philosophers', such as Thomas Hobbes, Baruch Spinoza and René Descartes, who 'rejected the whole concept of incorporeal substances as a contradiction in terms'.[80] While these thinkers did not, in print at least, go so far as to rule out the possibility of spirits completely, they asserted the view – in various ways and to different extremes – that spirits could not assume material form or directly influence the material world. As a consequence, Descartes, Hobbes et al. did not only throw out the old idea that spirits did not possess bodies and therefore could not appear bodily in dreams and visions, but they also threw out the idea that they could manip-ulate the imagination to make themselves *seem* to appear in bodily form. Here, the umbilical cord between visionary experience and the world of the spirits, which had survived over a thousand years of rationalism, was finally severed. The swing towards the material end of the classical divine/mundane spectrum which we now occupy so completely in the twenty-first century, had begun in earnest. As Barbara Tedlock claims, with regard to the dream: 'while dreaming was already depressed in value within the West by the time of the emergence of naturalistic or scientific thought, it was not until the development of Cartesian mechanistic dualism in the seventeenth century that dreams were finally placed totally within the realm of fantasy or irrational experience'.[81]

An Uncommon Scepticism

But vigorous as these sceptical ideas were, in Isobel's lifetime they still represented a minority view. Despite the fact that materialist paradigms and the epistemological status of spirits were hot topics that, as Clark notes, were 'regularly debated in theo-logical and philosophical faculties of Europe's universities and by some of the most prominent scholars of the age' the majority of the population did not relinquish their belief that objectively-real spirits existed and that they could be encountered, either in bodily form, assumed bodily form or seeming bodily form, through visionary experi-ence.[82] The wide range of polemics and pamphlets published to counter the 'new atheism', as materialist theories were often termed, are ample testament to this. While most of these authors would not have denied that some visionary experiences were symptomatic of psychological or somatic disturbance, their core brief was to assert the reality of spirits through amassing persuasive incidents of genuine spirit-encounters and other supernatural happenings: of which Baxter's *Certainty of the World of Spirits*, Sinclair's *Satan's Invisible World Discovered* and Lavater's *Of Ghostes and Spirites Walking by Nyght* are classic examples. The general indignation roused by the materialist philosophies is summed up by minister of Kirkcudbright Alexander Telfair, in the preface to his pamphlet on *A True Relation of an Apparition, Expressions, and Actings, of a Spirit*. Here, Telfair claims that his text provides: 'conviction and confutation of that prevailing spirit of atheism and infidelity in our time, denying, both in opinion and practice, the existence of spirits, either of God or Devils; and consequently a heaven and hell; and imputing the voices, apparitions, and actings of good or evil spirits to the melancholik disturbance or distemper of the brains and fancies of those who pretend to hear, see or feel them.'[83]

But on the other hand, despite this vigorous resistance to the new atheism there is no doubt that in this period this cornucopia of ideas about visionary experience represented confusion for many. Even in tribal cultures, where belief constructs are relatively homogeneous and closed, the task of interpreting dreams and visions is not an easy one, without the additional challenge of distinguishing between 'true and false', 'real and not real', 'good and evil', 'mundane and sacred', 'physical and spiritual' and so on. This uncertainty was openly articulated in an early eighteenth-century pamphlet detailing supernatural events in Kinross, where the author, after challenging the materialist claim that there are no 'spirits and angels good and bad', goes on to admit that 'what is the essence of spirits . . . is hard to determine'.[84] You can detect similar anxieties in the mind of Alexander Brodie, when he describes his struggle to understand Cathrin Hendrie's visions of the Devil. Faced with her obviously earnest tales about the latter appearing 'in the shape of a cat with burning fiery eyes', Brodie mused: 'I desird to enquir and consider, what may be from ordinar natural causes, or what may be from extraordinarie, unknown, spiritual causes; what is from a troubld imagination and fancie, melancholie or her complexion; or what may be external from Sathan: Whatever it be I have desir'd to lay it befor the Lord.'[85] Similarly, with regard to ghosts, Peter Marshall claims that 'meanings of ghostly apparitions were open, hazardous, and uncertain, both at the level of official theology, and among those who actually found themselves confronted in the night with a "questionable shape"'.[86]

As a consequence of this confusion, it is hardly surprising that by the seventeenth century the role of the visionary specialist had become an extremely ambiguous one, at all levels of society. Rationalist paradigms, of the kind we have been discussing here, had been quietly eating away at the status of the visionary experience for many centuries prior to the Reformation. Despite the fact that the medieval church fostered mystical traditions with a strong visionary component that required adherents to follow detailed spiritual exercises specifically designed to generate and deepen internal imagery, it still viewed the visionary experiences their monks and nuns gained with extreme wariness, and was forever on the lookout for the signature of the Devil or the slightest suggestion of heresy. Similarly, the ambiguity surrounding dream interpretation meant that, despite the fact that dream books and 'interpreters of dreames' usually claimed religious orthodoxy, they were often condemned by the church, both in the Middle Ages and increasingly so in the early modern period.[87] With regard to visionaries themselves, caution was even more pronounced. The medieval church had not only nurtured its contemplatives in cloisters because the reclusive lifestyle was conducive to visionary experience, but also because the ambiguous status of the latter was such that it was best monitored within a curtailed and theologically orthodox environment. The aim was, as John Cohen writes with regard to Teresa of Ávila, that the mystic 'pursued her path close beneath the shadow of her Church's dogma, and by continually dwelling on it unconsciously shaped the imagery of her visions and locutions to suit its teaching'.[88] Both before and after the Reformation, those who experienced visions outside the cloister, even if they were clergy, were viewed with added suspicion, with Todd noting, in relation to seventeenth-century Scotland, that 'The preachers who reported their own prophecies and miracles, visions and voices, knew the danger of their claims' and were quick to defend themselves against accusations of papism or demonic delusion.[89] Lay visionaries found themselves in an even more ambiguous position. Because millers, weavers and farmers' wives experienced dreams and visions that seldom conformed to theological orthodoxy; and because their lifestyles seldom lived up to their pretensions as divine mouthpieces; and because their claims to spiritual intelligence represented a shift of power from clerical into lay hands, the church viewed them with distrust. More often than not, particularly after the Reformation, the ecclesiastical authorities attributed lay visionary encounters to the Devil, even when they were experienced by the otherwise godly. Although the visions of the educated and pious Janet Frazer (1691), for example, were filled with informed biblical messages from Christ and his angels, they were unsettling enough for the presbytery to encourage her to confess 'That she pretended to prophecying and seeing of visions, and that she had sinned greatly in being deluded by Satan, causing her prophecie and see things future.'[90] Similarly, the strong visionary component running through the godly writings of ardent and independent-minded Stirling covenanter Elizabeth Cairns, 'caused some to express concern about the nature of her piety'.[91] The Glasgow revivalists of the early-eighteenth century, for whom conversion was often precipitated by vision, were similarly condemned by the church. As Hindmarsh has recently emphasized, when editing the conversion narratives of converts for publication local ministers often qualified or avoided references to 'sensible manifestations' (that is, the sense impressions, which often included visual imagery, that emerged during prayer). Some could be rendered acceptable by inserting a simple phrase such as 'it seemed to me' where the narrator reported 'hearing things or seeing things'; but others, being more extreme, were avoided altogether. After reading Jean Hay's description of how she had opened her eyes to see a marvellous light, for example, one minister concluded that 'This woman's case may be passed by and not published'.[92]

While zealous Protestant visionaries were thus condemned, for those whose dream and vision experiences drew on magical belief matrices that lay outside the official umbrella of reformed Christianity, suspicion and censure was even more severe. Here, the inherent ambiguity of the visionary experience was magnified even further by the ambiguity of the doctrines that moulded and contextualized it. As a consequence the visionary practices of both elite and popular magical practitioners were legislated against: the former, because their visions were a product of a literary corpus of heretical doctrines, the latter because their visions were the product of an amorphous body of orally-inherited superstitions. By the middle of the seventeenth century, a cunning woman who claimed to have discovered the whereabouts of lost goods through encounting a spirit of the dead was, if she had the misfortune to be hauled up before church or secular authorities, almost inevitably told that she had experienced, at best, the somatic disturbances of her own brain or, at worst, the manipulations of Devil.

A Culture in Transition

This brief overview of attitudes towards visionary experience in early modern Europe has given us a picture of a culture with one foot in its animist past and another in its rationalist future. A multi-layered and complex society in which perspectives on dreams and visions spanned a vertiginous continuum from those found in contemporary tribal cultures (that is, they are direct encounters with an objectively real spirit world vital to the survival of the community) and perspectives found in the modern West (that is, they are subjective manifestations of the unconscious mind, of no relevance to the survival of the community). This overview has also illustrated that, according to the 'reasonably narrow and precise' definition of shamanism being used here, in this period a wide range of individuals, both inside and outside the curtilage of orthodox Christianity, can be said to have fulfilled shamanistic-type roles, with the function being more comprehensively modelled in the magical traditions. This overview has also illustrated that, in response to the growing ambiguities surrounding visionary experience, all shamanistic traditions and practitioners – whether partial or comprehensive, elite or popular, orthodox or folkloric – were peripheral to both church and state, particularly after the Reformation. In other words, while shamanistic practitioners in culturally homogeneous tribal societies represent the ideological norm and stand at the centre of community life where they function – or closely support those who function – as religious and political authorities, in culturally and ideologically diverse seventeenth-century Europe the shamanistic role was less central, less significant, more differentiated and far more subversive.

The Missing Sources

This overview of attitudes towards visionary experience in early modern Scotland has been constructed, thus far, without reference to the wealth of source material relating to fairy-related and demonological encounter-narratives taken down in interrogations for witchcraft and sorcery. It now remains to examine how these narratives fit into the picture we have constructed, and explore whether they modify it in any way.

In the Introduction to Part II we noted that scholars working with the shamanistic paradigm have argued that trial-derived accounts of meeting spirits (whether fairies, demons or the dead etc.) and travelling into spirit worlds (whether fairyland or the witches' sabbath), may have been representative of shamanistic beliefs and practices of folkloric origin. We also noted that this paradigm is hotly contested, and that while many scholars admit that these encounter-narratives could represent the existence of shamanistic beliefs, they tend to skirt around the question of how far they represented shamanistic experience, often assuming – in the absence of any evidence to the contrary – that they did not.

But what is immediately apparent here is that, in the context of the overview of tribal and early modern European attitudes toward visionary experience presented in this chapter thus far, this shamanistic hypothesis does not appear at all unreasonable. Indeed, given the fundamental link between the belief in spirits and visionary experience, it could be argued that it would in fact be unreasonable to approach any contemporary narrative purporting to describe an encounter with spirits or journey into spirit worlds without considering the possibility that some kind of visionary experience was involved; and unreasonable to explore any individual's claim to have encountered these spirits on behalf of their community without reference to peripheral shamanism.

Fairy-Related Narratives

Bearing these perspectives in mind, we will begin with the fairy-related encounter narratives. As it is used in this context, the term 'fairy-related' is a broad one, covering events associated with both those spirits defined as fairies and those who behaved like or fraternized with them. In the overwhelming majority of sources, the two latter spirit-types are identified as the dead. As we have already seen, in this period it was widely believed that the deceased could find themselves dwelling, or trapped, in fairyland, and many cunning folk claimed that the helping spirit who guided them through fairyland and interceded with the fairies on their behalf was a spirit of the dead. Other cunning folk overtly claimed that fairies were themselves the dead.[93] Conversely, it is also not uncommon for encounter-narratives to describe spirits defined as the dead acting like fairies and taking the visionary to fairyland-like places in the absence of any references to fairies at all.[94] Taken together, these allusions suggest that on a popular level matrices of belief surrounding fairies and the dead were inextricably entwined and that one cannot be discussed in isolation from the other.

Although most contemporary historians discuss fairy beliefs without any reference to visionary experience, in the nineteenth century there emerged a body of scholarly thought linking the two phenomena, as expressed in Evans-Wentz's claim, in 1911, that 'the living Fairy-Faith depends not so much upon ancient traditions, oral and recorded, as upon recent and contemporary psychic experiences'.[95] Such views developed in response to contemporary fascination with the congruities between European and non-European magical traditions, but they also developed in response to the fact that a significant minority of fairy-related encounter-narratives are strongly suggestive of visionary experience. The most overt make direct references to 'visions' or 'dreams'. The trial dittays of Fife cunning woman Alison Peirson, for example, state that her trips to fairyland were facilitated through the help of a 'spreitis of the Devill' who appeared 'in the *visioune and forme* of ane Mr William Sympsoune, hir cousing and moder-broth-eris-sone [my italics]'.[96] An event recorded by Thomas Pennant, when he was passing through Perthshire nearly 200 years later, is equally explicit:

> I was in the county of *Breadalbane*. A poor visionary, who had been working in his cabbage-garden, imagined that he was raised suddenly into the air, and conveyed over a wall into an adjacent corn-field; that he found himself surrounded by a crowd of men and women, many of whom he knew to have been dead some years, and who appeared to him skimming over the tops of the unbended corn, and mingling together like bees going to hive: that they spoke in an unknown language and with a hollow sound: that they very roughly pushed him to and fro; but on his uttering the name of GOD, all vanished but a female sprite, who seizing him by the shoulder obliged him to promise an assignation, at that very hour, that day sevenight: that he then found that his hair was all tied in double knots, and that he had almost lost the use of his speech: that he kept his word with the spectre, whom he soon saw come floating thro' the air towards him: that he spoke to her, but she told him at that time she was in too much haste to attend to him, but bid him go away, and no harm should befall him; and so the affair rested when I left the country. But it is incredible the mischief these *Aegri Somnia* [ill dreams] did in the neighbourhood: the friends and relations of the deceased, whom the old Dreamer had named, were in the utmost anxiety at finding them in such bad company in the other world: the almost extinct belief of the old idle tales began again to gain ground, and the good minister will have many a weary discourse and exhortation before he can eradicate the absurd ideas this idle story has revived.[97]

A significant minority of fairy-related narratives also contain references to trance states, or the behaviours associated with them. A local man reported that when Perthshire farmer Donald McGrigor's daughter experienced a series of 'wonderful revelations' and 'trances' during which she believed she was carried to heaven by a group of angels, several of her neighbours 'said to her that she was taken away with the fairies'.[98] The behaviours associated with cataleptic trance also emerge strongly from contemporary sources. In his *Daemonologie* James VI famously referred to women who encountered the fairy queen's 'glistering courts and trains' while succumbing to 'that imaginar ravishing of the spirit forth of the body . . . in the meantime, their bodies being senseless'.[99] Similarly, Kirk claimed that the Scottish seer, when learning to negotiate the second sight, was 'put in a rapture, transport, and sort of death, as divested of his body, and all it's Senses, when he is first made participant of this curious piece of knowledge'.[100] The various accounts of women who 'went with the fairies' at night, sleeping on hills and in ditches, are also suggestive here. Kirk claimed to have examined a forty-year-old woman named 'Mc Intyre', who was famous for her fasting, and had 'tarry'd in the fields over night, saw, and convers'd with a people [the fairies] she knew not, having wandred in seeking of her sheep, and slept upon a hillock, and finding hirselfe transported to another place befor day'.[101] Alternatively, in 1647 Elgin woman Janet Cui was arraigned by the session for 'having bein for a whole night out off hir own hous from hir husband and returning in the morning wher hir husband was be 4 or 5 hours in the morning hir husband demanded hir wher she had bein, [and she] answered the fairie had taken hir away to Messindiu wher she slept all night'. The fact that the session minutes then go on to state that Janet was 'divers tyms found half dead lying in the Grayfriers and other places neirby' suggests that catalepsy, as opposed to adultery or some other illicit activity, was behind her absence from the marital bed.[102]

That individual fairy-related encounter-narratives may have been rooted in visionary experience is also suggested by the fact that a significant proportion contain anomalous details. Descriptions of fairy-encounters that occur in company, but can only be seen by one person present, are suggestive here, with Stirling cunning woman Isobel Watson claiming, as did her Ayrshire contemporary, Bessie Dunlop, that when she was in the market place she had encountered fairies 'quhome na uthir folk will ken bot sic [such] as hes bein in the court'.[103] Similarly evocative are the fantastic, dream-like details that pepper many narratives, such as: 'he was raised suddenly into the air, and conveyed over a wall into an adjacent corn-field'; 'they spoke in an unknown language and with a hollow sound'; 'thair come th[air]efter first ane grit blast lyke a quhirll wind and th[air]efter thair come the schaip of ane ma[n]'; and 'the elphis will mak the appeir to be in a fair chalmer, and yit thow will find thy selff in a moss on the morne'.[104]

The fact that suggestive details, ranging from direct references to vision and trance to more subtle narrative anomalies, can be found in a large proportion of fairy-related narratives is highly persuasive. But our argument gains further support from the fact that, as anthropological research into shamanism indicates, with regard to visionary experience even those encounter-narratives in which suggestive detail is minimal or completely absent should not be dismissed. Wherever they emerge in the world, tribal encounter-narratives seldom contain references to trance or vision, and when these references do occur they tend to have been made by the recording observer or commentator, usually the anthropologist, as opposed to the shaman himself. The shaman says 'I met my familiar' not 'I met my familiar in a vision' or 'I met my familiar in a trance'. This emphasis does not reflect the fact that visionary experience did not occur, but instead, reflects the fact that for the shaman and his community the physical and visionary modalities are so unified and interactive that they have little interest in the epistemological status of vision or trance experience, as it would be analyzed in Western terms. With regard to Turkic shamanism, Kira van Deusen notes:

[Turkic languages] have no words for the altered states of consciousness that shamans and storytellers enter. How to interpret this? It is clear that they enter states quite different from what we consider 'ordinary.' Siberian shamans and storytellers do not pay as much attention to their states of consciousness as do those Western researchers who believe that these states are unusual and difficult to attain, and whose research is focused largely on cultures using hallucinogens. For shamans and storytellers, as I suspect for any creative person, the state of consciousness is not as important as the task to be accomplished. Musicians concentrate on the music, artists on the work they are producing. Storytellers enter into their tales and shamans concentrate on the journey, the soul to be brought back, and the help and hindrance they encounter on the way. Not that alteration doesn't happen, allowing the inner senses to function, but it is incidental to the work.[105]

There is no reason to assume that early modern visionaries would have been any more interested in identifying and recording their altered states of consciousness than contemporary Siberian shamans, and as a consequence we cannot rule out the possibility that even the most matter-of-fact and prosaic-sounding fairy-encountering narrative may have nurtured a visionary experience at its core. In the last analysis, we must put aside knee-jerk scepticism, and approach the visionary dimension of the fairy-related encounter-narrative as the cosmologist approaches the black hole: having no sight of the phenomenon itself, but speculating as to its existence and building up a picture of its characteristics and function by virtue of the way that things behave around it.

Fairy Shamanism

Although these perspectives do not enable us to estimate, with any confidence, how many early modern fairy-related encounter-narratives may have reflected visionary experience, they certainly invite us to speculate that a percentage – and perhaps a significant percentage – were constructed around an experiential core. And as we have already done with regard to the angel-encountering experiences of early modern visionaries like William Rutherford and Janet Frazer, we can also argue that, according to the definition of shamanism being employed here, these fairy-related experiences can be termed 'shamanistic'. But if we move more deeply into the fairy-encountering experience we can take this line of inquiry one step further and argue that on a functional level these envisioned fairy-encounters may have more consistently and fully resembled shamanism, as it emerges in contemporary tribal societies, than any other category of visionary experience we have identified in early modern Scotland thus far.

To qualify as shamanistic, a visionary experience must generate some kind of community benefit. In tribal societies, where the struggle for physical existence is paramount, shamans are generally petitioned for basic survival aid. In early modern Britain, where staying alive and getting enough food to eat were also major concerns, shamanistic practitioners on all levels of society were similarly petitioned, and demands for healing of both humans and animals, divination (of the future and for lost goods), help with agricultural and domestic processes and protection against enemies were common. But those practitioners who concerned themselves with fairy-encounters were particularly active on this level. Visionaries who worked higher up the social scale often experimented with more varied pallets. Godly Christian visionaries, so far as the church was concerned at least, were more likely to be preoccupied with, and petitioned for, spiritual as opposed to worldly aid. The questions that McGrigor's daughter was asked were primarily concerned with religious scruples such as whether it was right to accept the indulgence or whether unbaptized babies went to heaven, while visionaries like Rutherford and Brightly were concerned with reinforcing godliness through prophetic warnings of God's imminent wrath. Alternatively elite magicians, while more likely than their godly counterparts to be petitioned for basic survival aid, also responded to requests for comparatively frivolous items such as treasure, sexual conquest and political advancement (these being linked to the fact that they serviced the wealthier sectors of society). At their most abstruse, these magical practitioners dispensed with community care altogether and focused on the personal benefits to be gained from the acquisition of magical power or (like their cloistered medieval counterparts) the union with God.

But like their tribal counterparts, fairy-encountering cunning folk seem to have endured a closer remit. While they could just as easily exploit their perceived magical power for personal gain, or be distracted by the promise of mystical ecstasy, or seek financial reward through negotiating luxuries for the moneyed – they more closely resembled tribal shamans in the extent to which they focused on basic survival aid. In addition, although they employed their visionary skills to a wide range of activities in this respect – from the finding of lost goods to the furthering of animal or crop fertility – they also more closely resembled tribal shamans in the extent to which their primary focus was the diagnosis and cure of sickness. For Stirling cunning woman Isobel Watson, any beauty, power or pleasure-dispensing abilities that the fairy queen possessed seem to have been less important than the fact that she could give her practical magical aids, such as a piece of woollen cloth with which to cure the toothache.[106] Similarly, Bessie Dunlop was overtly unimpressed by her familiar's access to the riches of fairyland, but was very grateful for the fact that when she approached him for advice about a sick animal, or 'ane barne that was tane away with ane evill blast of wind' he was able to tell her 'Quhat mycht help thame'.[107] Kirk session records and trial dittays are filled with references to women like Ayrshire cunning woman Jonat Hunter (1604) who claimed to possess healing powers because she 'gaid out with out with the fair folk', or Marion Or (1602) who professed 'to ride with the fair folk and to have skill' or Steven Maltman (Gargunnock, 1628) who confessed 'that he had the healing abilities of the fairy folk'.[108] Moreover, despite the hostile conditions in which they were elicited and recorded, a substantial minority of these references – such as those pertaining to Jonet Rendall, Janet Trall, Isobel Haldane, Alison Peirson and Andro Man – provide us with depictions of shamanistic healing practices that are as lengthy, detailed, coherent and persuasive as many of those found in contemporary anthropological sources. This strong link between fairy aid and practical survival benefits may have been rooted in the fairies' pagan characteristics (this, in turn, deriving from their origins in pre-Christian British animism), but it would also have been rooted, more pragmatically, in the fact that cunning folk primarily serviced the needs of the poor. As we shall explore in more depth in CHAPTER SIXTEEN, there is some evidence to suggest that before the Reformation (and to a certain extent afterwards) shamanistic practitioners invoked envisioned saints, angels, and even Christ himself, in a similarly pragmatic way.

Popular fairy-related shamanism also seems to have closely resembled tribal traditions in the degree to which the visionary experiences involved were intentioned and controlled. As we have seen earlier, many visionary accounts from the early modern period, whether found in theological and intellectual treatises, pamphlets or witchcraft confessions, describe experiences that were spontaneous and temporary: either occurring as isolated incidents or short series of visions. In addition, a large proportion of these accounts, particularly those given by alleged victims of bewitchment, seem to have been emotionally overwhelming and out-of-control, typically depicting terrified, uncomprehending protagonists unable to do anything but passively witness the strange hallucinatory events that unfolded before their eyes. While fairy-related encounter narratives contain their fair share of terror, confusion and passivity, they also contain lucid, precisely observed, descriptions of self-determined thought, speech and action that suggest the visionary had remained calm and retained an element of control throughout the experience. Although the cunning woman's initial visit to fairyland was often unintentional or spontaneous, she commonly developed the capacity to voluntarily encounter the fairies at specific times of the year. Stirling cunning woman Isobel Watson first encountered the fairies at the age of eighteen, when she fell asleep minding sheep near Tullibardine, and was 'takin away be the fair folk and hauldin with thame 24 houris'. But subsequent to this seemingly-spontaneous visitation, Isobel's encounters were more controlled, for she told the presbytery that she regularly joined the fairy gatherings 'at each change of the moon'.[109] Similarly, the first meeting between John Stewart, a cunning man tried for witchcraft in Irvine in 1618, and the fairy king seems to have been a sudden and dramatic one, for it deprived him of his sight and ability to speak. But after these faculties had been restored three years later, he pragmatically and punctually 'met with the fairies every Saturday at seven o'clock'.[110] By the same token, although initial encounters with a fairy familiar were often frightening (the latter often aggressively forcing its attentions on the reluctant visionary), as the working partnership developed cunning folk became increasingly empowered and often developed the capacity to ask or even demand that the spirit come to them when they needed its help. According to her 1572 trial dittays, for example, in an effort to heal a sick client Edinburgh cunning woman Jonet Boyman 'maid I[n]cantatioun and a[n]notatioun of the evill spreitis quhome ye callit upoun for to come to yow and declair quhat wald becum of that ma[n]'. And her commands did not stop here, for once the spirit had duly appeared (emerging out of 'ane grit blast lyke a quhirll wind' in the 'schaip of ane ma[n]') Boyman allegedly faced it and said 'I charge the in the name of the fader and the sone king artho[u]r and quene elspeth . . . that ye owthir gif him his health or ellis tak him to yow and releif him of his pane'.[111] The exchanges of information that took place during these commanded familiar appearances were often measured and workmanlike. Alison Peirson claimed that her fairy familiar, William Simpson, 'tauld hir of ewerie seiknes, and quhat herbis scho sould tak to haill thame, and how scho sould use thame; and gewis hir his directioune att all tymes'.[112] Bessie Dunlop asserted that when she needed to cure a sick animal her familiar 'wald pull ane herb, and gif hir out of his awin hand; and baid hir scheir [strain] the samin with onye uthir kynd of herbis, and oppin the beistis mouth, and put thame in; and the beist wald mend.'[113] By contrast, Perthshire cunning man John Gothray's deceased brother came to him regularly once a month, from fairyland, in order to show him 'such and such herbs' and tell him 'for what use they serve'.[114]

The ability to initiate, develop and control visionary experience in this manner was not, of course, exclusive to fairy-encountering cunning folk. Both medieval contemplatives and early modern elite magicians received detailed instruction on how to manage and deepen visionary skill, and the accounts given by mystics such as Birgitta of Sweden indicate the attainment of vivid, richly detailed and controlled imaginal experiences. But where the latter's skills were developed under formal or semi-formal tutelage (either within or without the curtilage of an institution), and drew on elite intellectual traditions long-encoded in literary canons, the shamanistic skills of fairy-encountering cunning men and women were developed more informally among the non-literate communities of the fermtoun and drew on orally-inherited belief and superstition. As a consequence of this derivation, in fairy-related shamanism these visionary skills were consistently combined with survival-based imperatives; and as we have seen in relation to tribal shamanism, these imperatives would have affected the nature of the experiences evoked. For the popular magical practitioner attempting to heal a sick patient, the practical need to find a specific cure for their physical ailment would have infused their visionary experiences with a high level of intention and accountability, and this focus would often have been sharpened by the seriousness of the problem they were required to resolve. The motivations driving a cunning woman immersed in the treatment of a mortally-ill child, for example, who also knew that her reputation and therefore livelihood depended upon whether she ended up with a dead child or a living one at the end of it, would have been very different from those of the elite magician who sought treasure for a client who already carried a fat purse; or those of the nun who knew that, whether or not she attained a vision of the Crucifixion, her dinner would still be on the table when she rose from prayer and that she would not be excluded from the monastery on the basis of an unsuccessful meditation.

This analysis of fairy-related encounter-narratives requires us to readjust the general picture of visionary experience in early modern Scotland sketched out earlier in this chapter. It suggests that although, in general, the role of the shamanistic practitioner was peripheral and his or her function only partially or semi-shamanistic, among the self-reliant micro-cultures of the poor this role was less peripheral and less partial than it was in contemporary society as a whole. We can also conclude here that distinctly folkloristic shamanistic beliefs and practices, such as those relating to fairies and the dead, persisted on a village level into the seventeenth century, despite the disapproval of the church, because there was a clear need for them. Although the number of physicians, surgeons and apothecaries was on the increase in this period, and the reformed church attempted, with varying degrees of success, to provide social welfare, these resources were not accessible or efficient enough to consistently meet the needs of the masses. Many of the poor could not gain access to, or afford, a physician if their child became sick, or enjoy the benefits of gifted grain if their crops failed. For the majority of people, the abiding directive was the same as it had been for their ancestors in the Middle Ages, and before that the Dark Ages, and before that the Iron, Bronze and Stone Ages. Either they found solutions to their own problems or they did not survive. And folkloric shamanistic traditions, even as late as the seventeenth century, provided just such a solution.

The fact that popular experiential traditions of this kind could have resisted the combined force of ecclesiastical and legal prohibition can be attributed both to the power of cultural patterning and the nature of the shamanistic experience itself. For the non-literate majority, rural life contained all the criteria necessary for culture-patterned visionary experience. As we saw in CHAPTER EIGHT, in the largely closed, close-knit micro-culture of the farm hamlet, the verbal and physical rituals so crucial to the transmission of shared beliefs and aspirations would have been the currency of every hearth, every working hour, every birth, death and sick bed. And since infancy, young minds would have been progressively moulded by the vivid fairy lore encoded in story, song, ballad, anecdote and ritual. These collective impressions would not only have shaped world-view, but also visionary experience. From this perspective, the fact that so many fairy-related narratives taken down during witchcraft and sorcery interrogations contain themes from fairy stories is not because desperate suspects frantically attempted to fill out their false confessions with half-remembered fairy tales, but because these themes were active on an experiential level, and reflected a living reciprocal interchange through which fairy lore fed into visionary experience and visionary experience fed into fairy lore. Similarly, the skills to conjure, control, and utilize these fairy-related visionary experiences could have emerged without access to formal training. As anthropologists and psychologists frequently reiterate, shamanism is not a set of doctrines or rules, but an experience-derived method, and for those who possess the natural ability and inclination, mental imagery cultivation can be developed to a high level in the absence of a fully-fledged teacher and pupil relationship.[115] It is because shamanistic skills depend so heavily on natural abilities and oral teachings, as opposed to book learning, that neither illiteracy nor poverty has ever been an obstacle to its success, either in tribal societies or early modern Europe. As we shall explore more deeply in CHAPTER THIRTEEN, this self-determining characteristic of shamanism has enabled it to flourish in an incredibly wide range of culturally hostile environments.

Witchcraft as Shamanism

If we can argue that some of the fairy-related encounter-narratives found in early modern witchcraft and sorcery records may have been representative of shamanistic visionary experiences, then the next question that arises is, can we argue the same for the far higher number of demonological encounter-narratives (that is, descriptions of meeting the Devil, making the demonic pact and attending the witches' sabbath) that emerge out of the same sources? The congruities between the two types of narrative make such a conclusion tempting. Thematically, both fairy-related and demonological narratives share the same shamanistic template: the protagonist meets a spirit that appears in the form of a human or animal; the spirit offers them magical aid in return for allegiance; a contractual working relationship ensues; and they periodically travel, sometimes in flight, to a place where other spirits, including the dead, congregate. The fact that demonological and fairy-related encounter-narratives are often intertwined within the same testimony is further evidence of their close relationship, as is the fact that both often share the same narrative tone: an ambiguous combination of fantastic imagery and prosaic realism delivered in language that is both emotionally intense and matter-of-fact at the same time.

But despite these similarities there are also fundamental differences between the two types of narrative. Fairy-related accounts draw primarily on traditional oral lore passed down within the micro-cultures of rural peasant life, while their demonological counterparts draw on theological stereotypes developed in elite writings and disseminated primarily through the pulpit and print. In addition, demonological narratives were more likely than their fairy-related counterparts to be delivered in response to interrogatorial suggestion, and elicited through psychological and physical coercion, with both factors making it more difficult to entertain the idea that they may have reflected any genuine experiences – visionary or otherwise – of the accused. Furthermore, unlike their fairy-related equivalents, demonological narratives challenge us to provide convincing explanations for text-embedded accounts of the witches' sabbath and the demonic pact before we can even begin to entertain notions of their visionary status. They also challenge us to find meaning. According to the definition of shamanism being used here, shamanistic traditions emerge and persist because they benefit their community, and on a grass roots level, shamanistic practitioners are primarily concerned with the alleviation of human suffering and the furthering of human survival. Fairy-related encounter-narratives, being largely focused on the acquisition of cures and divinations, fit snugly into this rationale, but the demonological narrative's concern with maleficent magic, apostasy and subversion, is more difficult to rationalize in this context.

As we saw in the Introduction to Part II, with regard to the shamanistic paradigm, historians have split themselves into two camps. On the one side are those who believe that demonological encounter-narratives were primarily the result of a fusion between elite ideas superimposed by the interrogators and retrospective fiction-making on the part of the accused, and that if shamanism played any role in proceedings it was largely in the form of folkloric themes, ideas and beliefs as opposed to experiential traditions. On the other side are the scholars who acknowledge all the above, but also maintain that the references to shamanistic experiences found in demonological narratives can, like fairy-related narratives, reflect visionary encounters experienced prior to interrogation, with Pócs, for example, going so far as to assert that: 'Those accused of witchcraft also had the common faculty for trance, as mentioned earlier in connection with the visionary experiences of injured parties. A significant proportion of the documented confessions referring to trance or visionary experience concerns witches who spoke about the way they came to be part of the company or present at the gatherings.'[116]

Although Pócs's assertion may be too confident for some, the argument that some demonological encounter-narratives may have been representative of prior visionary encounter is supported by compelling evidence. Not only do we have the fact, emphasized above, that the latter closely resemble their fairy-related counterparts both thematically and stylistically, but we also have the fact that they also contain the perennial signatures of visionary experience. Although, as with both fairy-related and tribal narratives, these indications are seldom direct, they are nevertheless consistent with their less demonological equivalents. Notably, a good proportion of these accounts contain anomalous details. Phrases such as '[the Devil came] into her house like a shadow and went away like a shadow'; 'as he went away she did not hear his feet on the stubble'; 'he vanished away like a whirlwind'; '[the witches'] language wes not our ordinarie language'; and '[the coven went] threw in at a little hole like bies, and took the substance of the aile' strongly suggest that the being encountered, or the event described, was not a physically real one.[117] Similarly, descriptions of the shape-shifting activities of the Devil often evoke the vivid emotions and constantly changing impressions characteristic of dream or vision experience. In a classic example from Bute, in 1662, which concludes with a dramatic anomaly, Margaret NcWilliam stated that:

> The yeire before the great Snaw about 28 yeires syne quhen she was dwelling in Corsmoire about Candlemes about 12 hours of the day [a traditional fairy-encountering time] she went owt to a fald beneath her hous called Faldtombuie and out of a furz in the mids of the fald ther apeared a spreit in the lyknes of a litle brown dog and desyred her to goe with it which she refused at first, it followed her downe to the fitt of the fald and apeared in the lyknes of a wele favored yong man and desyred her agane to goe with it and she should want nothing ... [and then] went away *as if it were a grene smoak* [my italics].[118]

A significant percentage of accounts describing the witches' sabbath are similarly fantastic and dream-like. In 1649 Eyemouth woman Helene Tailyear confessed to her minister that:

> shee was at ane meitting with Issobell Broun, Allison Cairns, Margarit Dobson, and Beatrix Young, and that thai all went along to William Burnitts hous, he lying seik, and that, coming to the hous, Margarit Dobsone was in the liknes of ane blak hen and went in at the chimley heid, and Beatrix Young was in the liknes of ane littill foall, and that hir selff was in the liknes of ane littill quhelp; Issobell Broun was in hir owen liknes with a long taild courtshaw upon hir heid, and Allison Cairns was in hir owen liknes.[119]

Also suggestive of dream or vision encounters is the simple fact – often inexplicably overlooked by those sceptical of the shamanistic paradigm – that throughout the period of witch-prosecutions in western Europe a good proportion of elite commentators and prosecutors specifically stated that they believed witches' sabbath experiences to be rooted in dream or vision experience. Indeed, by the late-sixteenth century even those who asserted the reality of bodily travel to witches' meetings often concluded that a visionary element may have been involved: Stuart Clark noting that 'by this time many writers of witchcraft were fudging the issue ... conceding that while many cases of nocturnal transvection to the witches' sabbat (and the sabbat itself) were undoubtedly true occurrences, others were indeed the product of dreaming'.[120] Scottish witch-interrogators were no different in this respect. In 1634, after much argument, a court threw out Elisabeth Bathgate's claim that 'shee and other witches were conveyed into George Huldie's ship, which they sank, with several persons therein' on the grounds that 'the

Images of saints or holy men and women receiving visions are a staple of medieval art and iconography. In this serene and spiritual painting, executed in Cologne between 1485–1515, Saint Ursula is visited by an angel as she lies in bed.

This unusually direct portrayal of the sabbath experience as visionary encounter is found in a 1719 German translation of John Webster's *Displaying of Supposed Witchcraft*, with the caption translating into English as 'Here you clearly see that there are witches in the world of which a dreamer's head easily hosts a thousand'. As in the painting of St Ursula above, the image portrays a woman encountering spirits whilst lying in bed, but here the artist clearly associates her experiences with chaos and delusion as opposed to serenity and spiritual revelation.

sinking of the ship looked like a dream and idle vision, rather than the serious article of a criminal indictment, neither condescending on the time when, and the means by which, the ship cast away, not even so much as a pretended raising a storm, or the witches being seen flying about like crows round the ship'.[121] Similarly in June, 1662, after reading Isobel's confessions, alleged witchcraft expert Alexander Colville told Brodie emphatically that the latter 'could not realli transport themselves whither they pleased, for they would be oft at that sam instant in other places visiblie lying on ther back or faces, quhil they seim'd in their imaginations to be caried to other places farr off'.[122] Sixteen years later Hugh Rose's university colleague, George Mackenzie, dramatically claimed that 'many' witchcraft suspects 'confess things which all Divines conclude impossible, as transmutation of their bodies into beasts, and money into stones, and their going through walls and closs doors, and a thousand other ridiculous things, which have no truth nor existence but in their lunacy'.[123] In the late-eighteenth century Thomas Pennant described the Breadalbane visionary, whose experiences we recounted in full earlier in this chapter, as an 'old Dreamer', and it is interesting to note that nearly 100 years earlier Sinclair had applied the same sobriquet to his maleficent counterparts, noting that: 'Many deny that there are any such as Witches . . . but call them Dreamers'.[124]

Witchcraft suspects whose narratives were dismissed as imaginary were not, of course, considered innocent of demonic allegiance in this period, for as we have seen earlier in this chapter, contemporary views concerning the epistemological status of the imagination were deeply intertwined with beliefs about the Devil. Although inter-rogators were capable of attributing their suspect's visionary experiences to madness or guiltless fantasy with no spiritual agency involved, they frequently attributed them to the Devil's imagination-manipulating skills. Given the fact that no lesser an authority than John Calvin claimed categorically that witches' sabbaths were 'imaginary' assemblies 'to which unhappy men, whom the devil has bewitched, fancy themselves to be transported' it is no surprise to find that Alexander Brodie, as a good Calvinist, concluded his reading of Isobel's and Janet's testimony with the judgement that 'the Devil's deluding of silli wretches, working on their imaginations, making them apre-hend, and beleev fals things . . . and yet tho' they see he cannot giv a counter or a sexpence, but bits of stons or brass, yet poor wretches beleev in him'.[125]

Also suggestive of shamanistic visionary experience are the debates that took place between interrogator and suspect concerning the reality of the experiences under discussion. Many witchcraft suspects seem to have genuinely believed, or been persuaded to believe, that they had covenanted with the Devil and attended the witches' sabbath. In the last chapter we argued that these self-incriminatory testimonies could have been rooted in false confession, either taking the form of a coerced-compliant response (the suspect caving in and believing the crimes alleged against them or pretending to be guilty in the hope of leniency), or false-memory construction (in response to suggestive questioning the suspect generating demonologically-themed memories that seem so vivid and real they are convinced they are genuine). But this explanation is not so plausible when we try to apply it to those cases where witchcraft suspects claimed that their experiences were real while their interrogators tried to

persuade them that they were not. In 1563, for example, the interrogator and demonologist Johann Weyer complained that witch-suspects 'openly acknowledge as their
own crimes [those] which are known to them only by dreams and images' and that
'They are devoutly confident that all the forms imposed by him [the Devil] upon their
powers of imagination and fantasy *exist truly* [my italics]'.[126] Nearly one hundred years
later, while perusing Isobel's trial confessions, Brodie echoed Weyer's observation in
his lament that the Devil makes them 'aprehend, and *beleev* fals things'.[127] Similarly, at
a trial in Tolna, Hungary, the interrogator asked the suspect: 'Perhaps you are simply
dreaming, and go to bed without prayer, that's why you have such funny dreams' only
to engender the tart reply 'But I don't dream because it's all so real.'[128] The claims of
these suspects cannot automatically be dismissed as false confession because, as we
explored in CHAPTER NINE, both coerced-compliant responses and false-memory recollections are nurtured through closed, suggestive questioning and a high presumption
of guilt. As such, it would be inconsistent for a suspect to have been sufficiently influenced by her interrogator's beliefs and desires to develop complex fictions or false
memories concerning the demonic pact or the witches' sabbath to then, at the last
hurdle, resist his relatively benign assertion that her experiences had been imaginary
ones.

This thesis is supported by the fact that a similarly heartfelt belief in the reality of
the envisioned experience was expressed by those who encountered fairies, and who
delivered their spirit-encountering narratives outside the false-memory-inducing
interrogatorial arena. In 1651, for example, the materialist philosopher Hobbes
claimed:

> From this ignorance of how to distinguish dreams and other strong fancies from vision and
> sense did arise the greatest part of religion of the gentiles in the past that worshipped satyrs,
> fauns, nymphs, and the like, and nowadays the opinion that rude people have of fairies,
> ghosts and goblins and of the power of witches.[129]

Hobbes's claim that 'rude' people could not 'distinguish dreams and other strong
fancies from vision and sense' reflects the view, noted by other contemporaries and since
reinforced by historians, that both belief in the objective reality of spirits and the disinclination to make epistemological distinctions between the 'real' and 'visionary' realms
were particularly widespread among the uneducated poor. Jo Bath noted recently that
the literal interpretations of the dead so plentifully described in the works of seventeenth-century anti-sadducean writers like Glanvil and Bovet, 'may well have been
close to that found in the folk belief of the period; indeed, it may have needed to be in
order to have communicated with its intended audience and achieved its purpose'.[130]
Similarly, as late as 1805, folklorist Arthur Edmondston reported that in the Shetland
Islands:

> A belief in the existence of these supposed beings, acquires confirmation among the credu-
> lous, by the statements of those who are said to be the objects either of their attention or
> their malignity. They believe in it themselves, and every dream or reverie of the imagina-

tion is related as an actual occurrence. Some persons have the reputation of having resided many years among the fairies, pretend to be familiar with their habits; and even assert that they can recognize individuals among them at a distance.[131]

That nineteenth-century Scots were capable of holding on to such beliefs even when confronted by educated opposition is attested to by the fact that, as one of J. F. Campbell's informants recounted, a contemporary local minister 'had some difficulty in convincing' a man whose wife had died in childbirth 'that his son, a boy twelve years of age, must have been under some hallucination when he maintained that his mother had come to him, saying she was taken by the fairies to a certain hill in Muckairn, known to be the residence of the fairies'.[132]

The popular conviction that envisioned spirits were objectively real entities, as opposed to manifestations of the imagination, suggests that ordinary people were generally closer to the tribal end of the attitudes-towards-visionary-experience continuum than their educated contemporaries, who were more likely to have been influenced, through written texts, by the rationalist paradigms developed by classical, medieval and early modern thinkers. As a corollary of this, a non-literate witchcraft suspect was, on balance, more likely to believe that an envisioned encounter with a spirit or flight to fairyland was an objectively real experience than a university-educated minister or laird. The fact that these 'old ways of seeing' were stronger on a popular level supports our prior conclusion that shamanistic traditions survived in a more comprehensive form and were more culturally significant among the non-literate poor than among early modern society as a whole. It also supports the view that some demonological encounter-narratives, as depictions of encounters with objectively real spirits (that is, the Devil and his demons), may well have been expressions, however convoluted, of these popular shamanistic traditions.

Journeying to the Sabbath

One of the strongest indicators that some demonological encounter-narratives may have contained an experiential core can be found in contemporary debates surrounding soul or spirit travel. Ginzburg's exposition on the shamanistic origins of the witches' sabbath articulated travel into spirit worlds in terms of the separable spirit or soul leaving the body in ecstasy. This choice of terminology was probably influenced by his original source material, the records of the interrogations of the Friulian *benandanti*, where it is overtly stated that 'the spirit [of the suspect] leaves the body and goes wandering'.[133] It may also have been influenced by anthropological writings, where it is commonly employed in relation to shamanistic experience. As we saw earlier, for example, the observer who recorded the trance states of Paiute shaman Bobby Dodd stated that 'The doctor's spirit flew up after the spirit of the sick person, leaving his body behind'.[134] The abandoned body, without the animating force of the soul or spirit, is often described as 'asleep' or 'as if dead'; these descriptions reflecting the standard physical characteristics of shamanistic catalepsy. Ginzburg's choice may also have been influenced by the fact that this terminology was clearly employed in many parts of Europe in the early modern period. James VI of Scotland claimed, in 1597, that 'some saith that their [the witches'] bodies lying still as in an ecstasy, their spirits will be ravished out of their bodies and carried to such places'.[135] Similarly, with regard to a selection of witch-records from early modern Germany, Behringer notes that 'As usual the witches' flights took place mainly during the quarterly Ember days, and usually we find the customary detail that only the soul travelled forth, leaving the body behind, as if dead in bed.'[136] These terms were also used to articulate encounters with fairy-type spirits, with sixteenth-century apothecary Renward Cysat, for example, recording that when he questioned a Swiss woman about her divinatory trips with the *säligen lütt*, she claimed that she did not travel in her body, 'for her body remained lying there in bed, and only her spirit or soul went traveling out in this way.'[137]

But we must set against this evidence the fact that overt references to spirit or soul travel are not uniformly found in contemporary demonological encounter-narratives. Many of the latter, and particularly those from Scotland, contain no comment, from either suspect or interrogator, as to whether the journey to the sabbath was believed to have been undertaken in body or spirit. The situation is further complicated by the fact that in a significant minority of cases not only are references to soul or spirit travel absent but this absence is reinforced by the claim that the journey was undertaken physically or 'in body'. Some of these instances may have been the result of elite superimposition, for as we have seen earlier a good proportion of witch-prosecutors and demonologists asserted the reality of bodily travel to the witches' sabbath and are likely, when faced with a suspect, to have tried to persuade them that they had travelled in this way. But the cases where witchcraft suspects claimed that their travel was in body when their interrogators were demonstrably trying to convince them that they were not, clearly indicates that this belief was also active on a popular level. Moreover, medieval sources suggest that this conviction was deeply rooted and of popular origin. As early as the tenth century, with regard to women who 'believe and say that they go out at night with the goddess Diana, or with Herodias', the French cleric, Réginon de Prüm, advised priests to 'preach to the men of their parishes that all this is absolutely false and that such fantasies in the minds of the faithful come not from the spirit of God but from Evil . . . Man wrongly thinks that everything happens not in spirit [*in animo*] but corporally [*in corpore*]'.[138] Similarly, in the following century, Burchard, the bishop of Worms, stated emphatically:

> Have you believed what many women, turning back to Satan, believe and affirm to be true; as that you believe that in the silence of the quiet night, when you have settled down in bed, and your husband lies in your bosom, you are able, while still in your body, to go out through the closed doors and travel through the spaces of the world . . . If you have believed this, you shall do penance on bread and water for fifty days . . . [139]

In the medieval and early modern centuries, many demonologists recounted stories that depicted frustrated inquisitors trying to convince witchcraft suspects that they did not travel to the witches' sabbath in bodily form, with the most famous being recorded by the Italian doctor and demonologist, Giambattista Della Porta. In the first edition of his *Magiae naturalis* Della Porta claimed that he and his companions, irritated by a witch's insistence that she travelled bodily to the sabbath, beat her when she was in a state of catalepsy so that they could show her the bruises when she regained consciousness. But the experiment was to no avail, for when the battered woman woke up she still insisted, despite all evidence to the contrary, that she had made her journey physically.[140] That this view survived into seventeenth-century Scotland is indicated by a number of witchcraft records, one of the most vivid coming from Caithness in 1719, in which Margaret Nin-Gilbert argued closely, and against all logic, that she had bodily attended a meeting of witches. After describing how Margaret confessed to having been 'bodily present' with others in a local house in the form of a 'feltered catt', the dittays go on to state: 'Being interrogat, How she could be bodily present, and yet invisible? Declares, She might have been seene, but could give no account by what means her body was rendered invisible.' When later pressed, Margaret claimed that 'The devil did hide and conceall' herself and her companions 'by raising a dark mist or fog to skreen them from being seen.'[141]

At first glance, such claims to have travelled bodily to the sabbath could be seen to contradict Ginzburg's argument that shamanistic visionaries travelled 'in spirit' and thereby challenge the shamanistic hypothesis in general. But on closer inspection such assertions could be interpreted, in fact, as a more accurate reflection of traditional shamanistic mentalities than the claim to have travelled to the sabbath in spirit only. The articulation of travel into spirit worlds in terms of the separable spirit or soul leaving the body, is dependent upon a conceptual distinction between spiritual and material that, as we have seen earlier, was introduced into Western culture by classical thinkers working with rationalist dualism. Tribal cultures, who work with monist conceptions of the universe, do not carve up and categorise reality in this way, perceiving it as the expression of a network of inter-relating dimensions or a fusion of different modalities, as opposed to a conjunction of opposites. As a consequence, tribal ideas about what the body is and what the soul is are very different from those held by rationalist thinkers, and it is this conflict of ideas that lies at the root of early modern confusions surrounding travel to the witches' sabbath.

Theories of Subtle Body

In many tribal cultures man is not simply divided into 'material body' and 'spiritual soul', but into a variety of ways of being that are generally referred to, in anthropological literature, as types of soul, and in western esoteric writings, as 'subtle' or 'astral' bodies. Although we are severely restricted here by the fact that we must discuss this phenomena using the same dualist paradigms we are trying to discard, put simplistically, subtle bodies can be seen as modes of self which exist somewhere between the two extremes of physical and spiritual and which possess, in varying degrees, both physical and spiritual characteristics and capacities. According to the visionary-experience-gave-rise-to-the-belief-in-spirits hypothesis, the genesis of subtle-body beliefs is inherently logical and would have arisen out of early man's attempts to rationalize visionary experiences in which he felt embodied, but capable of a superior range of action than normal (such as metamorphosing into animals and flying). By the same token, the fact that during these experiences early man encountered other entities, whether defined as non-human spirits, the dead, or the living, who also possessed similar-seeming bodies and similar-seeming supra-normal abilities, can be seen to have generated early man's belief, still current in many tribal cultures today, that through subtle-body activity these different entities could share and interact in the same modality.

But despite the fact that the body/soul paradigm has been dominant in Western thinking since classical times, as Éva Pócs and Claude Lecouteux have recently emphasized, beliefs surrounding subtle bodies that can 'detach from, leave, or during trance be sent by its owner, and after death live on as a dead soul' persisted throughout medieval and early modern Europe on both an elite and popular level.[142] In orthodox theology, these beliefs occupied an ambiguous position. A variety of notions concerning 'spiritual bodies' can be found in both Testaments (being notably discussed by St Paul) and they subsequently emerged particularly strongly in theologies of resurrection. In some hands, these Christian speculations could come very close to tribal notions of subtle bodies, with seventeenth-century Protestant mystic and philosopher Pierre Poiret claiming, for example, that: 'the body which the soul parts with at death is only of the nature of an outer bark or envelope, beneath which is a real body of subtle matter to which the soul is inseparably united' and that it was 'these subtle bodies made visible which appeared to the favoured disciples who beheld Moses and Elias discussing with Jesus at the Transfiguration'.[143] But although orthodox theology retained a place for theories of subtle bodies, it parted company from tribal world-views in its assertion that no part of the human could separate from the body and return to it during life and that souls or subtle bodies could only emerge, or be created, after death. It was for this reason that the men who questioned the Italian *benandante*, Battista Moduco, took great pains to bring him to confess, in his written abjuration, that 'I confess and believe that our spirit and soul cannot leave the body nor return to it at will. I also declare and admit that I grievously sinned by never unburdening myself of these errors in confession.'[144]

But despite orthodox disapproval, the belief in the existence of separable subtle bodies persisted on all levels of early modern society. Although filtering into main-stream Christian discourse, they characteristically flourished in less orthodox contexts: notably esoteric and heretical Christian traditions, elite magical traditions and, perhaps more surprisingly, medical theory (where they were linked to ideas about animal spirits). On a popular level, and among the people with whom we are primarily concerned here, beliefs in roving subtle bodies were primarily tied up with the nexus of beliefs surrounding the fairies, witches and the dead. Pócs and Lecouteux, who have both explored these folk beliefs in some depth, argue that two main types of subtle body – or as they term it, 'double' – feature in popular belief from the medieval period onwards, both of which are capable of appearing in either human or animal form. The first, being 'spiritual and psychic', appears most commonly in dreams while the second, being 'material and physical', manifests in either dreams or waking life. With regard to the latter, the belief that an entity possessing a tangible level of materiality and physicality could enter into the visionary sphere was, according to the popular world-view of the time, entirely logical. Pócs argues that early modern man, being immersed in the belief that the physical and visionary modalities were inter-connected, would have considered it 'just as likely that somebody would enter the other-world in their physical reality (that is, with the use of a physical double) as it was for the "manifested" dead to come here'.[145] The belief that the physical double could also appear in waking reality underpinned the widespread belief that an encountered animal could be a witch in disguise, and that by injuring the animal's body you simultaneously injured the material body of the witch.

Unsurprisingly, just as it is uncommon to find direct references to vision or trance in both early modern and tribal encounter-narratives, it is also uncommon to find direct references to subtle-body travel (that is, references that are more epistemologically specific than just 'I went in the form of an animal'). Nevertheless, as is also the case with visionary experience, the few examples that do exist are both unequivocal and striking. The reference, in a Hungarian witchcraft record, to an individual who, as paraphrased by Pócs, 'sensing a vision, felt him or herself to be "in the body of a phantom"' is highly evocative, as is Erzsébet Hampa's claim (Iharosberény, 1737) that she bewitched a cow in 'the form of a soul' that emerged in the 'image' of a 'very tiny' person.[146]

The False Body

The evidence suggests that this matrix of popular beliefs concerning the subtle body or double may have been culpable, in large part, for the disputes between witchcraft suspects and interrogators over the manner of travel to the witches' sabbath. It is not difficult to see how a suspect's belief that she could rove the world and negotiate with spirits in her physical double could have led her to maintain that she had bodily attended the sabbath. It is also not difficult to see that a witchcraft prosecutor may have had problems persuading her that her powerfully embodied visionary experiences were wholly imaginary. This line of enquiry, if pursued a little further, also helps us to shed light on those almost-burlesque cases where witchcraft suspects maintained their assertion to have travelled physically to the sabbath even when irritated interrogators, such as Della Porta, beat their senseless bodies and presented them with the resultant bruises on their return from trance. Anthropological studies indicate that in tribal societies in many parts of the world it is believed that the form left behind when an individual journeys in subtle form into the spirit realm, is not the real body but some kind of 'empty', 'partial' or 'false' body. Malinowski illustrates that among the South Pacific Trobriand Islanders the *yoyova*, or witch, 'casts off her body (literally, peels off her skin), she lies down and sleeps, we hear her snoring. Her covering (i.e. her outward body, her skin) remains in the house, and she herself flies . . . here the real personality is located in the flying part, whereas what remains is the "covering."'[147] Alternatively, according to Junod, the South African Basuto believe that the shaman travels to the spirit world 'entire, soul and body', while the Thonga believe that 'When he [the *noyi*, or shaman] flies away his "shadow" remains behind him, lying down on the mat. But it is not truly the body that remains. It appears as such only to the stupid uninitiated. In reality, what remains is a *wild beast*, the one with which the *noyi* has chosen to identify himself.'[148]

Traces of similar beliefs can be found in early modern Europe. As we have seen earlier, one of the stereotypical motifs emerging out of the witch hunts was that of the witch leaving an inanimate object, such as a piece of wood or broomstick, in her bed at night to replicate her body while she travelled to the witches' sabbath. That this motif reflected, and perhaps even originated in, popular mentalities is suggested by the fact that throughout Europe, from the early modern period through to the nineteenth century, it was widely believed among the uneducated that when the fairies stole human children or adults they left a replica or imitation body, often termed a 'fairy stock', in its place. Even as late as 1809, Edmonston related an account, taken from an eye-witness, in which 'to the last moment of her life' the distraught father of a mortally sick child from the Shetlands 'obstinately persisted in declaring that the fairies had taken possession of his daughter, and left an inanimate mass in her stead'.[149] That popular beliefs in fairy stocks were linked to beliefs and experiences associated with shamanistic catalepsy is further confirmed by the fact that these stocks were frequently likened to pieces of wood. This metaphor, which vividly articulates the bodily stiffness characteristic of catatonic trance, is frequently found in anthropological narratives; as we have seen earlier, during his soul flight Paiute shaman Bobby Dodd's body was 'stiff as a log'. The same metaphor occasionally appears in early modern witch-testimonies, with Hungarian witch Kata Barta (1721) claiming that when she was 'taken . . . away' she was 'seized in her heart and soul as if for a couple of days and nights, her body being as a piece of wood'.[150]

Even more specifically, some early modern sources also clearly indicate that the concept of 'false bodies' was associated, in the popular mind, with trance-journeys to the witches' sabbath. Pócs claims that Hungarian witches 'who went [to the sabbath] in their own image left an empty body at home'; and that this 'empty' body was some-times seen as a false or partial form, as opposed to merely a physical body without an animating soul, is clearly indicated in the following dialogue, taken from a trial in the Tolna region of Hungary. The conversation focuses on how the protagonist, while trav-elling in subtle body, believed that she would be aware of what was happening to the body she left behind, but it is equally clear that she believed the body to be a false one:

> 'Neither is it Mrs. Fiand who lies beside her husband on those nights but the exchanged body, which can be treated and done with just as the one in the real body.'
>
> 'But see, if you got a good beating up that night [while at the sabbath] it would show on you, your body would get blue and I bet you'd moan too.'
>
> 'It would moan too just as if it were me who was beaten, it would do all that it should but I'd not feel but know all that would be happening to me.'[151]

Similar beliefs are clearly indicated in other records. The following, again cited by Pócs, referring to the false body of a witness as opposed to the witch herself: 'Sophi Kapta and Mrs. Csanadi (A) carried in the image of a witch and they took [the soul of the witness] with them in a barrel, and although the body seemed like it was lying there, it was not the witness's but only its image. They put something there that stood for it.'[152]

We can see that for the witchcraft suspect who held such beliefs, a sceptical interrogator's assertion that he had seen her body remain lying on the floor while she was in trance would hold little weight because from her perspective, the interrogator had merely been looking at her false or exchanged body as opposed to her real one. As a consequence, we can speculate that when Italian demonologist Della Porta branded his witchcraft suspect ignorant for maintaining that she travelled bodily to the sabbath, the suspect herself may have believed, conversely, that Della Porta's assumption that the body she left behind was a real one was a testament to his ignorance, not hers. Like the nineteenth-century Thonga shaman, she may have assumed that when she flew to the spirit world it was 'not truly the body that remains. It appears as such only to the stupid uninitiated.' Indeed her condescension, in this respect, may have resembled that of the nineteenth-century Shetlander we met earlier who, despite the fact that medically-trained doctors made 'Every effort to convince him' that his daughter's dead body was not a fairy stock, merely 'smiled at the folly of those who could themselves believe, and endeavour to persuade him of the truth of a contrary opinion'.[153]

Subtle-Body Confusions

The evidence surrounding subtle-body belief in early modern Europe supports the view that demonological encounter-narratives could have been rooted in shamanistic visionary experience. Not only does it illustrate that the belief systems necessary to underpin these experiences were widespread but also, in the absence of other explanations, it illuminates those paradoxical instances where witchcraft suspects tenaciously clung to the belief that their experience was an embodied one despite vehement interrogatorial objections. But nevertheless it is important to remember, with regard to subtle-body beliefs, that we are not talking about a homogeneous body of belief and practice of the type that can exist in traditional tribal contexts. Early modern Europe, though primarily pre-industrial, was a highly-complex society that supported a number of contradictory belief systems simultaneously. And as a consequence, ideas about subtle bodies – as with ideas about a good many other things – were likely to have been multifarious and often contradictory. Regional differences alone would have generated variety, with Lecouteux stating that by the Middle Ages 'Every ethnic group and every civilisation thought of the Double in its own way'.[154] Similarly, the close links between the two basic types of double (that is, spiritual and physical) would have meant that, even within the same locality, beliefs would have been obscure; Lecouteux lamenting that 'It is difficult to distinguish precisely between the physical alter ego and the psychic Double, given that even our distant ancestors confused them'.[155] In the interrogatorial arena, witch-prosecutors would have further contributed to this ambiguity by attempting to interpret and express these already-confused ideas using theological terminology. It is likely for example that, like anthropologists 200 years later, witchcraft interrogators used the orthodox terms 'soul' or 'spirit' to signify what may have been, in the popular mind, a matrix of complex beliefs about subtle bodies. For example, references in the *benandanti* trial records to the fact that suspects went 'invisibly in spirit and the body remains behind', were almost certainly simplified allusions to the physical double. Embodied visionary experience is implied by Battista Moduco's claim that he travelled on a horse, hare and cat, and felt physical pain when he was beaten by angry witches; and by his companion Paolo Gasparrutto's claim that 'These benandanti assert that when their spirit leaves the body it has the appearance of a mouse, and also when it returns'.[156]

To these interpretative ambiguities we can also add experiential ones. As anyone who has ever had a dream knows from personal experience, some visionary experiences feel more embodied than others. And it is often difficult, either during or after the event, to make epistemological assessments about the status of the self-that-experienced. Even the most accomplished Christian mystics found themselves challenged on this issue, with St Paul famously stating, in relation to mystical experience, that 'I was caught up even to the third heaven, whether in the body, I know not, or whether out of the body, I know not: God knoweth'.[157] These confusions were just as acute in Scotland more than 1,500 years later, with seventeenth-century Stirling covenanter Elizabeth Cairns lamenting, after a particularly profound visionary experience, that 'I was so raised in my soul, that in some measure I may say, whether in the body, or out of the body, I cannot tell'.[158] If mystics as godly and experienced as Cairns could be challenged on this issue, we can assume that contemporary cunning folk, particularly when forced to define their experiences using unfamiliar terminology and under the interrogatorial spotlight, could have become equally confused.[159]

Isobel's Confession as Visionary Narrative

This overview of contemporary beliefs surrounding subtle-body travel is particularly helpful when we come, as we finally do now, to assessing the shamanistic status of Isobel's testimony. As is the case with the majority of both fairy-related and demonological encounter-narratives, Isobel's confessions contain no direct indications that prior dream or vision experience was involved. Neither she, nor her interrogators, nor the notary John Innes, stated that she travelled to the 'elfes houssis' or flew with the host 'in a vision' or while 'in a trance'. But, like many encounter-narratives, the confessions contain highly suggestive elements. On a general level, we have the fact that most of the fairy-related events Isobel described – such as yoking a plough with frogs, riding through the air on corn straws and feasting with the king and queen of the fairies – were clearly imagination-derived. Obviously, as we explored in CHAPTER NINE, Isobel could have conjured up these events during interrogation as either coerced-compliant fictions or, more probably, false-memory constructs generated in response to questions about demonological subjects such as the witches' sabbath. But, as we also argued in CHAPTER NINE, the fact that, where fairy belief was concerned, Isobel's interrogators are unlikely to have pestered her with the type of persistent, close and suggestive questioning that characteristically generates false confession reduces (though of course does not obviate) the likelihood that these events were wholly fictional and raises the possibility that they were constructed around dream or vision encounters experienced prior to her arrest and interrogation.

This possibility is further supported by the fact that – uniquely among Scottish encounter-narratives – Isobel's fairy-related passages contain several unusually direct references to subtle-body lore. The fact that the latter appear on only three brief occasions, and that they are not elaborated upon when they do appear, makes them more, as opposed to less, significant: suggesting that they were not of interest to the interrogators and therefore came largely from Isobel herself. The first two references are very similar, with the most detailed appearing in Confession Two, where it is unceremoniously sandwiched between a fairy-levitation charm and a charm designed to bring success at market:

> and immeditialie we flie away whair (*damaged – words missing*) and least owr husbandis sould miss vs owt of our bedes, we put in a boosom or a thrie (*damaged – words missing*) and say thryse ower I lay down this boosom or stooll in the divellis nam let it not ste . . . (*damaged – words missing*) com again: and immeditialie it seims a voman: before our husbandis . . . (44/5)

As we have already seen, such references were not unprecedented: only the year before Isobel made her confession, a woman named Isobel Cuming told the Elgin kirk session that 'she knew a woman in this toune that when she went from hir husband to her randivoues in the night she leaves a bisome in the bedd in hir place'.[160] This belief was clearly linked to folklore concerning fairy stocks, which was in turn rooted in shamanistic ideas about the false bodies left behind when a visionary enters the spirit world in catatonic trance.

The third reference to subtle-body lore, which appears in Confession One, is more ambiguous:

> and q[uhe]n any sies thes strawes in whirlewind, and doe not sanctifie them selves, they we mey shoot them dead at our pleasur, any th[a]t ar shot be us, their sowell will goe to hevin bot ther bodies remains w[i]th ws, and will flie as hors to ws als small as strawes. (40/1)

This passage is unique among British witchcraft records and is at first glance, obscure. Here, we have the seemingly conventional Christian distinction between body and soul, but the context is unworkable. The fact that Isobel believes that when she kills someone their soul 'will goe to hevin' is standard, but the fact that she believes that their body 'remains w[i]th ws' is not. It seems unlikely here that Isobel was referring to the physical body: Isobel, as well as anyone else, would have known that physical bodies decay upon death and do not go about transforming into animals and flying on horses 'als small as strawes'. We cannot rule out the possibility that Isobel made this claim because she was insane, but this conclusion does not only run contrary to our assessments of her mental state explored earlier, but also to the fact that Isobel's folkloric references were, by and large, consistently accurate representations of contemporary popular belief.

But in the context of subtle-body lore, Isobel's comments are immediately decipherable. Although the ordinary physical body could not fly on corn straws in the form of an animal, the physical double could. In other words, if we assume that by the word 'body' Isobel was not referring to flesh and blood, but to the popular belief that a 'material, physical' part of the human could separate from the normal body, either during life or on death, and move about in spirit worlds, then her comments make complete sense. Indeed, in this context, it is now Isobel's originally unproblematic claim that the souls of her victims 'go to heaven' that appears obscure. If, as this passage intimates, Isobel believed that the soul that went to heaven was not the only part of the human being to survive death, then her concept of the afterlife was very different from that of the reformed church.

But for Isobel, who like many people in this period had one foot in folk belief and residual Catholicism and the other in reformed Protestantism, this contradiction may have been accommodated relatively comfortably. As we have seen earlier, scholars have noted that although beliefs concerning physical and spiritual doubles were widespread, they were subject to regional variation and could, owing to their similarities, easily become confused. We can therefore speculate that for Isobel, who was a Christian and possibly attended Auldearn church regularly, the notion of the non-material Christian soul could readily have merged with that of the semi-material spiritual double. Through this unconscious fusion, Isobel created a hybrid belief that enabled her to adhere to the Christian view, promulgated from the pulpit, that we have a spiritual soul that ascends to heaven on death while still retaining the folkloric beliefs about roving subtle bodies that underpinned popular conceptions surrounding walking spirits of the dead and the existence of fairyland.

While these references to subtle-body belief may, like all fairy-related elements in the confessions, have been produced as a kind of false-confessional by-product to focused questioning on demonological matters, their contextualisation and relevance, when taken in conjunction with the perspectives on visionary phenomena outlined in this chapter, suggests that they could have emerged as an articulation of dream or vision experience. It suggests that Isobel's claim to have left behind an imitation body, in the form of a stool or broom, when she travelled to fairyland with her coven was not just the recounting of a local belief (as may have been the case for her Elgin neighbour, Isobel Cuming), but a genuine attempt to rationalize, in the only way she knew how, visionary experiences that had occurred prior to her arrest, as she lay in bed at night beside her husband.

But Was it Shamanism?

Of course, fact that Isobel may have experienced vivid, fairy-related nocturnal visions does not automatically indicate that her experiences were shamanistic, or that by virtue of them she worked as a shamanistic practitioner. As we saw earlier in the chapter, in the pre-industrial early modern period it was not unusual for physiological stresses, caused by factors ranging from bereavement and malnutrition to ergot-poisoning, to precipitate spontaneous visions that were not connected, or were only marginally connected, to any magical or spiritual practice or community function. Although unprovoked and temporary, such visionary episodes could have been powerful and memorable enough for a witchcraft suspect like Isobel to have drawn on them many years later during imprisonment and interrogation.

But in Isobel's case, the evidence weighs in favour of shamanistic practice. For example, while it is possible – given the disease's prevalence in the Auldearn area – that Isobel had experienced ergot-induced hallucinations at some point in her life, it is unlikely that they would have been solely responsible for any visionary component to her confessions. First, as a symptom of severe infection, ergot-induced hallucinations would necessarily have been accompanied by acute physical symptoms, but Isobel's fairy-related experiences are narrated as occurring over a period of many years, within a normal round of activity, and at no point are any painful or distressing physical symptoms described in association with them. Secondly, Isobel's confessions, like most contemporary encounter-narratives, are filled with realistically-contextualized, 'formed', persons, spirits and events that conform accurately to contemporary folk-loristic imagery and belief. But as psychologists Gottlieb and Spanos point out (in their refutation of Linnda Caporael's ergotism-was-the-cause-of-the-Salem-witchcraze theory) the psychoactive component of the ergot mycotoxin, like LSD to which it is chemically related, characteristically causes more generalized perceptual disturbances (particularly in subjects whose eyes are open) such as colours, haloes and moving shapes as opposed to 'formed persons or objects which they believe are actually out there'.[161] Thirdly, ergot-induced hallucinations, as with those caused by any powerful drug, are frequently uncontrollable, nonsensical, confusing and frightening (aka the proverbial LSD-induced 'bad trip') with Charles Sharpe noting in 1819 that some Scottish cunning folk made it their speciality to cure 'persons mad, distracted, or possest with fearfull apparitions, as St. Antonie's fire'.[162] While we could conceivably attribute isolated scenes such as being beaten by the Devil as illustrative of ergot-induced nightmare, in general Isobel's fairy-related and intermediary passages, being largely coherent and accessible, do not lend themselves to this interpretation.

It is also possible that, given the time and place in which she lived, at some point in her past, and perhaps more than once, Isobel had experienced periods of physical or psychological stress sufficiently extreme to provoke temporary psychoses that were accompanied by vivid hallucinations. But again, this can only ever amount to a partial explanation. The fact that Isobel's experiences conform in many ways to classic fairy-related encounter-narratives and that they seem to have occurred over a long period (fifteen years, according to her own reckoning), is not suggestive of temporary psychosis. Also counter-suggestive is the fact that over this period of time Isobel's experiences seem to have consistently maintained their congruity and rationale. They also seem to have been deliberately invoked (Isobel leaving a broom in bed beside her husband and 'calling' her coven members out); intentioned (Isobel going out on her flights with specific aims, such as feasting in cellars, hunting, stealing milk and so on);

and relatively controlled (Isobel having a certain amount of say over where she did things and when). These elements, combined with the fact that Isobel, by her own admission, seems to have worked as a magical practitioner, strongly suggests that the visionary component of her narrative, if it existed, would have been representative of a long-term, ongoing shamanistic vocation.

Taking all these perspectives into account, we can entertain the possibility that Isobel was not only a magical practitioner and oral performer, but that her healing practices and storytelling skills were enhanced and informed by the fact that on certain nights of the year she lay down next to her husband in their cottage in Lochloy and fell into deep catalepsy. And that while she lay there, with her body as stiff as a 'boosom', she experienced intense fairy-related visionary experiences in which the places and characters she described so vividly in fireside stories and ballads, quite literally came to life. And that these characters took her on supernatural journeys, instructed her in the ways of the spirits, showed her magical techniques and taught her songs and poems that she could bring back to waking consciousness and use to inform her magical practice. We can further speculate that some of these experiences, recollected during her long interrogation and imprisonment, were woven – thread by thread – into her complex narrative testimony. False confession was still highly likely to have been involved, but these perspectives suggest that in formulating her coerced-compliant responses and false memories Isobel did not only draw on real-life experiences, remembered fairy lore and interrogatorial suggestion, but also mined some of the emotive shamanistic experiences that had so vividly punctuated her life up to this point.

More Questions

But although this hypothesis is compelling, it raises as many questions as it answers. Stating that prior shamanistic experiences may have informed Isobel's confessions is all very well, but can we ascertain, with any accuracy, which parts of her narrative were likely to have related to visionary events, and which were not? And can we identify, with any more precision, how these visionary elements may have been interwoven with non-visionary elements during the construction of the confessions? More challenging still, what implications does this hypothesis have for the darker aspects of Isobel's testimony? If the fairy-related passages represented shamanistic visionary experience, and if such experiences are typically entered into for the benefit of the practitioner's local community, then why do they depict Isobel performing so much maleficent magic, and performing it so enthusiastically? Moreover, if the fairy-related passages were informed by prior shamanistic experience, then to what extent might the demonological passages – with which they were so deeply entwined – have also possessed a visionary core? In the remainder of this book we will be attempting to answer some of these questions from a variety of different angles. In doing so, we will not only gain fresh insights into the way Isobel's confessions may have been constructed, but will also find that the Isobel-as-shamanistic-visionary theory becomes progressively strengthened. Equally importantly, we will find that, approached from these angles, Isobel's confessions function as a portal through which we can gain new perspectives on some of the deeper problems that have perennially dogged the shamanistic hypothesis as a whole.

11

Isobel Follows the Goddess

We shall begin our enquiry by looking at Isobel's fairy-related passages and their hypo-thetical visionary component in their European context. Although scholars have suggested that a wide variety of shamanistic beliefs and practices of folkloric nature may have operated in many parts of Europe in the early modern period, trying to assess their nature and prevalence is a real challenge. First, the assortment of folkloric belief and practice that comes under the definition of 'shamanistic' is astonishingly diverse: Pócs's and Klaniczay's work into Hungarian sources is testament to the range that could exist in one region of central Europe alone. Secondly, our analysis is hampered by the fact that our source material, which ranges from canons of church law and theological literature to court records, seldom stipulates how far these shamanistic phenomena emerged as belief and physical ritual, and how far as visionary experience. This problem is further compounded by the fact that our most important evidence regarding visionary experience comes from encounter-narratives found in witch-testimonies that were elicited through coercion, and filtered through a nexus of elite demonological ideas. While some detailed and relatively undistorted documentation exists, most famously in relation to the Friulian *benandanti* and the Sicilian *donas de fuera,* the majority of references to folkloric shamanistic beliefs and practices are highly contam-inated, fragmentary and epistemologically problematic.

In this chapter we will attempt to ameliorate some of these difficulties by employing the following terms. All accounts of shamanistic belief and practice of folk-loric origin, wherever they are found and whatever form they take, will be termed 'shamanistic narratives'. Though not ideal, this term carries the benefit of confirming belief while only raising the possibility of, as opposed to assuming, an experiential component. We shall also be making a distinction between those shamanistic narra-tives concerned with encounters with individual spirits and those concerned with encounters with groups of spirits, with the latter being termed 'spirit-group narratives'. Although many shamanistic narratives combine these two elements, with contact with a group of spirits, for example, often being precipitated by contact with an individual spirit, in most cases one or the other is usually dominant. Isobel's fairy-related passages clearly fall into the 'spirit-group narrative' category, and therefore it is here that we will focus our attention.

Spirit-Group Narratives

Spirit-group narratives are primarily concerned with participation in supernatural activities with groups of spirits. These activities can range from processions and festive meetings to full-scale battles with enemy spirit groups, and are usually led by one or more figures that are frequently supernatural, but sometimes human. Group member-ship commonly includes, in differing combinations and proportions, spirits of non-human provenance variously described as fairies, demons, deities and so on; the dead; and the subtle bodies of living humans. Under this broad definition, the term spirit-group narratives covers documentation relating to traditions as diverse as those of the Sicilian *donas de fuera*, the Friulian *benandanti*, the Hungarian *táltos*, European werewolves and the corpus of beliefs and practices associated with the Wild Hunt.

Many spirit-group narratives, though they might be geographically and temporally distinct, display strong correspondences, both in terms of theme, motif, etymology and rationale. From the early medieval period to the present, scholars have attempted to classify them in various ways, with distinctions being made between those describing activities led by women and followed by women, those involving nocturnal canni-balism, those involving battle with neighbouring spirit groups and so on. Many scholars have also attempted to trace the historical and cultural connections between these narratives and narrative-categories, with Ginzburg famously asserting a funda-mental distinction between those depicting (what he termed) *following the goddess* shamanism and those depicting (what he termed) *warrior shamanism*, and arguing that both categories were rooted in a single archaic matrix – 'the ecstatic journey of the living into the land of the dead' – that possessed a clear line of historical evolution from pre-history through to the early modern centuries. Although deep belief matrices clearly connect many of these narratives, and although we shall be making a brief foray into the pre-Christian origins of some of Isobel's confessional material in the next chapter, the search for cultural links and historical origins does not fall within the remit of this book. Unless stated otherwise, all terms relating to spirit-group narratives or narrative categories will denote shamanistic beliefs and practices brought together on the basis of manifest similarities alone.

Female-Led Spirit Groups

One of the most prominent shamanistic narrative categories to emerge from the medieval and early modern sources is, what shall be termed here, the 'female-led spirit group'. In many parts of pre-modern Europe, from the ninth century onwards, we find written references to the belief that at certain times of the year a supernatural female figure, sometimes accompanied by a male consort, roamed the world at night with a large company of spirits, the latter sometimes appearing in animal form or riding on animals. This figure went under a variety of names. Elite writers usually affiliated her to one of the core pagan deities such as the classical Diana and Hecate, the Germanic Holda and Perchta and, less commonly, the Celtic Matrae or Matronae. But individual testimonies from witchcraft and sorcery trials reveal that she was often known to her followers by more derivative or regionally-sourced epithets such as 'Richella', 'Good Mistress', 'Mistress of the Good Game', 'Madona Horiente', 'Wise Sybil' or simply, 'the Lady'.[1] Some scholars have postulated that female-led spirit-group narratives were underpinned by a single archaic matrix, with Ginzburg, as we saw above, famously terming them *following the goddess* traditions and claiming that they were rooted in visionary rites surrounding the pre-Grecian Mediterranean goddess. However, while Ginzburg's hypothesis has much to recommend it, more recent scholars have urged caution: Hans Peter Broedel claiming, in reference to his theory, that 'the available evidence is scattered and contradictory, and suggests a group of more or less related components rather than a single, coherent belief-system'.[2]

According to the written sources, the female spirit-group leader did not just aim-lessly wander about the night skies, but was associated with specific activities, the most prominent of these being the house-to-house procession. The leader and her spirit train slipped into buildings (down chimneys, through keyholes and between the chinks in walls) after the householders had gone to bed, and once inside they began to make themselves at home. Feasting on the food and drink stored in cup-boards and cellars characteristically formed the core of these festivities, but dancing, music-making and the performance of magic were also relatively common. In the thirteenth century the bishop of Paris, Guillaume d'Auvergne, lamented that local peasants believed that 'ladies of the night' visited private homes, 'under the leader-ship of their mistress Lady Abundia, who is also called Satia. If they find food and drink ready for them, they partake of them, but without diminishing the quantity of either . . . Inspired by this belief, foolish old women, and some equally foolish men, open up their pantries and uncover their barrels on the nights when they expect a vis-itation.'[4] Meanwhile in sixteenth-century Switzerland, as Behringer notes, many claimed to have seen the *säligen lütt* – a fairy-like society that, though not specifically linked to a goddess figure, was clearly affiliated to the female-led corpus – 'moving through the streets of Lucerne "playing delightfully on stringed instruments." Many also averred that they had been visited by the *Säligen Lütt* in their houses, where they cooked and feasted even though on the next day no one noticed any decrease in the food supplies.'[5]

But the spirit procession did not only congregate in people's houses: it could con-duct its festivities and perform its magic in fields, beneath hills, on mountains and in distant countries. In the Italian town of Bressanone, in 1457, three old women from Val di Fassa confessed that during the four Ember weeks they participated in noctur-nal meetings with a 'good mistress' named Richella who took them to 'a place crowded with people who danced and made merry'.[6] Over a hundred years later, a Sicilian fisherman's wife claimed to have ridden a goat to a meeting where she encountered both the goddess and her male consort, stating grandly that: '[it was] a country called Benevento that belongs to the Pope and lies in the kingdom of Naples. There was a great plain there on which there stood a large tribune with two chairs. On one of them sat a red young man and on the other a beautiful woman; they called her the Queen, and the man was the King.'[7] These traditions were commonly associated with significant times of the year, such as feast days and holy days, particularly the Ember days and Yule.

The nocturnal processions and meetings of the supernatural female and her train were not perceived as idle amusements. Throughout medieval and early modern Europe it was believed that these wandering spirits possessed supernatural powers, and that if you received their visits hospitably and obeyed their laws and taboos, they would reward you with health and prosperity. According to Guillaume d'Auvergne, thirteenth-century French peasants believed that 'if they find food and drink ready for them' Lady Abundia and her procession would 'reward the hospitable household with an abundance of material goods'.[8] Similarly, in the same century Vincent of Beauvais recounted a jocular tale in which a peasant, being fooled by some youths who had dressed up as the goddess and her followers, tells his wife 'Keep quiet and shut your eyes; we shall be rich. These are the good women, and they will increase our wealth a hundred-fold.'[9] Two centuries later the Italian women from Val di Fassa claimed that they followed their 'good mistress' Richella because she was 'the 'mother of riches and good fortune'; while, a century on again, the Swiss still 'considered it a considerable honour' to host the *säligen lütt* and believed that such visits would leave them 'blessed'.[10]

But while many people swept their kitchens clean and left out food and drink in order to please the female-led spirit train, a minority of individuals took their devotions one step further. As we have seen, the group that followed the female supernatural figure typically consisted of non-human spirits (like the leader herself) and the human dead, but it also consisted of living humans in subtle-body form. This human participation was vividly described in a famous passage in the *Canon Episcopi* (as it was later known) which, though composed by bishop Réginon de Prüm in 906, was probably of earlier origin:

> One cannot allow that certain wicked women, perverted and seduced by Satan's illusions and mirages, believe and say that they go out at night with the goddess Diana, or with Herodias, and a great crowd of women, riding astride certain animals, covering large amounts of ground in the night silence and obeying Diana like a mistress.[11]

And it is here, in the narratives that describe people not only seeking to play host to the supernatural female and her spirit train, but also leaving their beds and joining her, that we find the shamanistic dimension of female-led spirit-group beliefs.

The Followers

The shamanistic rationale behind following the female spirit-group leader was simple. By becoming her adherent and joining her nocturnal processions, the shamanistic practitioner facilitated and enhanced the latter's good fortune and prosperity-bringing effects. This participation, which was often described in the language of feudal allegiance and service (with de Prüm claiming that Diana's followers obey her 'like a mistress'), could simply involve participating in the travelling festivities. In early seventeenth-century Sicily, as Henningsen tells us, an Alcamo journeyman's wife claimed that her company of *donas de fuera,* led by 'the Matron', toured around the town and:

> When they went into a house with their songs and music and fine clothes they would say: 'With God's blessing let the dance increase!', and, when, after taking a look into people's clothes' chests – and eating some of the food, if there was a festive gathering in progress – they left to go on somewhere else, their parting salute was: 'Stop the dance and let prosperity increase!'[12]

But enhancing general prosperity and good fortune were not the only benefits to be gained. Many sources reveal that in return for services rendered, the female leader or one of her spirits rewarded her human followers with specific magical knowledge or power, these gifts being most commonly associated with healing and divination. In the late-fourteenth century a Milanese woman, named Petrina, told an inquisitor that she and the other members of her society (termed the '*bona gens*' or 'good people'), served a fairy-like figure named Madona Horiente. The latter did not only lead her followers in prosperity-bringing house-to-house processions, but also personally gifted them with magical powers. The records state:

> And you [Petrina] have said that the Mistress teaches you members of this society the efficacy of herbs and shows you through signs everything you want to be shown and teaches you everything you want to know about sicknesses, thefts, and bewitchings, and also she teaches you the Art [*das Werk*] and you find out the truth about everything she shows you.[13]

For many shamanistic practitioners, the pursuit of healing and divinatory knowledge seems to have been a primary motivation for joining the female-led spirit group, and some clearly participated in their processions and meetings to order, in response to client demand. Henningsen claimed that in Sicily a *dona de fuera* would, after establishing the cause of an illness 'explain to her patient that the fairies can be mollified by an offering, and that she personally will attend the nocturnal meeting in company with her "Ladies" and persuade them to make the sick person well again'.[14] This motive is also found in other categories of spirit-group narrative, with some *benandanti,* for example, claiming that they were approached by clients who believed that they could identify whom had been bewitched and how to cure them through their visionary experiences.[15]

When the interaction between a magical practitioner and the spirits becomes this intimate, the line between the two becomes very blurred, and it is hardly surprising to find that in many traditions the shamanistic practitioner was not only believed able to gain access to the powers of the spirits, but also to possess these powers herself. Folklorist Giuseppe Pitrè noted that the Sicilian *dona de fuera* was 'something of a fairy and something of a witch although one cannot really distinguish which is which'; while Henningsen noted that although the term was used to denote the 'supernatural, fairy-like creatures (of both sexes) who accompanied the witches on their nocturnal excursions' several of the accused witches 'also stated that they themselves were *donas de fuera*'.[16] A similarly ambiguous status is also intimated in spirit-group narratives from contemporary Germany, with Juliana Winkerin, from Umes on the Schlern, claiming that on one occasion, while engaging in festive activities with a nocturnal company, the resurrection of a baby had been performed by local maidservant Anna Jobstin, who had 'been chosen Queen of Angel Land (also Queen of the Angels, Queen of the Elves)'.[17] The fact that in sixteenth-century Switzerland living persons who traveled with the *säligen lütt* 'were regarded as holy and blessed' and 'enjoyed a reputation for semi-sanctity' is also suggestive here.[18]

The Scottish Parallels

It is clear that many of the accounts of fairy-related beliefs and practices that have come down to us from early modern Scotland fall into this Europe-wide female-led spirit-group category. Among contemporary scholars, the Scottish fairy queen and her train or host are generally agreed to represent a version of the 'European nocturnal goddess' commonly associated with these narratives.[19] This link is also reflected by the fact that educated Scots linked the fairy queen with Diana, one of the deities identified with the female spirit-group leader as early as the first decade of the tenth century. James VI referred to 'That fourth kind of spirits, which by the gentiles was called Diana and her wandering court, and amongst us was called the fairy or "our good neighbours"'; while Scottish minister William Hay claimed, in 1564, that 'there are certain women who do say that they have dealings with Diana the queen of the fairies'.[20]

Conformity with female-led spirit-group narratives is also evinced by the fact that the Scottish fairy queen and her 'wandering court' are composed of the same kinds of spirits, and engage in the same kinds of activities as their Continental counterparts. Like the latter, their company is made up of non-human spirits, the dead, and the subtle bodies of the living; their primary preoccupation is feasting, dancing and revelry; and these festivities generally occur during house-to-house processions or in the country-side. Sometimes, as on the Continent, fairy processions were associated with Yule and the Ember days. As we saw in CHAPTER FOUR, in 1616 Orkney cunning woman Katherine Jonesdochter claimed that the 'Trowis' left their hills and churchyards to come to any house where there was 'feasting, or great mirrines and speciallie at Yule'.[21]

As did their Continental contemporaries, the pre-modern Scots also swept their kitchens and put out food and drink to please the wandering court; these beliefs being vividly encapsulated in the following nineteenth-century anecdote from the Isle of Man:

> This used to happen about one hundred years ago, as my mother has told me: Where my grandfather John Watterson was reared, just over near Kerroo Kiel (Narrow Quarter), all the family were sometimes sitting in the house of a cold winter night, and my great grandmother and her daughters at their wheels spinning, when a little white dog would suddenly appear in the room. Then every one there would have to drop their work and prepare for *the*

company to come in: they would put down a fire and leave fresh water for *them*, and hurry off upstairs to bed. They could hear *them* come, but could never see them, only the dog. The dog was a fairy dog, and a sure sign of their coming.[22]

Like their fellow Europeans, the Scots also believed that by joining the fairy queen and her train they could acquire magical benefits, with kirk session records and witch-testimonies frequently containing references to those people who, like Marion Or in 1602, were hauled before the authorities for professing themselves to 'ride with the fair folk and to have skill'.[23] As in spirit-group narratives Europe-wide, the powers gained were often associated with divination and healing.

Although, on the basis of these correspondences, it is clear that shamanistic beliefs and practices surrounding female-led spirit groups existed in early modern Scotland, the relative paucity of evidence makes them difficult to reconstruct. While witchcraft and sorcery trials from some areas of Europe, such as the Balkans and Sicily, provide us with a wealth of relatively undemonized documentation in this respect, Scottish records, in comparison, are often heavily demonized or lacking in detail. While we have a handful of descriptive accounts of meetings with the fairy queen, the majority of records simply state, 'I went with the fairies' or 'I got my skill from the fairies' and so on. It is for this reason that Isobel's rich and detailed confessions are particularly valuable.

Isobel Follows the Goddess

Isobel's claim to have feasted with the king and queen of the fairies under the Downie Hill securely places her narrative within the female-led spirit-group category: and it is easy to see why Ginzburg was persuaded to cite her case, along with that of Aberdeenshire cunning man Andro Man (1597), as evidence that *following the goddess* traditions were extant in seventeenth-century Britain.[24] Although Ginzburg did not explore any other aspects of Isobel's confessions in this context, her claims to have flown through the air in the form of an animal, to have engaged in house-to-house processions and danced on hilltops are also suggestive of female-led spirit-group activities. Additionally suggestive is the fact that, in keeping with similar groups throughout Europe, Isobel's companions were an assorted mixture of non-human spirits (the king and queen of the fairies, the elves, the Devil); the dead (the 'bodies' that 'remains w[i]th ws' after they have been shot and killed by elf arrows); and the living (Isobel and her neighbours). Furthermore, as we shall explore in more detail in CHAPTER EIGHTEEN, Isobel's term 'coven', though now predominantly associated with the demonological witches' sabbath, can be seen to reflect the fact that terms such as 'company' or 'society' were frequently used to define female-led spirit groups throughout Europe, from Scotland to the Balkans to Sicily.

When considered in the context of European female-led spirit-group narratives the cultural origins and rationale behind some of Isobel's confessional claims become clear, particularly with regard to the house-to-house processions. Isobel frequently mentions the fact that she and her coven 'wold goe s[eve]rall howses in the night tym'. At Robert Donaldsone's house they 'went in at the kitchen chimney, and went down wpon the crowk' in order to feast on 'beiff and drink'; at Grangehill, they 'got meat and drink enough'; at the Earl of Moray's house they 'gott anewgh ther and did eat and drink of the best, and browght pairt w[i]th ws;' and at Bessie Hay's house in Auldearn they consumed an ox that they had killed previously, presumably with elf arrows. Although Isobel does not make specific reference to the fact that these visits conferred prosperity or good fortune, they seem to have been generally benign. Barring one reference to a maleficent grace recited at Grangehill, not only does she fail to report the performance of any *maleficium* at these events, but her claim, in the first confession, that 'q[uhe]n ve goe to any hous we tak meat and drink, and we fill wp the barrellis w[i]th owr oven pish (*piss*) again', could be interpreted as a reference to the female group-leader's powers of magical increase, reflecting the fact that in Nairnshire, as in Switzerland, 'no one noticed any decrease in their food supplies' after a visit from the fairy train. In the context of female-led spirit-group narratives Europe-wide, this reference raises the possibility that Isobel may have consciously interpreted these house-to-house visits as communally beneficial.

Taken as a whole, these European perspectives suggest that we need not only interpret Isobel's claims to have feasted in houses as compensatory fictions, dreamt up in a courtroom to satisfy a chronically hungry and powerless woman, nor interpret them solely as folkloric themes produced to titillate and distract a curious audience because she had to say something. We can, instead, see them as testaments to the fact that, like many of her contemporaries across the Channel, Isobel periodically lay down in bed and entered into deep dreams or trances in which she participated in lucid and intentioned visionary experiences. Experiences in which she believed herself to join the house-to-house processions and nocturnal revels of the fairy queen and her train in order to bring prosperity and good fortune to both herself and her community.

The Unexplained *Maleficium*

But while this neat conclusion may well represent a partial truth, with regard to Isobel, matters were clearly a little more complicated. Although parts of her confessions contain discernible links to female-led spirit-group narratives, in the sense that they describe house-to-house processions and (through the refilling of barrels) the bringing of magical increase, taken as a whole both the processions and all the other activities Isobel performs with her coven seem to have been less concerned with the bringing of prosperity than with the bringing of misfortune and death. Although Isobel's house-to-house visits may have been generally beneficent, the fact that she followed her claim to have 'got beiff and drink' at Robert Donaldsone's house with the ominous observation that they then 'did no mor harme' suggests that some of her coven's attentions may have been less benign. This leads us to speculate that the variety of overtly maleficent acts that Isobel and her companions performed in houses, such as taking the strength of the ale from one barrel and transferring it to another and sabotaging Alexander

Cumming's dye vats, may well have been an integral feature of these inter-house perambulations. The picture is further darkened and complicated by the fact that the
company that feasted on beef and drink in the houses of Isobel's neighbours was the
same company that travelled to fairyland in order to watch elf arrows being forged,
before embarking on bloodthirsty human-hunting expeditions.

We could assume that both these hunting escapades and the malevolent variations
on the traditionally beneficent house-to-house procession theme were created by Isobel,
in the courtroom, in response to the pressures of interrogation. But such an interpretation is only partially satisfactory. The fact that these maleficent acts appear in the
first confession, fully-formed, wholly undemonized and interwoven into fairy-related
passages points to their authenticity, as does the fact that Isobel's interrogators, who
were primarily interested in her dealings with the Devil, and any *maleficium* performed
against her eminent neighbours, the Laird of Park and Harry Forbes, are unlikely to
have produced the close and suggestive questioning necessary to generate false confession in this regard. Most persuasive of all, however, with regard to the authenticity of
Isobel's maleficent accounts, is the fact that if we now move on to spread our net a little
wider, they can be rationalized within the wider context of European shamanistic spirit-
group narratives as a whole.

The Maleficent Hosts

Despite the fact they are predominantly associated with beneficence, the performance
of *maleficium* has, in fact, featured in a wide variety of shamanistic spirit-group narratives from the ninth century onwards, emerging particularly prominently in the
Europe-wide corpus of mythology and belief surrounding what is widely known as the
'Wild Hunt'. Although appearing in many variants, the Wild Hunt was essentially
depicted as an aggressive, night-roaming spirit horde, often appearing airborne and/or
on horseback and primarily composed of the dead. In many traditions, these dead souls
were identified as unbaptized children, or those who died an unnatural, premature or
violent death. Many Wild Hunt narratives, particularly in later centuries, emphasize
the leadership of a male chthonic deity, such as Odin, Woden, or some locally-signif-
icant figure. But the close links between the Wild Hunt and the female-led
spirit-group corpus are suggested by the fact that from its earliest known appearance
nocturnal goddesses such as Diana, Perchta and Holda have also been named as leaders
of the Hunt, with some scholars identifying the classical goddess Hecate as the leaders' common ancestor.[25]

There also seems to have been an experiential dimension to Wild Hunt beliefs,
although it emerges as less prominent and is less frequently documented than that of
traditional female-led spirit-group narratives. Many accounts describe how the Hunt
could sweep up living people to temporarily join their company; sometimes just giving
them a ride and sometimes pressing them to participate in their supernatural activities. Folklorist Lotte Motz has noted, in relation to early modern Germany, that:

A man brought to a witch's trial in 1630 confessed that he had become part of Dame Holle's retinue and had followed her on New Years Day into the Venusberg, the mountain from which issues in legend the Wild Host of the Lady. A woman was exiled from the town of Bern in the sixteenth century after she admitted to having ridden with the 'frow Selden' in the *wüttisheer*.[26]

Occasionally, in this context, we even have direct references to abductions occurring during shamanistic catalepsy. Quoting nineteenth-century folklorist Magnus Landstad, Kveldulf Gundarsson notes that the Norweigan Wild Hunt variant known as the *oskoreia* was associated with:

> people undergoing a sort of involuntary separation from their bodies, which lie as if dead while their souls are faring with the oskorei, as Landstad describes: 'She fell backwards and lay the whole night as if she were dead. It was of no profit to shake her, for the Asgardsreid had made off with her.' The woman then awakes to tell how she had ridden with the host 'so that fire spurted under horse-hooves'.[27]

Like their more beneficent female-led counterparts, Wild Hunt spirit groups were often associated with Yule and the Ember days, house-to-house processions and beneficent magical effects. Hilda Ellis Davidson notes of the Norweigan *oskoreia*, for example, that 'These riders were certainly regarded as dangerous, but their coming was sometimes said to secure a good year for the farm'.[28] While Gundarsson echoes that 'Those who help the [*oskoreia*] Hunter or members of his train, however, are often rewarded with gifts; often mundane objects which later turn to gold'.[29]

But despite this intermittent beneficence, Wild Hunt groups differed from their female-led equivalents in the sense that they were predominantly associated with negative activities and effects. In its death-bringing capacity, the Hunt characteristically roamed the countryside on horseback in search of prey, killing those in its path, particularly the young, and gathering them up to join its grim host of the dead. Similarly, its house-to-house processions were not characterized by good fortune and prosperity, but by misfortune and malevolence. In reference to the Norweigan *oskoreia* again, Davidson notes:

> [they] made much noise, and could be heard whistling, ringing bells, clashing weapons or making music, accompanied by their dogs. They might ride through a house, fling their saddles on to the roof, and play mischievous tricks on the occupants such as drinking their ale and filling up the casks with water, or taking horses from the stable, galloping them all night, and leaving them in a sorry state in the morning. Occasionally they carried off a child or someone who rashly ventured outside after dark, and left them a long way from home; there were even tales of people being murdered and then seen riding in their company.[30]

We find the same narrative template appearing over and over again throughout Europe, in a variety of different guises. To take just one region, in her analysis of the links between fairy and witch beliefs in south-eastern and central Europe, Pócs identifies an

This nineteenth-century depiction of the Wild Hunt, as imagined by Heinrich Heine, vividly evokes the fear, excitement and epic imagery associated with this belief matrix. bpk/Staatsbibliothek zu Berlin – PreuBischer Kulturbesitz, Foto: Dietmar Katz.

astonishingly wide array of fairy-type beings and demons who can be incorporated under the Wild Hunt umbrella, or which display Wild Hunt characteristics. The most dramatic of these, the 'winter demons' (that is, the 'demons who call on people in winter') include the Balkan *karakondzuli* and some types of werewolf demons, the Rumanian *sântoaderi* and the Serbian *tordorci* and were characteristically composed, in large part, of 'hostile living people' and souls of the dead who had died unbaptized or 'in the wrong way'. Like the Norweigan *oskoreia*, the winter demons could be generous toward their human helpers, and some types were linked to healing and fertility, but they were predominantly associated with maleficent effects, from famine and bad weather to the hunting and killing of humans and animals, with children often being their favoured prey. They also proceeded 'from house to house, [and] from wine cellar to wine cellar', where they did not only feast and dance, but also disrupted household tasks (turning 'everything upside down'), urinated over house contents, ravished women, destroyed buildings and brought sickness.[31]

Female-Led Maleficence

But while shamanistic spirit-group malevolence was perhaps at its most dramatic in the Wild Hunt corpus, it was also found in other arenas. Particularly relevant to Isobel is the fact that there are a number of remarkable, often-quoted, but still unexplained, accounts of maleficent activities, also centred around killing, embedded in specifically female-led spirit-group narratives from different parts of Europe from as early as the beginning of the eleventh century. First, we have the famous passage that appears in the fifth chapter of Burchard of Worm's *Corrector*, composed around 1008–12. This passage does not mention either female leaders or spirit trains (this leaving Cohn to deduce that it was linked to the tradition of the solitary night witch or 'Strix') but the allusion to the fact that the practice is performed 'together with others who are similarly deceived' and, as we shall see later, its theme of resurrection, suggests that it can be provisionally included under the female-led spirit-group narrative category:

> in the silence of the quiet night . . . [these women go] through the closed doors and travel through the spaces of the world, together with others who are similarly deceived; and that without visible weapons, *you kill people* who have been baptized and redeemed by Christ's blood, and together cook and devour the flesh; and that where the heart was, you put straw or something of the sort; and that after eating these people, you bring them alive again and grant them a brief spell of life? If you have believed this, you shall do penance on bread and water for fifty days.[32]

The theme of cannibalism, but this time clearly linked to female-led spirit-group beliefs, is echoed in the following century by John of Salisbury, who claimed that contemporary French peasants believed:

> a certain woman who shines by night, or Herodias, or the mistress of the night, summons

gatherings and assemblies, which attend various banquets. The figure receives all kinds of homage from her servants, some of whom are handed over for punishment, while others are singled out for praise, according to their deserts. Furthermore, they say that infants are exposed to the *lamiae*; some of them being dismembered and gluttonously devoured, while the mistress takes pity on others and has them put back in their cradles.[33]

Moving on a couple of centuries, we find similar themes of killing and resurrection in some of the narratives that, paradoxically, we employed earlier in this chapter to illustrate the female-led spirit-group's beneficence. We have already noted, for example, that in the South Tyrolean Alps in the first decade of the sixteenth century Juliana Winkerin claimed to have been a member of a 'good society' that met during the Ember nights to enjoy 'good food and beautiful music'. And that she claimed that one of her members had 'fulfilled her role as queen of the fairies' by bringing a dead child back to life, after gathering together its bones. But what is significant here is not the fact that the 'good society' brought the child back to life, but the fact that, according to Winkerin, it was the 'good society' who had killed (and then eaten) the child in the first place.[34] A similar ambivalence occurs in the testimony of the late fourteenth-century Milanese woman, Petrina, whom we also met earlier. As we have seen, Petrina claimed that she and her companions accompanied the goddess 'Horiens' on her house-to-house processions and that the latter both blessed her hosts and taught her followers everything they needed to know 'about sicknesses, thefts and bewitchings'. But these statements must be considered alongside the fact that Petrina also asserted that during these nocturnal adventures she and her companions 'kill animals and eat their flesh, but that they place the bones back into the skin, and the Mistress herself strikes the skin of the slaughtered animals with the staff that she holds in her hand with the apple, and that these animals at once revive, but that they are never much good for work thereafter'.[35]

The malevolent activities cited in these cases are dramatic but they are not anomalous. Once we start looking, we find that malevolence of some kind is present in most spirit-group narratives, however beneficent they may appear at first glance. The Friulian *benandanti*, for example, are generally lauded as a shining example of a benign shamanistic cult: securing fertility, cures and divinations for their community though battling witches and enemy sorcerers. But their function is somewhat complicated by the fact that after their fighting sprees, the *benandanti* joined their opponents for communal drinking bouts that could, on occasion, be uncannily redolent of the disruptive house-to-house processions of the Norweigan *oskoreia* or the Balkan winter demons. The *benandanti* who described these events characteristically distanced themselves from their maleficent dimension: Paolo Gasparutto and Battista Moduco, for example, claiming that it was their witch companions, not themselves, who would 'go into the cellars and overturn all the wine' and 'urinate in the casks' and ruin their contents by 'throwing filth in the bungholes' if they did not find clean water to drink.[36] But these protestations of innocence are undermined by the fact that, at times, the dividing line between the *benandanti* and their malign opponents seems to have been very thin. Not only did the two groups share post-battle drinking bouts, but the *benandanti* also knew some of the witches by name and could consciously ally themselves with them against the outside world, with Battista Moduco claiming, for example, that he would not reveal the names of the witches he fought because 'we have a life-long edict not to reveal secrets about one side or the other'.[37] The testimony given by Michele Soppe, meanwhile, suggests that such controversial alliances could even be rooted in affection; the *benandante* asserting that when he 'begged' a witch to lift a spell she had cast on a sick child she 'did it for love of me'.[38] Similar ambiguities underpin the ostensibly beneficent activities of the Sicilian *donas de fuera*. Although the shamanistic activities of the *donas* were largely benign, as Henningsen notes, 'their *donas de fuera* complex was ambivalent: fairies and "witches" could exercise both good and ill'.[39] Notably, some *donas* claimed that they attended nocturnal meetings to persuade their fairy allies to cure illnesses that they themselves had caused.[40]

Isobel's Wild Hunt?

Earlier in this chapter we asked whether the maleficent aspects of Isobel's house-to-house processions and other coven-related activities could be contextualized within European shamanistic spirit-group narratives as a whole. And in the light of the perspectives explored over the last few pages, we can now answer this question with an affirmative 'yes'. Many of the maleficent acts performed by Isobel's coven – such as disrupting dye processes, stealing milk and corn, killing oxen, causing storms and taking away the fertility of the land – can be thematically linked to the malign aspect of shamanistic spirit-group narratives. These seemingly arbitrary acts of vandalism are little different to those of the Balkan winter demons who enter houses and disrupt domestic processes, ruin crops and bring bad weather, and the Norweigan *oskoreia*, who spill barrels and steal horses. Even more specifically, Isobel's arrow-shooting escapades can be clearly linked to the central theme of the Wild Hunt, in which the malevolent and death-bringing capacity of the group leader and his train manifests as an overt hunt for living souls. As we saw in CHAPTER FOUR, although most of Isobel's arrow-shooting passages do not contain references to fairies, it is clear that they are inspired by contemporary beliefs surrounding the hunting escapades of the baby-stealing, dead-encompassing fairy host, or *sluagh*, which folklorists have long identified as a specifically western European variant of the Wild Hunt corpus.[41]

But while, on a thematic level, we can equate Isobel's fairy-related passages with the malign aspect of shamanistic spirit-group narratives, once we move on to consider their experiential dimension things become a lot more complicated. If, as we argued earlier in this chapter, her benign spirit-group activities may have been rooted in shamanistic visionary experiences, then can we speculate the same for the many malevolent activities with which, on a narrative level, they were so deeply entwined? Such a claim is problematic because, as we briefly explored in the previous chapter, almost all definitions of shamanism, whether broad or narrow, emphasize the fact that the shaman enters into trance and participates in envisioned activities for the benefit of his or her community. And while it is easy to see how this community-benefit rationale underpinned Isobel's beneficent spirit-group activities, with regard to the maleficent it is much more elusive. All attempts to track it down, moreover, are hampered by the fact that we cannot circumvent this issue by assuming, as historians often do with regard to the more conventional demonological encounter-narratives, that claims to have performed maleficent spirit-group activity were false confessions stimulated by interrogators seeking to superimpose stereotypical notions about the performance of maleficent magic and attendance at the witches' sabbath. Although this was undoubtedly the case in many instances, the fact that the maleficent activities cited in both Isobel's and many other ambivalent spirit-group narratives so frequently fail to conform to standard elite demonological norms (with cannibalism, for example, sometimes containing typically folkloric shamanistic features like bone collection and resurrection); plus the fact that this maleficence emerges as deeply embedded in those narratives long before the preoccupation with demonological witchcraft became widespread, challenges such a simplistic conclusion.

It could be argued that it is not difficult to see why *beliefs* concerning maleficent spirit-group activities persisted into the early modern age, for they would have provided an explanation for the ubiquitous sickness and suffering and concomitant preoccupation with death and the afterlife, that characterized life in the harsh and unpredictable pre-industrial world. It is also not difficult to explain the persistence of the belief that humans could participate in these harm-bringing activities, for according to psychoanalytic theories of witchcraft, accusing rival communities or problematic community members of participating in malevolent magical activities serves as an efficient method of both resolving community tension and reinforcing societal mores. We can also understand how, as a result of such widespread beliefs, some unwitting individuals may have been surprised by spontaneous and terrifying culture-patterned visionary experiences in which they believed they had been swept up by the Hunt, forced to participate in their malevolent activities and then left, as in the case of the Norweigan *oskoreia*, 'a long way from home'. But it is another matter altogether to try and understand why, with the exception of those who may have pretended to such experiences in order to intimidate or impress their neighbours, women throughout Europe, from the ninth century through to the seventeenth, might have chosen to willingly and repeatedly participate in envisioned malevolent spirit-group activities.

Several leading scholars faced with the malevolent/benevolent spirit-group dilemma have argued that benign and malign aspects of these beliefs and practices emerged as distinct, on a popular level, at an early – possibly pre-Christian – stage in Europe's history. In 1971 Cohn suggested that the 'cannibalistic night witch' traditions depicted so vividly in the *Corrector*, and the 'beneficent and sustaining' traditions of those following Diana, were 'kept quite separate from one another' in the popular mind, being only conflated in the minds of the elite.[42] More recently, in 1996, Behringer claimed that in early modern Switzerland the 'blessed society' and the Wild Hunt were distinct. With reference to research undertaken in the Upper Valais Valley he notes that:

> A few old storytellers . . . produced a charming explanation [of Wild Hunt-type legends]: This army of spirits was simply 'the evil society' (*böse Gesellschaft*). If we can reject the possibility that this phrase was just a euphemism, the idea that there was an 'evil society' that stood in sharp contrast to 'good people' or to the 'good society' is immediately persuasive. We have seen that the fairy appearance of the night people does not fit at all well with the demonic qualities of the furious army . . . [43]

This good/evil spirit-group conflation hypothesis fits well with the growing historical perception that, from the early Middle Ages, folkloric beliefs concerning maleficent spirit-group activities fed into (and perhaps even underpinned) elite demonological stereotypes surrounding the Devil-worshipping, baby-eating, maleficium-performing, witches' horde which, through being fed back to the popular mind through pulpit teachings and witch-hunts, gradually re-modelled and demonized the folkloric ideas that had originally energised it.

But in many other respects, this hypothesis is unsatisfactory. In the first place, it does not adequately explain why so many spirit-group narratives display such deep ambivalence at such an early period in Europe's history. Nor does it explain why this ambivalence exhibits itself as such a profound and seamless amalgam between maleficent and beneficent aspects, as modelled in the simultaneous power to both heal and kill displayed by figures like Oriente, Richella, the *donas de fuera* et al. This hypothesis also fails in that it expects us to accept that this complex ambivalence, which appears in such a wide range of traditions in so many different ways, must be attributed to an elite conflation of two wholly distinct traditions that were then tortuously, over a period of centuries, filtered back into the popular mind. But perhaps most persuasively of all, it fails in that it asks us to accept that spirit-group narratives were fundamentally at odds with the wider corpus of European mythology and folklore that contextualised them. With regard to the female spirit-group leaders, for example, the poems, stories, songs and anecdotes that evolved around these figures throughout Europe, depict supernatural figures that are deeply ambivalent. Whether defined as goddesses, fairy women or 'fate women', these figures are neither wholly good nor wholly bad, but like nature itself embrace, in varying degrees, the spectrum of opposites. Although they can bring fertility, prosperity and life, they can also bring want and death; although they can heal, they can also harm; and although they can be compassionate mistresses who bring their followers joy, they can also be cruel tyrants who 'instill terror' when they roam the night skies at the head of their ghostly trains.[44] Given the fact that, as argued in the last chapter, shamanistic traditions characteristically evolve through a dynamic interchange between mythology and visionary experience (with the two constantly feeding each other in cycles of innovation and conservatism), it would be highly illogical if female-led spirit-group narratives did not reflect the duality of the folkloric goddess-figures that inspired and were inspired by them.

But the good/evil spirit-group conflation hypothesis is not only unsatisfactory because it fails to accommodate these levels of ambivalence, but also because it inadvertently obstructs the enquiry into the experiential dimension of maleficent shamanistic activities in the wider sense. Once we accept that the co-existence of malign and benign aspects in spirit-group narratives was likely to have been rooted in an elite conflation, as opposed to an inherently folkloristic ambivalence, then it is all too easy to fall into default scepticism and assume that while accounts of beneficent activities may have related to visionary experience, malign activities were more likely to have been the result of prosecutorial superimposition. We can clearly see this process at work in Cohn's analysis. While the latter acknowledges that 'some women believed they were cannibalistic night witches' a number of times, he does not allow this to affect his central thesis that the traditions of Diana were fundamentally beneficent and sustaining and that any malevolence was the result of an elite conflation. Similarly, although Behringer discusses a wide range of maleficent spirit-group activities, including the Wild Hunt and the activities of the followers of Horiente, with regard to the experiential dimension of shamanistic belief he focuses on the largely beneficent experiences of Chonrad Stoeckhlin, whose periodic journeys with the 'phantoms of the night' were initiated by 'a truly helpful spirit' who led him to 'progress in spirituality'.[45]

Several scholars working with the shamanistic paradigm have acknowledged that the maleficent aspects of spirit-group encounter-narratives may have represented visionary experience, but their inquiry into the nature of this 'envisioned maleficium', as we can term it here, still leaves questions unanswered. Éva Pócs, whose need to explain the moral ambivalence of magical systems and practitioners so evident in contemporary Hungarian sources has provoked her to grapple with the issue more seriously than most, begins her impressive *Between the Living and the Dead* with the following challenge:

> The question will arise about whether these archaic, quasi-shamanistic witches functioned in reality, participated in supernatural communication as black shamans, and were self-conscious black magicians in this sense. Or were these activities simply attributed, in the sense that Evans-Pritchard meant? The obvious and automatic answer here would be that they did not function in reality, but as we shall see, [later in the book] the issue is more complex than that.[46]

But despite posing these questions, Pócs only succeeds in producing clear conclusions with regard to certain types of envisioned *maleficium*. She argues that the malefice performed by largely beneficent shamanistic cults such as the Hungarian *táltos* was underpinned by the community-benefit rationale in the sense that it was undertaken as a form of group protection or defence. Cult members believed that the health and survival of their community depended upon visionary combats against enemy beings (generally spirits or the subtle bodies of humans) that were seeking to harm the town or village. If the *táltos* did not fight the 'bad dead', for example, then the latter would bring rain to destroy 'the seedling crops and grapes around the town'.[47] Pócs also claims that envisioned community-defending battles could take place within the arena of individual healing practices. As in tribal cultures worldwide, some Hungarian cunning folk or 'good witches' seem to have effected their cures through visionary battles with the evil spirits or evil subtle bodies that were responsible for the disease: in one document an accused witch claiming, 'Oh, tonight they wanted to kill Mrs. István Kis, there were five of them. They all went for my arm, and now I cannot even lift it up so much they have hurt it'.[48] A similar bias is visible in Ginzburg's work. While being the first to draw attention to the community-benefit rationale underpinning the envisioned *maleficium* performed by the *benandanti* (claiming that the latter 'do battle, armed with stalks of fennel, against analogous companies of male witches for the fate of the season's crops'), once he moves away from the Friulian cult he is less forthcoming.[49] Though stating categorically, for example, that 'the goddess demands' visionary rituals involving 'battles, [and] murders, followed by acts of cannibalism', Ginzburg never explores why she may have made such bloodthirsty requests; generally passing over the issue of envisioned *maleficium* in favour of exploring the more general question of the existence of the 'ecstatic journey into the land of the dead'.[50]

The problem here, in large part, is the fact that while the shamanistic community-defence rationale works in cases such as those of the *benandanti* or *táltos*, many spirit-group narratives containing maleficent activities do not immediately lend themselves to this explanatory hypothesis. While we can understand why, in the interests of a good harvest, a *benandanti* warrior may have attacked his envisioned enemy with a fennel stalk, it is not at all clear why, for example, the women described in the *Corrector* hunted down people in 'the silence of the night', killed them, consumed them, and then stuffed their chests with straw by way of resurrection.[51] Neither is it clear why Juliana Winkerin, from Umes, claimed at the turn of the fifteenth century that her company had 'killed and eaten a baby' but then one of them, taking on the role of the fairy queen, had gathered the bones together and had 'brought the child back to life'.[52] Moving further into the early modern period, we find that the community-defence rationale even struggles, at times, to fully explain the ambiguities of the *benandanti* and *táltos* narratives. It is hard to understand, for example, why some of the *benandanti* developed such strange, quasi-intimate relationships with the witches they fought; nor why the 'bad dead' battled by Hungarian *táltos* Erzebet Toth 'appeared as the enemies of her *táltos* battles as well as her summoning companions'.[53] Any rationales that may have lain behind the more malevolent spirit-group narratives, such as those in the Wild Hunt category, are even further from our grasp.

This lack of clarity lies in the fact that envisioned *maleficium*, like basic *maleficium*, is very resistant to analysis. As we saw in CHAPTER EIGHT, any witchcraft suspect's claim to have performed harmful magic of any kind cannot, owing to the likelihood of interrogatorial contamination, be necessarily assumed to relate to any *real* experiences they may have had prior to the interrogation, whether visionary or otherwise. Moreover, for the modern scholar, any movement toward analyzing these claims on the premise that they may have been genuine is inhibited, just as it is with regard to basic *maleficium*, by the challenge to understand the mindset that would consider it acceptable to harm another human being through magical means. And it is here that we find ourselves at the Achilles heel of the shamanistic paradigm. The place where it is most ambiguous and vulnerable to criticism. It is one thing to argue that experiential shamanistic traditions survived into early modern Europe, but unless we can argue, more widely and convincingly, that the malevolent aspects of spirit-group narratives represented shamanistic experience then the hypothesis will always be of limited use. Unless we can ascertain what possible benefit, on either a community or personal level, could be derived from the envisioned spoiling of domestic processes, raising storms, stealing milk or, more gravely, causing sickness and death through the abduction and murder of innocent men, women and children, the shamanistic hypothesis cannot and should not challenge the widespread historiographical view that shamanistic traditions survived into early modern Europe largely on the level of belief and motif as opposed to experience.

But despite these many problems, we cannot do justice to Isobel's confessions, nor fully explore the epistemological dilemmas raised by the maleficent activities described in them, unless we rise to this challenge and attempt to tackle this question in more depth. Therefore, in the next chapter we will attempt to assess, in some detail, the shamanistic credentials of some of the spirit-group *maleficium* featured in Isobel's confessions. This analysis will largely concentrate on one activity: the arrow-shooting. This focus reflects the fact that the latter does not only represent Isobel and her coven at their most maleficent, but also that, of all her coven-related *maleficium*, it displays the firmest links with the perennially malevolent Wild Hunt nexus. As the chapter unfolds, it will become apparent that this analysis also has wider relevance. By shedding light on the shamanistic status of Isobel's spirit-group malevolence we simultaneously shed light on the shamanistic status of this malevolence per se, as it appears in spirit-group narratives throughout medieval and early modern Europe. And by doing so, we also gain some new perspectives on the perennial debate as to whether, and to what extent, more conventional demonological encounter-narratives may have contained a visionary component.

12

'His hour was pursuing him'

As we saw in CHAPTER FOUR, Isobel's claim to have shot elf arrows at humans and animals in the company of an airborne group of spirits was not a unique one. The belief that the fairy host, or *sluagh*, swept up men and women and coerced them to join their hunting forays was a consistent element of Scottish folklore from the seventeenth through to the nineteenth century, and can be subsumed under the European Wild Hunt corpus. Moreover, the possibility that these beliefs, as they appeared in Scotland, possessed a visionary dimension is raised by the fact that we have extant first-hand encounter-narratives emerging from throughout this period. Later examples emerge out of ordinary discourse – in the sense that they were recorded by folklorists questioning Highlanders about their fairy beliefs – and earlier ones generally appear embedded in witchcraft and sorcery records, with this divergence reflecting the fact that in the seventeenth century fairy-related magical practices were frequently prosecuted and demonized.

The latter sources suggest that in the early modern period elf-arrow damage was widely associated with witches, with Edward Cowan recently noting, for example, that 'Witches were often implicated for directing these particular assaults [fairy-arrow shootings], with or without the assistance of the fairies. Isobell Young of Eastbarns (1629), Katharine Oswald in Niddry (1629), Alison Nisbett from Hilton, Berwickshire (1632), John Burgh at Fossoway (1643), and Jane Craig in Tranent (1649) were all alleged to have the ability to cast elfin darts.'[1] While the majority of witchcraft records do not state where, or in whose company, the suspect was when she or he shot the arrows, a small number make the specific link between arrow shooting and participation in fairy host-related activities that emerges strongly in nineteenth-century accounts, and of course in Isobel's confessions. This link appears most prominently in the Bute records of 1662. Here, cunning woman Jonet Morison claimed that the Devil caused her to shoot elf arrows, but also claimed that 'she met with the devil quhen he was goeing by with a great number of men [and] that she asked him quhat were these that went by who answered they are my company and quhen she speired where they were going he answered that they were *going to seek a prey* [my italics]'.[2] Jonet's frequent references to supernatural fairy attacks, through elf-shot or being blasted in a whirl-wind, clearly link this 'great number of men' to the fairy host or *sluagh*; and her reference to the fact she saw her accomplice, Jonet McNicoll, in their company further points to her belief that humans could participate in the host's hunting activities.[3] Jonet's companion Margaret NcLevin did not mention the hunt so specifically, but like Isobel, described participating in a roaming group that shot at victims with elf arrows and then carried away their bodies, with fairy associations being implicated through reference to false bodies or fairy stocks. Margaret claimed that she and her companions 'went to Birgadele broch and in a window [where] Margret NcWilliam shot James Androws son and that Marie More NcCuill was appointed by them to take away the body and leave the stoke of a tree in his place quhich she gat nocht done, she not being so skilfull as she should have been . . . [at a later meeting it] was purposed to shoot one of Robert More McKemies bearnis (haveing taken two of them before) but was disappointed that night'.[4]

The Reasons Why

Examples such as these are suggestive of visionary experience, but if we are to argue that they represented evidence of shamanistic practices, as opposed to merely elaborate false confessions, or one-off dream or vision encounters that just happened to draw on folkloric host-related themes, then we need to establish a shamanistic rationale. But at first glance, such a rationale seems impossible to find, particularly with regard to Isobel. The confessions suggest that at the time of her interrogations both Isobel and the men who questioned her believed that elf-arrow shooting was morally wrong. Indeed, Isobel seems to have reserved her deepest contrition for her hunting activities, not only claiming that 'alace I deserw not to be sitting heir, for I haw done so manie ivill deidis, espe[ci]allie killing of men etc' but also lamenting that her murder, by arrow shot, of William Bower of Moynes 'griews me mor th[a]n any thing th[a]t ewer I did'. But this picture is complicated by the fact that prior to arrest (and perhaps for as long as fifteen years, since she first met the Devil) Isobel seems to have had rather less qualms, and willingly participated in arrow shooting, and all the other types of host-related *maleficium* described in the confessions. She did not, like the *benandante* Paolo Gasparutto, attempt to exonerate herself by claiming to have merely watched, or tried to prevent, her spirit-companions performing *maleficium*. Nor did she mollify her interrogators, as the followers of the Italian Richella seem to have done, by emphasizing that she joined processions in order to gain healing and divinatory knowledge (a trade-off that could be seen to eventually benefit the community). Although Isobel seems to have performed healing charms and rituals, her host-related *maleficium* appears to have been blithely unconnected to either them or their acquisition. She performed rituals to raise winds, steal milk and reduce fertility simply, it would seem, in order to raise winds, steal milk and reduce fertility. And she appears to have performed all her *maleficium* with unabashed gusto. As she set out on her arrow-shooting escapades she shouted enthusiastically, 'horse and hattok in the divellis name'; when she and her companions shot arrows they did so 'at our pleasur'; and most blatantly of all, when Margaret Brodie's arrow missed Harry

Forbes, Isobel's desire to see the job done was so ardent that she begged the Devil to give her a second shot.

In a general sense, the fact that Isobel depicts her host as morally ambiguous is not anomalous. Twentieth-century folklorists sometimes note that in traditional Scottish folklore a distinction was made between good and evil fairy hosts: the *seelie court* being predominantly good and the *unseelie court*, or *sluagh,* being predominantly malevolent.[5] This distinction may have existed and can be seen to reflect the good and evil spirit-group narrative categories that, as Behringer and Cohn have argued, emerged in other parts of Europe. But with regard to Scotland, its influence is debatable. The distinction is largely absent from the works of many nineteenth-century folklorists such as Stewart, Campbell (both J. G. and J. F.), MacGregor and Carmichael, with the latter, for example, flexibly using the term *sluagh* to describe 'a multitudinous host of [hunting] spirits' that, although they were the 'spirits of the departed' and 'put fear and fright, and more than enough, on the men and calves of Clanranald', were also a 'bright heroic' troop who were followed by 'luck of game' and 'fortune'; and whose passing left the air 'filled with music like the tinkling of innumerable bells'.[6] This distinction is also absent from our earliest and richest account of early modern fairy belief, Kirk's *Secret Commonwealth*. Although Kirk claims that some fairies make 'better Essays for Heroick actions then others', this is a general not typological distinction and, like Carmichael, he uses the term *sluagh*, as in *sluagh-maith,* to denote 'the good people' in general and claims that they have 'the same measurs of Virtue and Vice as we'.[7] Equally significantly, this 'good fairy host' versus 'bad fairy host' distinction does not, to my knowledge, emerge from the witchcraft trials. All in all this absence can be seen to support the argument, put forward in the last chapter, that although 'more evil' and 'less evil' examples emerged, on a Europe-wide scale shamanistic spirit-group narratives were characterized by, as Pócs puts it, an 'archaic ambivalence'.[8]

Because no clear conception of 'good fairy host' or 'bad fairy host' emerges from the period, it is difficult to ascertain how Isobel envisaged her host-related activities. The possibility that she self-consciously allied herself with a specifically malevolent fairy host, as opposed to a benevolent one, is contradicted by the fact that she seems to have drawn no clear line between her beneficent activities, such as feasting with the fairy queen, and her maleficent, such as sabotaging dye vats and drawing milk from her neighbour's cows. But on the other hand, even taking into account the demonizing influence of her interrogators, the sheer amount of maleficent magic Isobel claims to have performed with the host suggests that Isobel's fairies were far more malevolent than many described in this period; their exploits contrasting markedly with the more benign activities performed by the fairy-like spirits described by cunning folk like Donald McIlmichall and Andro Man.

But whatever the moral status of Isobel's fairy host, the fact that Isobel participated willingly in their arrow-shooting activities must still be explained, and in respect of the shamanistic hypothesis, a rationale found. As we shall explore in the next chapter, some of Isobel's airborne aggression can arguably be linked to personal vendetta. We know that she was likely to have nurtured grievances against both Harry Forbes and the Laird of Park, and in this context it is pertinent that both men were targets for her arrow-shooting attacks. But putting these cases aside for the moment, it is notable that the overwhelming majority of the arrow-shooting performed by both Isobel and her fellow coven members has a distinct air of arbitrariness, with the attacks seeming to be indiscriminate and directed at no-one in particular. The confessions provide us with frequent lists of the victims, but interestingly many of these are unnamed or only briefly named, with no reason given for why the victims should have provoked such an attack, as illustrated in Isobel's claim that 'margret brodie killed an vowman washing, at the burne of tarres, Bessie wilsone killed an man at the bushe of strutheris Bessie hay in aulderne killed an prettie man, called dunbar at the eist end of the town of forres as he wes coming out at ane gaitt, margret brodj in aulderne killed on david blak in darn-vay', and so on. Isobel's assertion, in the first confession, that her airborne coven shot those passers-by who 'sies thes strawes in whirlewind, and doe not sanctifie them selves', does little to mollify this impression, the punishment being so severely dispropor-tionate to the size of the crime. That this randomness was no accident is suggested by the fact that it is also a characteristic feature of much of the other host-related *malefi-cium* described in the confessions. In the majority of instances, when Isobel draws milk from her neighbour's cows, takes strength from their ale, diverts fish from their nets and helps herself to the food and drink stored in their kitchens and cellars, she does not name the neighbours exploited or indicate that any kind of personal grievance was involved. This broad-spectrum *maleficium*, of which the arrow-shooting forms the apotheosis, seems so pointless and meaninglessly subversive that it roundly challenges us to confront the question: if it represented some kind of shamanistic activity, then what purpose did it serve?

Dark Shamanism

In order to answer this question, we need to move more deeply into the question of visionary aggression. In the last chapter we noted that although scholars working with the shamanistic paradigm have argued that envisioned *maleficium* was a feature of some shamanistic activity in early modern Europe, their findings do not seem immediately relevant to narratives like Isobel's. Envisioned *maleficium* has generally been discussed in relation to specific, well-documented, central, southern and eastern European shamanistic cults such as the *táltos* and *benandanti*, and as a consequence emerges from these studies in the context of epic battles fought in grand arenas (storm-ridden skies, great fields, the pit of hell) with majestic archetypal symbols (shining crosses and dragons) motivated by noble, community-benefiting aims such as obtaining fertility of the fields, protecting towns against earthquakes and so on. But Isobel's seemingly-indiscriminate hunting escapades do not seem to be obviously related to any effort to secure resources for the community, nor to work within a mythological narrative evolved specifically for this purpose.

But this inconsistency may be more to do with scholarly bias, than with any incon-gruity on Isobel's part. What has been under-emphasized, in the field of witchcraft studies as a whole, is the fact that historians working with the shamanistic paradigm generally reflect the contemporary Western preoccupation with the positive aspects of the phenomenon. In the nineteenth and early-twentieth century the shaman was frequently dismissed by scholars as either a neurotic or charlatan, but over the past few decades he has undergone a process of rehabilitation. Among both scholars and popular writers the shaman is now commonly applauded as a person of superior intellect and strength of character. His role as healer, protector of his community and mystic are increasingly emphasized and in respect of these abilities many have lauded him as a mentor who can reveal metaphysical insights to the spiritually-impoverished West. 'It is almost as if a king who had been banished for his folly were reclaiming his realm' enthuses German ethno-psychologist Holger Kalweit: 'Shamanic experiences bring us once again closer to the sacred dimension of nature, and profane science, sacred inspiration, and genuine wisdom are beginning to unite, giving birth to a new kind of metarational science. In other words, the gaping wound of duality is beginning to heal.'[9]

But while this re-framing catches many truths and is a welcome antidote to formerly condescending colonialist attitudes towards tribal communities and their religico-magical belief systems, in the context of shamanism as a whole, it is not accurate. First, it makes it all too easy to sentimentalise the shaman's role, as vividly articulated in the following anecdote by anthropologist Piers Vitebsky:

> A shaman from Nepal met a Westerner who remarked how good it must be to live in harmony with the cosmos. The shaman replied, 'The main part of my job is killing witches and sorcerers. I am terrified every time before I perform a big ritual because I know that each time, one of us has to die.'[10]

More pertinently, recent research in the field emphasizes that much traditional shamanism was, and is, far more aggressive and violent than previously supposed, with an increasing number of scholars eschewing references to 'sacred inspiration' and 'genuine wisdom' in exchange for terms such as 'assault sorcery' and 'ritual predation' to articulate the shamanic experience. Some of the most exciting contemporary studies are emerging from field work undertaken in the Amazon region of South America, with anthropologists Neil Whitehead and Robin Wright noting, in the preface to their 2004 work *In Darkness and Secrecy*, that:

> there has been a marked tendency in the past two or three decades to emphasize the positive, therapeutic and socially integrative dimensions of shamanism . . . [but the] ethnographic experience of Amazonian dark shamanism pointedly contradicts this imagery and, while issues of the politics of representation cannot be ignored, it is obviously the role of anthropology to provide a more adequate interpretation and presentation of actual Amazonian practices. Although recognized, [until now] the 'dark' side – the shamans' power to destroy or inflict harm through sorcery and witchcraft – has received little in-depth attention.[11]

With regard to our exploration into Isobel's envisioned arrow-shootings, what is particularly interesting about these emerging anthropological perspectives is the fact that they emphasize that a significant number of tribal shamanistic practices revolve around the ritual act of killing or, as it is often termed, 'ritual predation'. Also notable, with reference to these 'dark shamanistic traditions' (as they are commonly referred to by anthropologists), is the fact that the envisioned killings undertaken are, like Isobel's arrow-shooting attacks, not easy to fit into the epic, altruistic and aesthetically-pleasing community-defence template sketched out in analyses of the *benandanti, táltos* et al. The trance-killings allegedly performed by Amazonian Yanomamö shaman Wyteli, recorded in powerful detail by the author and researcher Mark Ritchie, may have been undertaken in order to defend his community against a rival tribe, but they were clearly as utilitarian, expedient and ruthless as many other kinds of military endeavour; the shaman's course of action, in this case, being directed by his belief that one of the most powerful ways to weaken an enemy tribe is to kill their male children, both because their deaths prevent them from growing up into warriors and, more pragmatically, because the young are the 'easiest to kill'. According to Ritchie's informant, Wyteli returned from trance one evening, gathered the village around him and told 'story after story of the things he had been doing with his spirits':

> Everyone was very quiet when he talked; no one wanted to miss a word. 'You know that story we heard about the man who just died? I sent my spirits to kill him.' The crowd of warriors, women and children were excited to hear it. 'Remember those babies that died over in Sandy place? My spirits and I traveled over there and blew alowali powder all over them. Within a few days they were all dead. We can be happy that we won't have to worry about those babies growing up and coming back to kill us.' Everyone cheered when they heard what he had done to the babies. They laughed when they heard how helpless their enemies were against his spirits.[12]

The unrepentant brutality of these shaman-narratives, as recorded by Mark Ritchie, have caused some scholars to question their authenticity, although others have acknowledged that they provide an unprecedented, if disturbing, insight into the Yanomamö mind.[13] Whatever one's opinion of Ritchie, however, there is no doubt that in tribal societies throughout the world shamanistic activity is associated with aggression and that when death or sickness strikes, enemy shamans from neighbouring villages or tribes are usually among the prime suspects. Pollock claims that among the Brazilian Kulina 'The shaman's role in illness is not limited to the treatment of the *dori* [illness-causing agent]. He also identifies the enemy shaman who is presumed to have caused the illness, normally (with nonfatal illnesses) a shaman from another village.'[14] Across the other side of the world, in Queensland, Australia, an early observer noted that 'death is always caused by a *turrwan* (great man) of another tribe'.[15]

Anthropological sources suggest that envisioned shamanistic aggression is believed, by those who practice it, to carry a number of benefits. In the first instance, it is energy-efficient, with Yanomamö shaman Jungleman stating pragmatically of his envisioned baby-killing antics: '[it was] so much easier than travelling all the way [there] . . . and trying to kill someone. But the effect was the same.'[16] Another perceived advantage is the fact that because these shamanistic assaults are performed on a visionary level, they are more difficult to detect and counter than physical attacks. In locations as far apart as Australia, South America and Africa it is believed that while the shaman is travelling in subtle-body form during his trance-induced visionary journeys, he can attack and kill either physical bodies, or the subtle bodies of victims who are travelling in a similar way. Frequently the latter deaths are not immediate, but take some time to manifest on the material level. Moreover it is highly pertinent, in the light of our explorations into female-led spirit-group malevolence in the last chapter, to note that the time lag between the moment of the envisioned killing and that of physical death is generally explained through the concept of resurrection. The shaman, in other words, is believed to kill his victim but then, for an unspecified but usually brief length of time, bring him back to life.[17] With regard to the Indians of Bolivia, for example, anthropologist Lévy-Bruhl notes that after killing a man the shaman:

> considers it advantageous for himself to restore to them the appearance of life for a longer or shorter time. At first nothing in them has changed, although he has deprived them of an essential appurtenance without which they cannot continue to live long, that is, according to a current expression, he has 'eaten their soul.' As a matter of fact they are already dead, but their friends and relatives, and often they themselves, do not realize it. They are, as it were, 'respited' dead, and their position may be likened to that of the shell to which a time-fuse has been applied.[18]

The victim, blithely unaware that he has actually been killed on a visionary plane, goes about his normal life in his resurrected form but soon weakens and dies, often from a minor illness.[19] The inevitability of such a death, and the difficulty of tracing its occult cause, renders dark shamanistic aggression the ultimate stealth weapon.

But even more pertinent to our analysis of Isobel's envisioned arrow-shooting activities is the fact that a considerable number of dark shamanistic traditions are even more difficult to link to the community-defence rationale because they involve seemingly arbitrary killings against members of one's own tribe. As anthropologist Johannes Wilbert has recently highlighted, Amazonian Warao shamans who serve Hoebo, the bloodthirsty macaw god of the underworld, hunt and kill men and women in order to feed them to their spirit-master and his people. To this end, the shamans stalk vulnerable members of their 'own or of a neighbouring community' and then, with the aid of spirit familiars, and using a proboscis located in their chest, they suck out the victim's blood before killing them. After the death, the shaman carries the corpse to the underworld and:

> dangling them head down on his back, their heads knocking against his heels with every step he takes in spiteful mockery of his victims . . . the sorcerer carries his victim to the netherworld, following the blood-sodden road along the firmament. After emptying the blood into the trough, the victim is butchered and cooked to feed the shaman's *hoebo* sons [spirit familiars] and local denizens, reserving the heart and liver for the supreme macaw.[20]

326

Recent anthropological studies have revealed that the ritual killings of the *kanaimà*, a dark shamanistic cult from the Amazonian Guyana Highlands, are similarly non-personal. Under instruction from mentors or *kanaimà'san*, the *kanaimà* are believed to ritually stalk, kill and mutilate their human victims by inserting various objects into their mouth and anus and then, some time later, 'return to the dead body of the victim in order to drink the juices of putrefaction'. The cult's bloodthirsty reputation is further intensified by the fact that they are believed to hunt in 'packs' and commonly assume animal form, with nineteenth-century missionary William Brett noting, dramatically, that 'To enjoy the savage delight of killing and devouring human beings, such a person [the *kanaimà*] will assume the shape, or his soul animate the body, of a jaguar, approach the sleeping-places of men, or waylay the solitary Indian in his path.'[21] But as Neil Whitehead notes, these grisly attacks are essentially non-personal:

> Kanaimà . . . was traditionally pictured as a form of vendetta or vengeance and the victims were portrayed as, in some sense, offenders of social norms; but there were many cases, even some cited directly as examples of kanaimà attack, that did not on examination bear that interpretation. It is therefore critical to appreciate that the selection of victims is ultimately a matter of indifference, in the sense that *anyone will do* . . . The phraseology repeatedly used by kanaimàs is to the effect that they are 'hunting for their food' and that means, as with any subsistence hunter, they will take the easiest opportunity [my italics].[22]

In the case of these seemingly-arbitrary killings on members of one's own community the shamanistic rationale is, at first glance, difficult to find. As Whitehead has recently pointed out, not only have anthropologists studying shamanism 'tended to shy away from issues connected to violence', but the secrecy of such traditions, and confusion surrounding their workings and significance even within the host cultures themselves, means that it is only through exceptionally sensitive and impartial inquiry that the deeper logic underpinning them can come to light.[23] But nevertheless, analysis of Wilbert's pioneering study of dark Warao shamanism (1993) reveals that beneath all the dramatic blood-sucking and corpse-carrying there lies a community-defence rationale; with the threat, in this case, not being another tribe, but Hoebo, the macaw god of the underworld himself. According to Warao mythology, since the dawn of time Hoebo has required human flesh and blood to enable himself and his 'macaw people' to survive and if not satisfied in this respect he has the means to completely annihilate human kind. Through a series of historic events a compromise was reached through which the dark shamans took on the responsibility of managing the macaw god's human food supply. By acting as a kind of intermediary between their tribe and the deity the shamans perform a protective function. Not only do they prevent Hoebo from destroying the Warao people by providing him with the food he needs, but they also minimise his destructive effects by regulating his appetite, acting like a keeper who throws a caged beast just enough meat to prevent it breaking out of its compound in a frenzied search for food. As Wilbert notes, the Warao belief that these shamans, following their ancestors the *'hoa* fathers', are 'empowered to ration the macaw people's food supply and manage their survival is certainly of great (psychological) benefit to

327

humans and makes tolerating dark shaman sorcerers in their midst more bearable'.[24]

Although it is harder to identify, the ritual killings of the *kanaimà* seem to have a similarly cosmos-balancing and dark-force allaying rationale at their root. Whitehead notes that after their murders the *kanaimà* give some of their *maba* and body parts to their mentors (*kanaimà'san*) and that by virtue of the latter's special relationship with Makunaima, the creator of plants and animals, this exchange has a culturally-beneficent effect:

> These 'gifts of death' from the kanaimàs to their kanaimà'san are part of and historically drive the undending exchanges between divine animals and mundane humans in the guise of hunter and prey. It is this relationship that the kanaimà'san claims to sustain or influence through his special access to Makunaima, ultimate creator of animals and plants. This key role in the creation and management of the predatory interrelation of humanity, animality, and divinity through koumi-based magic is why the kanaimà is the source of powerful shamanic techniques.[25]

On a more pragmatic level, the beneficial aspect of the dark shaman's practice is even more tangibly expressed in the fact that, through their intimacy with the predatory forces of sickness and death, they are often believed to possess particular kinds of healing ability. After noting the Warao shaman's role in rationing the macaw people's food supply, Wilbert also notes that, 'to the Warao it is equally redeeming that predation by the netherworld is reined in even more through the healing power of dark shamans, conversely ensuring the survival of humanity'.[26] Through their role as Hoebo's helpers, Warao dark shamans are uniquely qualified to cure the diseases that the macaw deity persistently leashes on mankind, with Wilbert claiming that 'As soon as adults or children suffer from sharp pain in their bodies or experience internal bleeding . . . people send for a dark shaman healer to cure them of what they presume is *hoa* sickness.'[27] The relationship between the *kanaimà* and healing is more ambigious, however the intimate link between the power to kill and the power to cure is reflected in the fact that a *kanaimà* can also be a *piya* (that is, a shaman who can both heal and harm), and that in some traditions *piya* can act as tutors to novice *kanaimà*, or guard their bodies while they are out hunting and heal them if injured (with this mutually-protective alliance being redolent of the paradoxical intimacy between the *benandanti* and the Friulian witches).[28] Finally, as we shall explore in later chapters, both *kanaimà* and dark Warao shamans can employ their dark magical powers to defend their tribe, or an individual client, against enemies.[29] In the last analysis, shamans who possess this kind of intimacy with the forces of sickness and death are like the proverbial guns in the cupboard: nobody wants them to be there and nobody wants to have to use them – but at certain times, for better or for worse, they are simply very useful.

The Corsican *Mazzeri*

With regard to Isobel's arrow-shooting passages, the literature on dark shamanism is clearly pertinent and we must explore it in more depth. But we shall begin this analysis, paradoxically, by moving away from anthropological studies and focusing on a body of research compiled closer to home. While most of the literature relating to dark shamanism arises from the study of non-European tribal societies, in the nineteenth and mid-twentieth century historians and folklorists compiled a small, but compelling, body of evidence surrounding a dark shamanistic cult that existed in Corsica until recent times. Known as the *mazzeri*, this cult (which enjoys a predominantly – but not exclusively – female membership) has been most comprehensively explored, in the English language, by folklorist Dorothy Carrington in *The Dream-Hunters of Corsica* (1995).

The existence of the *mazzeri,* which is extraordinary on many counts, has been noted by some scholars working with the shamanistic paradigm, but primarily in passing. Ginzburg mentions them in *Ecstasies* but, en route to bigger things, he merely gives a brief description of their activities and notes that their tradition, though 'unusual' in many ways, still betrays a 'morphological proximity' to the *warrior shamanism* of the *benandanti, táltos, kresniki* and werewolf traditions. But here, in regard to our analysis of Isobel's confessions, the *mazzeri* merit closer attention. Research into the Corsican cult is extremely valuable, not only because it represents detailed and relatively impartial analysis of dark shamanistic practice, but also because the tradition under analysis is of European – and allegedly archaic – origin.[30] As such, this research provides us with the most in-depth and unbiased insight into a dark shamanistic cult, as it may have existed in early modern Europe, to have come down to us in the modern age.

The *mazzeri* believed that their spirits periodically left their bodies and roamed the countryside, sometimes alone but more commonly in packs, in pursuit of animals: either barehanded or armed with basic weapons such as sticks, stones or cudgels. When the animals were tracked down, they were killed and eaten, with the women usually 'tear[ing] their prey to death with their teeth, like hounds'.[31] The most notable aspect of this chain of events, however, is the fact that after the *mazzere's* quarry had been wounded or killed, it was recognized by its aggressor as a human relative or neighbour. Dorothy Carrington explains that 'Having killed an animal the *mazzere* rolls it onto its back, stares at it closely, and for a brief moment, "in a flash" as I have heard say, he recognizes the face of someone known to him, nearly always an inhabitant of his village, who may also be one of his kin.'[32] Significantly, the animal's death almost always presages the death of its human counterpart, a chain of events that constitutes, in effect, murder on a visionary plane. According to Carrington again, 'the spirit of the *mazzere,* when hunting, meets the spirit of his victim, a human being who has assumed animal form. When he kills the animal he severs spirit from body; the body may linger on for some time afterwards, but this life is only a reprieve and inevitably the body will sicken and die.'[33] Less commonly, a *mazzere* might only wound an animal, in which case its human incarnation merely becomes sick or meets with an accident. Carrington speculates that the *mazzeri* traditions are very old, and that its essential amorality and central theme of hunting as opposed to fertility put its origins at the hunter-gatherer stage of human evolution.[34]

As with Isobel's visionary adventures, it is difficult, at first glance, to detect the

This sixteenth-century woodcut by a European traveller to the Amazon depicts men being attacked by aggressive spirits of the Tupi, some of which are in animal or human/animal hybrid form. Contemporaries described these spirits as 'ferocious, cannibalistic, kidnappers of women, and assassins of men', but anthropologists have suggested that these early depictions were simplistic interpretations of dark shamanistic practice, as found among the Guyanese *kanaimà* (Whitehead 2002: 48–50). The John Carter Brown Library at Brown University.

This sixteenth-century woodcut by Lucas Cranach the Elder contains all the sensationalism associated with werewolf activity in the early modern age. But torn clothes and scattered body parts aside, it is notable that the werewolf's core activities – hunting, killing and consuming human beings – are no different to those calmly confessed to by Corsican *mazzeri* four hundred years later.

shamanistic rationale that lay behind the activities of the *mazzeri*. The visionary events were primarily concerned with bringing sickness and death to one's own community and we cannot detect either the prosperity-generating rationale that underpins house-to-house processions or the community-defending rationale that underpins battles for fertility and good weather. As with Isobel's fairy-related malevolence, it is not at all apparent, at first glance, how perfectly sane people could have considered themselves to have participated in such activities on a regular basis, nor how these bloodthirsty traditions could have benefited, or been tolerated by, the Corsican community.

But a key to this question can be found in the issue of volition. One of the most notable features of the *mazzeri* tradition is the fact that the visionaries claimed that their murderous behaviour was largely out of their control, with Carrington noting that the latter were:

> to use the Corsican expression, 'called' to hunt, 'called' to kill; the order was absolute; they could not even choose their victims. *Mazzeri*, it seems, have no animosity towards the animal they have to kill, nor towards the human being it represents.[35]

The nature of this call to kill is vividly described in Carrington's account of a personal meeting with a female *mazzere*, in the Sartenais region of Corsica:

> 'It still happens that I go out at night' she [the *mazzera*] began, 'over there, on that mountainside.' (She was pointing across the valley.) 'I tear my flesh and my clothes.' (Her clothes were in fact torn and there was clotted blood on her legs and hands.) 'It is stronger than I (the need to hunt), 'the blood wills it so. I have rendered my daughter exactly as I am' . . . 'It is better ,' she concluded, 'to die in my way than like those they cut down in the wars.' She had been speaking almost without pause, in melodious, rhythmic phrases, verging on music; now she passed naturally into song. In that high, thin poignant voice in which Corsican women mourn the dead, she began to chant . . . Then, abruptly, she disappeared. With the dynamic vitality that characterized all her movements she suddenly strode away, into the maquis, out of sight.[36]

After the woman had disappeared, Carrington's companion, a native Corsican, told her 'I think she's gone hunting . . . You saw how tense and restless she was, and how she was hovering on the edge of the village when we arrived. I think she's been called.'[37]

This uncontrollable urge to engage in ecstatic violence can be likened to a form of battle-frenzy, and was clearly so powerful and indiscriminate that some *mazzeri* felt deep remorse and sorrow after their nocturnal killing sprees. On one occasion a *mazzeru* told Carrington that his grandmother, who was herself a *mazzera* 'informed a female member of the family [in the morning] that she had killed her child, that night, in a dream. She regretted what she had done, but it was not she who had committed the act, but something that had entered into her. She would make amends.'[38] On another occasion, a native Corsican named Jean Cesari told the folklorist that he had once encountered a *mazzere* while visiting his cousins in the mountains. Cesari noted that:

The look in his eyes was very strange. The night before, he told us, he had taken part in a boar hunt in the forest of Ospedale. He had shot a boar in the shoulder, the boar got away but he thought he had killed it. About a week later I met the old man again. He was distressed. He had just received news that his nephew in Marseilles had died of a cancer of the lung. Then I knew that the old man was a *mazzere*. I shall never forget the look in his eyes.[39]

Telling here, is the fact that the experience of being taken over by an irresistible power is not exclusive to the *mazzeri*. It is common feature of shaman narratives worldwide; being particularly prominent in accounts of initiation, where the spirit-encountering experiences can be so spontaneous, overwhelming and uncontrollable that they characteristically manifest as a form of temporary psychosis. As we have seen in CHAPTER TEN, even when the individual accepts the shamanic vocation and learns how to control and manipulate his visions, this process is less a matter of taking total command than learning how to surrender to the inevitable and manage and negotiate his visions through a reciprocal process of give and take. Moreover, while the shaman learns how to induce visionary experience at will, the urge to enter into these states that initially propelled him into the shamanic vocation often continues to have a life of its own and it is not uncommon for shamans to depict the visionary impulse as an accumulation of psychological tension that has to be released, by 'shamanizing', in order to restore physiological equilibrium and avoid becoming either physically or mentally sick. According to Holger Kalweit, 'The Yakut shaman Tüsput, who was critically ill for more than twenty years, could only find relief from his suffering whenever he conducted a seance during which he fell into a trance. In the end he fully regained his health by this method. However, if he held no seances over a period of time he once again began to feel unwell, exhausted and indecisive.'[40] Alternatively, Van Deusen claims of Turkic Khakass shaman Slava Kuchenov that: 'If he doesn't perform [a shamanic séance], Slava feels ill – the spirits are bothering him', adding that when he has no other alternative, the shaman makes his wife 'sit down and listen' to him summon his spirits just so he 'won't get really sick'.[41] This compulsion can also be seen in early modern sources. The sixteenth-century century German visionary Chonrad Stoeckhlin claimed that on regular occasions an angel appeared before him and 'commanded' him to leave his body and travel with the 'phantoms of the night', with Behringer emphasizing that, 'He had no choice about taking part in his trip with the phantoms . . . Shortly before he was to go off travelling he would be overcome by a lethargy, an unconsciousness.'[42] Similarly, Ginzburg refers to the *benandanti's* motivation to participate in the Ember battles as an 'irresistible' urge.[43]

The *mazzeri's* claim that it was not only the entry into visionary experience, but also the acts of predation and killing that were propelled by this irresistible compulsion is paralleled in dark shamanistic traditions in other parts of the world. The dark shaman of the Amazonian Warao does not kill men and women because he wants to but because, as Wilbert notes, 'his macaw folk will keep prodding him for sustenance. Thus, with compulsive intermittent regularity, the veteran shaman must continue carrying blood and corpses to the netherworld'.[44] The following account suggests that, as with shamanistic compulsion in general, the tension that finally expresses itself through ecstatic violence builds up over a period of time:

> The ancient Hoebo (as red macaw) and his parrot retinue have an insatiable appetite and keep asking for human fare. They do this mostly via the dark shaman's spirit sons, who appear to him in dreams . . . the shaman stalls and propitiates them at least four times with palm starch and tobacco before agreeing to comply. But when the spirit children appear a fifth time to demand their proper food, he can no longer turn them away unsatisfied.[45]

The same compulsion is even more clearly spelt out in the following account of ritual trance-killing among the South American *kanaimà*, in which an initiate claims that after being taken into the forest and given some herbs to drink, 'he lay there some time [after which] he feels his spirit moved out and then he saw a woman in her farm . . . He killed her with his hands and stopped her up . . . He didn't really know what he was doing.'[46] Spreading our net wider, Cohn cites at length a testimony from west Africa in which a sane woman freely confesses to having ridden by night on animals, in the company of others, in order to kill and subsequently eat a number of people, including her husband. Part of her account states:

> Two days later I went to visit the accused [a fellow witch] in chief Maranda's area. I went at night on a hyena's back. I stood outside the hut where the accused was sleeping. The infant was in the accused's arms. We pulled the baby and later I rode off on my hyena . . . We wanted to bewitch the child – I cannot tell the reason because it only came to us as if we were dreaming. We fought over the child. We wanted to bewitch the child so it would die. We wanted to eat it.[47]

Compulsion in Scotland

With regard to our analysis of the shamanistic status of Isobel's fairy-related *maleficium*, what is highly pertinent here is the fact that this kind of shamanistic compulsion can be clearly detected in Scotland's host-related arrow-shooting narratives, as they have emerged from the seventeenth through to the nineteenth century. The following account, told to Victorian folklorist J. F. Campbell by a local doctor, for example, contains something of the urgency and expectation that characterized Carrington's accounts of the Sartenais *mazzera* (with both protagonists seeming to sense that their 'call' was coming through a build-up of psychological tension). Campbell claimed that, after pointing to a particular hill, the doctor told him:

> "Do you see that kind of shoulder on the hill? Well, a man told me that he was walking along there with another who used to 'go with the fairies', and he said to him – 'I know that they are coming for me this night. If they come, I must go with them; and I shall see them come, and the first that come will make a bow to me, and pass on; and so I shall know that they are going to take me with them.' 'Well,' said the man, 'we had not gone far when the

man called out, "'Tha iad so air tighin.' These are come. I see a number of 'sluagh' the people; and now they are making bows to me. And now they are gone." And then he was quiet for a while. Then he began again; and at last he began to cry out to hold him, or that he would be off.' "Well," said the doctor . . . "he was fairly lifted up by the 'sluagh' and taken away from him, and he found him about a couple of miles further on, laid on the ground. He told him that they had carried him through the air, and dropped him there. And," said the doctor, "that is a story that was told me as a fact, a very short time ago, by the man whom I was attending."[48]

The compulsive quality of host participation is even more evident in anecdotes depicting men or women consistently reluctant to accept their call. Campbell's contemporary Alexander Carmichael claimed that a Uist woman told him about a Benbecula man to whom the fairies were unfortunately 'partial':

His friends assured me that night became a terror to this man, and that ultimately he would on no account cross the threshold after dusk. He died, they said, from the extreme exhaustion consequent on these excursions. When the spirits [the *sluagh*] flew past his house, the man would wince as if undergoing a great mental struggle, and fighting against forces unseen of those around him.[49]

As with the *mazzeri*, the same kinds of visionary impulse that drove the Highlanders into trance also seems to have driven them to kill. Those who believed themselves to have been swept up by the fairy host never claimed to have shot elf arrows willingly, but emphasized that they had been forced or commanded to do so by the fairies, with Carmichael noting dramatically that the host 'commanded men to follow them, and men obeyed, having no alternative. It was these men of earth who slew and maimed at the bidding of their spirit-masters.'[50] The following anecdote from Campbell is also illustrative:

An old highlander declared to me that he was once in a boat with a man who was struck by a fairy arrow. He had the arrow for a long time; it was slender like a straw for thickness. He himself drew it out of the temple of the other man, where it was stuck in the skin through the bonnet. They were then miles from shore, fishing. A man, whom the fairies were in the habit of carrying about from island to island, told him that he had himself thrown the dart at the man in the boat by desire of *them*: '*they* made him do it.' My informant evidently believed he was speaking truth . . . [51]

A letter written by Welsh cartographer Edward Lhuyd in 1699, regarding his recent travels through Scotland, suggests that the same psychological dynamics occurred, with regard to arrow shooting, two hundred years earlier: Lhuyd claiming that the 'Vulgar throughout this Country' related 'many Instances' of fairy-arrow shooting, and that 'As to this *Elf-stricking*, their Opinion is, that the Fairies (having not much Power themselves to hurt Animal Bodies) do sometimes carry away Men in the Air, and furnishing them with Bows and Arrows, employ them to shoot Men & Cattle, &c.'[52]

That this belief was widespread in the early modern period is further supported by the fact that wherever contemporary first-hand accounts of participation in host-related arrow-shooting emerge (which is usually, as we saw earlier, in witchcraft records) the protagonists claim, like their descendants 200 years later, that they were ordered or coerced to shoot and kill their victims by the host or host leader; generally defined in these cases as the Devil, as opposed to a fairy. The power of these kinds of visionary impulses and the degree to which they could subsume personal will, is clearly and painfully indicated in the records given by Bute woman Margaret NcWilliam (1662) who, as we have seen earlier, participated in a coven that engaged in host-related arrow-shooting:

> [she claimed that] about 18 yeires syne being dwelling in Chapeltoune the devill apeired to her at the back of the Caleyaird and she haveing sustained losse by the death of horse and kye was turneing to great poverty he said unto her be not affrayed for yow shall get ringes eneugh and requiring . . . he sought her sone William a child of 7 yeires old which she promised to him and he gave her ane elf arrow stone to shott him which she did ten dayes therafter that the child dyed immediately therafter which grieved her most of anything that ever she did.[53]

In the context of our discussion concerning dark shamanism, we can speculate that during a period of intense physical and psychological suffering, Margaret succumbed to a visionary impulse that caused her to participate in a host-related hunt during the course of which she aimed an arrow at her own son. And that when the experience was over, or in other words, when she had regained normal consciousness, she looked back in horror at what she had done. Although it does not specifically mention arrow-shooting, cunning woman Janet Trall's (1623) account, given to the Perth session in 1623, describing how the leader of what appears to have been the fairy host commanded her to harm people, is also strongly suggestive of the same visionary dynamic. Trall stated:

> 'When I was lieing in child bed lair, I was drawn forth from my bed to a dub near my house door in Dunning, and was there puddled and troubled.' Being asked by whom this was done? She answered, 'by the fairy folks, who appeared some of them red, some of them grey, and riding upon horses. The principal of them that spake to me was like a bonny white man, riding upon a grey horse.' She said, 'He desired me to speak of God, and do good to poor folks' . . . Being asked the cause why she was so much troubled by them? She answered, that the principal of them had bidden her do ill, by casting sickness upon people, and she refused to do it.[54]

The notion that the visionary impulse can have been so overpowering that it caused individuals not only to harm innocent people but also, as in Margaret NcWilliam's case, to harm their own children may seem far-fetched, but clear parallels can be found in both the *mazzeri* and Amazonian material. Claiming that 'The *mazzeri* could be ordered to kill those they loved the most', Carrington cites the case of a woman who was possessed by an 'irresistible impulse' to attack a dog, despite knowing that it was the representation of her husband, with his death duly following a few days later. On another occasion Carrington claimed that a *mazzeru* told her 'Once I had to kill a bull with a knife . . . Imagine my horror when I recognized the animal as my poor father! I did no more than strike it, and I withdrew the knife immediately. My poor father broke his leg. He was very ill, but he recovered.'[55] Similarly, in the contemporary Amazonian village of Paramakatoi, a 'widely respected' local nurse, when describing the activities of the *kanaimà* sect to Neil Whitehead, maintained that 'the kanaimàs are hunting during certain points of the year, when they can get access . . . If you learned to kill you must then kill – they have the urge to kill and it might even be a brother or sister.'[56]

Through these cross-comparisons between anthropological studies, *mazzeri* research, nineteenth-century narratives and early modern witchcraft testimonies, we can begin to make sense of the experiences that may have underpinned Isobel's arrow-shooting descriptions. Although, as noted earlier, Isobel's confessions contain indications that she willingly participated in, or even relished, her bloodthirsty experiences, in the context of our discussion about compulsion it is highly significant that on at least five occasions Isobel specifically states that she had been encouraged, and even at times commanded, to shoot her arrows by the Devil. Early in the second confession, she claims that the Devil oversaw the arrow-making process after which he 'giwes them [elf arrows] to ws each of vs so mony . . . [and] Qwhen (*damaged – words missing*) giwes th[e]m to ws he sayes shoot thes in my name'; while later, she confessed that 'the divell gaw me an arrow, and cawsed me shoot an vowman in that fieldis: q[uhi]lk I did and she fell down dead'. In the third confession Isobel emphasizes that when her coven came across Harry Forbes going to Moynes 'the divell gaw margret brodie an arrow to shoot at him' and that 'the divell cawsed me to shoot at the Laird of park as he wes croceing the burne of the boath'. And in the fourth confession she reiterates that 'the divell dightis th[e]m & the elf boyes quhytis them, we got ewrie on ws so many of th[e]m from the divell to shoot at men'. The fact that the Devil was in command of the arrow-shooting process is most clearly indicated in the fact that, as in the cases of Forbes and Park, he could also prevent, as well as encourage, coven members from shooting. In the context of our analysis into dark shamanism, these perspectives invite us to speculate that Isobel's arrow-shooting passages may have reflected compulsive acts of shamanistic aggression experienced prior to arrest. Like her Victorian counterparts 200 years later, she may have been periodically seized by an irresistible impulse that propelled her into an envisioned bloodlust, or battle-frenzy, during which she loosed elf arrows at the men, women and animals that became, during the course of her deep dreams or trances, identified as prey. On recovering from these experiences, Isobel may have looked back in horror at what she had done. Certainly, her heartfelt claim that 'th[a]t q[uhi]ch trowbles my conscience most is the killing of sewerall persones, with the arrowes q[uhi]ch I gott from the divell' evokes, as do the lamentations of child-shooting Bute woman Margaret NcWilliam, the retrospective, post-vision remorse of the Corsican *mazzeri*.

The Rationale

But while these perspectives give us an insight into the psychological mechanisms that may have propelled Isobel into her envisioned arrow-shooting experiences, for the experience to be defined as shamanistic the question of rationale still remains. What community benefit could possibly have emerged from these strange bouts of ecstatic violence? How could Isobel's contemporaries have profited from the fact that she, and others like her, felt intermittently compelled to enter into trances and kill or wound the innocent inhabitants of their local towns and villages?

Here again, the *mazzeri* provide us with a clue. As a result of her research into the Corsican cult, Carrington concluded that their visionary rites were linked to ancient beliefs concerning knowledge of death. Crucially, the *mazzeri* did not keep their violent experiences to themselves, but always informed those they had either killed or seen killed, of their impending death, with Carrington claiming that 'The next day he [the *mazzeru*] will tell what he has seen, and the person mentioned invariably dies in the space of time running from three days to a year'.[57] Similarly, with regard to the annual battles between the *mazzeri* of different villages, Carrington notes, 'The *mazzeri* killed in combat were condemned to die within a year; sometimes they were found dead in their beds on the very morning of the next day. The village that lost most *mazzeri* would lose more lives in the coming year than the opposing village of the victorious *mazzeri*. The inhabitants of the villages were deeply concerned by these phantom battles, [and] even participated in them.'[58] Carrington emphasizes that in serving 'to lift a fragment of the veil that covers the mystery of dying' the actions of the Corsican visionaries were more explanatory and predictive than causative. In other words, at its root the *mazzeri* experience was a shamanistic act of death-divination.[59]

Can we suppose that the envisioned arrow-shooting experiences of Isobel and her contemporaries mirrored the same rationale? And can we suppose that their violent envisioned rites were valued because, like the rites of the *mazzeri*, they offered their communities the opportunity to lift 'a fragment of the veil that covers the mystery of dying' and gain valuable knowledge of those who were about to die? Interestingly, that something like this may have been the case gains support from a number of quarters. First, we have the fact that although the content of their grisly dreams and visions was sensitive, to say the least, Scottish arrow-shooting visionaries – as they emerge from the seventeenth century onwards – were clearly not shy about publicizing them. The anecdotes and eyewitness accounts found in the collections of nineteenth-century folklorists make it clear that in this period the men and women who joined the fairy hunt broadcast their experiences both to their victims and to the community at large. Two of the anecdotes recorded by J. G. Campbell are illustrative here. In the first, after the sudden death of a 'handsome, strong, healthy woman of the name of MacLean' from Saalun, on the Isle of Tiree, an Uist man named Neill Sgrob was reputed to have 'said himself' that he had had been compelled by the fairies to shoot the woman with an elf arrow through an open window.[60] And in the second, a cooper named Donald, from Gorthan Dubh, in Lorn, was digging when an elf arrow hit his spade. Several days later a local man named 'Calum Clever', who was 'frequently carried about by the Fairies', told the cooper that he had shot the arrow 'at the instigation of the Fairies, who wanted to take Donald himself' in order for him to work for them.[61] That such admissions were the stuff of real life and not just anecdote is suggested by J. F. Campbell's claim, seen earlier in this chapter, that an 'old highlander' who 'evidently believed he was speaking truth' told the folklorist that while out fishing he witnessed his companion be shot and wounded in the head by an elf arrow only to be told later, by a man 'whom the fairies were in the habit of carrying about from island to island', that 'he had himself thrown the dart at the man in the boat by desire of *them*: "*they* made him do it"'.[62]

With regard to the early modern period, where arrow-shooting accounts generally appear in witchcraft records, our assessment must be more speculative, but we can nevertheless assume that something comparable occurred. The testimonies taken down in witchcraft trials make it abundantly clear that during the interrogations themselves the suspects' alleged arrow-shooting activities and the identity of their victims, were often well-known to all of the participants involved, although of course it is difficult to be certain as to how far this knowledge was revealed as a result of the interrogation process and how far it had been pre-trial currency. That the latter was the case in seventeenth-century Nairnshire is suggested by Isobel's claim, in her third confession, that 'Janet breadheid spows to Jon taylor told me a litl befor she wes apprehendit th[a]t margret wilsoen in aulderne shot allexr hutcheon in aulderne'. That arrow-shooting experiences were shared outside the courts is also intimated by Lhuyd's claim, in 1699, that beliefs surrounding enforced elf-arrow-shooting activities were believed by the 'Vulgar throughout this Country'.[63]

But although these perspectives suggest that the pronouncements of early modern and later arrow-shooting visionaries were 'divinatory-like', it is difficult, on the basis of so few sources, to ascertain how far they were circulated merely as ghoulishly-themed anecdotes (to be passed from fireside to fireside to chill the bones but not be taken too seriously) and how far they were circulated as active, formal death-divinations that included the all-important transmission between envisioned killer and victim. It is also difficult to ascertain how far the Scottish visionary interpreted his aggressive visionary impulses, as did his *mazzeri* counterpart, as a prophetic vocation undertaken in service to his community.

However, although direct evidence is hard to find, the death-divinatory hypothesis becomes more probable when considered in the light of the fact that the prediction of future death was a major concern for the pre-industrial Scots. A wide variety of signs and portents of death were known – and warily watched out for – by the general population: visions of funeral processions or coffins being made; eerie sounds of glasses rattling at wakes; apparitions of the wraiths or physical doubles of the about-to-die; encounters with crows or ravens and so on. Interest in this area was so great that death-divination was one of the core preoccupations of popular visionaries, from the early modern period through to the nineteenth century, with folklorist Isabel Grant claiming that 'The visions of people who had the Second Sight *were largely concerned with a future death* [my italics]'.[64] Moreover, the sobriety of the death-divination and the seriousness with which it was received, is evinced by the fact that in many cases it was not delivered as hysterical doom-mongering, but as precise and considered assessments based on specific visible signs. With regard to the seer's ability to determine the time of a man's demise by the position of his death shroud, Kirk noted:

> [the seer] saw a winding-shroud creep up on a walking healthfull persons legs, till it came to the knee, and afterwards it came up to the midle, then to the shoulders, and at last over the head, which was visible to no other person. And by observing the spaces of time betwixt the several stages, he easily guess'd how long the man was to live who wore the shroud, for when it approached his head, he told that such a person was ripe for the Grave.[65]

The fact that a culture can be obsessed with knowing the nearness of death is, at first glance, difficult for the modern Western mind to understand. For those who live in a world where the average life expectancy exceeds seventy years, such a desire seems unnecessarily pessimistic and morbid. But in pre-industrial communities, where death is frequent, heartbreakingly indiscriminate and often fearfully sudden, the desire to know the nearness, date, and manner of the event assumes an ominous importance. Medieval and early modern images depicting the allegory of the Dance of Death (some of which we have seen in CHAPTER SEVEN, page 152), and in which the skeletal representation of the grim reaper walks beside the farmer's plough, tugs at the nobleman's sleeve or pulls the young child from the arms of his helpless mother, are vivid pictorial representations of how, in the pre-industrial European mentality, neither status, youth nor dilligent labour were a defence against mortality's ever-present threat. In regions at war, or where violence was endemic, as was the case in both seventeenth-century Nairnshire and pre-modern Corsica, this menace was further exaggerated. In these contexts, the fore-knowledge of death offered many comforts: it enabled men and women to be ready for their enemy; empowered them to set their houses in order; and inspired them to make the most of their remaining time on earth, whether through readying their souls for God or throwing themselves into some kind of bittersweet 'monster's ball'. Equally importantly, the fore-knowledge of death could also offer the opportunity for evasion: Kirk claiming that after looking into a sheep bone, a seer would not only be able to divine 'if any will die out of that house for that moneth' but also, as a consequence of this, 'prescribe a preservative and prevention'.[66] Death-averting divinations could also occur at the moment of vision itself: Kirk again recording an account in which a seer 'perceivd a person standing by him (sound to others veiw) wholy gored in blood, and he – (amazed-like) bid him instantly flee: the whole man laught at his art and warning, sinc there was no appearance of danger: he had scarc contracted his lips from laughter, when unexpectedly his enemy [the fairies] leapt in at his side and stab'd him'.[67]

Agents of Death

But compelling as these perspectives are, the objection could easily be raised that, however conducive the cultural conditions, if Isobel's envisioned arrow shooting was part of a death-divinatory tradition then it differed radically from others operating in

Scotland in the period in that death was not merely predicted through the interpretation of envisioned events, but was predicted because an individual underwent a visionary experience in which they were the agent of death themselves. Unlike Kirk's seer described above, Isobel did not just claim to have observed the fairy host attacking a man with elf arrows, but claimed that she herself, in the company of the host, loosed the arrows from her own hand.

However, looked at through a long lens, this contradiction is not as illogical as it may at first seem. Fairies were perceived as powerful agents of supernatural harm in the period to the extent that, second to that of bewitchment, fairy-malevolence was one of the most common explanations for death and sickness offered by contemporary cunning folk. But despite the threat they posed, the fact that men and women from all walks of life, and particularly magical practitioners, propitiated, and in the latter case conversed and openly negotiated with, the fairies indicates that they were not universally shunned as spiritual murderers or cosmological pariahs, to be avoided or condemned at all costs. This cultural condonation of 'fraternizing with the enemy' worked, in large part, on the premise that the beings who were best informed about death and sickness were the agents of death and sickness themselves. Kirk, for example, attributed the seers' death-divining shroud-visions to 'the operations of these forecasting invisible people among us (indulg'd thorow a stupendious providence to give warnings of som remarkable events, either in the Air, Earth, or Waters)'; while Ayrshire cunning woman Bessie Dunlop (1576) claimed that when she wished to cure sick animals or humans she would directly proposition her fairy familiar, Tom Reid, for advice and aid, even when the sickness was believed to be fairy-derived.[68] But even more significant, with regard to the question in hand, is the fact that in this period it was not only acceptable to converse with death-bringing fairies but also to be surprisingly intimate with them. As we have seen many times already, witchcraft records, kirk session minutes, stories, anecdotes and ballads are filled with accounts of people not only petitioning the fairy folk for divinatory knowledge and healing advice, but entering into fairy hills and feasting, dancing and making music with them, participating in their house-to-house processions and airborne cavalcades, acting as midwives and wet nurses to their children and, most notably of all, becoming their sexual partners or spouses. These sources suggest that, as opposed to being fastidious about the fairies' moral nature, the pragmatic Scots believed that if becoming the drinking buddy, lover, husband or wife of a fairy enabled a magical practitioner to better protect their community against the spirit's ill effects then such activities should be encouraged, or at least tolerated. Given this high level of intimacy and involvement, on an imaginative level the step between the claim to have ridden with the host while they were shooting arrows, and the claim to have ridden with the host while they were shooting arrows and to have also shot arrows oneself, does not seem so significant.

But while Isobel and her contemporaries may have been able to take this step on an imaginative level, on a moral level it must have been highly problematic. In order for a society to tolerate an arrow-shooting divinatory tradition it must not only accept that a visionary might feast, drink, make alliances with or marry the agents of sickness and death, but also accept that they might help them attack and kill members of their own community. However much an individual maintained – as arrow-shooting protagonists seem to have frequently done – that they were coerced into performing these violent acts, the fact that they participated in them at all put them in a very dangerous position. In the closed arena of inter-personal village tensions, where even a look, touch or muttered phrase coming from the wrong person could be identified as an act of witchcraft, it is difficult to see how death-divinatory traditions that involved people waking up in the morning and confessing to their relatives and neighbours that they had shot and killed them with elf arrows the night before, and that as a consequence they would soon sicken and die, could have escaped both local community censure and church prohibition. Given the fact that in the early modern period court records clearly indicate that those who confessed to, or were accused of, shooting elf arrows (whether independently or in the company of a host) were frequently condemned as witches, both by the authorities who led the investigations and the neighbours who provided the witness statements, it is also hard to understand how such a tradition could have persisted through this period, with its integrity intact, to emerge, largely undemonized, in the arrow-shooting beliefs and experiences recorded by the nineteenth-century folklorists. But it is here, where our rationale seems to fail us, that we can usefully return to the Corsican *mazzeri*.

The *Mazzeri* and Fate

Dorothy Carrington emphasizes that although *mazzeri* traditions involved nocturnal killing sprees, during which the participants believed themselves to attack, kill and even eat members of their own community, they were largely tolerated by ordinary Corsicans. In part, this toleration was rooted in the fact that their divinatory abilities were valued, with Carrington noting that although the *mazzeri*'s role as agents and harbingers of sickness and death meant that they were often feared and avoided, they were frequently 'looked on with respect because they possessed exceptional gifts'. At its most esteemed, the *mazzeri* vocation could even be worn as a badge of honour, with a Corsican psychoanalyst telling the folklorist that some of his patients 'were proud of having a *mazzere* in their families'.[69] The *mazzeri* also escaped censure because, despite the savagery of their visionary activities, they were not unduly aggressive or antagonistic, Carrington claiming that 'in daily life they are inoffensive and steer clear of hostilities.'[70]

But while practitioner-inoffensiveness and a societal need for divinatory skills may have contributed towards the Corsicans' acceptance of the *mazzeri* traditions, scholars have argued that, at its deepest level, this acceptance was motivated by the simple, but profound conviction that the *mazzeri* were innocent of the murders they committed. The research suggests that the Corsicans believed that the victims of the *mazzeri* did not die because the latter chose to kill them, but because God had decided that it was their time to die. And that because the victim's death had been dictated by a higher agency and would occur with or without the participation of an individual *mazzere*, it was meaningless to attribute any blame to them. This same logic enabled the *mazzeri* to indulge in their killing frenzies without feeling accountable: Carrington noting that the 'Mazzeri are so much aware of being governed by an unseen power that they may feel guilty for what they have done although not responsible for doing it.'[71] The beliefs that underpinned this reasoning are more fully explored in the folklorist's analysis of the Sartenais *mazzera* we met earlier:

> [she claimed that] God ordained all she did, all that happened to herself and to others, the Christian God of her ancestors, to whom she owed obedience. It was He, she believed, who determined the day of the death of each one. She had been chosen to convey this news; she could only submit to His will. Though persecuted, she was also privileged, for she was spared the sense of guilt that has tormented many *mazzeri*. Paradoxically, her Christian faith preserved her from any feeling of wrongdoing. Her creed, which might be described as 'fatalistic Christianity', is adhered to by many Corsicans. The Christian teaching of freedom of choice and personal responsibility has made little imprint on the Corsican psyche; the majority are convinced, like the *mazzera*, that every life is programmed from birth to grave by a supreme power variously defined as God, as Providence or as Destiny.[72]

Carrington concludes that, in general, the *mazzeri* were tolerated because they were believed to be messengers who were 'chosen to convey this news' of death as opposed to being the force of death itself: as servants of providence or destiny they were merely 'instruments of fate'. In other words, we can argue that the societal dynamics that enabled the *mazzeri's* bloodthirsty traditions to survive were rooted in a profound cultural fatalism.

Carrington's belief that fatalism underpinned the dark shamanistic practices of the Corsican *mazzeri* is supported by wider anthropological comparisons. Although scholars of anthropology do not necessarily articulate dark shamanistic rationales in terms of fatalism, in the sense that the shaman's death and sickness-bringing visionary rites generally reflect or attempt to mitigate sickness and death-bringing forces that are intrinsically unavoidable, their traditions can be interpreted in this way. The Warao god of the underworld who commands his shamans to kill, for example, has not only 'existed since the universe began' but has also created human kind, in the sense that he decreed 'that spiritual humans were henceforth to become embodied mortals'. To try and prevent Hoebo from feasting on human flesh and blood would be like trying to remove the sun from the sky, change the order of the seasons or, in Christian terms, override the will of God. According to the logic of the cosmos as laid out in the primordial creation myths, Hoebo needs to claim human lives whether an individual shaman is involved or not and, as Wilbert emphasizes, the traditionally enculturated members of the Warao know that in 'facing an enemy of catastrophic power' their shaman ancestors 'had no choice' but to 'uphold the primordial covenant of contingent predation'; this acceptance enabling them to tolerate their grisly journeys up and down the 'bloodsodden road along the firmament' to the netherworld, weighed down by the corpses of their mothers, husbands and children.[73] A similar fatalism underpins traditional toleration of the ritual murders and mutilations of the Amazonian *kanaimà*, with Whitehead noting that 'Whatever tragedy, distress, and death that dark shamans and allied ritual specialists may perform on humanity they are nonetheless an *inevitable*, continuing and even necessary part of the cosmos [my italics].'[74]

Scottish Fatalism

The idea that concepts of fate can be powerful enough to absolve an individual of envisioned murder, whether in the Corsican mountains or the Amazonian jungle, is difficult for the modern Western mind to appreciate. But it becomes easier to understand if we examine the nature and significance of fatalism, as it emerges in pre-industrial societies, in a little more depth. Fatalistic beliefs are a 'cultural universal' and, in whatever part of the world or period of history they appear, evolve in response to two of humanity's most abiding and painful questions: 'Why do we suffer and die?' and 'Why is suffering and death so unjust?'[75] Since the earliest times, men have asked themselves these questions over and over again in a myriad different ways: Why does one child die in infancy while another does not? Why is one man born beautiful and another born disfigured? Why did that fatal accident happen on that day, on that part of the road, in that way and to those particular people? Why must one man spend his life laboriously digging ditches or pushing pens just to earn enough money to feed his family while another spends his life lazily squandering a fat inheritance? Why does a woman who loves and longs for children remain barren, while another, who does not care for them, carelessly produces child after child, year after year? And why is the life of a man who has endeavoured his whole life to be honourable and kind prematurely ended by a crippling disease, while another, who has seldom given thought to another's feelings his whole life, continues hale and hearty into old age?

Within human culture as a whole, the fatalistic beliefs that have emerged to rationalize this existential injustice have taken, and continue to take, a wide variety of forms. A man's fate can be caused by impersonal forces or by the actions of spirits, including the creator God. A man's fate can be mapped out for a reason, or be completely meaningless. A man's fate can be altered through behaviour and ritual or can be uncontrollable and inescapable. Most magical and religious systems embrace these three polarities in varying degrees, with the more developed religions favouring concepts of fate as a meaningful moral force, responsive to human behaviour such as ritual and prayer, and the more archaic belief systems favouring concepts of fate as an amoral, immutable force, unresponsive to the actions of man. But whatever form fatalistic beliefs take, they perform the same function in that they support the psychological mechanisms that enable individuals to cope with suffering and the injustice of suffering. Because they emphasize that the span of the human life is mapped out by a higher force, whether benign or ambivalent, intentioned or random, flexible or fixed, they situate the seeming futility and arbitrariness of the individual life within the vast, internal logic of the cosmos. By giving these perennial human burdens some kind of 'belonging', fatalistic beliefs help to bring the individual to the profound place of mental and emotional surrender or acceptance that enables them to endure.

But while suffering, and an awareness of the injustice of suffering, is endemic to the human condition, and all individuals draw on fatalistic beliefs to help them deal with it, where people living in the modern West differ profoundly from those of pre-industrial societies is in the degree of suffering and injustice that they are exposed to and therefore the levels of acceptance and fatalism they are required to develop in response. Every year of their lives, since early childhood, individuals living in pre-industrial communities witness siblings, relatives, friends or acquaintances suffer painful, and often very sudden, deaths. And in addition to enduring this ongoing rolling bereavement they must also greet every new day in the knowledge that at any given moment they, too, might succumb to an accident or infection that will have them 'ripe for the Grave' by the next.[76] For the woman going into labour in a pre-industrial society, the prospect of death looms as large as the prospect of a new child (and in this context the anticipation of pain that is such a marked feature of modern Western birthing experiences barely merits consideration). The stoicism and levels of acceptance necessary to survive such a hostile environment means that in pre-industrial societies fatalistic beliefs assume an importance and potency difficult for the modern Western mind to appreciate. Only a profound conviction, nurtured since the earliest years of childhood, that beyond all rhyme, reason and effort of man 'What will be will be' and 'All will be as God wills' can enable pre-industrial peoples to endure these levels of trauma.

Fatalism in Seventeenth-Century Scotland

Can we speculate then, as Carrington has done with regard to the *mazzeri*, that the toleration of arrow-shooting divinatory traditions in early modern Scotland was rooted in a profound cultural fatalism? Such speculations are frustrated by the fact that ordinary people from this period have left little written evidence of their subjective beliefs and experiences. They are also frustrated by the fact that, although ubiquitous, fatalistic beliefs can be difficult to identify because they are ultimately rooted in emotional states, as opposed to intellectual commitments, and can therefore work their way into a wide range of belief systems in a bewildering variety of guises and into the world-views of people who would never consciously define themselves as fatalistic.

But despite these difficulties, the evidence that does exist is suggestive. As we explored in CHAPTER SEVEN, seventeenth-century Scotland was still a pre-industrial society. Up to 50 percent of children died before they reached the age of ten, disease was ubiquitous, medical care limited and hunger an ever-present threat. Violence was also endemic and social injustice high. As we saw earlier in this chapter, high levels of physical and psychological hardship are highly conducive to the prospering of fatalistic beliefs. Men such as Walter Stewart (Bute, 1662), for example, who was forced to watch helplessly while his son, David, 'took a sudden disease with cryeing and dyed within 8 days [while] the day he was buryed his dochter took ane very unaturall disease her face sying and growing black quhair of she dyed in a short space' would have been in grievous need of explanation and comfort.[77] Given the fact that experiences like Stewart's would not have been uncommon, we can assume that for the early modern Scots, as for the twentieth-century Corsicans, aspirational Christian teachings about 'freedom of choice and personal responsibility' would have flourished alongside more pragmatic fatalistic convictions that 'every life is programmed from birth to grave by a supreme power'.[78]

That this was the case is supported, in a more concrete sense, by the fact that although Protestant theologians would not have wanted to interpret their Christian beliefs in such terms, as defined in their broadest sense fatalistic beliefs were fundamental to the reformed world-view. The doctrines of predestination ('the belief that the final salvation of some of mankind is foreordained from eternity by God') and providence ('God's foreseeing protection and care of his creatures') were pillars of Protestant thinking and certainly by the nineteenth century the folklorist Alexander Nicolson could emphasize that the 'ordinary' Scots' religion 'is distinctly a Necessitarian system, implying a fixed belief that there is a Fate or Providence that shapes our ends, rough hew them how we will'.[79] Similar observations were made in Auldearn, just over 100 years after Isobel's trial, with minister John Paterson noting, with regard to local parishioners: 'the general gloominess of their faith, which teaches them, that all diseases which afflict the human frame are instances of Divine interposition, for the punishment of sin; any interference, therefore, on their part, they deem an usurpation of the prerogative of the Almighty'.[80] That these elite observers were correct, and that 'gloomy' fatalism genuinely flourished in popular mentalities is suggested by the enduring popularity of Gaelic proverbs, such as 'The fated will happen', 'For whom ill is fated, him it will strike', 'All will be as God wills' and 'What God has promised no man can baulk'. Even more interestingly, in the context of the present discussion, is the fact that many fatalistic proverbs were concerned with the manner and time of a man's death, as illustrated in the pithy observations that: 'No man can avoid the spot, where birth or death is his lot', 'Where folk's fate is to go, ford or hill won't prevent', 'Who is born to be hanged cannot be drowned', 'He whose destiny is cast sits on a sharp cope' and, most pertinently of all, 'His hour was pursuing him'.[81]

That host-related arrow-shooting traditions may have been somehow linked to this corpus of fatalistic beliefs is suggested by the fact that, as in Corsica, seers involved in death-divinations of many different kinds seem to have, outside the church at least, escaped moral censure. Although, like the *mazzeri*, they were often approached warily and feared, they were not considered to be personally responsible for their grisly visions, nor blamed for the grave messages they brought to their fellow men. Indeed, their inability to resist their dark calling seems to have elicited a certain amount of sympathy: seventeenth-century ministers Kirkwood and Kirk claiming of the second sight, respectively, that 'It's so very troublsome to many, that theyd be gladly free from it' and '[seers] find such horrour and truble by the entercourse [with visions and precognitions granted by fairies] that they would often full gladly be as free from them, as other men'.[82] Barring those accounts that appear in witchcraft records, exactly the same explanatory dynamic emerges in sources describing arrow-shooting experiences. From Lhuyd's comments of 1699 through to Evans-Wentz's of 1911, it is clear that in every account, almost without exception, the farmers, lairds and weavers who claimed to have been forced to participate in the fairy hunt were considered to be innocent participants who were in no way responsible for the murders they were required to commit. The fairies 'made them do it'.[83] Although the early modern Scots would not necessarily have articulated host-related arrow-shootings specifically as acts of 'fortune', or 'destiny', nor have linked their tolerance of human participation in these events to these matrices of belief, taken as a whole the evidence suggests that their attitudes toward these traditions were rooted in a profound cultural fatalism.

The Fate-Woman Connection

Interestingly, we can find further support for this hypothesis by tracing these early modern beliefs and practices back through time. Although the search for the cultural origins or roots of any early modern shamanistic tradition is fraught with difficulties and any such attempt can only be highly speculative, the fact that, on the level of both etymology and narrative motif, an association between fairy host-related arrow-shooting and the dispensation of fate can be traced back to the pre-Christian period is highly suggestive here, and cannot be passed over without a brief acknowledgement.

As scholars have frequently emphasized, among the Celtic, Scandinavian and Germanic societies that left their mark on Scottish culture in the pre-Christian and early medieval period, concepts surrounding fate were highly prominent. Ronald Grambo notes, for example, that 'Within the old Norse culture area, belief in the power of fate was strong', while Katharine Morris goes so far as to state that 'The importance of fate in Germanic mythology and literature cannot be over stressed'.[84] But in these cultures, notions of fate differed from those purveyed by Christianity in the sense that they were not associated with a male creator God but with a collection of female figures ranging from goddesses and other supernatural women to mortal seers. These 'fate-women' or 'fate-goddess' figures, as we can term them here, often appeared in triplicate (the three *parcae* of the Romans, the three *moirai* of the Greeks, the three *nornir* of the Scandinavians) and were characteristically amoral or ambivalent. The belief in supernatural fate-dispensing female figures clearly survived into the Christian period. In the tenth century the German bishop, Burchard of Worms, claimed that 'certain people have the habit of believing . . . that women whom the vulgar call the Fates exist or possess the powers that are attributed to them; that is, at the birth of a man, they do with him as they please'.[85] Pócs, meanwhile, claims that in central and south-eastern Europe, even up to the modern age, fate-women 'are not only the characters of *fate legends* popular in the whole region, but . . . they are also known as "real" belief figures determining the life of the new-born . . . They also have a role at marriages, while the "third Moira [fate-woman variant]" is often the leader of souls, the angel of death, too'.[86] These fate-women figures also have close links with the capricious European and Mediterranean nocturnal goddess who is depicted in the mythology as having the power to bestow or take away life on a whim and who – as we have seen in the last chapter – features so strongly in the female-led spirit group narratives emerging from medieval and early modern Europe.

Given our premise that the arrow-shooting activities of the fairy host may have been conceptualized as expressions of fate, it is pertinent here that among folklorists the

European fairy is etymologically and functionally related to the fate-woman/goddess nexus. As we have seen, in a general sense the fairy queen has been identified with the European nocturnal goddess, of which the fates are an aspect. But more specifically, as Jacqueline Simpson recently noted:

> It is generally accepted by both French and English etymologists that the Latin *fata*, 'destiny,' gradually evolved into the words *fee* and 'fairy,' through a central concept of 'fatedness,' though the details of this process are obscure. Some fusion or confusion between the personified classical Fates and the triple mother goddesses of Celtic and Germanic belief may have assisted this development.[87]

A similar link between the triple fate-goddess figure and the fairies emerges in Norse mythology, with Snorri Sturlusson (quoting *Reginsmal*) claiming that:

> Of different origins
> are the Norns, I think,
> not all of one kindred;
> some come from Aesir-kin,
> *some from the elves*
> and some are the daughters of Dvalin [my italics].[88]

This connection was still overt in some parts of the European continent, many centuries later, with Pócs claiming that in south-eastern and central Europe, even up to the modern age, 'These beings [fate-women] are similar to the fairies in appearance and bring blessing or illness to the people. In many places they are identified with the fairies themselves.'[89]

The *Wið færstice*

But while we can trace a general connection between the fate-dispensing activities of early modern fairies and the fate-dispensing activities of pre-Christian fate-women or goddesses, this connection becomes even more interesting and specific when considered in relation to the host-related arrow-shooting nexus with which Isobel was so deeply involved. A significant number of Anglo-Saxon charms bear testament to the fact that in this period people were very worried about spirits and other types of supernatural beings who wandered the world at night causing harm – harm that included inflicting sickness or death through the shooting of arrows or spears. These beliefs are accumulated, to greatest effect, in a remarkable charm supposed to cure 'violent, stabbing pain', known as the *Wið færstice*. Composed, according to recent estimates, in the late-tenth century, the charm (which has, according to linguist Alaric Hall, 'intrigued and challenged scholars since the nineteenth century' and is 'among the most remarkable of its kind in medieval Europe') depicts a variety of spirits and beings – described variously as *ēse* (the pagan gods, or *æsir*), *ælfe* (elves), *hægtessan* (roughly translated in the period as 'supernatural females') and 'mighty women' – shooting and harming people with specially-forged spears. Hall's recent translation (with my additions in square brackets) is quoted in full here:

> They were loud, yes, loud, when they rode over the (burial) mound; they were fierce when they rode across the land. Shield yourself now, you can survive this strife. Out, little spear, if there is one here within. It stood under/behind lime-wood (i.e. a shield), under a light-cloured/light-weight shield, where those mighty women marshalled their powers, and ?they sent shrieking spears. I will send another back, a flying arrow ahead in opposition. Out, little spear, if it is here within. A craftsman sat, forged a knife/knives; ?small as swords go, violent the wound. Out, little spear, if it should be here within. Six craftsmen sat, wrought slaughter-spears. Be out, spear, not in, spear. If there is here within a piece of iron/swords, the work/deed of *hægtessan*, it must melt. If you were *scoten* in the skin or were *scoten* in the flesh, or were *scoten* in the blood, or were scoten in the limb (?joint), may your life never be harmed. If it was the *gescot* of *ēse* [the pagan gods] or it was *gescot* of *ælfe* [elf] or it was the *gescot* of *hægtessan* [hags], now I want to (?will) help you. This is for you as a remedy for the *gescot* of *ēse*; this is for you as a remedy for the *gescot* of *ælfe*, this for you as a remedy for the *gescot* of *hægtessan*; I will help you. Fly around there on the mountain top. Be healthy, may the Lord help you. Then take the knife; put it in (the) liquid.[90]

In his recent work, *Elves in Anglo-Saxon England*, Hall concludes that the similarities between this charm and the arrow-shooting passages in Isobel's confessions are so compelling that we can speculate a direct link, in terms of belief-transmission, between the two. Although Isobel's terms of reference are different, in the sense that she talks in terms of 'elf arrow heidis' as opposed to 'slaughter spears', and refers to these weapons being shot by coven members as opposed to by gods, elves, *hægtessan* or mighty women, the similarities are clear. Most persuasive of all, as Hall points out, is the fact that both Isobel and the *Wið færstice* make reference to the arrows being manufactured by elven smiths. It is worth reproducing Hall's comments here in full:

> These hints [regarding the links between the elves and the smiths] are arguably consolidated by a remarkable parallel in the Scottish witchcraft trials, in the four confessions to witchcraft of Issobel Gowdie, tried in Nairn in 1662 . . . [Isobel] recounted material about *Fearrie* which commentators agree is too unusual to have come from her inquisitors; although there was a great gap of time and space between the writing of *Wið færstice* and Issobel's confessions, charm-texts and related traditions were demonstrably transmitted across this gap with little alteration. At various times, Issobel confessed to riding through the air on straws with her coven; shooting her victims with 'elf-arrow-heidis' or 'elf-arrows' which she acquired from the Devil, in 'the Elfes howssis', the Devil shaping them 'with his awin hand' before passing them on for finishing to 'Elf-boyes'; and visits to the king and queen of *Fearrie*. Drawing this material together to reconstruct a set of underlying concepts is problematic, but prominent in Issobel's confessions is a conception of witchcraft involving groups of witches riding out, gaining magical projectiles from the *elvis* who manufacture them, and using them to shoot people. Besides the general similarities of this material to

Wið færstice, Issobel portrayed one smith (in her account the Devil) in a group of smiths, as the charm does. The relevance of these parallels to the whole of the Old English charm consolidates literary arguments for its coherence, and their existence shows that *Wið færstice* is not a unique imaginative blooming. Issobel's use of *elf* links her narratives lexically to the history of *ælf*, and supports the inference on internal evidence that *Wið færstice's ælfe* are identical with its *smiðas*.[91]

Hall's claim that Isobel's confessions confirm a continuity of 'charm-texts and related traditions [that] were demonstrably transmitted across this gap [between the tenth and seventeenth centuries] with little alteration' is persuasive, and we can posit, on this premise, a degeneration of the 'high mythology' of the Eddaic poems into the culturally more peripheral 'lower mythology' of the early modern fireside: the *æsir* having been subsumed into the category of elf or fairy and *hægtessan* into cunning folk or witches.[92]

But equally importantly, Hall's treatment of the *Wið færstice* also supports our hypothesis that Isobel's arrow-shooting passages reflect shamanistic beliefs and practices focused on the death-bringing attributes of fate-spirits. The crucial reference here is the term *hægtessan*. Hall emphasizes that this term, which appears for the first time halfway through the charm, 'almost certainly corresponds' to the 'mighty women' described in the first ten metrical lines: women who 'were fierce when they rode across the land' and 'sent shrieking spears'.[93] He also emphasizes that the motif of 'mighty women' was a relatively common in contemporaneous texts, claiming that it 'compares well with other instances in medieval north-west European texts, both antedating and postdating *Wið færstice*, of martial supernatural females riding out in groups and causing harm'.[94] This motif can, of course, be linked to the warrior women that appear in both Celtic, Germanic and Scandinavian mythology under a variety of guises, such as the valkyrie or *valkyrja* (Norse) the *wælcyrige* (Germanic) and the *morrigan* (Celtic). Although there are differences between these figures as they emerge in their different cultures, their similarities suggest a common origin: all three act as, or serve, gods and heroes of war (most prominently the Norse Odin or his Germanic equivalent Woden); all three ride or fly onto battlefields and direct proceedings; all three are associated with the raven or crow; and all three are, like Isobel, unashamedly bloodthirsty and preoccupied with slaughter. According to the twelfth and thirteenth-century *Sturlunga saga*, the most famous incarnation of these warrior women, the *valkyrja*, rides at the head of a company, crying in battle-frenzy:

> I move with bloody cloth,
> I strike men into fire,
> I laugh when I see them go.
> To that loathly place I know.[95]

In their depictions of mounted, airborne combat-seeking troupes who also act as guardians, attendants and feasting companions of Odin and the slain heroes of Valhalla, mythological accounts of *valkyrjur* activity closely resemble the Wild Hunt category of spirit-group narratives into which, as we have already seen, the activities of the

Scottish fairy host or *sluagh* also fall. This connection is made all the more specific by the fact that in Scandinavian mythology Odin is commonly cited as the leader of the Hunt, and by the fact that after death the hunters' victims, like those of the Norse *valkyrja*, are reputed to rise up and join the god's train of the dead.[96]

But what is highly relevant to the shamanistic fate-dispensing and death-divining hypothesis being developed here is the fact that these archaic warrior women figures, whether found in Celtic, Germanic or Norse cultures were, like the fairies to whom they were so closely related, specifically linked to the concept of fate. The *valkyrjur* have been seen as personifications or aspects of the *nornir*, who 'were the shapers of fate, the women who determined the past, present and future of men and events': and in this context, the role of the *valkyrja* was not only to kill but also to decide who was to die.[97] This role finds dramatic confirmation in the fact that the term *valkyrja/wælcyrige* is translated, quite literally, as 'chooser of the slain'. Traces of this association between the supernatural female warrior figure and the dispensation of fate can also be found in Scottish and Irish fairy belief, most notably in the complex figure of the banshee or *bean sidhe*; a figure long believed by scholars to be derived, in part, from the Celtic *morrigan*.[98] Like other fairy-type spirits, the banshee predicted, and in some cases determined, man's fate, but she was also aggressive and concerned primarily with death; filling the houses of the soon-to-be-bereaved with sorrowful keening and being encountered, in her role as *bean-nighe*, in desolate places, often before a battle, washing the clothes of those about to die. Some scholars have also linked the banshee, or 'death-messenger', with the crow, although this link is disputed.[99] We also find these themes closer to home. Shakespeare's fierce, death-divining 'weird sisters', who met on the heath east of Auldearn, half a mile from where Isobel feasted and danced with the king and queen of the fairies, were etymologically linked to the Fates: the term arriving with Shakespeare, via Holinshed, from earlier Scottish sources and evolving out of the Old English *wyrd*, which means, quite literally, 'fate'.[100] Although this route is a literary, as opposed to historical, one, it brings the matrix of beliefs surrounding aggressive fate-dispensing goddesses right to the foot of Isobel's Downie Hill.

The Human Participation

As they stand, the similarities between the *Wið færstice* and Isobel's arrow-shooting passages, when taken in conjunction with wider mythological themes and narratives, support the hypothesis that Isobel's arrow-shooting accounts may have been somehow related to divinatory shamanistic practices linked to the death-bringing aspect of fate. But the relevance of this thread, with regard to our understanding of Isobel's narrative, is even further emphasized when we take into account the question of human partici-pation. Although the warrior women of the early mythologies and charms seem to have been generally identified as supernatural beings, from the earliest sources there are scat-tered references to the belief that the role could be assumed by humans, such as the daughters of kings or the wives of heroes. In a quatrain ascribed to ninth-century Irish poet Flann Mac Lonáin, it was the wife of Tethra, chief of the Fomorians, who – seemingly in the form of a crow or raven – flew over the battlefield 'longing . . . for the fire of combat'; while in the *Helgakviða Hundingsbana I*, the *valkyrja* Sigrún – who flew on horseback 'under helmets on Sky-plains' with her coat of mail 'spattered with blood' – was a mortal woman, 'the daughter of Hogni'.[101] This dual incarnation is also reflected in the fact that, as Hall notes, in Old English texts the word *hægtessan* – which, as we saw earlier, was put to such dramatic effect in the *Wið færstice* – is used to gloss both supernatural and human females: being employed, for example, in reference to both the Classical *parcae, furiae, phinotissa* (mortal prophetesses) and the 'more ambiguous *striga*'.[102] These dual incarnations have led Hall to speculate, as others have done before him, that popular beliefs surrounding 'martial supernatural females riding out in groups and causing harm' may offer us 'a glimpse into the non-intellectual cultural sources for witchcraft beliefs attested in the early-modern witchcraft trials'. Even more specifically, Hall speculates that 'it is possible that the *hægtessan* of the *Wið færstice* were deemed potentially, like Issobel Gowdie, to be enemies from within the community'.[103] Whether or not this was the case, this evidence pointing to human participation in warrior-women groups certainly strengthens Hall's case that the *Wið færstice* and Isobel's arrow-shooting narrative represent the continuance of beliefs and motifs through charm texts, and it encourages us to speculate that the inherited belief that humans could participate in these spirit-group hunts underpinned Isobel's dramatic claim that she had joined the host's hunting expeditions.

But these correspondences regarding human participation also tempt us to take these speculations one step further. In the context of the shamanistic paradigm, the thread we have traced here raises the tantalising possibility that Isobel's claim to have participated in the host's arrow-shooting raids is evidence that a dark shamanistic tradition, in which female visionaries participated in the fate-pronouncing activities of death-bringing warrior women, had survived from the pre-Christian period into seventeenth-century Scotland. Such a heady speculation is highly tenuous and merits far more research than is possible here, but it would certainly shed light on a textual anomaly that has puzzled scholars of Norse mythology and early medieval history from the nineteenth century to the present. In the eleventh century the Anglo-Saxon bishop, Wulfstan, in his famous *Sermo Lupi*, recounted a list of sinners as follows: 'and here are harlots and infanticides and many foul adulterous fornicators, and here are witches and valkyries, and here are plunderers and robbers and despoilers, and to sum it up quickly, a countless number of all crimes and misdeeds'.[104] Although, as we have seen earlier, mythological texts sometimes describe the role of *valkyrja* being assumed by a mortal woman, the fact that Wulfstan included the term in a workmanlike list of mundane and unambiguously human sinners has long challenged historians and folklorists, with Hilda Ellis Davidson noting that this comment was curious because 'All the other classes [of sinners] whom he mentions are human ones, and it seems unlikely that he has introduced mythological figures as well.'[105] Various speculations have been proffered to explain the anomaly, with Davidson concluding, as others have done, that Wulfstan may have been referring to 'a memory . . . of the priestesses of the god of war, women who officiated at the sacrificial rites when captives were put to death after battle'.[106] But Isobel's confessions invite us to speculate that in this ambiguous passage the bishop may have been referring to a contemporaneous and predominantly female shamanistic tradition surrounding fate-dispensing, death-bringing warrior spirits. After all, in doing so, Wulfstan would have behaved no differently from the early medieval ecclesiastics who condemned other, more famous, female-led spirit-group traditions in sources like the *Canon Episcopi*.

The Reluctant *Valkyrja*

These speculations as to pre-Christian antecedents are very tentative. But even without taking them into account we can argue that the shamanistic fate-dispensing hypothesis sketched out here explains many of the inconsistencies and incongruities of Isobel's arrow-shooting passages in one fell swoop, without the need for wholesale recourse to theories of mental illness and false confession. It accounts for the seemingly arbitrary nature of her arrow-shooting aggression; her surprisingly compliant acquiescence to the seemingly irrational and bloodthirsty demands of the Devil as host leader; and the chillingly specific and matter-of-fact way in which she narrated her envisioned murders. From this perspective, Isobel would have believed that the host-related hunts in which she was compelled to participate represented an immutable force that chose each victim on the simple grounds that, as the old proverb states, 'His hour was pursuing him' and he was 'ripe for the Grave'.[107] She would have been able to kill men and women against whom she bore no personal grievance because, being press-ganged into the host's service, she believed that she was merely acting out their ineffable dictates. And she would have been able to walk away from these crimes without any sense of personal responsibility because it was the elf boys who had whittled the arrows and the Devil who had put them into her hands and told her where to aim.

This hypothesis is not incompatible with the fact that, when she was finally hauled up for interrogation in 1662, Isobel seems to have expressed genuine contrition for her host-related killings. As we have seen earlier, although they did not generally consider themselves directly responsible for their actions, the *mazzeri* could often feel uncomfortable or sorrowful about their death-bringing role and this sadness could, in some cases, come very close to guilt. Living in a vigorous covenanting parish, it is likely that during her period of service to the fairy host, Isobel was well aware that the church condemned such activities but, tucked away from the scrutiny of ministers in the cottages, barns and fields of her fermtoun, she managed to maintain some kind of internal truce between her church-derived consciousness of sin and her conviction that, according to the inchoate fatalism of the fireside, her activities were somehow justified. This truce, which must have been a delicate one at the best of times, may have quickly broken under the articulate persuasions of men like Hugh Rose and Harry Forbes. Finding herself at the gates of the afterlife, and being forced by her interrogators to divide her life's works into black and white, Isobel could have found herself experiencing a dramatic change of heart and her latent misgivings concerning her arrow-shooting experiences could have been fully-activated and transformed into intense and perfectly genuine guilt.

The shamanistic fate-dispensing hypothesis also concurs with what little we know of Isobel's life. Violence was endemic in seventeenth-century Nairnshire, with clan disputes and Highland/Lowland antipathies causing the peoples along the Moray Firth to live in frequent fear of attack from the mountains to the south. In the 1640s and 50s these threats were compounded by the civil wars, when royalist and covenanting armies marched back and forth across the north-east plundering lands and besieging houses. In such violent times the consciousness of death and the need to understand its movements may have been high, and magical practitioners such as Isobel may have felt called upon to meet this need. The fact that Isobel became associated with host-related arrow-shooting traditions, as opposed to any other kind of shamanistic practice, also tempts us to posit personal trauma. As we saw in CHAPTER SEVEN, Isobel's likely proximity to the Battle of Auldearn, and to the successive raiding parties of Huntly and Montrose, invites us to speculate that at an impressionable age she may have witnessed, at close quarters, the battle-frenzy of the *valkyrjur* or *wælcyrigan* through the incomprehensible horror of large-scale human slaughter. She may have seen longbows drawn and flocks of whistling arrows darken the sky; she may have heard the screams and clash of steel as ranks of soldiers fell; she may have picked her way through the corpses looking for friends or family members; and she may have watched the mass burials in the patch of waste ground near the battlefields that later became known as Dead Men's Wood. Struggling to accommodate these events, Isobel could have felt compelled to relive her terrible experiences over and over again in a myriad of different ways, in a manner that has, in the twentieth century, been so conclusively linked to conditions like post-traumatic stress disorder. These preoccupations would not necessarily have made her, as they did not make the *mazzere*, an overtly-aggressive person, but they may have intensified her capacity for envisioned violence and increased the likelihood that she became attracted to what was, perhaps, the darkest and most ambiguous of the contemporary fairy-shamanism traditions.

The Wider Picture

Our assessments of Isobel's arrow-shooting passages have been brief and highly speculative, but even in this rudimentary state their relevance for our wider understanding of early modern witchcraft is immediately evident. As we have seen earlier, many scholars accept that encounter-narratives found in witchcraft and sorcery records in early modern Europe contained shamanistic themes and motifs of folkloric origin, but remain uncertain as to how far these narratives represented experience as opposed to belief. The small percentage of narratives that contain prominent folkloric themes and clearly defined community-benefit rationales (such as those relating to the *benandanti*) are generally considered to have possibly contained a visionary dimension; but the remaining majority, which include both demonological encounter-narratives and folkloric spirit-group narratives emphasizing malevolent activity, are viewed with caution, despite the fact that they often contain allusions to visionary experience through textual anomalies, references to subtle-body travel, and interrogatorial acknowledgements that the events described were imaginary ones. As we have explored in the last chapter, scholarly caution with regard to the latter narratives is largely rooted in two main concerns: the first being the fact that they lack a clear shamanistic rationale (frequently containing high-levels of seemingly meaningless and cold-blooded *maleficium* that cannot be clearly linked to the community-benefit paradigm); and the second being the fact that they display evidence of interrogatorial contamination (the presence of elite demonological themes, such as the demonic pact, shedding doubt on the reliability of the texts as reflections of the words and experiences of the accused).

But the analysis of Isobel's arrow-shooting passages undertaken in this chapter enables us to resolve the first of these two concerns. Although we have been focusing specifically on shamanistic aggression in relation to host-related arrow shooting, our Corsican, Amazonian and African material illustrates that dark shamanistic attacks could incorporate just about any form of violence, from blood-sucking, to beating with cudgels, tearing apart with the teeth and suffocating with the bare hands. It is therefore not unreasonable, in the face of this diversity, to entertain the possibility that any early modern spirit-group narrative, whether folkloric or demonological, that contains accounts of seemingly arbitrary, meaningless and savage killing could, like Isobel's arrow-shooting passages, reflect extant dark shamanistic practices characterized by ecstatic compulsion and underpinned by profoundly fatalistic beliefs concerning death. Though slender, suggestive evidence certainly exists. The following account, taken from a trial that took place in Hungary in 1756, is remarkably redolent of the testimonies of the *mazzeri*, Warao and *kanaimà* in its depiction of compulsion, killing, and retrospective remorse. It is also notable for its overt reference to 'the will of destiny'. Pócs writes:

> In 1756, Katalin Szabó from Nagyvázsony talked about her bewitching nocturnal round trips and 'being totally deprived of my senses, I became an exile . . . during the night, to the will of destiny. I should have set fire to the houses of four inhabitants: István Már, Cseke, Széderi, and Baranyai.' Squeezing through the smoke hole, she set fire to two of them, but then she felt bitterly sorry. Why had God allowed her to 'carry out such evil deeds?'[108]

Returning closer to home, these perspectives invite us to re-evaluate Scottish witchcraft records. Although most demonological encounter-narratives do not feature host-related arrow shooting, it is notable that a significant minority conform to Isobel's confessions in the sense that they describe groups of individuals, mainly women, who roam around the countryside, sometimes in the form of animals, entering houses and killing humans and animals in seemingly random and matter-of-fact ways. The confessions of Margaret Duchall, made at Alloa in 1658, are typical:

> Sche confest ane meiting in the Cuningar of all the sevine with the divell in the likeness of catts, who went to the – and destroyed ane kow to Edward Burnes. Ane other meitting one night and they went to Tullibodie and killed ane bairne. Anoyr meitting and went to bow house and killed ane horse and ane kow to William Monteath. Ane other meitting and they

went to Clakmannan and killed ane child to Thomas Bruce. Ane other meitting and they went to Caldone's and was the death of two bairnes of his.[109]

Through the interpretative lens constructed here, we can speculate that beneath the seemingly-arbitrary, death-bringing perambulations of the Alloa witches lay compulsive shamanistic practices rooted in beliefs concerning the predatory dictates of fate. Just as Isobel may have been compelled, on certain nights of the year, to participate in death-bringing arrow-shooting hunts, so Duchill and her companions may have also been swept up and compelled to participate in death-bringing house-to-house processions, fulfilling, in these strange visions and dreams, their dark shamanistic role as messengers and agents of the forces of death.

Resurrection and Compulsion

Although not relating directly to Isobel, our general argument is strengthened here by the fact that the narrative theme of killing followed by resurrection which, as we saw earlier, so frequently and problematically emerge in earlier (and particularly female-led) folkloric spirit-group narratives, can also be absorbed into this shamanistic fate-killing nexus. We can speculate that the women who, according to Burchard's *Corrector*, murdered their victims, ate them and then stuffed them with straw or wood to 'grant them a brief spell of life'; and the women who, according to Milanese inquisitor Fra Beltramino da Cernuscullo, killed and ate animals and then resurrected them though 'they are never much good for work thereafter'; and the women from the Dolomite Alps who, according to their interrogators, claimed to have 'cooked and eaten a baby' before collecting the bones together and bringing the child 'back to life', may have all been performing compulsive and possibly divinatory fate-killings of the type described by the *mazzeri*; subtle-body attacks where the visionary's victims did not die immediately after they had been killed and eaten but lingered on 'for some time afterwards'.[110] We can also cautiously speculate that the flesh-eating and cannibalistic elements that appear in some of these narratives – and which are so commonly attributed to either false confession or conspiracy theories surrounding marginal social groups – may have represented visionary rites that were, as they still are for dark shamans in Amazonia, contingent elements of these practices. Like the corpse-eating, blood-sucking practices of the *kanaimà* and dark Warao shamans, the animal-eating and cannibalism described by Burchard, John of Salisbury, da Cernuscullo and others may have represented the existence of deeply fatalistic – though by this date largely inchoate – shamanistic beliefs and practices concerning 'the unending exchanges' between the spiritual world and the human world 'in the guise of hunter and prey'. Beliefs that give the dark shamanistic practitioner a 'key role in the creation and management of the predatory interrelation of humanity, animality and divinity'.[111] Progressing into the period of the witch hunts, we can entertain the idea – though here much more cautiously – that some of the demonological encounter-narratives displaying overt cannibalistic themes, such as those from the towns of Nordlingen and Warzburg in late sixteenth-century Germany, may also have represented this nexus of dark shamanistic practice.[112]

More Fate-Women

There are further reasons for suspecting that some of Europe's more conventionally demonological encounter-narratives could have been rooted in shamanistic fate-killing practices. Earlier in this chapter we argued that the fate-woman figure of pre-Christian European and Mediterranean mythology was thematically linked with both the female fairy and arrow-shooting warrior women like the *valkyrja*. But what we have not yet addressed fully here is the fact that this figure was also linked to the nexus of beliefs surrounding the proverbial witch. By the early modern period the term *hag*, from the Old English *hægtesse* (which we have earlier linked – through the *valkyrja/wælcyrige* thread – to fate-dispensing martial supernatural females) was widely used to denote 'witches and evil spirits'.[113] As a reflection of this, Shakespeare's appropriation of the word *wyrd* or 'fate' to describe Macbeth's death-divining witches was not an arbitrary one. In his alleged source, *Holinshed's Chronicles*, it states that the three women 'in strange and wild apparell, resembling creatures of elder world' who met the laird as he travelled to Forres were 'either the weird sisters, that is (as ye would say) the goddesses of destinie, or else some nymphs or feiries, indued with knowledge of prophesie by their necromanticall science'.[114] The fact that Shakespeare followed Holinshed in defining the three women as 'weird sisters', but also embellished them with stereotypical 'Double, double toil and trouble' witch-characteristics, may have been a dramatic device, but it would have been a device that could only have worked if his audience accepted the link between divinatory witches and the pronouncements and function of fate. The strength of the link between fate-women and the proverbial witch has more recently been vividly confirmed by Pócs's research into Hungarian witchcraft records, with the latter confidently asserting that there was 'a very definite "fate goddess" aspect in the Hungarian witch in the whole of the language area and from all three centuries of the witch hunts'.[115]

Pócs' research into the fate-goddess aspect of the Hungarian witch is complex, but what is particularly significant, with regard to our analysis of the experiential dimension of demonological encounter-narratives, is her claim that for the early modern Hungarians this witch figure with 'fate-goddess features' did not only exist as an object of belief, but also as an aspect of dream or vision experience.[116] Pócs claims that witchcraft records in which a witness claims to have encountered an 'apparition' of a witch predicting a harmful event (some of the former specifically stating that the latter was a double, or perceived in a dream) are evidence that individuals experienced witches performing their fate-determining function on a visionary level. Pócs also emphasizes that in this role witches could sometimes appear before their victims in threes, reflecting the legendary theme of the triple judgement and possibly (though she does not mention this) the traditionally triplicate nature of the fate-goddess. As we shall touch on later, Pócs claims that witches generally pronounced harm-to-come as judgements meted out for specific sins, as a form of 'norm control'. But their function comes closer to the more arbitrary shamanistic fate-dispensing nexus we are postulating here in the records where witches pronounce fate without explanation. As Pócs notes, 'Apparitions [of witches] were even more fatelike when maleficium was presented as a judgement without a stated reason, or when the bewitched person's proximity to death, or often their fate – such as whether or not they would recover from an illness – was laid before them.'[117] In some witch-apparitions, the role of announcer of fate and dispenser of fate was fused, as we are proposing it to have been in Isobel's case, with Pócs claiming that 'In some of the narratives they [the fate-witches] not only condemned the injured party to [the fated] bewitchment but carried out the maleficium as well'.[118] Of the cases where the fate-witches appear in threes, Pócs writes:

> one of the creatures in the apparition, generally the third, announced the course of a type of maleficium as fate . . . Two astonishing documents verify the presumption about death meted out by fate in ancient Europe, where hanging is viewed as fate without any justification in the given context of witchcraft. In the example from 1731, it seems that witches that appeared in apparitions had wanted to hang a maiden from Nagybarom, in Sopron County: they left a noose on her bed when she was ill. Her family interpreted this as a message from the other world and feared that their daughter would indeed die through hanging.[119]

The fact that the subtle bodies of witches were believed, by those who encountered them, to determine, pronounce and enact the dictates of fate raises the possibility that those magical practitioners who believed themselves to go out in subtle body to pronounce and perform *maleficium* may have interpreted, and even initiated, their experiences according to the same rationale. Of course, it is unlikely that all, or even many, of these practitioners consciously identified their destiny-pronouncing or death-bringing role with fate-women figures, or even with the more generalized forces of fate, for by the early modern period these archaic associations seem to have been, at least in western Europe, very deeply absorbed into the nexus of beliefs surrounding demonological witchcraft. But for some practitioners this link may still have been as concrete as it clearly was for some of the victims of fate-witch apparitions. Hungarian witch Katalin Szabó's claim in 1756 that she 'became an exile' during the night and performed her 'evil deeds' according to the 'will of destiny' is suggestive here. We can of course surmise that the phrase 'will of destiny', if it came from Szabó herself, was merely used by her in a general sense to articulate the experience of shamanistic compulsion. But in the context of the perspectives developed here, we can also speculate that she may have employed it with more precision: articulating, as did the Corsican *mazzeri*, the experience of being compelled to serve or personify the inexorable dictates of fate.

The Image of the Witch

These perspectives are also supported by, and contribute to, contemporary debates

A woodcut from Ulrich Molitor's *De Lamiis et phitonicis mulieribus* (1500) depicts a witch harming a man through shooting arrows.

In this early sixteenth-century Flemish tapestry, which illustrates a poem by Petrarch, the three fates are depicted in their classical pose, carrying a spindle with which to measure out the length of human lives. Their association with mortality is further emphasized by the fact that they represent death as it celebrates over the fallen body of Chastity. As a reflection of this, the image is often titled *The Triumph of Death*.

A witch carrying a spindle in Albrecht Dürer's *Witch Riding Backwards on a Goat*. Through this motif, Durer's witch figure echoes the fates in the Flemish tapestry on the left. Photograph © 2010, Museum of Fine Arts, Boston.

concerning the visual representation of witchcraft in early modern Europe. Historians have emphasized that early images of witches (found largely in engravings and wood-cuts) are particularly valuable because they contain information about attitudes towards witches and witchcraft current before the demonological stereotype was fully formed in the later sixteenth and seventeenth centuries. With reference, for example, to Albrecht Dürer's *Witch Riding Backwards on a Goat*, which was executed sometime between 1500 and 1507, Charles Zika has recently stated that: 'the detail of the engraving has been remarkably resistant to any widely accepted interpretation. This is hardly surprising, given the lack of agreement at the turn of the sixteenth century as to how a witch and a witch's activities should be visually represented . . . Given that the witch's cultural meaning as a societal enemy was still so new, so ill-defined and also disputed at the turn of the sixteenth century, this image can tell us much about the range of meanings with which the figure of the witch was invested by those not directly involved in its legal and theological elaboration.'[120]

In this context, it is notable that a handful of late fifteenth and early sixteenth-century images – including Dürer's *Witch Riding Backwards on a Goat* – depict the witch carrying a distaff and spindle. Given the fact that spinning paraphernalia was the tradi-tional symbol of fate-women and goddesses throughout Europe since pre-classical times, the most obvious interpretation here is that they represent a link, in the artist's mind, between the witch and the dispensation of fate. But for reasons as yet unclear (but which may be linked to the fact that there is a dearth of supporting evidence) the few historians to have addressed this problem display a marked reluctance to settle for this fate-symbol explanation. Though they acknowledge it as a possibility, the acknowledgement is generally given in passing and fast followed by an attempt to find alternative interpretations. In 1931, in reference to Dürer's witch, Grillot de Givry noted that as the distaff and spindle are 'emblematic of the Fates, they perhaps signify here that she holds the fate of humans in her hands through her maleficent powers' before adding the caveat: 'A simpler interpretation may be that they are a straightfor-ward symbol of very Woman.'[121] Within the last decade Charles Zika has expressed a similar ambivalence, claiming of the same image that 'the distaff and spindle might conceivably have been read [by Dürer's contemporaries] as an allusion to the thread of life over which the classical Fates have control' before moving on to concentrate his attentions on alternative meanings associated with gender and sexuality.[122] Elsewhere, in an examination of how early modern artists drew on classical imagery to depict contemporary witches, Zika links Dürer's distaff-holding witch to the classical goddess Circe, whom Virgil depicts spinning as she sits on her remote island, but without emphasizing the fact that this symbolism could reflect Circe's fate-linked function as 'the goddess who gives form to life and the goddess who takes it away'.[123]

Obviously, in the early modern period, as in any period, visual symbols possessed complex and multi-layered meanings, but the arguments developed in this chapter suggest that historians need not be so hesitant in their speculation that the distaff and spindle found in early witch-images functioned – at least in part – in their classic role as emblems of fate. If the archaic idea that the witch's 'evil deeds' were performed according to the 'will of destiny' could still have burned in the minds of peasant women like Katalin Szabó well into the middle of the eighteenth century, then it is reasonable to assume that 250 years earlier, when ideas surrounding the witch were still emerging out of their folkloric past and into their stereotypically demonological future, the archaic link between the witch and the fate-goddess still flickered in the minds of some of the educated elite. This thesis gains further support from Pócs's assertion that in early modern Hungary – where, as we have seen, witches were clearly identified with fate-goddess figures throughout the period – trial documents sometimes recorded 'apparitions of witches spinning, weaving, or simply carrying a spindle'; with examples emerging as late as 1734.[124] The fact that the distaff and spindle largely disappeared from western European witchcraft iconography post-1500 need not challenge this hypothesis. It is reasonable to speculate that as the witchcraze progressed, learned commentators would have avoided such elevated associations. Both Catholic and Protestant reformers, anxious to purge superstition of its numinosity, would have been anxious to emphasize that the role of dispenser of fate could not be appropriated by ragged and malicious peasant women, but could only be assumed by God.

13

The Choosers of the Slain

But although the fate-killing hypothesis developed in the last chapter answers some of the questions raised by Isobel's confessions, and indeed demonological encounter-narratives in general, as an explanation it is not completely satisfactory. For we cannot argue that Isobel's arrow-shooting activities were compulsive trances in which she felt compelled to perform a series of seemingly impersonally-motivated envisioned murders, without addressing the fact that the shooting of Harry Forbes and the Laird of Park clearly do not come into this category. Here, Isobel's eagerness to succeed, when taken in conjunction with the fact that, as we argued in CHAPTER SEVEN, relations between Isobel and these men were likely to have been tense, strongly suggests that these victims were sought out and that the shootings were motivated by personal griev-ance. With regard to Harry Forbes, Isobel claimed in Confession Three that:

> Bessie and margret wilsones in aulderne Johne taylor and his wyff margrat brodie and I and the divell, wer togither and mr harie forbes minister of aulderne goeing to moynes the divell gaw margret brodie an arrow to shoot at him q[uhi]lk she did, bot it cam short & the divell cawsed tak it up again, and desyrit to shoot again bot the divell s[ai]d no: we wold not get his lyff at th[a]t tyme. (48/9)

With regard to the Laird of Park, in Confession Four Isobel claimed:

> I shot at the Laird of park as he ves crossing the burn of boath bot thankis to god now th[a]t he preserwit him, Bessie hay gaw me a great cuff becaws I missed him. (51/25)

Obviously, given the fact that these killings involved the two men who featured most prominently in Isobel's interrogations as a whole, we must consider the fact that they represent false confession. It is quite possible that when Isobel provided her interroga-tors with her long list of the arbitrarily arrow-slain, the former asked her whether Forbes or Park were among her victims and, caving-in under interrogatorial pressure, she obligingly acquiesced. It is also possible that during her long imprisonment Isobel developed false memories in which specific arrow-shooting attacks against Forbes and Park became seamlessly integrated into genuine memories of generalized fate-killing assaults. The fact that the Forbes and Park do not emerge as arrow-shot victims until the third confession – after her memories had had four weeks to mature – supports this hypothesis.

Specific *Maleficium* and the Tribal Shaman

But on the other hand, we cannot rule out the possibility that these accounts of specific and personally-motivated arrow-shootings may also have been representative of prior shamanistic practice. Anthropological sources make it quite clear that the shaman was believed to be capable of performing envisioned *maleficium* to satisfy personal vendetta: thus transgressing, as Márnio Teixeira-Pinto states with regard to the Brazilian Arara, the 'moral imperative to use his skills only for the benefit of others'.[1] Although the Yanomamö shaman, Jungleman, for example, frequently led or sent out his child-killing spirits in defence of his tribe, when a neighbouring shaman named Toucan – who was 'a fierce warrior who had killed many men' – murdered his son, he went to the same spirits for advice on how to gain recompense. Their instructions were clearly effective, for Jungleman claimed that: 'The next day I followed [my spirit] Snakeman's directions and soon I had my revenge. It was so much easier than travelling all the way to Toucan's area and trying to kill someone . . . A child in their village died. I lay in my hammock thinking how nice the revenge was. But I still missed my son so much.'[2] Similarly, with regard to the Guyanese *kanaimà*, Whitehead notes that although the 'selection of victims is ultimately a matter of indifference' and that 'anyone will do' this arbitrary hunting method 'does not rule out at all "trophy" hunting, as it were'. He also claims that a Patamuna informant (whose great-grandfather was a *kanaimà*) told him that 'if a kanaimà is jealous of somebody doing something, if that person has more things than them, they would become so jealous that they could even kill their own families, their sisters or brothers'.[3] We find a similar ambiguity among the Netsilik Inuit shamans, with Asen Balikci writing that 'The most striking characteristic of Netsilik shamanism and associated beliefs was the fusion of good and evil elements. Although the Netsilik distinguished clearly an evil shamanistic act from its positive counterpart, it was the same shaman who was capable of both. Thus, although most shamans were good, at some time in their career they committed aggressive acts.'[4] The shaman's ability to prey on victims in response to personal affront means that he is always treated warily, even within his own community, and those who are deemed persistently guilty of such crimes can be ostracized or killed, with the role of shaman here merging, as it so often does, into that of the proverbial witch. But unless a shaman's 'dark side' gets out of hand his capacity for malevolence is often tolerated. Just as the modern Westerner going into a hospital for a heart operation does not care whether his surgeon is a nice person or not, but only whether he has the technical skills for the job, so a tribe under threat from a neighbouring village or a hungry god does not esteem its shaman for his moral stability or empathic qualities but for his ability to defeat or propitiate its enemies quickly and decisively through assault sorcery.[5]

Specific Fairy Attacks

Though it may seem so at first glance, this revised picture of shamanistic malevolence is not incompatible with the arrow-shooting-as-impersonal-fate-killing hypothesis developed in the previous chapter. We have already noted that fairy attacks could be unerringly specific, as illustrated in Bute cunning woman Jonet Morison's claim, in 1662, that 'blasting is a whirlwinde that the fayries raises about that persone quhich they intend to wrong and that tho ther were twentie present yet will it harme none bot him'. Her later claim that these fairy blasts 'harme none bot him quhom they were set for' also clearly indicates the prior selection of individual prey.[6] This perceived selectivity may have been rooted in the fatalistic conviction that the fairies brought death to those whose time had come – as expressed in popular proverbs like 'For whom ill is fated, him it will strike' and 'No man can avoid the spot, where birth or death is his lot' – and that as such, though specific, they were impersonally motivated.[7] But conversely, a wide range of early modern and later sources suggest that fairy attacks could be initiated in response to personal affronts: if food and drink had not been left out for them at night; if they found someone sleeping on a fairy hill; if a human ally had betrayed their confidences; if a man or woman had strayed across their path without having blessed themselves first and so on. That a man's fate could be dispensed through the capricious revenge-attacks of ambivalent and touchy spirits – as opposed to some kind of wise and compassionate God-figure – reflects the conviction, characteristic of many non-developed religions, that the spiritual forces that arbitrate fate are not necessarily benevolent, wise or just.

From this perspective, it is not unreasonable to speculate that when Isobel participated in the envisioned arrow-shooting activities of the fairy host and became – to all intents and purposes – an honorary fairy, that she too, did not only select victims in response to some kind of inscrutable higher command, but also, more pragmatically, in response to personal grievance. As we saw in the last chapter, legal records indicate that it was not uncommon for witchcraft suspects to be accused of shooting elf-arrows at neighbours with whom they were in dispute, and a small number of these incorporate host-related references. In the following account, in which mid seventeenth-century East Lothian woman Isobel Thomasone claims to have been shot by her neighbour, Jenet Millar (with whom she had recently quarrelled), the host is intimated by the presence of the 'person who is dead':

> When she [Isobel] was lying awake with a pain in her arm, she perceived her thumb to be shot through with the thing that is called an *elf-stone*, and the blood of her thumb sprang out along the bed. And looking from there to the floor she saw her [Jenet] standing upon it with another person, who is dead.[8]

We find even clearer references to host-related arrow-killings being motivated by personal vendetta in the documentation relating to the Bute witches whose testimonies, as we have seen earlier, clearly refer to host-related activities. The declaration given by Jonet Morison states:

NcLevin, Margaret NcWilliam and Katharin Moore her dochter did by witchcraft shoot to deid William Stephen and that the cause therof was because a long space before John Stephen was blasted with ane evill ey quhen he dwelt in Balskye. NcLevine offered to heale him of that blasting bot he would not, saying till her that he would have none of the devils cures which was her quarrell with him and that he was shott underneath the short ribbs and that quhen she found him there was a hole in it that ye might put your neive [fist] in.[9]

The Psychological Dynamics

But while we can speculate that these kinds of personally-motivated attacks may have been performed, the psychological dynamics that may have lain behind them still require explanation. Earlier in this chapter we argued that for Isobel, as for many dark shamans, envisioned *maleficium* was performed during compulsive trance states characterized by a lack of personal volition. But then how do we equate this paradigm with the fact that personally-motivated attacks, of the kind allegedly performed by Millar and NcLevin, clearly required a certain level of autonomy and control? Once again, the material relating to the Corsican *mazzeri* is helpful here. Although our main source, Dorothy Carrington, emphasizes the compulsive aspect of these traditions, on closer inspection the *mazzeri* were not always as out of control as they might first appear. While they were unable to resist the 'call' to kill, and had little choice regarding the identity of their victims, they sometimes possessed the lucidity, self-control and independent-mindedness to withdraw from an attack. Carrington was told, by a 'reliable informant', of one such visionary who 'caught a trout in a pool with his hand and recognized it as one of his aunts. He promptly released the fish and the next day warned his aunt that she would be very ill, but would recover. And this is in fact what happened.'[10] Similarly, we have already seen the *mazzere* who, at the moment of killing a bull, identified it as his father, and told Carrington that 'when I recognized the animal as my poor father . . . I did no more than strike it, and I withdrew the knife immediately'. As in the previous case, the victim was wounded, but did not die.[11] These examples of averted death link do not only link the *mazzeri's* practices to sickness divination (with which, scholars have argued, their traditions may once have been more closely entwined) but they also reflect, more accurately than the compulsion-only accounts, the tension between being in control and being controlled that, as we saw earlier, lies at the very heart of the shamanistic visionary experience and is characteristic of associated phenomena like active imagination and lucid dreaming.[12]

That Isobel's personal-killings could have reflected a similar psychological dynamic is supported by the fact that this same shamanistic interplay between compulsion and control can also be identified in nineteenth-century arrow-shooting accounts. Evans-Wentz claims that Donald McKinnon, a ninety-six year old Scottish piper from the Isle of Barra, told him: 'I saw two men who used to be lifted by the hosts. They would be carried from South Uist as far south as Barra head, and as far north as Harris. Sometimes when these men were ordered by the hosts to kill men on the road they would kill instead either a horse or cow; for in that way, so long as an animal was killed, the injunction of the hosts was fulfilled.'[13] Similarly, Marian Maclean of Barra claimed that:

> There was a man who had only one cow and one daughter. The daughter was milking the cow at night when the hosts were passing, and that human being whom the hosts had lifted with them was her father's neighbour. And this neighbour was ordered by the hosts to shoot the daughter as she was milking, but, knowing the father and daughter, he shot the cow instead.[14]

In the following anecdote about the arrow-shooting experience of a weaver from the Western Isles, the participating human does not only resist the host's injunction to kill, but also possesses enough lucidity and presence of mind to turn the whole arrow-shooting experience to his advantage. J. G. Campbell, who collected the account, claimed that it was told to him by 'a shrewd enough person in ordinary life' who 'adduced it as proof of the existence of fairies, of which he said there could be no doubt [because] he had heard the story from his father, who knew the weaver':

> One clear moonlight, when thatching his house with fern, he [the weaver] heard the rushing sound of a high wind, and a multitude of little people settled on the housetop and on the ground like a flock of black starlings. He was told he must go along with them to Glen Cannel in Mull, where they were going for a woman. He refused to go unless he got whatever was foraged on the expedition to himself. On arriving at Glen Cannel the arrow was given him to throw. Pretending to aim at the woman he threw it through the window and killed a pet lamb. The animal at once came out through the window, but he was told this would not do, he must throw again. He did so, and the woman was taken away and a log of alder-wood was left in her place. The weaver claimed his agreement, and the Fairies left the woman with him at the Bridge of Awe, saying they would never again make the same paction with any man. She lived happily with him and he had three children by her.[15]

Can we speculate, on the basis of these indications, that Isobel's specific arrow-shootings represented this process in reverse? Could it be that while, in the cases of the Corsican *mazzeri* or the arrow-shooting Highland farmers, personal sympathies obstructed envisioned killing, in Isobel's case personal antipathies encouraged it? Can we suppose that during dream or vision Isobel sought out the visual representations or subtle bodies of those she wished to kill and that, like the shamans of the Amazonian Parkanã tribe, her enemy's double, as encountered in dreams, became her 'magic-prey'?[16]

Sending out Subtle Bodies

That something like this may have been the case is supported from other quarters. In CHAPTER EIGHT we drew attention to the fact that two statements from Janet Breadheid's confession suggest that she may have believed that a pair of local women,

Agnes Grant and Katherine Sowter, had been commissioned to perform specific *malefi-cium*. In neither statement is the type of *maleficium* detailed: the first merely claims that, 'Agnes grant who wes brunt on the (*damaged – words missing*) hill of (*blank*) gott hyre from elspet monro to destroy the Lairdis of park and lochloy' while the second, which appears a few lines further down, reads: 'and it wes keathren sowter th[a]t wes brunt th[a]t (*verb missing here?*) w[illia]m hay the Last Laird of parkis broth[e]r for on (*at the instigation of*) gilbert kintey' (544/44). But although the *maleficium* allegedly used is not specified, what is pertinent here is the fact that in his 1833 transcription, Pitcairn surmised that the verb missing from the second statement was 'shot', rendering the sense as follows: 'Kathrin Sowter that was burnt *shot* William Hay the last Laird of Park's brother at the instigation of Gilbert Kintey.'[17] This insertion amounts to nothing more than an educated guess and it could be argued that any word pertaining to the performance of *maleficium*, such as the earlier 'destroy', could just as easily have taken its place. But on the other hand, given the fact that Isobel's confession is so preoc-cupied with the performance of harm through arrow shooting and given the fact that Janet claimed earlier that 'we shoat noat in plewghes', it is easy to see why Pitcairn made the assumption and it is worth briefly exploring its implications for the argu-ments being developed here.

If Isobel's arrow-shooting narratives were rooted in shamanistic visionary experi-ences then Pitcairn's gloss would imply that in seventeenth-century Nairnshire women did not only perform envisioned arrow-killings for themselves, but also performed them on behalf of others, with Sowter and Grant, in this case, attacking the Lairds of Park on behalf of clients Kintey and Monroe. At first glance, such a hypothesis seems far-fetched. Although we argued in CHAPTER EIGHT that in this period individuals could employ cunning folk to perform maleficent magic against enemies, to my knowl-edge no evidence of commissioned arrow-shooting visionary rites emerge from either early modern or later sources (although, as we saw earlier, the 1590 Katharine Ross case indicates that commissioned arrow-shooting attacks of a non-visionary nature, that targeted an image of the desired victim, could take place). And yet, when considered within the shamanistic paradigm as a whole, such a conclusion is not illogical. First, we have the fact that the fairies' harm-bringing abilities could clearly be employed self-defensively in this period. Although the extent of this practice is difficult to assess – not least because the use of fairy malevolence, when it emerged in witchcraft trials, was frequently overlaid with demonologically stereotypical material – the fact that cunning folk as geographically diverse as Isobel Haldane (Perthshire), Jonet Rendall (Orkney) and Isobel Watson (Stirling) employed their fairy familiars to revenge themselves against enemies suggests that it may not have been unusual.[18] Certainly, on the other side of Europe, Hungarian *táltos* Andras Bartha (1725) allegedly confessed that in an attempt to evade repaying a deposit paid for unsuccessful magical work she 'apparently "sent" three fate women after the aggrieved client'.[19]

Given the fact that fairies could be employed to attack enemies, it is not illogical to speculate that those individuals who spent time with the fairies, participated in fairy activities and – for the duration of the time they spent with them – possessed fairy powers, could also have been called upon to perform the same function. If a woman could commission a cunning woman who was good with her hands, such as Janet Grant (Aberdeenshire, 1587), to make a *corp creadh* in order to kill a man, then she could feasibly have commissioned a cunning woman who was good at 'going with' the fairies, like Isobel Gowdie, to join the host's arrow-shooting hunts in order to accomplish the same end. Certainly, those who worked with fairy-derived healing, like Ayrshire cunning woman Bessie Dunlop, seem to have made little moral or epistemological distinction between an act of healing based on a practical herbal cure and an act of healing based on visionary intervention. In this context, although Katharine Ross employed cunning women to kill her stepson through shooting elf arrows at an image moulded out of butter or clay, she could just as logically have employed them to perform the murder through shooting elf arrows at an image conjured during dream or vision experience. In both cases ritualised arrow-shooting precipitating the desired effect.[20]

In the absence of enough contemporary evidence, these suppositions remain tentative, but it is worth pointing out that they do receive considerable support from anthropological sources. Many tribal cultures believe that dark shamans can not only be commissioned by the tribe to perform envisioned *maleficium* against community threats, such as enemy villages, but also by individuals wishing to resolve more personal disputes. During his residence with the Brazilian Xinguano, anthropologist Michael Heckenberger claimed (here conflating the term dark shaman with witch) that: 'A threat more insidious than witches, because there is virtually no way to retaliate, comes from the witches' accomplices: people who contract witches to avenge some perceived threat or slight from their political rivals.'[21] Similarly, Whitehead notes that when a mining frontier threatened the Amazonian Patamuna territory, it 'provided another vector for *kanaimà* activity, particularly in the guise of "contract killers"' and that a Wapishana tribesman (here emphasizing the involvement of plants and plant spirits in *kanaimà* ritual) told him that:

> Say a person [feels he has been wronged and wants to get even]. He makes a contract with the [kanaimà] who kills with the plant. The kanaimà travels in the wind. He takes the plant and passes it over the soles of the [seeker of revenge], from heel to toe. The person closes his eyes and in a minute he travels miles and miles with the kanaimà. He hides in the farm with the kanaimà and points out the man he wants to kill.[22]

There is no scope in the present book to explore how far these 'contract killings' were attributed – that is, socially constructed – and how far they reflected shamanistic practice, despite the fact that such a task immediately presents itself as fundamental to our understanding of early modern witchcraft. But it is sufficient to note here that, even as they stand, the existence of such beliefs raises the possibility that Isobel, like Sowter and Grant, may have been hired by clients to despatch specific victims through the use of envisioned *maleficium*. And with regard to Forbes and Park, this possibility is further enlivened by the fact that, given the former's complex fundamentalism and the latter's financial difficulties, it is unlikely that Isobel was the only Auldearn parishioner to bear the two men a grudge.

That this kind of tension could have existed, on a visionary level, between the non-personal dispensation of fate and specific killings performed in response to personal or community grievance is reflected in wider sources. As we have seen in the last chapter, Pócs has argued that Hungarian witches, in their role as envisioned fate-women, presented *maleficium* 'as a judgement without a stated reason'. But she also argues that it was even more common for them to employ their fate-dispensing capacities as a form of 'norm control'; in these cases predicting or dispensing *maleficium* as a judgement in response to perceived affront, made either against themselves or members of their community:

> Witches would sometimes explain their maleficium through speech and would talk about their conflict with the victim as well as the root of their bewitching revenge, as if it were the conscience of the injured party that had spoken out loud. For example, the creatures in apparitions talk about how the offenders had broken the norms of coexistence: 'we came to bewitch you because you gave no sack,' as in refusing to lend it. Type A conflict [concerned with neighbourhood disputes] is named as the reason for a type C maleficium [relating to the conflict between human and supernatural worlds]. In this the witch that represented the dead and the souls of fate, who regulated behaviour, became adapted to the social system of witchcraft, practically in front of our eyes [my brackets].[23]

Moving closer to home, it is also notable that a significant minority of Scottish encounter-narratives describe, as do Isobel's confessions, the malign house-to-house processions that we have identified with shamanistic experience and arbitrary, non-personal fate-dispensation, alongside specific maleficent acts clearly performed in response to personal or community dispute. In the same year that Isobel was tried, for example, Renfrewshire witch Marie Lamont confessed:

> that shee, Kettie Scot, and Margrat Holm, cam to Allan Orr's house in the likeness of kats, and followed his wif into the chalmer, where they took a herring owt of a barrell, and having taken a byt off it, they left it behind them; the qlk herring the said Allan his wif did eat, and yairefter taking heavy disease, died. The quarrel was, because the said Allan had put Margrat Holm out of the houss wher shee was dwelling.[24]

The Transference Rationale

But the plot thickens yet further. We have argued thus far that Isobel may have used her shamanistic skills to combine compulsive non-personal fate-killing visionary experiences with controlled specific-killings motivated by personal or client-derived grievance. But before we leave this subject for good, we must introduce a third factor into the equation. As we have seen in CHAPTER EIGHT, many contemporary cunning folk worked with the belief that when they were called upon to cure human or animal sickness, they did not attempt to eliminate the malady but merely to divert or transfer it onto something else. The most common recipient for transferred sickness seems to have been an animal, with Isobel herself claiming that in order to cure a bewitched child she diverted its ailment, via a cradle belt, onto a dog or cat. But sickness could also be transferred from person to person. This more controversial act of transference was not always believed to be unethical. As we have seen earlier, in the case of the evil-eye-averting charms misfortune was neatly reflected back to the man or woman who had sent it. But more pertinent in the present context is the fact that sickness could not only be mirrored back to its malevolent source, but also diverted onto the innocent. In 1616 Orkney cunning woman Katherine Jonesdochter was alleged to have 'wisheit in her mind' that 'her husband's infirmities might be transferred to a stranger'. Meanwhile the trial dittays of her fellow Islander, Katherine Bigland, who was tried for witchcraft in the previous year, indicate that strangers were not the only recipients of transferred sickness. Here, we have the almost burlesque description of an ailment being transferred from one man to another and then back to the first man again:

> Item fylit the said Katherene in laying of the seiknes the said William had upone Robert Broun his servand quha continewit therin almost mad tuo dayis quhill schoe cam and graippit his pulses and brow and straikit his hair backwards and saying he wald be weill. And casting of the same seiknes immediatlie upon the said William Bigland. And the said Katherene being challengit within the said Ile therfor for taking of the said seiknes af the said Robert and casiing the same agane upon the said William.[25]

Such skills were clearly dangerous; but they could become even more so. A number of sources suggest that contemporary magical practitioners did not only attempt to transfer sickness, but also death itself, with late seventeenth-century minister James Kirkwood claiming that 'Sometymes they [those with the second sight] bring back life to these who are giving up the Ghost; but another dies in his place, and it always provs fatal.'[26] That Kirkwood's claims were based on genuine folk practice, as opposed to elite fantasy, is suggested by a number of contemporary references. Although this entry from the Thurso session records (from around 1654) is open to a variety of interpretations, it strongly suggests that the protagonist, a cunning woman named 'Graycoat', claimed that the only way she could cure a woman's sick husband was through taking another human life; an admission that seems to have frightened off the prospective client:

> Isobel Groate declairs yt. when George Groat was on his deathbed, she comeing from his house weeping, mett Graycoat in the way, who asked if it was for him she was weeping, and she answered it wes. Therfore she desyred to sie what they wald give her and she wald mak him weill, for he was witched. They said if she would have cow or horse they would give, and she ansred she would not have yt., but lyffe for lyfe. Whereupon she told Catherine Davidsone, she said she wald not medle wt. her, but if it were the Lord's pleasure that he suld die lett him die.[27]

Specific Transference

A number of sources suggest that in death-transferral, as in sickness-transferral, the choice of victim was often arbitrary. It was widely believed, for example, that the unwanted misfortune could randomly alight on the first person entering the sick room after a transferral ritual had been performed, as illustrated in the following excerpt from the Elgin kirk session records, which cites the charges brought against cunning woman Elspet Watsone in 1631:

> the said Elspet being useing a charme upon a seik bairne of Agnes Donaldsones there and his dochter being the first that cam in upoun hir and met hir and that the said Elspet said to hir that the bairns seiknes would licht upoun hir, becaus scho was the first that cam in at the dore, the treuth wheroff he tuke him to prove be witnesses. His dochter therefter taking bed died . . . [28]

But more interestingly, in respect of our enquiry into Isobel's specific killings, is the fact that victims could, in some cases, be individually chosen. In the following account, paraphrased by Peter Maxwell-Stuart from Aberdeenshire trial dittays recorded in 1590, an arbitrary transferral is followed by a very specific one. Cunning women Janet Clerk and Janet Grant were allegedly performing a healing ritual at the house of Margaret Ross, when her neighbour, Elspeth Reid:

> 'came in to the houss be accident, and ye [the cunning women] keist the haill seiknes on hir'. Such a transference of sickness was standard magical practice and Elspeth became seriously ill. Janet Clerk then had the nerve to offer to cure her [Elspeth], provided she and Janet Grant were paid, and again a bargain was struck. Once the fee had been handed over, however, it was explained to Elspeth that her daughter would have to die in her place, 'and then scho ansrit to yow that scho had rather abyid godis will nor that hir barne suld die for hir causs': as a result of which refusal, Elspeth slowly wasted away and died. [29]

That these chilling beliefs – which were so foreign to the reformed church – were of archaic origin is suggested by the fact that human-to-human sickness and death transferral is a common feature of shamanistic practice in many parts of the world. Among the Panoan Shipibo of Brazil, according to anthropologist Elsje Lagrou, 'it is the nature of the shamanic healing act itself that "to remove *nihue* [the illness causing agent] from a sick body"' means "to cast it on another living being who doesn't possess enough *xinan* [knowledge, power] to repulse it. Thus, in curing one, he is always bewitching another"'. [30] Beliefs surrounding death-transferral are also clearly redolent of tribal beliefs concerning soul-retrieval. In many cultures throughout the world it is believed that sickness occurs when the soul, or one of the souls, separates from the body and becomes caught in the spirit worlds, with death occurring if the trapped soul cannot find its way back. In these cases of soul-loss, as it is often termed, the shaman is charged to effect a cure through retrieving the soul from the spirit world and reuniting it with its body. But in some cultures, if this exercise is not successful, the shaman can solve the problem by taking the soul of a healthy man to restore life to a sick one; Van Deusen noting that some Turkic shamans 'might be able to bring back somebody whose soul has already gone to the land of the dead. Sometimes these black shamans can steal a person's soul and give it to someone else to save a life.'[31]

Arrow-Shooting Transference

Of particular significance here, with respect to Isobel, is the fact that we have a contemporaneous witch-testimony that strongly suggests that some practitioners believed that they could effect death-transferral through host-related arrow shooting. As we have seen earlier, some of the 1662 records from Bute closely resemble Isobel's in the extent to which they emphasize participation in the fairy hunt. In one of these, the most articulate of the Bute suspects, Jonet Morison, describes how she attempted to cure a local man named Adam Ker, who had recently died after a period of sickness caused by bewitchment. She also claims that the second time she met the Devil he told her:

> I will free the of all the poverties and troubles thou art in and learn the a way how to bring hom Adam Ker . . . [then] the first service he [the Devil] imployed her in was to bring home Adam Ker and to put Niniane Ker baylie in his stead by shooting of the said Niniane.[32]

What Morison meant by the terms 'bring hom' and 'in his stead' are unclear, although two more of Morison's comments, made later on the same day, bring us closer to a possible explanation:

> [She claimed that] the devill desyred her to tak the lyfe of John Glas proveists dun horse by shooting him and to put him for William Stephen who was lying sick sore payned which she refused to doe. Item that the devill desyred her to tak William Stewart, bayly, his lyfe, by shooteing him to put him for ane nighbour of his that dwelt in the highlands which she refused to doe.[33]

These passages are obscure and therefore open to a variety of interpretations, but in the absence of any obvious alternative it can be argued that they suggest that Jonet Morison believed that her prospective victims (Niniane Ker, John Glas's horse and William Stewart the bayley) were to be killed – on the orders of the Devil – in exchange for the lives of Adam Ker, William Stephen and the Highland neighbour; with the phrases 'to put . . . in his stead' and 'to put him for' meaning 'to kill him in the place of'. From this perspective, bringing Adam Ker 'home' would mean bringing him back from sickness or death and, given Morison's concern with fairy 'blasting' and 'elf-shot', we can even speculate that she believed the sick or dead Ker to have been trapped in fairyland.

Armed with this explanation, we can re-evaluate one of the statements found in Janet Breadheid's confession. Earlier in this chapter we noted that her claim that 'it wes keathren sowter th[a]t wes brunt th[a]t (*shot/harmed*) w[illia]m hay the Last Laird of parkis broth[e]r for on gilbert kintey' could be interpreted as evidence of client-demanded revenge killing. But we also noted that this speculation depends upon accepting Pitcairn's glossing of the term 'for on' as 'at the instigation of'; an interpretation which was presumably influenced by Janet's considerably clearer statement, recorded several lines above, that Agnes Grant 'gott hyre from elspet monro to destroy the Lairdis of park and lochloy'. But in the light of Morison's testimony, we can also speculate that Pitcairn was mistaken, and that the ambiguous term 'for on' did not mean 'at the instigation of' but was in fact a shortened equivalent of Morison's phrase 'put him for ane', that is, 'to put him in the place of'. According to this interpretation, Breadhead's statement could be read to mean, not that 'Katherine Sowter shot/harmed William Hay *at the instigation of* Gilbert Kintey', but that 'Katherine Sowter shot/harmed William Hay *in the place of (or in exchange for)* Gilbert Kintey [my italics]'.

Such an interpretation may seem far-fetched, but it is supported by the fact that in the early modern popular mind, death or sickness transference was firmly linked to the arrow-shooting activities of the fairy host. As we have noted earlier, fairies were believed to roam the skies wounding and killing humans and animals with their elf arrows, either arbitrarily or in response to an affront, in order to feed on their 'spirituous liquor' and/or claim their souls to swell their airborne host. But some sources make it clear that although the host was soul-hungry, it was not always particular with regard to the identity of its victims and this lack of discrimination was negotiated to human advantage. In nineteenth-century arrow-shooting narratives, as we have seen earlier, human participants frequently attempted to divert fairy arrows away from one victim and onto another. When the men described by Donald McKinnon 'were ordered by the hosts to kill men on the road they would kill instead either a horse or cow; for in that way, so long as an animal was killed, the injunction of the hosts was fulfilled'; similarly, Marian Maclean claimed that she had heard of men who shot 'a horse or cow in place of the person ordered to be shot.'[34] In these nineteenth-century cases, the participating humans seem to have diverted fairy malevolence simply because they knew – and were presumably fond of – the victims. But other sources suggest that similar diversions were performed to cure those suffering from fairy-derived sickness; it being believed that if the fairies had 'blasted', 'grippit' or 'shot' an individual, and effectively earmarked him as their prey, they could be persuaded to loose their grip and move on if they were offered someone, or something, else in exchange. Kirk specifically states that many of the common folk believed that if the Highland *eug* or 'deaths Messenger' (an ontologically-obscure entity with fairy connections that 'somtimes [appears] as a litle rough dog') is 'crossed, and conjur'd in tim [it] will be pacified by the death of any other creature instead of the sick Man'.[35] Stirling cunning woman Isobel Watson, meanwhile, links these beliefs even more securely to the fairy nexus: Maxwell-Stuart noting that she claimed that 'she gave the *sithean* her own child, aged two, *in exchange* for their curing her husband of a long illness brought on because he had fallen asleep on a fairy hill [my italics]'.[36] These beliefs are reflected in nineteenth-century anecdotes, such as the following from Whiteness, Orkney, where a man asked a cunning woman who could 'do curious things with the assistance of the "trows"' to come and cure his sick wife. The woman stated:

'Yae, I Can set her . . . fit again, but what haes du ta gie?' There happened to be in the house at the time an old silly kind of man who used to wander about, begging among the neighbours. 'I kno no,' replied the husband, 'excep du taks da auld man at's i' da but-room yundru at da fire.' . . . Next morning the old wandering man was found dead on the hillside not far from the cottage, and from that time the wife got quickly better.[37]

Isobel's Transferral

Given the fact that Isobel was a magical practitioner who claimed to work with sickness transferral, and given the fact that the aforementioned statements in Janet Breadheid's confession can be interpreted as suggestive of death-transferral practices, we can tentatively entertain the possibility that some of Isobel's arrow shootings may have represented visionary rites through which she attempted to cure clients through diverting their sickness or oncoming death onto others. Should something like this have been the case, Isobel may have chosen her victims randomly, at the moment of vision, as the *mazzeri* seem to have done. For as we have seen, Katherine Jonesdochter's claim to have wished 'in her mind' that 'her husband's infirmities might be transferred to a stranger' clearly indicates that in this period the victims of sickness and death transferral could be arbitrarily chosen. But we can also speculate that Isobel's victims may have been specifically sought out. And if the latter were the case, her victim-choice may have been stimulated by a variety of factors. Both anthropological and early modern sources suggest that in magical healing practices the motivations behind the selection of transferal-targets can vary widely. The high proportion of children chosen in the few Scottish rites to have come down to us, as in the cases of Elspeth Reid and Isobel Watson, suggests that among the early modern Scots, as among the Amazonian *kanaimà* or the shamans of the Brazilian Shipibo, the physically vulnerable or burdensome presented themselves as obvious targets. But other sources indicate that motivations could be more complex and expedient. In 1590 Hector Monroe, second son of the Baron of Fowlis (who owned considerable lands in Ross, Sutherland and Inverness), was charged with witchcraft. His dittays state that when he was gravely ill, his foster-mother, Cristian Neill, came to his bedside and discussed treatment with cunning woman Marion McIngaruch: with one passage suggesting that McIngaruch aimed to heal Hector through specifically 'choosing' a death transference or exchange victim (here named as his stepbrother, George Monroe):

> [When Cristian] come agane to the graif, quhair ye was lyand, and inquyrit at the said Witch, 'Quhilk wes hir schois?' Quha answerit and said, that the said 'Mr Hector wes hir schois to leif, and your brother George to die for yow.'[38]

But another account of this incident, recorded earlier in the text, suggests that McIngaruch did not make her decision in isolation. When the ailing Monroe first sent for the cunning woman she allegedly:

gaif yow [Monroe] thre drinkis of walter furth of thre stanis, quhilkis sche had; and eftir lang consultacioun had with hir, sche declarit, that thair wes na remeid for yow to recover your health, without the principall man of your blude sould suffer death for yow; and ye and your complices [his foster mother, Cristian Neill and her daughter], haifing raknit with your selffis, quha this sould be, ffand that it wes George Monroe, eldest sone to Katherene Roiss Lady Fowles.[39]

Wider analysis of Hector Monroe's case reveals that his family was a hotbed of intrigue at the time, with sons and stepsons, stepmothers and foster mothers (including Monroe's stepmother Katharine Ross) vying with each other for inheritance and power, and allegedly hiring witches and using *maleficium* to achieve their aims. The sources strongly suggest that George Monroe's death would not only have saved Hector's life, but would also have benefited his family materially. In this context, it is highly likely that McIngaruch's choice – notably arrived at after 'lang consultacioun' with the client and other members of his family – was influenced by political expediency, with the need for death-transference dove-tailing, in this case, with her client's need for self-advancement. From this perspective, Monroe's case implies that the magical act of death or sickness transference teetered on an ethical knife-edge and reflected, perhaps more than any other type of traditional healing activity, the complexities of the human conscience.

These perspectives encourage us to speculate that the personal killings depicted in Isobel's confessions may have been provoked by similarly complex stimuli, although in the last analysis her precise motivations must elude us. While we can surmise that Isobel may well have deliberately attempted to kill Park and Forbes through envisioned arrow shooting, we cannot presume to know how far her endeavours were motivated by personal vendetta; how far they were motivated by client demands for magical defence or revenge; and how far they were motivated by her attempts, as a healer, to distract death's capricious attentions away from her clients, family and friends. But we can presume, reasonably safely, that whatever Isobel's motivations, these activities would have placed her in a very difficult position. However urgent the client demand and however just the cause, if Isobel joined the envisioned fairy hunt with pre-determined victims in mind then she stepped over the invisible line from being an instrument of fate to being a manipulator of fate. And as such, she would not only have deserved the title of 'chooser of the slain', as worn by her archaic Anglo-Saxon counterpart the *wælcyrige*, but she would also – so far as many of her contemporaries were concerned – have deserved the rather less distinguished sobriquet of evil sorcerer or witch.

PART III
The Demonological Elements

'Should not a righteous Christian prefer a thousand times
to be ill and in hardship with God, than be
healthy with the Devil?'
Bernhard Albrecht,1628

Introduction to Part III

I

In the last two chapters we have constructed an interpretative lens that, when turned onto Isobel's obscure and seemingly irrational arrow-shooting passages, causes them to come into focus and begin to make sense. Through this lens, these passages represent a complex nexus of dark shamanistic belief and practice underpinned by the community-benefit rationale, with rites ranging from that of death or sickness divination to that of death or sickness transferral and personal or client-commissioned revenge killing. As we touched on at the end of the last chapter, these practices, should they have taken place in seventeenth-century Auldearn, would have been highly controversial. Anthropological research suggests that all cultures nurturing dark shamanistic practices, whether touched or untouched by the developed world, view them with deep ambivalence. It also indicates that the more contact these cultures have with the world's major religions (and latterly modern Western culture) the more likely it is that this ambivalence will swing toward blanket condemnation. Recent studies in South America, for example, have illustrated how, in the hands of early missionaries and colonialists, the nuanced assessments of dark shamanism inherited by traditionally enculturated Amazonians could easily degenerate into simplistic denunciation.[1] As a consequence we can assume that – however acute their need for magical aid – for most men and women living in post-Reformation Scotland dark shamanistic practices would have been synonymous with witchcraft.

Pending further research, these conclusions must of course remain highly speculative, but even as they stand they have relevance for our understanding of early modern demonological witchcraft as a whole. They suggest that once we enlarge our positive view of shamanism to incorporate concepts of dark practice, many of the difficulties that have traditionally plagued the shamanistic paradigm dissolve. They also suggest that when we approach a given demonological encounter-narrative we should not automatically tell ourselves that 'this does not relate to visionary experience'; but that 'this *may* relate to visionary experience'. In many, indeed perhaps the large majority of cases, we may go on to conclude that on the basis of either insufficient evidence or incontrovertible counter-evidence (such as exists in the famous case of Johannes Junius of Bamberg, 1628) we cannot assert that visionary experience was involved. But importantly, the question has at least been asked.[2]

Moreover, with regard to the shamanistic paradigm, the fact that it is difficult to assess precisely what percentage of demonological encounter-narratives may have been rooted in visionary experience is less significant than it may at first appear. It would not have needed a high incidence of dark shamanistic practice to fuel the alarm that underpinned the witch-hunts, on both an elite and popular level. As with crimes like paedophilia today, fear of perceived practice undoubtedly exceeded actual practice; and for every genuine confession (that is, every confession that referred to actual dark shamanistic activity) there are likely to have been many more that were false. But nevertheless these hypotheses indicate that, as we concluded with regard to basic *maleficium* in CHAPTER EIGHT, the elevated hype that accumulated around demonological witchcraft may have been accumulating around something that was essentially 'real'.

II

But although such speculations are tempting, in entertaining them at this stage we are running a little too far ahead of ourselves. Even if we provisionally acknowledge that some of the *maleficium* found in some demonological encounter-narratives could have reflected dark shamanistic activity, before we can argue that they were rooted in actual visionary practice, as opposed to merely the recounting of shamanistic beliefs, themes and motifs, we still need to confront the problem of stereotypical demonological content. Witchcraft suspects did not just stand up in courts of law and claim to have performed *maleficium* in the company of elves, under fairy hills, and in festive cavalcades led by fairy kings and queens. They also stood up and claimed to have performed *maleficium* in the company of the Devil, at witches' sabbaths, and according to the chilling dictates of the soul-demanding, Christianity-renouncing demonic pact. As a consequence, before we can convincingly argue that demonological encounter-narratives were in any way related to shamanistic visionary experience, we need to explain how and why these stereotypically demonic ideas managed to weave themselves so deeply and coherently into the heart of suspects' testimonies.

And it is here, at the foot of this new challenge, that Isobel can help us once again. Her confessions are not only interesting because they contain fairy-related content suggestive of shamanistic visionary experience, but they are also unique in the extent to which this suggestive content is interspersed with stereotypically demonological references. In many places, this demonological material emerges as distinct from its surroundings. Indeed, the polarity between the passages depicting the demonic pact in Confessions One and Two, and the passages describing flight in fairy whirlwinds or feasting in fairy hills has been sufficiently marked to persuade us, in previous chapters, to argue that two different processes of narrative formation may have been occurring during their creation (in the former cases, false confession only, and in the second, false confession plus visionary experience recall). But conversely, this simplistic conclusion is challenged by the fact that these passages are seamlessly connected to each other by sections of intermediary material in which demonological and fairy-related elements emerge in such subtle combinations that it is not easy to argue for one or the other narrative genesis. It is also challenged by the fact that certain themes and characters, like the witches' coven, the performance of *maleficium*, and of course the Devil, seem to span the demonological/fairy lore continuum from one extreme to the other with effortless continuity. As a consequence, Isobel's confessions offer us a uniquely magnified perspective, as if gained through a microscope, onto the places where the stereotypically demonological elements found in witch-narratives may or may not have fused into shamanistic experience.

III

Of all the elements in Isobel's confessions that span the demonological/fairy lore continuum, none do so with as much panache as the figure of the Devil. And it is for this reason that we shall begin our analysis here. Like many confessional elements, Isobel's Devil figure presents us with an epistemological challenge. If he only appeared in the demonological passages, then we could neatly write him off as a coerced-compliant or false-memory response to interrogatorial pressure. But this tidy assessment is challenged by the fact that he is also a dominant presence in the intermediary and fairy-related passages. The Devil does not only surprise Isobel with unsolicited encounters on the lonely road between Drumduan and the Heads, or invite her to meet him in Auldearn churchyard to enter into a demonic pact; but he also sits with her as she roasts the *corp creadh* at Janet Breadheid's hearth, leads the paddock-drawn plough as it swings up and down the Breadley's land and takes her to the elves' house to give her arrows out of his own hand. Similarly, although the Devil behaves differently in different parts of the confessions, elements of his nature and performance are consistent throughout, to the extent that if Isobel's confessional narrative were a novel or play script you might argue that he was a relatively coherent piece of characterization.

The fact that Isobel's Devil straddles the continuum between the demonological and fairy lore passages with such consummate ease demands explanation. It challenges us to explore how far he was a figment of the interrogators' imaginations, how far he was a product of false confession, and how far he was constructed around shamanistic encounters experienced prior to arrest. And in trying to answer these questions we will gain further insight into the genesis, epistemological status, and 'shamanistic credentials' of demonological encounter-narratives per se.

14

Lady Isobel and the Elf Knight

The first problem to be faced when attempting to understand Isobel's Devil is the fact that, of all the figures described in her confessions, he represents the one most likely to have been influenced by her interrogators. Although the confessions do not contain any direct indications of the questions that Isobel was asked in this respect, if we look at some of the few Scottish records that retain prosecutorial dialogue, we can gain a rough idea. The trial dittays of Ayrshire cunning woman Bessie Dunlop (1576) are the most illustrative here. Although Bessie clearly believed that her familiar spirit, Tom Reid, was a spirit of the dead with fairy affiliations, her interrogators defined him as a 'spirit of the Devil' and plagued her with the following questions (here modernized and changed into direct speech):

> What kind of man was this Tom Reid?
> How and in what manner of place did the said Tom Reid come to her?
> Did she seek anything from Tom to help herself, or any other?
> How did she know this man was Tom Reid who had died at Pinkie?
> What time of the day or night did he come to her?
> Did she say anything to him?
> Did she never ask him why he came to her more than anyone else?
> Had she ever spoken to him at a loch or waterside?
> When did she last speak with Tom?
> Did she never ask him what trouble should come to her for being in his company?[1]

The questions concerning commerce with demonic spirits put to Appin cunning man Donald McIlmichall one hundred years later, show that although the demonological stereotype of the witches' sabbath was now more established in northern Scotland, the general tenor of the questioning was not, in this case at least, very different. McIlmichall was asked:

> What night did he first meet them, and where did he go after he parted with them?
> What time did he continue his meeting?
> With whom did he engage and what did he judge them to be?

Was he asked for his name and was he given a new name?

Did he meet with them in other places?

Did he consult the Devil and these evil spirits about stolen goods?[2]

Although we know that Isobel was likely to have been asked these kinds of questions about the Devil throughout her interrogations, we can speculate that in the parts of her narrative where her Devil figure most closely resembles theological stereotypes (as in the pact passages), he was most likely to have emerged through intense and specific-closed questioning, and in the parts where he differs most markedly from these stereotypes (as in the fairy lore passages), he is the least; with his genesis in the intermediate passages falling somewhere in between. Given this distinction, we will be best served here by dividing our analysis into two parts. In the present chapter we will explore Isobel's Devil figure as he appears in the fairy lore and intermediate passages, where he will be termed the 'folkloric Devil', while in the next chapter we will move on to explore him as he appears in the demonic-pact passages, where he will be termed the 'theological Devil'. The all-important connections between the two Devil figures, as they may have existed for both Isobel and her interrogators, will emerge as the analysis progresses.

Devils and Fairy Men

In recent years, historians have begun to focus more closely on the role of fairy belief in Scottish witchcraft confessions, and as a consequence it is becoming increasingly clear that there was a strong link, in both the popular and elite mind, between the Devil and the male fairy. A number of witch-records from different parts of Scotland clearly illustrate that although interrogators defined the spirits their suspects described as the Devil or a demon, the suspects themselves clearly believed him to have been a fairy or elf. Nowhere is this interrogatorial superimposition more clearly represented than in the blunt assertion, found in the trial dittays of Orkney cunning woman Elspeth Reoch (1616), that she met *'the devell quhilk she callis the farie man* [my italics]'.[3] Other fairy-related confessions contain no direct references to the fairy status of the spirit defined in the text as the Devil, but the latter's behaviour or appearance makes it clear that he was a fairy who had been demonized by the interrogators (or the accused, at their instigation) before his original identity was recorded on the page. Even in confessions that make no direct allusions to fairy belief at all, the character of the Devil can be strongly redolent of his fairy counterparts. Witchcraft records from early modern Fife, for example, do not contain many overt fairy-related references but, as Stuart Macdonald notes, in many passages describing the Devil, 'Instead of the details we would expect in a portrait of the great enemy of God and humanity, what we find are elements that in places are suggestive of a fairy or an elf.'[4] These observations are supported by the fact that, as the Survey of Scottish Witchcraft has recently shown, in the records between 1563 to 1736 that specify the colour of the clothes worn by the Devil or his demons, second to black, the most common colour cited was the traditional fairy green, with blue (also a coloration favoured by the fairies) coming a close second, with the three colours gaining fifty-one, twenty-three and twenty-one references respectively.[5]

In this context, what is immediately telling is the fact that, with the significant exception of feasting with the fairy king and queen at the Downie Hill, the Devil appears in nearly every fairy-related and intermediate passage in Isobel's trial. He is present at her house-to-house processions, oversees the manufacture of arrows at the elves' house, directs her host-arrow-shooting activities and is the 'maister' of the fairy-type servitor spirits described in the second and fourth confessions. In all of these different scenarios, he comes across as an authoritarian spirit with ultimate control over proceedings. That this Devil figure may have been fairy-derived is additionally supported by the fact that many other fairy-related encounter-narratives from the period clearly feature a fairy-man-in-authority figure. Sometimes, as in the case of Margaret Alexander, Isobel Watson et al., this figure is overtly defined as the king of the fairies, but in the majority of cases his precise identity is not specified. When Appin cunning man Donald McIlmichall (1677) entered a fairy hill he saw 'ane old man as seemed to have preference above the rest . . . [and who] seemed to be cheif being ane large tall corporal Gardman and ruddie'.[6] Perthshire cunning woman Janet Trall (1588) claimed to have met the fairy folk 'who appeared some of them red, some of them grey, and riding upon horses. The principal of them that spake to me was like a bonny white man, riding upon a grey horse . . . [and at a later meeting] the principal of them appeared, clad in green.'[7] Isobel's fellow countrywoman Alison Peirson (1588) met 'ane lustie mane' who appeared before her while she lay sick 'cled in grene clathis' and 'apperit to hir att ane uther tyme . . . with mony mene and wemen with him'; while Orkney cunning woman Katharine Caray (1616) claimed that 'ane great number of fairie men mett her' when she was wandering through the hills 'at the doun going of the sun', and that this 'great number' included 'a maister man'.[8] The folkloric origin of the fairy-man-in-authority, as he emerges in these narratives, is further supported by the fact that in contemporary and later oral literature, fairy society emerges as a reflection of the human, with a social hierarchy presided over by both male and female authority figures.

Mercy! Our Lord!

Although Isobel's folkloric Devil is never defined as a fairy man, his behaviour is consistent with the fairy-man-in-authority figure, as depicted in both early modern encounter-narratives and contemporary and later folklore. One of his most prominent characteristics, for example, is his temperamental and physical aggressiveness. He is quick to anger, controlling, sexually predatory and physically abusive, with Isobel claiming, in the third confession, that she and her companions would be 'beattin if ve wer absent any tym' and that 'he wold be beating and scurgeing ws all wp and downe, w[i]th tardis & uth[e]r sharp scurges . . . he wold haw neither pittie nor mercie, whan he vold be angrie at ws, he wold girne at ws, lyk a dowge, as iff he wold swellow ws wp'.

As we explored in CHAPTER SEVEN, seventeenth-century Scotland was a violent and patriarchal culture, and therefore we can assume that, whatever her Devil's epistemological status, Isobel drew on memories of real-life encounters with aggressive and authoritarian men to craft him. But violent, domineering behaviour was also associated with the fairies. The host who crowded around Pennant's Breadalbane seer as he worked in his garden 'very roughly pushed him to and fro'; Appin cunning man Donald McIlmichall (1677) was 'reproved and stricken' by the fairies 'in the cheik and other parts'; while Stirling cunning woman Isobel Watson (1590) claimed that she sought 'to keip hir fra all straikis [blows] of the fair folk (quha usit to straik hir sair) in the chainge of the mone' – allegedly drawing the presbytery's attention to 'a mark on the middle finger of her left hand where one of the *sithean* [fairies] had bitten her, and another mark on her arm, also caused by a *sith*'.[9] The dead, with whom the fairies commonly lived and travelled, were also associated with physical violence. A late seventeenth-century pamphlet recording the haunting of Kirkcudbright man Andrew Mackie and his family describes how a ghost (which appeared variously as a young man 'red faced, with yellow hair' and a boy 'with grey cloths, and a bonnet on his head') plagued the family by 'throwing stones, and beating them with staves'. The pamphlet also alleges that on one occasion the spectre 'gripped him [Andrew] so by the hair, that he thought something like nails of fingers scratched his skin. It [also] dragged severals up and down the house by the cloaths.'[10] Fairy violence also emerges prominently in nineteenth-century folklore. Just as Isobel and her companions were 'beattin [by the Devil] if ve wer absent [from coven meetings] any tym, or neglect any thing', the men who entered into magical partnerships with fairy women were punished harshly by their spirit-allies if they reneged on their commitments, with J. G. Campbell describing how 'On meeting her [his Elfin mistress] first he is put under spells to keep appointments with her in future every night. If he dares for one night to neglect his appointment, she gives him such a sound thrashing the first time she gets hold of him that he never neglects it again.'[11] The *brùnaidh* or brownie was also notoriously violent if angered, Campbell again claiming that in Cantyre it was 'much addicted to giving slaps in the dark to those who soiled the house; and there are some still alive who can testify to receiving a slap that left their faces black'.[12] As a consequence of this violence, both fairies and the dead were associated with bruises and marks (the latter's attentions being termed 'the dead man's nip') and further research is likely to prove that these beliefs were associated with, and to a certain extent underpinned, demonological notions concerning the witches' mark.[13] Traditional stories and ballads known to have been extant in early modern Scotland also emphasize this aspect of fairy nature. In the ballad of 'Tam Lin' the fairy queen is depicted as petulant and aggressive (in one version wishing the heroine an 'ill death' for stealing away her mortal abductee), while Hind Etin, the eponymous fairy hero who had 'neer got christendame', tied his human heroine to a tree, threatened her with death and then imprisoned her in a cave 'monie fathoms deep' for merely collecting nuts in his woods.[14] Similarly, 'The Red Etin' and 'Child Roland' both contain a supernatural authority figure – specifically defined, in the latter, as the king of the fairies – who was as angry and capricious as the fe-fi-fo-fumming giant featured in their more well-known variant, 'Jack and the Beanstalk'.[15]

The Amorous Elf Man

But Isobel's relationship with her demonic overlord was more complex than that of domineering master and frightened servant. As he emerges from the confessions, the Devil figure was not only aggressive but also deeply amorous, both towards Isobel and other members of her coven. At first glance, the fact that this aspect of the Devil's behaviour is largely concentrated in the demonological passages points to the super-imposition of elite stereotypes. Since the Middle Ages, learned writers and demonologists had drawn attention to the Devil's predatory sexuality and his proclivity to seduce or coerce witches into carnal union in order to seal the demonic pact. Although the presence of idiosyncratic elements in Isobel's sex-with-the-Devil passages suggest that she contributed to their genesis and quite probably drew on real-life sexual experiences in order to do so, their wealth of conventional references, such as the Devil's cold penis and the fact that intercourse occurred right after the pact in a business-like way, suggests that the interrogators fed Isobel stereotypical ideas about demonic sex. The likelihood that Harry Forbes would have been particularly interested in this aspect of the Devil's work supports this thesis.

But it is equally likely that in contributing to these passages Isobel may also have drawn on contemporary beliefs concerning fairies. A number of the individuals accused of witchcraft or sorcery during the early modern period confessed to having sex, or having seen others have sex, with fairy men, in some cases claiming that it was through this act that magical powers were gained. Orkney cunning woman Elspeth Reoch was allegedly approached by a fairy man in green who spent time 'persuading hir to let him ly with hir'; while Livingston witch Margaret Alexander (1647) claimed to have gone from Calder to Linton with a group of fairies, after which one of them, whom she iden-tified as the fairy king, 'laye with her upone the brige'.[16] Similarly, the daughter of Aberdeenshire cunning woman Isobel Strachan (1597) maintained that 'quhat skill so ever scho hed scho hed it of hir mother; and hir mother learnit at ane elf man quha lay with hir', and Stirling cunning woman Isobel Watson asserted that 'There was a woman in Stirling . . . with whom she saw the fairy king have sexual intercourse'.[17] These accounts are brief, and are compromised by the fact that they emerged in interrogato-rial arenas, but they undoubtedly reflected popular belief. Robert Kirk makes several references to the amorous nature of the female fairies who 'tryst with men', while the following extract from Jo Ben's *Descriptio Insularum Orchadiarum*, which was compiled sometime in the sixteenth century, vividly illustrates how ideas about sexual relation-ships between humans and spirits thrived outside the elite demonological mind. Here the supernatural protagonist, allegedly encountered on the Orkney Island of Stronsay, seems to be some kind of water horse; a fairy or 'trow [troll]' believed to frequent lochs, rivers and coastal waters and have a taste for human blood. With his large testicles and horse-like limbs the troll is uncannily redolent of Isobel's long-limbed Devil who, with his 'hodg nature', pursued the Auldearn coven members 'lyke a weath horse amongst mearis':

A great monster, called Troicis, often associates with women living here, which when I resided there a beautiful woman that was married to an able-bodied farmer, was much tormented by a great spirit, and were seen, against the husband's will, lying in one bed. The woman at last became emaciated through sorrow. I advised that she might get freedom by prayer, alms giving, and fasting, which she performed; the duration of the trouble lasted a year. The description of the monster is this. He was covered with sea-weed over his whole body, and resembled a dark horse with wrinkled skin, had limbs [or a penis?] like a horse and [large testicles].[18]

It is also significant, with respect to the Isobel-as-oral-performer hypothesis, that fairy sexuality is a consistent feature of traditional Scottish songs, stories and ballads. Buchan has noted that the majority of the ballads collected from women in the north-east of Scotland in the eighteenth and nineteenth centuries were concerned with romantic relationships, and that in many cases these relationships occurred between humans and a fairy or other type of supernatural being: the most common themes being the abduction of a human woman by a fairy man or the abduction of a human man by a fairy woman.[19] Notably, amatory relations between humans and fairy-like spirits occur in well-known and widely-circulated ballads such as 'The Elphin Knight', 'Alison Gross', 'Thomas Rhymer', 'Tam Lin', 'Hind Etin', 'Clerk Colville', 'The Earl of Mar's Daughter' and 'King Orfeo'. A similar emphasis can be found in traditional tales like 'The Mermaid Wife', 'The Tale of the Hoodie', 'The Daughter of the Skies' and 'The Fair Gruagach'; with this Europe-wide theme being immortalized, south of the border, in Shakespeare's 'A Midsummer Night's Dream'. As a female oral performer from the north-east of Scotland Isobel was, like her fellow countrywomen in subsequent centuries, likely to have favoured material of a romantic nature, and we can reasonably suppose that she had committed to memory a range of songs, stories and ballads concerning amorous encounters between human women and fairy men. We can also suppose that it would have been easy for her to consciously or unconsciously draw this folkloric material into her depiction of the sexually predatory Devil. That something like this may have transpired is supported by comparative analysis. In Confession Three Isobel states how:

> he wold com to my hows top in the shape of a crow, or lyk a dear or in any uther shap now and then, I wold ken his woice at the first heiring of it, and wold goe furth to him and hav carnall cowpula[tio]n w[i]th him . . . (46/31)

What is interesting here is the fact that although the Devil as lover in crow form does not emerge prominently from demonological works, the 'lover in bird-shape' was, as nineteenth-century folklorist Child noted, 'a very familiar trait in [Scottish] fiction, particularly in popular tales'.[20] In Child's north-eastern ballad 'The Earl of Mar's Daughter', for example, a young woman is so enamoured of a magical lover who transforms from a bird into a beautiful young man in order to seduce her every night, that she refuses the attentions of 'a lord o high renown': claiming obstinately 'I'm content to live alane/ Wi my bird, Cow-me-doo'.[21] The sexuality of Isobel's Devil is also closely mirrored in two further north-eastern ballads, also recorded by Child, known as 'The

Elfin Knight' and – coincidentally given our subject here – 'Lady Isabel and the Elf Knight'. These ballads are of undoubted archaic origin and appear in many variants throughout Europe, with Child claiming of the latter that 'Of all ballads this has perhaps obtained the widest circulation'.[22] Both feature a girl being seduced by a sexually predatory male fairy, but 'Lady Isabel and the Elf Knight' is particularly notable for the fact that the supernatural protagonist is not only as amorous as Isobel's Devil, but also as morally ambivalent and death-seeking. The adventure begins when the heroine is filled with longing at the sound of the elf knight's horn:

> Fair lady Isabel sits in her bower sewing,
> Aye as the gowans grow gay
> There she heard an elf-knight blawing his horn.
> The first morning in May

> 'If I had yon horn that I hear blawing,
> And yon elf-knight to sleep in my bosom.'
> This maiden had scarcely these words spoken,
> Till in at her window the elf-knight has luppen.

The elf knight then invites Isabel to travel with him, on horseback, to 'yon greenwood side'; a place that, though not specifically defined as fairyland, is clearly a region falling under his jurisdiction. Then subsequent verses reveal that, like most fairy folk, he has a chilling potential for malevolence and can operate as an agent of death:

> 'Light down, light down, lady Isabel,' said he,
> 'We are come to the place where ye are to die.'

> 'Seven king's-daughters here hae I slain,
> And ye shall be the eight o them.'

Here Isabel pleads with the elf knight to spare her life, with her cries of 'hae mercy' being uncannily similar to those uttered by Isobel Gowdie and her fellow coven members as they were beaten by the Devil:

> 'Hae mercy, hae mercy, kind sir, on me,
> Till ance my dear father and mother I see.'

When mercy was not forthcoming, the Lady Isabel did not give up and succumb to the elf knight's superior powers. Just as some of Isobel's coven members were prepared to stand up to the Devil when he beat them (with Bessie Wilson speaking 'croslie w[i]th hir tow-nge' and 'belling again to him stowtlie'), she used her wits to defend herself against her spirit-lover's bloodthirsty demands. The ballad describes how, after sweet-talking and charming the knight into sleep:

Wi his ain sword-belt sae fast as she ban him,
Wi his ain dag-durk sae sair as she dang him.

'If seven king's-daughters here ye hae slain,
Lye ye here, a husband to them a'.'[23]

Epistemological Status

The fact that popular lore surrounding fairy-men-in-authority resonates so strongly
with Isobel's Devil figure, as he is depicted in both the fairy-related and intermediate
passages, is strongly suggestive of folkloric influence. But our understanding of how,
when, and to what degree this influence occurred depends upon our assessment of the
Devil's epistemological status. As with all Isobel's confessional content, we have three
main options to choose from here, all of which could have occurred singly or in combination. (1) We can assume that the folkloric Devil was a coerced-compliant fiction,
created through psychological cave-in, or in an attempt to please her interrogators. (2)
We can assume that he was a coerced-internalized response, that is, a false-memory
recollection created in response to close questioning. (3) We can assume (on the basis
of our speculations in the previous three chapters) that he emerged out of shamanistic
visionary encounters experienced prior to arrest.

The analysis of the mechanics of false confession undertaken in CHAPTER NINE suggests that options one and two are very likely to have played a role here, and given the
idiosyncratic nature of Isobel's folkloric Devil and the fact that she did not (so far as we
know) retract her depiction of him during her long imprisonment, points to false-memory generation as the most likely option of the two. The interrogators were likely to
have pursued Isobel with questions about a stereotypical theological Devil who made
demonic pacts and led witches' covens and it is not difficult to envisage a situation in
which Isobel, left to ponder over and dream about these suggestions during her long
weeks of solitary confinement, began to generate false memories in which the Devil of
the interrogators did not only fuse with vivid memories of the real men she had encountered in her life, but also with the colourful images of violent fairy kings, shaggy-haired
trolls, seductive elves and cold-fingered ghosts that she had absorbed, since she was a
child, from the songs, ballads, stories and memorates passed around the fermtoun firesides.

But our analysis into shamanistic visionary experience in CHAPTERS TEN to
THIRTEEN also encourages us to consider the possibility that in creating her false
memories about the Devil, Isobel's imagination did not only draw on real-life physical events and remembered folklore, but also on prior shamanistic experience.
Although far-fetched at first glance, this possibility is supported by Continental comparisons. As we saw in CHAPTER ELEVEN, the male authority figure emerges in many
of the shamanistic spirit-group narratives of folkloric origin found in medieval and
early modern sources. This figure appears either in isolation or in conjunction with a
female consort and is described, like his female counterpart, as either a spirit or a

human in subtle body who directs proceedings and bestows magical powers. The Sicilian *donas de fuera* followed a goddess figure (defined variously as 'The Queen of the Fairies', La Matrona and so on) but some of them claimed that their leader was accompanied by a male consort. One *dona* from Palermo claimed that she attended meetings on a 'great plain' where there stood 'a large tribune with two chairs. On one of them sat a red young man and on the other a beautiful woman: they called her the Queen, and the man was the King', while her fellow *dona* Vicencia la Rosa, simply stated that she belonged to a company headed by a 'Prince' from whom she gained her healing knowledge.[24] Hungarian *táltos* Erzsébet Tóth claimed that she fought her 'heavenly battles' alongside the Christian God while Erzsébet Balási claimed that when she and her *táltos* troop fought at the hill of Szendelik, 'their chief was János Nagy'.[25] Similarly, a variety of male authority figures (often bearing the title of 'captain'), ranging from the supernatural to the human, oversaw the battles of the *benandanti*, with the young visionary, named Gasparo, claiming that his meetings were headed by a man and that 'I do not know him, but when we are all together, we hear people say, "this is the captain," and almost in a dream we see a man larger than the others'.[26] In Balkan werewolf belief, the humans who roam the countryside in the form of animals to fight the beings who steal fertility are led by a 'master of the animals' or 'wolf shepherd' who, according to Pócs, 'is able to summon the wolves from all over the world, and, as their chief, he allots to them their tasks; whom each of them must tear apart, which flocks they must attack.'[27] These traditions come even closer to Britain in the werewolf traditions of France, where suspects interrogated in Bordeaux at the beginning of the seventeenth century referred to their leader (who gave his followers wolf-skins so that they could transform) as 'the Lord of the Forest'.[28] Even the Corsican *mazzeri*, when engaged in their annual battles, organized themselves into a 'milizia' and elected captains.[29]

Even more pertinent, with regard to Isobel, is the fact that by the seventeenth century, spirit-group narratives that came under the Wild Hunt corpus were frequently associated with male command. Woden, or his Norse equivalent Odin, is widely believed to be one of the earliest and most long-standing Hunt leaders, although semi-supernatural or human characters as varied as Arthur, Charlemagne, King Herla, Wild Edric, Herne the Hunter and more local figures, have also been associated with the role.[30] Similarly, male authority figures also appear in narratives relating to the Scottish *sluagh*. In 1895 an old Arran crofter told Carmichael a story about a man who 'used to observe the ways of the fairies and to do as they did', claiming that when he and his spirit-companions had mounted their ragwort stalks one of those present chanted a rhyme which began 'My king at my head', after which the king of the fairies cried 'Follow me' and the whole company flew 'pell-mell' across the Irish ocean.[31] This male command, and the aggressiveness with which it could be executed, is also intimated by Carmichael's observation that host-abducted men 'slew and maimed at the bidding of their spirit-masters, who in return ill-treated them in a most pitiless manner'.[32] Also interesting, in the context of Isobel's confessions, is the fact that these male host leaders were identified with the Devil or his demons from the early medieval period through to the nineteenth century, with Jeffrey Russell noting, in reference to the Middle Ages, that 'In widely credited stories, the Devil leads the wild hunt surrounded by his demonic dogs' and, more generally, that 'The image of the Devil as a hunter with souls as his game was a popular metaphor of the medieval encyclopedists'.[33] In his role as leader of the Wild Hunt, handing elf arrows to Isobel's coven members and telling them who to shoot, Isobel's folkloric Devil acts little differently from the mythological Odin who 'commands' his *valkyrjur* 'while the battle rages, giving victory according to his will'; or from the Balkan werewolf chief who distributes tasks to his followers and tells them 'whom each of them must tear apart'; or from the pitiless Highland 'spirit-masters' who 'command' nineteenth-century weavers and farmers to slay men and cattle with their 'unerring venomous darts'.[34] Taken as a whole, these perspectives invite us to entertain the possibility that Isobel's folkloric Devil was, at his core, an envisioned shamanistic phenomenon.

Isobel's Perspective

But if we entertain the possibility that Isobel's folkloric Devil was constructed around an envisioned core, then a more complex question immediately arises. What, at the moment of visionary encounter, did Isobel herself believe her supernatural male leader to have been? And did her assessment of his identity change during imprisonment and interrogation? Isobel's is not one of those confessions, like those of Bessie Dunlop or Elspeth Reoch, in which it is clear that although the interrogators believed the suspect's spirit helper to have been the Devil, the suspect themselves believed him to have been a fairy man or spirit of the dead. With the exception of a brief reference to the 'weill favoured and broad faced' king of the fairies during the first interrogation, Isobel's male-spirit-in-authority figure is consistently defined as 'the Devil' in all four confessions. This uniform definition leaves us with a variety of interpretative options.

First, we can speculate that the term 'the Devil' was bluntly superimposed upon Isobel's description of a fairy or fairy-related figure by John Innes, in response to the opinions of the court. In other words, when Isobel made a comment such as 'the fairy man shapes elf arrows with his own hand' Innes wrote down '*the Devil* shapes elf arrows with his own hand' and so on. But this scenario is not congruent with what we know of the Auldearn notary. While the associations between fairies and the Devil could, in the minds of some witchcraft interrogators, have justified this linguistic manipulation, and it may well have taken place in some cases, Innes's scrupulousness and the care he seems to have taken in recording descriptive terms and names make such a blatant superimposition unlikely.

Secondly, we can take a directly opposing position and speculate that the consistent use of the term 'the Devil' in the confessions reflects the fact that Isobel herself defined the fairy host leader as such from the first confession onwards, and that she also employed this definition during any prior-to-arrest visionary encounters that may have informed them. The possibility that Isobel consciously brought the Devil to the Auldearn tolbooth, which seems highly unlikely at this point in our analysis, will be examined in more detail in CHAPTER SEVENTEEN.

Our third, and at this stage most likely, option lies somewhere between these two extremes. Here, we can speculate that the term 'the Devil' was, as in the first option, derived from an interrogator-led linguistic conflation between the terms 'fairy man' and 'Devil' but that in this case the conflation was more subtle. As we have noted before, the term 'devil' as in '*a* devil', was used to designate fairies on both a popular and elite level. In 1677, for example, a Scottish clergyman observed that the common folk termed brownies 'white deviles', while over one hundred years earlier William Hay noted how 'there are certain women who do say that they have dealings with Diana the queen of the fairies. There are others who say that the fairies are demons, and deny having any dealings with them'.[35] There is no doubt that this cross-definition was exploited by witchcraft interrogators, as illustrated by the trial dittay of Kirkcudbright cunning woman Bessie Carnochan (1657). According to witness reports paraphrased in the dittay, Carnochan had boasted to one neighbour that 'she had some skill indeed, but that she had got it from the fairies', and to another that 'The king of all the devils is my god'. Given Carnochan's intimacy with the fairies, and the synonymy of the terms 'devil' and 'fairy', it is likely that by the term 'king of all the devils' she referred to some kind of fairy-man-in-authority or perhaps even the fairy king. But the fact that Carnochan's dittay is prefaced by the statement, '[you have] many years bygone taken yourself to the service of *the* Devil, the enemy of Man's salvation, [and] entered in paction with him' strongly suggests that her interrogators defined her 'king of all the devils' as *the* Devil.[36]

We can speculate that something similar occurred in Isobel's case. In her second confession Isobel provides a long list of spirits with fairy-like characteristics, but concludes it by specifying that 'ther wilbe many uther divellis waiting wpon (*damaged – words missing*) maister divell bot he is bigger and mor awfull th[a]n the rest of the divellis and they all reverence him'. In this reference to a 'maister divell' Isobel may have, like Bessie Carnochan, been referring to '*a* devil' who was in fact a fairy-man-in-authority figure. And again, as in Carnochan's case, her interrogators may have re-defined him as '*the* Devil'. This possibility is supported by the fact that the only overt reference to a fairy-man-in-authority in Isobel's narrative – the 'king of fearie' – emerges relatively early in the first confession and in relation to one of the small number of coven-related activities at which the Devil seems to have been absent. This positioning leads us to speculate that at this early stage in the interrogations, Forbes et al. interpreted Isobel's fairy king as '*the* Devil' and reflected this interpretation back to her. Then, as the questioning intensified, Isobel gradually internalized this re-definition until she finally offered it up herself, voluntarily, to be duly recorded by Innes. We can certainly see this re-defining process at work in a number of other European witchcraft records, including those relating to envisioned shamanistic figures. At one interrogation the Friulian *benandante* Paolo Gasparutto, for example, claimed that he had been initiated into his work by 'The angel of God'; but one week later (having spent the intervening time in prison) he told his examiners that the spirit 'was really the devil tempting me, since you have told me that he can transform himself into an angel'.[37] This process of re-definition would have been all the more powerful, and Isobel all the more sincere, if it had been incorporated into false memories generated during imprisonment. In response to suggestive interrogatorial questioning regarding the presence of the Devil at various fairy-related events, Isobel may have gradually and unconsciously incorporated him into her memories of envisioned hunts and subterranean feasting, just as Beth Rutherford, in response to the insinuations of her counsellor, increasingly wove the figure of her father into her erotic dreams and memories.

15

The Devil and the Covenant of Grace

Although we can speculate that Isobel's Devil, as he emerges in the fairy-related and intermediate passages, evolved out of some kind of fairy-man-in-authority figure, we must set against this the fact that a very different kind of Devil emerges in the more demonological sections of the confessional text. As we noted in CHAPTER FOUR, in these passages Isobel provides us with some of the most detailed, vivid and in many ways stereotypical depictions of the demonic pact to have come down to us from any contemporary British witchcraft record. Here, the elfin knights and 'maister men' of popular folklore melt away into the background and the Devil of the demonologists moves centre stage.

There are many reasons for assuming that these passages were heavily sculpted by interrogatorial interest. As Christina Larner has emphasized, in order to convict an individual of witchcraft Scottish prosecutors often invested much energy and time into obtaining evidence of the demonic pact:

> [ministers and elders] were well aware of the type of evidence that would convict a witch in the High Court or obtain a commission from the Privy Council. Malefice alone would not normally be enough . . . The main purpose of the preliminary informal inquisition was to extract a confession of the Demonic Pact, which was regarded by the courts as the essence of witchcraft . . . The courts were properly satisfied only by a statement that the accused had renounced her baptism and become the Devil's servant.[1]

That Larner's assertions are correct in Isobel's case is confirmed by the fact that, in his comments scrawled on the back of her second confession, justice depute Alexander Colville makes it clear that he considered the pact passages seminal:

> hawing read & considered the confessions of Isabel gowdie within conteaned as paction with Sathan Renunciation of Baptisme, with dyvers malefices, I find that a co[m]mission may be verie justlie (*word unreadable*) for hir last tryall Acoluille. (45/37)

That Forbes, Rose, Innes et al. also considered the pact to be of extreme importance is evinced by the fact that they return to it again and again and place it at the forefront of each confession. Similarly, that their questioning on the subject was specific and leading is indicated by the fact that Isobel's pact contains many stereotypical elements: she met the Devil when alone; he invited her to the sabbath; she renounced her Christianity; she was given a new name; she received the witches' mark; she had sex with the Devil and his penis was cold. Close interrogatorial questioning is also suggested by the fact that, as the following excerpts illustrate, Isobel's first 'pact passage', as we can term it here, was very similar to the one made by her accomplice, Janet Breadheid, on the following day:

> ISOBEL: he marked me in the showlder, and suked owt my blood at that merk and spowted it in his hand, and sprinkling it on my head said I baptise the . . . he wes a meikle blak roch man werie cold and I faund his nature als cold w[i]thin me as spring wall vater. (39/6)
> JANET: the divell (*damaged – words missing*) in the shoulder, and suked out my blood w[i]th his mowth at th[a]t place, he spowted it in his hand & (*damaged – words missing*) on my head, he baptised me th[e]rvith . . . he was a meikle roch blak man, cloven footed, werie cold and I fand his nature w[i]thin me als cold as spring well water. (544/21)

These similarities suggest that Janet was probably asked the same questions – and with the same precision – as Isobel. But they also suggest, as we touched on in CHAPTER FIVE, that Janet's pact account, like her description of the making of the *corp creadh*, may have been produced through some kind of read-out-and-assent process whereby interrogators dictated the confession given by Isobel the day before and asked Janet if she had done the same. That contemporary interrogators made these kinds of short cuts is suggested by the records relating to the trial of Culross suspects Catherine Sands and Isabel Inglis, which took place thirteen years later. While Sand's testimony contains a relatively detailed stereotypical pact, the testimony given by Inglis, who was interrogated after her, contains the terse statement: 'Isabel Ingglis confest that . . . the Devil . . . caused her resign herself to him . . . *in the way and manner confessed by Catherine Sands* [my italics].'[2]

But on the other hand, we cannot blithely assume that Isobel and Janet were merely parroting assents to a preordained list of stereotypical questions, nor that the pact-passage creation process was a simple one. As we have touched on earlier, although there are significant similarities between the two women's accounts, there are also significant differences. Janet's pact does not appear at the beginning of her confession as it does in Isobel's. Similarly, her stereotypical statements are not presented together, or in the same order, as they are in Isobel's testimony, and they are interspersed with details absent from Isobel's version of the day before. Even more interesting is the fact that some of the latter exclusive-to-Janet details pop up in Isobel's later confessions. Reference to the Devil's promiscuity, for example, is mentioned in Janet's confession ('[he] lay with them all abowt') but does not emerge in Isobel's until over a month later, at her third interrogation. Similarly it is Janet, not Isobel, who first makes mention of sitting at the table next to the Devil, receiving money from him (he 'gaw me an piece of mo[ne]y lyk a testain') and worshipping the Devil upon her knees with her hair hanging loose and 'looking stedfastlie wpon (*him*)'. But the most significant difference of all, with regard to these passages, is the fact that Janet describes a demonic pact that was made on a different date, in a different place, and in the company of a different coven to Isobel. While Isobel made her pact in Auldearn church, Janet made hers in the church at Nairn; while Isobel's was made in the presence of twelve other coven members, Janet's was made in the presence of forty; while Isobel made her pact when 'John yownger of mebiestowne' was the officer and Jean Martin the maiden, Janet took care to point out that hers was made before Young took the post, when her husband held the position and when Bessie Wilson's daughter (name obscured in the MSS), not Martin, played the role of maiden.

Taken together, these factors suggest that even if parts of Janet's pact passage was produced through some kind of read-out-and-assent process, she was nevertheless actively involved in its creation. They suggest that she offered up new details that were carefully logged by Forbes et al. and then reflected back to Isobel at subsequent interrogations, where the latter obligingly seized the baton and enlarged upon them in more detail. From this perspective, both Isobel's and Janet's pact accounts emerge as the result of a complex and dynamic three-way interaction between the two women suspects and their interrogators.

That both women were actively involved in the genesis of the pact passages is also indicated by the fact that, as explored in CHAPTER FOUR, even at their most stereotypical, their accounts contain unconventional and highly idiosyncratic details. While it is likely, judging by the few extant records containing interrogatorial questions, that Isobel was asked something along the lines of 'Did you receive the witches' mark from the Devil and did he give you a new name?', it is unlikely that she was also asked whether, while the Devil was doing these things, he 'sucked out your blood and then spouted it in his hand and sprinkled it on your head and said "I baptise thee Janet"'. Similarly, while we can fairly safely assume that Isobel was asked whether the Devil's penis was cold, it is far less probable that she was asked whether his penis was 'as cold as spring-well water'. In other words, the general references to the witches' mark, new name and cold penis were likely to have come from the interrogators, but the specific references to sucked, spouted, sprinkled blood, the choice of new name received and the metaphor concerning spring-well water were not. That Isobel and Janet should have woven their own words and images into their pact passages is also supported by other witch-records. Although most accounts of the pact provide us with little indication as to how they were created, we occasionally gain glimpses of the interrogatorial exchanges that generated them. The trial dittays of Christian Grieve, for example, who 'freely confessed' to witchcraft at the Crook of Devon in the same month as Isobel, state that:

> upon the 19th day of June 1662, the minister posing you upon the foresaid particulars especially anent the renunciation of your Baptism, ye answered that Sathan speired at you if ye would do it and ye answered 'I warrand did I,' *and desired to put it in your own words*, this ye did in presence of Mr Alexander Ireland minister etc. [my italics][3]

But if we acknowledge that Isobel contributed to the pact passages, we must now negotiate the issue of how much. Did she merely enliven the formal stereotype presented to her by the interrogators with a few vivid metaphors, or was she more deeply involved in the construction and emotional charge of the narrative? While we can assume that she brought idiosyncratic details such as blood-spurting and sprinkling to the table, what involvement did she have with the more demonologically-conventional details associated with this event, such as the receiving of the Devil's mark and the crown-sole ritual through which she gave herself, body and soul, over to him? Similarly if, as we have speculated above, Isobel brought the alias 'Janet', and the metaphor likening the Devil's penis to spring-well water to the interrogation, how far did she concur with the fact that the name was bestowed as part of a Christianity-renouncing ritual, and that the sexual act was symbolic of her willing subjugation to the Devil? These are tricky questions, and in order to answer them we need to examine Isobel's world-view in a little more depth. Most importantly, we need to take a step back and explore what kinds of ideas and beliefs about the demonic pact she herself may have brought to the interrogations at the Auldearn tolbooth.

Church Teachings

In the seventeenth century the majority of the Scottish population, being either illiterate or only partly literate, would have formally absorbed elite ideas about the demonic pact through church teachings. But the extent to which these ideas were circulated is unclear. Contrary to popular misconception, we cannot assume that contemporary congregations were constantly subjected to thundering tirades from the pulpit about the dangers of demonological witchcraft. Few ordinary sermons from this period survive, but it is notable that many of the keynote addresses given by prominent covenanting ministers such as Andrew Cant, Alexander Henderson, Phillip Nye and Thomas Coleman in the first half of the seventeenth century, barely mention the Devil let alone the demonic pact.[4] Contemporary catechisms present us with a similar picture. In the 1563 Heidelberg Catechism (that was, according to one commentator, 'much beloved in Scotland' well into the seventeenth century) the Devil was overtly mentioned only twice, in a text that ran to at least 2,500 words. Similarly, the Westminster Larger Catechism, which was dominant in Scotland from 1649 onwards and ran to twice the length of its Heidelberg predecessor, only elevates the number of references to seven, with most of these being in passing.[5] With regard to direct references to the demonic pact the catechisms are even less forthcoming. Only the Larger Catechism mentions it, and here only once, the instance being hidden halfway down the long list of sins included under the first Commandment.[6] This mysterious absence also seems to have been reflected on a parish level, with Julian Goodare recently drawing attention to the fact that in this period those Scottish ministers who were moved to put pen to paper wrote little about witchcraft, demonological or otherwise.[7] Certainly, in the writings of Nairnshire covenanters like Alexander Brodie and Hugh Rose the pact is not mentioned and the Devil, though present, is by no means the ubiquitous, immediate personality that emerges from Isobel's confessions.

Such evidence cannot be taken to indicate that ideas about the demonic pact were not disseminated by the reformed church, but merely that circulation was not consistent or uniform, and that its extent probably depended heavily upon the predilections of regional kirk authorities; particularly the local minister who, in a period where the church lacked a centralized teaching system, possessed a considerable degree of pedagogical freedom. As a general rule, as Goodare has pointed out, ordinary ministers were far more likely to apply themselves to the theological problem of witchcraft than high-profile and politically-active divines like Andrew Cant, because they would have come into contact with it far more frequently and directly than their ivory-towered or often-travelling superiors. Being approached for help by parishioners who believed they had been bewitched, ministers would have been compelled to take up a position in response; whether that be to 'endorse their belief or else offer them a more theologically-sophisticated alternative', such as divine providence. They would also have had to reinforce this position from the pulpit and in private explanations of the catechism.[8]

But while many ministers are likely to have responded to the general threat of witchcraft, how vigorously and frequently they sermonized on and discussed the demonic pact is more difficult to assess, not least because, as we mentioned earlier, so few ordinary sermons survive. The fact that, as the Survey of Scottish Witchcraft has recently shown, only 15 percent of Scottish witchcraft records taken down between 1563 and 1736 mention the pact, could be interpreted as lack of ministerial concern in the subject. But because these figures include cases, such as commissions, where it was not necessary to mention the pact (even if it did emerge during interrogations) this is not a meaningful statistic here.[9] Some micro-studies do suggest that the incidence may have been relatively low, particularly in certain areas. For example, as a result of his detailed research into witch trials in Fife, Stuart Macdonald noted in 2002 that 'the presence of the Devil and the notion of the demonic pact are relatively rare' and that:

> Most remarkably, when confronted with clear elements of what could be interpreted as a sabbat, the clergy seemed unaware of what they were witnessing. The meeting by the lake of the unruly women where Andrew Patrick claimed to have seen Elspet Seath, should have been transformed by members of the presbytery of Cupar into a sabbat . . . The obvious, if surprising, answer is that these elite notions of the sabbat had not strongly taken hold, not only among the populace but even among the clergy.[10]

But in other locations ministers were clearly better informed. During the 1697 Paisley trials, James Hutchison delivered a sermon that indicates that he had given considerable thought the demonic pact and was well acquainted with demonological theory. Here, he discusses 'what constitutes formally a person to be a witch':

> It requires that there be a reall compact between Satan & that person either personally drawn up & made, or Mediately by parents immediat or mediat having power of the person; adding y^r unto his mark. The Ground of my assertion is this, there is no Less requisite to the constituting a person a visible professor of christ, then a personal compact and the external signe of Baptism super-added . . . No Less doth Satan require of them that will follow in his way

then either personal covenanting with him, and receiving his mark upon y^r flesh, or that the parent give their children to him and they receive his mark . . . [11]

In addition to the sermon, ministers like Hutchison could have used a variety of other tools to raise awareness of the pact. Although, as we have seen, reformed catechisms made little reference to it, as Stuart Clark has recently shown, in the plethora of texts that emerged to explain and elaborate on the catechisms the pact could be more heavily emphasized. The Heidelberg Catechism of 1563, he notes, merely states vaguely that the first Commandment requires parishioners to 'avoid and flee all idolatry, sorcery, [and] enchantments'. But in published lectures on its provisions, one of the theologians who probably drafted the catechism emphasizes that the first Commandment extended to 'Magike, Sorcerie, and Witchcraft,' since all these involved 'a league, or covenant with the divel the enemy of god, with certain words or ceremonies adjoined, that the doing and saying this or that, shal receive things promised, of the devil, and such things which are to be asked and received of god alone'.[12] These published explanations clearly indicate that a motivated minister, when clarifying the catechism to his parishioners through sermons and individual interviews, could easily have brought the demonic pact to the fore.

Such a minister could also have drawn on biblical passages depicting the perils of demonic temptation to drive his point home, with the most dramatic of these being the seminal New Testament scene where the Devil attempts to seduce Christ – whom he has swept up to a mountaintop – into an alliance by promising him worldly riches and power. The impact of these teachings on the popular mind would have been intensified by the fact that temptation scenes were a common feature of the medieval saints' tales that, although generally avoided by reformed ministers, remained popular at seventeenth-century firesides. Oral versions collected in the nineteenth century, for example, depict how the Devil appeared to St Anthony in his cell and offered him gold and jewels if he would return to the world; how he appeared in the form of a woman to St Dunstan as he toiled in his forge and tempted him to break his vow of celibacy; and how he approached St Servanus when he was 'lying upon his couch after matins' and tried to draw him away from God by challenging orthodoxy through theological disputation. These themes, in turn, were reflected in the plethora of popular tales and legends, extant from the medieval period onwards, that depicted a variety of unfortunates, from learned magicians to servant girls and hapless young farm boys, being coaxed into sin by the Devil.[13]

The Auldearn Pulpit

Given the fact that ministers had a degree of influence in this respect, we can assume that Isobel's ideas and beliefs about the demonic pact would have been shaped by the two men who held the Auldearn incumbency during her lifetime: John Brodie, minister from 1624 to 1655, and his successor, Harry Forbes, who held the post from 1655 until 1663. We have little insight into whether, and to what extent, the former may have concerned himself with the matter. Although a large number of his sermons were recorded in shorthand by his erudite nephew, Alexander Brodie the diarist, and are to this day held in the archives at Brodie Castle, they have not, as yet, been deciphered. But if we assume that his world-view was not so very different from that of his nephew, with whom he was very close and to whom he acted as a spiritual mentor, we can conclude that his interest was active but not prodigious. As we saw in CHAPTER SEVEN, although Alexander Brodie was consistently condemnatory of 'blind addictedness of men to superstition, charming and divelrie' and asked God to be 'instructed and guided in the reproving, suppressing, and punishing thes things'; and despite the fact that he discussed witchcraft with his peers as early as 1655; his diary entries suggest that when he was called upon to help with Isobel's and Janet's investigation in the spring of 1662 he felt a little out of his depth. When the news of (what we have assumed was) Isobel's case first reached his ears he lamented 'what does this say to me? Oh teach, teach for thy nam's sake! Discover in the mean tyme mor'. And two days later, after having examined the confessions, he wrote: 'I desird to look into this mysterie of wickednes and to be instructed.'[14] This 'desire to be instructed' is likely to have underpinned his meeting with Colville five days later, and the fact that Brodie recorded the latter's advice on how to assess witch-testimonies in his diary suggests that the information was new to him. Though inconclusive, these comments suggest that even at this late stage Brodie's knowledge concerning the specifically demonological aspects of witchcraft were not extensive. If, as we have argued, John Brodie's position was likely to have been similar to that of his nephew, we can assume that although he was likely to have been concerned about witchcraft and quite possibly broached the subject of the demonic pact from the pulpit, he is unlikely to have immersed himself deeply in demonological texts. And as a consequence, we can assume that that had he been at the helm during the 1662 interrogations he is unlikely to have engineered pact passages as demonologically stereotypical and precise as Isobel's.

But with regard to Harry Forbes, we can draw very different conclusions. As we have seen in CHAPTER SEVEN, Forbes considered himself to have been the victim of a maleficent magical attack as early as 1655 (although whether he believed it to have occurred in Caithness or Auldearn is unclear). We also know, from the case of Cathrin Hendrie, that even at this early date he was quicker to diagnose witchcraft than Brodie, and we have speculated that the increasing concern with witchcraft visible in the latter's diaries, coinciding as it does with his contact with Forbes, was attributable to the new minister's influence. The evidence strongly suggests that although the awareness of demonological witchcraft was probably relatively strong in Auldearn before his arrival, Forbes elevated this awareness to new heights. We can assume that, like other similarly motivated ministers, he expounded the dangers of maleficent magic through sermons, explanations of the catechism and intimate discussions with both individual parishioners and local authority figures such as Brodie. We can also assume that he fanned any smouldering community fears into flame by taking any witchcraft allegations brought to him very seriously; conducting his own interviews and investigations and repeatedly urging for information about witches from the pulpit. But even more significantly, we can speculate that, as an educated and curious man capable of spending long evenings discussing 'the mani mysteries ther ar in religion', Forbes nourished his interest in the subject through reading demonological works and that, like his Paisley counterpart James Hutchison, he seasoned his sermons and teachings with emotive and detailed expositions of the threats posed by the stereotypical demonic pact.

In his attempts to raise awareness in this regard, Forbes would have been aided by the fact that once formal accusations had been made and the judicial machinery set in motion, this process would have been fostered by the trials themselves. Many people witnessed witchcraft interrogations first-hand. In Isobel's and Janet's cases, for example, Innes recorded that in addition to the score of named witnesses there were, respectively, 'many utheris' and 'a great multitud of all sortis of uther persones' present. In response to both eye-witness accounts and general hearsay, the wider population would have discussed the charges levelled against the suspects and the statements given in response as avidly as people discuss criminal cases today. Janet Breadheid, for example, seems to have been well-acquainted with the cases of local women Agnes Grant and Katherine Sowter, despite the fact that the former had been tried nearly twenty years earlier. No doubt many witchcraft allegations that did not reach the courts provoked similar levels of interest and comment.

From these perspectives we can see how a zealous, demonologically-informed minister, such as Forbes, could have dramatically raised parish-awareness of stereotypical beliefs concerning the demonic pact. But it is still difficult to understand precisely how these beliefs made the transition from the minds of learned men like Forbes to the minds of their uneducated parishioners, particularly in cases such as Isobel's, where these beliefs seem to have been accommodated so firmly that an individual could be persuaded to confess that they had performed a demonic pact themselves. In Isobel's case some kind of process must have occurred, either before or during interrogation and imprisonment, through which her (what must have been) often inchoate beliefs concerning witchcraft and the temptations of the Devil were transformed into the exquisitely detailed, dramatic and stereotypically precise demonic bargains described in the confessions. But what kind of process this may have been is much harder to ascertain.

Spiritual Covenants

In trying to find some answers to these questions, we gain little help from traditional witchcraft scholarship, for although historians have explored the issue in various ways, confession-embedded (as opposed to obviously superimposed) accounts of the demonic pact still remain largely a mystery. More recently, Ildikó Kristóf and Soili-Maria Olli have shed some welcome light on this area, with both arguing – in relation to Hungary and Sweden respectively – that popular abilities to construct convincing pact-accounts may have been assisted by contemporary legal practice. Throughout early modern Europe the making of contracts – whether verbal or written – was the standard method of cementing business and personal transactions on all levels of society, from the village market-place to the royal courts. Given our exploration, in CHAPTER NINE, into the ways in which life-experience can be woven into false confession we can certainly support Kristóf's suggestion that, under coercion, witchcraft suspects wove memories of having made, or witnessed others make, real-life legal contracts into their fictional accounts of the demonic pact.[15] But equally relevant – and as yet, to my knowledge, largely unexplored in this context – is the fact that in constructing their pact accounts witchcraft suspects may not only have drawn on beliefs and experiences surrounding legal practice, but also on beliefs and experiences surrounding, what we can loosely term here, 'spiritual covenanting'.

Up to the present day, the demonic pact – as a negotiation through which an individual renounces her Christianity and gives herself over to the Devil – has retained such uncanny and chilling emotional connotations that it is easy to forget that ideas about the benefits to be gained through contracting with supernatural beings were fundamental to Protestant theology. Although pacts with the Devil were unequivocally condemned by the reformed church, other kinds of human/spirit pacts were not. Indeed, you could go so far as to argue that at no other time in the history of Scottish Christianity, either before or since, has the church made such efforts to encourage its parishioners to enter into formal negotiations with spiritual beings.

Beliefs surrounding the importance of making spiritual covenants with God, or God through Christ, are prominent in both the Old and New Testaments, being illustrated most dramatically in the covenant made between Yahweh and the Israelites in the Sinai Desert. Though certainly not absent from Catholicism, beliefs surrounding covenants assumed a special pre-eminence in reformed theology, with Calvin, the father of Scottish presbyterianism, being lauded by some as 'a critical formulator in the development of covenant theology'.[16] Calvin and many of his contemporaries used the term 'covenant' in a confusingly fluid way, with different thinkers conflating various kinds of covenant under different headings, to the extent that modern theologians still argue with regard to the distinctions between different types as they were understood in the period. But in early modern Scotland, as in other Protestant nations, the belief and practice subsumed under the umbrella of the 'covenant of grace', which emphasized the role of Christ as intermediary and the function of the sacraments as its sign and seal, was the most prominent. As we have seen in earlier chapters, in the late-sixteenth and early-seventeenth centuries, covenanting theology had a direct impact on the political arena when leading presbyterians drew up a series of written National Covenants, with the two most prominent occurring in Isobel's lifetime. In 1638, in a gesture of defiance and solidarity against English attempts to impose a new liturgy, they revived the National Covenant originally drawn up in 1581 by John Craig; and in 1643 the Solemn League and Covenant was devised to cement an alliance between the Scottish reformed church and the English parliament. In both cases, commitment to the articles of the covenants was confirmed through signatures.

Historians have frequently noted that covenanting theology influenced elite ideas about the demonic pact, although there is debate as to what form this influence took, with Stuart Clark claiming, on the one hand, that 'Covenant theory . . . gave extra inversionary meaning to the demonic pact, especially in its implicit form', and Julian Goodare noting, on the other, that 'The demonic pact could be considered as a covenant – but if it was, then theologians of covenanting did not usually say so.'[17] But whatever the connections between the covenant and the pact in elite discourse, scholars often overlook the possibility that covenanting theology may also have directly influenced popular ideas about the demonic pact. And that through exploring this influence we may be able to gain fresh insights into confessional material such as Isobel's.

Public and Private Covenants

With regard to the role that this theology may have played in Isobel's case, we can make several assumptions. First, given the fact that she was probably past puberty in 1647, we can speculate that she possessed some awareness of the 1638 and 1643 National Covenants. Although the latter were high-profile political documents intended to secure the signatures of those who held command or office, copies were circulated widely throughout Scotland and every member of the Scottish church, right down to the most theologically-ignorant peasant, were encouraged to subscribe. On a parish level, these signing events are likely to have been busy and memorable affairs. In Forfar in 1643, for example, minister Richard Brown gave a sermon and 'the Sermon being endit befor noone, he read the Covenant and explained the doubts, and took ane oath of all the people by holding up ther hands, that they wald sweare to the Articles of the said Covenant; and the blissing being given, he desyrit all that could wryt, to stay and subscryve the samyn, and those that could not wryt to come to the Reader that he might subscryve for them.'[18] Although tailored to meet different needs, both the 1638 and 1643 covenants required their subscribers to pledge allegiance to the reformed church and reject the Pope and Catholic doctrines, the former abjuring, among other things, 'his blasphemous opinion of transubstantiation', 'his devilish mass' and 'his profane sacrifice for sins of the dead'.[19] Given the covenanting sympathies of the Nairnshire lairds we can assume that public subscriptions to the covenants occurred at Auldearn church in both 1638 and 1643, under the auspices of John Brodie, and that a good proportion of the people mentioned in Isobel's confessions and perhaps even Isobel herself, may have been present when these signings took place.

One the one hand, with regard to the discussion in hand, we cannot read too much into this. As big, public events these National Covenant-signings bore little immediate resemblance to the intimate, often one-to-one and face-to-face pacts made between witches and the Devil. But on the other hand, their relevance becomes more marked when we take into account the fact that they were reinforcing, in a formal and theatrical way, a wide range of less dramatic covenanting practices that were taking place in this period. Scholars exploring the relationship between demonological witchcraft and covenanting theology have paid little attention to the fact that although the post-Reformation covenant with God or Christ could be undertaken in church amid great pomp and ceremony, it could also be a private affair, performed either alone or in a small group as a means of renewing personal commitment. Such covenants could be specifically tailored to meet the individual concerns of their creators and although, like the National Covenants, they could be drawn up in a document and signed (with Mullan stating that the late-seventeenth century saw 'the increasingly popular pious practice of writing out personal covenants'), they could also be made purely verbally or, as we shall explore in more detail later, could take the form of purely spontaneous experiences generated 'in the heart'.[20]

Particularly relevant to our analysis of Isobel's beliefs concerning the demonic pact is the fact that the private spiritual covenant was widespread among the pious Nairnshire covenanters. On 31 January 1654, for example, soon after Glencairn's royalist forces had 'burnt the corns and houses of leathin' a group of local families, including Alexander Brodie and his uncles John and Joseph, gathered at Lethen House for what they termed a 'solemn Humiliation'. Brodie writes that after John (who was still at this point minister of Auldearn) had sermonized on Joel 2, and his brother Joseph on Job 22, the company then:

> closed the exercise with a solemn engagement of ourselves to God, and did come under a new, firm, inviolable Covenant with God, that we should be his, and he should be ours. We gave up and surrendered our soul, body, estates, lands, rents, houses, families, wives, children, servants, wit, parts, endowments, friends, wealth, and all that we had, or ever should have or attain unto in this world, to be the Lord's for ever; that he might call for, make use and dispose of it, and mark it as his own. We besought the lord to accept the free-will offering of our lips and of our hearts, and not to permit us to depart from him.[21]

At other times Brodie records smaller-scale covenanting exercises. In April the following year, for example, Brodie records how the Laird of Park (who later rose to such prominence in Isobel's confessions) came to visit him:

> He [Park] made som acknowledgement of his soul's condition, and pray'd. I heard what the Lord was doing to his sister and familie, and from my soul did bless the Lord for what I saw about him in that place. I did stirr up and exhort, as the Lord gave utterance, and he resolved to engadg and give up himself wholli to the Lord, both soul and bodie, and to bind himself to be the Lord's, to his last breath. Oh! That the Lord may accept, and seal his acceptance on the soul of his poor creatur.[22]

What is notable about these, and other covenants made by the Nairnshire lairds, is that they bore more than a passing resemblance to Isobel's demonic pact. Not only did they involve verbally 'surrendering' oneself and all that one possessed to God or Christ, but interestingly, the most significant possessions to be surrendered, in every case, were the body and soul. Similarly, although these private covenants were characterized by dramatic self-abasement, there was no doubt that they functioned as bargains through which the supplicant hoped to gain something in return for his sacrifices. Those made at Lethen on the day of the Humiliation, for example, concluded with telling clauses such as '[so] that we should be his, and he should be ours'; '[so] that he might be his servant, and the Lord be his God'; and '[so] that the Lord shall be mine, and I shall be his, so long as I live'.[23] Nowhere is this negotiatory aspect more clearly expressed than in Brodie's account of the covenant made, at the same gathering, by his neighbour Katherine Donaldson:

> [she] burst forth in the complaint of her woful, sad, deserted case . . . [claiming that] if he would accept, there was not anything in all the earth which should so content and satisfy her, as that the Lord would condescend to that bargain, to become her God, and to take her, and accept of her as his for ever. It was replied, The bargain was sure enough, if she were willing for her part . . . [24]

The Private Covenant and the Pulpit

Although these private covenants were performed by the Nairnshire gentry and took place in the privacy of their castles and strong-houses, they could have impacted upon ordinary parishioners such as Isobel in a variety of ways. We can assume it likely, for example, that when Glencairn's forces threatened the region in 1654, John Brodie did not only preach on Joel 2 at Lethen, but also declaimed the same verses – which urge that 'whosoever shall call on the name of the LORD shall be delivered' – from the pulpit in order to comfort his frightened parishioners. And that he encouraged his anxious congregation – as he encouraged his anxious peers – to strengthen themselves in the face of this adversity through renewing their spiritual vows. Even in less stressful times, John Brodie and his successor, Harry Forbes, were likely to have extolled the virtues of spiritual covenanting as part of their ongoing remit to bring their parishioners closer to God, with Brodie's diaries clearly attesting to the fact that in 1653 William Falconer, minister of Dyke, had sermonized on the covenant of grace.[25] By translating the private covenants made by the Nairnshire lairds into the third person, we can get an idea of what parishioners like Isobel may have heard thundering down from the local pulpits:

> Engadg and give up yourself wholli to the Lord, both soul and bodie, and bind yourself to be the Lord's, to your last breath!

> Renounce yourself, and give up yourself, soul, mind, body, spirit, parts, abilities, learning, and all that you have or should attain unto, to the Lord!

> Give up, and surrender your soul, body, estates, lands, rents, houses, families, wives, children, servants, wit, parts, endowments, friends, wealth, and all that you have, or ever should have or attain unto in this world, to be the Lord's for ever!

Ideas about spiritual covenanting would also have imprinted themselves on the minds of the Auldearn parishioners in other ways. The psalms chanted religiously every Sabbath would have repeatedly reminded them, in a myriad different ways, that in times of hardship and self-doubt, relief could be gained through covenanting with God, as encapsulated in phrases such as: 'I have made a covenant with my chosen'; 'My mercy will I keep for him for evermore, and my covenant shall stand fast with him'; 'He hath

remembered his covenant for ever, the word which he commanded to a thousand generations'; and 'Have respect unto the covenant: for the dark places of the earth are full of
the habitations of cruelty.'[26] Covenants also featured prominently in both the Larger
and Shorter Westminster Catechisms of 1648 (the catechisms with which Isobel was
most likely to have come into contact), with the former devoting several pages of exposition to the covenant of grace, where it claims that God delivers his elect out of sin
and misery and 'brings them into a state of salvation by the second covenant, commonly
called the covenant of grace' and that 'The only mediator of the covenant of grace is the
Lord Jesus Christ'.[27] Given the fact that ministers were encouraged to reinforce these
seminal church doctrines during their annual catechizing examinations, we find
ourselves facing the intriguing possibility that at some point during their incumben-
cies John Brodie and Harry Forbes met privately with Isobel and her family in her
cottage or at the church, and that during these interviews they impressed upon her the
urgent necessity of making a sacred covenant; a covenant that would be sealed by
surrendering her body and soul and all that she possessed, to a higher spiritual
authority.

The Marriage-Covenant with Christ

The possibility that covenanting theology, as dispensed through the catechisms and
pulpit, influenced Isobel's ideas about the demonic pact also gains further credence
when we take on board the fact that, among contemporary theologians, the covenant
of grace was often represented allegorically as a marriage contract. Among scholars, this
allegory (which could be applied both to the relationship between an individual soul
and Christ or between Christ and the church) is more widely associated with
Catholicism, where it rose to particular prominence in medieval mystical traditions,
but the role it played in Protestantism is often under-emphasized. A number of
reformed theologians devoted whole books to the subject. For example, in addition to
producing a translation of the psalms subsequently taken up by the Scottish church
(*The booke of Psalmes in English meeter*, 1638), Francis Rous, member of Cromwell's privy
council and speaker of the House during Barebone's Parliament, published *The Misticall
Marriage: Or, Experimentall discoveries of the heavenly marriage betweene a Soule and her
Saviour* in 1631. Similarly, ten years after Isobel's death the nonconformist divine,
Edward Pearse, wrote *The Best Match: Or, the Soul's Espousal to Christ*, which passed
through numerous editions and was reprinted at least four times between 1673 and
1688. Indeed, Pearse considered the subject so important that he declaimed: 'A new
Covenant-relation to Christ is certainly a concern of the greatest weight, and highest
importance to the Sons of Men of any in the World; 'tis what lies at the foundation of
all true happiness both in Time and Eternity; without it (as a learned Divine hath well
observed) *we are not Christians; we are only the carkasses of Christians*'.[28]
    It is also clear that ideas surrounding the marriage-covenant, as with those
surrounding the National Covenants and the covenant of grace in general, were disseminated through sermons. Edward Pearse was moved to write his treatise on the subject

precisely because he was, through ill-health, prevented from sermonizing on it in church. 'So great did the desire of doing good to Souls remain in him' waxes John Rowe, in his introduction to *The Best Match*, 'and such were the yearnings of his Bowels towards them, that being not able to speak to them any longer out of the Pulpit, he could not satisfie himself, but he must needs speak to them in this small Tract, wherein his great Scope and principal Design is to allure and draw Souls unto Christ'.[29] Stirling covenanter Elizabeth Cairns describes hearing a number of sermons on the marriage-covenant in the early-eighteenth century, while several decades before, Argyllshire noblewoman Henrietta Lindsay was clearly deeply moved by what seems to have been a particularly passionate declaration on the subject:

> O that this day may never be forgot, quherin the liveliest of offers was held forth, and closing with gospel terms with the Son of God, powerfully urged, and the terms on quhich a covenant marriage relation to the Son of God was to be founded . . . and next, to hear of this design to win Christ spoken of was made marvellous, being held forth as a purchase of such an invaluable treasure and that enriching price of purchase was attainable and to be win at, and likewise quherin their work and duty did lye who had such a design, and in this it was to have a propriety in his glorious person by a marriage relation . . . Let not the Lord be gracious if I have not made an entire resignation of myself and my all to him . . . [30]

That people took these writings and sermons to heart, and that ideas about the marriage-covenant influenced lay spirituality in this period, is also amply confirmed by the fact that, as we shall explore in more depth later, they emerge prominently in many godly diaries and writings.

The Marriage-Covenant in Nairnshire

We have firm evidence that at least three of the men involved in Isobel's case were familiar with the allegory of the marriage-covenant. The term 'Bridegroom of Souls' – a sobriquet for Christ frequently employed in writings on the subject – emerges in Brodie's diaries; Sir Hugh Campbell of Cawdor, one of the men commissioned to try her, discusses the allegory in his 1704 *Essay on the Lord's Prayer*; and Hugh Rose, minister of Nairn, devotes over six pages of his *Meditations on several interesting subjects* to the topic.[31] We also know that the subject was addressed in local sermons. Morayshire covenanter Lilias Dunbar's claim that, after hearing a sermon on conversion by James Urquhart at Moiness in the 1670s, she approached him to discuss her personal experiences of 'the blessed marriage knot' that was 'cast betwixt Christ and myself', suggests that he did not only preach on the theme, but that his exposition was a moving one.[32] Given Urquhart's spiritual affinity with the local lairds and clergy (he not only took refuge in Nairnshire after being deposed as minister of Kinloss, but also worshipped privately with men like Brodie, Hogg and Harry Forbes and held illegal conventicles at safe houses like Pennick), we can assume that his fellow ministers at Auldearn and Nairn were equally eager to 'woo and allure poor Souls into an espousal, or Marriage-Covenant with this Blessed Husband, the Lord Jesus Christ'.[33] That the allegory was disseminated from local pulpits is also suggested by the fact that in his 1704 essay, in which he argues that the Lord's Prayer should be used in divine service, Campbell of Cawdor exploited parishional devotion to covenant teachings to drive his point home, claiming that because the prayer had been taught to the people by Christ, it was a 'Love-token design'd to be convey'd to the ear by Ministers of the Gospel, and lay'd up in the heart to keep us ever in mind if the matchless Love of the bridegroom of our Souls'.[34]

The Embodied Covenant

What is particularly significant, with regard to the present discussion, is the fact that contemporary writings on the marriage-covenant with Christ contained a number of emphases not always present in other forms of covenanting discourse. Most notably, working with the allegory of marriage between a man and a woman, they employed language and metaphor that evoked a level of realism and, for want of a better word, 'embodiment' absent from other covenant-templates. As the Bridegroom of Souls, Christ was not described as an abstract metaphysical principle or a remote presence or voice, but as a man with tangible physical and psychological characteristics who engaged in realistic human-like activities. Metaphors used to describe the Bridegroom were frequently drawn from the Old Testament Song of Songs: Henrietta Lindsay, for example, emphasizing that Christ's 'cheeks are like a bed of spices, as sweet flours; his lips like lilies, dropping sweet-smelling myrrh . . . his countenance is as Lebanon, excellent as the cedars'; and Hugh Rose echoing that 'his spouse describes him in generals, negatives, and metaphors: My love is fair and ruddy, the chiefest among ten thousand; his countenance is as Lebanon, excellent as the cedars; his mouth is most sweet; he is altogether lovely.'[35] Descriptions of the marriage-covenant with Christ are also filled with emotive references to love, both of Christ for his human spouse and the spouse for Christ. Lilias Dunbar claimed that 'when I was seeking the Lord in secret, I found the Lord Jesus manifesting his love to me with all his kingly power so that my soul was ravished with love to him'; while Katharine Collace echoed that 'I love him with all the little heart I have. I love him, and it is my exercise to love him'.[36]

But even more pertinent, in the context of the present discussion, is the fact that in the marriage-covenant context this love was often expressed through physical and pseudo-sexual imagery. Rous's *Misticall Marriage* is peppered with statements such as: 'She that loveth Christ much, may embrace him much, and kisse him much, and holde him much'; 'let the soul lust mightily for him, and let her lusts and desires ascend up to him in strong cries & invocations'; 'the soul may pant to be united to him in a perfect and consummate marriage'; and '[the] bridegroom kisseth and embraceth her [his mortal spous] with spiritual visitations [when he visits her] in the bed of love'.[37] Similarly John Welsh, minister of Ayr and son-in-law to Knox, claims of Christ: 'Thou, O full of Delights, my heart is ravish'd with thee, Oh when shall I see thy face?' He also claims, 'What can be troublesome to me, since my Lord looks upon me with so loving and amiable a countenance, and how greatly do I long for these embracements of my Lord'; and, most dramatically of all: 'Oh that he would kiss me with the kisses of his mouth.'[38] Closer to home, Hugh Rose eulogises that Christ 'is altogether lovely and useful: his conversation is most sweet; his embraces are comfortable and ravishing'.[39]

Working with the allegory of marriage, descriptions of the contractual exchanges made between Christ and his spouse are similarly embodied and realistic. In the following passage from Pearse's *Best Match*, Christ seduces his spouse-to-be just as a man might seduce a woman, or a merchant a client, or more pertinently, the Devil a witch:

> Now he comes, and tells over the stories of his love to them, how much he has done and suffered for them, how much his desire is towards them, what great things he will bestow upon them, and inflate them into, and all to win and allure them to himself, to gain their love and consent to accept of him, and to be his in a Marriage-Covenant.[40]

The following passage from Hugh Rose's *Meditations* suggests that similarly realistic and vivid depictions were dispensed from the Nairnshire pulpits:

> [Christ will] draw sinners into a marriage-covenant with himself . . . It is a wonder he should ever make such a love-proposal . . . He opens their eyes, and displays his beauties and excellencies before them, enabling them to see them. He acts upon their hearts and souls to accept and contract with him. He leads their hearts and hands in subscribing the marriage covenant. He spreads out his double fairly written, and sealed with his blood . . . None ever that married Christ had reason to rue the bargain; they find him so good and sweet a husband, that they wonder at their folly in standing out; they think it strange how any should deny him.[41]

The descriptions of the contractual commodities exchanged are equally concrete. As in direct covenants with God, the marriage-covenant with Christ required the surrender of the whole self and all that belonged to the self, with the primary emphasis being on the soul as the ultimate bargaining chip. Rose, for example, pleads 'Let my soul, my darling, be dear to thee [Christ], and keep it from the power of the destroyer. None can take thine out of thy hand; there I put it; there intrust it, and ever resolve to leave it. Keep me as the apple of thine eye; lodge me with thy lambs in thy bosom.'[42] Pearse, meanwhile, emphasizes that in return for this surrender the earthly lover gains the spiritual pleasures of union with Christ, including 'all Grace needful for the Soul, Righteousness, Remission of Sins, Sanctification, Renovation of the Spirit, and the like'.[43] The realism of the marriage-contract also expressed itself in the fact that according to some writers, Christ's mortal lover could – like any sharp bargainer – openly specify the type of benefit they wished to gain from the alliance, with Rous claiming, rather flamboyantly, that 'these seasons of love [between spouse and Christ], are seasons of prayer. If thou want any thing now ask it, for in these heats of love, thy husband will deny thee nothing. These be the moments when the spirit moveth the

The relationship between a witch and the Devil was often depicted as very immediate, down-to-earth and tactile. Here, in Ulrich Molitor's *De Laniis et phitonicis mulieribus* (1500), the Devil's realism is only betrayed by the fact that, like Isobel's Devil, he had monstrous feet.

THE MYSTICALL MARIAGE Betweene CHRIST and His CHURCH.

by Fran: Rouse.

the 2d. Edition.

London
Printed for
Iasper Emery
at the Eagle &
Child in Paules
Church yard.
1635.

A figure from the second edition of Francis Rous's *Misticall Marriage* (1635). Although this image depicts the marriage between Christ and his church as opposed to Christ and the soul, it illustrates the fact that the spiritual union with Christ was commonly articulated as a marriage or love-match between a man and woman.

St Teresa of Àvila's descriptions of the sacred marriage with Christ are arguably the most powerful to have come down to us from any period, and this mid seventeenth-century engraving, which depicts Teresa interceding for a woman trapped in purgatory, clearly evokes the embodiment of her interactions with Christ. Appearing as a handsome, virile young man, the saint's spiritual bridegroom is so tangible that it seems like she only has to reach out her hand to touch him; while the affectionate look she bestows on him, like that which Molitor's witch bestows on the Devil (*see* left), expresses all the intensity of the love-match. According to the definition of shamanism employed in this chapter, we can argue that this engraving depicts Teresa shamanistically negotiating with Christ.

waters, therefore cast in thy petition, and whatsoever grief it hath in it, thou shalt be cured of it.'[44]

Listening to local ministers like Rose using the flowery, metaphorical language of the marriage-covenant with Christ, Nairnshire congregations would have gained a very different impression of spiritual covenanting than might have been gleaned from a sermon on the National Covenant, the covenant of grace in general, or the less prominent covenant of works. This language would have painted a picture of an intimate and physically affectionate relationship between the supplicant and a handsome young man with a strong, sensual presence, to whom it was possible to surrender up the soul in return for specifically-demanded benefits. It would also have painted a picture of a spiritual covenant that was not an official document drawn up by theologians or a public event performed in front of congregations or kings, but an inner commitment entered into in private and witnessed only by the supplicant and Christ. It is hard to see how such language, dispensed widely and passionately from pulpits and through readings and explanations of the catechism, could not have influenced the ways in which seventeenth-century congregations in general, and Isobel in particular, absorbed ideas concerning the demonic pact.

The Covenants of the Fireside

But while we can speculate that ideas surrounding spiritual covenants may have influenced Isobel's notions of the demonic pact, the nature and extent of this influence is more difficult to determine. The fact that ministers like Rose and Falconer expounded the virtues of spiritual covenants from the pulpit, and the fact that the Nairnshire elite wrote about them in their essays and diaries, still does not tell us whether, and to what degree, these ideas were absorbed and understood by ordinary people like Isobel, nor the role they may have played in popular spirituality. Although the scarcity of documentary evidence concerning the latter means that any conclusions reached on this subject must be highly speculative, by spreading our net wide and moving beyond our period we find evidence to suggest that ordinary Scots did not only absorb elite ideas about spiritual covenants, but that they also took them to heart.

Our primary source material here emerges from the nineteenth-century charming traditions that we have already mined, in CHAPTER EIGHT, in reference to evil-eye-reversal beliefs. Of the wide range of popular charms and prayers collected by folklorists in this period, many of which are believed to be of pre-Reformation origin, a surprisingly large number are concerned with the request for protection from spiritual agencies. Examples of these 'protection charms', as they are generally termed, have also been found, in much smaller numbers, in seventeenth-century sources.[45] On closer inspection, it is clear that although these charms are often crude and repetitive when considered side by side with the elegant rhetoric of *The Misticall Marriage* or *The Best Match*, they nevertheless reflect the basic spiritual-covenant template as it is found in both Catholic and Protestant texts. Time and time again they articulate a process through which the individual gains protection from a spiritual agency, most frequently identified as God or Jesus, through placing themselves into its care. Even more significantly, a good percentage of these charms, which we can here sub-categorize as 'surrender-protection charms', involve the teller explicitly giving over or surrendering themselves and/or something that belongs to them, to the spirit. Like the covenants made by Brodie and his fellow evangelists, surrender-protection charms involve a direct plea to the spirit involved and frequently contain a verbal itemization of the possessions that are to be given over to the them: with the most prominent possessions on the list usually being the body and soul. The following 'night shielding' charm, taken from Carmichael's *Carmina Gadelica*, is standard:

My God and my Chief,
I seek to Thee in the morning,
My God and my Chief,
I seek to Thee this night.
I am giving Thee my mind,
I am giving Thee my will,
I am giving Thee my wish,
My soul everlasting and my body.[46]

At first glance, these popular covenanting traditions seem to differ from reformed teachings about the covenant of grace and the marriage-covenant in the sense that they emphasize predominantly material, as opposed to spiritual rewards. While elite writers emphasize that those who enter into marriage-covenants with Christ can hope to enjoy benefits such as 'Righteousness, Remission of Sins, [and] Sanctification', the wording of popular protection charms makes it clear that those who used them were seeking more prosaic benefits like the avoidance of disease, the deflection of the evil eye, protection when embarking on a journey or in conflict with enemies and, very frequently, safety for the soul during sleep. But if we look at covenanting texts more closely, it is clear that this difference is one of degree not substance. Although writers on theological covenants, both in the medieval and early modern periods, emphasized the spiritual benefits to be gained from union with the divine they did not categorically preclude material rewards. Rous, for example, tells his readers that they can ask for 'anything' during the moment of union, before going on to caution:

therefore now cast in thy petition, and whatsoever grief it hath in it, thou shalt be cured of it . . . [but] thou maist come down in thy petitions from the greater, to the lesser, and having desired the main petitions, that the King of glory may be glorified by the coming of his kingdom of grace, with the richteousness thereof, then after maist thou petition for daily bread to be given thee.[47]

Although Rous downplays the materially-beneficial aspect of the marriage-covenant (telling his readers that they should request spiritual benefits, such as the 'coming of the kingdom of grace' first, and only subsequently trouble him with requests for 'lesser' privileges such as 'daily bread') the fact that he concedes that such benefits were theoretically available is significant. Listening to teachings such as these, parishioners who were less theologically fastidious and more materially needy than their ministers would undoubtedly have focused on the daily bread that could be gained from such a covenant, however 'lesser' it may have been. These materialist interpretations are likely to have been inadvertently fuelled by the fact that covenant teachings, and marriage-covenant teachings in particular, frequently allegorised the spiritual benefits to be gained from Christ in terms of worldly protection and provision. It would have been very easy for a hungry parishioner, who struggled with the threat of insufficient food on a daily basis, to respond to Rous's claim that Christ 'filleth the hungry with good things' literally.[48] Similar responses may have been provoked by Pearse's claim that when Christ 'makes love . . . [he] offers himself with all his treasures and riches to poor sinners'; Welsh's claim that when Christ brings his lovers into his 'banqueting house' he feeds them with 'Flaggons' and 'Apples'; and Rous's promise that Christ rewards his 'workers' with 'a penny, even with a reward, favour, and a good eye'.[49] In the same vein, it is not diffi-cult to imagine the impact that the following words from Rose's *Meditations* (drawn from the Book of Isaiah) would have had as they echoed down from the Nairn pulpit in the mid-seventeenth century:

> Has he [Christ] not proclaimed, Ho, every one that thirsteth, come ye to the waters, and he that hath no money; come buy and eat; yea, come buy wine and milk without money, and without price. Incline your ear, and come unto me; hear, and your soul shall live; and I will make you an everlasting covenant . . . If she be poor, he [Christ] can enrich her; if drowned in debt, he will defray it; if naked, he can clothe her with white raiment; if diseased, he can heal her; if foolish, he can, in his wisdom, govern her; he comforts, and bears with her infir-mities . . . He provides for her temporally and eternally . . . He exalts her from the dunghill to a throne.[50]

The fact that protection charms frequently involve surrendering the self to God or Christ in return for defence against enemies is also congruent with covenant-teachings. In *The Misticall Marriage* Rous claims that through the marriage-covenant with Christ an individual could receive a 'great power' which:

> can do a great work . . . if thou have some mighty enemy, that hath been too hard for thee, even some raging and wasting concupiscence, fear, distrust, or other tentation, now set upon him mightily, for now canst thou best see the way to conquer him, and now hast thou most might to effect this conquest, and to do what thou seest. Having tasted his honey, thy eyes shall be opened, and thy strength revived, wherefore make thou now a more mighty slaughter of the Enemies of God, and thy soul.[51]

Although Rous undoubtedly intended this passage allegorically and used the phrase 'mighty enemy' as a metaphor for sin, it is possible that when such passages were dispensed from reformed pulpits, illiterate parishioners like Isobel were beguiled by its realism. In envisaging Christ as some kind of warrior spirit who could grant them the means to conquer mortal enemies, they would have behaved no differently from the beleaguered King David of the psalms, who saw the Old Testament God as an ally through which to visit 'mighty slaughter' on rival kingdoms; or from the covenanting armies who marched into battle at Tippermuir armed with the chilling war cry: 'Jesus and no quarter!'[52]

Although there is no scope to go into the issue in any depth here, it is reasonable to argue that extant protection charms, and particularly surrender-protection charms, represent a popular articulation of the theological beliefs and practices concerning spiritual covenants that were disseminated from Scottish pulpits and catechisms from the Middle Ages onwards. And given the fact that such a wide variety of surrender-protection charms were still being used well into the nineteenth century, we can also conclude that this form of spiritual covenanting continued to play an important role in popular spirituality through the intervening early modern centuries. We can also argue that although these charms were expressed in simple language and emphasized material reward, they did not necessarily indicate a lack of religiosity or emotional commitment. They merely reflected the fact that the desire for immediate physical survival, as opposed to godliness and learning, dominated the pragmatic spirituality of the masses.

More Fireside Covenanting

Popular covenanting traditions would also have been vigorous in early modern Scotland because they were nourished, from below, by a wide matrix of folkloric beliefs surrounding contractual relationships with fairies and saints. As I have explored in depth in a previous work, witchcraft records, contemporary elite writings and later folk-loric collections of tales, songs, charms and ballads make it abundantly clear that from the early modern period through to the nineteenth century, interaction with the fairies was believed to be reciprocal.[53] If you were hospitable and accommodating when the fairy queen and her train swept through your house at night, or when you were approached by a solitary fairy wishing to forge an alliance, they would favour you with good fortune and prosperity; but if you were inhospitable or inattentive, or if you broke fairy taboos by sleeping on fairy hills, farming fairy acres or divulging fairy confidences, you would be punished with misfortune, sickness and death. As we shall explore in more detail in the next chapter, the contractual nature of fairy-relations was a Europe-wide phenomenon, with Pócs, for example, arguing that in south-eastern Europe there existed a clearly defined popular matrix of beliefs surrounding overt paction with fairy-related spirits.[54] Beliefs surrounding contractual relations with ambivalent spirits are also characteristic of tribal cultures and, as I have explored elsewhere, we can assume their presence in seventeenth-century fairy belief to have been rooted in pre-Christian animism.[55]

A similar contractual template is visible in the beliefs and practices surrounding the saints that survived into early modern Scotland from the medieval period and which, to a certain extent, represented a Christian appropriation of the same bedrock of indigenous animism that underpinned fairy belief. John Arnold notes that in medieval Europe both clerics and lay people fostered very personal relationships with certain saints, particularly those to whom their parish church was dedicated, and could address them as they would a benevolent master, parent or friend. Significantly, the relationship was also inherently reciprocal, with Arnold claiming that:

> The sense of negotiation with the individual saint is strengthened by the bargaining with which people engaged in seeking aid. Saints did not work for free: one had to do a little something for them . . . Most usually a vow was made, involving a future gift: heal me, and I'll give you this coin, or these candles, or another votive offering . . . In a set of miracles recorded soon after the death of Louise of Anjou in 1297, almost 90 per cent involved conditional promises.[56]

This contractual element to human/saint relations endured through the early modern period and into the eighteenth and nineteenth centuries, with folklorist James Macpherson noting that 'for well-nigh two hundred years after the Reformation' men and women frequented chapel wells like St Mary's, in the old parish of Dundurcus, on Speyside, 'seeking health from its waters and offering at its shrine their propitiatory gifts'.[57] Women like Isobel Car, who was accused by the Elgin session, in 1627, of 'going supersticiously to a well at Speysyde' where she 'kneillit about the Chappell and drank of the water' were unlikely to have done so without taking a coin, a cake, a pin, or making a prayer or vow, to seal their request.[58] Unsurprisingly, pre-modern beliefs and practices surrounding contractual relationships with both fairies and saints also displayed the same concern with practical reward that we find in the God and Christ-invoking protection charms. Both types of spirit were primarily associated with healing, but could be petitioned to help with almost any kind of problem, from protection against enemies to success in farming or love.

With regard to the questions posed at the beginning of this section, these perspectives enable us to safely assume that in seventeenth-century Nairnshire, elite teachings about spiritual covenants, dispensed from the pulpit and in private examinations, would have interacted with a vigorous groundswell of popular belief concerning contractual relationships with a wide range of spirits that included not only God, Christ and the Devil, but also fairies and saints. They also suggest that the interaction between elite and popular notions of covenanting may have been potent, particularly during the century of Protestant extremism between the Reformation and the Restoration. Well-expressed and passionately-delivered sermons and explanations about the importance of National Covenants, the covenant of grace and the marriage-covenant with Christ may have brought ideas about contracting with spiritual beings to such prominence in the minds of the congregation and imbued them with such immediacy and significance, that even if men and women accused of witchcraft had not been specifically schooled in the demonic pact before they entered the courtroom they would, when it was presented to them, have responded with an instant and deep affinity. Such a dynamic suggests that although historians have traditionally focused on covenanting theology as it influenced elite ideas about the demonic pact, with regard to the history of witchcraft, the way that this theology worked in the hearts and minds of uneducated suspects like Isobel Gowdie may have been equally significant.

Protection Charms and Polytheism

But while it is not difficult to see how, in this climate, notions about the demonic pact could have quickly and easily taken root in the popular mindset, it is much harder to identify the specific mechanics through which a matrix of general ideas about contracting with God, Christ, saints or fairies could have been woven, during interrogation, into the stereotypically-precise accounts of demonic pacts (complete with renunciations of baptism, crown-sole rituals, witches' marks and so on) that provide such a marked component of many confessions; particularly when, as in Isobel's case, these accounts are so vivid and text-embedded. But if we return to the protection charms, we find that this gulf may not have been so wide or difficult to bridge as it first appears. The large numbers of charms collected in the nineteenth century and earlier are remarkable not only because they represent popular ownership of ideas about spiritual covenanting but also because, as derivations of medieval Catholicism, they do so in an essentially quasi-polytheistic framework. God and Christ are the most commonly named spiritual protectors, but they frequently share the stage with a wide range of other spiritual agencies. The Virgin Mary emerges as singularly prominent, angels are relatively common and Ossian heroes, such as Fionn, Diarmaid and Brianan, also make occasional appearances. But particularly significant in the context of the present discussion is the frequent emergence of a colourful variety of saints, most notable of these being Brigit, Columba and – though not officially a saint – the saint-like Archangel Michael. In the following short charm, for example, no less than three saints and one angel are invoked:

> I pray and supplicate
> Cuibh and Columba,
> The Mother of my King,
> Brigid womanly,
> Michael militant,
> High-king of the angels,
> To succour and shield me
> From each fay [fairy] on earth.[59]

In the following, we have apostles and more angels joining the fray:

> The holy Apostles guarding,
> The gentle martyrs' guarding,
> The nine angels' guarding,
> Be cherishing me, be aiding me.
>
> The quiet Brigit's guarding,
> The gentle Mary's guarding,
> The warrior Michael's guarding,
> Be shielding me, be aiding me.[60]

Saints could also be prominent in surrender-protection charms. In the following, the supplicant does not yield his soul and body up to God or Christ, but to St Brigit and Mary:

> I am placing my soul and my body
> Under thy guarding this night, O Brigit,
> O calm Foster mother of Christ without sin,
> O calm Foster mother of the Christ of wounds.

> I am placing my soul and my body
> Under thy guarding this night, O Mary,
> O tender Mother of the Christ of the poor,
> O tender Mother of the Christ of tears.[61]

These types of charms were not just parroted phrases, repeated on a 'To whom shall I bequeath my soul in order to be safe today?' basis. They involved genuine commitment, often of long-standing, to particular saints with whom people felt particularly intimate, and to whom they felt personally bound. The medieval *Life of Saint Wulfstan* contains a pertinent story in which a man, angry not to have received a cure, harangues his local saint, with his diatribe sounding uncannily similar to the way in which some magical practitioners, such as Agnes Sampson and Bessie Dunlop, harangued the Devil when he had disappointed them. But what is also clear from this account is that the man's relationship with St Stephen was structured according to the surrender-protection charm template:

> Oh blessed Stephen, Stephen! Long time have I laboured in thy service; yet now, I think, in vain. For if I had served the Earl of [Mortain] . . . so faithfully as I have long served you, he would have enriched me with many gifts; but you, to whom I have committed myself and my whole soul and all that I possess, give me now over to torture![62]

Given the fact that the veneration of saints persisted on a popular level from the medieval period through to the nineteenth century, we can assume that saint-invoking protection charms – that is, charms in which individuals surrendered themselves into the protection of a saint as opposed to that of God or Christ – survived through, and were employed during, the early modern period. While this fact is of little import in itself, when it is considered in the light of the fact that during most of these two centuries all invocations of saints were associated with the Devil, then we suddenly find ourselves looking at something that is much more significant.

As we have noted in earlier chapters, one of the elements of Catholicism most vociferously and bitterly rejected by Protestants was the emphasis on the intercessionary powers of the saints. According to reformed interpretations of the first Commandment (*Thou shalt have no other gods before me*) to supplicate any being other than God or Christ was 'idolatry', and the worshipping of 'false gods'. This emphasis was maintained in all the catechisms circulated in reformed Scotland. As we have seen, the influential

Heidelberg Catechism of 1563 stated that 'on peril of my soul's salvation and happiness, I must avoid and flee all idolatry, sorcery, enchantments, invocations of saints or of other creatures, and rightly acknowledge the only true God'.[63] Over eighty years later, in the Larger Catechism of 1648, the worship of saints (along with that of angels) was lumped together in the same sentence and given the same weight as covenanting with the Devil, the text stating that the 'sins forbidden in the first commandment are . . . praying, or giving any religious worship, to saints, angels, or any other creatures: all compacts and consulting with the devil, and hearkening to his suggestions'.[64] Similarly, the National Covenant of 1638 roundly condemned the practice of 'calling upon angels or saints departed'.

We can see that in the early modern centuries, sandwiched as they were between the lenient polytheism of the Middle Ages and the lenient disinterest of the Enlightenment, any parishioner who claimed to not only have prayed to or worshipped a saint or angel such as Michael or Columba, but also to have placed their soul into its protection, would clearly have found themselves in an ambiguous position. For it is not difficult to see how, seen through the eyes of a particularly zealous or antagonistic minister, such a charm could have been easily viewed as something demonic. Nor is it difficult to see how suspects like Isobel, becoming conscious of the ambiguous identity of their supernatural protectors through the interrogatorial lens, would have been vulnerable to confessing, or being persuaded to confess, to have covenanted – not with a saint or an angel – but with the Devil.

From the Crown of my Head to the Soles of My feet

Paradoxically, one of the ways in which this transformation from protection charm to demonic pact may have taken place can be highlighted by turning the microscope onto one of the most stereotypical features of the Scottish pact. Isobel begins her first confession by claiming that as she walked 'betuixt the townes of drumdewin and the headis' she met the Devil and promised to meet him later at the church of Auldearn. She then goes on to confess that, 'the first thing I did ther th[a]t night I denyed my baptisme, and did put the on of my handis to the crowne of my head and the uth[e]r to the sole of my foot, and th[e]n renuncet all betwixt my two handis ower to the divell' (39/1). In making this claim Isobel was being wholly conventional. This 'formula', as Larner put it, for the renunciation of baptism appears in many confessions and indictments, with George Mackenzie's claim, in *The Laws and Customes of Scotland*, that 'the solemnity confest by our Witches, is the putting one hand to the crown of the head, and another to the sole of the foot, renouncing their Baptism in that posture' indicating that by the mid-seventeenth century Scottish witchcraft interrogators considered the 'crown-sole ritual', as we can term it here, to be a standard feature of the demonic pact.[65]

But the origins of this ritual are obscure. The fact that it is not prominent in demonological texts and that, as Goodare points out, it appears in a witness statement as early as 1597 suggests that it may have drawn, at least in part, upon popular roots.[66]

The latter is also suggested by the fact that non-demonized rituals involving simultaneous ceremonial contact with heads and feet were clearly practised among magical practitioners in the early modern period; although here they generally involved person-to-person contact and were concerned with the gaining of second sight. In his *Secret Commonwealth* Robert Kirk claimed that if an individual wished to gain a glimpse of the subterranean people (that is, the fairies) they must 'put his foot on the Seers foot, and the Seers hand is put on the Inquirers head, who is to look over the Wizards right shoulder . . . then he will see a multitude of Wights'.[67] That Kirk's rather sensational description reflected wider popular practice is supported by the fact that similar rituals were described by contemporaries like James Kirkwood and James Garden, and also appear in the works of nineteenth-century folklorists.[68] Even more interestingly, analogous semi-demonized rituals also make an occasional appearance in witchcraft records, the most notable being found in the trial dittays of Aberdeenshire man Thomas Leys (1597). Here, the latter is charged with persuading his lover, Elspeth Reid, to 'gang withe the to [ ] quhilk scho did, and tak the man be the lug [ear] that was standen befoir hir . . . Thaireftir thow commandit hir to putt on hir futt on that mannis futt'.[69] But although these correspondences are interesting, crown-sole rituals designed to gain second sight still exhibit considerable differences, both in terms of form and rationale, to crown-sole rituals designed to effect surrender to the Devil, and it is perhaps for this reason that the links between the two have not been exploited by scholars exploring the Scottish demonic pact.

But if we return to popular charming traditions, we find that these differences are not so significant as they may at first appear. Scholars of witchcraft have largely overlooked the fact that many of the requests for magical aid found in the wide array of charms collected by the nineteenth-century folklorists (whether coming under the category of blessings, work charms, protection charms or evil-eye-reversal charms) contain, what we can term here, 'crown-sole' statements: the latter ranging from the more pact-stereotypical 'From the crown of thy head and thy forehead to the very sole of thy foot' to variants such as 'From the brow of my face to the edge of my soles' and 'From the top tablet of my face to the soles of my feet' and so on.[70] In this context, the crown-sole statement emerges as just one of the many oppositional statements that feature so prominently in popular Scottish charms. Here, in verse after verse, we do not only find people and objects being blessed, protected or harmed between 'crown and sole' but also between 'sole and throat', 'pap and knee', 'back and breast', 'chest and sole', 'eye and hair'; or in the case of buildings, between 'site to stay', 'beam to wall', 'ridge to basement', 'balk to roof-tree' and 'found to summit'.[71] But although, in the traditional charming context, the crown-sole statement emerges as just one oppositional statement among many, in the light of our earlier suggestion of links between the demonic pact and the popular protection charm it seems strangely coincidental that the former should be disproportionately common among the category of traditional charms concerned with human protection. The following nineteenth-century version is standard:

God, and Spirit, and Jesus,
From the crown of my head

To the soles of my feet;
Come I with my reputation,
Come I with my testimony,
Come I to thee, Jesu;
Jesu, shelter me.[72]

To draw the net even tighter, we have direct evidence that crown-sole statements also featured in protection charms used in Scotland in the seventeenth century. According to the records of the presbytery of Islay and Kintyre (1697) the following words were used by a cunning man in an attempt to cure a case of bewitchment and rickets; the practitioner clearly believing that by placing, or invoking God to place, a protective shield about his sick patient, the evil emanations that were causing his distress could be deflected:

I place the protection of God about thee,
Mayest thou be shielded from every peril,
May the Gospel of the God of grace
Be from thy crown to the ground about thee.
May men love thee
And women not work thee harm.[73]

While the presence of the crown-sole statement in protection charms is pertinent, it gains even more significance from the fact that it can be found in variants that involve placing the self into the care, not only of God and Christ, but also of saints, apostles and angels:

Be the cowl of Columba over thee,
Be the cowl of Michael militant about thee,
Christ's cowl, beloved, safeguard thee,
The cowl of the God of grace shield thee;

To guard thee from thy back,
To preserve thee from thy front,
From the crown of thy head and thy forehead
To the very sole of thy foot.[74]

We have already argued that memories of performed surrender-protection charms, and particularly those addressed to spirits such as saints and angels, may have been manipulated by interrogators into confessions to having performed the demonic pact. The fact that some of these surrender-protection charms may have actually involved verbally relinquishing the self 'from the crown of the head to the sole of the foot' to the suspect spirit, makes this hypothesis even more compelling.

The Physical Ritual

But it could be argued that, compelling as this hypothesis is, as it stands, it does not take sufficient account of the fact that in the majority of relevant pact passages the crown-sole element emerges as a physical ritual as opposed to a purely verbal one. The witch does not just say that she is surrendering herself to the Devil; she places one hand on her foot and another on her head to confirm the deal. But this difference is not as problematic as it may at first appear. Folklorists have often observed that although most pre-modern charms have come down to us as words only, as recorded on the page, in practice they were seldom performed without some form of accompanying ritual, however minimal. Even the simplest prayer or curse was intensified through being performed on the knees, while the shortest blessing was empowered and sealed through simultaneously signing the cross. Significantly, in the context of the present discussion, popular protection charms seem to have been little different in this respect. In the following passage, nineteenth-century folklorist Alexander Carmichael describes the ritual that accompanied 'encompassing charms', that is, protection charms in which the teller asked to be surrounded or 'encompassed' by the protection of a spiritual agency:

> *Caim* (encompassing), is a form of safe-guarding common in the west. The encompassing of any of the Three Persons of the Trinity, or of the Blessed Virgin, or of any of the Apostles or of any of the saints may be invoked, according to the faith of the suppliant. In making the *caim* the suppliant stretches out the right hand with the forefinger extended, and turns round sunwise as if on a pivot, describing a circle with the tip of the forefinger while invoking the desired protection. The circle encloses the suppliant and accompanies him as he walks onward, safeguarded from all evil without and within. Protestant or Catholic, educated or illiterate, may make the *caim* in fear, danger, or distress.[75]

If it was 'common' in the nineteenth century for those wishing to be encompassed by protective forces to symbolically draw a circle around themselves when speaking relevant charms then it is reasonable to entertain the possibility that in the early modern period, those wishing to be shielded by protective forces 'from the crown of their head to the soles of their feet' would have, through placing their hands on their head and feet, symbolically represented their desires in a similar manner. Certainly, in some parts of Britain today, people use the gesture when hearing or seeing an ambulance, in conjunction with the words, 'Touch my head and touch my toes, God save me from being in one of those'.[76]

Although direct evidence is hard to find, some contemporary accounts suggest that something like this may have been the case. In Orkney in 1643, James Halco claimed that when he was 'heavily diseased' Marion Peebles touched him and 'his pein and diseas was desolvit frae the crown of his head to the sole of his fute'. Similarly, in Edinburgh in 1597, Bessie Aitken was accused of attempting to cure a sick woman by collecting 'nyne sopis of salt watter' and washing her 'frome the croune of hir heid to the soill of hir fute, being haldin up betwix twa sisteris; and syne scho did that in Geillis [St

Giles's] name'.[77] Neither account specifies whether the references to crowns and soles came from the suspects, witnesses or accused, but both suggest that the magical practitioners performed healing rituals incorporating some kind of crown-sole ritual component. In the light of these sources, we can speculate that when the Islay cunning man (1697) we met earlier attempted to heal a client from bewitchment and rickets by invoking the 'Gospel of the God of grace' to place a protective shield 'from thy crown to the ground about thee', that he accompanied this charm with symbolic crown-sole encompassing gestures.[78] The records of the trial of Edinburgh cunning woman Jean Weir (1670) are also suggestive here. Weir's account is complex, and there is no scope to explore it in any detail in this book, but at one point in her narrative she claims to have been visited by a 'little woman' who 'did lay ane cloth upon the floor near the door, and caused the declarant set her foot upon the samen, and her hand upon the crown of her own head, and caused the declarant repeit these words thrice, viz. "All my cross and trubles goe to the door with the;" which accordinglie she did'.[79] This ritual is open to a variety of interpretations, but in the light of the perspectives developed in this chapter we can argue that it was a physically-enacted surrender-protection charm, in this case Weir gaining magical protection through abandoning all her 'cross and trubles' to her mysterious helper. This interpretation enables us to speculate that because many of those accused of performing the demonic pact were, like Weir, suffering in some way (whether from hunger, grief, loss of livelihood or oppression by others); and because their commonest justification for having resigned themselves to the Devil was that he offered to alleviate their suffering (most frequently through bringing them 'freedom from want' or the ability to avenge themselves on enemies), the crown-sole component of the demonic pact may have derived from folkloric charms and rituals rooted in the classic surrender-protection-charm template.

The Pact and the Second Sight

If we now come back full circle, and re-examine the second sight-procuring crown-sole rituals that we examined earlier (and put aside because they display 'considerable differences' to the stereotypical demonic pact) we find that this hypothesis becomes even more convincing. At first glance these rituals seem to have differed from classic protection charms in the sense that although they involved placing oneself into the keeping of a higher authority – in this case the magical practitioner – this implicit surrender was made in return for magical power, as opposed to supernatural protection. But although this distinction is significant, it becomes less so when we take into account the fact that in this period the getting of magical protection and the getting of magical power were often two sides of the same coin. Magical skill was in itself inherently protective. Orkney cunning woman Jonet Rendall (1629), for example, clearly believed that the healing skills she gained from her fairy familiar preserved her from starvation, as evinced by her familiar's assurance that 'He sould learne yow to win almiss be healling of folk'.[80] Other skills were specifically identified with protection. Through her commerce with the king and queen of the fairies, Stirling cunning woman Isobel

Watson (1590) gained both a magical bone with which to heal the sick and a magical oil that, so long as it 'was on hir, na mane suld haif powar to do hir skayth [harm]'.[81] A comparable dual function is visible in the magical benefits Jean Weir gained from the woman for whom she performed a crown-sole ritual; Weir claiming that the latter did not only relieve her of all her 'cros and trubles' but also gave her a magical root by virtue of which 'she wold be able to doe what she should desyre'. Similarly, although Thomas Leys's (Aberdeenshire, 1597) trial dittays do not directly specify why he urged his lover, Elspeth Reid, to 'take the man be the lug' and 'putt on hir futt on that mannis futt', taken as a whole they suggest that this, and similar rituals he urged Elspeth to perform, were attempts to gain magical aid that would help the couple avoid the destitution they feared would result from their planned elopement to Moray. In this context, it is telling that many demonic pact narratives display similarly multiple purposes, with witches not only claiming to have performed crown-sole rituals in order to gain freedom from want or revenge upon enemies, but also in order to gain more general magical abilities often loosely defined as giving the suspect 'the ability to do whatever they want'. In a standard example from the 1597 Aberdeenshire trials, Helene Fraser was accused of encouraging a neighbour 'to put hir ane hand to the croune of hir heid, and the other to the soile of hir fute, and so beteich quhatevir wes betwein hir handis, to the Devill, and sche suld want nathing that sche wald wiss or desyir'.[82] The association between rituals designed to forge allegiance with the Devil and rituals designed to gain magical skills such as second sight is reinforced by the fact that, as we shall explore in more detail in CHAPTER SEVENTEEN, the Devil was widely believed to reward those who covenanted with him with healing and divinatory powers. Aberdeenshire cunning woman Jonet Lucas (1597), for example, was only one of many who were 'indytit and accusit for being in companie and societie with thy maister the Devill, *of quhome thow lernit all thy sorcerie* [my italics]'.[83]

Of course we cannot, on the basis of this brief analysis, claim to have traced the popular origins of the demonic pact. But the perspectives outlined in this chapter suggest there may have been a strong link between crown-sole rituals, as they appeared in demonological encounter-narratives, and a collection of more indistinct and variable non-demonized crown-sole rituals of purely folkloric origin. Rituals that ranged from words and actions performed to gain general magical abilities, such as the second sight, to words and actions specifically performed to gain magical protection; and which could be performed by the self on the self or through physical contact with others. Certainly these correspondences were noted, by some, in the early modern period itself. Soon after sending her 'cros and trubles' to the 'little woman', Jean Weir 'did set bye her wheile, and did shut the door, and did stay within her house for the space of twentie dayes or thereby, and was exceedinglie trubled, and weeped becaus she thought what she had done in manner forsaid was in effect the renuncing of her baptisme'.[84] Similarly, Kirk noted that the crown-sole ritual through which a novice gained the second sight 'hes an ill appearance, as if by this ceremonie, an implicite surrender were made of all betwixt the Wizards foot and his hand ere the person can be admitted a privado to the art.'[85] In the white heat of interrogation, being closely questioned about demonic pacts, any individual who had performed any kind of folkloric crown-sole ritual, toward any kind of spiritual entity and for any purpose what-soever, would have been very vulnerable to coercive-compliant response or false-memory generation. From this perspective we can easily see why so many witch-craft suspects, hounded with the question 'Did you put one hand on your crown and the other on your foot and surrender yourself, body and soul, to the Devil?', seem to have answered 'yes'.

16

Crafting the Bridegroom

The analysis of contemporary beliefs and practices associated with spiritual covenanting undertaken in the last chapter certainly makes it much easier to understand how Isobel may have been persuaded, through a process of close and suggestive questioning, to produce coerced-compliant responses or false-memory fictions surrounding the stereotypical demonic pact. But before we leave this issue entirely, we need to address one final question: the epistemological status of the event itself. Many pact narratives differ from conventional depictions of prayer or charming in that the spiritual protagonist is not merely named, but is also depicted as being physically present. The Devil stands right in front of the witch as she surrenders herself to him (sometimes even placing her hands onto her head and feet himself) and participates directly in the ritual by bestowing the witches' mark and enticing his supplicant into sexual relations.[1]

In the light of our analyses into false confession in CHAPTER NINE, we can assume it likely that in these cases the Devil figure, conforming so closely as he does with elite demonological stereotypes, was an elaborate fiction forged during interrogation. But this is not our only option. In CHAPTER FOURTEEN we concluded that although Isobel's folkloric Devil figure, as he appears in the intermediate and fairy-related parts of the confessions, was likely to have been sculpted by coerced-compliant responses and false-memory generations, these false confessions may have been built around genuine recollections of prior visionary experience. We can now move on to argue that the high degree of narrative coherence between this folkloric Devil and the theological Devil of Isobel's pact passages invites us to entertain the possibility that the latter figure – stereotypical, demonological and falsely-confessed as he was – may also have been constructed around some kind of envisioned core. Although this may seem like the 'question too far', it merits consideration here.

Shamanistic Pacts

As I have explored in more detail in a previous work, anthropological sources indicate that in most tribal shamanistic traditions there is a definable point at which an individual agrees to become a shaman.[2] This moment, which can also be described as an initiation, can take many forms, be more or less explicit and be more or less ritualized, but it is always inherently contractual and frequently occurs at the instigation of an individual spirit. Appearing before an individual either before or after they have travelled into the spirit world, the latter offers the shaman-to-be magical knowledge or help in return for some form of commitment. This commitment can be expressed in many ways – from a simple acceptance of the spirit's offers of knowledge or help to more overt promises of service or marriage – but is essentially an articulation of the individual's alliance with the spirits and acceptance of the shamanic vocation. As Holger Kalweit notes, 'the shaman's contact with his spirit companions goes beyond a mere encounter because he establishes a permanent relationship with them. He enters into a covenant, as it were, and remains connected to them for the rest of his life.'[3] When the individual's shamanistic practice commences, the spirit that engineered this initiation usually goes on (as their 'familiar' or 'helping' spirit) to facilitate their practice, either through appearing individually before the shaman when he needs magical help or inviting him on and helping him during soul journeys.

In this context, it is not surprising to find that this helping-spirit initiatory pattern is prominent in many of the folkloric spirit-group narratives emerging from early modern Europe. Here, the dominant male or female authority figure either assumes the role of initiatory spirit or sends an emissary to assume it on their behalf. The angel who appeared before German visionary Chonrad Stoeckhlin 'one night around Our Lady's Birthday at Reicherberg Lake . . . dressed in white with a red cross on his (or her) forehead' told the herdsman that if he followed it into the other world he would gain knowledge of life after death. And after this meeting the spirit became, as Behringer articulates it, Stoeckhlin's 'soul-guide' and regularly took him – while he was 'in a rapture' – on nocturnal journeys with 'the phantoms of the night'.[4] Similarly, *benandante* Battista Moduco claimed that 'the first time I was summoned that person led me to the field of Mazzone and the captain took me by the hand and said: "Will you be a good servant?" and I replied, yes . . . He did not promise me anything, but did say that I was carrying out one of God's works and that when I died I would go to heaven.'[5] Alternatively, one of the *donas de fuera* from Palermo, Sicily, told her interrogators that when she first went to the meetings she was told she must:

> kneel and worship this king and queen and do everything they told her, because they could help her and give her wealth, beauty, and young men to make love with . . . So she took an oath to worship them, the King as God and the Queen as Our Lady, and promised them her body and soul . . . And after she had worshipped them like this, they set out tables and ate and drank, and after that the men lay with the women and with her and made love to them many times in a short time. All this seemed to be taking place in a dream, for when she awoke she always found herself in bed, naked as when she had gone to rest.[6]

In her paper *The Popular Foundations of the Witches' Sabbath and the Devil's Pact in Central and Southeastern Europe*, Pócs describes a wide range of undemonized or semi-demonized contracts or pacts made between early modern magical practitioners and their familiar spirits, concluding that although the specifically demonological variant of the pact was 'clearly a product of orthodox demonology and legend-literature', the evidence suggests that 'certain "popular" concepts of the Devil's pact are present in the area under survey' and that 'These concepts were, in the final analysis, built upon the contact-making rituals of shamanistic magicians.'[7]

But although these and other examples furnish us with persuasive evidence that envisioned pacts of folkloric origin took place in early modern Europe, their usefulness in Isobel's case is compromised by the fact that they derive primarily from the central, southern and eastern regions of the Continent. And even Pócs – our prime proponent of the shamanistic-rituals-underpinned-the-demonic-pact theory – is hesitant to extend her conclusions outside her research area and into western Europe. Cautioned by the fact that elite demonological ideas were far more influential in the West, and that most of the latter's potentially-shamanistic narratives emerge from witchcraft testimonies that are heavily demonized, Pócs merely hazards that with regard to Western trials the demonic pact '*may* have something to do with shamanistic helping spirits [my italics]'.[8]

But research into contemporary Scottish fairy belief suggests that Pócs is unnecessarily cautious. As we saw earlier in this chapter, beliefs surrounding contractual relationships with fairies were widespread in the early modern period and later. Furthermore, that this contractual dimension may have manifested experientially is suggested by the fact that a significant proportion of the fairy-related encounter-narratives that can be identified as suggestive of visionary experience contain descriptions of face-to-face contractual negotiations between their human protagonists and the fairy men or women encountered. Alison Peirson claimed that a fairy man in green told her 'Gif scho wald be faithfull, he wald do hir guid'; Donald McIlmichall stated that when he went to a fairy hill the spirits there 'wold have him promise and engadge to come ther againe that night' and that 'it wes a woman among them that took the promise of him'; Pennant's Breadalbane 'dreamer' claimed that after he had been approached by a group of fairies and the dead 'all vanished but a female sprite, who seizing him by the shoulder obliged him to promise an assignation, at that very hour, that day sevenight'; and Bessie Dunlop claimed that her fairy-related familiar Tom Reid told her that he would help her if she would 'trow [trust] in him' and that she, in return, 'promeist to be leill and trew to him in onye thing sche culd do'. Perhaps most compellingly of all, Aberdeenshire man Thomas Leys allegedly told his lover, Elspeth Reid, that: 'Thair is ane hill betuixt this and Murray, and at the fute thairof thow suld gar ane man ryse and plene appeir to hir, in ony lyiknes scho pleisit; and that thow suld speik the man first thi selff and that scho suld nocht feir, and becum that manis servand, and do as he commandit hir, and scho suld newir want.'[9] Many other fairy-related encounter-narratives, though they may not include the term 'contract' or 'promise' also depict this exchange between devotion, service or trust and magical power or protection.

Envisioned Marriage-Covenants

The hypothesis that envisioned pacts of folkloric origin were being experienced, not only by the members of seemingly bona fide shamanistic cults, such as the *benandanti* or the *donas de fuera*, but also by contemporary Scots like Bessie Dunlop and Donald McIlmichall may seem far-fetched, but gains additional support from some unlikely quarters: the most surprising of these being reformed literature concerning spiritual covenants and, in particular, the marriage-covenant with Christ. As we have argued earlier, in covenanting discourse the teachings surrounding the marriage-covenant were unique in the extent to which they emphasized the physical presence of Christ. This linguistic emphasis on embodiment was partly an expression of Christ's unique role as an intermediary between man and God; a being in whom, by virtue of his spiritual father and earthly mother, 'Godheid dwels bodilie'.[10] But it was simultaneously and perhaps more fundamentally rooted in the fact that the marriage-covenant with Christ, above all other kinds of covenant, was not a written pledge or renewed intellectual commitment or public act – but an inner experience. Writings describing the marriage-covenant emphasize, more fervently than writings on any other type of spiritual covenant, that the pledge made between a supplicant and the Bridegroom of Souls was an articulation of the *unio mystica* or mystical union with the divine. There is also no doubt that this emphasis reflected genuine experience, and the spiritual writings of seventeenth-century Protestant mystics clearly reveal that moments of mystical illumination, occurring either during prayer or when going about the business of daily life, were frequently interpreted and described using the allegorical concepts and language of the marriage-covenant.

On the one hand, we cannot jump ahead of ourselves and assume that these mystical experiences all involved visionary encounters. In most cases it is impossible to determine how far the mystic employed the language of the marriage-covenant purely allegorically, as a method of expressing a psychological event that would otherwise be impossible to put into words, and how far it was employed because, during their moments of illumination, they genuinely experienced visionary phenomena representative of their embodied bridegroom. This task is further complicated by the fact that mystics of all denominations generally downplayed these aspects of their experiences, should they have occurred, being only too aware, as we noted in CHAPTER TEN, that the church disapproved of the 'sensible manifestations' of prayer. Because of these smoke-screens, when we read Rous's description of the joys of seeing the 'beloved [Christ] clearly, and plainly, even face to face', or Elizabeth Cairns's claims to have experienced 'the light of his countenance, and sensible manifestations of his love', it is difficult to judge whether the mystics used these phrases as metaphors or as accurate depictions of something they had visually witnessed.[11]

But on the other hand, despite these ambiguities, a significant minority of accounts strongly suggest that for some people envisioned encounters with Christ were a prominent feature of the experienced marriage-covenant. As Mullan has argued, the spiritual diaries of covenanting women such as Elizabeth Cairns, Grizall Love and Barbara Peebles all point, in varying degrees, toward auditory and/or visual phenomena, with

Cairn's writings, according to Mullan, being 'marked more than any other of the works of this genre by a visual element which caused some to express concern about the nature of her piety'.[12] The memoirs of Morayshire covenanter Katharine Collace are similarly suggestive, the latter claiming that while she was living in Auldearn in the 1650s 'for nine months together I had constant communion with Christ, wherein all my spiritual sense were satisfied. I saw, felt, I heard his voice'.[13] The few detailed accounts of 'sensibly-experienced' covenants to have come down to us reveal that for some covenanting women the encounter resembled a conversation in which Christ approached the supplicant with offers of comfort and the two exchanged promises in the intimate, pragmatic manner redolent of both demonic and fairy-related pacts. Recalling her young adulthood in the late-seventeenth century, Edinburgh covenanter Elizabeth Blackadder described how, while mourning the deaths of several children within the space of a few years, she experienced a spontaneous covenant initiated by a voice:

> when I was at the [sacramental] table or coming from it, that word came into my mind with as great power as if it had been proposed by an audible voice: 'What is thy petition? and it shall be given thee.' To which my soul was made to reply, Lord, my petition is that the work of sanctification may be by thy Spirit carried on till it be perfited [perfected] in me. I was then enabled by grace to make a very free and full resignation of myself and all my concerns to be entirely at the disposal of my infinitely wise and kind Lord.[14]

That Christ could be encountered visually during the experienced marriage-covenant is supported by the fact that sensible manifestations of Christ clearly occurred in other arenas of reformed spirituality. As both Landsman and Hindmarsh have observed, the Christ-encountering experiences of the early eighteenth-century Glasgow revivalists often incorporated auditory and visual hallucinations. Glasgow weaver Jean Robe surprised her congregation when she 'cried out at the peak of her conversion that God had made covenant with her in person, and that Christ would glorify in her redemption'; Catherine Jackson, daughter of one of the church elders, claimed that during her conversion she 'had seen a vision of Christ with her "bodily eye"'; and Catherine Cameron announced that one night she saw 'Christ standing with outstretched arms ready to receive her'.[15] Such experiences could also occur in more orthodox congregations, with mid seventeenth-century parishioner John Broun allegedly seeing 'Christ physically present at communion'.[16] There is also no doubt that, despite church disapproval, such experiences were cherished. Although an 'experienced Christian' criticized Elizabeth Cairns when she described how, during a recent spiritual experience, she had 'got a sight of his [God's] glory', and reminded Cairns that 'sensible manifestations were reserved for eternity', the woman's disapproval did not prevent the Stirling mystic from maintaining that 'nothing will quench, or satisfy, but a new sensible enjoyment of his [Christ's] manifested presence'.[17]

With regard to the visionary status of folkloric pacts, these sources are highly significant. If envisioned spiritual covenants of this realism and vividness were being experienced by pious men and women fully cognisant of the fact that the sensible manifestations of mystical experience were not condoned by their mother church, then we cannot dismiss the possibility that ordinary people like Isobel, who were less inhibited by theological dictates and who were, via their dependence on magical practitioners, more committed to the significance of dream and vision encounters, also did not experience contracting with envisioned spirits in this way. In Isobel's case, entertaining the possibility that her demonic pact scenes were constructed around some kind of visionary core certainly solves some of the problems inherent to her confessions. It accounts for the integrity of her Devil figure and the way he strides confidently through demonological, intermediary and fairy-related passages without once coming out of character or dropping a line. It also obviates the need to accept that two different processes of narrative formation were going on during the interrogation and enables us to speculate that both false confession (whether in the form of coerced-compliant responses or false-memory recollection) and visionary experience recall were occurring consistently throughout the process of narrative formation, with one or the other being prominent at any given time. Given the overall coherence and continuity of Isobel's narrative, this option seems to make most sense.

The Outer Signs

In order to explore the hypothesis that Isobel's accounts of covenanting with the theological Devil were constructed around an envisioned core, we need to step back from our examination of the demonic pact and look, in a more general sense, at the ways in which encounters with spirits were interpreted in early modern Scotland. As we have seen in CHAPTER TEN, while it was believed that spirits either possessed a form, or assumed a form, or manipulated the imagination in order to simulate a form, which could then be encountered by humans during visionary experience, there was nevertheless ongoing dispute over the correct identification of the spirits encountered. To a certain extent this problem, which had been with the church since its inception, was rooted in the fact that there was no definitive consensus on how spirits were supposed to look, nor the context in which they were supposed to appear. Until the Reformation ecclesiastical iconography – in the form of paintings, statues and windows – along with written and oral descriptions found in the Bible, legends of saints, folk epics and ballads etc all provided general guidelines. With regard to colour, for example, saints and angels were associated with white and gold, the Devil was associated with black, fairy men with green and so on. But in reality spirits could appear in any colour they wished: an angel could appear in green, the Devil in white, a fairy man in black. Similar flexibility surrounded form. Although there were conventions (angels, for example, were usually beautiful and demons ugly) many spirits, including Christ himself, could assume almost any kind of semblance and the Devil, as the undisputed master of disguises, was the most skilled shape-shifter of them all. In a recent study Joyce Miller noted that 'an exact description of the [Scottish] Devil is difficult to find' and that although he could appear as the stereotypical 'man in black' he could also appear in colourful clothes, 'be old or young, handsome or ugly, or grim or gentlemanly in appearance. The demon might wear a hat or bonnet, a shawl or hood, or carry a staff . . . [he] could appear in female form, albeit quite rarely, or take the form of an animal'.[18] To make matters worse, the small element of consistency that church iconography did contribute toward popular ideas about spirit forms, would have been lost after the Reformation when zealous Protestants like Alexander Brodie white-washed wall paintings, broke statues and tore down rood screens in protest against idolatrous representations of the sacred.

The belief in the ability of envisioned spirits to appear in a wide variety of forms and the enduring problems surrounding how these forms should be identified, are likely to have historically emerged, in large part, in response to the way the way the human imagination works. Envisioned spirits would have been the visible result of what we can term here an 'autonomous psychic amalgam' – a process through which the psyche, independently of the conscious mind, draws on a combination of influences, both intellectual, physical and emotional, in order to create a visionary conflation unique to the individual. As a result, regional lore would have been very influential. The fierce water horse from Cromdale, on the Spey, whose 'coat was as black and glossy as the raven's wing' looked and behaved differently from the 'quiet and steady' one who appeared as a 'handsome grey mare' at Loch Frisa, on Mull; and the fairy queen who appeared to Isobel 'brawlie clothed in whyt linens' at the head of her glittering court under the Nairnshire hills, or to Andro Man 'riding a white hackneyis', contrasted vividly with the 'stout' fairy queen who sat down on a settle next to Ayrshire cunning woman Bessie Dunlop, as she lay in labour, and asked her for a drink.[19] Depending upon which encounter-narratives were told in which cottages, images of how a brownie or a troll or a saint may have looked would have varied from fermtoun to fermtoun even within the same area. Personal experience and temperament would also have played a role here. Without the benefit of iconography peering down at them from the church walls, every member of the congregation standing in Nairn church listening to Hugh Rose sermonizing on the marriage-covenant with Christ would have had their own mental picture of Christ's 'bed of love' and 'fair and ruddy' face, influenced by the men they had known and the love affairs they had experienced. And during the visionary encounter itself, their own particular pattern of suffering would have dictated what Christ promised them and what they gave in return when he acted 'upon their hearts and souls to accept and contract with him'.[20]

To regional and temperamental differences we can add a further factor. The psychic conflations that emerge in visionary experience, as anyone who has ever had a dream is aware, are the result of an autonomous process largely beyond our conscious control. Dream figures unpredictably fuse elements of waking life: a man can look like your father but act like your mother; a woman can look like your mother but act like your child; a human can sound and move like an animal; an animal can have the aura or pres-ence of a God. The autonomy of the conflation process also means that the amalgam created does not necessarily conform to the conscious ideas and wishes of the beholder: no one chooses their nightmares, just as no one chooses who will be the object of an erotic dream. The writings of medieval and early modern mystics clearly illustrate that they frequently found themselves confronted by dreams and visions containing events and emotions – like eroticism, violence and blasphemy – that deeply unsettled them because they flew in the face of their most deeply-held moral codes and beliefs. Although, as we explored in CHAPTER TEN, experiential visionary specialists, such as the tribal shaman, characteristically develop a degree of control over their experiences, this control is only ever partial. Even to the most able shamans, helping spirits come 'of their own accord, strong and powerful', and the skill of the shamanistic calling is not in dictating their form and character, but in negotiating with them once they have arrived.[21]

Isobel's Conflation – The Arrow-Shooting Devil

Approaching Isobel's Devil figure from this perspective helps us to understand why he emerges from her confessions with such immediacy, coherence and multidimensionality. If, as we have argued, she constructed him around genuine memories of one or more envisioned helping spirits encountered prior to interrogation and if this visionary figure – both as it appeared before arrest and later, as part of false-memory recollections generated during interrogation – was an unconsciously and involuntarily assembled psychic amalgam, then we can expect it to have been composed of a complex fusion of influences. Precisely how complex this fusion may have been can be vividly illustrated by looking at Isobel's folkloric Devil as he appears in the arrow-shooting passages.

At first glance, we can immediately speculate that in creating the visionary amalgam that underpinned this figure, Isobel's psyche would have drawn on the same reservoir of influences identified in CHAPTERS NINE and FOURTEEN: real-life experiences involving aggressive and dictatorial men, folklore surrounding host-leading fairy-men-in-authority, and of course, demonological beliefs – absorbed from both fireside and pulpit – concerning the *maleficium*-performing, coven-leading Devil. But by spreading our net a little wider we can speculate that in creating her arrow-shooting Devil, Isobel may have also mined less obvious lodes. In earlier chapters we have argued that she may have attended church regularly and that the ministry in Auldearn, as led by both John Brodie and Harry Forbes, was likely to have been committed and passionate. We have also speculated that as an oral performer, Isobel would have possessed a vivid imagination, quick ear and developed verbal facility. Taking these factors together, we can assume that she would have readily absorbed (perhaps more readily than some more godly but less receptive parishioners) the vivid language, imagery and narrative of the Bible. In doing so, Isobel would not have been immune to the fact that one of the most prominent activities engaged in by God, as he was portrayed in the Old Testament, was that of warfare. The books of the prophets and the psalms are dominated by descriptions of beleaguered kings and holy men calling on God to defend them against their enemies through cursing, storm, flood, sword and arrow-fire. And we can be fairly certain that seventeenth-century ministers, living in beleaguered times themselves, would have emphasized these themes in their sermons and readings. It would have been no coincidence that when Nairnshire was threatened by Glencairn's royalist forces in January 1654, John Brodie chose to sermonize on Joel 2, whose verses remind the faithful that God 'shall utter his voice before his army: for his camp is very great', and that he 'will remove far off from you the northern army, and will drive him into a land barren and desolate, with his face toward the east sea'. For the wider congregation, the psalms would have been particularly influential in this regard. Recent scholars have argued that sung psalms were one of the most direct and intense methods through which the non-literate absorbed reformed teachings. Not only did the fact that they were repeated 'to the exclusion of other religious songs' mean, as Margaret Mackay has noted in reference to contemporary Calvinism, that people would have known the words of the psalms 'intimately', but being chanted over and over again in repetitive, hypnotic tones, their imagery and narrative would have been impressed upon minds and emotions in a way that the content of sermons or readings seldom could.[22] In his detailed study of the Glasgow revivalists, Landsman noted that 'references to the spirituality of psalm singing appear repeatedly in the narratives. Several converts maintained that they felt the stirring of convictions during the singing of psalms', while some even 'credited their awakenings to dreams or visions in which psalms played a prominent role'.[24] Even more interestingly, this subjective intensity may have often been fostered because, as Mackay notes, individuals from psalm-focused denominations can gain 'a close personal attachment to a certain psalm or groups of psalms, identifying closely with their content in the autobiographical way which the psalms *par excellence* are open to'.[25]

Given the fact that Isobel lived in a violent place in violent times, and given the fact that she seems to have been attracted, either by circumstance or temperament, to the death-bringing aspect of fairy host activities, we can speculate that she may have developed just such a close and autobiographical attachment to some of the more martial and bloodthirsty verses chanted by the Auldearn congregation. More specifically, her arrow-shooting passages invite us to speculate that she may have been particularly attached to the group of psalms that depict God riding through the air, at the head of his army, raining down arrows on the enemies of his followers. Psalm 18, as the most vibrant and memorable of this group, is particularly suggestive here. The first half (with verses here taken from a 1641 printing of the translation made by the author of *The Misticall Marriage*, Francis Rous) conjures up a dramatic image of an aggressive God who, armed with arrows, defends his supplicant, King David, with all the airborne panache of Isobel's folkloric Devil:

(9) The Lord descended from above,
and bow'd the heavens hie;
And underneath his feet he cast
the darknesse of the skie.

(10) Upon a cherub did he ride
in royall majestie;
And he did flie, yea on the wings
Of winds did swiftly flie.

(14) He shot his arrowes, and my foes
did scatter and affright:
He shot his fearfull lightnings out,
and them did put to flight.[25]

It would have been almost impossible for a receptive mind such as Isobel's, not to have been moved by such vivid imagery, and we can speculate that it worked its way deep into her imagination to later emerge, conflated with a range of folkloric and demonological beliefs and personal memories, to colour her envisioned characterization of the arrow-shooting Devil. That something like this may have occurred is further supported by the fact that we can, in places, make the cross-referencing between her confessions and Psalm 18 even more specific. We have referred several times in the book to the following passage from Isobel's second confession, in which the Devil gives her elf arrows and instructs her on how to use them:

> q[uhe]n I wes in the elfes houssis they will haw we . . . (*damaged – words missing*) them whytting and dighting, and the divellis giwes them to ws each of vs so mony . . . Qwhen (*damaged – words missing*) giwes th[e]m to ws he sayes shoot thes in my name and they sall not goe heall home, and q[uhe]n ve shoot thes arrowes (we say) I shoot yon man in the divellis name, he sall not win heall home, and this salbe alswa trw th[ai]r sall not be an bitt of him upon on lieiw. (43/21)

We have already speculated in CHAPTER TWELVE that this passage may have been linked, through oral transmission, to the tenth-century English charm, the *Wið færstice*, in which *hægtessan* or 'mighty women' are armed with 'slaughter-spears' by elven smiths. But we can also entertain the possibility that there may have been a more-than-coincidental similarity between this passage and the verses in Psalm 18 where, as James Limburg has noted, 'God is a trainer who prepares the feet, hands and arms of persons for warfare. God is [also] an equipper in the spiritual armory, furnishing people with weaponry, such as the "shield of your salvation".'[26]

(33) Like to the feet of nimble Hinds
my feet he maketh swift;
And then upon my places high
he me aloft doth lift.

(34) He doth instruct my hands to war,
he gives them strength to fight;
So that to break a bow of steele
mine armes from him have might.

(35) The shield of thy salvation
receiv'd I have from thee:
Thy right hand holds me up, thy love
Greatly exalteth me:

(39) For to the battell with great strength
me girded so hast thou,
That under me mine enemies
thou hast enforc't to bow.

(40) And thou has given me the necke
of those that with me fight;
That such as hate me causlesly
slay and destroy I might.[27]

The Arrow-Shooting Archangel

But the God of the psalms may not have been the only Christian figure to work his way into Isobel's arrow-shooting conflation. Of the many spiritual agencies celebrated in Scotland from the Middle Ages through to the nineteenth century, one of the most popular was the Archangel Michael, also colloquially (though inaccurately) referred to as 'Saint Michael'. While associated with a number of attributes, some of which we shall explore in more detail later, Michael's most striking characteristic was his militancy. It was Michael who, according to medieval tradition, led his airborne army of angels in battle against Satan and his followers during the Grand Rebellion, this mission earning him noble titles such as 'High King of the Holy Angels', 'Prince of the Celestial Army' and 'Supreme Commander of the Heavenly Hosts'; and causing Catholic iconographers to depict him fully armed with helmet, sword and shield.

We know that Michael's martial aspect made its mark on the early modern Scottish consciousness. He is the only saint-figure mentioned by Brodie in his copious diaries, and where the reference occurs, it pertains to his role as warrior ('Destroy this dragon [Satan]; for he fights against our Michaell').[28] Similarly, if the numbers of extant nineteenth-century charms containing references to Michael are anything to go by, we can assume that in the fields, cottages and barns of Auldearn, Isobel and her contemporaries would, like their Highland descendants 200 years later, have chanted protection charms and prayers celebrating the archangel's skills at arms. The following verses from a prayer collected from a Taynuilt crofter in the mid-nineteenth century, for example, state:

Oh Michael Militant,
Thou king of the angels,
Shield thy people
With the power of thy sword,
Shield thy people
With the power of thy sword . . .

Brighten thy feast
From heaven above;

Be with us in the pilgrimage
And in the twistings of the fight;
Be with us in the pilgrimage
And in the twistings of the fight . . .

Thou chief of chiefs,
Thou chief of angels,
Spread thy wing
Over sea and land . . . [29]

During long evenings by the fireside and in church, particularly around the time of the annual *Féill Micheil* or 'Feast of Saint Michael', Isobel may have listened to Michael's exploits described in legends and tales that had filtered their way down from the manuscripts of the Middle Ages into the oral lore of the fireside. In the following extract from Jacobus de Voraigne's medieval bestseller, the *Golden Legend*, Michael comes, like an avenging familiar spirit, to the aid of the Christian army at Spyinte:

> By the counsel of the bishop, the christian men took truce for three days that they might fast those three days and require their patron S. Michael unto their aid and help. In the third night [after three days of fasting] the holy S. Michael appeared to the said bishop and said that their prayers were heard, and promised them to have victory, and commanded them to run on their enemies at the fourth hour of the day without more tarrying. And when they ran against them the mountain of Gargan began strongly to tremble and a great tempest arose, so that lightening flew about and a dark cloud covered the mountain, so that six hundred of their adversaries died of the fiery arrows which came from the air. [30]

Given Isobel's claim that the coven accompanied the Devil on airborne corn straws that were as 'hors to ws', it is also pertinent to note that Michael was strongly associated with both supernatural flight and horses: his magical steed and his abilities in the saddle at the head of his army being celebrated in charms like the following, again collected in the nineteenth century:

> You were the warrior of courage
> Going on the journey of prophecy,
> You would not travel on a cripple,
> You did take the steed of the god Michael,
> He was without bit in his mouth,
> You did tide him on the wing,
> You did leap over the knowledge of nature. [31]

These verses and tales of a warrior angel who headed an aggressive, airborne, horse-riding, arrow-shooting supernatural host that could be called upon to protect an individual against their enemies could have impressed themselves on a verbally receptive listener such as Isobel, and easily been drawn, alongside the God of the Hebrews and the fairy-man-in-authority, into her envisioned conflation of the arrow-shooting Devil. That Michael made some kind of contribution in this vein is also supported by the fact that, despite his Christian pretensions, in his guise as leader of an airborne spirit-army he had deeply folkloric roots. Scholars often attribute Michael's early prominence in Christian worship not to his presence in the Bible – where he is a minimal figure, only mentioned a couple of times in Daniel and Revelation – but to the fact that he assumed the mantle previously worn by the pre-Christian warrior gods (Woden, Odin, Lugh etc.) And these gods, as we argued earlier, often assumed a leading role in the shamanistic spirit-group narratives that – to bring the line of inquiry neatly back to our ubiquitous fairy-man-in-authority – also emerged in Scottish folklore surrounding the hunting and processional activities of the fairy host. Michael's august folkloric origins are further intimated by the fact that, as folklorist Anne Ross has noted, Michael was 'spoken of as "the god Michael" right down to Carmichael's time' (the *Golden Legend*, noting that 'Michael is expounded sometimes as God') and the fact that the *Féill Micheil*, with its traditions of bareback horse-racing and bacchanalian fertility rituals, was 'one of the most blatantly pagan feasts of the Christian calendar'.[32] What the connection may have been, in Isobel's conscious mind, between the militant Michael who rode at the head of his angelic cohorts, the martial Yahweh who championed King David's armies, the bullying fairy-man-in-authority who led the arrow-shooting host, and the belligerent Devil who presided over the witches' coven, is beyond our grasp. But we can speculate that when forging its vivid envisioned amalgam of an aggressive, arrow-shooting, host-leading protector spirit, Isobel's unconscious mind would have mined this complex quadruplet indiscriminately.

Isobel's Conflation – the Pact-Making Devil

That Michael may have had something to do with Isobel's folkloric Devil, as he appears in the arrow-shooting scenes, draws further confirmation from the fact that he also emerges as a primary candidate for her theological Devil figure, as depicted in the pact passages. We argued earlier that accounts of demonic pacts found in witchcraft records may have, in some cases, reflected envisioned spirit-encountering experiences involving surrender-protection charms that were deemed unorthodox, and therefore demonized by the interrogating authorities. We have also observed that, third to God and Christ, the categories of spirit most commonly invoked in traditional protection charms collected in the nineteenth century were saints, and to a lesser extent, angels. It is therefore notable that the saint/angel who was most frequently invoked in these protection charms, and was consequently most vulnerable to redefinition as the pact-making Devil, was none other than the Archangel Michael.

Michael did not only gain prominence in these charms because his role as the militant leader of airborne spirit-armies made him supremely qualified to grant protection, but also because he was believed to be the spiritual being whose responsibility it was to escort or carry human souls to heaven; this role being further confirmation of his

Here the Archangel Michael and his heavily-armed host are depicted, high in the clouds, fighting the dragon. This engraving by Albrecht Dürer vividly evokes the angel's militant, airborne aspect. Photograph © 2010, Museum of Fine Arts, Boston.

links with pre-Christian gods of the dead such as Woden. The following verse, from a nineteenth-century 'death blessing', is standard:

> And be the holy Michael, king of angels
> Coming to meet the soul,
> And leading it home
> To the heaven of the Son of God.[33]

But Michael's soul-protecting capacities were not only valued at death. He was also invoked in more general protection charms, particularly those involving sleep when, according to popular belief, the soul was vulnerable because it could separate and wander from the body. One of the 'sleep prayers' collected by Carmichael states:

> Whilst the body is dwelling in the sleep,
> The soul is soaring in the shadow of heaven,
> Be the red-white Michael meeting the soul,
> Early and late, night and day,
> Early and late, night and day.[34]

With regard to Isobel's pact-making Devil figure, it is also notable that many Michael-invoking protection charms ask him to 'possess' or 'shield' the soul. The following surrender-protection charm, for example, states:

> And may Michael white kindly,
> High king of the holy angels,
> Take possession of the beloved soul,
> And shield it home to the Three of surpassing love,
> O! to the Three of surpassing love.[35]

Also pertinent, in this context, is the fact that many of these Michael-invoking charms also feature crown-sole statements. One reads:

> God and Mary and Michael kindly
> And the cross of the nine angels fair,
> Be shielding me all Three and as One,
> From the brow of my face to the edge of my soles.[36]

And another:

> The cross of the saints and of the angels with me
> From the top of my face to the edge of my soles.
>
> O Michael mild, O Mary of glory,
> O gentle Bride of the locks of gold,

Preserve ye me in the weakly body,
The three preserve me on the just path.[37]

Absorbing fireside lore surrounding the Archangel Michael, Isobel is likely to have seen no incongruity in a spirit that was an aggressive and militant leader of supernatural armies, but also a loving and compassionate familiar that could be encountered alone; and to whom one could, in moments of intense interpersonal intimacy, surrender the body and soul for safekeeping. Emerging unconsciously in dream and vision, both before and after arrest, these beliefs could have influenced her construction of an envisioned helping spirit figure that swept her through the air with the bloodthirsty fairy host one minute, and surprised her with intimate encounters and personal promises of protection the next. Through the Archangel Michael we can see more clearly how the gulf between Isobel's theological Devil and folkloric Devil could have been bridged, at its deepest level, by visionary experience.

The Hidden God

We have speculated that lore surrounding both the God of the psalms and Archangel Michael may have influenced Isobel's envisioned-Devil conflation. But if we now move on to study her sex-with-the-Devil scenes in more depth, we can speculate that another, even more unexpected, Christian figure may also have played a role here. Sex with the Devil was one of the stereotypical features of the demonic pact, and the following passage, taken from the Isobel's third confession, is the most detailed and sensational on that subject to emerge from any Scottish witchcraft testimony:

> the yowngest and lustiest woomen will haw werie great pleasur in their carnall cowpula[tio]n w[i]th him, yea much mor th[a]n w[i]th their awin husbandis, and they will haw a exceiding great desyr of it w[i]th him, als much as he can haw to them & mor, and never think shame of it, he is able for ws th[a]t way th[a]n any man can be, (alace th[a]t I sould compair him to an man) onlie he ves heavie lyk a malt seck a hodg nature, verie cold as yce . . . (47/3)

What is remarkable about this passage is not just Isobel's emphasis on the promiscuity of the Devil, but her repeated insistence (so unnecessary, incriminating and provocative that it tempts us to reach for the Isobel-was-crazy hypothesis) that his skills in this department were far superior to those of ordinary men. But, larger-than-life as her claims were, we cannot presume them to have been the result of interrogatorial superimposition. Although our analyses in CHAPTER SEVEN suggest that Forbes was likely to have emphasized the sexual component of the demonic contract, statements specifically denoting the sexual superiority of the Devil over that of mortal men are not conventional components of the pact stereotype and are therefore hard to categorically place at Forbes's door. That Isobel directly contributed to these passages is also suggested by the fact that Innes inserted the first-person statement, 'Alac th[a]t I sould compair him to an man' into the confessional text in parentheses; an unusual editorial manoeuvre that suggests that he found Isobel's utterance so notable that he was moved to reproduce it verbatim.

On the basis of our research in earlier chapters we can speculate that these comments, or at least Isobel's contribution to these comments, may have been informed by some combination of remembered real-life sexual experiences, fireside lore surrounding the insatiable eroticism of elfin knights or water horses, and demonological beliefs concerning the aggressive sexuality of the Devil. But our analysis into contemporary teachings on spiritual covenants also suggest that Isobel's comments may have been influenced by a different figure altogether. As we have seen earlier, as it was presented in reformed writings, the marriage-covenant was distinguishable from other forms of covenant in the sense that the relationship between Christ and the supplicant was not forged in a church or in heaven or in the distant deserts of Sinai, but 'panting' in a 'bed of love' where 'she that loveth Christ much, may embrace him much, and kisse him much, and holde him much'.[38] But also notable, in the context of the current discussion, is the fact that marriage-covenant teachings consistently emphasized, to the point of obsession, how the spiritual pleasures to be gained from Christ's embraces were far more intense and enjoyable than any other. This sentiment was often expressed in general terms, with Hugh Rose claiming, 'let other things be dross and refuse in comparison of thee [Christ]', and East Lothian covenanter Henrietta Lindsay stating rhetorically: 'are there not loveliness and beauty to be discovered in him [Christ] that cannot be found anywhere else?'[39] But what is particularly notable here, with regard to Isobel's depiction of the superior sexual satisfactions to be gained from the Devil, is the fact that these sentiments were also commonly expressed in the form of direct comparisons between the pleasure and love experienced with Christ and the pleasure and love experienced among men, or on earth. Pearse, for example, notes that: 'Surely there is more sweetness, more happiness, in one kiss of the mouth of this blessed Lord, in one imbrace in his bosom . . . than in all the delights of sin . . . one turn with him in his Galleries, is infinitely beyond all earthly delights watsoever'.[40] While Rous claims that through Christ's spiritual embraces the lover 'may forget the low and base griefs, and cares, & distractions, of carnal and worldy love, and by a heavenly excesse be transported into an heavenly love, to embrace her beloved, who is the Lord'.[41] Even more pertinent to Isobel's case, is the fact that when celebrating the superiority of Christ's marital attentions, these writers sometimes highlighted the comparative deficiencies of both mortal husbands and mortal marriages in order to drive their point home. Pearse, for example, claims of Christ that 'he and he alone is a never-dying Husband; the best Husband here below is mortal, and may leave you in a moment; but Christ is immortal . . . he will never leave you in the desolate state of Widdow-hood . . . Oh what an Husband is this!'[42] While Rous states, even more explicitly, that 'the joy of love and union in an earthly marriag, cannot express a heavenly joy that is spiritually pure and purely active'.[43] Theologically sophisticated as these various statements were intended to be, there is no doubt that they bear a strong morphological similarity to Isobel's claim that her spirit lover, the Devil, 'is (more?) able for ws th[a]t way th[a]n any man can be, (alace th[a]t I should compair him to an man)'; and her insistence that her coven members 'will haw werie great pleasur in their carnall cowpula[tio]n w[i]th him, yea much mor th[a]n w[i]th their awin husbandis'. And for this reason we can speculate that, despite their different contexts, there may have been a link between them.

That Isobel's depiction of the Devil could display such a phrase-specific resemblance to the language of the marriage-covenant is of course highly speculative, but it receives additional support elsewhere. After describing sexual intercourse with the Devil for the first time, Isobel does not only claim that he possessed cloven feet, but also that he 'vold be somtymes w[i]th ws lyk a deer, or a rae (*roe*)' (39/12). While it is not uncommon for witchcraft suspects to claim that the Devil appeared before them in the form of an animal, references to 'deer' or 'rae' are unusual and their appearance together is, to my knowledge, unique. In the absence of any obvious explanations for this statement, it is interesting to note that when describing the beauty of Christ, particularly in the context of the marriage-covenant, Protestant writers frequently drew on exactly the same dual metaphor to describe the Bridegroom of Souls; the phrase being taken, as was so much marriage-covenant language, directly from the Song of Songs, where it appears as: 'Make hast my beloved, and be thou like to a Roe, and a young Hart upon the mountains of spices'.[44] As would be expected, the phrase was familiar to Hugh Rose who exclaims to Christ, in his diatribe on the marriage-covenant: 'turn thou, my beloved, and be thou like a roo or a young heart upon the mountains of Bether. Come over these mountains of Bether and division, and be thou eternally united to me'.[45] We can assume that Rose, and his fellow Nairnshire ministers, used the same metaphor when preaching on the marriage-covenant from the pulpit, and that ordinary parishioners like Isobel would have been familiar with it.

The possibility that marriage-covenant teachings wove their way into Isobel's confessions is further supported by the fact that, in addition to a penchant for the 'bed of love' and a more-than-passing resemblance to the hero of the Song of Songs, Isobel's Devil and the Bridegroom of Souls shared other attributes. The Devil's entreaty to covenant, for example, strongly evokes the Christ who entices his human lovers with promises of the 'great things he will bestow upon them, and instate them into, and all to win and allure them to himself, to gain their love and consent to accept of him, and to be his in a Marriage-Covenant.'[46] His desire to confirm the covenant with his mark is redolent of the Christ who, in taking Hugh Rose to his bosom, put his 'mark' upon him to 'seal' him as his own.[47] His invitation to help Isobel avenge her enemies reminds us of the Christ who promised his lover that, through entering into a marriage-covenant with him her 'strength [should be] revived' and she should see the best way to conquer 'some mighty enemy, that hath been too hard' for her.[48] His generous gifting of meat and ale evokes the Christ who tempted his spiritual lovers with the promise: 'he that hath no money; come buy and eat; yea, come buy wine and milk without money, and without price'.[49]

The language and imagery of the marriage-covenant with Christ, as disseminated from the Nairnshire pulpits, could have worked its way into Isobel's Devil figure – as he appears in the sex scenes – both during and prior to interrogation. Being questioned closely by Forbes et al. about the sexuality of the Devil after arrest, and then left to ruminate over the subject during her long weeks of solitary confinement, remembered phrases and images concerning the loving embraces and superior satisfactions of the Bridegroom of Souls, previously absorbed during sermons and readings, could have risen to the surface of Isobel's consciousness and woven their way into the coerced-compliant responses and false-memory fictions she created around sex with the Devil. Alternatively, if Isobel had constructed her Devil-figure around memories of previous shamanistic encounters with sexually-affectionate helping spirits, then she would have drawn this marriage-covenant narrative and imagery into her prototypical Devil-conflation prior to arrest. Either way, this spirit-creating process, working as it did with the idiosyncrasy of the visionary imagination and, after imprisonment, the distorting effects of maltreatment and stress, seems to have blurred allegory and reality, sacredness and profanity, pornography and propriety to such a degree that any marriage-covenant influences involved became unrecognizable, both to Isobel and her interrogators.

In the last analysis, in the conscious mind of the Nairnshire covenanters, and possibly in the conscious mind of Isobel herself, the Devil was the Devil, Christ was Christ and God was God. But the unconscious psyche that nourishes the imagination abides by different rules. For shamanistic practitioners like Isobel, for whom the visionary capacity was an ardent and autonomous force, the parts of the mind that created envisioned images of spiritual helpers are likely to have blithely disregarded the distinctions of men and promiscuously woven together the Bridegroom of Souls and Old Testament God with god-like archangels, cloven-footed devils, elfin knights and flesh-and-blood men. This process would have been complex and subtle, and on the basis of the available evidence, reconstructing it can never be more than highly speculative. But by looking at our material from this angle we gain some unusual perspectives. Not least, we find ourselves presented with the tantalising possibility that the single most graphic and 'ungodly' sex-with-the-Devil scene to have come down to us from our British witchcraft records did not gain its ultimate emotional charge from the stereotyped imaginations of zealous interrogators, or the frightened ravings of a tortured witchcraft suspect, but from the experiential heart of covenanting spirituality.

Discretio Spirituum

In arguing that so many different images, narratives and beliefs could have influenced Isobel's visionary conflation of the Devil, as he appeared both before arrest (as a shamanistic helping-spirit figure) and after (as a false-memory recollection), we are highlighting the dilemma that lies at the heart of all visionary traditions: identification. The autonomy, and therefore unpredictability and idiosyncrasy, of dream and vision phenomena and the way it seamlessly conflates such a wide variety of influences, means that the recognition and classification of spirits has always been a perennial problem in magical and religious belief systems throughout the world. Even in homogeneous tribal cultures, where visionary experiences are culturally sanctioned and sought after, and where beliefs about spiritual agencies evolve within a shared and relatively coherent and closed world-view, the form and appearance of envisioned spirits are highly idiosyncratic and shamans can worry over their identity. When, for example, a novice Yanomamö shaman was warned by a more experienced practitioner that he might soon encounter the dangerous Deer Spirit, his first question was 'But how will I recognize him?'[50]

In an effort to negotiate this problem the Christian church has, since its inception, developed a wide range of criteria (many of them contradictory and none of them deemed foolproof) to help both visionaries and interested parties to judge the origin and identity of an envisioned spirit. These involve, among other things, assessments of the spirit's behaviour and appearance, examination of post-encounter physical signs of authenticity and observations on the moral behaviour and 'mood' of the visionary. In practice, among Christian visionaries, the *discretio spirituum* or 'discernment of spirits' seems to have been as concerned with the more general question as to whether the spirit was good (from God) or evil (from the Devil) as opposed to the precise identity of the spirit itself (a process which may have owed as much to a pragmatic avoidance of the futile attempts to establish spirit identity as to the dualism inherent in Christian thought). But even for the Protestants, with their black and white mentality and rigidly clear ideas of good and evil, this was a difficult challenge, and its ambiguities were present at the very heart of the experienced covenants. In *The Misticall Marriage* Rous devotes a whole chapter to 'The signs, and marks of the true and right visitations of the heavenly Bridegroom' in order to 'shew what these visitations are, and so to undeceive those that think they are not' and 'free those from error, who believe that they are, yet do mistake those that are not, for those that are'. These explanations, Rous goes on, are important because 'those who are yet but children, and not perfect in the art of discerning good and evill, must not be left to the dangers of errour and mistaking. The black Angel sometimes changeth himself into an Angel of light.'[51]

Given the fact that theologians and contemplatives found it hard to identify envisioned spirits and differentiate between them, it is no surprise to find that ordinary lay people grappled with the same problem. On the one hand, it is clear that some considered themselves capable of discriminating, to their own satisfaction at least, between spirits of good and evil origin. Dyke resident Cathrin Hendrie was in no doubt that the visions that oppressed her were of the Devil, telling Brodie that 'Sathan had oft appeared to her lyk an angel and enticed and tempted her to sin, and cited the New Testament for it'.[52] Similarly, the daughter of godly Perthshire farmer Donald McGrigor clearly distinguished the many spirits that appeared to her into those sent by the Devil, which were terrifying and included a 'black man' and several old women who performed maleficent rituals, and those sent by God: beautiful angelic beings who held 'white feathers in their hands like wings' and 'carried her in spirit to heaven'.[53] Similarly confident discernment could also occur among the less educated. Aberdeenshire woman Elspeth Reid (1597) claimed to have refused her lover's command to invoke and covenant with a spirit in order to 'get geir aneucht [enough]' because she feared that 'it was ane evill spreit'; while Alloa witch Bessie Paton (1658) claimed that the Devil (in 'gray cloathes, with ane blew bonnett') approached her at a meeting and 'took her by the hand and asked her if she wold be fied [feed]' but 'his hand wes cold, and when she fand it cold that she was fearid and took out her hand agayne. She thought he wes not righteous. She thought that it wes the divell, and she said that she sained [blessed] herself.'[54]

But it is also clear that for many lay people, both educated and uneducated, the task of distinguishing between good and evil spirits was not always so simple. In 1623 Perthshire cunning woman Isobel Haldane claimed that she was lifted from her bed and carried to fairyland though 'whether it was by God or the Devil, she knows not'; while in Bute nearly forty years later, cunning woman Jonet Morison claimed she heard the voice of a spirit asking her to open the bedroom window and let it come in, and that she told it, '[if you are] a good Spirit Ile [I'll] let the in bot and [i.e. if] thou be ane evill spirit God be between me and the[e]'.[55] Similarly, Appin cunning man Donald McIlmichall (1677), when describing a visit to a fairy hill, defensively told his inter-rogators that 'he cannot weill tell quhat persons they wer bot he judges them not to have bein worldie men or men ordayned of god'.[56] Moving on to the early-eighteenth century, Glasgow evangelist Alexander Bisland's claim that 'during the course of his conversion he had learned how to distinguish the voice of Christ from the voice of the Devil, when either gave him orders, as both often did' suggests that in the early stages of his spiritual awakening he did not deem his discriminatory skills so accurate.[57] A similar picture of uncertainty resolved through time is found in the records of the inter-rogations of Joan of Arc which, as we shall explore in more detail later, provide us with one of the most vivid and detailed insights into the process of *discretio spirituum* among the uneducated to have come down to us from pre-modern Europe. In reference to the frequent encounters with the Archangel Michael that underpinned her spiritual prac-tice, the records state that 'She said she would know well enough if it was Saint Michael or something disguised as him. She also said that the first time she was very unsure if it was Saint Michael. And the first time she was very afraid; and she saw him many times before she knew it was Saint Michael.'[58]

Isobel's Discerning

With regard to Isobel's Devil figure, these perspectives raise some interesting possi-bilities. They suggest that, owing to the subtleties of the psychic conflation process, and the concomitant difficulties surrounding identification, we cannot assume that, had Isobel indeed encountered some form of shamanistic helping spirit prior to arrest, she would automatically have known who or what she was encountering. Under the physical and psychological stress of subsistence living, military unrest, and the oppres-sive demands of a religiously-fundamentalist minister and financially-desperate landlord, Isobel's unconscious psyche may well have spontaneously manifested an aggressive warrior spirit, who appeared before her in her moment of need and offered to protect her and avenge her enemies. But at the moment of encounter, can we assume that she would have known instantly and for certain whether her envisioned saviour was God, Christ, the Archangel Michael, the Devil or the 'maister man' of the fairy hosts? All were great warriors with sharp arrows in their quivers and all were prepared to effect 'mighty slaughter' in exchange for her service and her soul. In the midst of her dream or trance, as she flew with an envisioned spirit-army hunting for prey, filled with the thrill of the chase, would she have been absolutely clear as to the identity of the spirit that placed the avenging weapons into her hand? Similarly, defending itself against a hard-hearted world, Isobel's unconscious psyche may well have spontaneously manifested a physically affectionate spirit that appeared before her when she was at her most emotionally desolate, and offered comfort and compassion. But in the midst of her dream or vision, as the spirit wrapped her in its arms and enticed her to its marriage bed to make a 'vow of love', would she have known whether she succumbed to the envisioned embraces of an amorous elf man or water horse, a shape-shifting Devil or the 'fair and ruddy' Bridegroom of Souls?

On a visionary level, this ambiguity as regards the definition of spirits would have been critical when it came to moments of compact. Initiatory dreams and visions are characterized by a state of heightened emotional arousal, reflecting the fact that they often occur at times of physiological intensity and stress. Here, the spirit appears suddenly, in a moment of crisis, and offers its help in the urgent atmosphere of the spontaneous envisioned encounter. In this context, the discernment between good spirit and evil spirit has to be made at the moment of experience and there is little time for rational thought. The records of Fifeshire cunning woman Alison Peirson (1588) vividly convey the emotional confusion and pressure of such encounters. When a man 'cled in grene clathis' came to her as 'scho lay doun seik alane' and told her that 'Gif scho wald be faithfull, he wald do her guid', Alison 'cryit for help, bot nane hard hir; and thane, scho chargeit him, "In Godis name and the low he levit one [the law he lived by]," that if he come in Godis name and for the weill of hir saull, he sould tell'.[59] In this case, Alison seems to have retained a modicum of composure, despite her disorientation, but other narratives suggest that in the heat of the moment visionaries could be less scrupulous. The trial dittays of Haddington cunning woman Agnes Sampson, who encountered the Devil when worrying about how to provide for her children after her husband's recent death, state that 'Before she knew what spirit it was she consented [to make the demonic pact]'; while Alloa witch Margaret Tailzour claimed to have covenanted 'by putting her one hand on her head and the other on her foote and renuncit her baptisme from God to that man which she knew not at first to be the divell'. Similarly, Paisley witch Margaret Lang maintained that 'when the Devil first appeared [and made a pact with her] she knew him not to be such till afterwards'.[60]

Spiritual Compassion

The very real problems inherent in the discernment of spirits are evinced by the fact that even among highly-educated churchmen and contemplatives, it was sometimes agreed that the unreliability of external indicators rendered affective response, that is, the 'feeling' a vision generates in the visionary, as the most reliable indicator of origin. The belief that the discernment between good and evil spirits could be based upon sensibility and emotion, as opposed to spirit-appearance or behaviour, was of long-standing, with William Christian noting, in *Apparitions in Late Medieval and Renaissance Spain*, that the man called to re-evaluate Joan of Arc's visions in 1449:

> cited Thomas Aquinas, who in turn cited the Life of Saint Anthony to the effect that 'the distinguishing of good from evil spirits is not difficult: If fear is followed by joy, we know that the help of God has come to us. The security of the soul is a mark of the presence of divine majesty. If, on the contrary, the fear remains, then the enemy is present.' This criterion was probably influenced by neo-platonic ascetic doctrines. Iamblichus in the third century showed how higher or lower spirits could be distinguished by one's subjective reaction.[61]

These beliefs were clearly present on a popular level in many parts of early modern Europe. The records of the interrogations of Joan of Arc state that: 'She also says that she has a great joy when she sees [Archangel Michael]: and she thinks that when she sees him, she is not in a state of mortal sin.'[62] Similarly, in Morayshire more than 200 years later it was the 'power, light and love and suitableness' of the mystically-encountered Christ's contractual promises, as opposed to anything more concrete, that left Lilias Dunbar 'no place . . . for doubting, but these were the words of the Spirit of God to me'.[63] Alternatively, in Cambuslang in the early-eighteenth century, comforting tones of voice convinced Catherine Cameron that her experiences were of godly origin, with Landsman noting that she 'was affected by repeated words and visions from Christ and the devil' until finally a voice 'soothed her' by telling her that she was 'not under the Law but under Grace'.[64]

Although the use of feeling as a method of *discretio spirituum* was more frequently challenged by intellectuals and theologians in the increasingly rationalist and materialist early modern period, it continued to flourish among the laity. Landsman writes that among the Glasgow evangelists in the second quarter of the eighteenth century:

> For the clergy, the principal confirmation of assurance was scriptural, the ability to relate one's experience to religious doctrine. Such concerns mattered little to their converts, who mentioned doctrinal matters in their accounts almost as rarely as they discussed meetings with the minister. Instead, they looked inward to their feelings . . . many of the narratives [of the converts] appear as day-to-day histories of the words and experiences that affected their emotional equilibrium.[65]

Encounter-narratives found in witchcraft records also reveal that relationships with envisioned spirits could be rejected or fostered on the basis of affective response. Many narratives, particularly those given by the victims of witchcraft, suggest that spirits were immediately and unequivocally rejected because they generated fear and emanated malevolence (with variants of Bessie Dunlop's phrase 'I was sumthing fleit [afraid]' running through many accounts).[66] But other narratives suggest that encounters with envisioned spirits were marked by positive emotion. Renfrewshire witch Janet Robertson allegedly called the Devil 'her Joy', while the pleasure that Forfar cunning woman Isobel Shyrie gained from the Devil is soundly evinced by her claim to a neighbour that 'it wold be ane great joy to hir to be in such [the Devil's] service'.[67] These comments, in turn, echo the claims of the Sicilian *dona de fuera* who, although she had been told by the church authorities that her visionary adventures were sinful 'went on doing it . . . And she went out joyfully because of the pleasure she took in it'.[68] The references to feasting, dancing, music-making and 'great miriement' that characterize Scottish sabbath and fairy-gathering accounts indicate similarly positive emotions. As George Mackenzie noted in 1678: 'witches desire to have these Dreams, and glory in them when they are awake'.[69]

It is also important to point out here that both demonological and fairy-related encounter-narratives suggest that the positive emotional response generated through contact with envisioned helping spirits was deeply linked to the relief concomitant upon the alleviation of suffering. As we saw in CHAPTER TEN, spontaneous spirit-encounters – even at their most demonologically stereotypical – typically occurred when an individual was in great physical or psychological distress. Indeed, as Goodare has recently pointed out, in 1643 the general assembly of the Scottish church even placed 'extremity of grief' at the head of their list of reasons as to why witches allied themselves with the Devil, with 'pinching povertie' also featuring prominently on the list.[70] In this context, we can speculate that spontaneous offers of help, as they were offered by envisioned spirits defined in witch-trials as the Devil, the dead, or some kind of fairy, were experienced as genuine gestures of spiritual compassion. A woman with a mortally sick child, or not enough food to see her family through the winter, would have been deeply comforted by a spirit's seemingly prosaic entreaty to 'be of good cheer' because he would see to it that she 'would get better Meat and better Cloaths, and she would not need to beg', or that she would have 'als much silver as will buy you as many corn as will serve you before Lammas' or '[as] good furrows as her neighbours'.[71] A woman in the pit of despair because she had lost her husband or her livelihood could not fail to have been moved by the Devil's promise that 'thou sall have geir aneuch, and sall nocht want sa lang as thow levis', and that he would 'never let a tear fall from their eyn so long as they served him'.[72] Indeed, the Devil's entreaty, in one encounter-narrative, to 'eat, drink and be blithe, taking rest and ease, for he should raise them up at the latter day gloriously' so skilfully spans the spectrum of human needs, from the material to the metaphysical, that it is difficult to see how anyone could have resisted it.[73] There is no reason to assume that these offers of magical aid and material comfort were not experienced as deeply as the spiritual compassion traditionally offered by Christ or God, as depicted in pious covenanting narratives. The gratitude, humility, and emotional intensity they provoked in the suffering witchcraft suspect could have been little different from that provoked in the learned covenanter who, equally burdened by privation, encountered an envisioned Christ figure who promised her that 'If she be poor, he can enrich her', and 'if [she is] diseased, he can heal her' and that if she 'cast in thy petition, and whatsoever grief it hath in it, thou shalt be cured of it'.[74]

Unlike godly writings and diaries, witchcraft records seldom make direct reference to the complex emotions that may have been generated during covenanting encounters. But nevertheless, in some narratives hints of this interchange between human suffering and spiritual compassion can be glimpsed between the lines. The testimony of Alloa witch Margaret Duchall (1658) states that the Devil came to her when she was 'in Isobell Jamesone's little house, qr sche dwelt herself all alone' and that he:

> asked hir what ailleth you, sche ansrit, I am ane poor bodie and cannot get qron to live. He said ye sall not want if you will doe my bidding, and he gave me fyve shilling and bade me goe buy ane pek of meill with it . . . [Later, after she made the pact] he gave me his mark on my eyebrie by an nip and bade me qunsoevir ye wold have me, call upon me by my name Johne and I sall nevir leave you, but doe anything to you that ye bide me . . . [75]

For women like Margaret Duchall, who were enduring extreme privation, a spirit was identified as good not because it accorded with some exterior criteria devised by the church, but because it offered – both precipitously and empathetically – to alleviate their suffering. In the following account from sixteenth-century Lorraine, it is clear that an earlier encounter with an envisioned spirit had made such a favourable impression on a witchcraft suspect that, even though she was not sure of its identity, she maintained her belief in its essential beneficence despite her interrogators' attempts to persuade her otherwise. As Robin Briggs paraphrases:

> In 1592 Laurence Jolbay of Sainte Marguerite rashly mentioned an encounter with a good angel, who had told her that if she would believe in him he would not abandon her, then was subjected to remorseless questioning on the subject. She said that the angel was dressed like a woman, was about four feet high, and spoke honestly in a clear voice, promising to give her bread when she was in need. The judges replied that this must have been an evil spirit, to which she responded she was sure it had been good, and if not an angel had been the soul of her father or another dead man come to comfort her. [76]

The emotional dynamics and the rationale behind the identification of the spirits encountered – as displayed in Duchall's and Jolbay's narratives – differ little, in essence, from those found in contemporary accounts of experienced covenants as recorded by godly diarists such as the Morayshire covenanter Lilias Dunbar:

> when I was cast out into the open field, lying in my blood to the loathing of my person, and there was no eye to pity me – then, even the time of my greatest necessity was his time of love, wherein he looked on me and did cast his skirts over me, and entered into an everlasting covenant with me, and I became his. I was made to receive particular promises accompanied with such power, light and love and suitableness, that there was no place in it for doubting, but these were the words of the Spirit of God to me . . . [77]

A Place for Compulsion

The possibility that demonological and fairy-related narratives depicting contractual negotiations or overt pacts may have represented shamanistic visionary experience also gains confirmation from another quarter. Until now, we have suggested that when visionaries found themselves confronting a help-offering spirit they had some kind of choice: if they liked the spirit they entered into a relationship with it, and if they disliked it they did not. But while this was clearly the case in some instances, a significant minority of encounter-narratives describe people allying themselves with spirits despite the fact that they were clearly reluctant to do so; with the spirits' offers of help, in these cases, often being combined with coercion or threat of punishment. We shall be exploring the issue of conscious alliance with evil spirits in more detail in the next chapter, but it is pertinent here to note that these 'narratives of reluctance' concord, as strongly as do those involving choice, with what we know of the dynamics of visionary experience. As we have seen in previous chapters, the experience of being compelled, against the will, to enter into trance and participate in envisioned ritual activities is often found in shamanistic narratives, being clearly identifiable in the futile attempts of Siberian Tofa shamans to resist the 'demands of the spirits' and avoid initiation; the Corsican *mazzeri's* uncontrollable urge to hunt; and the nineteenth-century Highlanders' inability to evade their host-directed arrow-shooting duties.[78] This compulsion, which can be likened to an unbearable build-up of physical and mental tension (often presenting as temporary psychosis or psychosomatic illness), can be stimulated by either psychological disposition and/or external factors such as bereavement or physical suffering.

It is wholly logical to speculate that this compulsive element was present in the contractual relationships between shamanistic practitioners and their helping spirits in early modern Scotland, and this thesis is supported by the fact that so many encounter-narratives describe individuals first meeting their helping spirits when suffering a period of severe emotional and physical stress. Some of these elements are clearly evident in the following encounter-narrative, which describes how Lanark woman Kathren Shaw (1644) encountered a spirit shortly after the death of her husband. The sense of Kathren's disorientation, vulnerability, fear, and ultimate surrender to the spirit's demands, despite the fact that she was obviously uneasy about its status, are all redolent of the psychological dynamics of shamanistic compulsion:

> shortlie efter he appeired to hir in lickness of a colt foill [foal] and followit hir home to hir hous, and being enterit into the hous appeired lyk ane Johnne Johnstoun, ane neichbour sone, and when she looked to him she said, 'Johnne, I sall tell your father ye are come to terrifie me.' He said, 'I am not Johnne.' 'Quhom then,' said she. He answerit, 'I am your husband, Johnne Clerk,' and when she said that hir husband was dead and lying in the kirk yaird of Lanerk, he said that he wes come to fetch hir to him and askit if she wald be his servant as he had bene speaking to hir befoir and she sould fair weill. 'Quhat would ye give me?' said she, 'for I have meall and keall.' He answerit, 'I sall mak ilk day [als] guid as thy yuill day'; and with that he grippit hir with his hand which wes cold as leid, [and] struglit with hir and, she haiffing no power to resist, he had carnall copulatioun with hir and [put] his mark upoun hir, quhilk she shew in hir richt arme.[79]

Shamanistic compulsion also goes some way towards explaining why some women – like Agnes Sampson and Bessie Dunlop – remained in long-term relationships with spirits that did not live up to their expectations, who they could not always control and who, on occasion, they did not even like.[80]

The Narrow Glass

It is clear from Continental sources that individuals who underwent these types of complex – and often unsettling – visionary experiences did not always share them with the men of the church. Joan of Arc's indictments state that: 'she firmly believes that those she sees are saints, although she has no sign and she has consulted no bishop, priest, or prelate about whether to believe them', while the men who interrogated the Friulian *benandante*, Paolo Gasparutto, claimed that over a period of years, 'while you were performing all these diabolical things [*benandanti* rites], you received the most sacred Eucharist and confession, but you chose not to reveal these crimes to your confessor'.[81] The fact that many cunning folk, such as Bessie Dunlop, seem to have nurtured relationships with their familiar spirits that had spanned many years before they revealed them to interrogators, suggests that visionaries could be equally secretive in early modern Scotland.

Such self-sufficiency may have been rooted in naivety, but it is more likely to have been rooted in canniness. The idiosyncrasies of psychic conflation, combined with the subjective directives of feeling and compulsion, would have prompted individuals to ally themselves with envisioned entities that they knew, rationally, would not have been acceptable to the local minister. That this was the case is supported by extant spiritual diaries indicating that even literate and godly women, whose mystical covenanting experiences were articulated – often almost word-for-word – through the language of the Bible, were not always keen to share their experiences with the men of the church. Elizabeth Cairns, whose childhood and adolescence as a solitary cattle herder caused her to develop a strongly individual spirituality, became increasingly unwilling to divulge her mystical covenanting experiences to her local minister because of his evident inability to comprehend or guide her through them. On one occasion she wrote:

> One time in particular, he [her local minister] was preaching on the covenant of grace, but what he advanced on that subject I could not join with, being contrary to what the Lord had made me experience of the freedom and fullness of his covenant: but at this time the Lord mercifully ordered in his wise providence, that the minister went from home for some time, and so next Sabbath I went to hear a neighbouring minister, who was directed to preach upon the same text and subject, and by his sermon my experiences were cleared up, and I was more confirmed, from the word of the Lord, in the former views I had gotten of God's covenant. And so I came away confirmed of my hope on the same foundation; blessing God for that sermon, and admiring his wise and wonderful providence in bringing me to hear it; resolving no more to try either my state or case by my own minister's doctrine.[82]

Elizabeth possessed enough confidence and independence of mind to respond to the inadequacies and condemnations of her minister by seeking out the opinions of another, but other men and women who found themselves in similar situations were not necessarily so fortunate or self-possessed. Landsman has shown that, in early eighteenth-century Glasgow, lay evangelists were reluctant to share their mystical experiences with their local ministers because they knew that they would be sceptical of their authenticity, claiming that 'Several converts avoided going to see either ministers or community leaders even after they felt they had approached the point of assurance of their salvation, precisely "for fear of speaking amiss", to use Anne Wylie's phrase, or for fear of being exposed as a hypocrite.'[83] Such attitudes generated confusion and hostility. The Lesmahago visionary, Jean Hay, was so upset by the scepticism of local minister Thomas Lining, and the fact that he defined her heartfelt mystical experiences as 'strange', that she later 'came to imagine that she saw Lining . . . in the image of the devil himself'.[84]

From this perspective, the question that immediately presents itself here is: if pious Christians like Anne Wylie and Jean Hay hesitated to approach their local ministers about their spiritual experiences, then how much more difficult would it have been for women like Isobel Gowdie? We can speculate that, unlike her educated Dyke neighbour Cathrin Hendrie, Isobel would not have been inclined to go to Harry Forbes or her local landlord, the Laird of Park, for guidance in understanding her visionary experiences. Like her Friulian counterpart, Paolo Gasparutto, she may have instinctively known that her spirit helper, and the activities she performed with him, were too unorthodox and morally ambiguous to fit their rigid presbyterian template. If parishioners did not, as kirk session records amply attest, rush to inform ministers that they had loaded peats on the sabbath, danced at a wake, or performed healing charms to cure their sick cows, then they would have been even less likely to have voluntarily offered up accounts of covenanting with envisioned spirits for magical aid, for which punishment was so much more severe. Moreover, if you were in open conflict with the minister and his views – as magical practitioners like Isobel would often have been – then this reluctance was likely to have been even stronger. As a consequence, we can assume that for Isobel, as for many of her contemporaries, shamanistic visions were managed within the 'secret, uncharted areas of peasant exchange'; and as long as they fulfilled their magical purpose both the visionary and the clients they served saw no need for the theological discernments of ministers or the spurious involvement of the law. In this context, any idiosyncrasies or unorthodox elements pertaining to the visions would not have presented any problems because they would never have emerged from the fastness of the popular imagination.

From this perspective, difficulties would only have arisen when, through accident or design, these shamanistic experiences were hauled out of the secret areas of peasant exchange and scrutinised through the narrow lens of the presbyterian glass. And then the problems would have come thick and fast. As we have seen in CHAPTER TEN, this lens was so narrow that even the most theologically informed visions seldom escaped condemnation. In the 1680s Janet Frazer, the pious minister's daughter who spent her spare time lying in fields reading the Bible, experienced a series of visions that were considered – both by herself and many in her community – to be godly and informative. But despite the fact that her encounters featured white-clad spirits who spoke 'by course, with Scripture notes, naming books, chapter, and verse' and gave sage responses to her theological concerns about the 'suffering remnant', when Janet was finally – after seven years – brought before the presbytery it persuaded her to confess that she had been 'deluded by Satan'.[85] From the presbytery's point of view, the theological and logistical challenges – not to mention the threat to church authority – concomitant upon acknowledging the girl's visions as authentic were just too challenging to negotiate.

But if the church could demonize the visions of a pious minister's daughter, whose envisioned helpers spouted scripture, chapter and verse, then how could they possibly condone the visions of women like Isobel Gowdie? Unlike the godly Janet Frazer, Isobel and her peers did not spend their days lying in fields reading the Bible, they spent them bent double in fields digging peat, stacking corn sheaves and weeding flax; and any godly beliefs they did possess scrambled for space alongside an undisciplined crowd of unorthodox notions and practices. Even if Isobel was convinced, at the time of her visionary encounters, that her Devil-figure was a largely benign and helpful fairy man or saint, or even the Bridegroom of Souls himself, how could Harry Forbes and Hugh Rose look favourably on a being that overtly demanded sexual favours, transformed himself into an animal and taught his human ally how to fly through the air in a fairy whirlwind and perform maleficent magic against godly members of the community? Time and time again we find trial records, from throughout early modern Europe, detailing how magical practitioners were forced, during interrogation, to concede that the spirit they previously believed to have been good, was in fact the Devil. As we saw earlier, Paolo Gasparutto was forced to re-define the angel who summoned him to fight for the *benandanti*, claiming that 'I believe that the apparition of that angel was really the devil tempting me, since you have told me that he can transform himself into an angel.'[86] Similarly, a Sicilian *dona de fuera* claimed of her nocturnal processions that 'she did not know at that time that it was devilment, until her confessor opened her eyes to her errors and told her that it was the Devil and that she must not do it anymore'.[87] In Scotland the same picture emerges. George Mackenzie's recommendation that suspects 'should be interrogat, if they knew him to be the Devil when they condescended to his service' indicates that a substantial proportion of women must have covenanted with spirits that they did not identify as the Devil until, during questioning, their godly interrogators labelled them as such. We can speculate that Margaret Tailzour's claim to have surrendered herself to a spirit that she 'knew not at first to be the divell', and Margaret Lang's insistence that she covenanted with a spirit but 'knew him not' to be the Devil 'until afterwards' were re-definitions produced in response to interrogatorial suggestion.[88] The depositions of Rydon witch Janet Kennedy, who was tried in Edinburgh in 1591, are particularly suggestive here. Janet claimed that thirty years previously a man had appeared to her, on more than one occasion, asking her to covenant with him in return for 'a good life'. The records indicate that, in the beginning at least, Janet had believed the man to be a good spirit, for he appeared 'like an old [?pa]lmer clad in white' and asked her to swear upon a book that 'she should take her to the judgement of God and forsake the foul thief'. But the fact that the Edinburgh clerk concluded

Janet's account with the ominous statement: 'Whereby the deponer grants that now she perceives it was an evil spirit appeared unto her in that likenes' suggests that during the process of questioning, the interrogators had succeeded in convincing Janet that her spirit should be re-defined.[89] This process of interrogatorial transformation is also illustrated in the records pertaining to Stirling cunning woman Isobel Watson, who was tried in 1590. Maxwell-Stuart notes that although Isobel claimed that 'Jesus Christ came to her in the likeness of an angel [to tell her the whereabouts of lost goods]' the presbytery 'must have been taken aback by this presumption and clearly sought to change Isobel's mind about certain details, for the record goes on to say that "eftir farder examinatione [scho] confessit that it was the devil quha schew hir the samen"'.[90]

With regard to spirit-encounters, then, seventeenth-century Scotland grappled with a profound irony. Perhaps never before, in the history of the Christian church in Britain, had ministers so fervently urged their congregations to seek succour and illumination through covenanting with spirits. And the climate of the times ensured that the imaginations of their parishioners – rendered receptive through physical hardship, military unrest and religious uncertainty – duly conjured up a range of envisioned figures that could, in return for devotion, offer them compassion and protection in their times of need. But for zealots like the Nairnshire covenanters, the enlightening of places like 'poor desolat Auldearn' must have seemed a sisyphean task. However hard ministers like Hugh Rose and Harry Forbes strove 'to woo and allure poor souls into an espousal, or marriage-covenant' with Christ, the Bridegroom of Souls they evoked in the hearts and minds of men and women like Isobel Gowdie seldom stood up to scrutiny.

17

'The De'il's aye gude to his ain'

In the last two chapters we have argued that Isobel's Devil figure, as he is depicted in both the fairy-related and demonological passages, may have been constructed around recollections of visionary encounters with some kind of shamanistic helping-spirit figure experienced prior to her arrest. We have also suggested that, at the moment of encounter, this figure may have represented a seamless conflation of diverse cultural influences absorbed both from the fireside and the reformed pulpit, with the strongest links pointing to folkloric lore surrounding the leader of the Wild Hunt. We have also argued that Isobel's memory of this figure would have been further developed during imprisonment and interrogation, through coerced-compliant responses and false-memory generation, to finally give rise to the complex composite figure described in the confessions. But if we entertain this hypothesis, the question that now presents itself is this: if Isobel's Devil figure was a genuine depiction, however distorted, of a once-encountered visionary figure, then did Isobel herself, at any point, either during or after these encounters, actually consider him to have been the Devil?

In CHAPTER FOURTEEN, where we briefly addressed this question, we argued that we can dispense with the unlikely possibility that a notary as scrupulous as Innes simplistically superimposed the term 'the Devil' onto a narrative concerned with another kind of spirit altogether. And we suggested that the most obvious scenario is that Isobel was persuaded to employ the term herself during interrogation. Like Edinburgh witch Janet Kennedy and Stirling cunning woman Isobel Watson, she may have defined her envisioned spirit helper as some kind of fairy man/saint/Christ amalgam during the pre-arrest encounters themselves but then, in response to the questions and insinuations of Forbes et al., redefined him as 'the Devil'. This redefinition would then have been reinforced, over the weeks, through progressively detailed coercive-compliant responses and false-memory recollections. The fact that the 'king of fearie' is named in the first confession, but does not appear subsequently, could be interpreted as evidence that Isobel made an association – still just visible here in the early interrogations – between the Devil and the fairy king. Moreover, as we have seen in CHAPTERS SIX and EIGHT, Isobel's verbal skills would have rendered her quite capable of contextualizing her newly-redefined protagonist by inserting the phrase 'in the Devil's name' extempore into the cursing charms that appear in Confessions Two and Three.

But on the other hand, we cannot assume this to be the only explanation. The argument that the interrogators persuaded Isobel to redefine her spirit helper as the Devil is weakened by the fact that a plethora of spirit-names, clearly provided by Isobel, seem to have been left wholly undemonized, by both herself and Innes, throughout the whole six-week interrogation period. The references to the saints in the healing charms are not tampered with, and neither are the references to elf boys in the arrow-shooting sequences or the names of the spirits ('Thomas the fearie', 'the read reiver' and so on) listed as serving at the coven meetings; in the latter case, an attempt to define these spirits as 'devils' merely being tacked onto the end. Moreover, although we cannot be sure that all of Isobel's confessional material was recorded in the order in which it was recounted, the argument that Isobel's Devil was a neatly-demonized fairy king is challenged by the fact that in the first confession the former had already made several appearances by the time the latter appeared.

All in all, these perspectives suggest that Isobel could quite possibly have defined her helping spirit as 'the Devil' from the beginning of her first interrogation, on 13 April. On the one hand, this likelihood does not rule out the possibility that her definition was still a retrospective one. As we have argued previously, it is likely that Isobel endured preliminary interrogations – either with Forbes in the tolbooth or at the kirk session or barony court – prior to this date and she may well have been encouraged to demonize her envisioned helping spirit at this very early stage. But on the other hand, the fact that Isobel seems to have defined him as the Devil so early in the proceedings also raises the possibility that she made an association between her helping spirit and the Devil prior to her arrest and interrogation; perhaps even at the moment of visionary encounter itself. And it is this possibility, however absurd it may seem, that merits further consideration here.

Isobel's Devil

With regard to Isobel's early use of the term 'Devil', we have two options. First, given the synonymy between fairies and devils in this period, we can speculate that Isobel arrived at her first interrogation defining her helping spirit as '*a* devil' and that Innes, in response to the reinterpretations of the interrogators, and with or without Isobel's co-operation, neatly transformed the term into '*the* Devil' before it hit the page. But there are problems with this. Given what we know of Innes, and his scrupulousness, we can assume that he would not have made such an alteration lightly. Even more pertinently, given the fact that Isobel seems to have been so exact about names (giving nearly every person and spirit described in the confessions a clearly defined name, often in conjunction with an idiosyncratic and character-specific nickname) it seems highly unlikely that she would have defined the core protagonist of her narrative, and the most powerful and compelling of all the personalities she describes, using a term as ambiguous as '*a* devil'. The evidence suggests, therefore, that if Isobel did associate her helping spirit with the term 'Devil' prior to interrogation, that she probably associated it, not with *a* devil, but with *the* Devil.

But to argue that Isobel believed herself to have visionally encountered, and covenanted with, '*the* Devil' as opposed to '*a* devil' is a huge distinction. Although the reformed church drew rigid lines between godly and demonic, with regard to the definition of, and policing of communication with, spirits on a parish level it often took a more lenient and pragmatic view. Although applications to 'saints, angels, and any other spirits' were condemned by the catechisms as 'devilish practices', and although fairies were officially 'devils', kirk session records – even in covenanting parishes such as Elgin – indicate that punishments for resorting to holy wells or claiming to have 'gone with the fairies' were often relatively light. Whether this lenience was rooted in folkloric or neoplatonic conceptions of the ambivalent status of fairies (as reflected in the popular notion that fairies were spirits trapped between two worlds; too evil to go to heaven and too good to go to hell), as was clearly the case for Aberfoyle minister Robert Kirk, or whether it was rooted in a pragmatic 'Rome wasn't built in a day' and 'we can't put everyone on trial every time they perform a fairy charm or the harvest wouldn't be brought in'-mentality, is hard to tell. When this official moderation is taken in conjunction with the fact that many ordinary people considered fairies, as did Kirk, to be 'of God' then we can see that a woman could consider herself to have contracted with '*a* devil' and still be a member of the godly community. But contracting with *the* Devil was a completely different matter. According to church teaching, *the* Devil could never simplistically be 'of God' because he was God's greatest enemy. His crimes could never be mollified by classical philosophy or folk wisdom because they were set out, in blazing technicolour, in biblical accounts of the Great Rebellion and Eve's Temptation. *The* Devil was, as Alexander Brodie lamented in June 1662:

> that evel spirit which fell from his place, the father of lies, a murtherer from the begining, the serpent, old crooked, the dragon, accuser, tempter, the leviathan, Lucifer, enemi to mankind and our salvation, the roring lion, the adversarie, head of his members and instruments, quhom he helps and strenthens to work all ungodliness and unrighteousnes, opposit to God and his natur purelie and perfectlie, the destroyer, keeper of the bottomless pitt, prince of darkness.[1]

The Prince of Darkness

How Isobel and others like her could have nurtured intimate, contractual relationships with the envisioned 'prince of darkness' is not at all easy to rationalize. But the possibility becomes more concrete if we step back and take a wider look at how the figure of the Devil was conceptualized on a popular level in Scotland in this period. Theological writings, personal diaries and kirk session records make it quite clear that in the mid-seventeenth century, educated Protestants considered the Devil to be responsible for anything that was not 'godly', or, in other words, anything not sanctioned by the church of Scotland. His responsibility extended to both the external and internal man. Externally, the Devil was responsible for both generally immoral activities, such as murder and adultery, and superstitious behaviour, such as Catholic doctrine and ritual, the use of magic, the worship of saints, fairies or angels and of course, witchcraft. Internally, he was responsible for thoughts, fantasies and bodily desires that did not conform to godly mores. From this perspective, the Devil was a ubiquitous spiritual or metaphysical force capable of influencing all aspects of human life, both physical and psychological. At his most abstract, he was a metaphor for evil itself.

But although the Church considered the Devil to be a ubiquitous metaphysical force, it also, paradoxically, maintained that he could assume, or appear to assume, visible form. Ideas about the embodied Devil had emerged from the earliest decades of the Christian faith, being found in the accounts of the Desert Fathers and in the legends of the early saints, where he is most frequently represented in narratives of temptation. In response to changing ideas about the materiality of spirits – which we discussed briefly in CHAPTER TEN – concepts of the embodied Devil became progressively less conspicuous in theological writings through the Middle Ages, only to re-emerge to prominence, rather mysteriously, in the early modern period just as the view of the Devil as a metaphysical force was gaining new strength from emerging rationalist thought.

But while elite ideas about the Devil are easy to access, owing to the general dearth of sources with regard to popular belief, it is far more difficult to determine how he was envisaged by ordinary men and women in this period. Scholars generally maintain that the popular Devil was closer to the embodied spirit of early hagiographical literature than the lofty, metaphysical principle of the theologians. They also often emphasize his burlesque character, as represented in folk drama, carnival and popular oral narratives, with Martin Luther's famous claim to have woken up to find the Devil hurling nuts at his bedroom ceiling being frequently cited to illustrate how he 'peddled all sorts of popular beliefs' about the Devil.[2] But until recently, scholarly knowledge has extended little further than this. In his 2000 monograph on the Devil, the French scholar Muchembled claimed that although, in the century between 1550 and 1650, the Devil had never 'been so present in the collective unconscious' we still 'cannot know precisely how he was conceived by the illiterate masses, since only the classical image linked to the sabbath emerges from the sources'.[3] Similarly, in 2006 Nathan Johnstone, author of *The Devil and Demonism in Early Modern England*, echoed that 'The vast majority of the population of sixteenth- and seventeenth-century England have left no record at all of their demonological beliefs. It is simply impossible to say with any certainty to what extent the Devil played a significant role in the lives of those who either lacked the education or the inclination to record their experiences.'[4] The situation is similar with regard to Scotland, with Normand and Roberts claiming, in their 2000 analysis into the North Berwick trials, that 'a popular view of the devil is still something that requires research'.[5]

It is here that witchcraft records, with their wealth of first-person accounts of meeting the Devil, play an important role. Until recently, in response to clear evidence of interrogatorial contamination, scholars have been wary of approaching these records as evidence of popular mentalities, but the growing acknowledgement that suspects co-authored their testimonies to an extent hitherto underestimated, means that descriptions of the Devil found in witchcraft records are no longer being peremptorily dismissed as largely elite fantasies. Increasing interest in the folkloric dimension of witchcraft beliefs is leading scholars to consider that confession-depictions of the Devil might be rooted in genuinely popular ideas about embodied folk spirits, such as fairies and the dead. And these ideas, in turn, are contributing to the growing speculations that the seemingly illogical Europe-wide increase in elite conceptions of the embodied Devil at the very time when the Devil-as-metaphysical-force theories were gaining vigour, may have been due to the fact that popular views of embodied folk spirits and the Devil were, via witch-interrogations, filtering up into the elite sphere.

The scholar who has – arguably – explored these ideas in most depth is Hungarian historian Éva Pócs. Through her analysis of a large number of witchcraft records from south-eastern and central Europe, Pócs has concluded that well before the witch-hunting centuries, popular culture in these regions supported a wide range of beliefs concerning evil or ambivalent spirits (incorporating helping spirits, incubus-type spirits and the leaders of spirit troops) which she terms 'folkloristic devil figures'.[6] She argues that in witchcraft records from south-eastern and eastern Europe, where elite demonology was far less developed than in western and central parts of the Continent, these beliefs can be very clearly identified:

> [In these regions] there was a lack of any demonological literature, of an acquaintance with the learned demonology contained in the Central and Western European manuals on witch persecution. In the absence of any knowledge relating to that, there was little expectation of the devil entering into a pact and of the witches' Sabbath, held in worship of Satan. In 1562, for example, Péter Méliusz Juhász, in the 'Debrecen Confession', writes about those who 'have surrendered themselves to the devil'; yet, nowhere do we find any detailed expla-nation as to how that might have happened. Thus the diabolism appearing in the trials cannot, in general, be derived from the demonological manuals which, after all, were unknown to the witch-hunters themselves. On the contrary: our trials are relatively untouched storehouses of popular notions on the devil and the witches' Sabbath.[7]

Pócs goes on to argue that even in central Europe, where the church developed a rich official demonology, popular beliefs surrounding these folkloristic devil figures were still easily identifiable, although here they interacted closely with elite demonological ideas. 'This much is certain,' she claims, 'that two-directional processes took place: Church demonology – while taking on board many folkloristic features and absorbing a whole host of the demons of folk belief systems – itself had an impact on folk belief. These popular devil figures stand somewhere in the middle of the crossfire of reciprocal influences.'[8] Pócs takes care to emphasize that popular beliefs were by no means the weaker partner in this process and that, with regard to Hungary at least, were so influ-ential that 'the increase of the power of Satan, characteristic of the age, manifested itself not so much in the diffusion of the standardized and definitively elaborated Satan figure of the Western Church but rather in the absorption of folkloristic elements into the devil concept of theology'.[9] Although Pócs does not extend her theories into western

Europe, we can assume that this matrix of beliefs surrounding 'folkloristic devil figures' did not miraculously peter out as it crossed the border into the western regions of the Continent, and that it is identifiable in Scottish beliefs concerning ambivalent and evil spirits such as fairies and the dead.

But despite this growing acknowledgement that the Devil-figure of witch-records was closely connected to popular beliefs about embodied folk spirits, the works of scholars exploring this area, including that of Pócs, still fail to explore in any depth to what extent this popular belief accommodated the notion of *the* Devil as opposed to devils in general. Among scholars mining British witchcraft trials, the conventional historical model of the Devil/folk spirit connection seems to be largely one of super-imposition: that is, the view that during questioning the suspect produced a narrative about an encounter with a devil, or a devilish folk spirit, which was then re-defined as *the* Devil by interrogators. Similarly, although Pócs emphasizes, more than most, the strength of suspects' participation in this demonizing process – claiming with regard to Hungary that 'both Catholics and Protestants tended to adopt a view under which all evil demons were devils' and that this 'must have influenced folk belief as well' – her conclusion that '"bad" demons became, in the eyes of the peasantry too, more or less the equivalent of the devil' still leaves us with a degree of ambiguity.[10] By and large, then, with regard to witch-testimony in general, the question as to whether the defin-ition of *the* Devil was ever brought into the interrogation by suspects themselves, remains largely unanswered. And as we have seen, the question as to whether the defi-nition was ever used by the suspect to define a shamanistic spirit helper, encountered during visionary experience prior to arrest, is seldom even asked.

The Devil: Envisioned Helping Spirit?

But although the question is seldom asked, it merits serious consideration. Pócs argues that despite the fact that the fusion between folkloric and theological ideas about the Devil intensified in central and south-eastern Europe during the witch-hunting period, it had been many years in the making: claiming that in both folk belief and 'Orthodox church demonology' folkloristic demon figures 'were more or less identified, a very long time ago, with the Christian devil'.[11] Given the fact that shamanistic helping-spirit figures frequently come under the 'folkloristic demon' category, and given the fact that, as we explored in CHAPTER TEN, shamanistic traditions evolve and survive through an ongoing dialectic between belief and experience, it would seem highly illogical for Pócs's fusion between folkloristic demon figures and the Christian Devil to have occurred on an ideological level without also occurring on an experiential one.

Working this vein further, we can speculate that over the thousand years since Christianity arrived in Scotland, there had been a profound and ongoing cultural amal-gamation between popular shamanistic traditions of folkloric origin and theological conceptions of the Devil, and that over this period of time popular variants of the shamanistic helping-spirit complex emerged which – though closely connected to beliefs surrounding the getting of magical help from envisioned fairies, ghosts, white

461

devils and so on – were specifically concerned with gaining magical aid from an envisioned spirit overtly defined as the Devil. We could suppose that these variant traditions emerged in response to a complex interchange between popular and elite ideas, and to the ebb and flow of religious and political interest. And that they developed at different intensities and in different ways according to region and historical period. We can also argue that these, what we can term here, 'fully demonic' variants of popular helping-spirit traditions experienced an unprecedented acceleration, in response to elite interest, during the Reformation. In other words, some people living in early modern Scotland may quite conceivably have willingly contracted with an envisioned spirit defined, at the moment of encounter, as the Devil.

The Church's Help

Such a hypothesis may seem far-fetched, but with regard to post-Reformation Scotland at least, it receives corroboration on a surprising number of levels. As we have seen in previous chapters, in many cultures the lack of consensus regarding a fixed set of external characteristics makes the identification of envisioned helping spirits a difficult task, and visionaries from all religious and magical traditions have to make a choice between any number of candidates when attempting to define them. In any society, the choice of candidates available reflects prevalent culture patterns and in early modern Scotland – surprising as it may seem – the Devil would have emerged as a prime contender for the role.

The Devil's advantage in this respect would have been fuelled, in large part, by the very institution that chose to eliminate him. As we have seen earlier, the reformed church undertook a concerted campaign to eradicate superstition and magical belief and practice from the populace; a campaign of such vigour and scrupulousness that, as some historians have argued, has not been replicated in Europe before or since.[12] But pertinent, with regard to the current discussion, is the fact that through its anti-magic propaganda – as dispensed from the pulpit, catechisms, kirk sessions, courts and in pamphlets and market squares – the church inadvertently talked up the beneficent magical powers of the Devil. Ministers and elders told their congregations that the Devil was associated with witchcraft, but they also told them, even more frequently, that the beneficent magic to which they were so erroneously attached, such as healing and divination, was equally facilitated through his help. The following passage from Craig's Catechism of 1581 is illustrative. Characteristically, it is not isolated in a dramatic polemic about the Devil or the demonic pact but represents the standard message that ministers would have imparted to their parishioners with regard to beneficent magic and those who practised it:

> Q. Are the wicked excused through their good works?
> A. No, for they work their own evil work.
> Q. Why are they not excused, since God's will concurs with them?
> A. They mean one thing and God another.

Q. What do they mean in their actions?
A. A contempt of God, and hurt of His creatures.
Q. What does God mean in using them, and their sin?
A. The trial of His own, or the punishment of sin.
Q. What should we learn by this discourse?
A. To fear the Lord our God alone.
Q. What shall we judge of them that use familiarity with Satan?
A. That they deny this first article of our belief.
Q. May we not conjure Satan to reveal secrets?
A. No, for he is the author of lies.
Q. But he often speaks the truth.
A. That is to get the greater credit in his lies.
Q. May we not remove witchcraft with witchcraft?
A. No, for that is to seek help from Satan.[13]

The prevalence of this beneficent-magic-is-of-the-Devil instruction is evinced by the fact that when an individual came before a court or kirk session charged with performing beneficent magic – even when, as occurred in the majority of cases, they seem to have made no claim to have directly invoked any kind of spirit – the authorities nearly always took the trouble to remind the accused that their magical abilities were derived from the Devil. Though he apparently made no mention of either devils or the Devil in his testimony, Culross charmer John Young (1693) was told by his interrogators that 'his cures were not effected without the help of the devil'; similarly, Fifeshire cunning woman Grissel Gardiner (1610) was condemned 'for af-taking of the saidis seiknessis and diseases, and be consulting with the Devill, and seiking of responssis fra him' despite the fact that her testimony contains no reference to curing with spirit aid. Aberdeenshire cunning woman Jonat Lucas (1597), though being similarly reticent in this respect, was categorically told by the court that when she attempted to diagnose and prescribe a cure for a neighbour's sickness she was 'inspyrit be the Devill they maister, of quhome thow leirnit all thy craft'.[14] Given this powerful exercise in public relations, any man or woman living in early modern Scotland who found themselves struggling to identify an envisioned spirit that offered beneficent magical aid is likely to have seen the Devil as a strong candidate for the part.

The likelihood that an individual might define their helping spirit as the Devil would have been considerably facilitated by the fact that the reformed church emphasized that the Devil, over and above any other type of spirit, could change himself into, or manipulate nature into a delusory representation of, any form. Through this insistence, the church effectively ensured that an unsure visionary could safely alight upon the definition of 'the Devil' no matter what their envisioned helper's appearance happened to be or how it behaved. And there is no doubt that people took church teachings at their word. The weird and wonderful incarnations of the Devil described in witch-records, some of them so strange that even the credulity of interrogators like George Mackenzie was stretched to breaking point, bear testament to the popular appreciation of the Devil's skills in this quarter.[15] As Joyce Miller has recently shown, between 1563 and 1736, depictions of the Devil as a demonologically stereotypical 'black man or dressed in black' were not ubiquitous (only appearing in 81 out of a total of 392 descriptions); and in the remaining 311 instances he appeared in guises as varied as 'ane bonnie young lad', 'ane agit man, beirdit', 'a littill crippill man', 'a dog with a sowis head', 'ane hen flichtering', 'like Flies dancing about the Candle', 'ane bisome [broom]', 'a black cloud' and even as a 'ruck of hay'.[16] Outside the witch trials, the Devil seems to have been equally versatile, with Brand noting in 1703 that when Orkney and Shetland fishermen encounter strange-looking fish they 'are affraid when they see them, which panick fear of their's makes them think and sometimes say, that it is the Devil in the shape of such Creatures'.[17] The Devil's shape-shifting abilities were also so sophisticated that he could appear before an individual in different forms from one day to the next, and even during the same encounter. The godly Cathrin Hendrie complained to Brodie in 1655 that 'Sathan approached to her somtyms in the shap of som freind, or her brother, sometym in the shap of a catt with burning fyri eys, sometyms in one and another', while as we saw in the last chapter, the rather less godly Bute cunning woman, Margaret NcWilliam (1662), claimed that the Devil shapeshifted from the 'lyknes of a litle browne dog', to that of a 'wele favored yong man' to that of a 'grene smoak' during a single meeting.[18] Living in Nairnshire, where the covenanting minds of the ministers and lairds ensured that the Devil's remit was very large, it is not unreasonable to assume that, being confronted with an envisioned spirit, and needing to alight on a definition, Isobel could have passed over that of fairy man, saint or archangel in favour of the Devil.

The Devil-in-Relief

But while we can see that these cultural influences may have persuaded a popular visionary to identify their envisioned helping spirit as the Devil, these perspectives do not at first glance explain why they would allow themselves to take the next step and contract with him; using protection charms or some other form of negotiation in order to gain magical help. While it is not difficult to understand why a visionary might contract with a spirit of whose identity they were unsure (giving it the benefit of the doubt in their hour of need) or why they might contract with a spirit if they thought it was a fairy, saint, angel or dead soul (these kinds of spirits, as we have seen, retaining a modicum of ambivalence despite the condemnation of the church), it is harder to understand why they would consciously allow themselves to forge an alliance directly with the Prince of Darkness himself.

But it is easy to overlook the fact that, strange as it may seem, the church's emphasis on the ever-present threat of the Devil actually may have served to encourage such alliances. As we have explored earlier, the reformed church did not only define beneficent magic as demonic in origin, but included under the of-the-Devil umbrella any belief, practice or aspect of human behaviour that did not conform to contemporary godly mores. Although the Christian church had been making this of-the-Devil versus of-God distinction since it first emerged in Britain, in the early modern period these discriminations were sharpened by what Stuart Clark has defined as the 'piebald mentality' of the Protestant reformer, as epitomized in John Knox's claim that 'In religion there is no middle; either it is the religion of god . . . or else it is the religion of the Devil'.[19] But not only were the church's distinctions sharp, they were also provocatively drawn. From the reformed perspective, the behaviours and beliefs that came under the of-God category were relatively limited, while those that came under the of-the-Devil category were disconcertingly large. While the Protestant church, like the Catholic, condemned extreme evils like murder and rape; relatively lesser evils such as theft and adultery; and more subtle psychological evils like vanity and avarice, it also, as we saw in Chapter Seven, condemned many of the beliefs and activities which, to a large proportion of the laity, did not seem evil at all – either extremely, relatively or even very slightly. We have already seen how the church condemned beneficent magic, but it also condemned dancing, processions, performing music, guising, drinking, singing, gambling, sports and storytelling. It also prohibited the observance of many of the saints' days and holy days on which these activities traditionally took place, with Yule and Lammas festivities, May Day and misrule celebrations, annual pageants and plays, wakes and marriage festivities all being frowned upon. At their most extreme, as we have seen from Brodie's diaries, reformed teachings could even denounce the act of taking pleasure in a flowering meadow, or in reading a book about history, as 'carnal temptations' of the Devil.[20]

In condemning these practices, the church may have succeeded in imposing discipline and a level of religious uniformity, and undoubtedly tempered many of the excesses – such as drunkenness, blood-feud and domestic violence – that contributed to human suffering in the period. But at the same time it swept away many of the pleasures and comforts that sweetened the lives of the pre-industrial poor. And nowhere was this deprivation felt more keenly than in the area of beneficent magic. Popular magical practices were complex solutions which had evolved out of generations of the management of human suffering. In condemning magical cures, for example, the church was not only denying people the practical benefits of herbal medicine and physical therapy, but also denying them a complex matrix of belief and ritual which brought psychological and spiritual comfort to both the sick and their carers. Some of the healing rituals described in witch-confessions leave us in no doubt that they were performed with the intensity of a religious rite, with Orkney cunning woman Katherine Bigland (1615) performing a magical cure that involved a combination of nocturnal pilgrimage, ritual washing and other physical rites enacted over a period of six days. Even 200 years later, the folklorist J. F. Campbell could note that a simple magical rite to cure a bewitched cow was performed with 'becoming gravity'.[21]

But what is particularly significant, in the context of our discussion about Isobel's Devil, is the fact that the church did not only condemn all these practices, but they did so through actively associating them with the Devil. Dances were not just dances, they were 'the Devil's dance'; a bagpipe player was not just a bagpipe player, he was 'the Devils Piper'; guising and sport were not just idle pastimes, they were 'the Devil's pastimes'; and cunning folk were not just cunning folk, they were 'instrumentis of the

Devill' and so on. This association was particularly marked with regard to magical practice. Here, the church did not only label beneficent magic as 'the divell's prescriptions' and 'devilische practices', but did so in conjunction with emphasizing the fact that by virtue of his angelic origins and consequent powers over the natural world, the Devil was uniquely qualified to confer specifically physical and worldy benefits.[22] When Christ was in the wilderness, the Devil did not approach him empty-handed, but offered him palaces and riches in return for his allegiance. Through emphasizing the Devil's material power, ministers and laity only served to make his services all the more attractive, as the following treatise – published by a Württemberg pastor in 1565 – makes clear: '[the pious] should prefer a thousand times to be ill and miserable in God, than to be bright and healthy with the devil, to die in God, than survive with the devil, to have sick horses, oxen and sheep or to have none at all, than to have strong, healthy, well-made horses and other beasts with the devil's help and by means of devilish conjurations and blessings'.[23] For a chronically-undernourished cottar's wife, with her hollow-eyed, starving child lying in her ragged lap, what part of this speech would have made an impact: the being 'ill and miserable in God' or the being 'bright and healthy with the devil'?

In this sense, then, the popular image of the helpful, powerful Devil was fed by the criticisms of the church. To put it simply, if you were to construct a picture of the Devil 'in relief', that is, out of all the things the reformed church condemned, then you created a complex and edgy, but ultimately very compelling personality. A personality that liked to dance, sing and feast; that could cure the sick, bestow 'freedom from want' and bring, for some, the consolations of mystical joy. These are crucial associations. This positive-in-relief characterization of the Devil meant that although the laity undoubtedly associated him with general evils like murder, rape and theft, and with more metaphysical evils like pride and vanity, as sold to them by the reformed church he possessed a sensational flaw: ambivalence. He may well have been associated with damnation, but he was also associated with dancing a reel; he may well have been associated with murder, but he was also credited with the miraculous ability to fill a fisherman's nets, heal a sick child or help cattle and crops to thrive. It is almost as if, by constantly complaining that the Devil's remit was so large, the church inadvertently cried wolf; for by over-emphasizing as devilish those elements of life which people knew, instinctively, were good, they diminished Satan's disciplinary effectiveness as a piety-inducing bogeyman. The old Gaelic saying 'The Bauchan [fairy] is still kind, though the Priest should burst' distils the same pragmatic logic, as does the proverb 'The De'il's aye gude to his ain'.[24]

With regard to visionary experience, this positive-in-relief characterization of the Devil would have been particularly significant. As we have seen earlier, shamanistic covenanting between visionaries and helping spirits was essentially a dialectic between human suffering and supernatural compassion. Even when an element of compulsion was involved, the decision as to whether to accept or succumb to a spirit's advances was dictated as much by feeling as by intellectualization: if a spirit possessed a positive numinous charge and made you feel good and gave you comfort and hope, then you condescended to enter into an alliance with it. Consequently, while some people may have resisted a spirit's advances once they suspected it was the Devil, for others the positive-in-relief picture of the Devil disseminated by the church may have created just enough moral breathing space to allow a positive response to be expressed, and an emotional surrender made. The likelihood of such a surrender would have been increased by the fact that emotional responses are far quicker than intellectual ones, and the affective response to the spirit is likely to have come before, or simultaneous with, any intellectual definition. In other words, by the time the intellect had rationalized the spirit as 'the Devil' it was too late, for the emotional commitment had already been made.

This was undoubtedly a complex area. As we have seen, a number of confessions suggest that some women, in calmer moments of reflection, seem to have regretted the decision made in the emotional heat of the visionary encounter and repented their compact with the Devil after the event. Other confessions suggest that the good feeling which justified the relationship with the Devil faltered over time, owing to a diminishing of beneficent effects, with cunning women like Agnes Sampson (Edinburgh, 1591), claiming they tried to terminate the relationship because they 'had never gotten good of him'.[25] But, given the fact that many confessions describe relationships with the Devil that endured for many years, we can suppose that the Devil's ambiguity was successfully accommodated in respect of benefits gained. These successful relationships would have played a central role in the development of popular demonological belief and practice. Positive experiences of working with an envisioned helper defined as *the* Devil would have fed into the local belief matrix; and this matrix, in turn, would have generated more Devil-as-spirit-helper experiences. The many instances in which magical practitioners are accused of persuading others to ally themselves with the Devil, and telling them how advantageous it is to be in his service, can be seen to reflect this process.

Friends of the Devil: Enemies of God?

But although these arguments seem reasonable, they still do not address the question – briefly raised earlier – of apostasy. We still need to explain how people who consciously allied themselves with the envisioned Devil managed to square this allegiance with their identity as Christians. We can see how a parishioner who enjoyed guising at Hogmanay might define his pleasures as the 'Devil's dances' but at the same time consider his allegiance to Satan so indirect as to not amount to renunciation of God. But it is more difficult to see how a magical practitioner who directly entered into an working partnership with an envisioned spirit they believed to be the Devil, rationalized the fact that by doing so they were overtly renouncing God and their Christian faith.

However, we can gain some insight into this question by looking at seventeenth-century Christian identity in a little more depth. A wide range of contemporary sources, from catechisms and theological writings to spiritual diaries, clearly indicate that in this period many people held Christian beliefs that did not conform to the godly ideal.

The explanatory passage accompanying the first Commandment in the Larger Westminster Catechism of 1648 is illustrative. After forbidding 'all compacts and consulting with the devil, and hearkening to his suggestions' the text condemns:

> atheism, in denying, or not having a God; idolatry, in having or worshipping more gods than one, or any with or instead of the true God; the refusal to have or acknowledge Him as God . . . hatred of God, self-love, self-seeking . . . vain credulity, unbelief, heresy, wrong belief . . . estranging ourselves and apostatising from God . . . slighting and despising God and His commands; resisting and grieving His Spirit, discontent and impatience at His dispensations, charging Him foolishly for the evils He inflicts on us; and ascribing the praise of any good we either are, have, or can do, to fortune, idols, ourselves, or any other creature.[26]

If Alexander Brodie and Hugh Rose are to be believed, many of the inhabitants of Nairnshire were similarly inclined. Brodie laments 'a land and a people that ar dround in sin and ingodliness'; and the 'decay of religion generally, so particularly in this place'. He also condemns the Dyke parishioners who 'worship not God in their family' and laments that 'tyms ar ill; [and] godlines litl regarded'.[27] Meanwhile Rose, after many decades as minister of Nairn, still found cause to mourn that 'men do not believe, they do not rest upon the word of God as true, nor upon God as the God of truth that cannot lie . . . They have many by excuses and shifts, but the very strength of all their carnal peace in wickedness is unbelief.'[28]

Much of this 'unbelief' and 'ingodliness' was attributable, not to a lack of self-identity as a Protestant, or to a specific allegiance to Catholicism, but to theological ignorance. As we have seen in CHAPTER ONE, a significant minority of people seldom attended church, while even regular attendees seem to have been able to participate in the key rituals of baptism, communion and repentance throughout their whole adult lives without possessing a firm grasp of the doctrines that underpinned their observances, with laments such as 'sundry within this congregation are found ignorant of the principles and grounds of religion' and 'the most part of the people wanted the commands, belief and Lord's Prayer' frequently being uttered by frustrated kirk authorities.[29] This theological ignorance was in large part linked to illiteracy. However emotional their attachment to their faith, those who were literate and possessed the leisure time to exploit this skill, would have absorbed much of their Christian doctrine systematically, statement by statement, logical step by logical step, through the pages of catechisms, theological writings and of course the Bible. But for those who were non-literate, knowledge of Christian doctrine was acquired through what they heard once a week from the pulpit, or what was read to them around the fire by a literate relative or neighbour. And here, the coherence of the doctrine assimilated would have depended solely upon the function of memory that, in turn, was highly influenced by character and circumstance. A minister would have had little power over what statements from a catechism, arguments from a sermon, images from a psalm or lines from a prayer an individual chose to memorize, take to heart and incorporate into their religious imagination. Nor would he have had any control over how those absorbed fragments were ordered, to which other beliefs they were annexed and how they were generally contextualised. As Ned Landsman has recently emphasized with regard to the Glasgow revivalists, the question is 'less whether or not the laity was hearing the [Christian] message than *how they heard it* [my italics]'.[30] Given the fact that the further down the social scale you went, the higher the likelihood of illiteracy, it is quite clear that in this period unbelief and ungodliness derived from theological ignorance was strongly associated with the popular mind.

This ignorance would have been further exaggerated by the fact that, as we have touched on in various points in the book, the doctrines absorbed piecemeal from church teachings were absorbed into world-views heavily influenced by the orally-transmitted lore and literature of the fields, barns and fireside; influences that had been generated, over many centuries, in the 'secret, uncharted areas of peasant exchange'. Historians often lament that the nature of this folkloric world-view and the way in which it interacted with that of the church, is difficult to recover, for the beliefs and traditions of the uneducated majority provoked little interest among the contemporary literate elite and were seldom recorded for their own sake. Although scholars increasingly recognize that witchcraft and sorcery records provide us with our most direct insight into this world-view, and that through them we can glimpse a complex network of beliefs concerning magical forces and the operations of diverse spiritual agencies, the value of these insights is compromised by the fact that trial evidence is fragmentary and distorted by the dictates of the interrogatorial arena.

But what scholars of popular belief and witchcraft in early modern Scotland generally under-emphasize is the fact that the huge wealth of oral literature collected in the nineteenth century, although gathered more than 100 years after our period, can also be used as a guide to the sixteenth and seventeenth-century popular world-view. Its survival is its qualification. While men and women could be told what psalms to sing in church and what prayers to learn in order to be able to receive the eucharist or get their baby baptized, they could not be told (though ministers certainly tried) what songs they should sing when reaping, what charms to whisper over a newborn calf as it lay in the byre to ensure that it didn't get taken by the fairies, or what stories to tell as they crowded around their cottage hearths on long winter nights. People chanted charms, told stories, recited poems and sang songs because they wanted to and because they meant something to them. As a consequence, although these nineteenth-century collections must be approached cautiously, they can nevertheless be seen as visible continuations of the core preoccupations of the popular mind in the early modern period. Indeed, it could be argued that the sympathetic conditions in which they were recorded means that they can, in some respects, provide us with a less contaminated and more holistic picture of this mind than many witch-records and elite observations recorded in the period itself.

Significant to present discussion is the fact that, when these later sources are considered as a whole, very definite patterns emerge. Scholars have emphasized that traditional Scottish literature is largely concerned with three prominent, and usually overlapping, themes: physical prowess, sexual attraction or love and the supernatural or fantastic. Literature concerned with physical prowess charts the fighting, hunting and adventuring exploits of heroes, such as Finn mac Coul or William Wallace, and the outcomes of famous battles, local clan feuds and memorable cattle-raiding expeditions. Literature concerned with sexual attraction and love generally depicts forced marriages or abductions, or grand and sometimes humorous love affairs that hold true across great social or metaphysical divides: with love blossoming between lairds and cottage-girls, Lowlanders and Highlanders, humans and spirits and the living and the dead. Literature concerned with the supernatural and fantastic charts human encounters with spirits, spirit worlds and the miraculous forces of magic in which protagonists wage war, fall in love, seek help from, and make deals with a wide variety of supernatural agencies and magical practitioners. In all three areas, these imaginary worlds operate according to very different moral and social mores from those approved by the reformed church or state. Normal social hierarchies and ethical codes are inverted: seers can be as powerful as kings; farm boys can marry noblemen's daughters; women can pull on breeches, disguise themselves as men and run off to sea for the sheer joy of it; siblings can pledge romantic love to each other; newly-widowed men dance on their wives' graves out of gratitude for their death; heroes can rob corpses and decapitate fallen men; and those who seek revenge through bloodshed can be honoured as they stand, their hearts full of hate, amid 'rivers of floating blood and hills of slain'.[31]

But what is additionally noteworthy about this world, particularly with regard to our analysis of popular conceptions of the Devil, is the fact that although it arose out of more than 1,000 years of Christianity, with the exception of the saint's tales, exempla and religious charms derived from medieval Catholicism, the Christian God and his entourage do not emerge as prominent. As early as 1567 John Carswell, bishop of the Isles, lamented:

> Great is the blindness and darkness of sin and ignorance and of understanding among composers and writers and supporters of the Gaelic in that they prefer and practice the framing of vain, hurtful, lying stories about the *Tuatha de Danann* and about the sons of Milesius and about the heroes and Fionn MacCumhail and his giants and about many others whom I shall not number or tell of here in detail, in order to maintain and advance these, with a view to obtaining for themselves passing worldly gain, rather than to write and to compose and to support the faithful words of God and the perfect way of truth.[32]

The lack of emphasis on the 'faithful words of God' was clearly maintained through the early modern period, for a hundred or so years later, when oral literature began to be widely recorded, a similar picture emerged. The nineteenth-century compiler of Highland proverbs and sayings, Alexander Nicholson, noted that the class of sayings 'more frequently quoted in the Highlands and referred to, since time immemorial' did not concern Christian deities or figures but 'Fionn, or Fingal and the people of whom he was the head, the *Feinne*'.[33] Meanwhile the faithful words of God were also conspicuously absent from both the Gaelic romances and international marchen so beloved by the pre-modern Scots. Alan Bruford claims:

> There is no reason to suppose that the Irish, or even their poets, despised God or the knightly

virtues, but they did not see fit to bring them into romances. The international *marchen* which, in many cases, were being composed, assembled or modified at about the same date are very similar: God and the saints when they appear act just like any helpful fairy, clerics are figures of fun, and the hero is rather less likely to fight fairly than the ogre . . . The most binding oath is by sun and moon, *grian agus éasga*; the most usual by one's own weapons.[34]

With regard to Christianity, songs and ballads are similarly insouciant. Aberdeenshire folklorist Gavin Greig, who worked with the Reverend James Duncan to collect more than 3,000 folk songs from the north-east of Scotland in the nineteenth century, noted that in this region the folk singer 'rarely makes appeal to divine sanctions' and that:

> The Scot has never cared to romance with sacred themes, or to introduce the religious element into his fireside minstrelsy . . . Sunday and the kirk and the Psalms stood clear away from the week-day evening and the ingle and the traditional minstrelsy, always purely secular, and not seldom frankly pagan. The Reformers of the sixteenth century tried to cope with the situation; but their attempt to travesty the popular ditties of the time in the interests of religion and to turn them into 'Gude and Godly Ballads' was a notorious failure . . . the inclination to make sharp differentiation between the sacred and the secular and to keep them in separate compartments of life is still strong in the Northern man.[35]

Traditional Literature and Popular Spirituality

If the traditional songs, ballads, stories and sayings of the north-eastern peoples were purely recreational, then the fact that they avoided sacred themes and seldom mentioned the Christian God and his entourage, would provoke little comment. The person today who seeks light relief or visceral thrills from the latest romantic blockbuster or supernatural thriller does not expect to be bombarded with religious proselytizing. But in the early modern period – and even into Greig's century – this was not the case. While people today know that Narnia is a fictional world and that the elven princess Arwen did not exist until she sprang from an Oxford don's pen – for many early modern Scots the intense, imaginary worlds depicted in traditional literature, and the beings who inhabited them, were alive in a sense that it is difficult for the modern Westerner to appreciate. As folklorists such as Katharine Briggs have pointed out, this aliveness was due to the fact that for many people living in pre-industrial Britain, some forms of fireside literature were not just entertainment, or a source of instruction, but possessed the status of 'Secondary Myths'.[36] And as such they were seen to represent people, supernatural beings, events and places that had actually existed and that, in many cases, continued to exist in other worlds or dimensions. For many, accounts of wandering into fairy hills and meeting the fairy court were not considered to be fictional representations of an alternate world, but factual accounts of a location that was as real as heaven or hell. Even 200 years after Isobel's lifetime, the folklorist J. F. Campbell could note that in the Highlands of Scotland fairy tales 'are not told as stories, but facts'; that 'amongst the unlearned, the legends are firmly

471

believed'; and that some of his collectors' informants were 'much offended if any one doubted these [fairy] stories'.[37] Similarly, just as Christ, Mary and the Devil were not fictional beings who remained trapped within the pages of the Bible, so Fionn, Cormac, the water horse and the elf knight could walk out of a story and into the world of men. Islay schoolmaster Hector MacLean claimed, for example, that the nineteenth-century inhabitants of Barra 'speak of the Ossianic heroes with as much feeling, sympathy and belief in their existence and reality as the readers of the newspapers do of the exploits of the British army in the Crimea or in India'.[38] Indeed, anthropologists have shown that in tribal cultures, where similar attitudes survive, the telling of stories and myths about supernatural beings is believed to effectively bring them 'to life', with the activity of storytelling thus merging into that of invocation. In Turkic Siberia, for example, as Van Deusen notes, 'Once the khai eezi [spirit?] has entered the teller and the spirits of the characters in stories have been brought present at the telling, they must complete their actions and be put back into their places of rest. If the teller takes a break in a long tale, he must leave the heroes at a feast. And if evil creatures are not dealt with by the story hero they will continue to plague humans.'[39] Though we cannot assume that early modern Scots approached their storytelling in such a literal way, there is no doubt that, for many, the art retained shades of this magico-religious significance. Certainly, the magical practice of 'telling out' sickness through narrative-based charms, which was often performed by magical practitioners in the period, reflects this intimacy between story and invocation.

Also significant is the fact that this world, as with any mythological reality, possessed a spiritual charge. Although Greig, in the passage we quoted earlier, separated fireside oral traditions and the beliefs and practices of the church into 'secular' and 'sacred', it would be more accurate to define this distinction as 'secular' and 'sacred as defined by the church'. As living entities enshrined in myth, many of the beings that inhabited the world of oral literature displayed all the characteristics of the Christian God and his cohorts: they possessed supernatural powers that influenced the world of men; they could be petitioned for spiritual aid; they dictated human behaviour and set taboos; they inhabited a spirit-realm to which the soul went after death and they were objects of devotion. That this realm possessed a sacred dimension is corroborated by the fact that although, as Greig maintained, Christian devotions made few inroads into traditional oral literature, traditional oral literature certainly made inroads into Christian devotions. As we have seen in the previous chapter, although the wide array of religious charms collected in the nineteenth century were largely concerned with Christian figures, it was not uncommon for epic heroes like Fionn, Diarmud and King Arthur, or even the Fates, to slip in through the back door to receive veneration alongside Christ, God, Mary, the Holy Ghost and the saints. The following driving charm, *An Saodachadh*, sounds like a strange mixture between a Gaelic epic poem and a classic Christian protection charm, and contains a cacophony of diverse supernatural beings. After a verse invoking 'Odhran the dun', 'Brigit the Nurse' and 'Mary the Virgin' the charm goes on:

The keeping of Ciaran the swart be yours,

The keeping of Brianan the yellow be yours,
The keeping of Diarmaid the brown be yours,
A-sauntering the meadows,
A-sauntering the meadows.

The safeguard of Fionn mac Cumhall be yours,
The safeguard of Cormac the shapely be yours,
The safeguard of Conn and Cumhall be yours
From wolf and from bird-flock
From wolf and from bird-flock.

The charm goes on for four more verses, invoking, along the way, the protection of 'Colum Cille' (Saint Columba), 'Maol Ruibhe', 'Maol Odhrain', 'Maol Oighe', 'Maol Domhnaich' and the 'king of the Fiann' before finally, in the last verse, concluding:

The sheltering of the king of kings be yours,
The sheltering of Jesus Christ be yours,
The sheltering of the Spirit of healing be yours,
From evil deed and quarrel,
From evil dog and red dog.[40]

In this sense, early modern men and women like Isobel juggled two distinct, but interconnected, world-views in their heads: one where God and Christ reigned supreme, and godly virtues were significant and another where God and Christ were barely visible and their moral codes often subverted. In this sense, the myths of the church had to constantly jostle alongside the half-myths of the fireside. And although the Christian God almost certainly remained – for the overwhelming majority of people – the most significant spiritual presence, in some minds he probably still had to fight for his spot in the limelight just like everyone else.

God versus the Devil

These perspectives enable us to hazard some speculations as to the mentalities that may have been able to accommodate both the Christian faith and the making of an envisioned pact with the Devil. They suggest that although all men and women would have been cognisant of the Devil's ongoing conflict with God, some of the non-literate laity may not have conceptualized this battle, as did the educated godly, as the ultimate metaphysical conflict between the spiritual principles of good and evil, wherein the human conscience was the primary arena and the human soul the prize. For some, the conflict between God and the Devil may have been inadvertently diminished by the fact that it was envisaged as only one – albeit the most important one – of the many battles that were constantly being played out on either a remote, mythic or quasi-mythic level. Through biblical stories, legends of the saints, sermons and fireside literature, people would have learnt, from a young age, that God was not the Devil's only adversary. He was also locked in combat with Christ, Michael the Archangel, St Anthony, St Dunstan, St Servanus and the countless kings, lairds, weavers, millers and farmers' wives that peopled popular anecdotes of temptation. Similarly, they would have known that God was not only concerned with besting the Devil, he was also preoccupied with defeating the Canaanites, the Egyptians, the Pope, the French, the English, the elves, the heathens of the New World and many of the historical and contemporary kings and queens of Europe. Moreover, these supra-normal battles were waged alongside those of countless other warrior heroes and spirits: Fionn mac Cumhaill fighting the fairy host at the Brugh of Slievenamon; Wallace sparring with the French pirate, the Red Reivar, in the English Channel; Red Hector of the Battles facing the Earl of Mar's armies at Harlaw; and Cuchulain the 'Hound of Ulster' challenging the Clan Calatin at Slieve Faud.[41] These confrontations, in their turn, were mirrored by the more intimate conflicts played out in songs and ballads concerned with sexual and romantic relationships; and which celebrated power struggles between adversaries such as Tam Lin's Janet and the fairy queen, Lady Isobel and her elf knight, May Colvin and False John, Lady Margaret and Hind Etin, and the Aberdeenshire maid who outwitted her unscrupulous lover at the 'bonnie broom-fields'.[42]

The way that people responded to these supra-normal battles is likely to have been similar to the way they reacted to more immediate antagonisms. In Scotland in this period, as we have emphasized many times, conflict was endemic: Protestants challenged Catholics, episcopalians challenged covenanters, Highlanders challenged Lowlanders, the English challenged the Scots, clan challenged clan and neighbour challenged neighbour. And we can assume that many of the poor, for whom physical survival often took priority over matters of conscience, would have taken a pragmatic, and at times opportunistic, approach to these disputes. As is the case in war-torn parts of the world today, such as Afghanistan, they would have supported whichever side put the bread on their table. A farmer wanting to get his barley dried and ground before winter did not have the luxury to quibble over theological niceties and he would, if necessary, take it to a drying kiln owned by an episcopalian and then transport it to a mill owned by a covenanter. As a consequence of this imperative, it is likely that in many cases, unless it touched their life directly, people would not have become too intellectually or emotionally involved in the politico-religious wrangling between countries, clans, lairds and religious denominations, ducking down beneath the line of fire and only emerging when they needed something from someone.

Particularly pertinent to our discussion here is the fact that this batting-for-both-sides mentality may also have been at work with regard to the supernatural conflict between God and the Devil. While everyone would have been aware that the battle was being fought, they may not have considered it necessary to engage with it unless it directly concerned them. And when, through hardship or aspiration, they needed to solicit supernatural aid, the most logical approach, for some, would have been to keep their options open and petition both. This pragmatic duplicity can be glimpsed in the witch-records themselves. On an implicit level, it can be seen in the fact that although cunning women like Agnes Sampson, and indeed Isobel herself, allegedly sought magical benefits from the Devil, they also sought magical benefits through charms that invoked God, Christ and the saints.[43] It can be seen more explicitly in the fact that witch-records frequently contain overt requests for help from both God and the Devil at the same time. Lanark resident Katren Shaw's (1644) dispute with a neighbour allegedly 'movit hir to [fall] out in a fearfull passioun and say, "Now aither God or the devill give me a sein mendis of her"'; Angus cunning woman Isobel Smyth (1661) supposedly met the Devil 'when shee [was] desyreing either God or the divell to reveng hir one James Gray, Bowman to my Lord Spynie'; and, after quarrelling with her spouse, Margaret Bryson allegedly 'went out in a passion to the door of her house in the night time and there did imprecat that God or the devill might take her from her husband'.[44] The rich and educated may have uttered similar imprecations, with the trial dittays of Invernesshire noblewoman Katharine Ross stating: 'thow art accusit, for saying to the said Cristian Roiss, that thow sould do [destroy her enemy], be all kyndis of meanis, quhair itt mycht be had, of God in heaven or of the Devill in hell'.[45] Of course we must always bear in mind the possibility that interrogators may have been responsible for some of these demonic references. But the fact that examples occur outside witch trials suggest that a proportion were genuine. We saw in CHAPTER EIGHT, for example, that Caithness fisherman John Gill was reproved by his local kirk session in 1655 because 'being at sea, the rest of the boat getting fishe and not he, Did throw over his hook, saying, "If thou slay not in God's name, slay in ye devill's name"'.[46] These accounts are also corroborated by evidence from other parts of Europe. In her recent analysis of church demonology and popular belief in early modern Sweden, for example, Soili-Maria Olli notes that:

> Within the popular classes it seemed, however, possible to pray both to God and to the Devil, one not eliminating the other. In a large number of the cases of blasphemy an ambivalent relationship to God and the Devil appears. Per Larsson, for example, who was accused of blasphemy in 1702, said that he would pray to God until he had visited the Holy Communion, but as soon as he returned home he would start praying to the Devil again.[47]

Returning to Scotland, similar sentiments are also encapsulated in later oral literature: with Robert Trotter's collection of nineteenth-century Galloway anecdotes containing some vivid examples of dual-allegiance on the part of those who were 'not very well acquainted with the inside of the kirk'.[48] Although dispensed with the tone of the contrived jocular tale, the following anecdote vividly evokes the practical common sense of a poor Scotswoman not too clear on her theology. It is additionally notable in that it portrays a woman actively praying to the Devil, on her knees, as Isobel Gowdie was supposed to have done, but in a context devoid of witchcraft or demonic pacts:

> Kirsty Dunbar was an aul' wife that lived in a wee house on The Boreland of Kirkinner, but it was before my time, and she was an awfu' religious buddy, and a terrible hand at Scripture. Yae Sunday afternoon yin o' her gran'-dochters cam' ower to see her, and found Kirsty on her knees ahint the hallan, prayin' away like mad; and as she didna like to disturb the grannie at her devotions she sat down on a stool at the fire till she finished. After listening awhile

she was astonished to hear that it wasna the Lord that Kirsty was praying to, and she was praying awfu fervently. When she was dune, the lass said till her, 'Gude guide us, grannie! D'ye ken ye wur prayin' tae the deevil?' 'Atweel was I, hinny!' was the reply, 'I do't regular; he's a desperate bad yin, ye ken, an' it's better tae be in wi him nor oot wi him; an yin never kens what's afore them, or wha they're behauden tae.'[49]

Kirsty Dunbar's claim that 'it's better tae be in wi him nor oot wi him' echoes the punchline of a legend, recorded in the nineteenth century, that grew up around the infamous battle between Sir James MacDonald of Islay and Sir Lachlan Mor MacLean of Duart in 1598. When MacLean was killed by an elf arrow during the battle the victorious MacDonald enquired who had killed him, whereupon a 'trifling looking little man', whom he had hired just before battle, stepped forward:

'It was I' said the little man, 'who killed your enemy; and unless I had done so he would have killed you.' 'What is your name?' asked MacDonald. 'I am called,' he said, 'Dubh-Sith (i.e. 'Black Elf'), *and you were better to have me with you than against you* [my italics].'[50]

If we accept that some men and women living in early modern Scotland may have nurtured this dual-allegiance mentality, then it is only a small step to accept that a number of witchcraft and sorcery records may have reflected a genuine truth. In some cases, shamanistic visionaries may have genuinely allowed themselves to accept protection from an envisioned spirit they believed to be the Devil, on the rationale that if this was the spirit who had answered their plea for help, then this was the help that would be accepted.

Elite Dual-Allegiances

Although such a capacity for contradiction may seem extreme, it would have been little different to that displayed in a very different contemporary arena. As we briefly touched on in CHAPTER EIGHT, ample documentation attests to the fact that throughout the medieval and early modern periods, elite magicians invoked spirits in order to procure magical benefits. Although the extent of these practices are still unclear, scholars recognize that these learned practitioners saw no contradiction between their magical activities and their identity as Christians, with Cohn claiming that conjuring spirits on this level was 'one long exercise in religious devotion' and that 'Throughout, the attitude is that of a devout man who can with confidence call on God for help in his undertaking. Indeed, all the books of magic stress that a magical enterprise has no prospect of success unless the magician worships God and believes absolutely in his infinite goodness.' This attitude was apparently maintained even when the latter's activities came under the general definition of *maleficium*, with Cohn again noting that 'even when his aims were thoroughly destructive, the magician felt himself a pious Christian or Jew'.[51]

Particularly relevant to our discussion here is the fact that although the invocations of magicians were generally uttered in the names of God, Christ, saints, angels and so on, in a significant minority of cases, the spirits from whom they sought to benefit did not come under the category of Christian sacred beings – or even under the more ambiguous category of fairies or the dead – but were, as Cohn notes, specifically defined as 'demons', that is, the 'fallen, evil angels' that belonged 'to the hosts of hell, as they were imagined by medieval Catholicism'. Moreover these demons were not just generic faceless spirits, but named entities, some of whom were specifically defined in the Bible as adversaries of God and his chosen people: among them being Baal ('the sun-god of the Canaanites'), Belial ('chief power of evil' in the 'Jewish apocalyptic'), and Berith ('mentioned in the Book of Judges as the god of the infidels').[52] This practice of specifically invoking demons emerges so strongly from late medieval sources that scholars have argued that 'demonic magic' can be defined as a 'textual genre'.[53]

Of additional interest, with regard to our analysis of popular conceptions of the Devil, is the fact that contemporary magical writings make it clear that elite magicians saw the overtly demonic identity of their spirit-helpers as no obstacle to their Christian allegiances; with texts like the fifteenth-century *Liber de angelis* quite calmly instructing the magician to make a wax variant of the *corp creadh* and subject it to various ritual procedures (including submerging it in running water and sprinkling it with dove's blood) in order to gain divinatory knowledge from Baal, the 'lord' of the demons, in the name of the 'creator of the heavens and earth'.[54] Such contradictions provoked fierce debate and generated a stream of argument and counter-argument in religious and magical writings from the early medieval period onwards. Magicians defended their actions, in large part, by arguing that although they gained magical benefit from the demons, they did so through commanding and coercing them, as opposed to making any kind of alliance and emphasized that their demands were all made in God's name. Unimpressed by these subtleties, the orthodox church condemned all demonic magic as fraternisation with Satan; arguing, among other things, that the sacrifice, supplication and worship that characterized many elite magical rituals did not reflect this simplistic magician-as-master and demon-as-servant template. These critical perspectives generated legends about magicians or their clients making overt alliances with the Devil (often renouncing Christ in the bargain) from as early as the fourth century onwards, with this plot being most famously immortalized in Christopher Marlowe's *Doctor Faustus*. As scholars have long pointed out, these beliefs and legends clearly influenced the development of elite ideas about the witches' pact.

This is a complex subject and there is no scope to explore it in any detail here, but even this brief analysis is sufficient to illustrate that these perspectives on elite ritual magic are highly relevant to our understanding of popular shamanistic practices involving the Devil or his demons, despite the fact that they have seldom been exploited, in this context, by historians of witchcraft. These sources confirm that in this period of history and in the face of overt church condemnation, a group of individuals could – through a series of rationalizations – justify magical interactions with spirits who, though not generally defined as *the* Devil, were certainly servants of the Devil and often named historical enemies of God. Although their arguments would have been

That demons could be seen as helpful in this period is vividly illustrated in this woodcut from Olaus Magnus's *Historia de gentibus septentrionalibus* (1555). Titled 'De ministero dæmonium' it shows demons performing a variety of services to man.

Solomon was perhaps the most famous historical figure to enlist the help of demons, though his predelictions in this area were generally celebrated in occult texts. Here, in Jacobus de Theramo's *Das Buch Belial*, the arch-demon Belial dances for the biblical patriarch.

less sophisticated, there is no reason why, in their magical spirit-invoking practices, popular magical practitioners could not have accommodated similarly vertiginous contradictions, and have been equally insouciant in the face of church opinion as they did so.

The Devil and Damnation

But although the arguments developed thus far in this chapter are reasonable, we cannot entertain them seriously without confronting one final question. If ordinary men and women like Isobel were capable of consciously making envisioned pacts with spirits defined as the Devil while still considering themselves to be Christians, then how did these ambiguous activities concord with their views on the afterlife? Whichever way you looked at it, for those who leaned toward traditional or Arminian views and believed that salvation was conditional upon keeping faith with Christ, overt commerce with the Devil increased your chances of damnation. Even the most uneducated peasant must have been aware that if the practice of everyday sins, such as adultery or blasphemy, could jeopardise their passage through the pearly gates, then the surrender of the soul to God's arch-enemy certainly swung the heavenly scales in the wrong direction. We have already seen how the minister, David Brown, when sermonizing to a group of unrepentant witchcraft suspects in Paisley, in 1697, told them in no uncertain terms that the Devil would be waiting at the 'gallows foot ready to harle you down into hell'.[55] And in this period such a prospect was no theological nicety. Ministers emphasized the horrors of hell as a deterrent to ungodliness and they did not mince their words when doing so. Brown told his suspects that 'by your obstinacy, you declare you are content to dwell with the Devil and everlasting burnings' while Hugh Rose, as we have seen in CHAPTER SIX, stood in the pulpit at Nairn church and warned his congregation that if they did not repent of their sins and abide by God's word they would be 'tormented by Devils throughout eternity' and that 'When thousand thousands and millions of millions of ages are passed, their torments will be no more ended, than at the first beginning'.[56]

But with regard to the present discussion, what is highly significant here is that although ministers emphasized the prospect of hell, some contemporary evidence suggests that this message was not always absorbed by congregations in the manner they may have hoped. Ned Landsman has recently shown that in the early-eighteenth century even the very religious could be surprisingly nonchalant about the eternal torments that supposedly awaited them. He notes that the minister of Cambuslang, William McCulloch:

> spent many months preaching the terrors of Hell to his congregation. On at least one occasion, he echoed Jonathan Edwards's 'Sinners in the Hands of an Angry God,' preaching on the frail thread that protected sinners from everlasting burning, in an effort to awaken his hearers. Yet the Cambuslang converts stated with near unanimity that the fear of damnation played little part in their conversions . . . Indeed, in several places in the manuscript,

we find the rather surprising spectacle of converts stating categorically that they did not fear Hell while their clerical editors argued just as strenuously in the margins that they really did.[57]

Other accounts suggest that the less religiously-minded, whether through temperament or circumstance, could be similarly insouciant. The dittays of a woman tried for witchcraft in 1572 cites how: 'Being desyred that scho wold forgive a man, that had done hir some offence (as scho alledged), refused; then when ane uther that stude by said, gif scho did not forgive, that God wald not forgive hir, and so scho suld be dampned. Bot scho not caren for hell or heavin, said opinlie, I pas [care] not whidder I goe to hell or heavin, with dyvers utheris execrable wordis.'[58]

Such nonchalance could have been rooted in a variety of factors. Landsman claims that the revivalists' lack of concern for the torments of hell was, in large part, connected to the fact that they were not so concerned with 'what might happen during an afterlife but [with] matters that were much more immediate and present'.[59] And this preoccupation with the life lived at the moment, as opposed to the life lived after death, can be traced from the medieval period through to the nineteenth century. In *Belief and Unbelief in the Middle Ages*, John Arnold argues that although religious historians have traditionally focused on the effect that ideas about the afterlife had on the minds of medieval Christians, there is evidence to suggest that the latter were less concerned about salvation and more concerned about immediate survival than has often been acknowledged.[60] Such sentiments were clearly expressed by 'bold and sturdy beggar' Alexander Agnew, who was hung for blasphemy at Dumfries in the mid-seventeenth century; for as Sinclair recounts, 'when he was interrogate by the Judges, whether or not, he thought there was a God, he answered, he knew no God but Salt, Meal, and Water'.[61] Similar views were expressed 200 years later by the pragmatic Galloway farmer who exclaimed to a visiting minister: 'Religion! 'wha wants tae talk about religion an' nae meal in the hoose?' And in the following century, by Raasay poet Sorley Maclean:

> My eye is not on Calvary
> nor on Bethlehem the Blessed,
> but on a foul smelling backland in Glasgow,
> where life rots as it grows;
> and on a room in Edinburgh,
> a room of poverty and pain
> where the diseased infant writhes and wallows till death. [62]

This preoccupation with physical survival means that it might not have been a rarity for an individual to take great spiritual chances in return for immediate, material safety. The individual who called on a cunning woman to try and cure her sick child might know that such an act prejudiced her chances of salvation, but on a basic process of risk-assessment, she would have been prepared to accept this long-in-the-future risk for the sake of the infant who was suffering, in the present moment, in front of her eyes. As has recently been claimed with regard to the famous nineteenth-century fairy doctor, Biddy Early: 'there is no doubt it was from the faeries she got the knowledge. But who wouldn't go to hell for a cure if one of his own was sick?'[63] In the same vein, few of the cottars and labourers living in crop-ravaged Nairnshire in the aftermath of Battle of Auldearn would have shared Brodie's lament that 'quher a famine of the word is sent. This is wors then a famin of bread.'[64]

'Better to Reign in Hell than Serve in Heaven'

It is also possible that, for some, this lack of concern for the terrors of hell may have had a more intellectual basis. Very occasionally, as John Arnold has shown with regard to the Middle Ages, it may have derived from a more profound scepticism about core articles of faith, such as whether God exists or whether there is any kind of afterlife or soul. Alexander Agnew's claim to know no God but 'Salt, Meal, and Water', if not illustrative of atheism proper, was certainly provocative in this respect.[65] However it is also possible that this apparent insouciance in the face of eternal damnation was rooted in an appreciation, as opposed to a rejection, of church doctrines.

As we have noted in earlier chapters, the reformed doctrine of predestination taught that God had already decided who was going to heaven and who was going to hell and that no-one could escape their predetermined fate: salvation could not be earned and damnation could not be averted. There is dispute among scholars as to what degree this absolute predestinarianism was taught from the pulpit, for we have very little information about parish-level ministry and the way it was interiorized by the laity. Some have argued that many ministers – being anxious not to deter their congregations from the pursuit of godliness – downplayed predestination when sermonizing, with this view being epitomised in the 'old ministerial proverb', here paraphrased by Knappen, that 'all are Calvinists when they pray but Arminians when they preach'. But others have argued that in the mid to late-seventeenth century, as Arminianism became increasingly feared as a threat to orthodoxy, many ministers focused their attentions on doctrinal preaching and would not have shied away from the complexities of predestination in the pulpit.[66]

If the latter were indeed the case, then it has considerable and as yet largely unexamined implications for the study of demonological witchcraft. And although there is no scope to explore this complex issue in the depth it deserves here, for Isobel's sake we must tender some preliminary observations. Obviously some parishioners would have either failed or refused to grapple with the doctrine of predestination, even when fervently preached. We have already seen how reformed congregations were quite capable of contesting their minister's version of Christianity, either not bothering to listen or standing up in church and questioning his teachings, with pithy Highland proverbs like 'God has not said all thou hast said' giving voice to these sentiments.[67] It would certainly not have been illogical for those who did not believe that the minister was the sole authority when it came to religious matters in general to also believe that he was not the sole authority when it came to judging theories of salvation in particular. This grass-roots scepticism is well-illustrated in the jocular orally-transmitted tales collected in the nineteenth century, which poked fun at the ridiculousness of predestinarianism and the ministers who attempted to propound it.[68] But we can also assume that a percentage of parishioners took the doctrine of predestination, or what they understood to be the doctrine of predestination, on board. The church's claim that mankind was separated into those who were saved and those who were damned was striking and unambiguous, and we can imagine the impact of tirades like the following, taken from English puritan John Preston's *The New Covenant* (1630), as they thundered down from the reformed pulpits: 'There is no middle sort of men in the world, all are either sheepe or goates, all are either within the Covenant, or without the Covenant, all are either elect, or reprobates: God hath divided all the world into these two, either they are the Lord's portion, or the Divel's portion.'[69]

Hearing such declarations, parishioners were bound to ask themselves: 'Am I a sheep, or am I a goat?' 'Am I elect or reprobate?' 'Am I the Lord's portion or the Devil's portion?' And however reluctantly, some may have opted for the latter options. Although the church taught that there was no certain way of knowing who were among the elect and who were not – such knowledge being deemed the sole preserve of God – it emphasized that godly impulses and behaviour were a sign that an individual was saved; the theory being that God gave his elect the strength to turn from sin. It does not seem unreasonable to assume, in the light of the overview of popular pastimes and mentalities given in this chapter, that this belief placed a large proportion of the population in a difficult position. Well aware of their love of the gillatrype, the violin, the magical charm or the curse, and well aware of their disinclination toward godly pursuits such as temperance, self-denial and introspection, many people may have pessimistically concluded that because they were obviously not blessed with the capacity to resist sinful activities they were almost certainly one of the damned. For such people, pessimistic fatalism in the face of damnation would have bred a sense of futility and the belief that it was pointless trying to avoid the inevitable, particularly when the more pressing concerns of physical survival were at hand. Such sentiments may have lain behind the brash claims of Reay piper Donald Gunne, who was summoned before the session in 1663 and 'appointed to stand in sackcloth for pypping at Lykewakes, and saying that if all the pypers in Caithness would goe to hell he would goe with them'.[70] More pertinently, in some this sense of futility may have translated into an overt disregard for the consequences of sin. Though they may not have been as learned as (speculated) antinomians like John Weir and Harry Forbes, astute and independent-minded parishioners would have been perfectly capable of following absolute predestinarianism to its logical conclusion and adopting the view that since damnation was predicted irrespective of worldy behaviour, then they did not need to worry about sin. Since they were the Devil's already, they need not fear God's curses.

With regard to our analysis into the demonic pact, what is significant here is that these attitudes would have made it much easier to justify commerce with the Devil for the purposes of magical healing, divination, self-defensive *maleficium* and so on. In hell, there was eternal suffering to come anyway, so men and women who considered themselves damned may well have decided to ease their present material sufferings, with the

Devil's help, while they could. This pragmatic pessimism may even have conspired to generate a certain intimacy with the Devil on a 'we're all in this together' basis. The accounts of the trial and execution of Edinburgh sorcerer John Weir (1670) indicate that, knowing that damnation was inevitable, he 'died obduredly, without any sign of repentance, and would not hear any minister pray to and for him, telling, his condemnation was sealed, and that now since he was to goe to the devil, he would not anger him'.[71] The Devil's positive-in-relief persona and the belief that he was 'aye gude to his ain' can only have served to encourage these subversive loyalties. It is also worth noting here that while this fatalistic pessimism was destructive, the more optimistic supposition that one was probably a member of the elect could have been equally dangerous in this respect. As we have seen in CHAPTER SEVEN, those of antinomian persuasion could hold the view that since salvation was non-conditional and granted irrespective of behaviour then as members of the elect they could 'do no wrong'. And if learned and pious men like Thomas Weir and Harry Forbes could twist these views to accommodate adultery and incest, then there is no reason why their less learned contemporaries could not have twisted them to accommodate commerce with the Devil.

These perspectives on predestinarian teachings are relevant to our understanding of popular conceptions of the Devil in early modern Scotland in the wider sense, but it is also worth bearing in mind that they may have particular relevance in Isobel's case. Like all ministers, Harry Forbes would have been interested in the question of salvation and election, with Brodie's claim that he and Forbes 'spok off Frie Will' at supper, in July 1655, directly intimating the minister's interest in the subject.[72] But as a covenanting divine whose views were so extreme that he could not accept episcopacy, we can also assume that he was one of those ministers least likely – when in the pulpit – to have shied away from the complexities of predestination. This supposition is supported by the fact that this unflinching position was certainly adopted by Thomas Hogg; the minister (later to be the Laird of Park's brother-in-law) who was instrumental in securing Forbes's instalment at Auldearn; who worshipped with him at Brodie Castle; and whose covenanting principles were so strong that he, too, was unable to stomach the bishops.[73] Murdoch Macdonald notes that Hogg's opinions about election were so forthright and stringent that even some of his contemporaries 'thought he pitched his standard too high', and that the minister 'would have difficulty in finding among hundreds of our modern converts thirty or forty who could give what he would regard "as a distinct account of the saving work of God's Spirit upon their souls"'.[74] Even the zealous Alexander Brodie lamented, of Hogg, that 'I thought him too rigid in the marks of saving grace and as to the state of men'.[75] If Harry Forbes maintained, or even just came close to, Hogg's position then Isobel would have gained a very concrete picture of a world divided – since the beginning of time – into that which belonged to the Devil and that which belonged to God.

The Bonny Road

The ability of some of Isobel's contemporaries, such as Donald Gunne and John Weir, to anticipate the terrors of hell with such seeming equanimity may not only have been fostered by live-for-the-moment philosophies or predestinarian doctrines, but also by the belief that with regard to the afterlife heaven and hell were not the only options. A significant number of fairy-related encounter-narratives indicate that in the sixteenth and seventeenth centuries some men and women believed that on death the human went on to live in fairyland. These accounts seldom indicate whether it was believed to be the physical body, subtle body or soul that existed in this realm, nor do they clearly indicate what links, if any, fairyland was believed to have with the newly-outlawed purgatory, but they nevertheless delineate a belief that was literal and heartfelt. Fifeshire cunning woman Alison Peirson (1588), for example, maintained that when she went to 'elphame' she saw 'mony guid freindis in that court'; Pennant's Breadalbane 'dreamer' claimed to have seen a 'crowd of men and women, many of whom he knew to have been dead for some years' among the fairies; and, as we have seen earlier, Isobel herself claimed that 'any th[a]t ar shot be us, their sowell will goe to hevin bot ther bodies remains w[i]th ws'.[76] Similar beliefs were found in the Orkneys, with sixteenth-century author 'Jo Ben' noting that the people of Stronsay 'relate that men dying suddenly afterwards live with them [the fairies]'.[77] Many accounts attest to the fact that these beliefs were still active 300 years later. J. F. Campbell, as we have seen earlier, received an account from one of his informants about a man who believed, despite all his minister's efforts to persuade him otherwise, that his dead wife had been 'taken by fairies to a certain hill in Muckairn, known to be the residence of the fairies'.[78]

The Protestant church, defining the fairies as devils, would have officially taught that fairyland came under the auspices of hell, but it is clear that for some people its status was a little more nuanced, with the realm representing – as purgatory once did – a kind of intermediary world or lesser hell. These beliefs were vividly reflected in the folkloric cosmology sketched out in the ballad of 'Thomas Rhymer', manuscript and oral versions of which were circulated around Scottish firesides from at least the medieval period onwards. The following version can be traced to the first half of the eighteenth century but its stylistic features indicate that, as Child notes, it 'must be of considerable age'. Here, the seductive fairy queen offers Thomas three choices:

O see not ye yon narrow road,
So thick beset wi thors and briers?
That is the path of righteousness,
Tho after it but few enquires.

And see not ye that braid braid road,
That lies across yon lillie leven?
That is the path of wickedness,
Tho some call it the road to heaven.

And see not yee that bonny road,
Which winds about the fernie brae?
That is the road to fair Elfland,
Whe[re] you and I this night maun gae.[79]

Whether a man or woman saw fairyland as an alternative to hell, or a version of hell itself, if contemporary accounts are anything to go by, as a substitute for heaven it was not a wholly unattractive prospect. Although the fairies were believed to be violent spirits who could abuse their human visitors, these beliefs ran alongside the conviction that those who took up residence in their realm would be treated well. Stirling cunning woman Isobel Watson (1590), as Maxwell-Stuart notes, claimed that the fairy queen had 'bidden her deny God and stay with the *sithean* [fairies], since she would have a better life with them'.[80] Similarly, 200 years later J. F. Campbell echoed the popular belief that the fairies 'never maltreat those they carry away'.[81] Oral literature collected in the nineteenth century also emphasizes fairy hospitality: 'pleasant is the fairy land' opines the ballad of 'Tam Lin', while the tale about the 'Miller o' Menstrie' describes how the fairy host swept the unfortunate man's wife up the chimney and 'carried her to Cauldhame – the palace o' the fairies – whaur she lived like a queen'.[82] From Isobel's confessions alone we can see that a resident of elphame could hope to feast beneath the Downie Hill in the company of the fairy king and queen; be waited on by Thomas Rhymer; dance in the wooded hills of Darnaway and Earleseat; and wander through the cellars and kitchens of local lairds and dignitaries eating fresh beef and drinking good ale. Such a prospect would have been even more enticing if the individual believed, as some clearly did, that when they chose the 'bonny road which winds about the fernie brae' they would be reunited with those friends and relatives – particularly dead children – who had followed the same path. Given the fact that, as we have seen earlier, qualification for heaven became an even more tenuous and ambiguous affair after the Reformation than it had been under Catholicism, such beliefs must have been strangely compelling. As Cowan and Henderson note:

> Anxiety about death is universal, but perhaps it had a particular sting in Reformation Scotland, where, while the good and the godly were predestined for salvation, there must have been legions of less fortunate and less confident souls who had severe doubts about what awaited them in the afterlife. For some the home of the fairies, imperfect though it was, provided some sort of an alternative, just as the very idea of Fairyland permitted some assuagement of the grief attending the death of a loved one. It is even quite possible that a number of disoriented Scots in this period really did believe, to cite the old adage, that it was better to reign in Hell than serve in Heaven.[83]

These beliefs merit far more examination in this context than it is possible to undertake here. Of particular interest, for example, is how far they were restricted to 'disoriented Scots' and how far they were part of widespread currency in the period, and held by rational individuals who knew exactly where they were going and what they deserved. Similarly, the links between fairyland and purgatory also call for more research. But although brief, what this overview successfully illustrates is that, for Isobel and her contemporaries, neither earthly life nor the afterlife were as black and white as they were for the godly covenanters. In the grey area between eternal bliss in heaven and eternal suffering in hell, as in the grey area between good and evil or God and the Devil, there was room for many mansions.

The Malevolent Devil

The perspectives outlined in this chapter make it easier to understand how an individual like Isobel may have allowed themselves to contract with an envisioned spirit they believed to be the Devil. But before we leave the subject altogether, we must address one outstanding issue. To date, the argument that Isobel and others like her may have entered into working relationships with the envisioned Devil has been constructed upon the premise that the latter was perceived as ambivalent (that is, he could do good as well as harm, particularly with regard to healing) and that he possessed a positive-in-relief persona. However, with regard to Isobel, and a large number of other witchcraft suspects, this was clearly not the whole picture. Like many witch-narratives, a considerable proportion of Isobel's confessions are not devoted to describing the ways in which the Devil helped her to perform beneficent magic, but to the ways in which he helped her to perform *maleficium*. Even if some of this magical harm can be rationalized, within the shamanistic community-benefit paradigm, as client-demanded self-defence or the attempt to heal through the transferral of sickness or death, it cannot be denied that the Devil, as described by Isobel, comes across as largely concerned with magical benefits specifically derived through bringing misfortune to others. Obviously this emphasis can be attributed, in large part, to the fact that witnesses and prosecutors, anxious for a conviction, would have focused on the maleficent magic they believed Isobel to have performed. But we can also speculate that it may have reflected genuine popular practice.

As argued in CHAPTER EIGHT, on a popular level the performance of maleficent magic in self-defence was, to a certain extent, culturally sanctioned. And as we have argued in CHAPTERS TWELVE to SIXTEEN, this sanction extended to the envisioned alliance with a range of spirits, from God and Christ to saints and fairies, who were believed capable of causing harm as well as good. In this context, it is wholly reasonable to suppose, as we have done in the current chapter, that an individual could petition the ambivalent Devil to harm an enemy in just the same way that he could petition the God of the Hebrews, the Bridegroom of Souls or the fairy 'maister man'. The scattering of witchcraft records in which suspects claimed to have sought vengeance from 'either God or the Devil' are testament to this lack of differentiation. But although in this period most types of supernatural being were considered to possess the capacity to do harm, church propaganda would have ensured that, on both an elite and popular level, the Devil, as the 'king of all the devils', was the specialist in this area: the practitioner of *maleficium* par excellence. And given the Devil's notoriety in this quarter, it is reasonable to assume that if a magical practitioner specifically sought to satisfy themselves, or a client, through the performance of envisioned *maleficium*, they might have opted for the Devil over and above any other type of spirit as their visionary helper of choice. Put another way, if an individual wished to magically heal or predict the future, then the Devil may have offered little more than the less ambiguous fairy or saint. But if they wanted to perform magical harm, or healing through the use of magical harm, then it may have seemed logical to seek out the best service and pitch for the man at the top.

Evil Spirits and the Dark Shaman

Although the petitioning of spirits on the basis of their capacity to do harm may sound far-fetched, it gains support from both elite magical traditions and anthropological sources. As we have seen earlier, the learned magicians of the Middle Ages called on both demons and more benign spirits, such as good angels, in order to procure magical effects. But the texts suggest that, while both types of spirit could often be employed to either beneficent or maleficent ends, the magical effects sought from demons were disproportionately malevolent. With regard to the category of magical practice loosely defined as 'demonic magic', Claire Fanger has recently noted:

> If the terminology is imprecise, demonic magic as a textual genre nonetheless has certain discernible common features. The magical effects sought for are often (if not invariably) of a rather spiteful and petty-minded sort – causing disease, harm or deformity in another person; manipulating the emotions of others to induce love or hatred between two people, or to get a person of the opposite sex to submit to the operator's desires.[84]

The possibility that both popular and elite magical practitioners specifically favoured demonic spirits when wishing to perform less morally-acceptable magical acts, gains further support from the fact that anthropological studies testify to such practices in tribal cultures throughout the world. From the Siberian tundra to the Amazonian rain-forest, when certain magical outcomes are desired, spirits veering toward the evil end of the continuum are considered the most effective. When his village was under pressure from enemy tribes, the Amazonian Yanomamö shaman, Jungleman, decided to try and weaken the enemy by killing their children. But when he asked his favourite helping spirit for aid she claimed 'I don't do that . . . but I can get you spirits who can', after which she introduced him to another, less scrupulous, spirit named 'Snakeman', who helped him to fulfil his gruesome task and thereafter became one of Jungleman's greatest spiritual allies.[85] Similarly, the dark shamans of the Amazonian Warao tribe are feared and disliked because, as Wilbert notes, 'Instead of decimating their [spiritual] enemies and keeping them at bay like light shamans do with their devastating idols, dark shamans collude with the insufferable enemy and carry destruction into their own camps.' But as we saw in CHAPTERS TWELVE and THIRTEEN, these acts bring their compensations, for the shamans who ally themselves with evil spirits in this way are uniquely qualified to cure *Hoa* diseases and defend their community through regulating the macaw god of the underworld's human food supply.[86] In Turkic Siberia, shamans can make similarly dark alliances, with Van Deusen claiming:

> In spite of their danger, or maybe because of it, evil spirits are sometimes the source of the shamanic gift. I asked ethnographer Vera Diakonova 'How can a shaman who takes ancestry from evil spirits do good?' She replied that those shamans with ancestry from evil spirits, specifically the *albys* or *almys*, have dealings only with the lower world. For example, they accompany the souls of the dead. It's possible that they might be able to bring back somebody whose soul has already gone to the land of the dead. Sometimes these black shamans

can steal a person's soul and give it to someone else to save a life. So in this way they are useful, but very dangerous. Some shamans say that taking ancestry from an evil spirit is analogous to the way we become stronger by overcoming difficulties – the difficulties are our teachers and bring us benefits.[87]

Isobel's relationship with the Devil may have been underpinned by similar rationales. If she sought, as we have argued, to perform envisioned *maleficium*-in-self-defence against her enemies, most notably the Laird of Park and Harry Forbes, she may have been well aware that of all the spirits potentially available to her, the Devil – both for his capacity to do harm and his lack of Christian scruples – may have been the spirit best equipped to carry out her wishes. And so when she encountered an envisioned helping spirit on the road 'betuixt the townes of drumdewin and the headis', or at the head of an envisioned arrow-shooting spirit troupe, she may have been strongly predisposed to define him as the Devil. By the same token if, through her arrow-shooting escapades, Isobel had been engaging, as we speculated in CHAPTER THIRTEEN, in the ambiguous magical practice of curing clients through human-to-human sickness and death transferral, the Devil may also have been her spirit helper of choice. Just as in Turkic Siberia the shaman who cures the sick through stealing a healthy person's soul does so with the help of specifically evil spirits, so in early modern Scotland a magical practitioner such as Isobel may have felt that her attempts to shoot an innocent man or woman dead with elf arrows in order to save the life of a client, would have been best aided by the only spirit unscrupulous enough to do it.

Such speculations are controversial, and merit deeper research than is possible in the present book. And most pressing of all, of course, is the question of extent. Although we have argued here that in Isobel's case – which was by all accounts exceptional – an individual may have specifically petitioned the Devil in order to perform *maleficium*, it is far harder to assess how common such practices may have been in the wider community, and how its levels of incidence reflected descriptions of commerce with the *maleficium*-performing Devil found in encounter-narratives. For the practice to have been anything other than anomalous, we must presume the existence of a certain degree of social toleration, but whether, and to what degree, the latter may have existed is hard to gauge. Anthropological comparisons are difficult here because among traditional tribal cultures, the acceptability or non-acceptability of consorting with evil spirits in order to perform *maleficium* varies widely from society to society, and in response to a diverse range of cultural, religious and political factors. Our task is also hampered by the fact that whatever their extent, and however they are perceived within their community, once a tribal religion comes into contact with a developed religion like Christianity, such practices quickly become demonized and run underground.

While we cannot explore this issue in any depth here, it is worth observing that, with regard to extent, some suggestive inferences arise directly from the witch trials themselves. The second most common type of magical help offered by the Devil in demonological narratives – after 'freedom from want' and the ilk – was that of vengeance. Edinburgh cunning woman Agnes Sampson, for example, was enticed by the Devil's promise that 'she and her bairns should be made rich, and [that he] should give her power to be revenged of her enemies', while Angus witch Isobel Shyrie covenanted with him on the condition that 'hee wold wrong those that wronged hir'.[88] When the Devil appeared before Lanark witch Katren Shaw in the form of a 'meikle rouch dog' he asked her 'what she would give to have ane mends of Issbell Haistie, promeising that, if she would becum his servant, he wold give hir ane mends'.[89] Of course such references can be attributed to interrogatorial superimposition, for the Devil's offer of revenge was commonly featured as a standard contractual enticement in demonological writings, and it was obviously in the interests of interrogators to associate commerce with the Devil with the troublesome and un-Christian revenge ethic. But in the context of the perspectives developed here, we could speculate that the chain of causation may also have run the other way, and that the association between the desire for revenge and the demonic pact filtered up into demonological writings from the trials themselves; this emphasis reflecting the fact that when magical practitioners wished to perform revenge-*maleficium* they were statistically more likely to call on – or define their spontaneously-appearing helping spirit as – the Devil. This emphasis would certainly concord with the growing historical conviction that learned demonological theory emerged out of a two-way dialogue between witch-testimonies and theological speculation. It could even be seen to support the more extreme view, as articulated by Clark, that 'It is simply not the case that witchcraft theory caused "witch hunts" or that its incidence influenced theirs; indeed, the reverse is much more likely to have been true'.[90]

All in all, these perspectives do not enable us to jump to any grand conclusions. We must still assume that most shamanistic practitioners seeking to find a definition for their *maleficium*-performing envisioned helping spirits would have commonly passed over that of 'the Devil' – despite his superior abilities in this respect – in favour of less dangerous and controversial spirits such as saints, fairies or the dead. But nevertheless, the arguments developed in this chapter enable us to tentatively entertain the idea that demonologists and witch-prosecutors like Alexander Brodie and Harry Forbes may not have been chasing shadows or tilting at windmills. Although, during the period of the witch-hunts in Scotland, many hundreds of men and women were clearly falsely accused of contracting with the Devil, an unknown minority, with perhaps Isobel Gowdie among them, may have genuinely sought to revenge themselves on their neighbours, ministers and landlords, through an alliance with an envisioned spirit they consciously identified as the Prince of Darkness himself.

18

Witches' Covens and Dark Dream Cults

In CHAPTERS TEN to THIRTEEN we have argued that the fairy-related elements of Isobel's confessions, although undoubtedly sculpted by coercive-compliant responses and false-memory generation, may have been drawing on a kernel, or *prima materia* of prior experience rooted in shamanistic visionary traditions of folkloric origin. In CHAPTERS FOURTEEN to SIXTEEN we have extended this hypothesis and argued that the demonological passages, and in particular the figure of the Devil, may also have been constructed around an experiential core. This explanatory model enables us to account for the fluidity and seamlessness of Isobel's complex narrative, the way it moves from fairy-related to demonological material in such an effortless manner and the way the figure of the Devil straddles all these contradictions with such ease.

But although this shamanistic hypothesis is helpful, before we can consider it a viable explanation in Isobel's case, we need to confront one final issue: all the other witches. With the exception of her encounter with the Devil on the road 'betuixt the townes of drumdewin and the headis', Isobel claimed that every single one of her core activities, whether it came into the fairy lore, demonological or intermediate category, was undertaken in the company of others. This group of men and women, which Isobel termed her 'coven', arranged itself into a hierarchy, converged at formal meetings and performed communal rituals. But the coven members were not elf men, devils, saints, fairy queens or the dead. They were Isobel's neighbours, with their names, the names of their spouses and their places of residence clearly recorded in the confessions. We can fairly safely assume, from cross-referencing with Janet Breadheid's testimony, Brodie's diaries and contemporary place names and surnames, that most – if not all – of these named men and women were likely to have been real people who lived in the Auldearn locality at the time. But if, as we have argued in the previous four chapters, Isobel's confessions were rooted in visionary experience, then how are we to explain their presence in her narrative?

Obviously we can assume that, as with the figure of the Devil, interrogatorial superimposition played a role here. It is clear from a wide range of written and visual sources that the collective imagination of the age was dominated by the 'devilische league and band' of witches who 'convened in the gloaming and did their turn in the night', and there is no reason to believe that the minds of Harry Forbes, Hugh Rose and Alexander

Brodie of Lethen were any different in this respect.[1] The men who wrote about witch-craft and prosecuted witches firmly believed that groups of individuals who lived near to each other and were personally known to each other congregated at meetings (termed 'witches' sabbaths' by later historians) where they performed communal rites in the presence of the Devil. As a consequence, second to establishing the performance of *maleficium* and the making of the demonic pact, the primary concern for most inter-rogators was to uncover the names of their suspects' fellow witches. This could be a painstaking process, in which alleged accomplices were brought face to face with their accusers in an effort to better establish guilt and their respective stories cross-referenced to ensure legitimacy. Care was also often taken to establish whether an accusation was a false one, based on envy or spite, and whether coven-members had been voluntarily present at the alleged gatherings.[2] Interestingly, concerns about witches' sabbaths were often as pressing among those who maintained that they were purely fantastical occa-sions, created through the imagination-manipulating powers of the Devil, as among those who maintained that they were physically real events.

Clearly the witch-meetings described in Isobel's confessions can be partly attrib-uted to interrogatorial suggestion. We have some direct evidence that Forbes, like many witch-prosecutors, was interested in the subject, as evinced by Brodie's claim that when Cathrin Hendrie confessed to being plagued by the Devil, the minister promptly detected the workings of witchcraft and told the woman that 'she oght to disclaim solemnlie that confederacie'.[3] Interrogatorial influence is also suggested by the fact that in many coven-related passages the sentence structure is such that it is not difficult to imagine the kinds of leading questions that may have sculpted them. The following, from the first confession, is illustrative (with some hypothetical questions being inserted in parentheses):

> q[uhe]n we tak cornes at lambes we tak (*crease in page – several words unreadable*) cornes ar full or two stokis of keall or therby and th[a]t giwes ws the fruit of the corn land or keal yaird whair they grew: and it mey be (*crease in page – several words unreadable*) yewll or pace, and th[e]n devyd it amongst ws (HOW MANY PEOPLE ARE THERE IN YOUR COVEN?) ther ar threttien persones in my coven, (WHERE DID YOUR COVEN LAST MEET?) the last tym th[a]t owr coven (*rest of line obscured*) wer daunceing at the hill of earlseat, and befor th[a]t betuixt moynes and bowgholl, & befor th[a]t we ves besyd the meikle burne, (DID YOU MEET WITH ANY OTHER COVENS?) and the uth[e]r coven being at the downiehillis we went from beyond the meikle burne and went besyd them to the howssis at the woodend of Inshoch and w[i]thin a qwhyll went hom to o[u]r howssis befor candlmas we went be east kinlosse and ther we yoaked an plewghe of paddokis. (39/20)

But although there is evidence that interrogatorial suggestion shaped Isobel's coven-related passages, we cannot assume that this was the whole story. It is clear that here, as in so much of Isobel's interrogation, questioning was coercive-open, and that Isobel was detailed and creative in her responses. With regard to the above-quoted passage, for example, although it is likely that the interrogators asked 'Where did your coven last meet?', and possible that they then asked 'Did you meet with any other covens?', it is virtually inconceivable that they should have followed this up with 'And did your coven yoke a plough of frogs east of Kinloss?' Similarly, that details concerning the coven came from Isobel herself is indicated by the fact that the coven is woven into the very heart of the fairy lore and lightly-demonized intermediate passages, with this conflation suggesting that – as we have noted many times before – Isobel's ideas about the witches' coven were strongly linked to folkloric ideas about travel with the fairy host.

The Murray Controversy

But in attempting to explore and explain Isobel's coven, we enter dangerous territory. The ideas and theories surrounding both the witches' coven and the witches' sabbath are perhaps the most problematic and widely debated in witchcraft studies, historically presenting even more problems than many of the other difficult issues we have covered in this book, such as the existence of self-conscious witches and the reality of envisioned pacts with the Devil. And hardly surprisingly, given the fact that they contain so much detail in this respect, Isobel's confessions have been at the centre of this debate. Although the witches' coven was of interest to historians and folklorists throughout the nineteenth century, it came to the forefront of scholarly discourse in 1921, in the wake of Margaret Murray's controversial book *The Witch-Cult in Western Europe*. As an Egyptologist and archaeologist, Murray was highly cognisant of the fact that in early cultures throughout the world religious observance frequently manifested as cult activity (the term 'cult' here indicating 'a sect devoted to a specific system of religious worship') and that when one religion officially superseded another, pre-existent cultic beliefs and rituals tended to persist on the fringes of the newly-established orthodoxy.[4] From this vantage point, Murray postulated that early modern witch-trial records were testament to the continued existence, throughout western Europe, of a pre-Christian fertility cult that had been consistently demonized by the church. This 'witch cult', as she termed and described it, met at significant dates in the year in order to participate in bacchanalian rites that included masquerading as animals and sexual intercourse. The cult was structured into a hierarchy presided over by the pagan Horned God and his female consort and admitted membership through complex initiation ceremonies and naming rituals.

In *The Witch-Cult* Murray noted that 'Isobel Gowdie of Auldearne gives the most detail concerning the Covens', and it is not surprising, therefore, that she cites Isobel's testimony more frequently than any other from the period (at least twenty-six times).[5] Moreover, Murray seems to have used Isobel's coven as a kind of template for her witch cult, for Isobel's coven-accounts contain more of the latter's structural and ritual elements than any other witch-testimony from the period: including the number of participants (thirteen), the initiation by the Devil, the presence of both male and female authority figures, the roles of maiden and officer, naming and marking rituals and the emphasis on sexual ritual. Most pertinently, via Murray, Isobel may have been largely responsible for the ubiquity of the word 'coven' itself. In early modern Scotland, groups of witches were referred to in various ways: 'league', 'band', 'army', 'conventicle' and so on, but to my knowledge the word 'coven' or 'covin' (an old Scots word meaning 'to gather' or 'to come together', deriving from from the Latin *convenire*) is employed consistently in only two sets of witchcraft records: those from Alloa, in 1658, and those from Auldearn in 1662. Although Murray was not (as is sometimes claimed) the first to seize on this term – for as early as 1888, in *The Proceedings of the Society of the Antiquaries of Scotland*, Burns Begg noted that 'thirteen formed the orthodox number of which a "covin" or organised company of witches consisted' – through employing it vigorously and consistently throughout her analysis Murray launched it onto the international stage, where it has since become the definitive term for a group of witches in both popular and scholarly arenas.[6] It is also worth pointing out that, by virtue of Murray's influence on the core founder of the neopagan Wiccan faith, Gerald Gardner, Isobel's confessions have probably influenced the genesis of modern witchcraft traditions more than any other witch-testimony on record.

But while Murray's theories were instrumental in forging a new faith on a popular level, they were received cautiously by many scholars from the beginning, and by the mid-twentieth century emergent theories about the predominantly elite origins of the sabbath overshadowed her hypothesis, which was finally discredited in 1975 when Norman Cohn (*Europe's Inner Demons*) demonstrated severe methodological flaws in her analysis. Hardly surprisingly, just as Isobel's confessions were so fruitfully mined by Murray to support her case, they were just as fruitfully mined by Cohn to demolish it. Cohn's central criticism was that Murray deliberately omitted the fantastic elements in sabbath accounts in order to 'give the impression that a number of perfectly sober, realistic accounts of the sabbat exist'; and her misrepresentation of Isobel's confessions forms the meat of nearly half of his famous analysis. In his most compelling example, Cohn illustrated how Murray distorted the sense of a passage found in Confession Three by inserting a dash to delete the passage beginning 'All the coven did fly like cats, jack-daws, hares and rooks, etc.' which inconveniently sat between two relatively realistic descriptions of sabbath feasts.[7] Although Murray nodded toward an explanation for these fantastic elements by referring to the 'undoubted fact that in many cases the witch confused dreams with reality and believed that she had visited the Sabbath when credible witnesses could prove that she had slept in her bed all the time', the reference was too undeveloped and too concealed (being buried in the book's introduction) to withstand Cohn's assault.[8] Since the dramatic rise and fall of Murray, the idea that early modern coven-accounts reflect the performance of physical cult rites has been largely dismissed by scholars.

Shamanistic Cults

But ironically, just as Murray's theories were being thoroughly dismantled by Cohn et al. in the 1970s, in Continental Europe new theories about witches' cults were beginning to emerge in their place. Anthropologists have long observed that shamanistic belief and practice can manifest in the form of cultic activity, particularly in cultures with more complex social structures, and have widely documented how, in locations as divergent as the Americas, Africa and South East Asia, shamans can be found operating in specialist groups in which membership is gained through the sharing of particular types of visionary experiences aimed at producing specific magical effects. Lee Irwin writes of the Native American Plains Indians that:

> Empowerment took its primary social manifestation in the various religious societies that an individual could join after having a certain type of visionary experience. Dreamers and visionaries tended to form societies (or sodalities) revolving around a visionary encounter with a specific dream-spirit; there were buffalo dreamers, elk dreamers, bear dreamers, and so on. Membership in these societies might enhance individual social identity and confer religious status on the dreamer.[9]

Historians exploring the shamanistic paradigm have observed that shamanistic practices, as they emerged in early modern Europe, were also frequently linked to cult-like activity. These ideas first achieved prominence in Ginzburg's *Night Battles*, in which he argued that those Friulian peasants who defined themselves as *benandanti* did not only undergo a specific culture-patterned visionary experience, but that, by virtue of these experiences, they self-consciously identified themselves as members of a select group of magical specialists. 'It is worth repeating', Ginzburg emphasized, 'that we are not dealing here with a fossilized superstition, a dead and incomprehensible remnant from a too distant past, but with an *actual living cult* [my italics].'[10] Other scholars have replicated Ginzburg's findings in different parts of Europe, with shamanistic cultic activity being identified in, among other places, Sicily, Corsica, Rumania and Hungary.

But these shamanistic-cult theories have thrown up as many questions as they have answered, with the debate being largely centred on the two hoary old issues of physical ritual and demonisation. When Ginzburg first publicized the cultic activities of the *benandanti*, some scholars assumed that he was supporting Murray's claim that magical cults congregated together, in body, to perform physical rites; an accusation which earned him, as he dryly put it, 'ex-officio enrolment in the phantom (but discredited) sect of "Murrayists"'. Ginzburg's response to these accusations was ambiguous. On the one hand, he challenged them by emphasizing that the *benandanti's* visionary rites occurred during catalepsy, while they lay at home in their beds, and that 'The physical reality of witches' assemblies receives no confirmation whatever, even by analogy, from the trials of the *benandanti*'. But on the other, his subsequent claim that 'The possibility that the *benandanti* would gather periodically before undergoing individual hallucinatory experiences, as described in their confessions, cannot be definitively proven', while being marshalled as defence against accusations of Murrayism, also continues to raise the possibility that these periodic gatherings did in fact take place.[11]

Others scholars in the field have been similarly ambivalent. Pócs, among others, has drawn attention to the fact that shamanistic cults using physical rites did in fact exist in central and southern parts of Europe in this period: prominent among these being the Balkan 'fairy societies', such as the *călușarii* and *rusalia*, which 'practised a kind of possession [healing] cult known in a variety of forms from the Mediterranean to the Near East'.[12] But despite arguing that 'a few references in our [witch] trials' also point to the presence of similar rituals 'in some form' in early modern Hungary, Pócs generally avoids the question of physical rites, particularly in reference to the more demonological spirit-group narratives.[13] Similar ambiguities are found in the work of Henningsen, who in one place states categorically that the ritual activities of the Sicilian fairy cult took place 'in an immaterial world of dream and vision', and in another records a detailed account in which a cult member performed a healing visionary ritual in a client's house in the company of others. Even Carrington, who has never been embroiled in the touchy debates surrounding the existence or non-existence of witch cults, states enigmatically that 'When speaking of the *mazzeri* [cult] the usual arbitrary distinctions between dreaming and "real life" must be laid aside . . . Some *mazzeri*, then, go out into the maquis [in trance] while others stay at home dreaming that they do so.'[14]

Similar ambiguity surrounds the relationship between shamanistic-cult activity and demonisation. Continental scholars have increasingly argued that the beliefs and practices surrounding shamanistic cults of pre-Christian origin, such as the Balkan fairy societies, affected the development of elite ideas about the witches' coven, although there is still much debate over exactly how this process may have taken place. One of the most compelling perspectives, developed most comprehensively by Pócs, is that the companies of supernatural beings (often defined as fairy-type spirits or the dead) who made up folkloric spirit groups (as they emerged in a wide range of shamanistic beliefs and narratives) became progressively translated, over a period of centuries and through ongoing interaction between elite and popular mentalities, into a company of living human witches; a process Pócs termed 'witchization'.[15] But far more difficult to determine however, as Pócs acknowledges, is how far beliefs and practices surrounding these folkloric spirit-groups merged with ideas about the witches' coven on an experiential level. Despite having undertaken what is arguably the most wide-ranging and detailed exploration of shamanistic cultic beliefs and practices (as they may have existed in early modern Europe) to date, Pócs largely avoids this question. Although she claims, as we have seen in CHAPTER TWELVE, that the performance of community-defending *maleficium* was an integral feature of some shamanistic-cult activity (as in the case of the *táltos*) she only occasionally concludes that individuals may have been 'self-conscious witches' and does not explore how far ideas and beliefs surrounding the demonologically stereotypical witches' coven may have become part of cult identity. Similarly, although Ginzburg's researches into the *benandanti* clearly indicate that some traditional shamanistic cults were re-cast as witches' covens by interrogators and that cult members could, as a result of questioning, produce demonized accounts of visionary experiences, he still maintains that it is difficult, if not impossible, to ascertain whether any of the *benandanti* internalized stereotypically demonological elements into their visionary experiences prior to imprisonment and interrogation.[16]

With regard to the study of Scottish witch-records these ambiguities have been particularly disabling. Here, the overwhelming majority of coven-accounts (or coven-narratives, as we can term them here) are heavily demonized. This distorting smoke-screen means that even if we accept that shamanistic cults existed in some parts of Europe in this period, and even if we accept that some Scottish accounts of meetings with individual spirits, such as fairies, may represent the survival of shamanistic traditions into early modern Scotland, we are still no closer to establishing for certain whether any given coven-narrative may have been rooted in cultic experience. Among British scholars, where the shamanistic paradigm in general has been viewed with caution, these ambiguities have usually been automatically translated into the negative. After all, those who find it difficult to accept that an encounter with an elf man may have been a visionary experience are unlikely to accept such an explanation with regard to the experience of participating in a witches' coven. But on the other hand, the growing realization that witch-testimonies reflected folkloric beliefs and experiences to a greater extent than has been hitherto supposed, is generating a need for new rationalizations, and this need is opening the doors to explanatory hypotheses linked to shamanism.

But with regard to the present exploration of Isobel's coven, these doors have not been open for long enough. Any proper analysis would need to take place alongside a broad-ranging study that cross-referenced both Scottish and Continental coven-narratives with shamanistic-cult accounts from both early modern Europe and contemporary tribal societies, and which analyzed these findings in relation to recent psychological and scientific research into dream and vision experience. In the absence of such a study, it is difficult to hypothesise about the epistemological status of Isobel's coven. But on the other hand, in order to provide a rounded analysis of her confessions, some attempt must be made to tackle the issue here. The following analysis will form what amounts to a brief perusal of some of the relevant lines of enquiry that have emerged during the course of research for this book. None of these avenues have been explored in enough depth to be conclusive, or even persuasive when considered individually, but taken together they amount to a tentative hypothesis as to how far Isobel's claim to have been a member of a coven may have been related to shamanistic-cult experience.

Isobel's 'Cult of One'?

In order to ascertain whether Isobel's shamanistic rites were wholly private experiences, or whether they were contextualized within some kind of cult practice, we need to first establish whether there is any evidence of cultic identity within her local community. On the one hand, it could be argued that this evidence is both copious and staring us in the face, in the sense that Isobel states quite clearly that she was a member of a clandestine, hierarchically-organised group that came together on certain nights of the year to perform fairy-related magical rituals, and provides us with a detailed list containing the names and places of residence of these members. But on the other hand, using this list as any kind of indicator of genuine cult activity is hampered by the fact that although Isobel's fairy-related coven-activities are relatively undemonized, her list of coven members – just by virtue of being a list of coven members – is articulated through the language of elite witchcraft discourse. And as such it must be viewed critically.

Although, for example, all of the coven members named by Isobel lived in the Auldearn area at the time, the little evidence we do have suggests that they were not all self-conscious members of any kind of cult. Doubts are cast, for example, by the sheer numbers of people involved. If Isobel is to be believed, no less than thirteen local men and women regularly participated in the activities relating to her coven, while her reference to 'the uth[e]r coven' that met them at the 'howssis at the woodend of Inshoch' implies at least the same number, totalling twenty-six participants in this region of Nairnshire alone. Janet Breadheid's claims are even more unbelievable. The Nairn witch claimed that at the time of her initiation her coven boasted a membership of forty, only ten of whom corresponded to those on Isobel's list, and even if Janet's list included the supposed members of other covens this is still a huge number. To these incongruities, we can add the fact that one of the allegations of coven membership was almost certainly false. Although both Isobel and Janet claimed that a woman from Auldearn, named Bessie Hay, was a prominent member of their coven, the evidence suggests that the woman they referred to – and whom Brodie claimed was being hounded, in 1662, by accusations of witchcraft – was 'the dame of the school' attended by the sons of the local lairds. As a pillar of the community, waged by the Roses of Kilravock and others, it is unlikely that Hay would have consciously participated in cultic meetings composed of subversive cottar's wives, however convinced they were of her presence there.[17]

That Isobel's list of coven members did not wholly reflect reality is further intimated – and here more soundly – by the fact that the interrogators themselves do not seem to have found it very convincing. So far as we know, with the exception of Janet Breadheid, none of the other named accomplices were charged at the time, although some may have been interrogated and then released. Certainly, the privy council issued a commission to try only Isobel and Janet during this period, while Bessie Hay, though roundly accused by both women, seems to have been walking free six months later.[18] This interrogatorial scepticism is also evident in the conversation held between Brodie and justice depute Alexander Colville around the time when Isobel's confessions were being presented to the privy council. Although the question of accomplice-allegation was clearly important to both men (as evinced by the fact that it headed Brodie's list of the topics discussed at the meeting) Colville nevertheless told Brodie that 'A deposition that they saw persons ther, cannot without other evidenc prov them present'.[19]

So if Isobel's long and detailed list of coven members did not reflect reality and the interrogators did not find it convincing, then we need to ask: why did she produce it? On the one hand, we cannot rule out the possibility that, in response to close and curious 'Who else was in your coven?'-type questioning, Isobel simply made the list up. But the research undertaken during the course of this book challenges such a simplistic conclusion. Any assumption that she made these allegations out of madness or spite must be tempered by the fact that, as we have argued in earlier chapters, there are no grounds for assuming that Isobel suffered from severe mental illness, or that she was unusually vindictive. The possibility that she may have produced the list of coven members as a with or without belief coerced-compliant false confession, in a bid for leniency, is more persuasive, but as we argued in CHAPTER NINE, it is hard to believe

that she would have maintained this elaborate fiction throughout the six-week interrogatorial period, seemingly without doubt or recantation. Indeed, the fact that Janet
Breadheid produced a list of coven members three times as long suggests that, if
anything, that Isobel employed some restraint in this matter. Most persuasive of all is
the possibility that Isobel's convictions surrounding coven membership may have
developed during imprisonment and interrogation, as a result of false-memory generated in response to close questioning; although the fact that both she and Janet
Breadheid gave such a full account of their fellow members during their first interrogations renders this hypothesis only partly satisfactory.

But while there is likely to be truth in some of these possibilities, particularly with
regard to false-memory generation, in considering them the question that immediately
presents itself is: was this really all there was to it? Was Isobel's list of coven members
purely constructed out of thin air? And here, we need to return to the question of
visionary experience. Given the fact that we have argued that the fairy lore, intermediate, and perhaps even the demonologically-themed activities allegedly undertaken
by Isobel's coven, such as feasting and dancing in the presence of the Devil and making
the demonic pact, may have been constructed around some kind of experiential shamanistic core, it would be illogical not to look at Isobel's coven membership from the same
perspective. In other words, we must explore the idea that Isobel's coven members were,
at their root, envisioned phenomena encountered prior to arrest.

The Spirit-Group Characters

If we gather together a wide selection of medieval and early modern spirit-group narratives suggestive of both folkloric origin and shamanistic visionary experience (ranging
from the accounts of the *benandanti* and *donas de fuera* to undemonized or only mini-
mally-demonized Scottish fairy-host narratives), we can identify six basic categories of
participant:

1. Non-human spirits.
2. Living humans known personally to the visionary.
3. Living humans 'known of', but not known personally to the visionary.
4. Dead humans known personally to the visionary.
5. Dead humans 'known of', but not known personally to the visionary.
6. Persons, either living or dead, unknown to and unnamed by, the visionary.

In the context of the present discussion, the most remarkable feature of this cast of characters is that it represents an accurate and sophisticated reflection of the behaviour of
the visionary mind. One of the trans-historical and trans-cultural features of the
visionary experience is that it does not discriminate between the living and the dead,
the unknown and the known, the human and the non-human. Any individual who has
ever dreamed or daydreamed will know that in these states it is possible to encounter
family and friends who have died alongside those still living, to see known people

mingling with the unknown, and to encounter persons only previously known through image or reputation.

But while this conflation of so many levels of human experience and memory is a universal feature of the visionary mind, the six character-categories cited above are additionally notable in the sense that they specifically reflect the preoccupations of the pre-industrial mentality. The prominence of non-human spirits reflects the contemporary belief that spirits congregated as groups or hosts and that humans, both living and dead, could participate in their activities. The prominence of the dead reflects the simple fact that in this period every man, woman and child would have known many family members, friends and acquaintances 'translated from life to eternity', and the frequency of bereavement would have ensured that most people, most of the time, would have gone about their business carrying vivid images of the recently-dead in their minds. The prominence of communal activity in these visions reflects the fact that the sense of self would have been linked more closely to membership of a group – whether family, fermtoun, estate or clan – than to identity as an individual. Most men and women would have spent every day of their lives engaged in communal activities, from reaping, washing and collecting peat to attending markets or church, and this commonality would have been replicated on the visionary plane. In other words, if an early modern individual underwent a dream or vision experience in which they travelled on a windlestraw through the air with the fairies; they were very likely to imagine that they had done so, as they did most things in waking life, in the company of others.

Spirit-Group Characters and the Demonological Narrative

With regard to our analysis of Isobel's coven, what is also notable here is that if we take this six character-category template – which has been constructed using folkloric spirit-group narratives – and superimpose it onto the more demonologically themed 'coven-narratives', we find both accordance and contrast. From the beginning to the end of the early modern period we find the latter containing more than one, and often many, of the six character-categories cited above. But these accounts differ from folkloric spirit-group narratives in general in the sense that they disproportionately emphasize the 'living humans known personally to the visionary' category at the expense of all others. This emphasis is no accident. If we look at Scottish spirit-group narratives as a whole, both fairy-related and demonological, we find that as a general rule the more demonological the narrative, the more likely it is that the 'known living human' category, as we can précis it here, will be heavily emphasized. For example, in the fairy-related and mildly-demonized spirit-group narratives given by Cristan Nauchty (Elgin, 1629) and Jonet Morison (Bute, 1662) the known living human presence is either absent or minimal, the former telling the Elgin session that there were 'above ane hundreth' present at her meeting but that she 'knew no man bot Johne Mowtra and ane Packman quho wer dead lang ago'; and the latter informing her interrogators that 'that tyme quhairin she spoke with the devil in the Ferne quhen the great army went by she knew none of the companie bot only Jonet McNicoll'.[20] But in the more heavily demonized and stereotypical account given by East Lothian cunning woman Agnes Sampson in 1591, by comparison, only known living humans and the Devil are listed as present at the coven meeting.[21] In this context it is interesting to note that the cast of characters described in Isobel's confessions, in keeping with the latter's status as narratives combining folkloric and demonological elements to an unprecedented degree, fully span this continuum. Like any narrative containing strong demonological themes, known living humans (that is, the coven-members) are very prominent. But as in many fairy-related narratives, other categories of participant also emerge as distinctive, including both non-human spirits (the Devil, elf boys, the king and queen of the fairies, the helping spirits); the known dead ('any th[a]t ar shot be us, their sowell will goe to hevin bot ther bodies remains w[i]th ws'); the 'known of by reputation' dead ('Thomas the fearie' and the 'read reiver') and the unnamed living (as in the members of the other covens).[22]

Envisioned Coven Members

These perspectives suggest that although coven-narratives characteristically emphasize known living participants more than their folkloric counterparts, it would be unreasonable to automatically assume that this difference denoted a difference in the epistemological status of the experiences described. If we are prepared to accept that a known living human appearing in a folkloric narrative may have been an envisioned phenomenon then we must concede that the same may have been true for the known living human appearing in a demonological one. And as a consequence, we cannot rule out the possibility that some coven-member allegations were rooted in prior-to-arrest envisioned encounters.

Moreover, in the light of out knowledge about contemporary attitudes toward visionary experience, this conclusion is, in fact, logical. Because visionary phenomena were still interpreted literally in the early modern period – particularly, as we have seen in CHAPTER TEN, on a popular level – if an individual encountered the likeness of a relative or acquaintance during a coven-related visionary experience they could quite conceivably have interpreted this encounter as evidence that the person was actually present and participating in events, whether in spirit, subtle body or physical body. Moreover, such a conviction would not have necessitated encountering an accurate visionary representation of the person involved. As we emphasized in CHAPTER SIXTEEN, visual signs are only one of many ways in which the mind identifies a visionary image: with sound, context and, most notably of all, feeling or sense playing an equally important role. In addition, in the early modern period this multi-layered approach to identification would have been further nuanced by the inherited belief that, like spirits, human subtle bodies possessed malleable properties and shape-shifting abilities that enabled them to theoretically appear in any likeness they wished. Taking these factors together we can speculate that an individual undergoing a spirit-group related visionary experience could have positively identified individuals present on the basis of the flimsiest visual evidence, the defining conviction being the fact that they merely felt or sensed that they were there. Such a detection process is intimated in Alloa witch Margaret Tailzour's allegation, in 1658, that Margaret Duchall had appeared before her at a sabbath meeting, despite the fact that she 'came to her in the likeness of ane catt'; and in Bute cunning woman Jonet Morison's claim, in 1662, that 'at that meeting with the devil at But Kyie she hard one speake to him like Donald McConochies wife in Ardroskadill, Margaret McIlduy. She saw hir bot she wold not know her wele bot she knew that it was hir voice.'[23]

These perspectives enable us to look at erroneous accomplice-allegations, that is, instances where individuals falsely accused their friends and neighbours of being present at coven meetings, in a new way. While there is no doubt that unfounded allegations were made in response to interrogatorial pressure, or out of malice, or as a result of false-memory generation, some may have been genuine in the sense that they were motivated by prior visionary experience. According to the dynamic between contemporary belief and visionary experience described above, an individual could have genuinely believed that they had encountered a particular woman at an envisioned coven meeting while the woman in question, not being privy to these visionary events, could have gone about her daily business completely unaware of her supposed involvement. From this perspective, we can see why a suspect like Lillias Adie (Fife, 1704) could claim that her neighbour's presence at her coven meeting was 'as true as the sun shines on that floor', while her neighbour, who had no recollection of the event, could have claimed, just as genuinely, that as surely as the shone on that floor she hadn't.[24] That this type of dynamic lay behind coven-membership allegations is supported by the fact that some of those witchcraft interrogators who gave credence to the 'sabbath as illusion' paradigm seem to have suspected as much. We have already seen that during their conversation in 1662, Colville told Brodie that coven-membership allegations could not always be proved, but it is interesting to note that the justice depute did not urge scepticism on this point because he believed that suspects made their allegations up, but because he believed that they were duped by visual illusion. The full entry, as it appeared in Brodie's diary, reads: '[Colville] told me, 1. A deposition that they saw persons ther, cannot without other evidenc prov them present, becaus *the devel can mak appeirances fals* [my italics].'[25]

Taking these perspectives together, we can hesitantly speculate that the tendency for stereotypical coven-narratives to emphasize known living persons, as opposed to any other category on our spirit-group character list, did not reflect epistemological divergence from folkloric spirit-group narratives so much as exposure to demonological propaganda. Witchcraft interrogators, armed with preconceptions about the stereotypical witches' coven, would have pressed their suspects hard for the identity of known living accomplices. The suspects, in turn, would have scoured their memories of prior spirit-group-related visionary experience in response, producing more living human names than they would have done in less coercive arenas. Additionally, as the early modern period progressed, the internalization of elite ideas about witches' covens among the general population would have generated reflective dreams and visions. In other words, people who anticipate that they are likely to encounter a group of known living persons, as opposed to predominantly fairies and the dead, during spirit-group experiences are both more likely to encounter them and more likely to subsume more indeterminate envisioned beings under the known living human category. Coming back to Pócs' thesis, this process can be seen to represent the experiential dimension of the 'witchization' of folkloric spirit-group narratives.

Isobel's Envisioned Coven

These perspectives enable us to speculate that although Isobel's list of coven members may not have reflected any kind of physical reality, it may have emerged out of a genuine conviction that she had encountered at least some of the named men and women during visionary experience prior to her arrest and interrogation. Furthermore, this hypothesis would convincingly explain, perhaps better than any other, why Isobel seems to have divulged her coven membership with such certainty, and yet why her interrogators seem to have taken so little notice of it. But although this explanation is plausible, it throws up many questions that must be answered before we can give it serious consideration. As we have seen previously, all the evidence suggests that Isobel was acquainted with Janet Breadheid, who lived at neighbouring Belmakeith. Indeed, the arguments developed in CHAPTER EIGHT (that is, that the two women, along with others, may have gathered in each other's cottages to perform basic *maleficium*) suggest that their acquaintance may have been intimate. But this simple fact begs the question: if Isobel genuinely believed, as we have argued here, that Janet was with her, either in body, subtle body or spirit, when she feasted with the king and queen of the fairies under the Downie Hill, covenanted with the Devil in Auldearn church and shot elf arrows with the fairy host, then how did she integrate this belief into her relationship with the real, physical Janet? Similarly, if Isobel genuinely believed that she had shared arrow-shooting and pact-making experiences with other friends and neighbours, with whom she may not have been so intimate but who she would undoubtedly have encountered at local markets, or the roads and beaches between Nairn and Lochloy, then how did she manage these convictions alongside her day-to-day interactions with them? Did Isobel share her visions with these men and women? Were they aware of the role they played in her inner life? Did they concede that they had, in some way, played a part in Isobel's visionary rites? And equally importantly: did they themselves experience visions similar to Isobel's? Did they believe that they had also convened at the quarters, feasted in fairyland, flown in fairy whirlwinds and made pacts with the Devil? And did they believe that they had participated in these events alongside either Isobel or Janet? At this juncture, what becomes immediately apparent is that by acknowledging that coven members could have been shamanistic envisioned phenomena, we have inadvertently taken a small, but highly significant step towards a different kind of hypothesis altogether. For if we answer 'yes' to any of the last three questions, we find ourselves suddenly looking at the possible existence of a shamanistic cult.

The Dream Cults

In exploring whether Isobel was a member of a shamanistic cult, we can immediately narrow our focus by excluding the question of communal ecstatic rites. While we cannot rule these out completely (there is firm evidence, for example, that in England and Continental Europe in this period groups of men and women performed visionary rites prohibited by the church), there is insufficient data to attempt to prove or disprove the matter here.[26] With regard to this question we must take the ambiguous 'probably not, but can't rule it out' position taken by Pócs, Ginzburg et al. But in dismissing the idea that Isobel and her companions engaged in communal physical rites we are not ruling out the possibility that they considered themselves to participate in cultic activity. As we have seen earlier, although historians acknowledge that some shamanistic cults (such as the Rumanian *cǎluṣarii*) were defined by collective physical rituals, they also acknowledge that in this period cult identity could also be forged through rites that seem to have been solely visionary in nature, with some scholars employing the evocative term 'dream cult' to define the phenomenon. Indeed, the documentation suggests that in early modern Europe, shamanistic-cult traditions were more likely to fall into the second category than the first.[27]

It is clear that Isobel's cult, if it is to be found anywhere, is to be found here. But any immediate understanding of Isobel's coven as 'dream cult' is thwarted by the fact that, even at its most fully documented, the phenomenon slips through the fingers like a handful of water whenever you try to grasp it. Although dream cults have attained a certain notoriety through the works of scholars like Ginzburg and Henningsen, the latter generally employ the term 'cult' as a given, and focus on dream or vision content as opposed to the social and psychological structures that may have underpinned cult membership. This emphasis has left many historians confused as to the exact nature and mechanics of these traditions, and this confusion, when combined with ongoing bewilderment surrounding the nature and definition of shamanism itself, has contributed substantially toward scholarly indifference to the shamanistic paradigm per se. But despite these problems, the need to find answers to the questions raised by Isobel's coven-narratives demands that we confront this issue, and therefore we will attempt here to construct a basic model of the way in which dream cults operated in early modern Europe. Owing to limitations of time and space, this will not be a comprehensive analysis, but will focus on those cults for which we have the most coherent and detailed documentation: the Sicilian *donas de fuera*, the Friulian *benandanti* and, although not investigated until 200 years later, the Corsican *mazzeri*.

First, the documentation confirms that dream cults undoubtedly existed as an objective phenomenon in some regions of Europe in the early modern period and that their members were recognized as such by their communities. The trial records of *benandante* Paolo Gasparutto (1575) state firmly that 'It is openly rumoured about Brazzano and other neighbouring places that this Paolo is one of the benandanti witches'; while, twenty-five years later, a letter written by an inhabitant of the Italian town of Valvasone stated that 'When my wife was in Morucis in April, thinking she would get some fun out of it, she mixed in with a crowd of gossiping women to see if she could discover who among them might be a witch or benandanti'.[28] This picture is reinforced by Henningsen's claim that in the sixteenth and seventeenth centuries 'poor Sicilians talked endlessly among themselves about the fairies, and that those of them who were themselves *donas de fuera* gladly described their wonderful adventures, even when this might be dangerous'. Carrington's observation that when she arrived in Corsica in the mid-twentieth century she was taken to visit several *mazzeri* who were 'known by reputation' is also illustrative here.[29]

But while there is evidence that cult members were known in their community, there is also evidence that they were identified as such by each other. Henningsen notes that one of the Sicilian *donas de fuera* 'entertained her friends (two of whom were themselves *donas de fuera*) with accounts of the company's tours around the houses of the town'.[30] Similarly, Carrington claimed that in mid twentieth-century Corsica 'Relations between *mazzeri* of the same village, I have heard, were friendly, if casual. They stuck together by day, conversing in a style that seemed rather brusque and unceremonious, like old drinking companions, I was told, who are inclined to bicker and argue when sober.'[31] In the light of these observations, it is hardly surprising that some Friulian *benandanti* also claimed to have been personally acquainted with each other. Although as we have seen earlier, when defending himself against accusations of Murrayism, Ginzburg emphasized that real-life sectarian relationships between *benandanti* 'cannot be definitely proven', it is clear that, in *The Night Battles* at least, he assumed them to have existed. With regard to the alleged friendship between Bastiano Menos and Michele Soppe, for example, he claimed that on the basis of shared details in the men's confessions, 'we have to suppose that the two had been in contact prior to the arrest' and that examples like these make it 'clear that the reciprocal accusations of complicity made by these benandanti and the relationships by which they themselves claimed to have been bound, were not invented. They were objective, real associations, of a sectarian type.'[32]

But the picture that emerges from documentation relating to both the *mazzeri*, *donas de fuera* and *benandanti* is that although only a small number of individual cult members may have been known to each other, they considered themselves to be part of a much bigger membership of people not known or only 'known of' to the visionaries. The *dona* Vicencia la Rosa claimed that there were no less than five 'companies' in her home town of Noto, while the *benandante* Battista Moduco said that at times the *benandanti* were 'a great multitude, and at times we are five-thousand and more' and that 'Some who belong to the village know one another, and others do not.' Similarly, the *mazzeri* from one village were well aware that there were many in others, and could encounter them during hunting expeditions or annual inter-village battles, though they did not necessarily know them personally.[33]

But whether relationships with other cult members were real or visionary, and whether they were intimate or not, the thread that bound all dream-cult members together was the fact that they periodically experienced intense dreams or visions in which they performed specific magical rites for the benefit of their communities. As we touched on in CHAPTER TEN, these experiences seem to have been predominantly solitary and to have occurred most commonly at night, while the visionary lay in bed.

The trial records of Paolo Gasparutto state that 'when he goes to these games his body stayed in bed'; one of the Sicilian *donas* reported that 'All this seemed to her to be taking place in a dream, for when she awoke she always found herself in bed, naked as when she had gone to rest'; while, according to Carrington, most *mazzeri* 'stay in their beds at night; [and] their more or less incredible hunting tales are the matter of dreams'.[34] But although their dreams and visions were experienced when they were alone, cult members believed themselves to be connected to each other by virtue of the fact that their envisioned experiences shared similar imagery, narrative and magical intent. The *benandanti* fought witches and evil sorcerers for the fertility of the fields; the *donas* participated in festive meetings and house-to-house processions in order to bring prosperity and health to their community; and the *mazzeri* engaged in pack-killing, or fighting with enemy *mazzeri*, as a form of death-divination and defensive assault sorcery. Cult members were also united by their shared belief that their experiences took place on the same nights of the year. The *benandanti* met on 'Thursdays during the Ember Days of the year'; the *donas de fuera* met, according to one informant 'in the month of March' or 'on Tuesday, Thursday and Saturday night'; while the *mazzeri* engaged in their big annual battle on the night between 31 July and 1 August.[35] As we shall explore in more depth later in this chapter, at its most esoteric, cult membership was forged by the fact that individuals believed themselves to have participated in the same ritual events, in the same place and at exactly the same time.

But while these perspectives from Corsica, Friuli and Sicily give us a relatively coherent view of the basic mechanics of the early modern dream cult and enable us to gain a sense of how cult identity was forged, there is still much about the phenomenon that eludes us. While we can negotiate ourselves into a position, as we did in CHAPTER TEN, where we can appreciate that an individual shamanistic practitioner might have induced, or succumbed to, culture-patterned visionary experience in order to achieve certain magical effects, it is more of a challenge to picture how this process may have worked communally. It is hard for the modern Western mind to understand how a group of individuals could have, completely independently of each other, evoked dream or vision experiences on the same nights of the year that were so congruent that they believed themselves to have participated alongside each other in the same rites. It is also hard to envisage the kinds of relationships that developed between these visionaries, and to understand how they bonded to form a cultic identity strong enough to maintain considerable form and integrity under decades of church prohibition and persecution. Because of these difficulties, before we move on to explore in more detail the pressing question of whether some kind of dream cult existed in seventeenth-century Auldearn, we will attempt to gain a deeper understanding of dream cults in general by taking a short diversion into some contemporary research into the phenomenon known as 'mutual dreaming'.

The Mystery of Mutual Dreaming

Like most subjective states of consciousness, visionary experiences are very difficult to study under laboratory conditions, but nevertheless over the last century there has been a steady trickle of research into a variety of dream states, including lucid dreams, out-of-body experiences, flying dreams, precognitive dreams, telepathic dreams and mutual dreaming. With regard to early modern dream cults these categories are all pertinent, but the one that is most relevant and yet which has, to the best of my knowledge, received no attention from historians, is that of mutual dreaming. Defined as the phenomenon whereby two people seem to share the same or a very similar dream, the term 'mutual dreaming' has only recently been coined by researchers, but the experience seems to be a trans-historical and trans-cultural function of human consciousness, being found in sources as diverse as the Bible, ancient Persian texts and modern anthropological studies.[36] It is relatively widely reported among the current Western population and researchers maintain that it actually occurs more frequently than is currently realized, with its under-recognition being linked to the fact that we do not routinely share our dreams.[37]

It must be said from the very beginning that analysis of this phenomenon is in its very early stages, and the research that does exist is not satisfactory, for a number of reasons. First, in academic circles mutual dreaming is generally classified as a form of telepathy and therefore falls under the category of parapsychology, a subject that, despite eminent beginnings in the nineteenth century (where it was strongly linked to folkloric research) has since fought to maintain its right to academic credibility. Secondly, the literature that explores this subject is largely directed towards the popular marketplace (where interest in parapsychology is high) and the sensationalist marketing strategies employed for works such as Linda Jane Magallón's *Mutual Dreaming* unfortunately serve to mask its potential value for academic researchers.[38] Thirdly, funding for dream research of this kind is scarce, and most studies into mutual dreaming to date have been small scale, and undertaken by a limited number of research groups in North America, resulting in very little scope for cross-comparison of findings. Fourthly, and this is more an aesthetic consideration than anything else, the accounts of mutual dreams derived from psychological trials often have a disappointing sense of banality and are, as psychiatrist and dream researcher Montague Ullman notes, 'less striking qualitatively' than those derived from anecdotal literature. This difference seems to be one of degree as opposed to substance, with Ullman emphasizing that they are likely to be related to the conditions surrounding working in a laboratory.[39] And lastly, research into mutual dreaming is hampered by the fact that there are currently no adequate, or even halfway adequate, hypotheses to explain the phenomenon and that, like most parapsychological events, it is largely immune to empirical analysis. But nevertheless, although these problems exist, the evidence that has emerged from the studies undertaken to date, and the terminology that has evolved to articulate it, is highly relevant to our understanding of both shamanistic dream cults and, by implication, the witches' coven. And faced with the decision to either abstain from using this evidence until it can be corroborated by further studies (which, given the lack of funding in this area, could be a long wait) or work with what we have, we are choosing the latter option here. But it must be emphasized that in using this evidence we are not commenting on the broader question as to whether mutual dreams

– and particularly those of the more dramatic 'meeting' kind – represent genuine extra-sensory communication or mere coincidence. Psychologists Ullman, Krippner and Vaughan have collated statistically significant experimental results to suggest that the content of a sleeper's dream can be influenced by the mental preoccupations of a waking individual, and this raises the possibility that similar communications can occur between two dreamers.[40] But much more work needs to be undertaken in this area before these results can be taken seriously. As a consequence, our analysis here works on the simple premise that, though scientifically unverifiable, mutual dreams are a well-documented and perennial feature of human belief and experience. And as such, we will be approaching them in the same way that a historian approaches belief and experience surrounding ghosts or God.

The American dream researcher Linda Lane Magallón, who has either participated in or analyzed most of the mutual dream research that has taken place in the United States over the last two decades, has concluded that there are two main types of mutual dream, both of which can occur either simultaneously or separated by time. The first type, which is less common, is termed the 'meeting dream', and shall be explored in more detail later in this chapter. The second type, which forms the bulk of mutual dream experience, is termed the 'meshing dream': defined by Magallón as a general correspondence between the dream experiences of two individuals in which 'Ideas, pictures, feelings, symbols, emotions, events, or the dreamscape can be shared between dreamers.' According to Magallón, the correspondence between meshing dreams is never exact, and that 'At times there may be the sharing of only a single symbol. At other times virtually an entire dream sequence will correspond with another dreamer's.'[41] As such, meshing dreams can be said to run along a continuum of mutu-ality which ranges from low-level (where dreams contain minimal similarities) at one end to high-level (where dreams share many similarities) at the other. The differences are illustrated here.

1. The following low-level meshing dreams were recorded by co-dreamworkers, sleeping separately, on the same night:

Dream A: *There were preparations for a large-scale dinner meal for 150 people. Some people felt the meal would be stereotyped and wanted more variety than could be arranged for so many.*

Dream B: *Food is laid out on several tables – varied gourmet foods. It seems as though this has been done in Tom's honor. I am there as his guest. I am sampling foods and they are deli-cious.*[42]

2. The following intermediate-level meshing dreams were experienced by a husband and wife, sleeping in the same bed, at around 5 a.m. on the same morning:

Dream A: *I am with my two sons and we are scrambling along a sea shore, over big boul-ders. I can sense a cliff rising beside me, to my right. The waves are crashing onto the rocks and there is a feeling of menace. My eldest son has gone in front and I cannot see him and am worried.*

Dream B: *I am walking with my two sons near the edge of a cliff, on a barren peninsula. My sons run ahead. I see my eldest son clambering down the rocky cliff and I am scared.*[43]

3. The following high-level meshing dreams were recorded by two sisters in Texas, with both women claiming that they occurred around 6.30 a.m. on the same morning in 1987. Both dreams share considerable narrative detail and emotion and feature the sisters' deceased father:

Dream A: *I am at my grandparents' house even though it doesn't look like their house. Mom, Dad (deceased), my two sons, Greg and Chris, and I are there expecting a tornado. My (deceased) grandfather's essence is around, too. Mom and I get some mattresses out, and we sit on the floor around a coffee table, all except Daddy, who sits on the couch, not worried about a thing. He has an extremely white appearance. Mom sits next to my oldest son and pulls a mattress over them. I sit next to my youngest son. We are on the couch with Dad, and we pull the mattress over us. We can see the tornado is enormous and coming our way. It takes up the whole view of the picture window. I can just imagine in my mind the grinding away at the house, and then I become frightened, for the first time, for our lives. Then the tornado is some distance from us, and I know it is going to pass by. I feel protected.*

Dream B: *I am with Mom, Dad, and my two kids at a restaurant. I look out the window and see a huge tornado coming toward us. I get the kids under the table and try to shield them with my body. I feel I can get a better hold on my little boy than on my little girl. I say a prayer of protection and know I will be protected. Sure enough, the tornado moves away from us.*[44]

Conducive Conditions

Through experiential research involving many groups of people over several years, Magallón, Ullman et al. have demonstrated that certain personalities and conditions are more conducive to the generation of mutual dreaming than others. First, as with the ability to shamanize, psychological propensity seems to play a role. According to Magallón, successful mutual dreamers are 'also likely to have frequent encounters with the "borderlands" between dreaming and waking. In addition to mutual dreams, they report experiences with false awakenings, astral projection, lucidity, hypnogogia, trance, and other altered states, which are not quite waking and not quite dream'. Also interesting, in the context of traditional witch lore, is the fact that successful mutual dreamers also report a higher-than-average incidence of flying dreams: with an astonishing 61 percent, in Magallón's research projects, experiencing mutual dream flight.[45]

But in addition to psychological propensity, the conditions in which dreams are generated are also significant. Ullman, Krippner and Vaughan have shown that the incidence of dream telepathy in experimental studies is responsive to a wide range of factors, including the types of stimulus used, the atmosphere generated in the laboratory and the relationship between the dreamer and the experiment leader.[46] With regard to mutual dreaming in particular, Magallón claims that the initial task for those wishing to share dreams is that of 'reducing the physical and mental distance between oneself and another'. This can merely be physical closeness, on the simple basis that living and sleeping together 'contributes to the discovery of mutual dreams, if not their production'; Magallón noting, in reference to published spontaneous mutual dreams, that 68 percent derive from intimates, particularly friends and family members.[47] But mental closeness is even more significant. Participants in mutual dream research projects are urged to increase intimacy through sharing both waking and dream experiences with other members of the group. Particular emphasis is placed on the sharing of dream symbols. If one participant dreams of a symbol that has also appeared in another participant's dream, they are encouraged to focus on the symbol and talk in depth around it. This process, which can be likened to the mental imagery cultivation undergone by traditional shamans, is termed by Magallón as 'priming the pump' with similar imagery and 'sharing what we have in common at the dreaming level, in order to invoke continuing similarities'.[48]

But the process does not end here. Magallón claims that once you have become intimate in this way with one or more dreaming partners, you then need to devise a formula to 'hatch a dream'. Magallón's hatching formulas are similar to those found in modern imaginal therapies and in many ways reflect ancient techniques of dream incubation and induction (that is, practices involving travel to a designated place to perform physical or mental rites in order to induce a dream for a specific purpose). According to Magallón, in order to successfully hatch a dream prospective dreamers, armed with the knowledge they have gained about each other, select a goal that is mutually significant, and once the goal has been established they immerse themselves in it: thinking about it, talking about it, and writing about or drawing it as much as possible. In order to successfully harvest the fruits of these labours, participants must also develop dream recall and recording skills, of the type used in contemporary imaginal therapies; enhancing the capacity for detailed recollection through memory exercises and increasing the number of dreams remembered through night-waking and writing up. As with any form of mental imagery cultivation, the more dreams are hatched and remembered the more vivid and controllable they become. And in the case of mutual dreaming, the more individuals share their dreams, the more they mesh, and the more they mesh the more dreamers are motivated to share them. This process is characteristically underpinned by a growing positiveness and camaraderie, with Ullman noting, at the conclusion of a pilot study, that 'Work carried out in this manner results in empathic and intimate bonding among the people involved and creates conditions that stimulate psi interactions among the participants'.[49] Of all these ingredients, however, intensity of meaning and intention consistently emerge as the most important: Magallón stating that 'you will have greatest success with those goals in which you have some emotional investment' and that 'As a mutual dreamer [participating in group research], one of the strongest reasons for you to recall your dreams is that your dreams have a place to go.'[50]

Mutual Dreaming in Early Modern Europe

Given the fact that mutual dreaming seems to be a universal feature of human consciousness, we can assume that it occurred among the peoples of early modern Europe. But what is also immediately apparent is that many of the conditions defined by Magallón, Ullman et al. as particularly conducive to their generation were, in this period, naturally present. Unlike the members of twentieth-century dream-research groups, the members of early modern communities did not come from diverse backgrounds or live many miles apart, and therefore they did not have to work hard to 'reduce the physical and mental distance' between each other. Physical proximity was a given, for people slept together, ate together, worked in the same fields and barns and gathered together around the same firesides in the evenings. As for mental proximity, mentalities were inter-connected to a degree that is very difficult for the individualistic modern Western mind to appreciate. The demands of subsistence-level farming meant that all individuals were primarily tied to the same fermtoun, performing the same activities, scanning at the same horizons, listening to the same storytellers and sermons and performing the same rituals for their whole lives. In the absence of alternatives, only a small minority of the poor would have been able to individualize their minds through reading a different book or listening to different stories or attending different churches to their family, friends and neighbours. This does not mean that personalities would not have been rich and diverse, nor that thinking could not have been original, but it means that individual mentalities were sculpted out of a relatively finite pool of symbol, imagery, narrative and experience. Given this pre-existent physical and mental closeness it is not unreasonable to speculate that the incidence of mutual dreams would have been higher among the general population of early modern Europe than it is today.

But we can also speculate that not only the incidence, but also the awareness of the incidence, of mutual dreaming would have been higher in this period. In large part, this awareness would have arisen out of the fact that dreams would have been shared more frequently than they are in the modern West. As in contemporary tribal cultures, communal sleeping arrangements, segmented sleep patterns and the enhanced memorization skills characteristic of oral cultures would have encouraged both dream recall and dream sharing in the dark hours of the night or early morning. This practice would also have been stimulated by the fact that, in a world with few books and no television, radio or computers, dream relation – like any other form of oral narrative – would have been a welcome form of entertainment. But most importantly of all, early modern Europeans would have been for more motivated to both tell and listen to dreams than their modern counterparts because they believed they were potential sources of spiritual power and aid. Through dreams, an individual was not only believed to encounter illusions of mind, but also objectively real supernatural entities that still walked the world and wielded influence over the affairs of men. Certain kinds of dream encounters and certain kinds of actions employed while having them were believed to dramatically and directly affect the physical world. A dream, well dreamt, could cure a mortally sick child, predict the future, avert famine, secure a good harvest, defeat enemies and even channel the word of God. Here, we have levels of 'emotional invest-ment' and places for dreams 'to go' that modern dream researchers can barely imagine, let alone replicate.

Mutual Dream Generation and the Early Modern Dream Cult

It is perhaps no coincidence that the early modern environment, being so conducive to mutual-dream generation, should have given rise to the phenomenon of the dream cult. And if we explore the phenomenon in more depth it is clear that – though they may not have deliberately set out to do so – dream-cult members engaged in activities that actively stimulated mutual-dream production. First, we have the fact that cult members shared their visionary experiences both between themselves and – to varying degrees – with their wider communities. As we have seen earlier, Henningsen records that in 1627 a Sicilian journeyman's wife, who was also a *dona de fuera*, was alleged to have 'entertained her friends (two of whom were themselves *donas de fuera*) with evoca-tive accounts of the company's tours around the houses of the town each Tuesday, Thursday and Saturday'.[51] In Italy at around the same period the *benandante* Menichino della Nota gave an evocative description of how he frequently found himself 'discussing them [the activities of the *benandanti*] like that at night, walking single file, as was customary' with 'many people' including fellow *benandanti*. While another cult member, Battista Moduco, claimed tellingly that he 'heard from that [*benandante*] friend of mine who is in prison that an angel appeared to him'.[52]

The impact that dream narratives, shared in this way, would have had on the imag-inations of listeners – whether they were dream-cult members or not – would have been intensified by the fact that they were often detailed and dramatic. According to Henningsen, despite being forbidden to speak of her experiences by the authorities, the colourful Sicilian *dona*, Vicencia la Rosa, provided her listeners with a veritable how-to and who's-who of the activities of the *donas de fuera*, in which she 'went on telling her friends about her familiar spirit, Martinillo, who took her to the sabbath three times a week, when she consulted her "Prince" about people's diseases and bewitchings; and she told them who belonged to the Company of the Noble, and who to the Company of the Poor.' Alternatively, the following *dona* narrative, dating from the late 1630s, would have gained additional bite through being delivered at the moment of encounter itself, as part of what appears to be a classic communal shamanistic healing ritual. In order to cure a sick client from Santa Ninfa, a 'wise woman' laid out a ritual feast and then:

> said that the people she had been describing, her 'Ladies', would soon be coming, and every so often she went out into the yard and acted as if she could see them, and waved her hand to them. Shortly after this she said that they had come. And she appeared to be taking them by the hand one by one and leading them to sit down on the chairs. But neither the witnesses nor the others who were present could see anything. Then she walked up and down near the sick person and played on a tambourine, and picking up food from the plates she made as

if to put it into the mouths of her friends. She then took ceremonial leave of her friends in the same fashion, and told [the occupants of the house] that they had shown her how the sick [woman] was to be cured, and that now she was well again, for those [Ladies] had touched her with their hands.[53]

These effects would have been further magnified by the fact that dream and vision accounts were believed, by both the teller and a significant proportion of their community, to represent literal events, with Henningsen claiming, in reference to Vicencia la Rosa, that 'both listeners and story-tellers in the main believed the tales [she told] and took them seriously'.[54] The belief that the experiences described could have generated practical magical effects – whether involving healing, fertility or community protection – would have further intensified the impact they made on the imaginations of listeners. Dream and vision sharing, in this much detail, and with this level of conviction, emotional investment and intensity of purpose, would have replicated the 'priming the pump' and 'dream hatching' techniques employed by modern dream researchers to generate mutual dreams. Similarly, the contemporary belief that particular spirits could be conjured in response to particular needs, and that in order to meet them a dreamer must invoke them at a certain time, could have generated the 'mutual goal' and 'intention to meet' necessary to ensure successful dream incubations.

Contemporary sources also suggest that, as modern research has found, close friend and family networks were particularly effective at promoting mutual-dream generation, with the men who interrogated the young *benandante*, Maria Panzoni, stating that, 'she had learned all these things, including the difference between benandanti and witches, from her godfather, Vincenzo dal Bosco del Merlo, himself a benandante, as, for that matter, her father had been also'.[55] Among close-knit family groups the accumulative process through which dream sharing generates mutual dreams which then stimulates further dream sharing, could have gained great momentum. The dream narrative given by one *dona* from Palermo – in which she claimed that when 'they [the *donas*] went into the houses it was like a wind, and that they opened the chests and dressed themselves up in the clothes they found, and they played the tambourine and the lute and sang very sweetly' – sounds so seductive that it is hardly surprising to find that her son, too, 'went out with' the *donas*. That his mother's experiences were also stimulated and honed through dream-sharing with family members is suggested by her claim that both her late husband and father-in-law also went with the *donas* before they died.[56]

Some dream-cult records even provide us with glimpses of the ways in which imagery may have passed from one receptive imagination to the other. During interrogation the cowherd Menichino della Nota recounted a lively conversation in which a seasoned *benandante*, Giambattista Tamburlino, predicted that in the near future Menichino would travel in spirit to Josaphat's field to perform the *benandanti* rites and that when he did so he would go 'as though in a smoky haze'. Further on in his testimony Menichino admits that a year after these conversations he did indeed dream that he was in Josaphat's field, and that whilst there:

it felt as if I was in a field, wide, large and beautiful: and it had a scent, that is it emitted a good odour, and there appeared to be flowers and roses in abundance . . . I did not see the roses, because there was a sort of cloud and mist . . . I had the impression there were many of us together as though in a haze but we did not know one another, and it felt as if we moved through the air like smoke and that we crossed over water like smoke.[57]

Tamburlino's influence on the visionary experiences of the less experienced Menichino is even more directly illustrated in the latter's claim that 'when the combat was finished, which lasted about an hour, we all had to return and be at home by cock's crow, or else we would die, *as the aforesaid Giovambattista Tamburlino told me* [my italics]'.[58]

Although there is no space to give this subject the attention it deserves here, on the basis of the perspectives developed in this chapter thus far we can construct a rough model of the role that mutual-dream generation may have played in the early modern dream cult. As in tribal cultures today, we can suppose that the majority of dreams experienced by cult members would have been individual as opposed to culture-patterned, drawing on mostly personal details as opposed to communally and culturally-significant themes and symbols. But we can also speculate that cult members may have been bound together through the intermittent experiencing and subsequent sharing of low-level meshing dreams (whether taking place on separate or, less commonly, the same dates). We can further speculate that these low-level meshing dreams may have been intermittently punctuated, and cult identity and conviction further invigorated, by occasional and highly memorable intermediate or high-level meshing dreams in which imagery, narrative and emotion were mirrored in a detailed and striking way. Both low-level and high-level meshing dreams could have caused individuals to believe themselves to have participated in the same magically-propitious meetings, processions, battles and hunts in the same places and on the same nights of the year. And this belief would have created, as it did with Ullman's twentieth-century dreamworkers, an 'empathic and intimate bonding among the people involved'.[59]

Meeting Dreams and Cult Identity

Through this analysis of meshing dreams we have identified some of the threads that may have bound early modern dream cults together, but if we now bring meeting dreams into the equation, then the weave becomes even tighter. Recent research suggests that although meeting dreams are less common than meshing dreams, they are still relatively frequent, with Magallón claiming that 'Out of 124 published classic mutual dream accounts, slightly more than a third (36%) are meeting dreams.' In these kinds of dream experience, she elaborates, individuals do not only have similar dreams, as in the meshing dream, but 'two or more dreamers recognize or encounter one another in their dreams . . . Each of us seems to have the same appearance as our physical bodies. We often act like we do in daily life: walking around, seeing each other, talking to one another, perhaps even touching one another.'[60] As with meshing dreams, meeting dreams can be simultaneous or separated by a number of hours, days, weeks or longer and they seldom share an exact correspondence – with each dreamer, as in waking life, describing a meeting from their own point of view. The following account is typical:

> A woman in England dreams she visits a friend who seems about to die. She takes his hand and comforts him, saying that he will live. As she speaks, she hears music fill the room. On his part, her male friend has been ill to the point of death. He dreams that he requests both his woman friend and a favourite sonata by Beethoven. While the music plays, he sees the woman enter his room and speak to him encouragingly. He lives.[61]

Some dreams can be meeting for one individual and only meshing for another. In other words, one person can consciously encounter another person in a dream but the encountered individual, though experiencing a very similar dream, is absorbed in the unfolding events and does not perceive their companion. Magallón records such an event shared between a sixty-year-old woman, Elizabeth, and her daughter Molly. The former had the following dream: 'I am crying because I know I am eight months pregnant. I stand by a window, gazing out into the distance, thinking sadly about my life'. After waking, Magallón notes, Elizabeth pondered her dream, 'concerned about what it might mean for her. But before she had a chance to relate the dream to any-one, her grown up daughter, Molly, came to visit. "Oh, mother!" exclaimed Molly, "I had a dream about you this morning! You were crying in front of a mirror. And when I looked at you, I knew you were pregnant!"'[62] Also significant, with reference to dream-cult and coven narratives is the fact that meeting dreams, like meshing dreams, can reportedly be shared by more than two dreamers, can be precognitive, and can be generated through intent: with Magallón claiming in respect of the latter that, 'It is claimed that in some Eastern traditions, any two people sharing a close bond can visit each other at will in dreams. Both will be aware the following morn-ing that the visit has taken place and will agree on what has been said. Tibetan Llamas trained in Highest Yoga Tantra assured researcher David Fontana that they had experienced such intentional dream visits.'[63]

It is difficult to isolate specific instances of meeting dreams in early modern sources, particularly those as contaminated and complex as witchcraft and sorcery records, but the accounts give by some dream-cult members are strongly suggestive. As we saw earlier, in seventeenth-century Italy Bastiano Menos and Michele Soppe, who were likely to have been acquainted with each other, were interrogated for alleged *benandanti* activities. When the former came before the interrogators in 1649, he claimed that:

> One night the aforesaid Michele called me by name and said, 'Bastiano, you must come with me'; and I, who was an ignorant youth, told him 'yes'; and he mounted a cock, and made me get on a hare, both animals being in attendance outside . . . and on these creatures, as though flying swiftly over the land, we reached the field of Santa Chaterina.[64]

Several weeks later Soppe, who had already been imprisoned for several months, named

Bastiano Menos as an accomplice and claimed that on a specific day, some time previously, the two men had arranged to travel together to the *benandanti* rites:

> I mounted my goat and went to find Bastiano who was in bed; I called him by name and said to him: 'Bastiano, do you want to come with me to the dance of the witches?' And he replied, 'Yes, I do.' I had another goat with me, and Bastiano mounted it, and together we rode off to the dance of the witches in Santa Catarina's field beyond the Cormor, on the road between Udine and Codroipo.[65]

It would be easy to suppose that the congruities found in the two testimonies (which afterwards diverge quite dramatically) were the result of interrogatorial superimposition. But according to Ginzburg, the men had not been in contact since Soppe had been imprisoned several months earlier; and Soppe named Bastiano and described their mutual travelling experience 'without the benefit of any prompting, or even hints, on the part of the inquisitor'. The inquisitor, meanwhile, was allegedly so 'visibly struck by the similarities and connections in the confessions of Michele Soppe and Bastiano Menos' that he was motivated to pursue the case further and arrest another *benandante* named by the men.[66] Ginzburg does not explore the roots of this, as he terms it, 'absolute agreement' between elements of Soppe's and Menos's confessions, but in the context of contemporary dream research we can speculate, tentatively, that it was rooted in prior meeting-dream experience. Interestingly, similar interrogatorial bemusement, in the face of improbably-similar testimonies, can be found in documentation relating to Scottish witchcraft trials, notable among these being the Renfrewshire prosecutions of 1697. A contemporary abbreviation of the commissioners' report for the trial of Elizabeth Anderson and James and Thomas Lindsay states that:

> It is to be noticed that the three confessants were separately apprehended upon several occasions, so they (after the obstinacy to discover was abated) did emit these confessions in several distinct places, without communication with, or knowledge of, another's confession in manner mentioned in the preceding narrative. The commissioners did examine them upon other trying questions that were new, thereby to make experiment of their consonancy or disagreement, but still found them strangely to accord.[67]

We also find anecdotes suggestive of precognitive meeting dreams in the documentation relating to European dream cults. In *Mutual Dreaming* Magallón cites the following dream, recorded by a fellow dreamworker:

> [My friend Alison dreamed that the door opened] and a totally strange but handsome young man entered. They greeted each other warmly, and were soon making passionate love. This dream was real and vivid; Alison was shaken by it. Within two weeks, at a dance she met this man. When they became better acquainted, each described the same vivid precognitive love dream. They are now married and the proud parents of two beautiful daughters. I suspect that this sort of preliminary meeting dream occurs rather frequently.[68]

The following account, recorded by Dorothy Carrington, and describing the mutual dream experiences of two Corsican *mazzeri*, is structurally identical to Alison's precognitive dream. Although, as a second-hand account, it is not evidence that these reflective dreams were actually experienced in mid twentieth-century Corsica, it is evidence that the idea of mutual dreaming existed in the *mazzeri* tradition:

> As so often happens in Corsica, a stranger came to join us. Without prompting he spoke to us of the *mazzeri*. A friend of his, he said, was a practising *mazzeru*; he hunted with others of his kind, all people of his village, save one, whom he had been unable to identify. Recently a Sardinian labourer had come to work in the district. The *mazzeru* at once recognized him as the unknown hunter of his dreams, while the Sardinian greeted him as the companion of his own hunting dreams whom he had never so far recognized.[69]

It is impossible to gauge how common meeting-dream experiences may have been in early modern Europe. Even if we speculate, as we have done with regard to meshing dreams, that in response to favourable conditions they were likely to have been more common, more intentioned and more specific than they are in the modern West, we must still be cautious with regard to extent. But however frequent, meeting dreams would undoubtedly have made their presence felt. As anyone who has ever experienced this type of dream will testify, such an experience need only happen once to profoundly alter an individual's world-view, and predispose them to a level of conviction and visionary experimentation that can last many years, if not a lifetime. In terms of early modern perceptions, a single meeting dream, if it were powerful enough, could have convinced two dreamers that they had genuinely encountered each other in the other world and generated the emotional resonance to nurture cult identity. Such experiences would then have reinforced their belief in the reality and effectiveness of the visionary rites experienced during the more common low and intermediate-level meshing dreams.

Dream Cults in Early Modern Auldearn

Armed with this more nuanced view of how the early modern dream cult may have operated, we can now return to our original task: that of determining whether such a cult may have existed in seventeenth-century Auldearn. Unfortunately, the main problem here is the lack of sources. In constructing a picture of the *benandanti*, *mazzeri* and *donas de fuera*, we have been able to draw on a wide number of testimonies, mostly undemonized or only partly demonized, that emerged out of the same region over a period of many decades. When spliced together these separate testimonies, though signifying little individually, form a relatively-coherent composite picture of the cult under analysis. In the case of the hypothetical Auldearn cult, we have only five semi-demonized confessions, with four of them relating to a single individual, and with all of them coming from a single point in time. Although we know that witchcraft allegations were made in this region both before and after 1662, with the first being as early as 1643; that by the mid-1650s the local lairds considered 'that desolat plac Auldearn' to be a veritable hotbed of witchcraft; and that some of those accused of the crime over these decades were aware of each other's existence, we have no documentary evidence with which to flesh out these scattered facts. Our analysis, therefore, must be highly speculative.

Having said this, both Isobel's and Janet's testimony contain suggestive elements. As we noted in CHAPTER TEN, Isobel makes specific reference to the fact that she and her fellow coven-members embarked on their spirit-group experiences at night, claiming that they left brooms or stools in their beds lest 'owr husbandis sould miss ws'. While this could, of course, be either a folkloric reference unrelated to visionary experience or a reference to non-cultic trance states, it clearly resembles the ways in which both the *benandanti*, *donas de fuera* and *mazzeri* visionaries described their nocturnal shamanistic raptures. Indeed, Isobel's evident concern about her husband's response to her nocturnal journeys reflects the challenges faced by other dream-cult members who were compelled to undergo their envisioned rites in the intimacy of the family bed. The wife of *benandante* Paolo Gasparutto told the court that 'one night, about the fourth hour before daylight, I had to get up, and because I was afraid I called to my husband Paolo so that he would get up too, and even though I called him perhaps ten times and shook him, I could not manage to wake him, and he lay face up'.[70] When challenged in the morning, Paolo admitted that his body had been 'without its spirit' because he had been participating in *benandanti* rites; but the fact that, during eight years of marriage, this was seemingly the only time that Gasparutto's wife had observed his catalepsy, suggests that it generally went unnoticed. We can see that Isobel's belief that she left a broom in her bed when travelling with her coven would have enabled her to rationalize the fact that John Gilbert – who, like Gasparutto's wife, does not seem to have been a visionary himself – did not always notice her nocturnal journeys. As we have seen in CHAPTER TEN, Isobel's choice of a stool or broom to function as a false body reflected the common observation that, when in shamanistic catalepsy, the body was 'stiff as a log'.[71]

The possibility that Isobel's coven-related activities may have represented cultic activity is also raised by the fact that both her's and Janet's confessions display that same awareness of both widespread membership (largely composed of unknown persons) and more localised membership (largely composed of known), that is such a feature of the testimony of the *benandanti* et al. As we have seen earlier, Isobel makes clear reference to the presence of other covens, stating in her first confession that while she and her accomplices were 'besyd the meickle burne' the 'uth[e]r coven' were 'at the downiehillis, (*and*) we went from beyond the meickle burne and went besyd them to the howssis at the woodend of Inshoch'. That she believed the number of local covens to be greater than two is indicated by her claim, in the third confession, that separate covens meet individually but that 'the multitud of owr all o[u]r coevens' congregate at certain times of the year for a 'grand meitting'. Janet Breadheid also talks of 'great meit-tings' when many were present and smaller gatherings 'qhen ther wold be bot fewar'. In her first confession and almost certainly in response to questioning, Isobel also iden-tifies two members of one of these alternative covens, the passage beginning 'margret kyllie in (*blank*) is on of the uth[e]r coven meslie hirdall spows to allexr ross in lonheid is on of th[e]m, hir skin is fyrie'. But after this reference she quickly returns to her own coven and the subject is not returned to again. As a general rule both Isobel's and Janet's allusions to other covens resemble the non-specific references made by *donas de fuera* to 'other companyes' and the *benandanti* to 'other armies' and the Corsicans to 'foreign *mazzeri*'.

The possibility that Isobel and Janet participated in cultic activity is also suggested, in a more general sense, by the general congruity between their confessions. As we have seen earlier, dream-cult membership is established through the experiencing of similarly-themed dream or vision rites, and Isobel and Janet both claimed to have participated in coven-related activities that included covenanting and having sex with the Devil, gathering at meetings presided over by an 'officer' and a 'maiden', feasting, elf-arrow shooting, transforming into animals, engaging in house-to-house visits and performing *maleficium*. Obviously we can attribute some of this congruence to elite intervention. It could also be argued that – even if the confessions reflected prior shamanistic experience – their similarities merely reflect the fact that, as visionary practitioners inhabiting same region, both Isobel and Janet would have drawn on the same pool of folkloric and demonological lore to fashion their personal dream or vision phenomena. In this case, non-cultic experiences that had occurred completely independently of each other would have been homogenized after the women's arrest for witchcraft, purely through interrogatorial cross-pollination.

But this hypothesis becomes less feasible, and the cult hypothesis stronger, when we take into account the fact that in this period the likelihood that a person could experience an encounter with a spirit 'completely independently' of anyone else, was very slim. In seventeenth-century Scotland, men and women who experienced culture-patterned dreams and visions were highly likely to have shared their experiences with others. Encounters with all kinds of spirits were widely publicized and talked about and fairies were no exception. In March 1660, for example, 'Rothesay kirk session was told that the *whole district* was talking about Jean Campbell because she was going with the fairies [my italics]'.[72] While this particular case was attributed to slander, it is clear that many fairy-related accounts came directly from the visionaries themselves. It took only a few 'smooth words and a piece of money' to persuade the mid seventeenth-century 'Fairy Boy of Leith' to freely divulge his experiences of feasting under the local fairy hill to the curious Captain George Burton; while a century later, according to Kirkmichael minister John Grant, a Banff clergyman who believed himself to have been swept away by a fairy whirlwind, did not keep his experiences to himself but 'often recited to the wondering circle the marvellous tale of his adventure'.[73] Fairy encounters were similarly hot currency in contemporary Perthshire where, as we have seen, Pennant noted of the visions of a Breadalbane seer: 'it is incredible the mischief these *Aegri Somnia* did in the neighbourhood . . . the almost extinct belief of the old idle tales began again to gain ground, and the good minister will have many a weary discourse and exhortation before he can eradicate the absurd ideas this idle story has revived'.[74] One hundred years later, as the works of J. F. Campbell et al. attest, Highlanders were equally eager to disclose details of their host-related house-to-house processions and arrow-shooting hunts. On a more formal level, dream disclosure was a compulsory aspect of the Scottish shamanistic practitioner's work. Seers gained their reputations through reporting both spontaneous and induced premonitions of danger and death to the persons concerned, while those who worked with envisioned familiars characteristically sought out their spirit's help before reporting their findings to their client, with Duns cunning man Harry Wilson (1669), whose familiar regularly appeared to him in the form of a woman, typically claiming that 'when anybody came to him to inquire anent things lost or stolen, that he gave no perfect answer, but appointed them to come to him some other day; and in the mean time, the said woman appeared to him in the night and informed him how to answer'.[75]

There is also evidence to suggest that in early modern Scotland, as in other parts of Europe in this period, visionary narratives could be both vivid and detailed. Given their immersion in the predominantly oral culture of the poor, it is hardly surprising that some of the men and women who narrated fairy-encounters deployed language and imagery worthy of the liveliest ballad or fireside epic. No-one could have listened to the evocative accounts given by Donald McIlmichall or Alison Peirson, for example, without failing to gain a powerful and viscerally-real picture of the elven folk as they feasted and danced in candle-lit halls beneath the green fairy hills. Such accounts could also contain detailed instructions on the generation and management of visionary experience, of the type passed between the *benandanti* and *donas de fuera*. Robert Kirk's description of how the seer guides his novices through vision-inducing crown-sole rituals, and 'conforts' them when struck 'breathles and speechless' by the 'multitude of Wights' invoked, reflects the precision noted earlier in the exchanges between Giambattista Tamburlino and Menichino della Nota.[76] We can also see this complex sharing process at work between Aberdeenshire cunning man Thomas Leys and his lover, Elspeth Reid. The latter claimed that on one occasion Leys instructed her to perform a variant of the crown-sole ritual described by Kirk, while on another, according to his trial dittays, he asked her:

> Will thou use my counsall and do as I command the, and sayid we suld gett geir aneucht. Quha [Elspeth] ansuerit to the and sayid, Quhat is that, that ye wald have me doing? And thou [Leys] sayid, Thair is ane [fairy?] hill betwixt this and Murray, and at the fute thairof thow should gar ane man ryse and plene appeir to hir, in ony lyiknes scho pleisit; and that thou suld speik the man first thi selff, that scho suld nocht feir, and becum that manis servand, and do as he commandit hir, and scho suld nevir want.[77]

The records of the interrogation of Perth cunning women Janet Trall and Isobel Haldane suggest that dream sharing could not only function as a source of entertainment and instruction in this period, but also as a source of emotional support. In 1623 Trall told the Perth sessions that although she healed using fairy-derived skill, she had sometimes been 'puddled and troubled' by her encounters with these spirits, claiming that on one occasion 'when she was going out of this town, they [the fairies] dang her down, and she was then beside herself, ready to eat the ground, and continued so until she came to Isabell Haldane's house, and got a drink from her'. That she sought refuge in Haldane's house was unlikely to have been mere coincidence. Not only did Haldane also have fairy-encountering experience – claiming to have gained healing skills from a man with a 'gray beard' whom she had met in fairyland – but the two women clearly enjoyed a working partnership that involved the sharing of magical knowledge; Haldane claiming, for example, that she had performed a healing ritual 'according to the direction of Janet Trall'. As a consequence of this working intimacy, we can assume that that when the frightened Trall took refuge in her neighbour's house she gained not only 'a drink from her', but also comfort and advice concerning the distressing fairy encounter that had driven her there.[78] In conclusion, although much of the Scottish evidence is frustratingly fragmentary and ambiguous, when taken as a whole and set alongside the more comprehensive evidence coming from Continental Europe, we can reasonably speculate that in early modern Scotland dream and vision sharing, occurring between those who 'believed the tales and took them seriously' would have 'primed the pump' sufficiently to effectively incubate mutual dreams.

Isobel and Janet: Cult Members?

With regard to Isobel and Janet, then, the stage was well set. We have speculated that the two women were acquainted. And we have speculated that they both regularly experienced spirit-group-related visionary experience. Given the fact that in this period those who underwent these kinds of experiences were highly likely to have recounted them to others, we can reasonably surmise that during the course of Isobel and Janet's day-to-day interactions, their dream and vision experiences were shared. And with this simple fact, we find ourselves, arguably, at the end of our search. For if we accept the possibility that both Isobel and Janet were shamanistic magical practitioners; that their confessions were rooted in prior visionary experience; that their respective visionary experiences were similar; and that they shared them with each other – we have, in effect, the core dynamics of a dream cult. Because visionary experiences were so closely associated with the getting of magical power in this period it is highly unlikely that, as magical practitioners, Isobel and Janet would have consistently shared dreams simply for idle entertainment, exchanging 'isn't that funny, our dreams are so similar' remarks while they were waiting for the corn to be dried and then passing onto something more interesting. It is much more likely that these exchanges were serious matters and that the women defined themselves as magical practitioners and identified themselves with each other by virtue of them.

Pertinently, a number of ambiguous statements in both women's confessions could be seen to support this view. As we have noted several times in the book, in her third confession Isobel states that 'Janet Breadheid spows to Jon taylor told me a litle befor she wes apprehendit th[a]t margret wilsoen in aulderne shot allexr hutcheon in aulderne'(48/1). This conversation, which is not mentioned by Janet, could have been a figment of Isobel's imagination that emerged as part of a coerced-compliant or false-memory response to interrogatorial demands to provide information about other coven members. But on the other hand, as a bald statement of fact it has a ring of truth. Whether Janet made the claim because she saw Margaret Wilson shoot the arrow during a visionary experience, or whether she made it because Margaret had herself told her about the event, is immaterial in this context. Both suggest a two-way, or even three-way (if Margaret was involved) conversation between visionaries regarding the details of dream and vision rites. That such conversations were not isolated occurrences and that they did not only occur between these three women, is suggested by Janet's further claims that 'it wes keathren sowter th[a]t wes brunt th[a]t (*verb missing here, speculated as 'shot'*) w[illia]m hay the Last Laird of parkis broth[e]r for on gilbert kintey' and 'Agnes grant who wes brunt on the (*damaged, words missing*) hill of (*blank*) gott hyre from elspet monro to destroy the Lairdis of park and lochloy' (544/43). Of course it is possible that these references originated in gossip freely available to anyone in the region. But it is equally possible, in the light of the three-way conversation we have speculated between Isobel, Janet and Margaret, that they also represented a sharing or – given the time scale involved – handing down of information between magical practitioners concerning the ritual performance of *maleficium*. And if we accept Pitcairn's assertion that the Sowter reference concerned an elf-arrow shooting, then these comments could be seen to support the view that women in the Auldearn region self-consciously allied themselves with each other in the belief that they experienced collective fairy-hunt related visionary rites.

In absence of firm evidence, this hypothesis can only be highly speculative, but it is indirectly supported by the fact that we occasionally find similar – equally fleeting but equally tantalising – references in other coven-narratives. As we have noted in CHAPTER TWELVE, though they do not specifically incorporate arrow shooting, the destructive child-killing house-to-house perambulations of the 1658 Alloa coven are strongly redolent of Isobel's maleficent coven activities and we can speculate that they, too, represented dream-cult rites that may have involved death or sickness divination or transferral and personal or client-commissioned revenge killing. In this context, the resemblance between Isobel's claim that Janet Breadheid 'told me a litle befor she wes apprehendit th[a]t margret wilsoen in aulderne shot allexr hutcheon' and Alloa coven-member Margaret Tailzour's claim that 'Jonet Black . . . said that she wes the death of ane bairne in Tullibodie of Marie Moreis and that Margaret Duchall told her that they were at Clackmannan and killed ane bairn to Thomas Bruce', is striking. Margaret Tailzour's subsequent claim that 'Jonet Millar in Tullibodie told her that the divell haid appeired to her' could also be interpreted as evidence of the dream or vision-sharing that may have served to both disseminate and reinforce cultic rites and strengthen cultic identity.[79]

In conclusion, these perspectives enable us to speculate that the similarities between Isobel's and Janet's confessions were not only rooted in interrogatorial intervention or coincidence. We can speculate that they represent, at their root, mutual culture-patterned visionary experiences that had been entered into with magical intent and forged through cultic discourse. As among the Continental dream cults, this discourse need not have been planned or formal. Although it could have occurred at clandestine meetings at Janet Breadheid's house, it could just as easily have taken place at the other places where the two women were likely to have met: on the shoreline between Nairn and Lochloy waiting for the fishing boats to come in, at the Laird of Park's mill at Millhill (situated equidistant between Lochloy and Belmakeith), at the mosses where the women and children gathered to dig peat, or at the Nairn and Auldearn markets, where the farmers' wives went to sell butter and exchange gossip. Similarly, as among the Continental dream cults, membership may not have been large or, for that matter, have corresponded to any great degree to the list of participants recorded in the women's encounter-narratives. As we have seen through research into the *benandanti* et al., dream-cult identity could thrive on a handful of real-life relationships, with the bulk of membership comprising of known, 'known of' or unknown individuals interacted with, in a cultic capacity, solely during visionary experience. In other words, the Auldearn cult could have consisted of thirteen, or it could have consisted of two.

Difference and Demonology

But if the Auldearn dream-cult hypothesis is to be considered seriously, we need to negotiate two further obstacles. First, scholars have sometimes noted, with bemusement, that coven-narratives from known intimates from throughout Scotland usually differ substantially, even when they refer to allegedly shared experiences. As Larner notes:

> It is also interesting to note that when we have the accounts of a group of accused who were alleged to have met together with the Devil there is little agreement between them as to his appearance . . . the collection of suspects at the Crook of Devon in Angus in 1661 had strikingly different coloured spectacles. Isobel Rutherford first saw three women with black heads and Satan with 'ane blue bonnet and grey clothes'. Bessie Henderson saw him as 'a halflong fellow with an dusti-coloured coat'; Janet Brough as 'an uncoath man with black cloathes and ane hood on his head'.[80]

Isobel's and Janet's accounts are no different in this respect. As we have explored at various points in the book, although the confessions display many similarities, they also display many differences. The coven rituals often diverge. For example, Janet's coven members do not enjoy the benefits of 'a sprit to wait wpon ws and ve pleas to call wpon him', nor are their magical 'acts and deeds' recorded in a book belonging to the Devil. Janet is also far less forthcoming than Isobel with regard to the folkloric and fairy-related activities of the coven, such as house-to-house processions and arrow-shooting with the host, her only direct reference to the latter being the abrupt, short sentence 'we shoat noat (*cattle*) in plewghes'. While the notorious passage in which Isobel claimed that, together with Janet and others, she had yoked a plough with frogs, is completely absent from Janet's testimony. Some of these differences can undoubtedly be attributed to the fact that, in reconstructing Isobel's coven ritual we have four confessions to refer to, while in reconstructing Janet's we have only one. But when considered alongside the fact that these kinds of inter-testimonial differences are commonly found in coven-narratives from known intimates, we can speculate that they also reflected divergence on an experiential level. As a consequence, it could be argued that even if the two women did exchange detailed accounts of their visionary narratives, any sense of cult identity would have been obviated by their awareness that their experiences were often so dissimilar.

But in terms of dream-cult cohesion, these differences would have signified less than might be imagined. As we have learnt, mutual-dream researchers have discovered that in both meshing and meeting dreams there is never an exact equivalence, with Magallón stating that 'At times there may be the sharing of a single symbol. At other times virtually an entire dream sequence will correspond with another dreamer's.'[81] In this context, it is interesting to note that no two early modern dream-cult accounts are the same. For example, those given by the *benandanti,* even when they come from known intimates, contain marked and sometimes extreme, differences. With regard to Michele Soppe and Bastiano, who claimed to have met socially, Ginzburg notes that while 'there are many significant similarities' between their accounts, there were also 'profound differences between the two. Menos declared that he fought witches and kept "God's faith", whereas Michele, from his very first appearance before the Holy Office, said that he participated in the witches' ball in the presence of the devil.' It is clear that each *benandanti*, as Ginzburg notes, 'relived [their traditional beliefs] in a different way'.[82] However heavily conditioned they may be, dream and vision experiences are intensely personal events, and the places and beings encountered in them are the result of psychic conflations unique to the individual.

But while, with regard to early modern dream cults, these differences may be a problem for the modern Western mind, anthropological evidence suggests that they were unlikely to have been a problem for the cult members themselves. In traditional shamanistic societies, experiences in the visionary world are not judged by the same criteria as those of waking life and the sharing of dreams is not concerned with a blow-by-blow dissection of similarities. As the anthropologist Gilbert Herdt claims of the Sambia of Papua New Guinea:

> Sambia genuinely believe that others have had some of the same dreams. Sharing this belief is an important sign of their sense of community . . . [but] they do not test each other's dream experience to verify whether the images, sensations, and ideas felt in each other's dreams are the same. Instead, Sambia assume that when someone shares a dream in which such-and-such images and actions seem to occur, that dream equates to ones they have had. Their interpretive system thus unites people's dreams on the level of iconic imagination (bogs, tree, fires, women) and metaphoric meaning (women are hamlet spirits; you'll catch a cassowary). Because these narrative equivalences seem to link thought and soul, conscious and unconscious, listeners assume an isomorphism between all levels of experience.[83]

For early modern visionaries, the knowledge that both spirits and human subtle bodies could assume different forms meant that nothing was 'fixed'; to the extent that a woman like Jonet Watson (Dalkeith, 1661) could quite earnestly confess that the Devil appeared to her 'in the liknes of ane prettie boy, in grein clothes . . . and [then] went away from her in the liknes of ane blak doug'; Thomas Leys could tell Elspeth Reid that a local hill-dwelling spirit could be invoked 'in ony lyiknes scho pleisit'; and Forfar witch Elspet Bruice could tell her interrogators that when her coven met on the beach near Barrie 'the divell wes there present with them all, in the shape of ane great horse' but that after going off to perform some *maleficium* 'they returned all in the same liknes as of befor, except that the divell wes in the shape of a man upone his returne'.[84] Similarly, in the shifting sands and mirages of the visionary realm it was quite reasonable to expect that different people would experience the same event in different ways. Both Isobel and Janet may have believed themselves to have attended the same 'grand meitting . . . [at] the end of ilk quarter'; but as we explored in CHAPTER SIXTEEN, in Isobel's case the appearance and behaviour of the envisioned Devil presiding over proceedings may have drawn on memories of her own husband or father, or a particular devotion to Psalm 18, or by an ongoing attachment to specific narratives concerning the Archangel Michael or the superior satisfactions of the Bridegroom of Souls; while Janet's Devil figure, being influenced by other real-life relationships and by an attachment to other religious or folkloric narratives, would have looked and behaved differently as a result. Contrary to weakening the visionary's belief in the shared dream or vision, this individuality would have given the experience its numinous core. The personal significance of the encounter generated its emotional intensity, and this intensity, fed back into the communal imagination through dream or vision recounting, invigorated both cultic and community mythology.

The second problem, with regard to the Auldearn dream-cult hypothesis, is the question of specifically demonological content. It is one thing to entertain the idea that the fairy-related passages in Isobel's and Janet's confessions may have been rooted in culture-patterned mutual-dream experiences generated through dream sharing, but another thing altogether to assume the same for the demonological passages. In order for the latter to have been the case, we must accept that Isobel and Janet did not only share experiences of animal metamorphosis or flying with the fairy host, but that they also shared experiences that pertained, in some way, to their confessional descriptions of encountering the Devil, making the demonic pact and participating in formal sabbath rituals. Such a prospect may seem unlikely, but in the context of the perspectives developed earlier in this book, it cannot be dismissed out of hand. In CHAPTERS FOURTEEN to SEVENTEEN we have argued that individuals were capable of believing that they had encountered and covenanted with spirits that were, either at the time or retrospectively, identified as the Devil. We also argued that in the popular mind, even '*the* Devil' himself could have been the spirit of choice for those who wished to embark on certain types of magical practice, from healing through to assault sorcery, and that seeking help from the Prince of Darkness may not have been as culturally taboo as contemporary historians like to think.

When these conclusions are taken in conjunction with the perspectives on dream sharing and mutual dreaming developed in this chapter, it does not seem unreasonable to entertain the possibility that if individuals were having Devil-related shamanistic experiences, then they would have shared them with others; and that this sharing could have generated mutual dreams on demonological themes. What is notable, in this context, is the fact that collections of coven-narratives from known intimates, such as those from Forfar, Bute and of course, Auldearn, all share a fusion of demonological and folkloric elements wholly unique to that place and moment in history. And we can tentatively speculate that, in some of these cases, these regional differences may not only have reflected belief, but also experience. It may only have needed one or two eloquent and persuasive people to undergo one or more overtly Devil-related shaman-istic encounters for this demonized variant of the regional helping-spirit template to have passed quickly from person to person, sowing imagery, symbolism and narrative – like living seed – into receptive imaginations, to be personally re-experienced on a visionary level again and again in many different guises.

We can glimpse this process at work in the 1658 Alloa records. Margaret Tailzour's claim (which we saw earlier) that 'Jonet Millar in Tullibodie told her that the divell haid appeired to her' concludes with the phrase 'yet the said Jonet knew not that she was ane witch'. This sentence is obscure and can be interpreted in a variety of ways, but we can speculate here that it reflects the fact that after suffering a troubling Devil-themed dream or vision Jonet – who was herself no stranger to magical practice, being 'a gret charmer, all hir lyftym' – had sought advice from the more experienced Margaret, who had told her that this experience confirmed her identity as a witch.[85] As a result of this exchange, the next time Jonet found herself encountering the envisioned Devil she would have negotiated her experience in a very different manner. In this way, through retrospective dream analysis, a confident visionary like Tailzour may have been able to turn a magical practitioner who had merely encountered the Devil into one who had entered into an alliance with him – and who was therefore drawn, under her guid-ance, to participate in coven-related rites from that date onwards. This process would have been advanced by the fact that when Margaret Tailzour – who was clearly an old hand when it came to participating in coven-related rites – informed Jonet that her experience of encountering the Devil meant that she 'was ane witch', it is unlikely that she would have stopped there. She would have followed up her assessment with an account of what witches' covens did, when they did it, and where. And drawn on her own demonologically-themed visions and dreams in order to do so.

Initiatory Rituals

The ways in which physical relationships and visionary experience may have interacted to bind the members of the Auldearn dream cult together can be illustrated more vividly through looking in a little more detail at initiatory experiences. Early modern demonological tracts consistently emphasize the fact that although their vocation was often inherited, witches were not automatically members of covens and generally had to be persuaded or coerced into participation. The stereotypical scenario, which was already well-developed in early texts such as the *Malleus Maleficarum*, depicts the young novice being lured to the 'dark side' by an older, more experienced woman.[86] This narra-tive – which we have already glimpsed above in the interaction between Margaret Tailzour and Jonet Millar – runs strongly through the Scottish witch records. And although we do not find it in Isobel confessions we find it in Janet Breadheid's claims that: 'it was he [her husband] and Elpeth Nishie, his mother, that entysed me to that craft'(543/14). Janet's claims, and those of other suspects, were of course likely to have been rooted in coerced-compliant responses and false-memory recollections elicited through leading questions of the 'Who enticed you into that craft?' and 'Who offered you up to the Devil to be baptized?' type. But anthropological perspectives suggest that this may not have been the whole explanation.

The experienced-magical-practitioner-entices-the-novice dynamic is not only a core feature of the early modern demonological stereotype, it is also a consistent feature of shamanistic initiation, as it is found in a wide range of tribal cultures throughout the world. Tribal shamans resemble early modern witches in the sense that although they can assume their vocations independently, they are usually helped along the way by a practising shaman, who is often a relative or close acquaintance. Where this vocation involves becoming a member of a shamanistic group or society then this help amounts to 'conversion to a cult'. The following account, which describes how a man from Kato, in the Guyana Highlands, was coerced into the aggressive *kanaimà* cult by his in-laws, is remarkably similar to Janet Breadheid's account of how she was 'entysed' into witch-craft by her mother-in-law:

> DA was very much smitten by a girl from Kaibarupai and to his joy married into the family and went to live with them. DA later said that when he first arrived at his father-in-law's house he wondered why it was that the family seemed always to be out in the bush. So the family decided to show him. What he then found out was that they were kanaimàs. Even women were kanaimà in this family. They told him that 'if he wanted to marry them he had to become like them as well,' so he allowed himself to be initiated.[87]

Similar dynamics seem to have occurred among early modern dream cults. Earlier in this chapter we observed how the visionary experiences of the *benandante* Menichino della Nota were heavily influenced by the dream-recountings of the more experienced Giambattista Tamburlino. But interesting in the present context is the fact that Tamburlino's recountings were not performed for Menichino's entertainment, but were part of a predatory attempt to persuade him, in this case quite coercively, into partic-ipating in the *benandanti* rites. Menichino claimed:

> I went on those three days because others told me to . . . the first one to tell me to go was Giambattista Tamburlino . . . he informed me that he and I were benandanti, and that I had to go with him. And when I replied that I would not go, he said, 'When you have to come, you will come.' And to this I declared, 'You will not be able to make me,' and he, in turn, insisted 'You will have to come anyway, one goes as though in a smoky haze, we do not go physically,' and said that we had to go and fight for the faith, even though I kept saying that I did not want to go. And a year after these conversations I dreamed that I was in Josaphat's field . . . [88]

Benandante Paolo Gasparutto seems to have been similarly evangelistic, as evinced by his interrogators' claim that: 'not only did you follow this diabolical sect during all the years you dedicated yourself to these works, but you also urged others to accompany you, and once they had promised, they were compelled in the future, whether they wanted to or not, to attend your spectacles and crimes'.[89] Comparable enticements also occurred in twentieth-century Corsica, with Carrington claiming that the process of becoming a *mazzere* is influenced by contact with others and that 'Whether or not the predisposition is inherited, it is undoubtedly stimulated by contact with practising *mazzeri*. *Mazzeri*, I have been told, are very insinuating, and will try by every means to win one's friendship. But any familiarity with them is dangerous, for inevitably they will draw one down to their realm of darkness and death.' As in shamanistic traditions worldwide, the young *mazzeru* can be called to initiation by a relative. Carrington elaborates:

> The initiated is likely to be 'called' by a relative, usually somewhat older: initiation seems to take place most often in adolescence. Corsicans insist on the hereditary nature of *mazzerisme* and speak of '*familles mazzeriques*'. I have indeed observed that *mazzerisme* runs in certain families: the *mazzeru* I met had originally been 'called' by an uncle: a *mazzera* confided to me that she had initiated her daughter . . . The *mazzeru* described by Marie-Madeleine Rotily-Forcioli was, one might say, born into *mazzerisme*: his father and aunt and a first cousin were all *mazzeri*.[90]

These accounts suggest that potential dream-cult members were precipitated into membership through spontaneous culture-patterned visionary experience instigated through intensive suggestions of the 'When you have to come, you will come' and 'You will have to come anyway' variety. The novice's imagination, being worked on in this way over a number of months or years, would finally produce the requisite mutual dream at the requisite time. After which they had no choice but to identify themselves as a dream-cult member. Those who lived in close proximity to other cult adherents, particularly if they were relatives (such as the son of the charismatic *dona* from Palermo) would have found it even harder to escape such influences. Similar psychological dynamics emerge in contemporary psychological research into dream telepathy. In a series of experiments designed to generate specifically-themed dreams on the basis of certain stimuli, psychologists Ullman at al. noted that 'the active involvement of the agent [that is, the individual who provides the stimuli] is an important ingredient for success', with 'emotional rapport' and romantic attachment between agent and subject also increasing positive results.[91]

Envisioned Summons

But the plot thickens yet further. In the *benandanti* narratives, where initiation plays a particularly prominent role, the novice's first visionary journey was often accompanied by an experience of being 'called' or 'summoned' by an envisioned entity. This entity was sometimes a non-human spirit, but it could also be a living human in subtle-body form. Paolo Gasparutto, for example, claimed that he was first called to the *benandanti* rites by a man named Battista Vicentio, who appeared before him one night and told him that 'the captain of the benandanti' was summoning him 'to come out and fight for the crops'. The fact that Battista was a visionary entity is suggested by the following exchanges:

> Q: When he [Battista] spoke to you were you awake or asleep?
> A: When Battista appeared before me I was sleeping.
> Q: If you were asleep, how did you answer him and how did you hear his voice?
> A: My spirit replied to him.[92]

We do not know whether Gasparutto was genuinely acquainted with Battista Vicentio, but other *benandanti* accounts make it clear that the individual who summoned in spirit could be the same individual who summoned on the physical plane. In 1619 Maria Panzoni claimed that her godfather enticed her to become a *benandante*, stating that 'he was around me all the time, saying such things as "if you had come you would have seen so many beautiful things"'. But as is clear from Ginzburg's summing up, when Maria's godfather took her journeying for the first time, he was in visionary form:

> The first time she went to the sabbat, conducted there by her godfather, she had gone in body and spirit, and she had been a 'young girl'. Her godfather, instead, had been *in the form of a butterfly*. He cautioned her 'not to speak': 'and he led me,' Maria related, 'to heaven, to the meadow of the Madonna and to hell . . . [my italics]'.[93]

This dynamic also emerges in the interactions between Michele Soppe and Bastiano Menos. Earlier, we claimed that the two seemed to have had a meeting-dream encounter, but when we re-read the passage in full we can see that the meeting was in fact a visionary summons following on from a previous physical summons:

> This Bastiano used to come with me to a pasture where his master's animals grazed; he became friendly, and I asked him in the pasture if he wanted to come with me and the witches to the dance; he said yes, he would come. I repeated this a second time when we were at the pasture; he told me that he would come, and then I said to him, 'I shall come to call you at night, don't be afraid, we shall go together.' And so I did: the following Thursday I mounted my goat and went to find Bastiano who was in bed; I called him by name and said to him: 'Bastiano, do you want to come with me to the dance of the witches?' And he replied, 'Yes, I do.' I had another goat with me, and Bastiano mounted it, and together we rode off to the dance of the witches in Santa Catarina's field . . . [94]

Interestingly, we find very similar accounts in Scottish witchcraft confessions. Here, the individual who persuades the novice witch into the craft often summons or carries them to the witches' sabbath, and/or plays a prominent role in coven ritual. In many cases it is difficult to tell, as with accounts from the *benandanti* et al., whether this human helper was a physical or a visionary presence, but some accounts are suggestive of the physical/visionary summons dynamic we have identified in the *benandanti* sources. For example, according to a pamphlet printed in 1697, Renfrewshire witch Elizabeth Anderson claimed that 'both the Devil and her Father invited her several times to the *Devil's Service*, Promising to Reward her for her paines. But that she altogether refus'd to Ingage therein'. She also described her father instructing her on witch-protocol, on one occasion forbidding her to 'tell any thing she saw, or else she would be Torn in pieces'. While there may have been a real-life physical component to these interactions (between Elizabeth and her father at least), other parts of the account are suggestive of visionary summons, with Elizabeth claiming on one occasion that 'one Night her Father raised her out of her Bed, and took her to the Ferry-Boat of *Erskin*, where he took her on his Back, and, in a Flight, carry'd her over the Water' to the sabbath; later adding that 'the Words that her Father spoke when he took her on his Back, and Flew with her, were *Mount and Fly*'.[95] Similarly, North Berwick woman Janet Kennedy (1591) claimed that the local 'great witch', Agnes Sampson, had sent her daughter to persuade her to come to coven meetings, but that on her refusal the latter:

> threatened her in Agnes Sampson's name and said that the said Agnes . . . would compel whether she would or not the pith of her body to come unto her, as after it fell or sorted out. For at divers times fra that time forth the said Agnes would by her enchantments, when this deponer was lying in her bed in the night, draw forth her spirit, as it appeared to her, and make it to be transported to the convention to assist at their deeds.[96]

Something similar seems to have occurred to Forfar suspect Agnes Spark, who appears to have been a teenager at the time of her interrogation. Spark's claim that a well-known local witch named Isobel Shyrie 'did cairie hir away to neir Litle milne, quhair shoe saw a duzen of people dauncing, and that they had sweet musick, quhich shoe thought was the musick of a pype' is suggestive of visionary experience. And her account of a conversation between herself and Shyrie on the following day suggests that this experience was linked to an ongoing real-life summoner/novice relationship:

> Shoe went to sie the said Issobell Syrie, and that shoe fand hir lying in hir bed, quhilk shoe did doe all that day, and that the said Issobell's handis wer verie sore, and that shoe plucked the skin affs them and made great moan, and said it was no wonder that shoe had so sore handis, seing shoe was so soir tosted up and doun; and that the said Agnes Spark answered her, Iff yow had not been at sutch work yisternight as yow was at, yow wold not have been lying in your bed that day; and that the said Issobell said, Have ye nothing to doe with that, and speik noething of it to any bodie; and usit many intysing wordis to draw hir to the divell's service, and said it wold be verie great joy to hir to be in that service, but shoe refused to harkin thairto.[97]

A similar dynamic may have underpinned Janet Breadheid's relationship with her husband, John Taylor and mother-in-law Elspeth Nishie, both of whom, according to Janet, first 'entysed me to that craft'. Janet's claim that John and Elspeth taught her to make and administer potion magic 'to lerne me', suggests that their encouragement was practical and physical. But her simultaneous claim that they played a prominent role in her first coven experience (taking her to the church of Nairn to meet the Devil, and, in the case of her husband, holding her up to be baptized by him), suggests that, for Janet, their enticements may also have been experienced on a visionary level.

We can speculate that the psychological mechanism at work behind this physical/visionary summons dynamic is rooted in the fact that mental imagery is intimately linked to emotional experience. If two individuals share an intense relationship, whether positive or negative, then this affective charge can manifest on a visionary level. This can be clearly seen in an encounter-narrative told to historian Gustav Henningsen by a twentieth-century Sicilian healer who claimed to journey 'all over the world in spirit' whilst her 'body remains in its usual place':

> Among the experiences she told us about was the following event, which is remarkable by beginning in the human world and continuing in the spirit world: Once she quarrelled with a young man in the neighbourhood 'who practised black magic', and the man said to her: 'If I meet you by night at a crossroads, I will kill you!' One night (some time later, when she was out in spirit) she met the same man, together with his mother-in-law, who was a Tunisian, and the man made ready to beat her. But his mother-in-law stopped him: 'Don't you see, that we must be three to go out (there was a third spirit with them), but she is able to do it alone [i.e. she was much stronger than them].'[98]

The emotionally-charged relationship between dream-cult summoner and novice could have expressed itself in a similar way. Just as individuals who were repeatedly told 'When you have to come, you will come' found themselves compulsively drawn to the visionary-cult experience; those who were told by an initiate that 'You will come when I call you' would have found themselves spontaneously generating initiatory visions in which their insinuating summoner played a central role. As with the identification of coven members generally, the novice would not have needed to encounter an accurate visual representation of the summoner in order to recognize them; for like all envisioned phenomena, the latter's presence could have been determined or guessed through a range of alternative indicators such as sound, context and, most importantly of all, feeling or sense. As with coven members generally, these non-visual factors could have been so persuasive that an envisioned summoner could have been identified positively even when they appeared in a completely different form. Maria Panzoni, for example, was convinced that it was her godfather who had come to take her to the *benandanti* rites for the first time, despite the fact that he came to her 'in the form of a butterfly'.[99]

As we have speculated with regard to dream-cult experiences in general, we can suppose that these summoning experiences occurred during predominantly low-to-intermediate level meshing dreams that were not necessarily simultaneous, or even very similar, but which were congruent enough to confirm to both novice and initiate that the summoning had taken place. But we can also suppose that summoning experiences also occurred during high-level meshing or (as may have been the case with Michele Soppe and Bastiano Menos) meeting dreams. If we transpose the following meeting dream, experienced by a pair of flatmates in the twentieth century, onto the early modern envisioned-summoning template, we can gain an idea of the emotional impact such experiences could have had. The first dreamer recounts:

> when she [my flatmate] started recalling the dream . . . my jaw literally dropped. She had dreamed of waking in the middle of the night and feeling fear because of a presence of something in her room. She got up from her bed and rushed down stairs to my room, she banged on the door and shouted my name but the door was locked and she had to return to bed. In my dream I was woken from sleep in the middle of the night by her banging on my door and shouting my name. This is where our dreams diverge as she found my door locked whereas I answered the door. My dream continued with her saying that there was a presence in her room and could I go and check the room . . . Then I woke (middle of the night 3–4 a.m.) my heart was racing and it took a long time to get back to sleep.[100]

This exploration into the physical/visionary summons dynamic also sheds light on some other cult mechanisms. It suggests that individual charismatic personalities may have been vitally important in the forging and sustaining of dream-cult traditions. Just as the *benandanti* of Latisana danced to the tune of Giambattista Tamburlino, so in Forfar they danced to that of Isobel Shyrie and in Auldearn to that of Elspeth Nishie and John Taylor. Filtered through the intensely-lived interior worlds of these human orchestrators, each dream cult would have been intimately responsive to local temperament and circumstance. It would have developed in response to things which were happening in particular fields and barns, to the stories which were told around particular fires and to the sermons preached by particular ministers – all these elements contriving to give each clutch of coven-narratives their own distinctive character. This exploration also suggests that, among dream-cult members, physical and visionary relationships were highly fluid and interactive; this dynamic explaining why coven-narratives seem to flow from seemingly concrete worldly events to fantastic supernatural events in such a seamless way, and why relationships between coven members seem to so effortlessly span this continuum. From this perspective, it is quite logical that John Taylor should be showing Janet Breadheid how to make a potion out of dog and sheep flesh in one sentence, and holding her up to be baptized by the Devil in the next. Dream-cult membership revolved around the fact that in the early modern period the wall between the physical world and the visionary world was very thin.

The Reasons Why

As we mentioned earlier in this chapter, to properly analyze the coven-related and cultic aspects of Isobel's confessions would require much more research than is possible in the present book, but on the basis of the perspectives sketched out above, we can draw up a preliminary hypothesis. According to the definitions used here, we can argue that some form of dream cult *may* have existed in mid seventeenth-century Auldearn. In physical reality, it would probably have represented a small, and perhaps even very small, group of individuals who experienced and shared intense culture-patterned visionary experiences and believed that through these experiences they magically altered the world around them. The membership of the Auldearn cult could have extended to only two individuals: Isobel and Janet. But it may also have included more, including Janet's mother-in-law, Elspeth Nishie, and others who appeared prominently in the two women's confessions, such as Margaret Brodie and Margaret Wilson. But although the real-life, physical cult network may have been relatively limited, on a visionary level Isobel and Janet may have experienced themselves as being members of a far larger group, including in their imagined coven a range of both known, 'known of' and unknown persons. Cult identity would have also been reinforced by the belief that similar groups, with whom they occasionally convened, existed elsewhere. The fact that Isobel identified two of the members of another coven by name suggests that some of these neighbouring cults may have been real, and their members known personally to Isobel. But it is also likely that, as with the *mazzeri* and *benandanti*, these alternate-cult participants were merely rumoured, presumed or imagined to exist.

Both women may have fallen into coven membership in a number of ways. They may have found themselves spontaneously experiencing culture-patterned visions concerning fairy processions, arrow-shooting hunts or sabbath-like feasts and may have sought out others reputed to have had similar experiences. Or they may have come into contact with a charismatic friend or family member, such as Elspeth Nishie, who 'primed their pump' and encouraged them to incubate an initiatory dream or vision. Either way, once the psychological process was started it was likely to have gained a momentum of its own. Conviction and motivation would have been progressively stimulated by the deepening vividness and intensity of experiences generated through ongoing mental imagery generation. It would also have been stimulated by the interpersonal intimacy developed through frequent dream sharing; the intermittent emergence of highly-memorable and life-altering high-level meeting or meshing dream experiences; growing attachment to the vocational satisfaction and social status to be gained through functioning as a shamanistic practitioner; and, perhaps most importantly of all, an increasing belief in the perceived magical effects of the cultic experiences themselves.

And what of these magical effects? We can speculate that the practices of the Auldearn cult were, like those of the *benandanti, donas de fuera* et al., rooted in shamanistic spirit-group traditions of folkloric origin. Although, unlike their Sicilian and Friulian counterparts, Isobel and Janet do not give a clear indication of what their cult's core magical rationale may have been, on the basis of the research undertaken in earlier chapters we can speculate that – as is the case with most shamanistic cults – it revolved around healing and divinatory rites designed to benefit the community. Some of these rites may have been physical and practical, as suggested by Isobel's descriptions of rituals and charms employed to heal fevers and the 'bean shaw'. But on a visionary level, they may have taken the form of host-related arrow-shooting hunts, and other supra-normal activities, designed to facilitate human-to-human sickness or death transferral and sickness or death divination. But despite this evidence of beneficence, and despite the fact that outside the interrogatorial arena the community-benefiting aspects of the cult's activities may have emerged as more prominent, it is also clear that many of the visionary rites performed by the Auldearn dream cult would, in anthropological terms, come under the category of 'dark' shamanism. Whether they were intended to heal the sick, divine the future or bring prosperity to households, our analysis suggests that any beneficial effects procured by Isobel's envisioned activities were gained largely through the causing of magical harm. This impression is further supported by our argument, developed in CHAPTER THIRTEEN, that Isobel and her companions may have performed defensive revenge killings in response to client demand. That dream cults centred around the performance of magical harm or *maleficium* could have existed in early modern Scotland may seem far-fetched but, as we argued earlier, anthropological research is increasingly testifying to the fact that in any culture where shamanistic practices exist, dark shamanistic practices are generally not very far away.

In arguing that a 'dark dream cult' of this nature may have existed in seventeenth-century Auldearn we are, of course, also arguing that similar cults may have existed elsewhere in Scotland in this period. But we must remain very cautious here. As the Survey of Scottish Witchcraft has recently shown, the majority of Scottish records report accusations relating to basic *maleficium* performed by individual witches. The numbers of records describing the activities of groups that could arguably fulfil some of the criteria for a dream cult – dark or otherwise – are relatively small and on closer analysis some of these could probably be dismissed. As a consequence, even taking into account the fact that some cults may have existed undetected by the law courts, without further research we cannot maintain that this was a widespread phenomenon. We can only speculate here that although individual shamanistic visionaries were probably relatively widespread, organised cultic activity, involving a regular exchange of experiences and communally-intentioned visionary journeys between individuals, if it did exist, would have been restricted to certain areas where the supporting traditions had managed to survive. And even here, it would have generally simmered away on a very low level, only emerging into more substantial cultic activity in response to particular social or political conditions or, just as significantly, the presence of one or more charismatic, highly motivated individuals, such as Elspeth Nishie, to set the ball rolling. As we have touched on at various points in this chapter, clusters of coven-narratives, such as those from Alloa (1658), Aberdeen (1597), Bute (1662), the Crook of Devon (1662), Forfar (1661), North Berwick (1591), Paisley (1697) and (though only one record survives in this case) Innerkip (1662), contain levels of confessional congruity, folkloric content (focusing on suggestive spirit-group narrative themes) and depictions of magical aggression against authority figures that qualify them as possible candidates for dark dream-cult status.[101] In the last analysis, however, only detailed further research, on a case-by-case basis, can establish whether or not we can hypothesise about these sources using the shamanistic paradigm. On the matter of dream cults, as with so many of the issues covered in this book, the analysis of Isobel's confessions proves valuable not so much for the surety of the conclusions reached, but in the vitality of the questions raised.

Darkening the Dark Cults

But although we are nearing the end of our analysis, with regard to the question of dark dream cults in seventeenth-century Scotland, Isobel's confessions have one last contribution to make. From the Middle Ages through to the early modern period, western European demonologists consistently argued that witchcraft (including both covenanting with the Devil and attending witches' sabbaths) was a direct threat to authority; both as it emerged through the church and state and as it was embodied in the figure of God. They also argued, with relative frequency, that this threat was on the increase, with Normand and Roberts noting that 'demonologists often claim in their prefaces that witches are now plentiful or multiplying "even as worms in a garden"'.[102] On the one hand, we can attribute these perceptions to self-fulfilling prophesy, in the sense that if you look for cracks in a wall long and hard enough you will find them. But on the other, there is no doubt that the dynamics underpinning dark dream cults – complex and ambivalent as they are at the best of times – would have been further complicated by the particular social and political conditions that evolved in many parts of late medieval and early modern Europe. And that in some places, these conditions may have conspired to make dark dream cults even darker.

This may seem unnecessarily sensationalist, but is supported by anthropological perspectives. Scholars emphasize that although religious cults of all kinds can draw on very ancient roots, they are not static structures, and can strengthen, re-define themselves and decay in response to social change. Of particular relevance to our discussion here is the fact that cults frequently coalesce and mobilize to protect the interests of their host community in response to external threat. This mobilizing process has frequently been reported in cultures undergoing military occupation or colonization. In reference to the Guyanese *kanaimà*, Whitehead claims that dark shamans are not only preserved because they are a 'necessary part of the cosmos' and 'ensure the continuing beneficence of [Makunaima] the creator of plants and animals' but also because, at times of trouble, they can become 'the source and even symbol of a potent indigenous society and culture that is capable of defending itself against the depredations of the outside world, be that a neighbouring village or even the national state'.[103] By the same token, in reference to an indigenous Amerindian Nagual cult that once extended over Southern Mexico and Guatemala, and which focused on communion with familiar spirits and the ritual use of the peyote cactus to attain 'union with divinity', anthropologist Hutton Webster notes that 'after the Spanish conquest of Mexico it [the cult] became political in its aims, and its members were inspired by two ruling sentiments – detestation of the Spaniards and hatred of the Christian religion'.[104] Similar resistance could occur many years after Christianization, with Ioan Lewis describing how the Rhodesian *Zezuru* cults waned in response to Western colonization that occurred in the nineteenth century, but re-emerged in the 1960s in response to governmental suppression of the African nationalist parties, this emergence taking the form of 'a self-conscious and deliberate rejection of Christianity and of European culture'.[105] Bringing the phenomenon closer to home, Carrington noted that in the twentieth century the Corsican *mazzeri* cult was invigorated by 'young people with nationalist

534

tendencies, who feel that their inherited culture has been too long derided and ignored'.[106] During these times of tension, the self-defensive function of the dark shamanistic cult does not only manifest in the form of strengthened cultural identity and an enhanced means of self-expression for the disaffected, but also, more bluntly, as a means through which to weaken or threaten the enemy through assault sorcery (aka *maleficium* in self-defence). Whitehead emphasizes, for example, that in the beginning of the nineteenth century *kanaimà* ritual predation functioned as 'a defensive magico-military technique to ward off the new and overwhelming gun violence and slave raiding' that threatened the Guyanese Indians, and that by the end of the century the 'pattern of killings by *kanaimàs* . . . shows that it was explicitly understood as a means to resist and reject the white man's materiality and spirituality'.[107] As we saw in CHAPTER EIGHT, when an individual, or in this case a society, is without effective arms, land or political power, magical attack becomes a tempting resource. And in these kinds of situations, the same capacity for causing envisioned harm that makes the dark shamanistic cult so feared and abhorred, emerges as its trump card.

In respect of the adaptive behaviour of dark shamanistic cults, it is pertinent here that in early modern Scotland the sector of the population from which most covens allegedly emerged, sought to defend itself against a variety of external threats. In the sixteenth and seventeenth centuries Scotland was a highly-complex stratified society in which, as we have seen in CHAPTERS SIX and SEVEN, there were large differences in power and culture between the rich and the poor, the landed and the landless and the educated and the non-educated. While these different sectors of society could exist in mutually harmonious interdependence, in response to the pressures of pre-industrial living, the uneasy status quo frequently broke down. And when it did, ensuing conflicts commonly gained expression through the perennial us-and-them dynamic. In this context, so far as a poor tenant or cottar was concerned, an unfair, selfish or oppressive landlord would have been an external threat against which they needed to defend themselves. This perennial social antagonism – which would have existed in some form or other since the early Middle Ages – would have been exacerbated after the Reformation by an altogether new factor. As touched on many times already, the reformed church differed from its medieval Catholic predecessor in the extent to which it attempted to reform popular culture. The ecclesiastical authorities strove tirelessly to eradicate deeply-rooted and widely-held unorthodox beliefs and practices and superimpose those of the Protestant church in their place. The difference between the superstitious and reformed mentality was often so great, and the reforming process so invasive and intense that although this conflict was played out between individuals of the same nationality and religion it can be likened, as it was in the period itself, to that which took place between the tribal cultures of the African and American continents and colonizing settlers from Europe. In reference to both Protestant and Counter Reformation reformers, Stuart Clark notes that:

> The cultural distance that separated the aims of the religious reformers (and their secular backers among the European states) from the ideas and behaviour of the mass of the laity seemed to be great enough to invite comparison with the colonial confrontations overseas.

The very broad extent of the popular beliefs and practices that the reformers hoped to eradicate, or drastically modify, also indicated the proscription of a whole culture, rather than
piecemeal or narrowly focused change. And the methods chosen for the task, including
surveillance, forcible conversion, repression, and punishment, as well as huge educational
programmes, suggested the imposition of cultural superiority by dominant elites on subject
populations . . . One of the most persistent images held by the European reformers was
precisely that they were faced by conditions like those in the New World or the Far East.[108]

As a consequence, it is reasonable to speculate that if in nineteenth-century colonies
like Guyana and southern Mexico the resentment of cultural oppression could be
expressed through an upsurge in visionary traditions tailored to both preserve cultural
identity and perform *maleficium* in self-defence through assault sorcery, then in early
modern Scotland, among the poor and superstitious, the resentment of cultural oppression may have been expressed in a similar way. Of course this magical response would
not have worked – as it did in the nineteenth-century Americas – with a simple 'let's
zap the invader with assault sorcery' dynamic, for in early modern Scotland, the enemy
came from within. The acculturation process set in motion by the reformed church
caused deep fractures within popular culture itself, with many people supporting the
changes, many rejecting them, and even more falling somewhere in between these two
extremes. Unlike the Guyanese Indian, who could clearly identify his enemy as a white-
skinned, Caucasian Christian who had sailed across the sea from Europe, Nairnshire
parishioners who wished to defend themselves against the oppression of the reformed
church may well have found themselves identifying a neighbour, friend, or even family
member as their enemy. In coven-narratives, for example, magical aggression is not
only directed towards authority figures like lairds and ministers but also towards individuals of similar social standing.

It is not difficult to see how these complex cultural conflicts could have gained
expression through the language and mechanics of witchcraft persecution. Whether
they were a laird, minister, merchant or cottar, if a contemporary parishioner wished
to protect themselves against the perceived threat of a dark dream cult then demonological witchcraft theory would have provided them with the justification and state
legislation with the means. Moreover, by articulating their fears through these chan-
nels these frightened individuals would have invigorated – or even in some senses
created – the very thing they feared. As argued in earlier chapters, the 'witchization' of
folkloric shamanistic cults that occurred in many parts of Europe in this period, though
most easily detectable in elite writings, is likely to have been reflected in the visionary
experiences of cult members themselves. In response to witchcraft accusations and prosecutions, pulpit teachings and local gossip would have focused on the nature and threat
of demonological magical practices. And in reaction to this dissemination of ideas and
concerns, oppressed dream-cult members – whose rites traditionally emerged out of
fireside mythologies surrounding fairies, folkloristic devils and the dead – would have
increasingly drawn beliefs surrounding the theological Devil, the sabbath and the
witches' coven into their dream and trance experiences in order to facilitate their envisioned self-defence and articulate their emotional distress.

536

Isobel's Cult

Obviously the hypothesis that reformed teaching and discipline exacerbated dark dream-cult activity in early modern Scotland is a tentative one, and requires more research than is possible here. But it is pertinent to point out that, if the evidence were to persuade anywhere, it would persuade in relation to mid seventeenth-century Auldearn. As particularly ardent covenanters, the lairds and ministers of this region of Nairnshire embraced a degree of religious extremism and lack of empathy toward popular culture that was unusually high, even by the standards of the reformed church, and in Auldearn the tense cultural stand off between the godly ministers or landowners and superstitious tenants seems to have been particularly acute. In the late 1650s and early 1660s, this empathy was further compromised by the fact that ministers like Harry Forbes and Hugh Rose, and lairds like Brodie of Brodie and Hay of Park, were being fenced into a political and religious corner by the growing threat of episcopacy. To these cultural tensions, we can also add more material ones. As we have seen in CHAPTER SEVEN, the inhabitants of Nairnshire did not only endure the intermittent threats posed by outlaws and a constant vulnerability to Highland raiding parties, but were also exposed to the sharp end of the civil wars. Their unstable position at the 'gateway to the Highlands', the drama of the Battle of Auldearn and the unwelcome raids of Huntly and Montrose brought bloodied corpses, burnt fields and heavily-armed garrisons to their very doorsteps.

Moreover, for the men and women who lived on the lands owned by the Hays of Park, these already considerable tensions were further compounded. As Brodie noted, despite – or perhaps also because of – their covenanting principles it was not unusual for the local lairds to be 'sever to tenants'. But in the Laird of Park's case this severity would have been sharpened by the fact that for at least three decades his family had been in financial straits so acute that within fifty years the estates they had enjoyed for over five centuries would dwindle away into nothing. In addition, the fact that, twenty years previously, the deaths of three lairds in quick succession had been attributed to witchcraft would have rendered the Hays of Park highly sensitized to both tenant hostility and any rumours of magical practice performed by the men and women who lived and worked their lands. These sensitivities would have come to a head in the late 1650s, both because the narcissistic young heir, now grown to manhood, began to produce precious sons for the first time and because the parish of Auldearn saw the arrival of zealous and witch-fearing minister Harry Forbes. As a consequence, if a poor, magic-practising tenant like Isobel Gowdie ever came, with a request or complaint, to the 'slippery flagstone' at the Inshoch Castle door, the Laird of Park would have found it difficult to muster a measured response. Cultural oppression, chronic violence, civil war, the spectre of bankruptcy and an exaggerated fear of witchcraft; if any parish in early modern Scotland could have nurtured a dark dream cult pre-occupied with defensive assault sorcery, then Auldearn, in 1662, would have been the perfect place.

Afterword

Coming to the end of our analysis, we can see that we have navigated a labyrinthine path through Isobel's confessions. With a landscape this dense and complex, the route taken has necessarily been a personal one. There have been many crossroads and many decisions to be made about what to explore and what to pass by. As a consequence, I will have emphasized elements that a different researcher would not, and overlooked elements that another might consider important. But nevertheless, we have made some progress.

I

One of the most important things to emerge from the book is the fact that, as was stated in the Introduction to Part I, the attempt to understand the confessions has necessitated developing hypotheses that have a wider significance than for Isobel alone, and give us fresh perspectives on the phenomenon of early modern witchcraft as a whole. The analysis of Isobel's maleficent charms in the context of contemporary revenge-ethics, in CHAPTER EIGHT, invites us to shift from the view that the performance of basic *maleficium* was generally attributed towards the possibility that it was regularly practised, by some people, as a form of self-defence. The analysis into the epistemological status of Isobel's narrative in CHAPTER NINE suggests that recent research into the phenomenon of false memory can go some way towards explaining why so many witch-testimonies present such an improbably-seamless fusion of real-life experiences and demonological stereotypes. The inquiry into Isobel's arrow shooting in CHAPTERS TWELVE and THIRTEEN suggests that recent anthropological research into the nature and prevalence of dark shamanism in contemporary tribal societies may help us to re-configure the way we rationalize stereotypical accounts of sabbath-related *maleficium*. The explorations of Isobel's demonological passages in the context of surrender-protection charms, covenanting mysticism and folkloristic Devil figures in CHAPTERS FIFTEEN to SEVENTEEN, suggest that witchcraft suspects may have contributed more to stereotypical accounts of the demonic pact than has been previously supposed. And finally, the analysis into Isobel's coven in CHAPTER EIGHTEEN suggests that folkloric dream-cult activity may not have been the exclusive preserve of exceptional central, eastern and southern European groups like the *donas de fuera*, *benandanti* or *táltos*, but may also have extended into Scotland and, by implication, other parts of western Europe. While we must take care not minimize the degree of false accusation and false confession that occurred throughout early modern Europe, taken together, these hypotheses both assert the relevance of the shamanistic paradigm in relation to demonological witchcraft and suggest that, on both a physical and visionary level, the practice of maleficent magic may have been more common and socially-tolerated in this period than historians often assume.

II

It is a testament to Isobel that her confessions contain sufficient depth and breadth to generate such a diverse collection of hypotheses. But meanwhile, at the end of all this, what of the woman herself? The need to travel far and wide in order to explain the content of her confessions may have enriched our understanding of early modern witch-craft in general, but it has also meant that at many times in the book, and sometimes for whole chapters at a time, the Nairnshire cottar's wife standing at the heart of them has been lost under a sea of theory and analysis. In the final instance, do we really know much more about 'Issobell gowdie spous to Johne gilbert in Lochloy', than when we started?

Here, we have both something and nothing. We can be fairly certain that Isobel was of at least thirty years of age and that, like most others living in this region of seven-teenth-century Scotland, she lived a life both culturally and physically restricted by the confines of the fermtoun, with her days tightly proscribed by a relentless round of domestic and agricultural tasks. As we have emphasized in the last chapter, we also know that, even by the standards of the time, she lived through unusually difficult and violent decades: surviving the carnage of the Battle of Auldearn, the raids of Montrose and Huntly and the stresses of military occupation. The evidence also confirms that she endured the ministry of a religiously fundamentalist, witch-fearing and morally hypo-critical minister; and that her husband leased or laboured on lands belonging to an equally fundamentalist and witch-fearing landlord who was haunted by the spectre of imminent financial ruin.

III

Beyond these facts, our picture of Isobel has been fleshed out through speculations of varying probability. We can now entertain the idea, for example, that she was an oral performer who diverted her friends and family with tales of the supernatural and led the extempore versifying in the fields and at the washing stones. We can also speculate that she was a magical practitioner and that, like others in the period, she worked shamanistically, gaining her magical skill and knowledge through 'going with the fairies'. Further to this we can also conjecture, though here more tentatively, that Isobel did not shy away from some of the darker magical practices. She may have gathered at the cottages of neighbours to make poisons and knead clay into *corp creadh* and – whether through the coercion of others and/or through irresistible psychological impulse – she may have lain down next to her husband John Gilbert on the quarter days in order to participate in the shamanistic assaults of the envisioned arrow-shooting hosts.

With regard to Isobel's mental health we can speculate that if she had suffered from some kind of psychiatric disorder it is unlikely to have been so overt or severe that she could not integrate into society and lead a relatively normal life. But we can also suppose that, as a shamanistic practitioner, she was probably an intense personality who struggled on a day-to-day basis to integrate the incursions of the visionary realm into her everyday world. And this psychological intensity, as with dark shamans worldwide, is likely to have been further strained by the fact that however many people she healed and however many enemies she vanquished, her intimacy with the forces of death meant that she was regarded with fear and suspicion by many in her community.

With regard to Isobel's character and temperament, the evidence can be interpreted in contrasting ways. We can see her as aggressive and malicious, roasting clay images of innocent children before fires and nonchalantly shooting people at her 'pleasur'. Or we can see her as brave and self-empowered, seeking to heal and defend herself and her community through magical means, despite the fact that such practices made her vulnerable to accusations of witchcraft. Or we can have her falling, as so many dark shamans seem to fall, somewhere in-between these two extremes.

Similarly we can suppose, as commentators have done since the nineteenth century, that Isobel recounted her attempted murders and sexual exploits with the Devil so openly and in such forensic detail, because she was proud, provocative and anti-authoritarian; adding to this old chestnut the new hypothesis that, as an oral performer brought before a rapt audience, her fluency may have been fuelled by artistic conceit. But we can also modify this Isobel-as-anti-hero stereotype by arguing that John Innes may have been right, and that her no-holds-barred narrative was motivated by genuine spiritual remorse. Finding herself facing the death penalty and pitching for a place in heaven, Isobel may well have decided to nail her colours to the covenanting post, passionately abjuring the elves, devils and dark magical practices that she had, for so many years, pragmatically accommodated alongside her devotion to God, Christ and the church.

IV

But whether they were motivated by pride, remorse, or some combination of the two, we can conclude that the palpable intensity of Isobel's confessions were almost certainly fuelled by the extremity of her situation. It is likely that she was deprived of sleep and beaten, and that during the six weeks between her first and last confessions she endured long periods of solitary confinement. We also know that the intermittent interrogatorial sessions in the Auldearn tolbooth were crowded and intense, and that Isobel was subjected to successive rounds of close and suggestive questioning. We can also fairly

THE CONFESSION OF ISOBEL GOWDIE

Isobel's swansong, as articulated by Scottish composer James Macmillan in his orchestral piece *The Confession of Isobel Gowdie*, 1990. Macmillan cites the work as 'the requiem Isobel Gowdie never had'.

safely assume that Isobel responded creatively to these questions by weaving remembered events from her own life – both actual and visionary – into a web of false-memory recollections that seemed to her, at the moment of recall, to be as vivid and real as anything else that had happened in her life up to this point.

The evidence also suggests that in Isobel's case the dark creativity of the early modern witch-interrogation process reached a kind of apotheosis. Her prosecution saw the chance coming together of a number of diverse people: the minister of Auldearn, Harry Forbes, with his covenanting zeal, developed listening skills, and desire to plumb 'the mani great misteries in religion'; the minister of Nairn, Hugh Rose, with his judicious, poetic nature and 'itchingly curious' mind; the notary, John Innes, with his literary flair and professional scrupulousness; and most importantly of all the suspect herself, Isobel Gowdie, with her oral fluency, emotional intensity and head full of half-remembered verses and visions. We can speculate that the interaction between this randomly-gathered group of people generated a profound alchemy: an artistic collaboration that gave rise to the richest and most unusual witch-testimony to have emerged from anywhere in Britain during the witch-hunting period.

V

But although these speculations about the kind of person Isobel was, the kinds of treatment she may have endured and the ways in which her confessions may have been constructed are interesting, ultimately they can only take us so far. In the last analysis, Isobel remains a mystery: resolutely dwarfed, as any author should be, by the substance of her own narrative. Whatever we judge Isobel or the epistemological status of her testimony to have been, through her confessions, she has given us something we can all understand. She has spoken to us of the suffering, and the awareness of the inevitability of death, that dominated the lives and minds of our early modern ancestors and that still oppress us today, though we gaze at them through the protective double-glazing of our industrialized world. She has shown us how every individual wrestles with their mortality within their own uniquely-personal inner landscape, whether inhabited by the loving embraces of Christ, the temptations of the Devil, the bloodlust of the fairy folk or the ordered forces of reason. And most of all, she has reminded us that in all parts of the world and in all ages, suffering, and the inexorable path toward the grave are sweetened by the glories of the human imagination.

Appendix

Janet Breadheid's Confession

Att Inshoch the fourteinth day of aprill 1662 yeiris in p[rese]nce of Patrik dunbar of belnaferrie S[he]reffe prin[cipa]ll of the S[he]reffdome of elgin and forres hew hay of newtowne Archbald dunbar of meikle penik archibald dunbar in lochloy walter chalmer in belnafeerie James cowper in Inshoche Johne weir in aulderne and a great multitud of all sortis of uther persones witnessis to the confessione and declara[tio]n efter sett downe spokin furth of the mowth of janet breadheid spows to Johne taylor in belmakeith

The quhilk day In p[rese]nce of me Johne Innes no[ta]r publict and witnessis abownamet undersub[scriv]and said Janet breadhead professing repentence for hir former sines of witchcraft & th[a]t she haid bein owerlong in the (*divellis?*) service w[i]thout any pressuris proceidit as followes, to witt, first:

I knew nothing of witchcraft untill I wes mari(*ed wit*)h my husband Johne taylor, and it wes he and elspet nishie his moth[e]r, th[a]t entysed me to th[a]t craft and the first (*thing?*) th[a]t we did wes we maid som rowgries of dowgs flesh and sheips flesh against Johne hay in the mure & therby took away his cornes and killed his horsis noat sheip & uth[e]r guidis and layed it abowt his hows to tak away his awin lyffe and therefter he shortlie died;

onlie my moth[e]r in law and my husband did this to learne me and this wes my first (*damaged – words missing*) from them etc when they gott me to consent to this craft, first they haid me to the kirk of nairne in the night (*damaged – words missing*) the divell ves in the readeris dask and an book in his hand, and at that meitting, Bessie wilsone in auld(*erne*) (*damaged – words missing*) (*m*)ergret wilsone spows to donald callam th[e]r margret brodie th[e]r barbara friece ther helen Inglis spows to willia(*m*) (*damaged – words missing*) th[e]r Janet burnet th[e]r elspet makkeith ther elspet nishie spows to Johne mathew in aulderne mariorie taylor (*spows?*) to robert borrie ther bessie hay th[e]r archbald man ther mariorie man his daughter th[e]r elspet mackhomie relic[t] (*of?*) umq[uhi]ll allexr hucheon th[e]r bessie friece spows to Johne gilbert th[e]r Issobell friece spows to androw millen th[e]r agnes corrie spows to w[illia]m yowng th[e]r elspet

543

chisholme spows to umq[uhi]ll (*blank*) mackhomie ther allexr elder in earlseat Janet finlay his spows elspet laird in miltoun of moynes Jon ro[ber]tson in leathin grissall sinklar his spows allexr sheipheard in miltoun of moynes Janet man his spows mariorie dunbar in brightmanney (*blank*) kyllie in vester kinstarj allexr ledy ther elspet gilbert in leathin bar agnes brodie in leathin Janet smith spows to ro[ber]t frasser in arr, bessie piterkin in torrich, allexr bell in drumdewin, a charmer, Issobell nicoll in lochloy bessie young ther elspet falconer spows to James Inglis in penick bessie and margret hutcheons ther walter ledy th[e]r wer all ther (*that?*) night Jon taylor my husband wes then officer, bot Johne yowng in mebestoune is now officer to my coe . . . (*damaged – words missing*) q[uhe]n I cam first ther, ('my' *crossed out*) the divell called th[e]m all be their names on the book, and my husband th[e]n (*damaged – words missing*) called them at the dore, and when th[a]t wes done bessie wilson in aulderne, sat down nixt the divell (*damaged – words missing*) hay th[e]r sat nixt him on the uth[e]r sid, Janet burnet sat nixt hir, and elspet nishie spows to the s[ai]d John (*damaged – words missing*) sat nixt bessie wilson hir moth[e]r, she wes th[e]n maiden to thir nwyris coeven, all the rest satt downe (*damaged – words missing*) they to cam, the nixt thing efter q[uha]t wes done th[a]t night (*word crossed out*) the divell lay w[i]th th[e]m all abowt & th[e]n (*damaged – words missing*) for me, my husband presented me, and he and margrat wilson in aulderne held me up to the (*damaged – words missing*) be baptized, and efter I haid put my on hand to the soallis of my foot and the uth[e]r hand to the (*damaged – words missing*) my head, and renunced my baptisme and all betuixt my two handis to the divell the divell (*damaged – words missing*) in the shoulder, and suked out my blood w[i]th his mowth at th[a]t place, he spowted it in his hand & (*damaged – words missing*) on my head, he baptized me th[e]rvith in his awin nam christain, & th[e]n immediatlie th[e]refter (*damaged – words missing*) each to ther awin howssis,

within fyw dayes th[e]refter he cam to me to my hows, q[uhe]n my husb(*and*) (*damaged – words missing*) in the morning at the plewgh, to sie the mark q[uhi]ch he gaw me, and he did lye w[i]th me in the naked (*damaged – words missing*) & haid carnall cowpula[tio]n w[i]th me, and gaw me an piece of mo[ne]y lyk a testain; he was a meikle roch blak man, cloven footed, werie cold and I fand his nature w[i]thin me als cold as spring well water, he promeisit to sie me again within eight dayes q[uhi]lk he did, and haid carnall cowpula[tio]n w[i]th me again and gaw me an uth[e]r piece of mo[ne]y lyk the first bot they both turned read and I got nothing for th[e]m (*damaged – words missing*) he cam again within twantie dayes and still once in the twantie dayes and lay w[i]th me at each tym continuallj

(*damaged – words missing*) met in the place of darnway nixt th[a]t & th[e]r we did at & drink etc eftir th[a]t we vold still meitt (*damaged – words missing*) ten twelw or twantie dayes continuallj; whan we haid great meittings walter ledy in penik my (*hus?*)band and allexr elder nixt to the divell wer ruleris, and q[uhe]n ther wold be bot fewar I my self the deceassit Jean suth[e]rland bessie hay bessie hay (*sic*) bessie wilsone and Janet burnet wold rule th[e]m

The first thing th[a]t we did except the taking of meat, wes taking of the corns of drumdewin, and (*damaged – words missing*) . . . airted th[a]t amongst ws, 2lj we shoat noat in plewghes, 3lj Agnes grant who wes brunt on the (*damaged – words missing*) hill of (*blank*) gott hyre from elspet monro to destroy the Lairdis of park and lochloy, & th[e]r (*damaged – words missing*) and then I and my husband, elspet nishie, and bessie and margret wilsones in aulderne, con . . . (*damaged – words missing*) our selws, w[i]th the divell in elspet nishies hows, and ther took dowgs flesh and sheips flesh, and (*damaged – words missing*) it werie small, w[i]th an aix, and seithed it an heall fornoon ina pot among water, & (*damaged – words missing*) I took it owt and the divell w[i]th his awin hand, did put it in a sheips bagg, and he steiring it still abowt w[i]th his handis, we wer wpon o[u]r kneyes owr hair about o[u]r eyes and our handis lifted up, and ve looking stedfastlie wpon the divell prayeing to him repeatting the vordis q[uhi]ch he learned us, th[a]t it sould kill and destroy the lairdis of park and lochloy & th[i]r meall children & posteritie and then we cam to Inshoch in the night tym and skatered it wpon and downe abow and about the gait & uth[e]r places q[uhai]r the Lairdis & th[e]r sones wold most haint (to be – *crossed out?*), and th[e]n ve in the liknes of crowes and rewkis stood abow the gait and in the treis oposit to the gait, it wes apointed so th[a]t if any of th[e]m suld twitch or tramp wpon any of it, als veill as it or any of it to fall on th[e]m it sould strik th[e]m w[i]th byllis etc & kill them, q[uhi]lk it did & they shortlie died, we did it to mak (*damaged – words missing*) howl (airles) it wold wrong non els bot they, and it wes keathren sowter th[a]t wes brunt th[a]t w[illia]m hay the Last Laird of parkis broth[e]r for on gilbert kintey, it wes only th[a]t bagg th[a]t wes the death of both the last lairdis of park,

Also ffour yeir since, I and my husband Issobell gowdie spows to Jon gilbert in lochloy and bessie and margret wilsones in (*word crossed out*) aulderne, maid (*an pic*)tur of clay, lyk the Laird of parkis eldest sone, my husband brought hom the clay in his plaid (*damaged – words missing*) ves maid in my hows and the divell himself w[i]th us, we brak the clay werie small lyk meal (*damaged – words missing*) sifted it w[i]th a seiw and powred in vater amongst it w[i]th wordis th[a]t the divell learned vs (*damaged – words missing*) divellis nam, I brought hom the water in a pig, owt of the rud wall, we wer all wpon o[u]r (*kneyes*) and o[u]r hair abowt owr eyes and o[u]r handis lifted vp to the divell & o[u]r eyes stedfast looking (*damaged – words missing*) praying and saying wordis which he learned ws thryse ower, for destroyeing of this Lairds (*maill?*) children and to mak his hows airles, it wes werie sore wrowght, Lyk rye bowt, it wes abowt the bignes of a feadge or pow, it wes just maid lyk the bairne it vanted no mark of any maill child, such as heid face eyes nose mowth lippes etc and the handis of it folded downe by its syds: it ves putt to the fyre first till it scrukned, and th[e]n a cleir fyre about it till it ves hard, & th[e]n we took it out of the fyre in the divellis nam, & we laid a clowt abowt it & did lay up on a knag, & somtyms under a chist, each day we vold vater it & th[e]n rost and bek it & turn it at the fyre, each uth[e]r day whill th[a]t bairne died, and then layed it up and steired it not untill the nixt bairn (*word crossed out*) wes borne, and then within half an yeir efter that bairn ves borne (*we?*) took it owt again out of the cradl and clowt, and vold dip it now & th[e]n among water, and beck and rost it at the fyre each uth[e]r day once, as ve did ag[ains]t the uth[e]r th[a]t ves dead untill th[a]t bairne (*damaged – words missing*)

also all quhilkis of the premissis swa spokin and willinglie confessit & declarit furth of the mouth of the s[ai]d Janet bread(heid) in all and be all things as is abow sett downe

I the s[ai]f Johne Innes no[ta]r publict & haw w[ritti]ne thir p[rese]ntis and w[i]th the witnessis abownamet in farder testimonie and witnessing of the premissis to be of veritie we haw sub[scrivi]t the samen w[i]th our handis (*damaged – words missing*) yeir and place abowspe[cife]it

    (*Here follows John Innes' docquet – not transcribed*)

    (*Page damaged –signatures unreadable*)   WSutherland of kinsterie
                                        ATTESTES the premissis confessed in my
                                            presence apryl 15 1662
                                            JCouper ATTESTES

Hew Rose Mini[ste]r
At Nairne ATTESTS the premisses
Confessed in my p[rese]ce Aprile 15
1662

                                         J Falconer witnes to the premisses
Mr Hary forbes minister of   confest in my presentis
the gospel at OldEarn ATTESTS   15 of apryle
Archibald du[n]bar witnes ATESTS   Hew Hay ATTESTES the premisses
                                         confest 15 appryll 1662

    . . . ir: in auldearne ATTEASTS

Notes

Introduction to Part I THE CONSTRUCTION OF THE CONFESSIONS

1 Wedeck 1961: 202.
2 Pitcairn 1833: vol. 3, 604; Black 1938: 70.
3 *The Confession of Isobel Gowdie* premiered at the Royal Albert Hall in August 1990; Brodie-Innes 1974; Forde 2005, and *also see* Maitland 2003; Lawson 2007. Radio broadcasts include 'It must be Witchcraft' by Gary Lachman, aired on Radio 3 in August 2006. Lectures include 'Witchcraft and Elfhame: Isobel Gowdie' by Dr John Callow, given at Treadwells Bookshop in September 2005.
4 Wicca is a nature-based, modern pagan religion that draws inspiration from beliefs and practices surrounding traditional British magic and witchcraft. Although it has many roots, it was first popularized by English civil servant and occultist Gerald Gardner in the 1950s. The last sixty years has seen the development of many different traditions coming under the general term 'Wiccan'.

CHAPTER ONE

The Cottar's Wife

1 Dennison 1999: 7.
2 Donaldson 1794: 31.
3 Withrington & Grant 1982: 581; Donaldson 1794: 8.
4 Withrington & Grant 1982: 712; Bain 1928: 463.
5 Franck 1694: 184.
6 *NAS*, legal and estate documents relating to Hay of Lochloy and Park, GD125/17: Rest dated 1677 re rents from Lochloy.
7 Ross 1992: 124.
8 Franck 1694: 86; Ward 1699: 8.
9 Donaldson 1794: 20.
10 Grant 1995: 162.
11 Campbell 1975: 25.
12 Grant 1995: 162.
13 Youngson 1974: 102.
14 Ibid., 102 & 89.
15 *Papers of Brodie*. Box 2, drawer 4: Rentals, 1724 Lochloy & Park/1743 Brodie, Penick, Inshoch and Lochloy; Box 9, bundle 4: Rentals, 1731–72 Inshoch & Lochloy/1749 Inshoch and Penick; Box 6, bundle 3: 1728 Rental of barony of Lochloy/1731–35 Rental of Inshoch & Lochloy.

16 Anderson 1996: 127–8.
17 Brodie-Innes 1974: 8.
18 This portrait of Margaret Innes is on display at Kilravock Castle, Nairn; Youngson 1974: 151.
19 Ward 1699: 8.
20 Youngson 1974: 116.
21 Franck 1694: 80; Youngson 1974: 115.
22 Ward 1699: 8; Youngson 1974: 54.
23 *NAS*, legal and estate documents relating to Hay of Lochloy and Park, GD125/17.
24 Houston 1996: 133–4.
25 Law 1818: 27.
26 Youngson 1974: 51–2.
27 Ibid., 51.
28 *NAS*, legal and estate documents relating to Hay of Lochloy and Park, GD125/17.
29 Grant 1995: 222.
30 Carmichael 1995: 524.
31 For examples of these and many other activities illegally undertaken on the sabbath *see Records of Elgin*, vols. 1 & 2.
32 Withrington & Grant 1982: 719.
33 Ross 1992: 91; Withrington & Grant 1982: 535.
34 Ibid., 722; Bain 1928: 99.
35 Ibid., 249.
36 Ibid., 253.
37 Dennison 1998: 25.
38 Bain 1928: 90.
39 Ibid., 90.
40 Ibid., 90.
41 Ibid., 94.
42 Ibid., 216.
43 Ibid., 222 & 219.
44 Brodie 1863: xvii, xxv–xxxiii; Bain 1928: 211–12.
45 MacDonald 1875: 92–3; Young 1992: 334.
46 *See* Rose 1762, Campbell 1704 and Brodie 1863.
47 Kerr 1895: 77.
48 Brodie 1863: 217.
49 Dennison 1999: 24–5.
50 Maxwell-Stuart 2005: 12.
51 Arnold 2005: 40; Brown 1987: 100.
52 Todd 2002: 83.
53 Torrance 1959: 97.
54 Ibid., 184.
55 Brodie 1863: 174–5.
56 *Records of Elgin*: vol. 2, 289, 302.
57 Todd 2002: 393; Kirton 1704: 8.
58 Brodie 1863: 309; Campbell 1704: 60; Rose 1762: 14.
59 Todd 2002: 82.
60 Brodie 1863: 148.

61 Ibid., 171 & 332; Rose 1762: 213.

62 Campbell 1704: 36.

63 *Records of Elgin*: vol. 2, 367.

64 Ibid., vol. 2, 380.

65 Brodie 1863: 191.

66 Sinclair 1685: 158.

67 *Records of Elgin*: vol. 2, 300–1.

68 Todd 2002: 40.

69 *Records of Elgin*: vol. 2, 223, 269.

70 Craven 1908: 101 & 3.

71 Arnold 2005: 39.

72 Brodie 1863: 333.

73 *See* Sanderson 1976; Larner 1981: 78–9.

74 Cowan & Henderson 2001: 2 & 12.

75 Todd 2002: 396.

76 Davies 2007: 82–4.

77 Sinclair 1685: 123.

78 Sharpe 1884: 118.

79 Maxwell-Stuart 2001: 30.

80 *Records of Elgin*: vol. 2, 369.

81 Goodare 2008: 56.

82 Ibid.,119.

83 *See* Macdonald 2002: 169–77.

84 Levack 1980: 91–3.

85 Macdonald 2002: 173–5.

86 Brodie 1863: 246.

87 *PSAS*: 242.

88 *NAS*, Isobel Gowdie's Second Confession, GD125/16/5/1/2r,v. Thanks to Alison Lindsay of the NAS for this transcription.

89 *RPC*: series 3, vol.1: 243.

90 Brodie 1863: 259–60.

91 Ibid., 259.

92 For examples *see* ibid., 76, 273, 274, 362.

93 *ODNB*: 98.

94 Brodie 1863: 274.

95 Dennison 1999: 20; Bain 1928: 243–5; Brodie 1863: 293.

96 Larner 1981: 118.

97 Brodie 1863: 274.

98 Ibid., 296.

99 *Nairnshire Telegraph*, 20 June, 1860 (Jurisdictia of the magistrates of Nairn 200 years ago).

100 Brodie 1863: 274.

CHAPTER THREE

The Shadow of the Interrogator

1 Briggs 1959: 100; Bain 1928: 464; Briggs 1959: 100; Robbins 1959: 232; Davidson 1949: 5; *ODNB*: 98; Maxwell-Stuart 2005: 215; Hutton 1999:100; Cowan & Henderson 2002:

134; Pitcairn 1833: vol. 3, 604; Maxwell-Stuart 2005: 217.

2 Black 1938:70; McPherson 1929: 147.
3 Maxwell-Stuart 2005: 217.
4 Briggs 1959: 39.
5 Larner 1981: 151.
6 Cowan & Henderson 2002: 134.
7 Larner 1981: 153; Maxwell-Stuart 2005: 215.
8 This figure includes three charms that were recorded twice. These repeated charms differ sufficiently from their originals to be counted separately here.
9 Pitcairn 1833: vol. 3, 604.
10 Macculloch 1921: 237; Davidson 1949: 54; Robbins 1959: 232.
11 Bain 1928: 464.
12 Harte 2004: 150; Cowan & Henderson 2002: 16.
13 *RPC*: series 3, vol. 1: 243.
14 Scott 1857: 281–2.
15 Macculloch 1921: 238; Robbins 1959: 232; Briggs 1978: 128.
16 Bain 1928: 464; Smout 1969: 205–6.
17 Black 2005: viii; Harte 2004: 149.
18 Barger 1931: 31–37 *passim*.
19 *NAS*, legal and estate documents relating to Hay of Lochloy and Park, GD125/17. *See also* Caporael 1976: 23–4.
20 Withrington & Grant 1982: 714.
21 *See* example in *PSAS*: 224.
22 *See* examples in *PSAS*: 218–241; Hallen 1895:49–52; Pitcairn 1833: vol. I, 49–58.
23 *Stirling Presbytery Minutes*, CH2/722/6, p. 90. My thanks to Diane Baptie for this transcription.
24 Maxwell-Stuart 2005: 73.
25 *SSW*: Introduction.
26 Pitcairn 1833: vol. 1, 377. This quote has been modernized.
27 Sinclair 1685: lxx.
28 Mackenzie 1678: 86–7.
29 Sinclair 1685: *Preface*, A3.
30 Mackenzie 1678: 87.
31 Brainerd & Reyna 2005: 255–6.
32 Larner 1981: 118; Maxwell-Stuart 2005: 21 & 45.
33 Sinclair 1685: lxx.
34 Sharpe 1884: 188.
35 *SSW*: Introduction; *RPC*: series 3, vol. 1, 206.
36 Sinclair 1685: 53–4.
37 Todd 2002: 247–8.
38 Ibid., 248.
39 *SSW*: Introduction.
40 Mackenzie 1678: 87–7.
41 Goodare 2008: 56; Goodare 2002: 171.
42 Sinclair 1685: 212.
43 Brodie 1863: 260.
44 *RPC*: series 3, vol. 1, 243.

45 For example, if we take ten pages either side of the *RPC* reference to Isobel (all dated 1662) we find that similar cautions were issued alongside commissions in 4 out of 14 witchcraft cases, with no indication as to why they were inserted (*see RPC*: series 3, vol. 1, 232–3). For a proper assessment of this issue a wider survey is needed.

46 Barrett 2006: 46.

47 Brodie 1863: 294.

48 Ibid., 273.

49 Ibid., 274.

50 Ibid., 296.

51 Ibid., 295–6.

52 Ibid., 293–4.

53 Ibid., 296.

54 Ibid., 260.

55 Ibid., 273 & 293–4.

56 Ibid., 246 & 259.

57 Ibid., 259.

58 Ibid., 261.

59 Ibid., 294.

60 Ibid., 296.

61 Ibid., 273.

62 Ibid., 276.

63 Ibid., 421.

64 Ibid., 296.

65 Ibid., 296 & 292.

66 Craven 1889: 330 & 224. Cosmo Innes also observes that Rose's *Meditations* were 'written in a gentle and pious' spirit (Rose 1848: 378).

67 *See* Rose 1762: 207–9 for examples.

68 Goodare 2002: 171.

69 Rose 1762: 79–81.

70 Ibid., 197.

71 Lang 1909: 39–47.

72 Rose 1762: 195–6.

73 Ibid., vi.

74 Brodie 1863: 317.

75 Ibid., 136.

76 Ibid., 171.

77 Ibid., 176–7.

78 Ibid., 296.

79 Bain 1928: 218 & 222; Brodie 1863: 350–2.

80 Bain 1904: 151–2.

81 Ibid., 274.

82 Ibid., 291.

83 Grange was a named commissioner in the case of Nic Ean Vane and Mc Gillivorich, and as minister of Auldearn, Forbes was likely to have been involved in their interrogation, just as Hugh Rose was involved in Isobel's case two months later. Forbes may also have been sent to counsel them, as he was to Dyke witches Elder and Simpson the following year. Meanwhile Grange, having been a named commissioner in previous Auldearn and Nairn

cases, was likely to have been similarly employed in Bandon's case, if she was tried at an ad hoc court.

84 Brodie 1863: 294.

85 Adapted from Brainerd & Reyna 2005: 229.

86 The confessions do not make it clear whether the term 'nature' referred to penis or semen, though in my opinion the former seems more likely.

87 Pitcairn 1833: vol. 1, 49–52; MacPhail 1920: 37–8.

CHAPTER FOUR
Interweaving Worlds

1 Sharpe 1884: 134; Sinclair 1685: xlv.

2 Maxwell-Stuart 2005: 120; *Records of Elgin*: vol. 2, 275.

3 Black 1903: 100.

4 MacPhail 1920: 8.

5 Maxwell-Stuart 2005: 128.

6 MacPhail 1920: 25–6; Kinloch 1848: 121.

7 Stuart 1841: 180.

8 Ibid., 136.

9 Sinclair 1685: 9–11.

10 *See* MacPhail 1920: 11; *PSAS*: 50.

11 Lockhart 1938: 46. The Brodies of Brodie were later said to be cursed with just such a malediction (*see* Gordon 1882: 236–7).

12 Black 1903: 154–5.

13 McPherson 1929: 239–40 & 248–50.

14 Pitcairn concluded that the first line of this passage related to a previous charm. The evidence is unclear either way, so I have reproduced the text here as is.

15 Sanderson 1976: 112.

16 McPherson 1929: 232.

17 Pitcairn 1833: vol. 3, 556.

18 Goodare 2008: 145.

19 *PSAS*: 234.

20 Simpkins 1914: 360; Kinloch 1848: 115; MacPhail 1920: 18.

21 Brodie 1863: 00.

22 *PSAS*: 50.

23 *See* confession text: 42/25; 48/42; 49/13; 49/6; 49/24–5; 46/25; 42/27; 39/31; 49/2.

24 Larner 1981: 151. *See also* Kinloch 1848: 113–142 and, to a lesser extent, Hallen 1895: 49–52.

25 Kinloch 1848: 131.

26 Normand & Roberts 2000: 418.

27 Simpkins 1914: 72–3.

28 *Records of Elgin*: vol. 2, 211.

29 For examples see Pitcairn 1833: vol. 3, 602 and Normand & Roberts 2000: 226.

30 Cowan & Henderson 2002: 160.

31 *Galloway Gossip* . . . 1878: 142–160.

32 Simpkins 1914: 316.

33 Levack 1992: vol. 7, 393.

34 Campbell 1960: vol. 2, 60; Black 2005: 34.

35 Hunter 2001: 153.

36 Ibid., 154.

37 Brodie 1863: 353.

38 Marwick 1975: 35. *See also* Saxby 1932: 65, where the phrase appears as 'Hupp holes handokes'.

39 MacPhail 1920: 23.

40 Sanderson 1976: 59–60; Black 2005: lxxiii & 47.

41 Black 2005: 304–5.

42 Harte 2004: 146.

43 Campbell 1860: vol. 2, 71–2.

44 Black 1903: 85.

45 Hunter 2001: 153; Simpkins 1914: 316–17.

46 MacPhail 1920: 87; Maxwell-Stuart 2001: 115.

47 *Records of Elgin*: vol. 2, 357; Maxwell-Stuart 2001: 115.

48 MacPhail 1920: 11.

49 *Records of Elgin*: vol. 2, 211; *NAS*, the trial of Janet Boyman, JC26/1/57.

50 Harte 2004: 146.

51 This confusion clearly occurs during the interrogation of Donald McIlmichall (MacPhail 1920: 37–8).

CHAPTER FIVE

Curious Minds

1   Black 1903: 61–2.

2   Pitcairn 1833: vol. 1, 161–5; Normand and Roberts 2000: 231–46; Pitcairn 1833: vol. 1, 49–58.

3   Ibid., vol. 1, 163; Stuart 1841: 121; MacPhail 1920: 21.

4   Normand & Roberts 2000: 261–74 & 224–230; Black 1903: 55–60 & 99–103.

5   *See* confession text: 00/00; 00/00; 00/00.

6   Maxwell-Stuart 2005: 216.

7   *Nairnshire Telegraph*, 20th June, 1860 (Jurisdictia of the magistrates of Nairn 200 years ago).

8   Mullan 2000: 209.

9   Brodie 1863: 85.

10 McLachlan 2006: 288.

11 Roper 1994: 204–5.

12 Todd 2002: 129.

13 Ibid., 162.

14 Rose 1762: 25.

15 Ibid., 147.

16 Anderson 1893: 186.

17 Brodie 1863:136, 290, 141.

18 Ibid., 305.

19 Ibid., 137.

20 Ibid., 138.

21 MacDonald 1875: 210.

22 Rose 1762: 185–6.

23 *NAS*, Notarial protocol Book of John Innes, Elgin, 1662–1664, NPI/110.

24 Thomas 1990: 23.

25 Bain 1904: 152. Dunbar was also a close friend of Thomas Hogg, while Campbell of Cawdor lauded him as 'one of the best men I ever knew' (Ibid., 151–2).

26 My thanks to John Finlay for emphasizing Innes's clerical role here. With regard to Dunbar, it is also worth pointing out that although his role as witness did not preclude his functioning in a clerical role, the inconsistency of his appearance makes it less likely.

27 *Ars Notariatus* 1740: 294–5.

28 Ibid., 294.

29 Fox 2000: 83.

30 Angus 1936: 294–5.

31 *PSAS*: 242.

32 Maxwell-Stuart 2001: 117–18.

33 Thanks to Diane Baptie for these observations.

34 Forbes 1864: 246.

35 Grimble 1989: 112.

36 Pitcairn 1833: vol. 3, 604; Maxwell-Stuart 2005: 216; Purkiss 1996: 88.

37 Maxwell-Stuart 2005: 217.

38 Black 1646: 321. For the Scandinavian link *see* www.gowdy.org/name.htm, and for the latin link *see* www.davidkfaux.org/shetlandislandsYdataDtoGa.htm.

39 Withers 1983: 72.

40 Ibid., 32 & 55.

41 Bain 1928: 194.

42 Withers 1983: 68.

43 Ibid., 37.

44 See *Records of Elgin*: vol. 2, 275.

45 Buchan 1972: 4.

46 Ibid., 5; Omand 1987: 313.

47 Briggs 1970: p. A, vol. 1, 183.

CHAPTER SIX

'Q[uhe]n I wes in the elfes houssis'

1 Buchan 1984: 9.

2 Carmichael 1992: 24.

3 Grant 1981: 10.

4 Grant 1995: 136.

5 Sinclair 1685: 127.

6 Campbell 1860: vol. 2, 302.

7 Nagy 1986: 272.

8 Grant 1995: 131.

9 Ibid., 132.

10 Ibid., 131.

11 Campbell 1860: vol. 2, 473.

12 Ibid., vol. 1, 217.

13 Ibid., vol. 2, 302.

14 Ibid., vol. 2, 256.

15 Ibid., vol. 1, lvi–lvii.

16 Nagy 1986: 272.

17 Buchan 1972: 51–61; Bruford 1969: 36.

18 Buchan 1984: 8; Bruford 1969: 33.

19 Campbell 1860: vol. 2, 174.

20 Buchan 1984: 180.

21 Bruford 1969: 34.

22 Buchan 1984: 20–33; Briggs 1970: p. A, vol. 1, 180–4.

23 Bruford 1969: 36.

24 Buchan 1984: 74.

25 Ibid., 28.

26 Buchan 1972: 16.

27 Campbell 1860: vol. 1, xxxiii.

28 Briggs 1970: p. A, vol. 1, 183.

29 Grant 1995: 136; Child 1904: 413.

30 Grant 1995: 107.

31 Bruford 1996: 63.

32 Houston 1982: 87.

33 Buchan 1984: 9.

34 Grant 1981: 16.

35 Child 1904: 393, 399–400.

36 Forbes 1864: 248.

37 Maxwell-Stuart 2001: 30–2.

38 Neat 2002: 229.

39 Ibid., 229.

40 Rose 1848: 350. Her function as 'dame' was assumed by Rose's editor.

41 Hamilton 1998: 198.

42 Stuart 1841: 121.

43 McKay 1891: 21; Cowan & Henderson 2001: 42.

44 *The Greig-Duncan Folksong Collection*: vol. 1, 302–7 & 527. The ballad has been recently performed at Aberdeenshire's Doric Festival.

45 Hayward 1992: 51–2. The cast list of the Galoshins play was often as vivid and improbable as Isobel's list of familiar spirits: one version recorded in Ayr in the early-twentieth century features not only Hector, but also St George, William Wallace, a 'Black Prince', Robert the Bruce and 'Beelzebub' (Hayward 1992: 207–12).

46 *Records of Elgin*: vol. 2, 212–13.

47 Cowan & Henderson 2001: 144.

48 Mackay 1905: xxix.

49 Todd 2002: 376.

50 Cowan 1991: 74; Buchan 1984: 91, 238. Child was the most prominent collector to overlook 'bawdry'.

51 Cowan 2001: 143.

52 Buchan 1984: 110.

53 Cowan 2002: 166.

54 www.lib.rochester.edu/camelot/TTEssay.htm. *Also see* Green 2007: 126.

55 *See Tom Thumb, His Life and Death* . . . 1682.

56   Stuart 1841: 121.
57   *The Famous History of Tom Thumb* . . . 1775: 37; Briggs 1970: p. A, vol. 1, 532.
58   Child 1904: 4.
59   Ibid., 67–9.
60   Ibid., 78.
61   Campbell 1860: vol. 1, 63–6.
62   Buchan 1972: 76.
63   Buchan 1984: 3–4.
64   Ibid., 3–4.
65   Goodare 2008: 95–118.
66   Brodie 1863: 165.
67   Evans Wentz 1977: xvi.
68   Carmichael 1992: 9–10.
69   Campbell 1860: vol. I, xxi.
70   Mackay 1905: xvii.
71   Ibid., xxxv.
72   Thanks to Diane Baptie for pointing this out to me.
73   Simpson 1995: 18; Buchan 1984: 12; Cowan & Henderson 2001: 165.
74   Ibid., 11–12.
75   Kirton 1704: 8.
76   Mackay 1905: xxxv.
77   Brodie 1863: 33 & 39.
78   Rose 1762: 166, 198, 190.
79   Ibid., 48.

CHAPTER SEVEN

The Men of Constant Sorrows

1   Cowan & Henderson 2001:16.
2   Black 1903: 103–11; Stuart 1843: x–xi.
3   Pócs 1999: 12.
4   Goodare 2008: 66.
5   Briggs 1996: 141.
6   Brodie 1863: 136, 103.
7   Dennison 1998: 21.
8   *See* Ross 1992.
9   Wormald 2008: 156–7.
10   Dennison 1998: 24; Ross 1992: 128.
11   Sibbald 1699: 3.
12   Dennison 1998: 26; Withrington & Grant 1982: lii.
13   Ibid., 723.
14   Brodie 1863: 350.
15   Ibid., 354; Mullan 2003: 62.
16   Rose 1762: 21.
17   Bain 1928: 230.
18   Constable 1859: 387.
19   Mackay 1905: xxix.

20 Bain 1928: 230.

21 Reid 2003: 64.

22 Barrett 2006: 48.

23 Reid 2003: *cover blurb*; Bain 1928: 205; Reid 2003:61. In the song recorded in Aberdeen the Battle of Auldearn was confused with an engagement that took place between Sir Thomas Livingstone and Colonel Buchan in 1690, as celebrated in 'The Haughs o' Cromdale' (Greig-Duncan 1983: vol. 1, 314, 528–9).

24 Reid 2003: 42.

25 Bain 1928: 206; Reid 2003: 61.

26 Bain 1928: 206–7; Reid 2003: 61.

27 Bain 1928: 205–6. Possibly the uncle of the young John Hay whose father died in 1640. Also see CHAPTER SEVEN, n. 74.

28 Brodie 1863: 139.

29 Ibid., 110.

30 Ibid., lxxv.

31 Ibid., lxix.

32 Barrett 2006: 50.

33 Brodie 1863: lxix.

34 Ibid., 112.

35 Bain 1928: 213; *Records of Elgin*, vol. 2, 366; Stevenson 1986: 73.

36 Levack 1980: 91–3.

37 Ward 1699: 13.

38 Brodie 1863: 168, 172.

39 Ibid., 196–7.

40 Ibid., 88.

41 Ibid., 112, 109.

42 Ward 1699: 8–9.

43 Nicholson 1881: xxix.

44 Brodie 1863: 79, 443.

45 Ibid., 496.

46 *NAS*, legal and estate documents relating to Hay of Lochloy and Park, GD125/17.

47 Ross 1992: 126.

48 Ibid., 123–4.

49 Brodie 1863: 281, 283.

50 Nicholson 1881: xxix.

51 Barrett 2006: 50.

52 Rose 1848: 312–13. The Spalding Club transcription cites the date as both 1625 and 1635. It is assumed here that the second date is a misprint.

53 Bain 1928: 269.

54 *RPS*, 1690/4/138; Young 1992: 334.

55 Brodie 1863: 485.

56 *RPS*, 1690/4/138. *See also* Brodie archives, Box 27, Bundle 5: Decreet of sale of lands of late John Hay of Park to George Brodie of Brodie, 22 June 1710.

57 Brodie 1863: 315-16.

58 *NAS*, Account resting by the Laird of Park to Mr Harry Forbes, GD/125/16/3/4/2.

59 *NAS*, Letter Alexander Dunbar to the Laird of Park, GD125/16/4/1/10.

60 Brodie 1863: 280.

61 Ibid., 447.

62 Ibid., 443-4.

63 In his 1882 updating of Lachlan Shaw's *History of Moray and Nairn,* James Gordon states that 'John Hay, of Lochloy, who deceased in July, 1640, left his body to be buried in the burial place of his forbearis within the quier of Aulderne, and ordained ane loft to be biggit within the Kirk of Aulderne, on the north syd therof, with the timber gotten of the chanrie Kirk of Elgin.' (Kilravock papers. Ed.) (Gordon 1882: 252). *NAS* GD125/16 contains many documents, dated around 1641, relating to John Hay of Knockandie, 'executor testamentar to John Hay of Park'.

64 For reference to a brother, *see NAS,* Account resting by the Laird of Park to Mr Harry Forbes, GD/125/16/3/4/2 and *NAS,* bond from David Stewart, Comissary of Moray, to John Hay of Park, GD/125/16/2/1/27. For reference to sisters, *see NAS,* marriage contract between Thomas Dunbar of Westfield, on behalf of Patrick Dhis 2nd son . . . ', GD/125/16/3/1/8, and Macdonald 1875: 93.

65 Brodie 1863: 315.

66 For an example *see* Scott-Moncrieff 1889: x-xi.

67 Rose 1848: 84.

68 *RPC:* series 3, vol. 1, 206, 221.

69 MacPhail 1920: 35, 31.

70 Sinclair 1685: 14–15.

71 *RPC:* series 2, vol. 7, 595.

72 Ibid., series 2, vol. 7, 596.

73 Brodie 1863: 325.

74 We can draw this conclusion based on the fact that in his *Genealogical Deduction* Hugh Rose claims that David Hay had three sons, John, William and 'Hugh Hay of Brightmonie, Tutor of Park, who dyed January 30, 1665' (Rose 1848: 84). Rose is likely to have been correct in his assertions, for he was clearly acquainted with this Hugh Hay of Brightmony (both men being present at Isobel's trial in 1662) and with John Hay, the heir of Park (Rose 1848: 85–6). Moreover, it would have been logical for the younger surviving son to take on the running of the estate until the heir came of age, while living on one of the minor Park estates like Brightmony; while a 'Tutor of Park' appears in a variety of legal documents up to the early 1660s (for examples *see* Rose 1848: 375 & Wodrow 1835: 274). However, this interpretation is contradicted by Bain's claim, in his *Lord Brodie: His Life and Times,* that the father of the 'Hugh Hay of Brightmony' alive in 1659 was killed at the Battle of Auldearn (Bain 1904: 85). The most likely explanation is that Bain was confusing his Hays, or that he was referring to a subsequent Hay of Brightmony, particularly given the fact that in his later *History of Nairnshire* he claims that it was 'Hay of Kinnudie . . . uncle of young Hay of Lochloy' who died at Auldearn in 1645 (Bain 1928: 205). Nevertheless, these contradictions emphasize the fact that, given the lack of genealogical information for this branch of the Hays in this period, we must exercise caution when drawing any conclusions.

75 *See* Sanderson 1976.

76 Mackay 1905: xvii.

77 Torrance 1959: 147.

78 Rose 1762: 122–3.

79 Brodie 1863: 179.

80 Nicholson 1881: xxiii.

81 Todd 2002: 378.

82 Ibid., 380–1.

83 Brodie 1863: 306.

84 Bain 1904: 62; Rose 1762: 163.

85 Brodie 1863: 128.

86 Ibid., 128, 132.

87 Ibid., 123.

88 Ibid., 135.

89 Ibid., 279.

90 Bain 1904: 151.

91 Macdonald 1875: 95–6.

92 Mullan 2003: 49–50.

93 *NAS*, Caithness Presbytery Minutes, CH2/47/1, August 22. Thanks to Diane Baptie for this reference.

94 Craven 1908: 109–10.

95 Ibid., 112.

96 Brodie 1863: 141.

97 Ibid., 136.

98 Craven 1908: 111.

99 *RPC*: series 2, vol. 8, 29–30.

100 Maxwell-Stuart 2005: 119.

101 Todd 2002: 377–8.

102 Maxwell-Stuart 2005: 79.

103 Brodie 1863: 136.

104 Ibid., 135.

105 Ibid., 136.

106 Ibid., 135.

107 Brodie 1863: 143; Bain 1928: 216.

108 *NAS*, Bond Forbes to Forbes, RD3/9p178-179.

109 Brodie 1863: 273, 279.

110 Ibid., 405.

111 Macdonald 1875: 102.

112 Macdonald 1875: 102. Collace's memoirs are reproduced in Mullan 2003: 39–94.

113 Mullan 2003: 49.

114 Ibid., 49–50.

115 Ibid., 49.

116 Ibid., 49.

117 Nicholson 1881: xxiii: Simpkins 1912: 414.

118 Macdonald 1875: 102; Brodie 1863: 167. *See also* Stevenson 1756 for a more detailed exposition of Hogg's spirituality.

119 Todd 2002: 361–9.

120 Brodie 1863: 306.

121 Donaldson 1990: 83.

122 Stevenson 1972: 168.

123 Ibid., 169.

124 Ibid., 169.

125 Mullan 2003: 50.

126 Stevenson 1972: 169.
127 Black 1903: 74.

CHAPTER EIGHT

The Ethics of Malevolence

1   Colville 1825: 217; Youngson 1974: 99.
2   Wormald 1981: 36.
3   Ibid., 35.
4   *RPC*: series 2, vol. 8, 225.
5   Hamilton 1998: xi.
6   Ibid., 71.
7   Ibid., 70.
8   The Sunday Review, *Sunday Independent*, 21 January 2007: 21–2.
9   Kirton 1704: 8.
10 Hamilton 1998: 36, 59.
11 Nicholson 1881: xxix.
12 Lockhart 1938: 3–4.
13 Torrance 1959: 211; Brodie 1863: 190–1.
14 Black 2005: 153–4.
15 Torrance 1959: 222.
16 Brodie 1863: 77.
17 *RPC*: series 2, vol. 8, 223; Black 1903: 74; *RPC*: series 2, vol. 8, 220, 222; McPherson 1929: 194.
18 Black 1903: 55.
19 McPherson 1929: 194; Black 1903: 125.
20 Black 2005: 154.
21 Mackey 1997: 189.
22 *Records of Elgin*, vol. 2, 357.
23 Brodie 1863: 314.
24 Kimura 2000: 11, 101.
25 Kieckhefer 2000: 82.
26 Black 2005: 204.
27 Carmichael 1992: 386.
28 Ibid., 13–18; Black 2005: 600.
29 Jolly 1996: 92; Black 2005: 451.
30 Maxwell-Stuart 2001: 17.
31 MacPhail 1920: 19; Dalyell 1834: 7.
32 Sanderson 1976: 112.
33 Simpkins 1912: 94.
34 Carmichael 1992: 429.
35 Cohn 1993: 212–13.
36 Maxwell-Stuart 2001: 27.
37 Cohn 1993: 212–13.
38 *Inverness Courier*, Thurs 17 July, 1879.
39 Black 1903: 72–4.
40 *See* Thomas 1971: 670–72 & Roper 1994: 206–218.

41 Stuart 1843: xi.

42 *RPC*: series 2, vol. 8, 75.

43 Stuart 1841: 105.

44 Black 1903: 95.

45 Pitcairn 1833, vol. 1: 201.

46 Black 1903: 66–73 *passim*.

47 Stuart 1841: 94–5.

48 Maxwell-Stuart 2001: 125. For the whole analysis, *see* 124–33.

49 Ibid., 129.

50 Pitcairn 1833: vol. 3, 618.

51 Ibid., vol. 1, 192.

52 Cohn 1993: 107.

53 Kieckhefer 1998: 71–2.

CHAPTER NINE

Wonderful Lies

1 Burwick 1996: 238–40; Barger 1931: 31–6.

2 Ibid., 36.

3 Ibid., 36–7.

4 Campbell 1860, vol. 1, 63.

5 Roper 1994: 52.

6 *See* Roper 1994: 199–241; Purkiss 2001a: 90–109; Purkiss 1996: 100–12. *Also see* Purkiss 2001b.

7 Roper 1994: 1.

8 Ibid., 226.

9 Ibid., 230–1.

10 Dennison 1998: 9; Ross 1992: 88.

11 Ross 1992: 88, 91.

12 Bochel 2003: 73.

13 Levine & Scudamore 1998: 24.

14 Ross 1992: 64.

15 Purkiss 2001: 113.

16 *ODNB*: 98.

17 Ibid., 98; Purkiss 2001: 113; Maxwell-Stuart 2005: 218–19.

18 Examples from seventeenth-century Nairn can be found in Dennison 1998: 25 and Bain 1928: 253.

19 Bain 1928: 254.

20 Todd 2002: 264.

21 Brodie 1863: 323.

22 Stevenson 1986: 72.

23 *RPC*: series 2, vol. 8, 206.

24 Todd 2002: 296–7.

25 Purkiss 2001: 88.

26 Roper 1994: 232.

27 Roper 2004: 58.

28 Todd 2002: 264.

29   Roper 2004: 6 & 77.
30   Purkiss 2001: 88; Briggs 1996: 339.
31   Brainerd & Reyna 2005: 253.
32   Ibid., 257.
33   Ibid., 256.
34   Ibid., *Preface.*
35   Ibid., 73–96.
36   Ibid., 410–12.
37   Ibid., 413.
38   Ibid., 414.
39   Ibid., 412.
40   Ibid., 415.
41   Ibid., 366–70 *passim.*
42   Ibid., 369.
43   Ibid., 370.
44   Ibid., 374.
45   *See* McLachlan 2006: 56–7.
46   Stuart 1841: 129.
47   Craven 1908: 104.
48   Child 1904: 19.
49   Fox 2000: 26.
50   Campbell 1975: 49.
51   *Galloway Gossip* . . . 1878: 223.
52   Fox 2000: 26.
53   Grant 1995: 132; Martin 1703: 13–14.
54   Buchan 1972: 52, 58.
55   Ibid., 59.
56   Grant 1995: 133.
57   Child 1904: xxiv.
58   Buchan 1972: 52.
59   *See* Hamish Henderson's critique in Cowan 1991: 68–74. *Also see* Bruford 1978.
60   Buchan 1972: 52.
61   Ibid., 53, 87, 87–144 *passim.*
62   Ibid., 61.
63   Child 1904: xxiv.
64   Campbell 1860: vol. 1, xliv–xlv.
65   The only elements of fairy belief which the interrogators seem to have consistently considered criminally relevant (as evinced by the fact that they were repeatedly returned to in depth and appeared in the fourth confession) were those involving the shooting of elf arrows (coming, as they did, under the umbrella of *maleficium*) and those involving servitor spirits (being defined as commerce with evil spirits).

Introduction to Part II SHAMANISTIC PERSPECTIVES

1   The English translation of Ginzburg's *Ecstasies* was first published by Pantheon Books in 1991. *See* Ginzburg 1992.
2   Stevenson & Davidson 2001: 399.

3　The English translation of Ginzburg's *The Night Battles* was first published by Routledge & Kegan Paul in 1983. *See* Ginzburg 1983.

4　Ginzburg 1991: 307, 23.

5　*See* Behringer 1998, Henningsen 1990, Klaniczay 1990, Klaniczay & Pócs 2005–8, Lecouteux 2003, Pócs 1991–2 & 1999, Wilby 2005.

6　Pócs 1991: 7, 95.

7　Kivelson 2000: 201. *See also* Klaniczay & Pócs 2008: 37–42.

8　Briggs 1996: 37.

9　Ibid., 37.

10　Barry & Davies 2007: 137; Dégh 1991: 760.

11　Briggs 1996: 56.

12　Kieckhefer 1992: 837.

13　Goodare 2008: 30.

14　Kieckhefer 1992: 838.

15　Pócs 1999: 96.

16　Muchembled 2003: 18.

17　Bailey 2003: 48; Thurston 2001: 55; Cowan & Henderson 2001: 45.

18　Todd 2002: 219.

19　Briggs 1996: 58.

20　Roper 2004: 117.

21　Cohn 1993: 175.

22　Ibid., 178.

23　*Records of Elgin*: vol. 2, 211.

24　Todd 2002: 356.

25　These problems were recently discussed by Carlo Ginzburg, Gustav Henningsen, Éva Pócs, Giovanni Pizza and Gábor Klaniczay, at a round-table debate in Budapest (*see* Klaniczay and Pócs 2008: 35–49).

26　Behringer 1998: 145; Kieckhefer 1992: 837–8; Behringer 1998: 143; Barry & Davies 2007: 135; Pòcs 1999: 13.

CHAPTER TEN
An Old Way of Seeing

1　Walsh 1990: 45–55, 161–5.

2　Lincoln 1970: 44–5.

3　Ibid., 28.

4　Tedlock 1987: 5.

5　Ibid., 6, 119.

6　Ibid., 62.

7　Ekirch 2001: 367.

8　Lincoln 1970: 39, 300.

9　Ibid., 40.

10　Ibid., 209.

11　Tedlock 1987: 171.

12　Lincoln 1970: 250.

13　Ibid., 250.

14　*Collins English Dictionary*; Walsh 1990: 9; http://oregonstate.edu/instruct/anth370/gloss.html.

15 Walsh 1990: 11.
16 Ibid., 12.
17 Ibid., 12.
18 Lyon 1998: 65–6.
19 Lincoln 1970: 72.
20 Balzer 1990: 57, 102; Van Deusen 2004: 122.
21 Gackenbach & LaBerge 1988: 353–87.
22 Balzer 1990: 29.
23 Walsh 1990: 119.
24 Ibid., 446.
25 Tedlock 2005: 105–6.
26 Ullman 1973: 37.
27 Tedlock 2005: 108.
28 Lincoln 1970: 194.
29 Tedlock 1987: 21.
30 Fortune 1969: 38–42.
31 Noll 1985: 449–50.
32 Van Deusen 2004: 132.
33 Ibid., xv, 19, 140.
34 Irwin 1994: 189–90.
35 Kruger 1992: 151.
36 Mullan 2003: 47–8.
37 Sharpe 1884: 218.
38 Ekirch 2001: 344, 364–74.
39 Devlin 1987: 80.
40 Campbell 1975: 35.
41 Pócs 1999: 93.
42 MacPhail 1920: 13.
43 Kruger 1992: 120, 179; *also see* Sharpe 1884: 214.
44 Erickson 1976: 29.
45 Campbell & Thomson 1963: 54; Simpkins 1912: 389.
46 Brodie 1863: 283.
47 Thomas 1973: 153.
48 Sharpe 1884: 101.
49 Brodie 1863: 134.
50 Shaw 1775: 306. Shaw does not specify a date here, but the latter was likely to have been between 1560 and 1700.
51 Ibid., 307.
52 Ibid., 307.
53 Marwick 1975: 97.
54 Walsham 1999: 203–14; Todd 2002: 393–6; Landsman 1989: 135.
55 Brodie 1863: 283.
56 Sharpe 1884: 203–4.
57 Clark 2007: 307.
58 *See* Landsman 1989.
59 Thomas 1971: 153; Brown 1999: 131.
60 Black 1903: 101.

61 *The Greig-Duncan Folksong Collection*: vol. 1, 47.

62 Sharpe 1884: 202.

63 Ibid., 203–4.

64 Ibid., 151–8.

65 Todd 2002: 399.

66 *See* Wilby 2005: 231–2. *See also* Klaniczay & Pócs 2005: 223–5.

67 Cohn 1993: 102–17. *See also* Kieckhefer 1998.

68 Ross 1976: 33–62.

69 Sanderson 1976: 75, 77; Davidson 1989: 13.

70 Black 1903: 74.

71 Sharpe 1884: 210.

72 Kruger 1992: 17–56.

73 Ibid., 119–22.

74 Sanderson 1976: 50.

75 Cohn 1993: 24.

76 Kruger 1992: 68.

77 Sahlin 2001: 68.

78 Cohen 1957: 304; Tedlock 1987: 185.

79 Thomas 1973: 151.

80 Ibid., 682.

81 Tedlock 1989: 2.

82 Clarke 2007: 216.

83 Sharpe 1884: 232.

84 Ibid., 178.

85 Brodie 1863: 132.

86 Bath & Newton 2006: 2.

87 Clark 1997: 493–500.

88 Cohen 1957: 15.

89 Todd 2002: 398.

90 Sharpe 1884: 166.

91 Mullan 2003: 47.

92 Hindmarsh 2005: 221.

93 Sanderson 1976: 58.

94 *See* Stuart 1843: x–xi for an example.

95 Evans-Wentz 1977: 477.

96 Pitcairn 1833: vol. 1, 162.

97 Youngson 1974: 134.

98 Sharpe 1884: 151–2, 156.

99 Normand & Roberts 2000: 419.

100 Sanderson 1976: 98.

101 Ibid., 70.

102 *The Records of Elgin*, vol. 2, 357.

103 Maxwell-Stuart 2001: 117.

104 Youngson 1974: 134; *NAS*, The trial of Janet Boyman, JC26/1/57; Stuart 1941: 121–2.

105 Van Deusen 2004: xii, 8, 138–9.

106 Maxwell-Stuart 2001: 116–18.

107 Pitcairn 1833: vol. 1, 53.

108 Todd 2002: 219; Cowan & Henderson 2001: 83.
109 Maxwell-Stuart 2001: 131.
110 Cowan & Henderson 2001: 131.
111 *NAS*, The trial of Janet Boyman, JC26/1/57.
112 Simpkins 1912: 73.
113 Pitcairn 1833: vol. 1, 53.
114 Todd 2002: 356.
115 Van Deusen 2004: 25–6.
116 Pócs 1999: 74.
117 Simpkins 1912: 103, 88, 326; Kinloch 1848: 121.
118 MacPhail 1920: 18.
119 *RPC*: series 2, vol. 8, 197.
120 Clark 2007: 313.
121 Maidment 1845: 65–6.
122 Brodie 1863: 260.
123 Mackenzie 1678: 87.
124 Youngson 1974: 135; Sinclair 1685: xcii.
125 Clark 1997: 461; Brodie 1863: 259.
126 Clark 2007: 317.
127 Brodie 1863: 259.
128 Pócs 1999: 39.
129 Noll 1985: 444.
130 Bath & Newton 2006: 9.
131 Black 1903: 37.
132 Campbell 1860: vol. 2, 51.
133 Ginzburg 1983: 154.
134 Lyon 1998: 66.
135 Normand & Roberts 2000: 389.
136 Behringer 1998: 135.
137 Ibid., 70.
138 Lecouteux 2003: 76.
139 Cohn 1993: 165.
140 Clark 1997: 238.
141 Sharpe 1884: 192.
142 Pócs 1999: 31.
143 Carr 1930: 85.
144 Ginzburg 1983: 165.
145 Pócs 1999: 93.
146 Ibid., 61, 96.
147 Lévy-Bruhl 1965: 169.
148 Ibid., 170.
149 Black 1903: 36.
150 Pócs 1999: 74.
151 Ibid., 39.
152 Ibid., 39.
153 Black 1903: 36.
154 Lecouteux 2003: 148.

155 Ibid., 148.
156 Ginzburg 1983: 159.
157 *Holy Bible*, King James Version.
158 Cairns 1762: 31.
159 As late as 1697 minister James Hutchison noted that some witches are 'carried and brought back again [from the sabbath] *they know not how* [my italics]' (Levack 1992: vol. 7, 394).
160 *The Records of Elgin*, vol. 2, 299.
161 Spanos & Gottlieb 1976: 1391.
162 Sharpe 1884: 101.

CHAPTER ELEVEN
Isobel Follows the Goddess

 1 Ginzburg 1991: 92–4; Behringer 1998: 59; Henningsen 1990: 204.
 2 Barry & Davies 2007: 132.
 3 Cohn 1993: 170.
 4 Ibid., 170.
 5 Behringer 1998: 69. For links with the female-led nexus *see* Behringer 1998: 47–71. Behringer also provides a good example of this tradition-matrix among the Waldensians in Klaniczay & Pócs 2005: 174.
 6 Ginzburg 1991: 94–5.
 7 Henningsen 1990: 196.
 8 Cohn 1993: 170.
 9 Behringer 1998: 69.
10 Ginzburg 1991: 94; Behringer 1998: 69.
11 Lecouteux 2003: 76.
12 Henningsen 1990: 198.
13 Behringer 1998: 54–55.
14 Henningsen 1990: 200.
15 Ginzburg 1983: 149–50.
16 Henningsen 1990: 195.
17 Behringer 1998: 59.
18 Ibid., 70.
19 Cowan & Henderson 2001: 136.
20 Normand & Roberts 2000: 418; Cowan & Henderson 2001: 135.
21 Black 1903: 85.
22 Evans-Wentz 1977: 122.
23 Todd 2002: 219.
24 Ginzburg 1991: 96.
25 Pócs 1989: 23.
26 Motz 1984: 154.
27 *See* Gundarsson 1992.
28 Davidson & Chaudri 2001: 172.
29 *See* Gundarsson 1992.
30 Davidson & Chaudri 2001: 171–2.
31 Pócs 1989: 22.
32 Cohn 1993: 165.

33   Ibid., 175.
34   Behringer 1998: 59.
35   Ibid., 54.
36   Ginzburg 1983: 148, 151, 150.
37   Ibid., 122.
38   Ibid., 155.
39   Henningsen 1990: 206.
40   Ibid., 200.
41   Davidson & Chaudri 2001: 173–4.
42   Cohn 1993: 169.
43   Behringer 1998: 80–81.
44   Morris 1991: 146.
45   Behringer 1998: 81.
46   Pócs 1999: 16.
47   Ibid., 138.
48   Pócs 1999: 113.
49   Ginzburg 1983: ix.
50   Ginzburg 1991: 90.
51   Cohn 1993: 165.
52   Behringer 1998: 59.
53   Pócs 1999: 138.

CHAPTER TWELVE

'His hour was pursuing him'

1   Cowan & Henderson 2001: 77.
2   MacPhail 1920: 23.
3   Ibid., 27.
4   Ibid., 10.
5   Briggs 1959: 194.
6   Briggs 1978: 173–4.
7   Sanderson 1976: 95, 49.
8   Pócs 1999: 153.
9   Kalweit 1988: xv.
10   Vitebsky 2001: 74.
11   Whitehead & Wright 2004: 10.
12   Ritchie 2000: 28.
13   Ibid., 253–7.
14   Whitehead & Wright 2004: 268.
15   Lévy-Bruhl 1965: 270.
16   Ritchie 2000: 66.
17   Lévy-Bruhl 1965: 270–2.
18   Ibid., 270.
19   Ibid., 272.
20   Whitehead & Wright 2004: 90–1.
21   Whitehead 2002: 14, 104, 66.
22   Ibid., 90–1.

23   Ibid., 202–3.
24   Whitehead & Wright 2004: 48.
25   Whitehead 2002: 97.
26   Whitehead & Wright 2004: 48.
27   Ibid., 42.
28   Whitehead 2002: 125–6, 163, 169, 217–8. For *benandanti* duplicity *see* Ginzburg 1983: 122–3, 155.
29   Whitehead & Wright 2004: 41–2, 45, 61–2; Whitehead 2002: 126.
30   Carrington 1996: 76–7.
31   Ibid., 58.
32   Ibid., 58.
33   Ibid., 63.
34   Ibid., 77.
35   Ibid., 67.
36   Ibid., 98.
37   Ibid., 98.
38   Ibid., 107.
39   Ibid., 59.
40   Kalweit 1988: 87–8.
41   Van Deusen 2004: 76.
42   Behringer 1998: 23.
43   Ginzburg 1983: 61.
44   Whitehead & Wright 2004: 40.
45   Ibid., 39.
46   Whitehead 2002: 114.
47   Cohn 1993: 178.
48   Black 2005: 303–4.
49   Carmichael 1928: 358.
50   Ibid., 357.
51   Campbell 1860: vol. 2, 71–2.
52   Black 2005: 305.
53   MacPhail 1920: 18–19.
54   Stuart 1843: xii.
55   Carrington 1996: 88, 110.
56   Whitehead 2002: 115, 117.
57   Carrington 1996: 58.
58   Ibid., 70.
59   Ibid., 107.
60   Black 2005: 37.
61   Ibid., 81.
62   Campbell 1860: vol. 2, 72.
63   Black 2005: 305.
64   Grant 1995: 366.
65   Sanderson 1976: 60–1.
66   Ibid., 68.
67   Ibid., 59–60.
68   Ibid., 60; Pitcairn 1833: vol. 1, 53.

69 Carrington 1996: 89.

70 Ibid., 89.

71 Ibid., 106.

72 Ibid., 99.

73 Whitehead & Wright 2004: 48, 41.

74 Whitehead 2002: 204.

75 Grambo 1988: 13.

76 Sanderson 1976: 61.

77 Macphail 1920: 29.

78 Carrington 1996: 99.

79 Nicholson 1881: xxii. For definitions see *Collins English Dictionary*.

80 Withrington & Grant 1982: 718.

81 Nicholson 1881: xxii.

82 Campbell 1975: 36; Sanderson 1976: 103.

83 This is a rephrasing of Campbell 1860: vol. 2, 72.

84 Grambo 1988: 11; Morris 1991: 29.

85 Lecouteux 2003: 110.

86 Pócs 1989: 32.

87 Simpson 1995: 11.

88 Jolly 1996: 134.

89 Pócs 1989: 32.

90 Hall 2007: 1–3.

91 Ibid., 114–15.

92 Ibid., 114–15.

93 Ibid., 113.

94 Ibid., 113.

95 Morris 1991: 108.

96 Davidson 1964: 61.

97 Morris 1991: 8.

98 Lysaght 1986: 130, 198, 396.

99 Evans-Wentz 1977: 305. Link challenged by Lysaght 1986: 105–7.

100 Simpson 1995: 11.

101 Jubainville & Best 1903: 110; Hall 2005b: 174.

102 Ibid., 172.

103 Hall 2007: 113, 116.

104 Morris 1991: 107.

105 Davidson 1964: 61–2.

106 Ibid., 61.

107 Nicholson 1881: xxii; Sanderson 1976: 61.

108 Pócs 1999: 96.

109 Simpkins 1914: 325.

110 Cohn 1993: 165; Behringer 1998: 54, 59; Carrington 1996: 63.

111 Whitehead 2002: 97.

112 *See* Roper 2004, Chapter Three.

113 Hall 2005b: 171.

114 Holinshed 1808: 268–9.

115 Pócs 1999: 65, 50.

116 Ibid., 65–6.

117 Ibid., 65.

118 Ibid., 66.

119 Ibid., 66.

120 Eichenberger & Zika 1998: 120.

121 Grillot de Givry 1971: 59.

122 Eichenberger & Zika 1998: 123.

123 Zika 2002: 16–17; Yarnall 1994: 194.

124 Pócs 1999: 152.

CHAPTER THIRTEEN

The Choosers of the Slain

1   Whitehead & Wright 2004: 239.

2   Ritchie 2000: 66.

3   Whitehead 2002: 91, 124.

4   Balikci 1967: 206.

5   Ritchie 2000: 66.

6   MacPhail 1920: 27.

7   Nicholson 1881: xxii.

8   Hall 2005: 30. Alaric Hall assumes this Jenet Millar to be the Linlithgow woman of the same name tried in Edinburgh in 1661 (Hall 2005: 34, *fn* 6).

9   MacPhail 1920: 24.

10   Carrington 1996: 58.

11   Ibid., 110.

12   Ibid., 148–9.

13   Evans-Wentz 1977: 106.

14   Ibid., 109.

15   Black 2005: 47.

16   Fausto 2000: 940.

17   Pitcairn 1833: vol. 3, 618.

18   Stuart 1843: x–xi; Black 1903: 103–11; Maxwell-Stuart 2001: 115–21.

19   Pócs 1999: 138.

20   Pitcairn 1833: vol. 1, 192–200.

21   Whitehead & Wright 2004: 196.

22   Whitehead 2002: 104 & 126.

23   Pócs 1999: 65.

24   Sharpe 1884: 133.

25   Black 1903: 85 & 73.

26   Campbell 1975: 36.

27   Craven 1908: 103.

28   *Records of Elgin*, vol. 2, 220.

29   Maxwell-Stuart 2001: 129.

30   Whitehead & Wright 2004: 268.

31   Van Deusen 2004: 62.

32   MacPhail 1920: 21–2.

33   Ibid., 23.

34 Evans-Wentz 1977: 106, 108.
35 Sanderson 1976: 58.
36 Maxwell-Stuart 2001: 115.
37 Black 1903: 54.
38 Pitcairn 1833: vol. 1, 203.
39 Ibid., vol. 1, 202.

Introduction to Part III THE DEMONOLOGICAL ELEMENTS
1 Whitehead 2002: 50, 53–76.
2 Levack 2004: 198–202.

CHAPTER FOURTEEN
Lady Isobel and the Elf Knight
1 Pitcairn 1833: vol. 1, 51–8.
2 MacPhail 1920: 37–8.
3 Black 1903: 114.
4 Macdonald 2002: 46.
5 Goodare 2008: 149.
6 MacPhail 1920: 37–8.
7 Stuart 1843: xii.
8 Pitcairn 1833: vol. 1, 163; Black 1903: 55.
9 Youngson 1974: 134; MacPhail 1920: 38; Maxwell-Stuart 2001: 117.
10 Sharpe 1884: 240.
11 Black 2005: 22.
12 Black 2005: 100.
13 MacPherson 1929: 131.
14 Child 1904: 66–9, 73–4.
15 Briggs 1970: p. A, vol. 1, 563–5, 180–3.
16 Black 1903: 113; Cowan & Henderson 2001: 61.
17 Stuart 1841: 177; Maxwell-Stuart 2001: 118.
18 Ben 1922: 6. The translators fastidiously omitted the reference to 'testiculo magnos' (large testicles) in this text. Similarly, they translated the word 'membrum' as 'limbs' as opposed to the equally-feasible 'penis'. The link between Isobel's Devil and the water horse also gains support from her references to the 'great bullis' that were 'crowtting and skrylling ther at the entrie' to the Downie Hill. In Isobel's period, as later, the water horse was closely associated with the 'water bull' (*see* Campbell and Thomson 1963: 55–7). Jonas Liliequist has recently compiled a collection of similar accounts of sex with water spirits and other fairy-types from early modern Sweden (*see* Klaniczay and Pócs 2006: 152-69). My thanks to Sigurd Towrie of the Orkneyjar website (www.orkneyjar.com) for his help with the Jo Ben passage.
19 Buchan 1972: 74–86.
20 Child 1904: 584.
21 Ibid., 584–586.
22 Child 1904: 4.
23 Child 1904: 5.
24 Henningsen 1990: 196–8.

25   Pócs 1999: 139.
26   Ginzburg 1983: 84.
27   Pócs 1992: 332.
28   Levack 1992: vol. 5, 141.
29   Carrington 1996: 68.
20   Davidson & Chaudri 2001: 178.
31   Carmichael 1928: vol. 2, 355.
32   Ibid., vol. 2, 357.
33   *See* Russell 1990: 73 & 69 & Davidson & Chaudri 2001: 167–8 for examples.
34   Davidson 1964: 61; Pócs 1992: 332; Carmichael 1928: 357; Gundarrsson 1992.
35   *See* Law 1818: lxxvi for an example.
36   Maxwell-Stuart 2005: 49–51.
37   Ginzburg 1983: 162.

CHAPTER FIFTEEN

The Devil and the Covenant of Grace

 1   Larner 1981: 107.
 2   Simpkins 1914: 100.
 3   *PSAS*: 239.
 4   *See* Kerr 1895.
 5   Torrance 1959: 69–96, 185–234.
 6   Ibid., 208.
 7   Goodare 2008: 5.
 8   Goodare 2005: 238–40.
 9   Goodare 2008: 64.
10   Macdonald 2002: 180.
11   Levack 1992: vol. 7, 393.
12   Clark 1997: 493.
13   Simpkins 1914: 245. *Also see* Russell 1990: 73 and Briggs 1971: p. B, vol. 1, 43–155.
14   Brodie 1863: 176, 259.
15   Klaniczay & Pócs 2006: 170–9; Ibid. 2008: 164–79.
16   *See* Garner 2002.
17   Clark 1997: 529; Goodare 2008: 6.
18   Kinloch 1848: 158.
19   Kerr 1895: 40–1.
20   Mullan 2003: 13.
21   Brodie 1863: 113.
22   Ibid., 128.
23   Ibid., 113–15.
24   Ibid., 116.
25   Ibid., 85.
26   *The Holy Bible*, King James Version: Psalms 89, 105 & 74.
27   Torrance 1959: 190–1.
28   Pearse 1673: 1–2.
29   Ibid., *see* preface 'To the Reader'.
30   Cairns 1762: 68–9; Mullan 2003: 283.

31 Campbell 1704: 26–7; Rose 1762: 101–6.
32 Mullan 2003: 142.
33 Brodie 1863: 286; Pearse 1673: 2.
34 Campbell 1704: 27.
35 Mullan 2003: 272; Rose 1762: 59.
36 Mullan 2003: 146, 153, 94.
37 Rous 1653: 114, 272, 59, 204.
38 Kirton 1704: 17–18.
39 Rose 1762: 103.
40 Pearse 1673: 39.
41 Rose 1762: 103.
42 Ibid., 105.
43 Pearse 1673: 13–14.
44 Rous 1653: 184.
45 *See* Ross 1976: 89 & Sinclair 1685: 217 for examples.
46 Carmichael 1992: 303.
47 Rous 1653: 184–6.
48 Ibid., 111.
49 Pearse 1673: 38–9; Kirton 1704: 17; Rous 1653: 160.
50 Rose 1761: 25, 103.
51 Rous 1653: 189–95.
52 Williams 1975: 155
53 Wilby 2005: 95–111.
54 Pócs 1992: 337–8.
55 Wilby 2005: 128–59.
56 Arnold 2005: 87.
57 McPherson 1929: 37.
58 *Records of Elgin*: vol. 2, 200–1.
59 Carmichael 1992: 237.
60 Ibid., 221.
61 Ibid., 296.
62 Arnold 2005: 89.
63 Torrance 1959: 89.
64 Ibid., 207.
65 Mackenzie 1678: 91.
66 Goodare 2008: 34, 47.
67 Sanderson 1976: 64.
68 Campbell 1975: 35; Hunter 2001: 147.
69 Stuart 1841: 100.
70 Carmichael 1992: 218, 59, 58.
71 Ibid., 132, 63.
72 Ibid., 53.
73 Ross 1976: 89.
74 Carmichael 1992: 218.
75 Ibid., 623.
76 I was taught this charm by my grandmother in the early 1970s.
77 Black 1903: 94; Pitcairn 1833: vol. 2, 28.

78 Ross 1976: 89.
79 Law 1818: 27.
80 Black 1903: 103.
81 Maxwell-Stuart 2001: 118.
82 Stuart 1841: 107.
83 Ibid., 149.
84 Law 1818: 27.
85 Sanderson 1976: 64.

CHAPTER SIXTEEN

Crafting the Bridegroom

1   Simpkins 1912: 102.
2   Wilby 2005: 128–38.
3   Kalweit 1988: 118.
4   Behringer 1998: 18–22.
5   Ginzburg 1983: 161.
6   Henningsen 1990: 197.
7   Pócs 1992: 350.
8   Ibid., 350.
9   Pitcairn 1833: vol. 1, 163; MacPhail 1920: 37; Youngson 1974: 134–5; Pitcairn 1833: vol. 1, 52; Stuart 1841: 98.
10 Brodie 1863: 00.
11 Rous 1653: 345; Cairns 1762: 46.
12 Mullan 2003: 47.
13 Ibid., 47.
14 Ibid., 391–2.
15 Landsman 1989: 143, 140; Hindmarsh 2005: 221.
16 Todd 2002: 399.
17 Cairns 1762: 46–7, 86.
18 Goodare 2008: 144–5.
19 McDougall 1910: 309; Black 2005: 110.
20 Rose 1762: 103.
21 Kalweit 1988: 111; Wilby 2005: 131–45.
22 Mackay 2002: 148.
23 Landsman 1989: 144.
24 Mackay 2002: 148.
25 Rous 1641: 10 25–6.
26 Limburg 2000: 57.
27 Rous 1641: 28–9.
28 Brodie 1863: 261.
29 Carmichael 1992: 235.
30 *The Golden Legend*: 180.
31 Ross 1976: 146.
32 *The Golden Legend*: 180; Ross 1976: 145, 147.
33 Carmichael 1992: 67.
34 Ibid., 57.

35   Ibid., 68.
36   Ibid., 59.
37   Ibid., 47.
38   Rous 1653: 114.
39   Rose 1762: 105; Mullan 2003:284.
40   Pearse 1673: 63.
41   Rous 1653: 169.
42   Pearse 1673: 84–5.
43   Rous 1653: 54.
44   Ibid., 169.
45   Rose 1762: 106.
46   Pearse 1673: 39.
47   Rose 1762: 89.
48   Rous 1653: 194.
49   Rose 1762: 25.
50   Ritchie 2000: 73.
51   Rous 1653: 225, 228.
52   Brodie 1863: 134.
53   Sharpe 1884: 154–6.
54   Stuart 1841: 98; Simpkins 1912: 327.
55   Stuart 1843: x; Macphail 1920: 21.
56   Ibid., 37.
57   Landsman 1989: 143.
58   Christian 1981: 189.
59   Pitcairn 1833: vol. 1, 163.
60   Normand & Roberts 2000: 139; Simpkins 1912: 328; McLachlan 2006: 294.
61   Christian 1981: 193.
62   Ibid., 193.
63   Mullan 2003: 151.
64   Landsman 1989: 143.
65   Ibid., 142.
66   Pitcairn 1833: vol. 1, 52.
67   McLachlan 2006: 362; Kinloch 1848: 130.
68   Henningsen 1990: 197.
69   Kinloch 1848: 120; Mackenzie 1678: 98.
70   Goodare 2008: 38.
71   Macdonald 2002: 111; *A Relation of the Diabolical* . . . : 10–11; *PSAS*: 219; Macdonald 2002: 111.
72   Stuart 1841: 164; Normand & Roberts 2000: 227.
73   Ibid., 227.
74   Rose 1762: 103; Rous 1653: 184–5.
75   Simpkins 1912: 322–3.
76   Briggs 2007:131.
77   Mullan 2003: 151.
78   Kalweit 1988: 77–8.
79   *RPC*: series 2, vol. 8, 156.
80   Pitcairn 1833: vol. 1, 53; Normand & Roberts 2000: 238.

81 Christian 1981: 190–1; Ginzburg 1983: 168.

82 Cairns 1762: 68–9.

83 Landsman 1989: 140.

84 Ibid., 137.

85 Sharpe 1884: 166.

86 Ginzburg 1983: 162.

87 Henningsen 1990: 197.

88 Simpkins 1912: 328; McLachlan 2006: 294.

89 Normand & Roberts 2000: 184.

90 Maxwell-Stuart 2001: 118.

CHAPTER SEVENTEEN
'The De'il's aye gude to his ain'

1   Brodie 1863: 261.

2   Muchembled 2003: 112.

3   Ibid., 153.

4   Johnstone 2006: 24–5.

5   Normand & Roberts 2000: 216.

6   Pócs 1992: 337.

7   Ibid., 306–7. Recent treatments of folkloristic devil figures can also be found in Klaniczay & Pócs 2006: 109–18, 139–80, 221–36.

8   Pócs 1992: 338.

9   Ibid., 339.

10 Ibid., 339.

11 Ibid., 337.

12 Clark 1997: 509–12.

13 Torrance 1959: 110.

14 Simpkins 1912: 111, 78; Stuart 1841: 148.

15 Mackenzie 1678: 86.

16 Goodare 2008: 149; *PSAS*: 223; Stuart 1841: 127, 164; Hallen 1895: 51; Stuart 1841: 159; Mackenzie 1678: 86; Simpkins 1912: 327; Sharpe 1884: 191; Normand & Roberts 2000: 146.

17 Brand 1703: 115.

18 Brodie 1863: 134; Macphail 1920: 18.

19 Clark 1997: 63. Knox.

20 Brodie 1863: 179.

21 Black 1903: 73; Campbell 1860: vol. 1, lxxv.

22 Cowan 1980: 41; Stuart 1841: 142; Sinclair 1685: 219; Pitcairn 1833: vol. 3, 512; Simpkins 1912: 111.

23 Clark 1997: 467.

24 Campbell 1860: vol. 2, 92; Simpkins 1912: 414.

25 Normand & Roberts 2000: 146.

26 Torrance 1959: 208.

27 Brodie 1863: 136, 309, 177, 89.

28 Rose 1762: 14.

29 Todd 2002: 82.

30   Landsman 1989: 121.
31   *The Greig-Duncan Folksong Collection*, vol. 1, 422, 487; Ibid., vol. 2, 166; Buchan 1984: 151–4, 114; Bruford 1969: 26; Hamilton 1998: 70.
32   Ross 1976: 17.
33   Nicholson 1881: xxx.
34   Bruford 1969: 25.
35   *The Greig-Duncan Folksong Collection*: vol. 2, 585, 578–9.
36   Buchan 1984: 19.
37   Campbell 1860: vol. 1, c; Ibid., vol. 2, 71, 51.
38   Ibid., vol. 1, xiii.
39   Van Deusen 2004: 78.
40   Ross 1976: 137.
41   Rolleston 1994: 284–6; Hamilton 1998: 140–3; Child 1904: 400–2; Rolleston 1994: 232.
42   Child 1904: 66–9, 4–7, 73–4; *The Greig-Duncan Folksong Collection*: vol. 2, 322.
43   Normand & Roberts 2000: 231–46.
44   *RPC*: series 2, vol. 8, 156; Kinloch 1848: 132; Sharpe 1884: 126.
45   Pitcairn 1833: vol. 1, 195.
46   Craven 1908: 104.
47   Klaniczay & Pócs 2006: 174
48   *Galloway Gossip* . . . 1878: 7.
49   Ibid., 10.
50   Black 2005: 53–4.
51   Cohn 1993: 107–8.
52   Ibid., 106.
53   Fanger 1998: viii.
54   Ibid., 55–6.
55   McLachlan 2006: 288.
56   Rose 1762: 48.
57   Landsman 1989: 137.
58   Simpkins 1914: 67.
59   Landsman 1989: 138.
60   Arnold 2005: 167–9.
61   Sinclair 1685: 76–7.
62   *Galloway Gossip* . . . 1878: 185; Mackey 1997: 195.
63   Jenkins 2007: 169.
64   Brodie 1863: 203.
65   Arnold and Sinclair 1685: 76–7.
66   Mullan 2000: 209. My thanks to Alasdair Raffe of Durham university for some helpful communication on this subject.
67   Nicholson 1881: xxiii.
68   *Galloway Gossip* . . . 1878: 37–41.
69   Clark 1997: 63.
70   Craven 1908: 137.
71   Law 1818: 23.
72   Brodie 1863: 141.
73   Macdonald 1875: 93, 100.
74   Ibid., 95.

75   Ibid., 95–6.
76   Pitcairn 1833: vol. 1, 162; Youngson 1974: 134.
77   Ben 1922: 6.
78   Campbell 1860: vol. 2, 51.
79   Child 1904: 65.
80   Maxwell-Stuart 2001: 117.
81   Campbell 1860: vol. 2, 65.
82   Child 1904: 68; Simpkins 1912: 316.
83   Cowan & Henderson 2001: 61.
84   Fanger 1998: viii.
85   Ritchie 2000: 64.
86   Whitehead and Wright 2004: 47.
87   Van Deusen 2004: 62.
88   Normand and Roberts 2000: 237; Kinloch 1848: 132.
89   *RPC*: series 2, vol. 8, 156.
90   Clark 1997: vii.

CHAPTER EIGHTEEN

Witches' Covens and Dark Dream Cults

1   Normand & Roberts 2000: 160.
2   Simpkins 1914: 366. The pains taken by those involved in the Renfrewshire trials of 1697 to argue that accusations of sabbath-attendance should be assumed real unless proved otherwise vividly highlights the contemporary vigour of the opposing view (*see* McLachlan 2006: 260–72).
3   Brodie 1863: 171.
4   *See* Murray 1921. The definition of 'cult' is taken from the *Collins English Dictionary,* 1994.
5   Murray 1921: 193.
6   Hallen 1895: 49–52; *PSAS*: 212.
7   Cohn 1993: 154–160.
8   Murray 1921: 15.
9   Irwin 1994: 152.
10 Ginzburg 1983: 84.
11 Ginzburg 1991: 8, 10.
12 Pócs 1999: 155.
13 Ibid., 156–7.
14 Henningsen 1990: 206; Carrington 1995: 61.
15 Pócs 1989: 9.
16 Ginzburg 1983: 135–45.
17 Rose 1848: 350.
18 Brodie 1863: 274.
19 Ibid., 260.
20 *The Records of Elgin*: vol. 2, 211; MacPhail 1920: 26.
21 Normand & Roberts 2000: 243–4.
22 Cowan and Henderson 2001: 134.
23 Simpkins 1914: 326; Macphail 1920: 27.
24 Simpkins 1914: 104.

25   Brodie 1863: 260.
26   Thomas 1973: 286.
27   Pócs 1989: 50–3; Henningsen 1990: 204.
28   Ginzburg 1983: 149, 80.
29   Henningsen 1990: 198; Carrington 1995: 56, 95–6.
30   Henningsen 1990: 198.
31   Carrington 1995: 68.
32   Ginzburg 1983: 133.
33   Henningsen 1990: 196; Ginzburg 1983: 154; Carrington 1995: 71–2.
34   Ginzburg 1983: 150; Henningsen 1990: 197; Carrington 1995: 61.
35   Ginzburg 1983: 1; Henningsen 1990: 198; Carrington 1995: 70.
36   Magallón 1997: 36–9, 27–8.
37   Ibid., 36–9.
38   *See* Magallón 1997.
39   Ullman 1981: 7.
40   Ullman, Krippner & Vaughan: 86–95.
41   Magallón 1997: 25, 28.
42   Ullman 1981: 5.
43   Dreams recalled by my husband and myself, in 2007.
44   Magallón 1997: 25–6.
45   Ibid., 99, 289–90.
46   Ullman, Krippner & Vaughan 1973: 210–18.
47   Magallón 1997: 38, 47.
48   Ibid., 151.
49   Ullman 1981: 7.
50   Magallón 1997: 165.
51   Henningsen 1990: 198.
52   Ginzburg 1983: 76, 160.
53   Henningsen 1990: 198, 201. Though it is in reference to the appearance of the Devil, and makes no mention of healing, an account similarly redolent of public visionary ritual is found in the dittays relating to the trial of Angus witch Bessie Wilson in 1662, which read: 'ye confessed that when ye was brought from the East Blair twenty years since or thereby be Robert Livingstone of Cruik Miln; umquhill John Livingstone, his brother; umquhill Andrew Dowie, in Cruik of Devon; and Thomas Dowie, in . . . , and others mae, that ye cried there three several times to the Devil to come and . . . (*sic*), and that the Devil appeared to you and gave you ane sair stroke on the right shoulder, but nane of the foresaid men saw him' (*PSAS*: 226).
54   Henningsen 1990: 198–99.
55   Ginzburg 1983: 103.
56   Henningsen 1990: 199.
57   Ginzburg 1983: 75.
58   Ibid., 76.
59   Ullman 1981: 7.
60   Magallón 1997: 16.
61   Ibid., 15.
62   Ibid., 31.
63   Ibid., 18, 37.

64 Ginzburg 1983: 130–1.
65 Ibid., 132.
66 Ibid., 132.
67 McLachlan 2006: 232.
68 Magallón 1997: 17.
69 Carrington 1995: 76.
70 Ginzburg 1983: 159.
71 Lyon 1998: 65.
72 Maxwell-Stuart 2005:164.
73 Bovet 1975: 104; Maxwell-Stuart 2005: 112.
74 Youngson 1974: 135.
75 Maxwell-Stuart 2005: 113.
76 Sanderson 1976: 64.
77 Stuart 1841: 98–100.
78 Stuart 1843: xii.
79 Simpkins 1914: 326–7.
80 Larner 1981: 148.
81 Magallón 1997: 28.
82 Ginzburg 1992: 132, 130, 133.
83 Tedlock 1989: 78–9.
84 Pitcairn 1833: vol. 3, 601; Stuart 1841: 98–100; Kinloch 1848: 122.
85 Simpkins 1914: 327; Hallen 1895: 52.
86 Summers 1928: 226.
87 Whitehead 2002: 113.
88 Ginzburg 1983: 75.
89 Ibid., 168.
90 Carrington 1995: 85–6.
91 Ullman, Krippner & Vaughan 1973: 212–13.
92 Ginzburg 1983: 156.
93 Ibid., 103.
94 Ibid., 131–2.
95 *A Relation . . . 1697*: 8, 13.
96 Normand & Roberts 2000: 184.
97 Kinloch 1848: 117–18.
98 Henningsen 1990: 214.
99 Ginzburg 1983: 103.
100 www.lucidcrossroads.co.uk/shared.htm. Thanks to Russell, of the Lucid Crossroads Network, for this permission to publish his dream-experience here.
101 In this case only one confession, that of Marie Lamont, survives. But we know that local prosecutors gained a commission to try seven local witches in addition to Lamont, two of whom (Kettie Scot and Jean King) were cited by the latter as accomplices. Another of Lamont's alleged accomplices, Jonet Holm, was tried along with five other witches three months later. The fact that the prosecutors chose to state, on three different occasions, and in relation to three different subject areas, that Lamont's confession (which she allegedly offered 'willingly') accorded with that of accomplice Kettie Scot points to a level of confessional congruity, while the strong folkloric themes are suggestive of shamanistic spirit-group narratives (Black 1938: 72; Sharpe 1884: 133–4).

102 Normand & Roberts 2000: 353.
103 Whitehead 2002: 222, 204.
104 Webster 1968: 124–5.
105 Lewis 1975: 141.
106 Carrington 1996: 56.
107 Whitehead 2002: 250; Whitehead & Wright 2004: 62.
108 Clark 1997: 509–12.

Works Cited

Manuscript Sources

National Archives of Scotland (NAS)

GD125/16/5/1/1 Isobel Gowdie's first confession.
GD125/16/5/1/2 Isobel Gowdie's second confession.
GD125/16/5/1/3 Isobel Gowdie's third confession.
GD125/16/5/1/4 Isobel Gowdie's fourth confession.
GD125/16/5/1/5 Janet Breadheid's confession.
GD125/16/3/4/2 Account resting by the Laird of Park to Mr Harry Forbes.
GD125/16/4/1/10 Letter Alexander Dunbar to the Laird of Park.
GD125/16/2/1/27 Bond from David Stewart, Comissary of Moray, to John Hay of Park.
GD125/16/3/1/8 Marriage contract between Thomas Dunbar of Westfield, on behalf of Patrick
    D his 2nd son.
GD125/17 Legal and estate documents relating to Hay of Lochloy and Park (uncatalogued).
NP 1/110 Notarial Protocol Book of John Innes, Elgin, 1662-64.
JC26/1/57 The trial of Jonet Boyman.
RD3/9P178-179 Bond Forbes to Forbes.

National Register of Archives (Scotland)

Papers of N.M.A. Brodie of Brodie, Brodie Castle, Forres

Box 2, drawer 4: Rentals, 1724 Lochloy and Park/1743 Brodie, Penick, Inshoch and Lochloy.
Box 6, bundle 3: 1728 Rental of barony of Lochloy/1731-35 Rental of Inshoch and Lochloy.
Box 9, bundle 4: Rentals, 1731-72 Inshoch and Lochloy/1749 Inshoch and Penick.
Box 27, bundle 5: Decreet of sale of lands of late John Hay of Park to George Brodie of Brodie,
    22 June 1710.

Printed Sources

In the case of books published before 1800 only the place and publication and date are given.
Dates given relate to the edition used by the author and referenced for quotations.

Anderson, Michael (1996) *British Population History: From the Black Death to the Present Day*. Cambridge: Cambridge University Press.

Anderson, Peter, J (ed.) (1893) *Officers and Graduates of University and King's College, Aberdeen, MVD–MDCCCLX*. Aberdeen: New Spalding Club.

Angus, William (1936) 'Notarial Protocol Books 1469–1700', in *Introductory Survey of the Sources and Literature of Scots Law*, vol. 1. The Stair Society.

Arnold, John, H. (2005) B*elief and Unbelief in Medieval Europe*. London: Hodder Arnold.

Ars Notariatus: or, the art and office of a notary-publick, as the same is practised in Scotland. In two parts . . . To which is added, by way of conclusion, an advice to notaries, touching the right discharging of their office. (1740). Edinburgh.

Bailey, Michael, D. (2003) *Battling Demons: Witchcraft, Heresy and Reform in the Late Middle Ages*. University Park: Pennsylvania State University Press.

Bain, George (1928) *History of Nairnshire*, Second edition. Nairn: Telegraph Office.

——(1904) *Lord Brodie: His Life and Times 1617–80. With Continuation to the Revolution*. Nairn: Telegraph Office.

Balzac, Marjorie Mandelstam (ed.) (1990) *Shamanism: Soviet Studies of Traditional Religion in Siberia and Central Asia*. New York: M.E. Sharpe Inc.

Barger, George (1931) *Ergot and Ergotism: A Monograph*. London: Gurney and Jackson.

Barrett, John and Mitchell, Alastair (2006) 'Elgin's Love Gift: Civil War and the Burgh Community', in *Scottish Local History* 68 (Winter 2006): 46–51.

Barry, Jonathan and Owen Davies (eds) (2007) *Palgrave Advances in Witchcraft Historiography*. Basingstoke: Palgrave Macmillan.

Bath, Jo and John Newton (2006) '"Sensible Proof of Spirits": Ghost Belief during the later Seventeenth Century', in *Folklore* 117 (1): 1–14.

Behringer, Wolfgang (1998) *Shaman of Oberstdorf: Chonrad Stoeckhlin and the Phantoms of the Night*, Trans. H. C. Erik Midelfort. Charlottesville: University Press of Virginia.

Ben, Jo (1922) *Descriptio Insularum Orchadiarum: A translation from the Latin version in Barry's History of Orkney . . .* Kirkwall: Proprietors of the 'Orkney Herald'.

Black, George F (1946) *The Surnames of Scotland: Their Origin, Meaning and History*. New York: New York Public Library.

—— (1938) *A Calendar of Cases of Witchcraft in Scotland 1510 to 1727*. New York: New York Public Library; reprinted Arno Press Inc., 1971.

—— (1903) *Examples of Printed Folklore Concerning the Orkney & Shetland Islands*. Ed. Northcote. W. Thomas. London: Folk-Lore Society; facsimile reprint, 1994, Llanerch Publishers.

Black, Ronald (2005) *The Gaelic Otherworld: John Gregorson Campbell's 'Superstitions of the Highlands and Islands of Scotland' and 'Witchcraft and Second Sight in the Highlands and Islands'*. Edinburgh: Birlinn Limited.

Bochel, Margaret (2003) *Salt Herring on Saturday: The Fishertown of Nairn Last Century*. East Linton: Tuckwell Press.

Bovet, Richard (1975) *Pandaemonium, or the Devil's Cloyster*. Wakefield: E. P. Publishing Limited.

Brainerd, Charles and Valerie Reyna (2005) *The Science of False Memory*. Oxford: Oxford University Press.

Brand, John (1703) *A New Description of Orkney, Zetland, Plightland Firth and Caithness*. Edinburgh.

Branston, Brian (1974) *The Lost Gods of England*. London: Thames & Hudson Ltd.

Briggs, Katharine, M. (1978) *The Vanishing People: A Study of Traditional Fairy Beliefs*. London: Batsford Ltd.

—— (1970–1) *A Dictionary of British Folk-Tales in the English Language, incorporating the F. J. Norton Collection*. Part A, vol. 1, Bloomington: Indiana University Press (1970). Part A, vol. 2 & Part B, vols. 1 & 2, London: Routledge & Kegan Paul (1971).

—— (1959) *The Anatomy of Puck*. London: Routledge & Kegan Paul.

Briggs, Robin (2007) *The Witches of Lorraine*. Oxford: Oxford University Press.

—— (1996) *Witches & Neighbours: The Social and Cultural Context of European Witchcraft*. London: HarperCollins.

Brodie, Alexander (1863) *The Diary of Alexander Brodie of Brodie, and of his son, James Brodie, consisting of extracts from the existing manuscripts, and a republication of the volume printed at Edinburgh in the year 1740*. Aberdeen: Spalding Club.

Brodie-Innes, J.W. (1974) *The Devil's Mistress*. London: Sphere Books Limited.

Brown, Callum (1987) *The Social History of Religion in Scotland since 1730*. London: Methuen.

Brown, Peter (ed.) (1999) *Reading Dreams: The Interpretation of Dreams from Chaucer to Shakespeare*. Oxford: Oxford University Press.

Bruford, Alan (1996) Workers, Weepers, and Witches: The Status of the Female Singer in Gaelic Society, in *Scottish Gaelic Studies* 17: 61–70.

—— (1978) 'Recitation or recreation? Examples from South Uist Storytelling', in *Scottish Studies*, Vol. 22

—— (1969) *Gaelic Folk-Tales and Medieval Romances* Dublin: The Folklore of Ireland Society.

Buchan, David (1984) *Scottish Tradition: A Collection of Scottish Folk Literature*. London: Routledge & Kegan Paul.

—— (1972) *The Ballad and the Folk*. London: Routledge & Kegan Paul.

Burwick, Frederick (1996) *Poetic Madness and the Romantic Imagination*. University Park, Pennsylvania: Pennsylvania State University Press.

Cairns, Elizabeth (1762) *Memoirs of the Life of Elizabeth Cairns, written by herself before her death*. Glasgow.

Campbell of Calder, Sir Hugh (1704) *An Essay on the Lord's Prayer*. Edinburgh.

Campbell, John Francis (1860) *Popular Tales of the West Highlands*, vols. 1 & 2. Edinburgh: Edmonston & Douglas.

Campbell, J. L. (ed.) (1975) *A Collection of Highland Rites and Customes: copied by Edward Lhuyd from the manuscript of the Rev James Kirkwood (1650–1709)*. Cambridge: The Folklore Society.

Campbell, J. L. and D. Thomson (1963) *Edward Lhuyd in the Scottish Highlands 1699–1700*. Oxford: Clarendon Press.

Caporael, Linnda, R. (1976) 'Ergotism: The Satan Loosed in Salem?', in *Science* 192 (4234): 21–6.

Carmichael, Alexander (1992) *Carmina Gadelica: Hymns and Incantations*. Edinburgh: Floris Books.

—— (1928) *Carmina Gadelica: Hymns and Incantations*, vol. 2. Edinburgh: Oliver & Boyd.

Carr, Herbert Wildon (1930) *The Monadology of Leibniz*. Los Angeles: University of Southern California.

Carrington, Dorothy (1995) *The Dream-Hunters of Corsica*. London: Phoenix.

Child, Francis James (1904) *English and Scottish Popular Ballads*, ed. Helen Child Sargent and George Kittredge. London: George G. Harrap & Company.

Christian, William, A. (1981) *Apparitions in Late Medieval and Renaissance Spain*. Princeton: Princeton University Press.

Clark, Stuart (2007) *Vanities of the Eye*. Oxford: Oxford University Press.

—— (1997) *Thinking with Demons*. Oxford: Clarendon Press.

Cohen, J. M (ed.) (1987) *The Life of Saint Teresa of Avila By Herself*. London: Penguin.

Cohn, Norman (1993) *Europe's Inner Demons: The Demonization of Christians in Medieval Christendom*. London: Pimlico.

Colcock, Charles (1908) *The Family of Hay: A History of the progenitors and some South Carolina descendants of Colonel Ann Hawkes Hay, with collateral genealogies, AD 500–1908*. New York: The Genealogical Association.

Constable, T. (ed.) (1859) *The Book of the Thanes of Cawdor*. Aberdeen: Spalding Club.

Cowan, Edward, J. (ed.) (1991) *The People's Past: Scottish Folk, Scottish History*. Edinburgh: Polygon.

Cowan, Edward, J and Lizanne Henderson (2001) *Scottish Fairy Belief: A History*. East Linton: Tuckwell Press.

Craven, J. B (1908) *A History of the Episcopal Church in the Diocese of Caithness*. Kirkwall: William Peace & Son.

—— (1889) *History of the Episcopal Church in the Diocese of Moray*. London: Skeffington & Son.

Chambers Scots Dictionary (1977), ed. Alexander Warrack. Edinburgh: W&R Chambers Ltd.

Davidson, Hilda Ellis (ed.) (1989) *The Seer in Celtic and Other Traditions*. Edinburgh: John Donald Publishers Ltd.

—— (1964) *Gods and Myths of Northern Europe*. Harmondsworth: Penguin.

Davidson, Hilda Ellis and Anna Chaudri (eds) (2001) *Supernatural Enemies*. Durham, North Carolina: Carolina Academic Press.

Davidson, Thomas (1949) *Rowan Tree and Red Thread*. Edinburgh: Oliver and Boyd.

Davies, Owen (2003) *Popular Magic: Cunning Folk in English History*. London: Hambledon Continuum.

Dégh, Linda (1991) Review of 'Fairies and Witches at the Boundaries of South-Eastern and Central Europe' in *American Anthropologist* 93: 760.

Dennison, E. Patricia and Russel Coleman (1999) *Historical Nairn: The Archaeological Implications of Development*. Edinburgh: Scottish Cultural Press.

Devlin, Judith (1987) *The Superstitious Mind: French Peasants and the Supernatural in the Nineteenth Century*. New Haven and London: Yale University Press.

Dictionary of the Older Scottish Tongue (1931–90), eds W. A. Craigie, A. J. Aitken *et al.*, Vols. 1–7. Chicago: University of Chicago Press; Oxford: Oxford University Press.

Donaldson, Gordon (1990) *The Faith of the Scots*. London: BT Batsford Ltd.

Donaldson, James (1794) *General View of the Agriculture of the County of Nairn*. London: B. Millan.

Eichberger, Dagmar and Charles Zika (eds) (1998) *Dürer and his Culture*. Cambridge: Cambridge University Press.

Ekirch, Roger (2001) 'Sleep We Have Lost: Pre-Industrial Slumber in the British Isles', in *American Historical Review*, Vol. 106: 343–386.

Erickson, Carolly (1976) *The Medieval Vision: Essays in History and Perception*. Oxford: Oxford University Press.

Evans-Wentz, W.Y. (1977) *The Fairy-Faith in Celtic Countries*. Gerrards Cross, Buckinghamshire: Colin Smythe Ltd.

Ewan, Elisabeth, Sue Innes, Sian Reynolds and Rose Pipes (eds) (2007) *Biographical Dictionary of Scottish Women*. Edinburgh: Edinburgh University Press.

The Famous History of Tom Thumb. Wherein is declared, his marvellous acts of manhood full of wonderful merriment. Performed after his first return from fairyland, Part the Second. London, 1775.

Fanger, Claire (ed.) (1998) *Conjuring Spirits: Texts and Traditions of Medieval Ritual Magic*. University Park, PA: Pennsylvania State University Press.

Fausto, Carlos (2000) 'Of Enemies and Pets: Warfare and Shamanism in Amazonia', Trans. David Rodgers, in *American Ethnologist*, 26 (4): 933–956.

Flinn, Michael (ed.) (1977) *Scottish Population History from the Seventeenth Century to the Present.* Cambridge: Cambridge University Press.

Forbes, Duncan (1864) *Ane Account of the Familie of Innes, compiled by Duncan Forbes of Culloden, 1698, edited by Cosmo Innes.* Aberdeen: The Spalding Club.

Forde, Catherine (2005) *The Drowning Pond.* London: Egmont Books.

Fortune, R.F. (1969) *Omaha Secret Societies.* New York: AMS Press.

Fox, Adam (2000) *Oral and Literate Culture in England 1500–1700.* Oxford: Oxford University Press.

Francke, Richard (1694) *Northern Memoirs, Calculated for the Meridian of Scotland.* London.

Gackenbach, J. I and S. LaBerge (eds.) (1988) *Conscious Mind, Sleeping Brain: Perspectives on Lucid Dreaming.* New York: Plenum.

Galloway Gossip Sixty Years Ago (1878), ed. 'Saxon', 2nd edition. Choppington: Robert Trotter.

Garfield, Patricia (1974) *Creative Dreaming.* New York: Simon and Schuster.

Garner, David, B. (2002) review of 'The Binding of God: Calvin's Role in the Development of Covenant Theology' by Peter Lilliback (2001), in *Trinity Journal* 23 (2): 291–94.

Gibson, Marion (2008) Review of 'Cunning Folk and Familiar Spirits' in *Magic, Ritual and Witchcraft* 3 (1): 115–8.

Ginzburg, Carlo (1992) *Ecstasies: Deciphering the Witches' Sabbath*, trans. R. Rosenthal. Harmondsworth: Penguin. Originally published in Italy, 1989.

—— (1983) *The Night Battles: Witchcraft and Agrarian Cults in the Sixteenth and Seventeenth Centuries*, trans. John and Anne Tedeschi. Baltimore, Maryland: The Johns Hopkins University Press. Originally published in Italy, 1966.

Goodare, Julian (2005) 'John Knox on Demonology and Witchcraft' in *Archiv für Reformationsgeschichte,* 96:221–45.

—— (ed.) (2002) *The Scottish Witch-Hunt in Context.* Manchester: Manchester University Press.

Goodare, Julian, Lauren Martin and Joyce Miller (eds.) (2007) *Witchcraft and Belief in Early Modern Scotland.* Basingstoke: Palgrave Macmillan.

Gordon, James (ed.) (1882) *The History of the Province of Moray*, by Lachlan Shaw, vol. 2. London: Hamilton, Adams, & Co.

Grambo, Ronald (1988) 'Problems of Fatalism: A Blueprint for Further Research', in *Folklore* 99: 11–29.

Grant, I.F. (1995) *Highland Folk Ways.* Originally published in 1961. Edinburgh: Birlinn Ltd.

—— (1981) *Everyday Life on an Old Highland Farm 1769–1782.* London: Shepheard-Walwyn Ltd.

Green, Thomas (2007) 'Tom Thumb and Jack the Giant Killer: Two Arthurian Fairytales?', in *Folklore* 118 (2): 123–140.

The Greig-Duncan Folk Song Collection (1981–3), vols. 1 & 2, eds Emily B. Lyle and Patrick Shuldham-Shaw. Edinburgh: Mercat Press for the University of Aberdeen.

Grillot de Givry, Emile (1971) *Witchcraft, Magic and Alchemy*, trans. J. Courtenay Locke. New York: Dover Publications Inc.

Grimble, Ian (1989) *Scottish Clans and Tartans.* London: Hamlyn.

Gundarsson, Kveldulf (1992) 'The Folklore of the Wild Hunt and the Furious Host' in *Mountain Thunder*, Issue 7.

Hall, Alaric (2007) *Elves in Anglo-Saxon England: Matters of Belief, Health, Gender and Identity.* Woodbridge, Suffolk: The Boydell Press.

—— (2005a) 'Getting Shot of Elves: Healing, Witchcraft and Fairies in the Scottish Witchcraft Trials', in *Folklore* 116: 19–36.

—— (2005b) *The meanings of Elf, and Elves, in Medieval England*. Phd. University of Glasgow.

Hallen, Cornelius (ed.) (1895) *The Scottish Antiquary, or Northern Notes and Queries*, vol. 9. Edinburgh: University Press.

Hamilton, William of Gilbertfield (1998) *Blind Harry's Wallace*. Edinburgh: Luath Press Limited.

Harte, Jeremy (2004) *Explore Fairy Traditions*. Loughborough: Heart of Albion Press.

Harvey, Graham (2003) *Shamanism: A Reader*. London: Routledge.

Hayward, Brian (1992) *Galoshins: The Scottish Folk Play*. Edinburgh: Edinburgh University Press.

Henningsen, Gustav (1990) '"The Ladies from Outside": An Archaic Pattern of the Witches' Sabbath', in B. Ankarloo and G. Henningsen (eds), *Early Modern European Witchcraft: Centres and Peripheries*. Oxford: Clarendon Press.

Hindmarsh, Bruce (2005) *The Evangelical Conversion Narrative: Spiritual Autobiography in Early Modern England*. Oxford: Oxford University Press.

Holinshed, Raphael (1808) *Holinshed's Chronicles of England, Scotland and Ireland*, vol. 5. London: Johnson et al.

Honko, Lauri (1964) 'Memorates and the Study of Folk Beliefs', in *Journal of the Folklore Institute*, 1: 5–19.

Houston, Rab (1982) 'The Literacy Myth? Illiteracy in Scotland 1630–1760' in *Past and Present* 96 (1): 81–102.

Hunter, Michael (2001) *The Occult Laboratory: Magic, Science and Second Sight in Late Seventeenth-Century Scotland*. Woodbridge, Suffolk: Boydell Press.

Hutton, Ronald (1999) *The Triumph of the Moon: A History of Modern Pagan Witchcraft*. Oxford: Oxford University Press.

Irwin, Lee (1996) *Visionary Worlds: The Making and Unmaking of Reality*, SUNY Series in Western Esoteric Traditions. New York: State University of New York Press.

—— (1994) *The Dream Seekers: Native American Visionary Traditions of the Great Plains*. Norman and London: University of Oklahoma Press.

Jacobs, Joseph (ed.) (1994) *Celtic Fairy Tales*. London: Senate.

Jenkins, Richard (2007) 'The Transformations of Biddy Early: From Local Reports of magical healing to Globalised New Age Fantasies' in *Folklore* 118: 162–82.

Johnson, Samuel and Boswell (1979) *A Journey to the Western Islands of Scotland: The Journal of a Tour to the Hebrides*. Oxford: Oxford University Press.

Johnstone, Nathan (2007) *The Devil and Demonism in Early Modern England*. Cambridge: Cambridge University Press.

Jolly, Karen, L. (1996) *Popular Religion in Late Saxon England: Elf Charms in Context*. Chapel Hill, NC: University of North Carolina Press.

Jubainville, M. H. d'Arbois de and Richard Irvine Best (1903) *The Irish Mythological Cycle and Celtic Mythology*. Dublin: Hodges, Figgis & Co, reprint by Kessinger Publishing Rare Reprints.

Kalweit, Holger (1988) *Dreamtime & Inner Space: The World of the Shaman*, trans. W. Wünsche. Boston & London: Shambhala.

Kerr, Rev. James (1895) *The Covenants and the Covenanters. Covenants, Sermons, and Documents of the Covenanted Reformation*. Edinburgh: R. W. Hunter.

Kieckhefer, Richard (2000) *Magic in the Middle Ages*. Cambridge: Cambridge University Press.

—— (1998) *Forbidden Rites: A Necromancer's Manual of the Fifteenth Century.* University Park PA: Pennsylvania State University Press.

—— (1992) Review of Carlo Ginzburg's 'Ecstasies', in *American Historical Review* 97 (3): 837–8.

Kimura, Doreen (2000) *Sex and Cognition.* Cambridge, Massachusetts: The MIT Press.

Kinloch, George. R. (ed.) (1848) *Reliquiae Antiquae Scoticae: illustrative of civil and ecclesiastical affairs. From original manuscripts.* Edinburgh.

Kirton, James (1703) *The History of Mr John Welsh, Minister of the Gospel at Aire.* Edinburgh.

Kittredge, George Lyman (1956) *Witchcraft in Old and New England.* New York: Russell & Russell.

Kivelson, Valerie (2000) Review of 'Between the Living and the Dead' by Éva Pócs in *Slavic Review*, 59: 200–1.

Klaniczay, Gábor (1990a) 'Hungary: The Accusations and the Universe of Popular Magic', in B. Ankarloo and G. Henningsen, (eds) *Early Modern European Witchcraft: Centres and Peripheries.* Oxford: Clarendon Press.

—— (1990b) *The Uses of Supernatural Power: The Transformation of Popular Religion in Medieval and Early-Modern Europe*, trans. Susan Singerman. Ed. Karen Margolis. Cambridge: Polity Press.

Klaniczay, Gábor & Éva Pócs (eds) (2005–8) *Demons, Spirits, Witches.* Vol. 1: *Communicating with Spirits* (2005); Vol 2: *Christian Demonology and Popular Mythology* (2006); Vol. 3: *Witchcraft Mythologies and Persecutions* (2008). Budapest & New York: Central European University Press.

Kruger, Steven, F. (1992) *Dreaming in the Middle Ages.* Cambridge: Cambridge University Press.

Landsman, Ned (1989) 'Evangelists and their Hearers: Popular Interpretation of Revivalist Preaching in Eighteenth-Century Scotland', in *Journal of British Studies* 28: 138.

Lang, Andrew (1909) *Sir George Mackenzie, King's Advocate of Rosehaugh, His Life and Times 1636–1691.* London: Longmans Green and Co.

Larner, Christina (1981) *Enemies of God: The Witch-hunt in Scotland.* London: Chatto & Windus.

Lavater, Ludwig (1929) *Of Ghostes and Spirites Walking By Nyght.* Reprint of 1572 version, ed. J. Dover Wilson and May Yardley. Oxford: Oxford University Press.

Law, Robert (1818) *Memorialls; or the Memorable Things that fell out within this Island of Brittain from 1638 to 1684*, ed. C. K. Sharpe. Edinburgh.

Lawson, John (2007) *The Witch of Auldearn.* Nairn: The Nairn Bookshop.

Lecouteux, Claude (2003) *Witches, Werewolves and Fairies: Shapeshifters and Astral Doubles in the Middle Ages*, trans. Clare Frock. Vermont: Inner Traditions.

Levack, Brian (2004) *The Witchcraft Sourcebook.* New York & London: Routledge.

—— (1992) (ed.) *Articles on Witchcraft, Magic and Demonology*, vols 5 & 7. New York and London: Garland Press.

—— (1980) 'The Great Scottish Witch Hunt of 1661–1662' in *The Journal of British Studies* 20 (1): 90–108.

Levine, Shar and Vicki Scudamore (1998) *Marbles: A Player's Guide.* New York: Sterling Publishing Co, Inc.

Lévy-Bruhl, Lucien (1965) *The Soul of the Primitive.* London: George Allen & Unwin Ltd.

Lewis, Ioan, M. (1975) *Ecstatic Religion: An Anthropological Study of Spirit Possession and Shamanism.* Penguin: Harmondsworth.

Limburg, James (2000) *Psalms* (Westminster Bible Companion). Westminster: John Knox Press.

Lincoln, Jackson Steward (1970/1935) *The Dream in Primitive Cultures.* New York and London: Johnson Reprint Corporation.

Lockhart, Gilbert (1938) *Curses, Charms and Talismans.* London: Geoffrey Bles.

Lyon, William S. (1998) *Encyclopedia of Native American Healing.* New York: W.W. Norton & Company.

Lucid Crossroads: www.lucidcrossroads.co.uk/shared.htm

MacCulloch, J. A (1921) 'The Mingling of Fairy and Witch Beliefs in Sixteenth and Seventeenth Century Scotland', in *Folk-Lore, The Transactions of the Folk-Lore Society* 32: 227–244.

MacDonald, Murdoch (1875) *The Covenanters in Moray and Ross.* Nairn: J.T. Melven.

MacDonald, Stuart (2002) *The Witches of Fife: Witch-Hunting in a Scottish Shire, 1560–1710.* East Linton: Tuckwell Press.

MacDougall, James (1910) *Folk Tales and Fairy Lore in Gaelic and English: Collected from Oral Tradition.* Edinburgh: John Grant.

McKay, Eneas (1891) *The Witch of Inverness and the Fairies of Tomnahurich.* Inverness: John Noble.

Mackay, Margaret, A. (2002) 'Folk Religion in a Calvinist Context: Hungarian Models and Scottish Examples', in *Folklore*, 113 (2): 139–149.

Mackay, William (ed.) (1905) *Chronicles of the Frasers: The Wardlaw Manuscript entitled 'Polichronicon Seu Policratica Temporum, or, The True Genealogy of the Frasers.'* 916–1674, by Master James Fraser. Edinburgh: Scottish History Society.

Mackenzie, Sir George (1678) *The Lawes and Customes of Scotland in Matters Criminal.* Edinburgh.

Mackey, James, P. (1997) *An Introduction to Celtic Christianity.* Edinburgh: T&T Clark.

McLachlan, Hugh, V. (ed.) (2006) *The Kirk, Satan and Salem: A History of the Witches of Renfrewshire.* Glasgow: The Grimsay Press.

MacPhail, J.R.N (ed.) (1920) *Highland Papers,* Vol. 3, 1662–1677. Edinburgh: The Scottish History Society.

McPherson, J. M. (1929) *Primitive Beliefs in the North-East of Scotland.* London, New York and Toronto: Longmans, Green & Co.

MacTavish, Duncan (ed.) (1943) *Minutes of the Synod of Argyll 1639–1651.* Edinburgh: Scottish History Society.

Magallón, Linda Lane (1997) *Mutual Dreaming: When Two or More People Share the Same Dream.* New York: Pocket Books.

Maidment, James (ed.) (1845) *Miscellany of the Spottiswoode Society,* Vol. 2. Edinburgh:

Maitland, Sarah (2003) *'On becoming a Fairy Godmother' Witch Woman.* Maia Press Books.

Martin, Martin (1703) *A Description of the Western Isles of Scotland.* London.

Marwick, Ernest, W. (1975) *The Folklore of Orkney and Shetland.* London: B. T. Batsford.

Maxwell-Stuart, Peter (ed.) (2005) *An Abundance of Witches: The Great Scottish Witch-Hunt.* Stroud: Tempus Publishing.

—— (2001) *Satan's Conspiracy: Magic and Witchcraft in Sixteenth-Century Scotland.* East Linton: Tuckwell Press.

—— (ed.) (2000) *Martin Del Rio: Investigations into Magic,* trans. P. Maxwell-Stuart. Manchester: Manchester University Press.

—— (ed.) (1999) *The Occult in Early Modern Europe: A Documentary History.* London: Palgrave Macmillan.

Miller, Joyce (2005) *Magic and Witchcraft in Scotland.* Musselburgh: Goblinshead.

Morris, Katherine (1991) *Sorceress or Witch? The Image of Gender in Medieval Iceland and Northern Europe.* Lanham: University Press of America.

Motze, Lotte (1984) 'The Winter Goddess: Percht, Holda, and Related Figures', in *Folklore* 95: 151–66.

Muchembled, Robert (2003) *The History of the Devil: From the Middle Ages to the Present.* Trans. Jean Birrell. Originally published in 2000. Cambridge: Polity Press.

Mullan, David (ed.) (2003) *Women's Life Writing in Early Modern Scotland: Writing the Evangelical Self c 1670–1730*. Aldershot: Ashgate Publishing Limited.

—— (2000) *Scottish Puritanism 1590–1638*. Oxford: Oxford University Press.

Murray, Margaret (1921) *The Witch-Cult in Western Europe*. Oxford: Clarendon Press.

Nairnshire Telegraph (1860) *Jurisdictia of the Magistrates of Nairn 200 years ago*.

Nagy, Joseph Falaky (1986) 'Orality in Medieval Irish Narrative', in *Oral Tradition* 1: 272–301.

Neat, Timothy (2002) *The Summer Walkers: Travelling People and Pearl-Fishers in the Highlands of Scotland*. Edinburgh: Birlinn Ltd.

Neihardt, John. G. (1988) *Black Elk Speaks: Being the Life Story of a Holy Man of the Oglala Sioux*. Lincoln and London: University of Nebraska Press.

Newall, Venetia (ed.) (1973) *The Witch Figure: Folklore essays by a group of scholars in England honouring the 75th birthday of Katharine M. Briggs*. London: Routledge & Kegan Paul.

Nicholson, Alexander (ed.) 1881 *A Collection of Gaelic Proverbs and Familiar Phrases*. Edinburgh: Maclachlan and Stewart.

Noll, Richard (1985) 'Mental Imagery Cultivation as a Cultural Phenomenon: The Role of Visions in Shamanism', in *Current Anthropology*, 26 (4): 443–461.

Normand, Lawrence and Roberts, Gareth (eds.) (2000) *Witchcraft in Early Modern Scotland: James VI's Demonology and the North Berwick Witches*. Exeter: University of Exeter Press.

Oates, Caroline (1992) *Diaries of a Teenage Werewolf*, . . . (1992) 'Witch-Hunting in Continental Europe: Local and Regional Studies', in *Articles on Witchcraft, Magic and Demonology*, vol. 5, 131–59. New York and London: Garland Publishing.

Omand, Donald (ed.) (1987) *The Grampian Book*. Golspie, Sutherland: The Northern Times Limited.

ODNB: Oxford Dictionary of National Biography: From the earliest times to the year 2000 (2004). Edited by H.C.G. Matthew. Oxford: Oxford University Press.

Pearse, Edward (1673) *The Best Match, or the Soul's Espousal to Christ opened and improved by Edward Pearse*. London.

Pitcairn, Robert (1833) *Ancient Criminal Trials in Scotland 1488–1624*, Vols. 1–3. Edinburgh: Bannatyne Club.

Pócs, Éva (1999) *Between the Living and the Dead: A Perspective on Witches and Seers in the Early Modern Age*. Trans. Szilvia Rédey and Michael Webb. Budapest: Central European University Press.

—— (1991–2) 'The Popular Foundations of the Witches' Sabbath and the Devil's Pact in Central and Southeastern Europe' in *Acta Ethnographia* 37: 305–370.

—— (1989) 'Fairies and Witches at the Boundary of South-Eastern and Central Europe', Helsinki: F.F. Communications, no. 243.

PSAS: Proceedings of the Society of Antiquaries of Scotland (1888) Vol. 22, 1887–8. Edinburgh.

Purkiss, Diane (2001a) *Troublesome Things: A History of Fairies and Fairy Stories*. London: Penguin.

—— (2001b) 'Sounds of Silence: Fairies and Incest in Scottish Witchcraft Stories' in Stuart Clark (ed.), *Languages of Witchcraft: Narrative, Ideology and Meaning in Early Modern Culture*. Basingstoke, Hampshire: Macmillan Press Ltd.

—— (1996) *The Witch in History: Early Modern and Twentieth-Century Representations*. London and New York: Routledge.

The Records of Elgin 1234–1800 (1903–8), 2 Vols. Compiled by W. Cramond. Aberdeen: The New Spalding Club.

RPC: Register of the Privy Council of Scotland, Series 2, Vol. 8 (1644–1660).

RPC: Register of the Privy Council of Scotland, Series 3, Vol. 1 (1661–1664).

Reid, Stuart (2003) *Auldearn 1645: The Marquis of Montrose's Scottish Campaign.* Oxford: Osprey Publishing.

Relation of the Diabolical Practices of Above Twenty Wizards and Witches of the Sherriffdom of Renfrew in the Kingdom of Scotland (1697). London.

Ringgren, Helmer (ed.) (1967) *Fatalistic beliefs in Religion, Folklore, and Literature.* Stockholm: Almqvist & Wiksell.

Ritchie, Mark, A. (2000) *Spirit of the Rainforest: A Yanomamö Shaman's Story.* Chicago: Island Lake Press.

Robbins, Rossell Hope (1959) *The Encyclopaedia of Witchcraft and Demonology.* New York: Crown Publishers Inc.

Rolleston, T.W. (1994) *Celtic Myths and Legends.* London: Senate.

Roper, Jonathan (2004) *Charms and Charming in Europe.* Basingstoke: Palgrave Macmillan.

Roper, Lyndal (2004) *Witch Craze: Terror and Fantasy in Baroque Germany.* London: Yale University Press.

—— (1994) *Oedipus and the Devil: Witchcraft, Sexuality and Religion in Early Modern Europe.* London and New York: Routledge.

Rose, Hugh (1848) *A Genealogical Deduction of the Family of Rose of Kilravock*, ed. Cosmo Innes. Aberdeen: The Spalding Club.

—— (1762) *Meditations on Several Interesting Subjects by the later reverend Mr Hugh Rose, Minister at Nairn.* Edinburgh.

Rosen, Barbara (ed.) (1991) *Witchcraft in England, 1558–1618.* Amherst: The University of Massachusetts Press.

Ross, Anne (1976) *The Folklore of the Scottish Highlands.* London: B.T. Batsford Ltd.

Ross, Sinclair (1992) *The Culbin Sands, Fact and Fiction.* Aberdeen: Centre for Scottish Studies, University of Aberdeen.

Rous, Francis (1653) *The Mistical Marriage. Or, Experimentall discoveries of the heavenly marriage betweene a Soule and her Saviour.* London.

—— (1641) *The booke of Psalms in English meeter.* London.

RPS: Records of the Parliaments of Scotland to 1707. William II and Mary II: Translation 16; Act in favour of John Hay of Lochloy [1690/4/138]/www.rps.ac.uk.

Russell, Jeffrey B. (1990) *Lucifer: The Devil in the Middle Ages.* New York: Cornell University Press.

—— (1972) *Witchcraft in the Middle Ages.* London: Cornell University Press Limited.

Sahlin, Claire, L. (2001) *Birgitta of Sweden and the Voice of Prophecy.* Woodbridge, Suffolk: The Boydell Press.

Sanderson, Stewart, (ed.) (1976) Robert Kirk's *The Secret Commonwealth of Elves, Fauns and Fairies.* Cambridge: D. S. Brewer for the Folklore Society.

Saxby, Jessie, M. E. (1932) *Shetland Traditional Lore.* London: Simpkin Marshall Ltd.

Scott, Walter (1857) *Letters on Demonology and Witchcraft*, 2nd edition. London: William Tegg & Co.

Scott-Moncrieff (ed.) (1889) *Narrative of Mr James Nimmo: Written for his own satisfaction to keep in some remembrance the Lord's way, dealing and kindness towards him, 1654–1709.* Printed for the Scottish History Society. Edinburgh: Edinburgh University Press.

Sharpe, Charles Kilpatrick (1884) *A Historical Account of the Belief in Witchcraft in Scotland.* London: Hamilton, Adams & Co.

Sibbald, Robert (1699) *Provision for the Poor in Time of Dearth and Scarcity.* Edinburgh: James Watson.

Simpkins, John Ewart (1914) 'Examples of Printed Folk-Lore concerning Fife with some notes on Clackmannan & Kinross-shires', *County Folk-Lore*, Vol. 7. London: Sidgwick & Jackson Ltd.

Simpson, Jacqueline (2006) Review of 'Cunning Folk and Familiar Spirits' in *Folklore* 117 (3): 343–4.

—— (1996) 'Witches and Witchbusters', in *Folklore* 107: 5–18.

—— (1995) '"The Weird Sisters Wandering": Burlesque Witchery in Montgomerie's "Flyting"', in *Folklore* 106: 9–20.

Sinclair, George (1685) *Satan's Invisible World Discovered*. Facsimile reprint edition, 1871. Edinburgh: Thomas George Stevenson.

Smith, J. Irvine (1972) 'Introduction' to *Selected Justiciary Cases 1624–1650*, 2 vols. Edinburgh: Stair Society.

Smith, John (1989) *Fermfolk and Fisherfolk: Rural life in Northern Scotland in the Eighteenth and Nineteenth Centuries*. Aberdeen: Aberdeen University Press.

Smith, Moira (2007) Review of 'Cunning Folk and Familiar Spirits' in *Journal of Folklore Research*

Smout, Thomas, C. (1969) *A History of the Scottish People 1560–1830*. London: Collins.

Spanos, Nicholas and Jack Gottlieb, (1976) 'Ergotism and the Salem Village Witch Trials' in *Science* 194 (4272): 1390–4.

Spence, Lewis (1945) *The Magic Arts in Celtic Britain*. London: Rider & Co.

Stevenson, Andrew (1756) *Memoirs of the Life of Mr. Thomas Hog: Minister of the Gospel at Kiltearn, in Ross. Containing some very signal displays of the divine condescension in him, and to others by him*. Edinburgh.

Stevenson, David (ed.) (1986) *From Lairds to Louns: Country and Burgh Life in Aberdeen 1600–1800*. Aberdeen: Aberdeen University Press.

—— (1972) 'Major Weir: A Justified Sinner?', in *Scottish Studies* 16: 161–73.

Stevenson, Jane and Peter Davidson (eds) (2001) *Early Modern Women Poets 1520–1700: An Anthology*. Oxford: Oxford University Press.

Stewart, William Grant (1970) *The Popular Superstitions and Festive Amusements of the Highlanders of Scotland*. Trowbridge & London: Wardlock Reprints. Originally published in Edinburgh, 1823.

Stuart, John (ed.) (1843) *Extracts from the Presbytery Book of Strathbogie*. Aberdeen: The Spalding Club.

—— (ed.) (1841) *The Miscellany of the Spalding Club*, Vol. 1. Aberdeen: The Spalding Club.

Sugg, Richard (2007) *Murder After Death: Literature and Anatomy in Early Modern England*. Cornell University Press.

The Survey of Scottish Witchcraft 1563–1736 (2003) J. Goodare, L. Martin, J. Miller and L. Yeoman (www.shc.ed.ac.uk/witches/).

Summers, Montague (ed.) (1928) *Malleus Maleficarum*. London: Arrow Books Ltd.

Tedlock, Barbara (2005) *The Woman in the Shaman's Body: Reclaiming the Feminine in Religion and Medicine*. New York: Bantam Books.

—— (1987) *Dreaming: Anthropological and Psychological Interpretations*. Cambridge: Cambridge University Press.

Thomas, Jane (1993) 'Elgin Notaries in Burgh Society and Government 1540–1660', in *Northern Scotland* 13: 21–30.

—— (1990) 'The burgh of Elgin in early modern times'. Unpublished M.Litt thesis: University of Aberdeen.

Thomas, Keith (1973) *Religion and the Decline of Magic*. London: Penguin.

Thomson, Thomas (ed.) (1825) *The Historie and Life of King James the Sext: Being an account of the affairs of Scotland, from the year 1566, to the year 1596; with a short continuation to the year 1617*, by John Colville. Edinburgh: The Bannatyne Club.

Thurston, Robert (2001) *Witch, Wicce, Mother Goose*. Harlow: Longman.

Todd, Margo (2002) *The Culture of Protestantism in Early Modern Scotland*. London: Yale University Press.

Tom Thumb, his Life and Death; Wherein is declared many marvellous Acts of Manhood, full of wonder and strange merriment: which little knight lived in King Arthur's time, in the Court of Great Britain. (1682). Edinburgh.

Torrance, Thomas (1959) *The School of Faith: The Catechisms of the Reformed Church*. London: James Clarke & Co Limited.

Ullman, Montague (1981) 'PSI Communication through Dream Sharing', in *Parapsychology Review* 12 (2):1–8.

Van Deusen, Kira (2004) *Singing Story, Healing Drum: Shamans and Storytellers of Turkic Siberia*. Montreal & Kingston: McGill-Queen's University Press.

Vitebsky, Piers (2001) *The Shaman*. London: Duncan Baird.

Voragine, Jacobus (1900) *The Golden Legend (as Englished by William Caxton)*, vols 4 & 5, ed. F.S. Ellis. New York: AMS Press, reprint of JM Dent & Sons 1900.

Wallis, Richard (2008) Review of 'Cunning Folk and Familiar Spirits', in *Journal for the Academic Study of Magic* 4: 360–66.

Walsh, Roger (1990) *The Spirit of Shamanism*. London: Mandala.

Walsham, Alexandra (1999) *Providence in Early Modern England*. Oxford: Oxford University Press.

Webster, Hutton (1968) *Primitive Secret Societies: A Study in Early Politics and Religion*. ****: Octagon Books.

Wedderburn, Robert (1979) *The Complaynt of Scotland* (c.1550). Edinburgh: Scottish Text Society

Wedeck, Harry, E. (1962) *A Treasury of Witchcraft: A Sourcebook of the Magic Arts*. New Jersey: Gramercy Books.

Whitehead, Neil, L. (2002) *Dark Shamans: Kanaimà and the Poetics of Violent Death*. Durham: Duke University Press.

Whitehead, Neil and Robin Wright (eds) (2004) *In Darkness and Secrecy: The Anthropology of Assault Sorcery and Witchcraft in Amazonia*. Durham: Duke University Press.

Wilby, Emma (2005) *Cunning Folk and Familiar Spirits: Shamanistic Visionary Traditions in Early Modern British Witchcraft and Magic*. Brighton & Portland: Sussex Academic Press.

—— (2000) 'The Witch's Familiar and the Fairy in Early Modern England and Scotland', in *Folklore* 111 (2): 283–305.

Williams, Ronald (1975) *Montrose: Cavalier in Mourning*. London: Barrie & Jenkins Limited.

Withers, Charles (1983) *Gaelic in Scotland 1698–1981: The Geographical History of a Language*. Edinburgh: John Donald Publishers Limited.

Withrington, Donald and Ian Grant (eds) (1982) *The Statistical Account of Scotland: Banffshire, Moray and Nairnshire 1791–1799*, ed. John Sinclair, Vol. 16. Wakefield: E.P. Publishing.

Wodrow, Robert (1835) *The History of the Sufferings of the Church of Scotland from the Restoration to the Revolution*, vol. 1, ed. Robert Burns. Glasgow: Blackie & Son.

Wormald, Jenny (ed.) (2008) *The Seventeenth Century 1603–1688*. Oxford: Oxford University Press.

—— (1981) *Court, Kirk & Community: Scotland 1470–1625*. London: Edward Arnold.

Yarnall, Judith (1994) *Transformations of Circe: The History of an Enchantress.* Urbana & Chicago: University of Illinois Press.

Young, Margaret (ed.) (1992) *The Parliaments of Scotland: Burgh and Shire Commissioners*, vol I. Edinburgh: Scottish Academic Press.

Youngson, A. J. (1974) *Beyond the Highland Line: Three Journals of Travel in Eighteenth Century Scotland by Burt, Pennant and Thornton.* London: Collins.

Zika, Charles (2002) 'Images of Circe and Discourses of Witchcraft 1480–1580', in *Zeitenblicke*, vol. 1. Translation available at: www.zeitenblicke.de/2002/01/zika/zika.html#zitierwise.

Index